WEBSTER'S
CONCISE EDITION
SPANISH–ENGLISH
ENGLISH–SPANISH
DICTIONARY

**GEDDES &
GROSSET**

List of Abbreviations
The following abbreviations are used throughout the dictionary.

	Abbreviation	**Abreviaturas**
abbrev	abbreviation	abreviatura
adj	adjective	adjectivo
adv	adverb	adverbio
art	article	artículo
auto	automobile	automóvil
aux	auxiliary	auxiliar
bot	botany	botánica
chem	chemistry	química
col	colloquial term	lengua familiar
com	commerce	comercio
compd	in compounds	usada en palabras compuestas
comput	computers	informática
conj	conjunction	conjunctión
excl	exclamation	exclamación
f	feminine noun	sustantivo femenino
fig	figurative use	uso figurado
gr	grammar	gramática
imp	impersonal	impersonal
interj	interjection	interjección
invar	invariable	invariable
law	law term	jurisprudencia
m	masculine noun	sustantivo masculino
math	mathematics	matemáticas
med	medicine	medicina
mil	military term	lo militar
mus	music	música
n	noun	sustantivo
pej	pejorative	peyorativo
pl	plural	plural
pn	pronoun	pronombre
poet	poetical term	vocablo poético
pref	prefix	prefijo
prep	preposition	preposición
rad	radio	radio
rail	railway	ferrocarilero
theat	theater	teatro
tec	technology	téchnica, tecnologia
TV	television	televisión
vi	intransitive verb	verbo intransitivo
vr	reflexive verb	verbo reflexivo
vt	transitive verb	verbo transitivo

Published 2003 by Geddes & Grosset,
David Dale House, New Lanark, ML11 9DJ, Scotland

© 2003 Geddes & Grosset

ISBN 1 84205 252 7

Printed and bound in Poland

Spanish–English Dictionary

A

a *prep* to; in; at; according to; on; by; for; of.
abacería *f* grocery.
abacero *m* grocer.
ábaco *m* abacus.
abad *m* abbot.
abadejo *m* cod.
abadesa *f* abbess.
abadía *f* abbey.
abajo *adv* under; underneath; below; ~ **de** *prep* under, below.
abalanzarse *vr* to rush forward.
abalorio *m* glass bead.
abanderado *m* (*mil*) ensign; standard bearer.
abandonado/da *adj* derelict; abandoned; neglected.
abandonar *vt* to abandon; to leave; ~**se** *vr* ~ **a** to give oneself up to.
abandono *m* desertion; neglect; retirement.
abanicar *vt* to fan.
abanico *m* fan.
abaratar *vt* to lower the price of.
abarca *f* sandal.
abarcar *vt* to include.
abarrancarse *vr* to get into difficulties.
abarrotado/da *adj* packed.
abarrotar *vt* to tie down.
abastecedor/ra *m/f* supplier, purveyor.
abastecer *vt* to supply, provide.
abastecimiento *m* supplying; provisions.
abasto *m* supply of provisions.
abate *m* French abbot.
abatido/da *adj* dejected, low-spirited.
abatimiento *m* low spirits *pl*; depression.
abatir *vt* to knock down; to humble.
abdicación *f* abdication.
abdicar *vt* to abdicate.
abdomen *m* abdomen.
abdominal *adj* abdominal.
abecé *m* alphabet.
abecedario *m* alphabet; spelling book; primer.
abedul *m* birch tree.
abeja *f* bee; ~ **reina** queen bee.
abejar *m* beehive.
abejarrón *m* bumblebee.

abejón *m* drone; hornet.
abejorro *m* bumblebee.
aberración *f* aberration.
abertura *f* aperture, chink, opening.
abeto *m* fir tree.
abetunado/da *adj* dark-skinned.
abierto/ta *adj* open; sincere; frank.
abigarrado/da *adj* multicolored.
abintestato *adj* intestate.
abismal *adj* abysmal.
abismo *m* abyss; gulf; hell.
abjuración *f* abjuration.
abjurar *vt* to abjure, to recant; * *vi:* ~ **de** to abjure, to recant.
ablandamiento *m* softening.
ablandar *vt*, *vi* to soften.
ablativo *m* (*gr*) ablative.
ablución *f* ablution.
abnegación *f* self-denial.
abnegado/da *adj* selfless.
abnegar *vt* to renounce.
abobado/da *adj* silly.
abobamiento *m* stupefaction.
abobar *vt* to stupefy.
abocado/da *adj* light (wine).
abocar *vt* to seize with the mouth; ~**se** *vr* to meet by agreement.
abochornar *vt* to swelter; ~**se** *vr* to shame.
abofetear *vt* to slap.
abogacía *f* legal profession.
abogado/a *m/f* attorney-at-law, counsel.
abogar *vi* to intercede; ~ **por** to advocate.
abolengo *m* ancestry; inheritance from ancestors.
abolición *f* abolition, abrogation.
abolir *vt* to abolish.
abolladura *f* dent.
abollar *vt* to dent.
abominable *adj* abominable, cursed.
abominación *f* abomination.
abominar *vt* to detest.
abonado/da *adj* ready; prepared; * *m/f* subscriber; season ticket holder.
abonar *vt* to settle; to fertilize; to endorse; ~**se** *vr* to subscribe; * *vi* to clear up.

abono *m* payment; subscription; dung, manure.

abordaje *m* boarding.

abordar *vt* (*mar*) to board; to broach.

aborigen *m* aborigine.

aborrecer *vt* to hate, to abhor.

aborrecible *adj* hateful, detestable.

aborrecimiento *m* abhorrence, hatred.

abortar *vi* to miscarry; to have an abortion.

abortivo/va *adj* abortive.

aborto *m* miscarriage; abortion; monster.

abortón *m* abortion (in animals).

abotagado/da *adj* swollen.

abotinado/da *adj* tied up.

abotonar *vt* to button.

abovedado/da *adj* vaulted.

abrasar *vt* to burn; to parch; ~se *vr* to burn oneself.

abrazadera *f* bracket; clasp.

abrazar *vt* to embrace; to surround.

abrazo *m* embrace.

abrebotellas *m invar* bottle opener.

abrecartas *m invar* letter opener.

abrelatas *m invar* can opener.

abrevadero *m* watering place.

abrevar *vt* to water (cattle).

abreviación *f* abbreviation, abridgement; shortening.

abreviar *vt* to abridge, to cut short.

abreviatura *f* abbreviation.

abridor *m* opener.

abrigar *vt* to shelter; to protect; ~se *vr* to take shelter.

abrigo *m* coat; shelter; protection; aid.

abril *m* April.

abrillantar *vt* to polish.

abrir *vt* to open; to unlock; ~se *vr* to open up; to clear the way; to be open.

abrochador *m* buttonhook.

abrochar *vt* to button; to do up.

abrogar *vt* to abrogate.

abrumador/ra *adj* overwhelming; annoying.

abrumar *vt* to overwhelm.

abrupto/ta *adj* abrupt; steep.

absceso *m* abscess.

absentismo *m* absenteeism.

absolución *f* forgiveness, absolution.

absoluto/ta *adj* absolute.

absolutorio/a *adj* absolutely.

absolver *vt* to absolve.

absorbente *adj* absorbent.

absorber *vt* to absorb.

absorción *f* absorption; takeover.

absorto *adj* engrossed.

abstemio *adj* teetotal.

abstención *f* abstention.

abstenerse *vr* to abstain.

abstinencia *f* abstinence.

abstinente *adj* abstinent, abstemious.

abstracción *f* abstraction.

abstracto/ta *adj* abstract.

abstraer *vt* to abstract; ~se *vr* to be absorbed.

abstraído *adj* absent-minded.

absuelto/ta *adj* absolved.

absurdidad *f* , **absurdo** *m* absurdity.

absurdo *adj* absurd.

abuela *f* grandmother.

abuelo *m* grandfather.

abulia *f* lethargy.

abultado/da *adj* bulky, large, massive.

abultar *vt* to increase, to enlarge; * *vi* to be bulky.

abundancia *f* abundance.

abundante *adj* abundant, copious.

abundar *vi* to abound.

aburrido/da *adj* boring, dull.

aburridor/ra *adj Lat Am* boring, dull.

aburrimiento *m* boredom.

aburrir *vt* to bore.

abusador/ra *adj Lat Am* greedy.

abusar *vt* to abuse.

abusivo/va *adj* abusive.

abuso *m* abuse.

abyección *f* abjectness.

abyecto/ta *adj* abject, wretched.

acá *adv* here.

acabado/da *adj* perfect, accomplished.

acabar *vt* to finish, to complete; to achieve; ~se *vr* to finish; to be over; to run out; * *vi* to finish; to die, to expire.

acabose *m*: **el** ~ the last straw.

acacia *f* acacia.

academia *f* academy.

académico/ca *m/f* academician; * *adj* academic.

acaecer *vi* to happen.

acallar *vt* to quiet, to hush; to soften, to appease.

acalorado/da *adj* heated.

acalorarse *vr* to become heated.

acampar *vt* to camp.

acanalado/da *adj* grooved; fluted.

acanalar *vt* to corrugate.

acanto *m* acanthus.

acantonamiento *m* cantonment.

acantonar *vt* to billet.

acaparar *vt* to monopolize; to hoard.

acápite *m Lat Am* paragraph.

acariciar *vt* to fondle, to caress.

acarrear *vt* to transport; to occasion.
acarreo *m* carriage, transportation.
acaso *m* chance; * *adv* perhaps.
acatarrarse *vr* to catch (a) cold.
acaudalado/da *adj* rich, wealthy.
acaudalar *vt* to hoard.
acaudillar *vt* to command.
acceder *vi* to agree; ~ a to have access to.
accesible *adj* attainable; accessible.
acceso *m* access; fit.
accesorio/ria *adj*, *m* accessory.
accidentado/da *adj* uneven; hilly; eventful.
accidental *adj* accidental; casual.
accidentarse *vr* to have an accident.
accidente *m* accident.
acción *f* action, operation; share.
accionar *vt* to work; *Lat Am* to bring a suit against.
accionista *m* shareholder.
acebo *m* holly tree.
acebuche *m* wild olive tree.
acechador/ra *m/f* spy, observer.
acechar *vt* to lie in wait for; to spy on, observe.
acecho *m* spying, watching; ambush.
aceitar *vt* to oil.
aceite *m* oil.
aceitera *f* oilcan.
aceitoso/sa *adj* oily.
aceituna *f* olive.
aceitunado/da *adj* olive-green.
aceitunero *m* olive seller.
aceituno *m* olive tree.
aceleración *f* acceleration.
acelerada *f Lat Am* acceleration.
aceleradamente *adv* swiftly, hastily.
acelerador *m* gas pedal.
acelerar *vt* to accelerate; to hurry.
acelga *f* (*bot*) chard (a variety of beet).
acento *m* accent.
acentuación *f* accentuation.
acentuar *vt* to accentuate.
aceña *f* water mill.
acepción *f* acceptation.
aceptable *adj* acceptable.
aceptación *f* acceptance; approval.
aceptar *vt* to accept, to admit.
acequia *f* canal, channel; drain.
acera *f* sidewalk.
acerado/da *adj* steel *compd*, made of steel; sharp; steely.
acerbo/ba *adj* rigorous, harsh; cruel.
acerca *prep* about, relating to.
acercar *vt* to move nearer; ~se *vr* ~ a to approach.

acerico *m* pincushion.
acero *m* steel.
acérrimo/ma *adj* staunch; bitter.
acertado/da *adj* correct, proper; prudent.
acertar *vt* to hit; to guess right; * *vi* to get it right; to turn out true.
acertijo *m* riddle.
acervo *m* heap, pile.
acetato *m* (*chem*) acetate.
achacar *vt* to impute.
achacoso/sa *adj* sickly, unhealthy.
achantar *vt* (*col*) to scare; ~se *vr* to back down.
achaparrado/da *adj* stunted; stocky.
achaque *m* ailment; excuse; subject, matter.
achicar *vt* to diminish; to humiliate; to bale (out).
achicharrar *vt* to scorch; to overheat.
achicoria *f* (*bot*) chicory.
achiquitar *vt Lat Am* to make smaller.
achisparse *vr* to get tipsy.
aciago/ga *adj* unlucky; ominous.
acíbar *m* aloes; (*fig*) bitterness; displeasure.
acicalar *vt* to polish; ~se *vr* to dress in style.
acicate *m* spur.
acidez *f* acidity.
ácido *m* acid; * ~/da *adj* acid, sour.
acierto *m* success; solution; dexterity.
aclamación *f* acclamation.
aclamar *vt* to applaud, to acclaim.
aclaración *f* clarification.
aclarar *vt* to clear; to brighten; to explain; to clarify; ~se *vr* to understand; * *vi* to clear up.
aclimatar *vt* to acclimatize; ~se *vr* to become acclimatized.
acne *m* acne.
acobardar *vt* to intimidate.
acodarse *vr* to lean.
acogedor/ra *adj* welcoming.
acoger *vt* to receive; to welcome; to harbor; ~se *vr* to take refuge.
acogida *f* reception; asylum.
acolchar *vt* to quilt; to cushion.
acólito *m* acolyte; assistant.
acometer *vt* to attack; to undertake.
acometida *f* attack, assault.
acomodadizo *adj* accommodating.
acomodado/da *adj* suitable, convenient, fit; wealthy.
acomodador/ra *m/f* usher, usherette.
acomodar *vt* to accommodate, to arrange; ~se *vr* to comply.
acomodaticio/cia *adj* accommodating; pliable.

acompañamiento *m* (*mus*) accompaniment.
acompañar *vt* to accompany; to join; (*mus*) to accompany.
acompasado/da *adj* measured; well-proportioned.
acondicionado/da *adj* conditioned.
acondicionar *vt* to arrange; to condition.
acongojar *vt* to distress.
aconsejable *adj* advisable.
aconsejar *vt* to advise; ~**se** *vr* to take advice.
acontecer *vi* to happen.
acontecimiento *m* event, incident.
acopio *m* gathering, storing.
acopiar *vt* to gather, to store up.
acoplamiento *m* coupling.
acoplar *vt* to couple; to fit; to connect.
acorazado/da *adj* armored; * *m* battleship.
acordado/da *adj* agreed.
acordar *vt* to agree; to remind; *Lat Am* to award; ~**se** *vr* to agree; to remember.
acorde *adj* harmonious; * *m* chord.
acordeón *m* accordion.
acordonado/da *adj* cordoned-off.
acordonar *vt* to tie up; to cordon off.
acorralar *vt* to round up, corral; corner.
acortar *vt* to abridge, to shorten; ~**se** *vr* to become shorter.
acosar *vt* to pursue closely; to pester.
acostado/da *adj* in bed; lying down.
acostar *vt* to put to bed; to lay down; ~**se** *vr* to go to bed; to lie down.
acostumbrado/da *adj* usual.
acostumbrar *vi* to be used to; ~**se** *vr* ~ **a** to get used to; * *vt* to accustom.
acotación *f* boundary mark; quotation in the margin; stage direction.
acotar *vt* to set bounds to; to annotate.
ácrata *m/f* anarchist.
acre *adj* acid; sharp; * *m* acre.
acrecentamiento *m* increase.
acrecentar *vt* to increase, to augment.
acreditar *vt* to guarantee; to assure; to affirm; to authorize; to credit; ~**se** *vr* to become famous.
acreedor *m* creditor.
acribillar *vt* to riddle with bullets; to molest, to torment.
acriminar *vt* to incriminate; to accuse.
acrimonia *f* acrimony.
acriollado/da *adj Lat Am* integrated.
acrisolar *vt* to refine, to purify.
acritud *f* acrimony.
acróbata *m/f* acrobat.
acta *f* act; ~**s** *fpl* records *pl*.

actitud *f* attitude; posture.
activar *vt* to activate; to speed up.
actividad *f* activity; liveliness.
activo/va *adj* active; diligent.
acto *m* act, action; act of a play; ceremony.
actor *m* actor; plaintiff.
actriz *f* actress.
actuación *f* action; behavior; proceedings *pl*.
actual *adj* actual, present.
actualidad *f* present time; ~**es** *fpl* current events *pl*.
actualizar *vt* to update.
actualmente *adv* at present.
actuar *vt* to work; to operate; * *vi* to work; to act.
acuarela *f* watercolor.
acuariano/na *adj Lat Am* Aquarian (zodiac sign).
acuario *m* tank.
Acuario *m* Aquarius (zodiac sign).
acuartelamiento *m* quartering of troops.
acuartelar *vt* (*mil*) to quarter (troops).
acuático/ca *adj* aquatic.
acuchillar *vt* to cut; to plane.
acuciar *vt* to urge on.
acuclillarse *vr* to crouch.
acudir *vi* to go to; to attend; to assist.
acueducto *m* aqueduct.
acuerdo *m* agreement; **de** ~ (*col*) OK, all right.
acumular *vt* to accumulate, to collect.
acuñación *f* coining.
acuñar *vt* to coin, to mint; to wedge in.
acuoso/sa *adj* watery.
acupuntura *f* acupuncture.
acurrucarse *vr* to squat; to huddle up.
acusación *f* accusation.
acusador/ra *m/f* accuser; * *adj* accusing.
acusar *vt* to accuse; to reveal; to denounce; ~**se** *vr* to confess.
acusativo *m* (*gr*) accusative.
acuse *m*: ~ **de recibo** acknowledgement of receipt.
acústica *f* acoustics *pl*.
acústico/ca *adj* acoustic.
adagio *m* adage, proverb; (*mus*) adagio.
adalid *m* chief, commander.
adamascado/da *adj* damask.
adaptable *adj* adaptable.
adaptación *f* adaptation.
adaptador *m* adapter.
adaptar *vt* to adapt.
adecuado/da *adj* adequate, fit; appropriate.
adecuar *vt* to fit, to accommodate, to proportion.

adefesio *m* folly, nonsense.
adelantado/da *adj* advanced; fast.
adelantamiento *m* progress, improvement, advancement; overtaking.
adelantar *vt, vi* to advance, to accelerate; to pass; to ameliorate, to improve; ~**se** *vr* to advance; to outdo.
adelante *adv* forward(s); **de hoy en** ~ from now on; **más** ~ later on; further on; ~ **de** *Lat Am* in front of; * *excl* come in!
adelanto *m* advance; progress; improvement.
adelfa *f* (*bot*) rosebay.
adelgazar *vt* to make thin/slender; * *vi* to lose weight.
ademán *m* gesture; attitude.
además *adv* moreover, besides; ~ **de** besides.
adentrarse *vr* to get inside; to penetrate.
adentro *adv* in; inside; ~ **de** *Lat Am* inside.
adepto/ta *m/f* supporter.
aderezar *vt* to dress, to adorn; to prepare; to season.
aderezo *m* adorning; seasoning; arrangement.
adeudado *adj* in debt.
adeudar *vt* to owe; ~**se** *vr* to run into debt.
adherencia *f* adhesion, cohesion; alliance.
adherente *adj* adhering to, cohesive.
adherir *vi*: ~ **a** to adhere to; to espouse.
adhesión *f* adhesion; cohesion.
adición *f* addition.
adicionar *vt* to add.
adicto/ta *adj*: ~ **a** addicted to; devoted to; * *m* supporter; addict.
adiestrar *vt* to guide; to teach, to instruct; ~**se** *vr* to practice.
adinerado/da *adj* wealthy, rich.
adiós *excl* goodbye; hello.
aditivo *m* additive.
adivinanza *f* enigma; riddle.
adivinar *vt* to foretell; to guess.
adivino/na *m/f* fortune-teller.
adjetivo *m* adjective.
adjudicación *f* adjudication.
adjudicar *vt* to adjudge; ~**se** *vr* to appropriate.
adjuntar *vt* to endorse.
adjunto/ta *adj* united, joined, annexed; * *m/f* assistant.
administración *f* administration.
administrador/a *m/f* administrator.
administrar *vt* to administer.
administrativo/va *adj* administrative.
admirable *adj* admirable, marvelous.
admiración *f* admiration; wonder; (*gr*) exclamation mark.

admirar *vt* to admire; to surprise; ~**se** *vr* to be surprised.
admisible *adj* admissible.
admisión *f* admission, acceptance.
admitir *vt* to admit, to let in; to concede; to permit.
admonición *f* warning.
adobado *m* pickled pork.
adobar *vt* to dress; to season.
adobe *m* adobe, sun-dried brick.
adobo *m* dressing; pickle sauce.
adoctrinar *vt* to indoctrinate; to teach.
adolecer *vi* to suffer from.
adolescencia *f* adolescence.
adolescente *adj, m/f* adolescent.
adonde *adv* (to) where.
adónde *adv* where.
adopción *f* adoption.
adoptar *vt* to adopt.
adoptivo/va *adj* adoptive; adopted.
adoquín *m* paving stone.
adoración *f* adoration, worship.
adorar *vt* to adore; to love.
adormecer *vt* to put to sleep; ~**se** *vr* to fall asleep.
adormidera *f* (*bot*) poppy.
adornar *vt* to embellish, to adorn.
adorno *m* adornment; ornament, decoration.
adosado/da *adj* semidetached, joined to another building by a common wall.
adquirir *vt* to acquire.
adquisición *f* acquisition.
adrede *adv* on purpose.
adscribir *vt* to appoint.
aduana *f* customs *pl*.
aduanero *m* customs officer; ~/**ra** *adj* customs *compd*.
aducir *vt* to adduce.
adueñarse *vr*: ~ **de** to take possession of.
adulación *f* adulation.
adulador/ra *m/f* flatterer.
adular *vt* to flatter.
adulterar *vt* to adulterate; * *vi* to commit adultery.
adulterio *m* adultery.
adúltero/ra *m/f* adulterer, adulteress.
adulto/ta *adj, m/f* adult, grown-up.
adusto/ta *adj* gloomy; stern.
advenedizo *m* upstart.
advenimiento *m* arrival; accession.
adverbio *m* adverb.
adversario *m* adversary; antagonist.
adversidad *f* adversity; setback.
adverso/sa *adj* adverse.

advertencia f warning, foreword.
advertido/da adj sharp.
advertir vt to notice; to warn.
Adviento m Advent.
adyacente adj adjacent.
aéreo/rea adj aerial.
aerobic m aerobics pl.
aerobismo m Lat Am aerobics pl.
aerodeslizador m hovercraft.
aerodeslizante m hovercraft.
aerogenerador m wind turbine.
aeromozo/za m/f Lat Am air steward/ess.
aeronauta m aeronaut.
aeronáutica f aeronautics.
aeronave f spaceship.
aeroplano m airplane.
aeropuerto m airport.
aerosol m aerosol.
aerostática f aerostatics.
afabilidad f affability.
afable adj affable.
afán m hard work; desire.
afanar vt to harass; (col) to pinch; ~se vr to strive.
afanoso/sa adj hard, industrious.
afear vt to deform, to misshape.
afección f affection; fondness, attachment; disease.
afectación f affectation.
afectadamente adv affectedly.
afectado/da adj affected.
afectar vt to affect, to feign.
afectísimo/ma adj affectionate; ~ suyo yours truly.
afectivo/va adj fond, tender.
afecto m affection; passion; ~/ta adj affectionate; disposed; reserved.
afectuoso/sa adj affectionate; moving; tender.
afeitada f Lat Am shave.
afeitar vt, ~se vr to shave.
afeite m make-up, rouge.
afeminado/da adj effeminate.
afeminar vt to make effeminate.
aferrado/da adj stubborn.
aferrar vt to grapple, to grasp, to seize.
afianzamiento m strengthening.
afianzar vt to strengthen; to prop up; ~se vr to become established.
afiche m Lat Am poster.
afición f affection; hobby; fans pl.
aficionado/da adj keen; * m/f lover, fan; amateur.
aficionar vt to inspire affection; ~se vr ~ a to grow fond of.

afiebrado/da adj Lat Am feverish.
afiladera f grindstone.
afilado adj sharp.
afilar vt to sharpen, to grind.
afín m related; similar.
afinar vt to tune; to refine.
afincarse vr to settle.
afinidad f affinity; analogy; relationship.
afirmación f affirmation.
afirmado m road surface.
afirmar vt to secure, to fasten; to affirm, to assure.
afirmativo/va adj affirmative.
aflicción f affliction, grief.
aflictivo/va adj distressing.
afligir vt to afflict, to torment.
aflojar vt to loosen, to slacken, to relax; * vi to grow weak; to abate; to relent; ~se vr to relax.
aflorar vi to emerge.
afluente adj flowing; * m tributary.
afluir vi to flow.
afónico/ca adj hoarse; voiceless.
aforismo m aphorism.
afortunado/da adj fortunate, lucky.
afrancesado/da adj Frenchified.
afrenta f outrage; insult.
afrentar vt to affront; to insult.
afroamericano/na adj, m/f African-American.
afrontar vt to confront; to bring face to face.
afuera adv out, outside; ~ de Lat Am outside.
afueras fpl outskirts pl.
agacharse vr to stoop, to squat.
agalla f gill; ~s pl pluck, guts; tonsils pl; tonsillitis.
agarradera f Lat Am handle.
agarradero m handle.
agarrado/da adj miserly, stingy.
agarrar vt to grasp, to seize; ~se vr to hold on tightly.
agarrón m Lat Am fight.
agarrotar vt to tie down; to squeeze tightly; to garrote.
agasajar vt to receive and treat kindly; to regale.
agasajo m graceful reception; kindness.
ágata f agate.
agazaparse vr to crouch.
agencia f agency.
agenciarse vr to obtain.
agenda f diary.
agente m agent; police officer.

ágil *adj* agile.
agilidad *f* agility, nimbleness.
agitación *f* shaking; stirring; agitation.
agitanado/da *adj* Gypsy-like.
agitar *vt* to wave; to move; ~se *vr* to become excited; to become worried.
aglomeración *f* crowd; ~ **de tráfico** traffic jam.
aglomerar *vt*, ~se *vr* to crowd together.
agnóstico/ca *adj*, *m/f* agnostic.
agobiar *vt* to weigh down; to oppress; to burden.
agolparse *vr* to assemble in crowds.
agonía *f* death throes *pl*.
agonizante *adj* dying.
agonizar *vi* to be dying.
agorar *vt* to predict.
agostar *vt* to parch.
agosto *m* August.
agotado/da *adj* exhausted; finished; sold out.
agotador/ra *adj* exhausting.
agotamiento *m* exhaustion.
agotar *vt* to exhaust; to drain; to misspend.
agraciado/da *adj* attractive; lucky.
agraciar *vt* to pardon; to reward.
agradable *adj* pleasant; lovely.
agradar *vt* to please, to gratify.
agradecer *vt* to be grateful for; to thank.
agradecido/da *adj* thankful.
agradecimiento *m* gratitude, gratefulness, thanks *pl*.
agrado *m* agreeableness, courteousness; will, pleasure; liking.
agrandar *vt* to enlarge; to exaggerate; to aggrandize; ~se *vr* to get bigger.
agrario/ria *adj* agrarian; agricultural.
agravante *f* further difficulty.
agravar *vt* to oppress; to aggrieve; to aggravate; to exaggerate; ~se *vr* to get worse.
agraviar *vt* to wrong, to offend; ~se *vr* to be aggrieved; to be piqued.
agravio *m* offence; grievance.
agredir *vt* to attack.
agregado *m* aggregate; attaché.
agregar *vt* to aggregate, to heap together; to collate; to appoint.
agremiado/da *adj* *Lat Am* unionized.
agresión *f* aggression, attack.
agresivo/va *adj* aggressive.
agresor *m* aggressor, assaulter.
agreste *adj* rustic, rural.
agriar *vt* to sour; to exasperate.
agrícola *adj* farming *compd*.
agricultor/ra *m/f* farmer.

agricultura *f* agriculture; ~ **biológica** organic farming.
agridulce *adj* sweet and sour.
agrietarse *vr* to crack.
agrimensor *m* surveyor.
agrimensura *f* surveying.
agrio *adj* sour, acrid; rough, sharp, rude, unpleasant.
agronomía *f* agronomy.
agropecuario/ria *adj* farming *compd*.
agrupación *f* group(ing).
agrupar *vt* to group, to cluster; to crowd.
agua *f* water; slope of a roof; ~ **fuerte** etching; ~ **bendita** holy water; ~s *fpl* waters *pl*.
aguacate *m* avocado pear.
aguacero *m* short, heavy shower of rain.
aguachento/ta *adj* *Lat Am* watery.
aguachirle *f* slops *pl*.
aguado/da *adj* watery; *Lat Am* weak.
aguador *m* water carrier.
aguatuerte *m* etching
aguamarina *f* aquamarine (precious stone).
aguanieve *f* sleet.
aguantador/ra *adj* *Lat Am* patient.
aguantar *vt* to bear, to suffer; to hold up.
aguante *m* firmness; patience.
aguar *vt* to water down.
aguardar *vt* to wait for.
aguardiente *m* brandy.
aguarrás *f* turpentine.
aguatero/ra *m/f* *Lat Am* water seller.
agudeza *f* keenness, sharpness; acuteness; acidity; smartness.
agudizar *vt* to make worse; ~se *vr* to get worse.
agudo/da *adj* sharp; keen-edged; smart; fine; acute; witty; brisk.
aguero *m*: **buen/mal** ~ good/bad omen.
aguijar *vt* to prick, to spur, to goad; to stimulate.
aguijón *m* sting of a bee, wasp etc; stimulation.
aguijonear *vt* to prick; to spur; to stimulate.
águila *f* eagle; genius.
aguileño/ña *adj* aquiline; sharp-featured.
aguilucho *m* eaglet.
aguinaldo *m* Christmas box, New Year gift, tip.
aguja *f* needle; spire; hand; magnetic needle; (*rail*) points *pl*.
agujerear *vt* to pierce, to bore.
agujero *m* hole.
agujetas *fpl* stitch; stiffness; pains *pl* from fatigue.

agustino *m* monk of the order of St Augustine.

aguzar *vt* to whet, to sharpen; to stimulate.

ahí *adv* there.

ahijada *f* goddaughter.

ahijado *m* godson.

ahijar *vt* to adopt (as one's own child).

ahínco *m* earnestness; eagerness.

ahogar *vt* to smother; to drown; to suffocate; to oppress; to quench; ~**se** *vr* to drown; to suffocate.

ahogo *m* breathlessness; financial difficulty.

ahondar *vt* to deepen; to study deeply; * *vi:* ~ **en** to penetrate into.

ahora *adv* now, at present; just now.

ahorcar *vt* to hang; ~**se** *vr* to hang oneself.

ahorrar *vt* to save; to avoid.

ahorrativo/va *adj* thrifty, careful with money.

ahorro *m* saving; thrift.

ahuecar *vt* to hollow, to scoop out; ~**se** *vr* to get pig-headed.

ahumar *vt* to smoke, to cure (in smoke); ~**se** *vr* to fill with smoke.

ahuyentar *vt* to drive off; to dispel.

airado/da *adj* angry.

airarse *vr* to get angry.

airbag *m* airbag.

aire *m* air; wind; aspect; musical composition.

airearse *vr* to take the air.

airoso/sa *adj* airy; windy; graceful; successful.

aislado/da *adj* insulated; isolated.

aislar *vt* to insulate; to isolate.

ajar *vt* to spoil; to abuse.

ajardinado/da *adj* landscaped.

ajedrez *m* chess.

ajedrezado/da *adj* checkered.

ajenjo *m* wormwood, absinth.

ajeno/na *adj* someone else's; foreign; ignorant; improper.

ajetrearse *vr* to exert oneself; to bustle; to toil; to fidget.

ajetreo *m* activity; bustling.

ají *m* red pepper.

ajo *m* garlic.

ajorca *f* bracelet.

ajuar *m* household furniture; trousseau.

ajustado/da *adj* tight; right; close.

ajustar *vt* to regulate, to adjust; to settle (a balance); to fit; to agree on; * *vi* to fit.

ajuste *m* agreement; accommodation; settlement; fitting.

ajusticiar *vt* to execute.

al = **a el.**

ala *f* wing; aisle; row, file; brim; winger.

alabanza *f* praise; applause.

alabar *vt* to praise; to applaud.

alabastro *m* alabaster.

alacena *f* cupboard, closet.

alacrán *m* scorpion.

alado/da *adj* winged.

alambique *m* still.

alambrada *f* wire fence; wire netting.

alambrado *m Lat Am* wire fence; wire netting.

alambre *m* wire.

alambrista *m/f* tightrope walker.

alameda *f* avenue; poplar grove.

álamo *m* poplar.

alano *m* mastiff.

alarde *m* show.

alargador *m* extension lead.

alargar *vt* to lengthen; to extend; to hasten; to stretch out; to spin out; ~**se** *vr* to get longer; to drag on.

alarido *m* outcry, shout; **dar** ~**s** to howl.

alarma *f* alarm.

alarmante *adj* alarming.

alarmar *vt* to alarm.

alarmista *m* alarmist.

alazán *m* sorrel.

alba *f* dawn.

albacea *m* executor.

albahaca *f* (*bot*) basil.

albañil *m* bricklayer.

albañilería *f* bricklaying.

albarán *m* invoice.

albarda *f* saddle.

albaricoque *m* apricot.

albedrío *m* free will.

alberca *f* reservoir; swimming pool.

albergar *vt* to lodge, to harbor; ~**se** *vr* to shelter.

albergue *m* shelter; ~ **de juventud** youth hostel.

albóndiga *f* meatball.

albor *m* dawn; whiteness.

alborada *f* dawn; reveille.

alborear *vi* to dawn.

albornoz *m* dressing gown.

alborotado/da *adj* restless, turbulent.

alborotar *vi* to make a row; * *vt* to stir up; ~**se** *vr* to get excited; to get rough.

alboroto *m* noise; disturbance, riot.

alborozar *vt* to exhilarate; ~**se** *vr* to rejoice.

alborozo *m* joy.

albricias *fpl* good news *pl*.

albufera *f* lagoon.
álbum *m* album.
albumen *m* egg white.
alcachofa *f* artichoke.
alcahuete/ta *m/f* pimp, bawd.
alcalde *m* mayor.
alcaldesa *f* mayoress.
alcaldía *f* office and jurisdiction of a mayor; mayor's office.
alcalino/na *adj* alkaline.
alcance *m* reach; bad balance.
alcancía *f* Lat Am money box.
alcanfor *m* camphor.
alcantarilla *m* sewer; gutter.
alcanzar *vt* to reach; to get, to obtain; to hit; * *vi* to suffice; to reach.
alcaparra *f* caper.
alcatraz *m* gannet.
alcayata *f* hook.
alcázar *m* castle, fortress.
alcoba *f* bedroom.
alcohol *m* alcohol.
alcohólico/ca *adj, m/f* alcoholic.
alcoholismo *m* alcoholism.
alcornoque *m* cork tree.
aldaba *f* knocker.
aldea *f* village.
aldeano/na *m/f* villager; * *adj* rustic.
ale *excl* come on!
aleación *f* alloy.
aleatorio/ria *adj* random.
aleccionar *vt* to instruct; to train.
alegación *f* allegation.
alegar *vt* to allege; to quote; * *vi* Lat Am to argue; to complain.
alegato *m* allegation; argument.
alegoria *f* allegory.
alegórico/ca *adj* allegorical.
alegrar *vt* to cheer; to poke; to liven up; ~se *vr* to get merry.
alegre *adj* happy; merry, joyful; content.
alegría *f* happiness; merriment.
alegrón *m* sudden joy; flicker.
alejamiento *m* remoteness; removal.
alejar *vt* to remove; to estrange; ~se *vr* to go away.
aleluya *f* hallelujah.
alemán/ana *adj, m/f* German; * *m* German language.
alentador/ra *adj* encouraging.
alentar *vt* to encourage.
alergia *f* allergy.
alero *m* gable-end; eaves *pl*.
alerta *adj, f* alert.
alertar *vt* to alert.

aleta *f* fin; wing; flipper; fender.
aletargarse *vr* to get drowsy.
aletazo *m* flap.
aletear *vi* to flutter.
aleteo *m* fluttering.
alevosía *f* treachery.
alevoso/sa *adj* treacherous.
alfabéticamente *adv* alphabetically.
alfabético/ca *adj* alphabetical.
alfabeto *m* alphabet.
alfalfa *f* (*bot*) lucerne.
alfarería *f* pottery.
alfarero *m* potter.
alféizar *m* window sill.
alférez *m* second lieutenant; (US navy) ensign.
alfil *m* bishop (at chess).
alfiler *m* pin; clip; clothes peg.
alfiletero *m* pincushion.
alfombra *f* carpet; rug.
alfombrar *vt* to carpet.
alfombrilla *f* mouse mat.
alforja *f* saddlebag, knapsack.
alga *f* (*bot*) seaweed.
algarabia *f* gabble, gibberish.
algarroba *f* (*bot*) carob.
algarrobo *m* (*bot*) carob tree.
algazara *f* din.
álgebra *f* algebra.
álgido/da *adj* chilly; crucial.
algo *pn* something; anything; * *adv* somewhat.
algodón *m* cotton; cotton plant; cotton wool; ~ azucarado *m* cotton candy.
algodonero *m* cotton plant; dealer in cotton.
alguacil *m* bailiff; mounted official.
alguien *pn* someone, somebody; anyone, anybody.
alguno/na *adj* some; any; no; * *pn* someone, somebody.
alhaja *f* jewel.
alhajera *f* Lat Am jewelry box.
alhelí *m* wallflower.
aliado/da *adj* allied.
alianza *f* alliance, league; wedding ring.
aliar *vt* to ally; ~se *vr* to form an alliance.
alias *adv* alias.
alicaído/da *adj* weak; downcast.
alicates *mpl* pincers *pl*, nippers *pl*.
aliciente *m* attraction; incitement.
alienación *f* alienation.
aliento *m* breath; respiration.
aligerar *vt* to lighten, to alleviate; to hasten; to ease.

alijo *m* lightening of a ship; alleviation; cache.

alimaña *f* pest.

alimentación *f* nourishment; food; grocery.

alimentar *vt* to feed, to nourish; ~se *vr* to feed.

alimenticio/cia *adj* food *compd*; nutritious.

alimento *m* food; ~s *mpl* alimony.

alineación *m* alignment; line-up.

alinear *vt* to arrange in line; ~se *vr* to line up.

aliñar *vt* to adorn; to season.

aliño *m* dressing; ornament, decoration.

alisar *vt* to plane; to polish; to smooth.

alistarse *vr* to enlist, to enroll; *Lat Am* to get ready.

aliviar *vt* to lighten; to ease; to relieve, to mollify.

alivio *m* alleviation; mitigation; relief; comfort.

aljibe *m* cistern.

allá *adv* there; over there; then.

allanamiento *m*: ~ de morada burglary.

allanar *vt* to level, to flatten; to overcome difficulties; to pacify; to subdue; to burgle; *Lat Am* to raid; ~se *vr* to submit; to tumble down.

allegado/da *adj* near; * *m/f* follower.

allí *adv* there, in that place.

alma *f* soul; human being.

almacén *m* warehouse, store; magazine.

almacenaje *m* storage.

almacenar *vt* to store (up).

almanaque *m* almanac.

almeja *f* clam.

almena *f* battlement.

almendra *f* almond.

almendrado/da *adj* almond-shaped; * *m* macaroon.

almendro *m* almond tree.

almiar *m* haystack.

almíbar *m* syrup.

almidón *m* starch.

almidonado/da *adj* starched; affected; spruce.

almidonar *vt* to starch.

almirantazgo *m* admiralty.

almirante *m* admiral.

almirez *m* mortar.

almizcle *m* musk.

almohada *f* pillow; cushion.

almohadilla *f* small pillow; pad; pincushion.

almohadón *m* large cushion.

almorranas *fpl* hemorrhoids *pl*.

almorzar *vt* to have for lunch; * *vi* to have lunch.

almuerzo *m* lunch.

alocado/da *adj* crazy; foolish; inconsiderate.

alocución *f* allocution.

áloe *m* (*bot*) aloes.

alojamiento *m* lodging; housing.

alojar *vt* to lodge; ~se *vr* to stay.

alondra *f* lark.

alpargata *f* rope-soled shoe.

alpinismo *m* mountaineering.

alpinista *m/f* mountaineer.

alpiste *m* canary seed.

alquería *f* farmhouse.

alquilar *vt* to let, to rent; to hire.

alquiler *m* renting, letting; hiring; rent; hire.

alquimia *f* alchemy.

alquimista *m* alchemist.

alquitrán *m* tar, liquid pitch.

alquitranado/da *adj* tarred.

alrededor *adv* around.

alrededores *mpl* surroundings *pl*.

alta *f* discharge from hospital.

altanería *f* haughtiness.

altanero/ra *adj* haughty, arrogant, vain, proud.

altar *m* altar; ~ mayor high altar.

altavoz *m* loudspeaker.

alterable *adj* changeable.

alteración *f* alteration; disturbance, tumult.

alterar *vt* to alter, to change; to disturb; ~se *vr* to get upset.

altercado *m* altercation, controversy; quarrel.

alternar *vt, vi* to alternate.

alternativa *f* alternative.

alternativo/va *adj* alternate.

alterno/na *adj* alternate; alternating.

Alteza *f* Highness (title).

altibajos *mpl* ups and downs *pl*.

altillo *m* hillock.

altiplanicie *f* high plateau.

altísimo/ma *adj* extremely high, most high; * *m* el A~ the Most High, God.

altisonante, altísono/na *adj* high-sounding, pompous.

altitud *f* height; altitude.

altivez *f* haughtiness.

altivo/va *adj* haughty, proud, high-flown.

alto/ta *adj* high; elevated; tall; sharp; arduous, difficult; eminent; enormous; * *m* height; story; highland; (*mil*) halt; (*mus*) alto; ¡~!, ¡~ ahí! *interj* stop!

altoparlante *m Lat Am* loudspeaker.
altramuz *m* (*bot*) lupin.
altura *f* height; depth; mountain summit; altitude; ~s *pl*: **las ~s** the heavens.
alubia *f* bean.
alucinación *f* hallucination.
alucinar *vt* to blind, to deceive; * *vi* to hallucinate; ~**se** *vr* to deceive oneself, to labor under a delusion.
aludir *vi* to allude.
alumbrado *m* lighting; illumination.
alumbramiento *m* lighting; illumination; childbirth.
alumbrar *vt* to light; * *vi* to give birth.
aluminio *m* aluminum.
alumno/na *m/f* student, pupil.
alunizar *vi* to land on the moon.
alusión *f* allusion; hint.
alusivo/va *adj* allusive.
aluvión *f* alluvium; flood.
alvéolo *m* socket; cell of a honeycomb.
alza *f* risc; sight.
alzacuello *m* dog collar.
alzada *f* height; appeal.
alzamiento *m* rise; elevation; higher bid; uprising.
alzar *vt* to raise, to lift up; to construct, to build; to gather (in); ~**se** *vr* to get up; to rise in rebellion; ~**se** *vr*: ~ **con algo** to make off with something.
ama *f* mistress, owner; housewife; foster mother; ~ **de llaves** housekeeper; ~ **de leche** nurse.
amabilidad *f* kindness, niceness.
amable *adj* kind, nice.
amaestrado/da *adj* performing.
amaestrar *vt* to teach; to instruct; to train.
amagar *vt* to threaten; to shake one's fist at; * *vi* to feint.
amago *m* threat; indication; symptom.
amalgama *f* amalgam.
amalgamar *vt* to amalgamate.
amamantar *vt* to suckle.
amanecer *vi* to dawn; **al ~** at daybreak.
amanerado/da *adj* affected.
amansar *vt* to tame; to soften; to subdue; ~**se** *vr* to calm down.
amante *m/f* lover.
amanuense *m* amanuensis, clerk, copyist.
amapola *f* (*bot*) poppy.
amar *vt* to love.
amargar *vt* to make bitter; to exasperate; ~**se** *vr* to be bitter.
amargo/ga *adj* bitter, acrid; painful; * *m* bitterness.

amargor *m* bitterness; sorrow, distress.
amargura *f* bitterness; sorrow.
amarillear *vi* to turn yellow.
amarillento/ta *adj* yellowish.
amarillo/lla *adj* yellow; * *m* yellow.
amarra *f* mooring rope.
amarrar *vt* to moor; to tie, to fasten.
amartelar *vt* to court, to woo; ~**se** *vr* to fall in love with.
amartillar *vt* to hammer; to cock (a gun/pistol).
amasar *vt* to knead; (*fig*) to arrange, to settle; to prepare.
amasijo *m* dough; mixed mortar; medley.
amateur *m/f* amateur.
amatista *f* amethyst.
amatorio/ria *adj* relating to love.
amazona *f* amazon; masculine woman.
ambages *mpl*: **sin ~** in plain language.
ámbar *m* amber.
ambición *f* ambition.
ambicionar *vt* to crave, to covet.
ambicioso/sa *adj* ambitious.
ambidextro/tra *adj* ambidextrous.
ambientación *f* setting; sound effects *pl*.
ambiente *m* atmosphere; environment.
ambigüedad *f* ambiguity.
ambiguo/gua *adj* ambiguous; doubtful, equivocal.
ámbito *m* circuit, circumference; field; scope.
ambos/bas *adj, pn* both.
ambrosía *f* ambrosia.
ambulancia *f* ambulance.
ambulante *adj* traveling.
ambulatorio *m* state-run clinic.
ameba *f* ameba.
amedrentar *vt* to frighten, to terrify; to intimidate.
amén *f* amen; so be it; ~ **de** besides; except.
amenaza *f* threat.
amenazar *vt* to threaten.
amenizar *vt* to make pleasant.
ameno/na *adj* pleasant; delicious; flowery (of language).
América *f* America; ~ **del Norte/del Sur** North/South America.
americano/na *adj, m/f* (Latin) American.
ameritar *vt Lat Am* to deserve.
ametralladora *m* machine gun.
amianto *m* asbestos.
amiga *f* (female) friend.
amigable *adj* amicable, friendly; suitable.
amigo *m* friend; comrade; lover; ~/**ga** *adj* friendly.

amilanar *vt* to frighten, to terrify; ~**se** *vr* to get scared.

aminorar *vt* to diminish; to reduce.

amistad *f* friendship.

amistoso/sa *adj* friendly, cordial.

amnesia *f* amnesia.

amnistía *f* amnesty.

amo *m* owner; boss.

amoblar *vt Lat Am* to furnish.

amodorrarse *vr* to grow sleepy.

amohinar *vt* to annoy; ~**se** *vr* to sulk.

amoldar *vt* to mold; to adapt; ~**se** *vr* to adapt oneself.

amonestación *f* advice; admonition; ~**ones** *fpl* publication of marriage banns.

amonestar *vt* to advise; to admonish; to publish banns of marriage of.

amoníaco *m* ammoniac.

amor *m* love; fancy; lover; ~ **mío** my love; **por ~ de Dios** for God's sake; ~ **propio** self-love.

amoratado *adj* livid.

amordazar *vt* to muzzle; to gag.

amorfo/fa *adj* shapeless.

amorío *m* love affair.

amoroso/sa *adj* affectionate, loving; lovely.

amortajar *vt* to shroud.

amortiguador *m* shock absorber.

amortiguadores *mpl* suspension.

amortiguar *vt* to mortify; to deaden; to temper; to muffle.

amortización *f* repayment; redemption.

amortizar *vt* to entail (an estate), to render inalienable; to pay, to liquidate, to discharge (a debt).

amotinamiento *m* mutiny.

amotinar *vt* to incite rebellion; ~**se** *vr* to mutiny.

amparar *vt* to shelter, to protect; to favor; ~**se** *vr* to claim protection.

amparo *m* protection, support; help; refuge, asylum.

amperio *m* amp.

ampliación *f* amplification, enlargement.

ampliar *vt* to amplify, to enlarge; to extend; to expand.

amplificación *f* enlargement.

amplificador *m* amplifier.

amplificar *vt* to amplify.

amplio/lia *adj* ample, extensive.

amplitud *f* amplitude, extension, largeness.

ampolla *f* blister; ampoule.

ampuloso/sa *adj* pompous.

amputación *f* amputation.

amputar *vt* to amputate.

amueblar *vt* to furnish.

amuleto *m* amulet.

amurallar *vt* to surround with walls.

anacoreta *m* anchorite, hermit.

anacronismo *m* anachronism.

ánade *m/f* duck.

anadear *vi* to waddle.

anagrama *f* anagram.

anales *mpl* annals *pl.*

analfabetismo *m* illiteracy.

analfabeto/ta *adj* illiterate.

analgésico *m* painkiller.

análisis *m* analysis.

analista *m/f* analyst.

analítico/ca *adj* analytical.

analizar *vt* to analyze.

analogía *f* analogy.

analógico/ca, análogo/ga *adj* analogous.

ananá *m* pineapple.

anaquel *m* shelf (in a bookcase).

anaranjado/da *adj* orange-colored.

anarquía *f* anarchy.

anárquico/ca *adj* anarchic, chaotic.

anarquismo *m* anarchism.

anarquista *m/f* anarchist.

anatema *f* anathema.

anatomía *f* anatomy.

anatómico/ca *adj* anatomical.

anca *f* rump.

ancho/cha *adj* broad, wide, large; * *m* breadth, width.

anchoa *f* anchovy.

anchura *f* width, breadth.

anciano/na *adj* old; * *m/f* old man/woman.

ancla *f* anchor.

ancladero *m* anchorage.

anclaje *m* anchorage.

anclar *vi* to anchor.

andaderas *fpl* baby walker.

andadura *f* walk; pace; amble.

andamio *m* scaffold.

andamiaje *m* scaffolding.

andanada *f* (*mar*) broadside.

andar *vi* to go, to walk; to fare; to act, to proceed, to work; to behave; to elapse; to move; * *vt* to go, to travel; * *m* walk, pace.

andariego/ga *adj* wandering.

andarín *m* fast walker.

andas *fpl* stretcher.

andén *m* sidewalk; (*rail*) platform; quayside.

andinismo *m Lat Am* mountaineering.

andinista *m/f Lat Am* mountaineer.

andrajo *m* rag.

andrajoso/sa *adj* ragged.

andurriales *mpl* byways *pl.*
anécdota *f* anecdote.
anegar *vt* to inundate, to submerge; ~**se** *vr* to drown; to sink.
anejo/ja *adj* attached.
anemia *f* anemia.
anestésico *m* anesthetic.
anexar *vt* to annex; to join.
anexión *f* annexation.
anexionamiento *m* annexation.
anexo/xa *adj* annexed.
anfibio/bia *adj* amphibious.
anfiteatro *m* amphitheater.
anfitrión/ona *m/f* host/ess.
ángel *m* angel.
angelical *adj* angelic, heaven-born.
angélico/ca *adj* angelic.
angina *f* angina.
anglicano/na *adj, m/f* Anglican.
anglicismo *m* Anglicanism.
angosto/ta *adj* narrow, close.
anguila *f* eel.
angula *f* elver.
angular *adj* angular; **piedra** ~ *f* cornerstone.
ángulo *m* angle, corner.
anguloso/sa *adj* angled, cornered.
angurria *f Lat Am* hunger; greed.
angurriento/ta *adj Lat Am* hungry; greedy.
angustia *f* anguish; heartache.
angustiar *vt* to cause anguish.
anhelante *adj* eager; longing.
anhelar *vi* to gasp; * *vt* to long for.
anhelo *m* desire, longing.
anidar *vi* to nestle, to make a nest; to dwell, to inhabit.
anillo *m* ring.
ánima *f* soul.
animación *f* liveliness; activity.
animado/da *adj* lively.
animador/ora *m/f* host(ess).
animadversión *f* ill-will.
animal *adj, m* animal.
animar *vt* to animate, to liven up; to comfort; to revive; ~**se** *vr* to cheer up.
ánimo *m* soul; courage; mind; intention, meaning; will; thought; * *excl* come on!
animosidad *f* valor, courage; boldness.
animoso/sa *adj* courageous, spirited.
aniñarse *vr* to act in a childish manner.
aniquilar *vt* to annihilate, to destroy; ~**se** *vr* to decline, to decay.
anís *m* aniseed; anisette.
aniversario/ria *adj* annual; * *m* anniversary.
ano *m* anus.

anoche *adv* last night.
anochecer *vi* to grow dark; * *m* nightfall.
anodino/na *adj* (*med*) anodyne.
anomalia *f* anomaly.
anómalo/la *adj* anomalous.
anonadar *vt* to annihilate; to lessen; ~**se** *vr* to humble oneself.
anonimato *m* anonymity.
anónimo/ma *adj* anonymous.
anormal *adj* abnormal.
anotación *f* annotation, note.
anotar *vt* to comment, to note.
anquilosamiento *m* paralysis.
ánsar *m* goose.
ansia *f* anxiety, eagerness, hankering.
ansiar *vt* to desire.
ansiedad *f* anxiety.
ansioso/sa *adj* anxious, eager.
antagónico/ca *adj* antagonistic; opposed.
antagonista *m* antagonist.
antaño *adv* formerly.
antártico/ca *adj* Antarctic; * *m*: **el A**~ the Antarctic.
ante *m* suede; * *prep* before; in the presence of; faced with.
anteanoche *adv* the night before last.
anteayer *adv* the day before yesterday.
antebrazo *m* forearm.
antecámara *f* antechamber.
antecedente *adj, m* antecedent.
anteceder *vt* to precede.
antecesor/ra *m/f* predecessor; * *m* forefather.
antedicho/cha *adj* aforesaid.
antelación *f*: **con** ~ in advance.
antemano *adv*: **de** ~ beforehand.
antena *f* feeler, antenna; aerial; ~ **parabólica** satellite dish.
antenoche *adv Lat Am* the night before last.
anteojo *m* eyeglass; ~ **de larga vista** telescope; ~**s** *mpl Lat Am* glasses *pl.*
antepasado/da *adj* passed, elapsed; ~**s** *mpl* ancestors *pl.*
antepecho *m* (*mil*) parapet; ledge.
anteponer *vt* to place in front; to prefer.
anteproyecto *m* sketch; blueprint.
anterior *adj* preceding; former.
anterioridad *f* priority; preference.
antes *prep, adv* before; * *conj* before.
antesala *f* antechamber.
antiaéreo/rea *adj* anti-aircraft.
antibalas *adj* bullet-proof.
antibiótico *m* antibiotic.
anticiclón *m* anticyclone.

anticipación *f* anticipation.
anticipado/da *adj* advance.
anticipar *vt* to anticipate; to forestall; to advance.
anticipo *m* advance.
anticonceptivo *m* contraceptive.
anticongelante *m* antifreeze.
anticuado/da *adj* antiquated.
anticuario *m* antiquary, antiquarian.
anticuerpo *m* antibody.
antídoto *m* antidote.
antífona *f* antiphony; anthem.
antiestético/ca *adj* unsightly.
antifaz *m* mask.
antigualla *f* monument of antiquity; antique.
antiguamente *adv* in ancient times, of old.
antigüedad *f* antiquity, oldness.
antiguo/gua *adj* antique, old, ancient; * *m* senior; ~s *mpl*: los ~s the ancients.
antílope *m* antelope.
antinatural *adj* unnatural.
antimonio *m* antimony.
antipatía *f* antipathy.
antipático/ca *adj* unpleasant.
antipasto *m Lat Am* antipasto.
antípodas *mpl* antipodes.
antirrobo *adj* anti-theft.
antisemita *adj* anti-Semitic.
antiséptico/ca *adj* antiseptic.
antítesis *f* (*gr*) antithesis.
antojadizo/za *adj* capricious, fanciful.
antojarse *vr* to long, to desire; to itch.
antojo *m* whim, fancy; longing.
antología *f* anthology.
antorcha *f* torch; taper.
antro *m* (*poet*) cavern, den, grotto.
antropófago *m* cannibal.
antropología *f* anthropology.
antropólogo/ga *m/f* anthropologist.
anual *adj* annual.
anualidad *f* annuity.
anublar *vt* to cloud, to obscure; ~se *vr* to become clouded.
anudar *vt* to knot; to join; ~se *vr* to get into knots.
anulación *f* annulment; cancellation.
anular *vt* to annul; to revoke; to cancel; * *adj* annular.
anunciación *f* announcement.
anunciante *m/f* advertiser.
anunciar *vt* to announce; to advertise.
anuncio *m* advertisement.
anverso *m* obverse.
anzuelo *m* hook; allurement.

añadidura *f* addition.
añadir *vt* to add.
añejo/ja *adj* old; stale, musty.
añicos *mpl* bits *pl*, small pieces *pl*; **hacer** ~ to shatter.
añil *m* indigo plant; indigo.
año *m* year.
añojo *m* yearling calf.
añoranza *f* longing.
aorta *f* aorta.
aovar *vi* to lay eggs.
apabullar *vt* to squash.
apacentar *vt* to graze.
apacible *adj* affable; gentle; placid, quiet.
apaciguar *vt* to appease; to pacify, to calm.
apadrinar *vt* to support, to favor; to be godfather to.
apagado/da *adj* dull; quiet; muted; listless.
apagar *vt* to put out; to turn off; to quench, to extinguish; to damp; to destroy; to soften.
apagón *m* power cut, outage.
apalabrar *vt* to agree to; to engage.
apalancar *vt* to lever.
apalear *vt* to cane, to drub; to winnow.
apañado/da *adj* skillful; suitable.
apañar *vt* to grasp; to pick up; to patch; ~se *vr* to manage.
aparador *m* sideboard; shop/store window.
aparato *m* apparatus; machine; ostentation, show.
aparatoso/sa *adj* showy; spectacular.
aparcamiento *m* parking lot.
aparcar *vt*, *vi* to park.
aparcería *f* partnership in a farm/other business.
aparcero/ra *m/f* partner; associate.
aparecer *vi* to appear; ~se *vr* to appear.
aparecido/da *m/f* ghost.
aparejar *vt* to prepare; to harness (horses); to rig (a ship).
aparejo *m* preparation; harness, gear; (*mar*) tackle, rigging; ~s *mpl* tools *pl*, implements *pl*.
aparentar *vt* to look; to pretend; to deceive.
aparente *adj* apparent; convenient.
aparición *f* apparition; appearance.
apariencia *f* outward appearance.
apartadero *m* (*rail*) siding.
apartado *m* paragraph; ~ **de correos/postal** PO Box.
apartamento *m* apartment.
apartamiento *m* isolation; separation; apartment.
apartar *vt* to separate, to divide; to remove;

to sort; ~se vr to go away; to be divorced; to desist.

aparte m aside; new paragraph; * adv apart, separately; besides; aside.

apasionado/da adj passionate; devoted; fond; biased.

apasionar vt to excite; ~se vr to get excited.

apatía f apathy.

apático/ca adj apathetic, indifferent.

apeadero m halt, stopping place; station.

apearse vr to dismount; to get down/out/off.

apechugar vt to face up to.

apedrear vt to stone; * vi to hail.

apegarse vr: ~ a to become fond of.

apego m attachment, fondness.

apelación f (law) appeal.

apelar vi (law) to appeal; ~ a to have recourse to.

apelativo adj (gr): nombre ~ m generic name.

apellidar vt to call by name; to proclaim; ~se vr to be called.

apellido m surname; family name; epithet.

apelmazar vt to compress.

apenar vt to grieve; to embarrass; ~se vr to grieve; to be embarrassed.

apenas adv scarcely, hardly; * conj as soon as.

apéndice m appendix, supplement.

apendicitis f appendicitis.

apercibido/da adj provided; ready.

apercibirse vr to notice.

aperitivo m aperitif; appetizer.

apero m agricultural implement.

apertura f aperture, opening, chink; cleft.

apesadumbrar vt to sadden.

apestar vt to infect; * vi: ~ a to stink of.

apetecer vt to fancy.

apetecible adj desirable; appetizing.

apetito m appetite.

apetitoso/sa adj pleasing to the taste, appetizing; tempting.

apiadarse vr to take pity.

apiario m Lat Am apiary.

ápice m summit, point; smallest part of a thing.

apilar vt to pile up; ~se vr to pile up.

apiñado/da adj crowded; pyramidal; pineshaped.

apiñarse vr to clog, to crowd.

apio m (bot) celery.

apisonadora f steamroller, roadroller.

apisonar vt to ram down.

aplacar vt to appease, to pacify; ~se vr to calm down.

aplanadora f Lat Am roadroller, steamroller.

aplanar vt to level, to flatten.

aplastar vt to flatten, to crush.

aplatanarse vr to get weary.

aplaudir vt to applaud; to extoll.

aplauso m applause; approbation, praise.

aplazamiento m postponement.

aplazar vt to postpone.

aplicable adj applicable.

aplicación f application; effort.

aplicado/da adj studious; industrious.

aplicar vt to apply; to clasp; to attribute; ~se vr: ~ a to devote oneself to.

aplique m wall light.

aplomo m self-assurance.

apocado/da adj timid.

Apocalipsis m Apocalypse.

apocamiento m timidity; depression.

apocar vt to lessen, to diminish; to contract; ~se vr to feel humiliated.

apócrifo/fa adj apocryphal; fabulous.

apodar vt to nickname.

apoderado/da m/f proxy, attorney; agent.

apoderar vt to authorize; to give the power of attorney to; ~se vr: ~ de to take possession of.

apodo m nickname, sobriquet.

apogeo m peak.

apolillar vt to gnaw/eat (clothes); ~se vr to be moth-eaten.

apología f eulogy; defense.

apoltronarse vr to grow lazy; to loiter.

apoplejía f apoplexy.

apoplético/ca adj apoplectic.

apoquinar vt (col) to fork out.

aporrear vt to beat up.

aportar vi to arrive at a port; to arrive; * vt to contribute.

aposentar vt to harbor; to put up.

aposento m room.

aposición f (gr) apposition.

apósito m (med) external dressing.

aposta adv on purpose.

apostar vt to bet, to wager; to post soldiers; * vi to bet.

apostasia f apostasy.

apóstata m apostate.

apostatar vi to apostatize.

apostilla f marginal note; postscript.

apóstol m apostle.

apostolado m apostleship.

apostólico/ca adj apostolic(al).

apostrofar vt to apostrophize.

apóstrofe m apostrophe.

apóstrofo m (gr) apostrophe.

apostura *f* neatness.
apoteosis *f* apotheosis.
apoyar *vt* to rest; to favor, to patronize, to support; ~**se** *vr* to lean.
apoyo *m* support; protection.
apreciable *adj* appreciable; valuable; respectable.
apreciar *vt* to appreciate; to estimate, to value.
aprecio *m* appreciation; esteem.
aprehender *vt* to apprehend, to seize.
aprehensión *f* apprehension, seizure.
apremiante *adj* urgent.
apremiar *vt* to press; to compel.
apremio *m* pressure, constriction; judicial compulsion.
aprender *vt* to learn; ~ **de memoria** to learn by heart.
aprendiz/za *m/f* apprentice.
aprendizaje *m* apprenticeship.
aprensión *f* apprehension.
aprensivo/va *adj* apprehensive.
apresar *vt* to seize, to grasp.
apresurado/da *adj* hasty.
apresuramiento *m* hurry.
apresurar *vt* to accelerate, to hasten, to expedite; ~**se** *vr* to hurry.
apretado/da *adj* tight; cramped;, difficult.
apretar *vt* to compress, to tighten; to constrain; to distress; to urge earnestly; * *vi* to be too tight.
apretón *m* squeeze.
apretura *f* squeeze.
aprieto *m* conflict; tight spot.
aprisa *adv* quickly, swiftly; promptly.
aprisco *m* sheepfold.
aprisionar *vt* to imprison.
aprobación *f* approbation, approval.
aprobar *vt* to approve; to pass; * *vi* to pass.
apropiación *f* appropriation, assumption.
apropiado/da *adj* appropriate.
apropiarse *vr* to appropriate.
aprovechable *adj* profitable.
aprovechado/da *adj* industrious; thrifty; selfish.
aprovechamiento *m* use; exploitation.
aprovechar *vt* to use; to exploit; to profit from; to take advantage of; * *vi* to be useful; to progress; ~**se** *vr:* ~ **de** to use; to take advantage of.
aproximación *f* approximation; closeness.
aproximado/da *adj* approximate.
aproximar *vt* to approach; ~**se** *vr* to approach.

aptitud *f* aptitude, fitness, ability.
apto/ta *adj* apt; fit, able; clever.
apuesta *f* bet, wager.
apuesto/ta *adj* neat.
apuntado/da *adj* pointed.
apuntador *m* prompter.
apuntalar *vt* to prop up.
apuntar *vt* to aim; to level, to point at; to mark; * *vi* to begin to appear/show itself; to prompt (theater); ~**se** *vr* to score; to enroll.
apunte *m* annotation; prompting (theater).
apuñalar *vt* to stab.
apurado/da *adj* poor, destitute of means; exhausted; hurried.
apurar *vt* to purify; to clear up, to verify; to exhaust; to tease and perplex; ~**se** *vr* to worry; to hurry.
apuro *m* want; pain, affliction; haste; jam.
aquejado/da *adj* afflicted.
aquel/~la *adj* that; ~**los/~las** *pl* those.
aquél/~la; *pn* that (one); ~ **los/~ las** *pl* those (ones).
aquello *pn* that.
aquí *adv* here; now.
aquietar *vt* to quiet, to appease.
aquilino *adj* aquiline.
aquilón *m* north wind.
ara *f* altar.
árabe *adj, m/f , m (ling)* Arabic.
arabesco *m* arabesque.
arado *m* plow.
arancel *m* tariff.
arándano *m* bilberry; blueberry.
arandela *f* washer.
araña *f* spider; chandelier.
arañar *vt* to scratch; to scrape; to corrode.
arar *vt* to plow.
arbitraje *m* arbitration.
arbitrar *vt, vi* to arbitrate; to referee.
arbitrariedad *f* arbitrariness.
arbitrario/ria *adj* arbitrary.
arbitrativo/va *adj* arbitrary.
arbitrio *m* free will; arbitration.
árbitro *m* arbitrator; referee; umpire.
árbol *m* tree; *(mar)* mast; shaft.
arbolado/da *adj* forested; wooded; * *m* woodland.
arboladura *f* rigging; masts *pl.*
arbolar *vt* to hoist, to set upright.
arboleda *f* grove.
arbusto *m* shrub.
arca *f* chest, wooden box.
arcada *f* arch; arcade; ~**s** *fpl* retching.
arcaico/ca *adj* archaic.

arcaísmo *m* archaism.
arcángel *m* archangel.
arce *m* maple tree.
archipiélago *m* archipelago.
archivador *m* filing cabinet.
archivar *vt* to file.
archivero, archivista *m* keeper of records, archivist.
archivo *m* file(s) (*pl*); archives *pl*.
arcilla *f* clay.
arcilloso/sa *adj* clayey.
arcipreste *m* archpriest.
arco *m* arc; arch; fiddle bow; hoop; *Lat Am* goalmouth; ~ iris rainbow.
arder *vi* to burn, to blaze.
ardid *m* stratagem, artifice; cunning.
ardiente *adj* burning; ardent, passionate; active; fiery.
ardilla *f* squirrel.
ardor *m* heat; valor; vivacity; fieriness, fervor.
ardoroso/sa *adj* fiery; restless.
arduo/dua *adj* arduous, difficult; high.
área *f* area.
arena *f* sand; grit; arena.
arenal *m* sandy ground.
arenga *f* harangue; speech.
arengar *vi* to harangue.
arenisca *f* sandstone; grit.
arenoso/sa *adj* sandy.
arenque *m* herring; ~ ahumado smoked herring, kipper.
argamasa *f* mortar.
argamasar *vi* to mix mortar.
argolla *f* large ring.
argot *m* slang.
argucia *f* subtlety.
argüir *vi* to argue, to dispute; * *vt* to deduce; to argue; to imply.
argumentación *f* argumentation.
argumentar *vt*, *vi* to argue, to dispute; to conclude.
argumento *m* argument.
aria *f* (*mus*) aria; tune, air.
ariano/na *adj* *Lat Am* Arien (zodiac sign).
aridez *f* drought, want of rain.
árido/da *adj* dry; barren.
Aries *m* Aries (sign of the zodiac).
ariete *m* battering ram.
ario/a *adj* Aryan.
arisco/ca *adj* fierce; rude; intractable.
aristocracia *f* aristocracy.
aristócrata *m* aristocrat.
aristocrático/ca *adj* aristocratic.
aritmética *f* arithmetic.
arlequín *m* harlequin, buffoon.

arma *f* weapon, arm.
armada *f* fleet, armada.
armadillo *m* armadillo.
armado/da *adj* armed; reinforced.
armador *m* ship owner; privateer; jacket, jerkin.
armadura *f* armor; framework; skeleton; armature.
armamento *m* armament.
armar *vt* to man; to arm; to fit; ~la to kick up a fuss.
armario *m* wardrobe; cupboard.
armatoste *m* hulk; contraption.
armazón *f* chassis; skeleton; frame.
armería *f* arsenal; heraldry; gunsmith's (premises).
armero *m* gunsmith.
armiño *m* ermine.
armisticio *m* armistice.
armonía *f* harmony.
armonioso/sa *adj* harmonious.
armonizar *vt* to harmonize; to reconcile.
arnés *m* harness; *pl* gear, trappings *pl*
aro *m* ring; earring.
aroma *m* aroma, fragrance.
aromaterapia *f* aromatherapy.
aromático/ca *adj* aromatic.
arpa *f* harp.
arpegio *m* (*mus*) arpeggio.
arpía *f* (*poet*) shrew.
arpillera *f* sackcloth.
arpón *m* harpoon.
arqueado/da *adj* arched, vaulted.
arquear *vt* to arch; to bend.
arqueo *m* arching; tonnage, capacity (of a ship).
arqueología *f* archeology.
arqueólogo/ga *m/f* archeologist.
arquero *m* archer; *Lat Am* goalkeeper.
arqueta *f* small trunk.
arquetipo *m* archetype.
arquitecto *m* architect.
arquitectónico/ca *adj* architectural.
arquitectura *f* architecture.
arrabal *m* suburb; slum.
arrabalero *m* suburbanite.
arraigado *adj* deep-rooted; established.
arraigar *vi* to root; to establish; * *vt* to establish; ~se *vr* to take root; to settle.
arrancar *vt* to pull up by the roots; to pull out; to wrest; to extract; * *vi* to start; to move.
arranque *m* sudden start; start; outburst.
arras *fpl* security.
arrasar *vt* to demolish, to destroy.

arrastrado/da *adj* miserable; painstaking; servile.

arrastrar *vt* to drag; * *vi* to creep, to crawl; to lead a trump at cards; ~se *vr* to crawl; to grovel.

arrastre *m* dragging.

¡arre! *excl* gee!, go on!

arrear *vt* to drive on; * *vi* to hurry along.

arrebañar *vt* to scrape together; to pick up.

arrebatado/da *adj* rapid; violent, impetuous; rash, inconsiderate.

arrebatar *vt* to carry off, to snatch; to enrapture.

arrebato *m* fury; rapture.

arrebol *m* rouge.

arrebujar *vt* to crumple; to wrap up.

arrecife *m* reef.

arrecirse *vr* to grow stiff with cold.

arreglado *adj* neat; regular, moderate.

arreglar *vt* to regulate; to tidy; to adjust; ~se *vr* to come to an understanding.

arreglo *m* rule, order; agreement; arrangement.

arrellanarse *vr* to sit at ease; to make oneself comfortable.

arremangar *vt* to roll up; ~se *vr* to roll up one's sleeves.

arremeter *vi* to attack; to seize suddenly.

arremetida *f* attack, assault.

arrendador *m* landlord.

arrendamiento *m* leasing; hire; lease.

arrendar *vt* to rent, to let out, to lease.

arrendatario/ria *m/f* tenant.

arreo *m* dress, ornament; ~s *mpl* harness.

arrepentido/da *adj* repentant.

arrepentimiento *m* repentance, penitence.

arrepentirse *vr* to repent.

arrestar *vt* to arrest; to imprison.

arresto *m* boldness; prison; arrest.

arriada *f* flood, overflowing.

arriar *vt* (*mar*) to lower, to strike; to pay out.

arriate *m* bed; causeway.

arriba *adv* above, over, up; high, on high, overhead; aloft; ~ de *Lat Am* above.

arribada *f* (*mar*) arrival (of a vessel) in port.

arribar *vi* (*mar*) to put into harbor.

arribeño/ña *m/f* *Lat Am* highlander.

arribista *m/f* upstart.

arriendo *m* lease; farm rent.

arriero *m* muleteer.

arriesgado/da *adj* risky; daring.

arriesgar *vt* to risk, to hazard; to expose to danger; ~se *vr* to take a chance.

arrimar *vt* to approach, to draw near; (*mar*) to stow (cargo); ~se *vr* to side up; to lean.

arrinconar *vt* to put in a corner; to lay aside.

arrobado/da *adj* enchanted.

arrobamiento *m* rapture; amazement.

arrobarse *vr* to be totally amazed; to be out of one's senses.

arrocero/ra *adj* rice-producing.

arrodillarse *vr* to kneel down.

arrogancia *f* arrogance, haughtiness.

arrogante *adj* arrogant; haughty, proud; stout.

arrojadizo/za *adj* easily thrown.

arrojar *vt* to throw, to fling; to dash; to emit; to shoot, to sprout; ~se *vr* to hurl oneself.

arrojo *m* boldness, fearlessness.

arrollador/ra *adj* overwhelming.

arrollar *vt* to run over; to defeat heavily.

arropar *vt* to clothe, to dress; ~se *vr* to wrap up.

arrostrar *vt* to face (up to).

arroyo *m* stream; gutter.

arroz *m* rice.

arrozal *m* paddy, paddy field, rice field.

arruga *f* wrinkle; rumple.

arrugar *vt* to wrinkle; to rumple; to fold; ~ la frente to frown; ~se *vr* to shrivel.

arruinar *vt* to demolish; to ruin; ~se *vr* to go bankrupt.

arrullador/ra *adj* flattering, cajoling.

arrullar *vt* to lull; * *vi* to coo.

arrullo *m* cooing (of pigeons); lullaby.

arrumaco *m* caress.

arsenal *m* arsenal; dockyard.

arsénico *m* arsenic.

arte *m/f* art; skill; artfulness.

artefacto *m* appliance.

arteria *f* artery.

artero/ra *adj* dexterous, cunning, artful.

artesa *f* trough; kneading trough.

artesanía *f* craftsmanship.

artesano *m* artisan, workman.

ártico/ca *adj* arctic; * *m*: el A~ the Arctic.

articulación *f* articulation; joint.

articulado/da *adj* articulated; jointed.

articular *vt* to articulate; to joint.

artículo *m* article; clause; point; (*gr*) article; condition.

artífice *m* artisan; artist.

artificial *adj* artificial.

artificio *m* workmanship, craft; artifice, cunning trick.

artificioso/sa *adj* skillful, ingenious; artful, cunning.
artillería *f* gunnery; artillery.
artillero *m* artillery man.
artimaña *f* trap; cunning.
artista *m* artist; craftsman.
artístico/ca *adj* artistic.
artritis *f* arthritis.
arzobispado *m* archbishopric.
arzobispo *m* archbishop.
as *m* ace.
asa *f* handle; lever.
asado *m* roast meat; barbecue.
asador *m* spit.
asadura *f* offal.
asalariado/da *adj* salaried.
asaltador/a *m/f* assailant.
asaltante *m/f* assailant.
asaltar *vt* to assault; to storm (a position); to assail.
asalto *m* assault, attack; stick-up.
asamblea *f* assembly, meeting.
asar *vt* to roast.
asbesto *m* asbestos.
ascendencia *f* ascendancy; ancestry.
ascendente *adj* ascending; (*rail*) **tren ~** *m* up train.
ascender *vi* to be promoted; to rise; * *vt* to promote.
ascendiente *m* forefather; influence.
Ascensión *f* feast of the Ascension.
ascenso *m* promotion; ascent.
ascensor *m* elevator.
asceta *m* ascetic.
ascético/ca *adj* ascetic.
asco *m* nausea; loathing.
ascua *f* red-hot coal.
aseado/da *adj* clean; elegant; neat.
asear *vt* to clean; to tidy.
asediar *vt* to besiege; to chase.
asedio *m* siege.
asegurado/da *adj* insured.
asegurador *m* insurer.
asegurar *vt* to secure; to insure; to affirm; to bail; ~**se** *vr* to make sure.
asemejarse *vr* to be like, to resemble.
asentado/da *adj* established.
asentar *vt* to sit down; to affirm, to assure; to note; * *vi* to suit.
asentir *vi* to acquiesce, to concede.
aseo *m* cleanliness; neatness; ~**s** *mpl* bathroom facilities *pl*.
aséptico/ca *adj* germ-free.
asequible *adj* attainable; obtainable.
aserción *f* assertion, affirmation.

aserradero *m* sawmill.
aserrar *vt* to saw.
aserrín *m* sawdust.
asertivo/va *adj* affirmative.
asesinar *vt* to assassinate; to murder.
asesinato *m* assassination; murder.
asesino *m* assassin; murderer.
asesor *m* counselor, adviser, consultant.
asesorar *vt* to advise; to act as consultant to; ~**se** *vr* to consult.
asestar *vt* to aim, to point; to strike.
aseverar *vt* to affirm.
asfalto *m* asphalt.
asfixia *f* suffocation.
asfixiar *vt* to suffocate; ~**se** *vr* to suffocate.
así *adv* so, thus, in this manner; like this; therefore; so that; also; ~ **que** so that; therefore; **así, así** so-so; middling.
asidero *m* handle.
asiduidad *f* assiduousness.
asiduo/dua *adj* assiduous.
asiento *m* chair; bench, stool; seat; contract; entry; residence.
asignación *f* assignation; destination.
asignar *vt* to assign, to attribute.
asignatario/a *m/f Lat Am* heir.
asignatura *f* subject; course.
asilado/da *m/f* inmate; refugee.
asilo *m* asylum, refuge; ~ **político** political asylum.
asimilación *f* assimilation.
asimilar *vt* to assimilate.
asimismo *adv* similarly, in the same manner.
asir *vt* to grasp, to seize; to hold, to grip; * *vi* to take root.
asistencia *f* audience; presence; assistance, help.
asistente *m* assistant, helper.
asistir *vi* to be present; to assist; * *vt* to help.
asma *f* asthma.
asmático/ca *adj* asthmatic.
asno *m* ass.
asociación *f* association; partnership.
asociado *m* associate.
asociar *vt* to associate; ~**se** *vr* to associate.
asolar *vt* to destroy; to devastate.
asolear *vt* to expose to the sun; ~**se** *vr* to sunbathe.
asomar *vi* to appear; ~**se** *vr* to appear, to show up.
asombrar *vt* to amaze; to astonish; ~**se** *vr* to be amazed; to get a fright.
asombro *m* dread, terror; astonishment.
asombroso/sa *adj* astonishing, marvelous.

asomo *m* mark, token, indication; conjecture.

asonancia *f* assonance; harmony.

aspa *f* cross; sail.

aspaviento *m* astonishment; fuss.

aspecto *m* appearance; aspect.

aspereza *f* roughness; surliness.

áspero/ra *adj* rough, rugged; craggy, knotty; horrid; harsh, hard; severe, austere; gruff.

asperón *m* grindstone.

aspersión *f* sprinkling; aspersion.

áspid *m* asp.

aspiración *f* breath; pause.

aspirante *m* aspirant, aspirer.

aspirar *vt* to breathe; to aspire; (*gr*) to aspirate.

aspirina *f* aspirin.

asquear *vt* to sicken; * *vi* to be sickening; ~se *vr* to feel disgusted.

asqueroso/sa *adj* disgusting.

asta *f* lance; horn; handle.

astado/da *adj* horned.

asterisco *m* asterisk.

astilla *f* chip (of wood), splinter.

astillero *m* dockyard.

astral *adj* astral.

astringente *adj* astringent.

astro *m* star.

astrología *f* astrology.

astrológico/ca *adj* astrological.

astrólogo/ga *m/f* astrologer.

astronauta *m/f* astronaut.

astronave *f* spaceship.

astronomía *f* astronomy.

astronómico/ca *adj* astronomical.

astrónomo/ma *m/f* astronomer.

astucia *f* cunning, slyness.

astuto/ta *adj* cunning, sly; astute.

asueto *m* time off; vacation, holiday.

asumir *vt* to assume.

Asunción *f* Assumption.

asunto *m* subject, matter; affair, business.

asustar *vt* to frighten; ~se *vr* to be frightened.

atacar *vt* to attack.

atajada *f Lat Am* (*sport*) save.

atajo *m* short cut.

atalaya *f* watchtower.

atañer *vi*: ~ a to concern.

ataque *m* attack.

atar *vt* to tie; to fasten.

atardecer *vi* to get dark; * *m* dusk; evening.

atareado/da *adj* busy.

atascar *vt* to jam; to hinder; ~se *vr* to become bogged down.

atasco *m* traffic jam.

ataúd *m* coffin.

ataviar *vt* to dress up, to trim, to adorn.

atavío *m* dress; ornament; ~s *mpl* finery.

ateísmo *m* atheism.

atemorizar *vt* to frighten; ~se *vr* to get scared.

atenazar *vt* to grip; to torment.

atención *f* attention, heedfulness; civility; observance, consideration.

atender *vi* to be attentive; * *vt* to attend to; to heed, to expect, to wait for; to look at.

atenerse *vr*: ~ a to adhere to.

atentado *m* terrorist attack; transgression, offence.

atentamente *adv* observantly; **le saluda** ~ yours faithfully.

atentar *vt* to attempt; to commit.

atento/ta *adj* attentive; heedful; observing; mindful; polite, courteous, mannerly.

atenuante *adj* extenuating.

atenuar *vt* to diminish; to lessen.

ateo/a *adj*, *m/f* atheist.

aterciopelado/da *adj* velvety.

aterido/da *adj* frozen stiff.

aterirse *vr* to grow stiff with cold.

aterrador/a *adj* frightening.

aterrar *vt* to terrify; ~se *vr* to be terrified.

aterrizaje *m* landing.

aterrizar *vi* to land.

aterrorizar *vt* to frighten, to terrify.

atesorar *vt* to treasure/hoard up (riches).

atestación *f* testimony, evidence.

atestado/da *adj* packed; * *m* affidavit.

atestar *vt* to cram, to stuff; to attest, to witness.

atestiguar *vt* to witness, to attest.

atiborrar *vt* to stuff; ~se *vr* to stuff oneself.

ático *m* attic.

atildar *vt* to punctuate with a tilde; to censure.

atinado/da *adj* wise; correct.

atisbar *vt* to pry into; to examine closely.

atizar *vt* to stir (the fire) with a poker; to stir up.

atlántico/ca *adj* Atlantic; * *m*: **el A**~ the Atlantic.

atlas *m* atlas.

atleta *m/f* athlete.

atlético/ca *adj* athletic.

atletismo *m* athletics.

atmósfera *f* atmosphere.

atmosférico/ca *adj* atmospheric.

atolladero *m* bog; obstacle; impediment.

atollar *vi* to stick; ~se *vr* to get stuck.

atolondramiento *m* stupefaction, consternation.

atolondrar *vt* to stun, to stupefy; ~se *vr* to be stupefied.

atómico/ca *adj* atomic.

atomizador *m* spray.

átomo *m* atom.

atónito/ta *adj* astonished, amazed.

atontado/da *adj* stunned; silly.

atontar *vt* to stun, to stupefy; ~se to grow stupid.

atormentar *vt* to torture; to harass; to torment.

atornillar *vt* to screw on; to screw down.

atosigar *vt* to poison; to harass; to oppress.

atracadero *m* landing-place.

atracador/a *m/f* robber.

atracar *vt* to moor; to rob; ~se *vr*: ~ (de) to stuff oneself (with).

atracción *f* attraction.

atraco *m* stick-up, robbery.

atractivo/va *adj* attractive; magnetic; * *m* charm.

atraer *vt* to attract, to allure.

atragantarse *vr* to stick in the throat, to choke.

atrancar *vt* to bar (a door).

atrapar *vt* to trap; to nab; to deceive.

atrás *adv* backward(s); behind; previously, hacia ~ backward(s); ~ de *Lat Am* behind.

atrasado/da *adj* slow; backward; in arrears.

atrasar *vi* to be slow; * *vt* to postpone; ~ el reloj to put back a watch; ~se *vr* to stay behind, to be late.

atraso *m* backwardness; slowness; delay.

atravesado/da *adj* oblique; cross; perverse; mongrel; degenerate.

atravesar *vt* to cross; to pass over; to pierce; to go through; ~se *vr* to get in the way; to meddle.

atrayente *adj* attractive.

atreverse *vr* to dare, to venture.

atrevido/da *adj* bold, audacious, daring.

atrevimiento *m* boldness, audacity.

atribución *f* attribution, imputation.

atribuir *vt* to attribute, to ascribe; to impute.

atribular *vt* to vex, to afflict.

atributivo/va *adj* attributive.

atributo *m* attribute.

atrición *f* attrition.

atril *m* lectern; music stand.

atrio *m* porch; portico.

atrocidad *f* atrocity.

atrochar *vi* to take a short cut.

atropellado/da *adj* hasty, precipitate.

atropellar *vt* to trample; to run down; to hurry; to insult; ~se *vr* to hurry.

atropello *m* accident; push; outrage.

atuendo *m* attire.

atroz *adj* atrocious, heinous; cruel.

atufar *vt* to vex, to plague; ~se *vr* turn sour; to get mad.

atún *m* tuna.

aturdido/da *adj* hare-brained.

aturdimiento *m* stupefaction; astonishment; dullness.

aturdir *vt* to stun, to confuse; to stupefy.

atusar *vt* to smooth.

audacia *f* audacity, boldness.

audaz *adj* audacious, bold.

audible *adj* audible.

audiencia *f* audience.

audífonos *mpl Lat Am* headphones.

auditivo/va *adj* auditory.

auditor *m* auditor.

auditoría *f* audit.

auditorio *m* audience; auditorium.

auge *m* boom; climax.

augurar *vt* to predict.

augurio *m* omen.

aula *f* lecture room.

aullar *vi* to howl.

aullido/aullo *m* howling.

aumentar *vt* to augment, to increase; to magnify; to put up; * *vi* to increase; to grow larger.

aumento *m* increase; promotion; advancement.

aún *adv* even; ~ así even so.

aun *adv* still; yet.

aunar *vt* to unite, to assemble.

aunque *adv* though, although.

¡aúpa! *excl* come on!

aura *f Lat Am* turkey vulture/buzzard.

áureo/rea *adj* golden, gilt *compd*.

aureola *f* glory; nimbus.

auricular *m* receiver; ~es *mpl* headphones *pl*.

aurora *f* dawn.

auscultar *vt* to sound.

ausencia *f* absence.

ausentarse *vr* to go out.

ausente *adj* absent.

auspicio *m* auspice; prediction; protection.

austeridad *f* austerity.

austero/ra *adj* austere, severe.

austral *adj* southern.

autenticar *vt* to authenticate.

autenticidad *f* authenticity.

auténtico/ca *adj* authentic.
autillo *m* brown owl.
auto *m* judicial sentence; car; edict, ordinance; ~ **de fe** auto-da-fé.
autoadhesivo/va *adj* self-adhesive.
autobiografía *f* autobiography.
autobús *m* bus.
autocar *m* bus.
autocracia *f* autocracy.
autócrata *m* autocrat.
autóctono/na *adj* native.
autodefensa *f* self-defense.
autodeterminación *f* self-determination.
autoedición *f* desktop publishing.
autoescuela *f* driving school.
autoestop, autostop *f* hitchhiking; **hacer** ~ to hitchhike.
autoestopista, autostopista *m/f* hitchhiker.
autógrafo *m* autograph.
autómata *m* automaton.
automático/ca *adj* automatic.
automatización *f* automation.
automedicación *f* self-medication.
automotor *m* diesel train.
automóvil *m* automobile.
automovilismo *m* motoring; motor racing.
automovilista *m/f* motorist, driver.
automovilístico/ca *adj* car *compd.*
autonomía *f* autonomy.
autónomo/ma *adj* autonomous.
autonómico/ca *adj* autonomous.
autopista *f* highway, superhighway, expressway; ~ **de la información** information superhighway; ~ **de peaje** turnpike.
autopsía *f* post mortem, autopsy.
autor/ra *m/f* author; maker; writer.
autoridad *f* authority.
autorización *f* authorization.
autorizar *vt* to authorize.
autorradio *m* car radio.
autorretrato *m* self-portrait.
autoservicio *m* self-service store; self-service restaurant.
autosuficiencia *f* self-sufficiency.
autovía *f* state highway.
auxiliar *vt* to aid, to help, to assist; to attend; * *adj* auxiliary.
auxilio *m* aid, help, assistance.
aval *m* guarantee; guarantor.
avalancha *f* avalanche.
avaluar *vt Lat Am* to value.
avance *m* advance; attack; trailer (for a film).
avanzada *f* (*mil*) vanguard.
avanzar *vt, vi* to advance.

avaricia *f* avarice.
avaricioso/sa *adj* avaricious, covetous.
avaro/ra *adj* miserly; * *m/f* miser.
avasallar *vt* to subdue; to enslave.
ave *f* bird; fowl.
avecinarse *vr* to be on the way.
avellana *f* hazelnut.
avellano *m* hazelnut tree.
ave maría *f* Hail Mary.
avena *f* oats *pl.*
avenencia *f* agreement, bargain; union.
avenida *f* avenue.
avenido/da *adj* agreed.
avenir *vt* to reconcile; ~**se** *vr* to reach a compromise.
aventajado/da *adj* advantageous, profitable; beautiful; excellent.
aventajar *vt* to surpass, to excel.
aventar *vt* to fan; to expel.
aventura *f* adventure; event, incident.
aventurado/da *adj* risky.
aventurar *vt* to venture, to risk.
aventurero/ra *adj* adventurous.
avergonzar *vt* to shame, to abash; ~**se** *vr* to be ashamed.
avería *f* breakdown.
averiado/da *adj* broken down; out of order.
averiarse *vr* to break down.
averiguación *f* discovery; investigation.
averiguar *vt* to inquire into; to investigate, to explore.
aversión *f* aversion, dislike; abhorrence.
avestruz *m* ostrich.
aviación *f* aviation; air force.
aviador/a *m/f* aviator.
avicultura *f* poultry farming.
avidez *f* covetousness.
ávido/da *adj* (*poet*) greedy, covetous.
avieso/sa *adj* irregular, out of the way; mischievous, perverse.
avinagrado/da *adj* sour.
avinagrarse *vr* to go sour.
avío *m* preparation, provision.
avión *m* airplane.
avioneta *f* light aircraft.
avisado/da *adj* prudent, cautious; **mal** ~ ill-advised.
avisar *vt* to inform; to warn; to advise.
aviso *m* notice; warning; hint; *Lat Am* advertisement.
avispa *f* wasp.
avispado/da *adj* lively, brisk; vivacious.
avisparse *vr* to worry.
avispero *m* wasp's nest.
avispón *m* hornet.

avistar *vt* to sight.
avituallar *vt* (*mil*) to supply (with food).
avivar *vt* to quicken, to enliven; to encourage.
avutarda *f* bustard.
axioma *m* axiom, maxim.
¡ay! *oxol* ouoh!; owl ¡~ de mí! alas!, poor me!
aya *f* governess, instructress.
ayer *adv* yesterday.
ayuda *f* help, aid; support; * *m* deputy, assistant.
ayudante *m* (*mil*) adjutant; assistant.
ayudar *vt* to help, to assist; to further.
ayunar *vi* to fast, to abstain from food.
ayuno *m* fasting, abstinence from food.
ayuntamiento *m* town/city hall.
azabache *m* jet.
azada *f* spade; hoe.
azafata *f* air stewardess.
azafrán *m* saffron.
azahar *m* orange/lemon blossom.

azar *m* unforeseen disaster; unexpected accident; fate; **por** ~ by chance; **al** ~ at random.
azaroso/sa *adj* unlucky, ominous; risky.
azogue *m* mercury.
azor *m* goshawk.
azorar *vt* to frighten, to terrify
azotaina *f* drubbing, sound flogging.
azotar *vt* to whip, to lash.
azote *m* whip.
azotea *f* flat roof of a house.
azteca *m/f* Aztec.
azúcar *m/f* sugar.
azucarado/da *adj* sugared; sugary.
azucarar *vt* to sugar, to sweeten.
azucarero *m* sugar bowl.
azucena *f* white lily.
azufre *m* sulfur, brimstone.
azul *adj* blue; ~ celeste sky blue.
azulado/da *adj* azure, bluish.
azulejo *m* tile.
azuzar *vt* to irritate, to stir up.

B

baba *f* dribble, spittle.
babear *vi* to dribble, to drool.
babel *m* bedlam.
babero *m* bib.
babia *f*: estar en ~ to be absent-minded/
dreaming.
baboso/sa *adj* dribbling, drooling.
babucha *f* slipper.
baca *f* (*auto*) roof rack.
bacalao *m* cod.
bache *m* pothole.
bachillerato *m* baccalaureate; a sermon
delivered to a graduating class.
báculo *m* stick.
bagaje *m* baggage.
bagatela *f* trinket, trifle.
bahía *f* bay.
bailador/ra *m/f* dancer.
bailar *vi* to dance.
bailarín/ina *m/f* dancer.
baile *m* dance, ball; ~ de disfraces fancy-
dress ball; ~ de gala prom.
baja *f* fall; casualty.
bajada *f* descent; inclination; slope; ebb.
bajamar *f* low water, low tide.
bajar *vt* to lower, to let down; to lessen; to
humble; to go/come down; to bend
downward(s); * *vi* to descend; to go/come
down; to grow less; ~se *vr* to crouch; to
lessen.
bajeza *f* meanness; lowliness.
bajío *m* shoal, sandbank; lowlands *pl*.
bajo/ja *adj* low; abject, despicable; common;
dull (of colors); deep; humble; * *prep* under, underneath, below; * *adv* softly; quietly; * *m* (*mus*) bass; low place.
bajón *m* fall.
bakalao *m* (*col*) rave music.
bala *f* bullet; lanzamiento de ~ *Lat Am*
shot put.
balacear *vt Lat Am* to shoot.
balacera *f Lat Am* shootout.
baladronada *f* boast, brag; bravado.
balance *m* hesitation; balance sheet; balance; rocking chair; rolling (of a ship).
balancear *vt*, *vi* to balance; to roll; to waver; ~se *vr* to swing.
balancín *m* balance beam; seesaw; balancing pole.
balanza *f* scale; balance.
balar *vi* to bleat.

balaustrada *f* balustrade, banister.
balazo *m* shot.
balbucear *vt*, *vi* to stutter.
balbuciente *adj* stammering, stuttering.
balcón *m* balcony.
baldar *vt* to cripple, to disable.
balde *m* bucket; de ~ *adv* gratis, for nothing; en ~ in vain.
baldío/día *adj* waste; uncultivated.
baldosa *f* floor; tile; paving stone, flagstone.
balear *vt Lat Am* to shoot.
baleo *m Lat Am* shootout.
balido *m* bleating, bleat.
balín *m* buckshot.
balística *f* ballistics *pl*.
ballena *f* whale; whalebone.
ballenato *m* calf of a whale.
ballenero *m* (*mar*) whaler.
ballesta *f* crossbow; a tiro de ~ at a great
distance.
ballestero *m* archer; crossbow-maker.
ballet *m* ballet.
balneario *m* spa; *Lat Am* seaside resort.
balón *m* ball.
baloncesto *m* basketball.
balonmano *m* handball.
balonvolea *m* volleyball.
balsa¹ *f* balsa wood; raft, float.
balsa² *f* pool, pond.
bálsamo *m* balsam, balm.
baluarte *m* bastion; bulwark.
bamba *f* fat; (*bot*) swelling; flabbiness.
bambolear *vi* to reel; ~se *vr* to sway.
bamboleo *m* reeling, staggering.
bambú *m* bamboo.
banana *f* banana; plantain.
banano *m* banana tree.
banasta *f* large basket.
banca *f* bench; banking; ~ electrónica electronic banking.
bancario/ria *adj* bank(ing) *compd*.
bancarrota *f* bankruptcy.
banco *m* bench; work bench; bank.
banda *f* band; sash; ribbon; troop; party;
gang; touchline.
bandada *f* flock; shoal.
bandearse *vr* to move to and fro.
bandeja *f* tray, salver.
bandera *f* banner, standard; flag.
banderilla *f* small decorated dart used at a
bullfight.

26

banderillear *vt* to plant banderillas in a bull's neck/shoulder.
banderillero *m* thrower of banderillas.
banderín *m* small flag, pennant.
bandido *m* bandit, outlaw.
bando *m* faction, party; edict.
bandolera *f* bandoleer.
bandolero *m* bandit.
bandurria *f* bandore (musical instrument resembling a lute).
banquero/ra *m/f* banker.
banqueta *f* three-legged stool; sidewalk.
banquete *m* banquet; formal dinner.
banquillo *m* dock; bench.
bañador *m* swimsuit.
bañar *vt* to bathe; to dip; to coat (with varnish); ~**se** *vr* to bathe; to swim; *Lat Am* to have a shower.
bañera *f* bath(tub).
bañero *m* lifeguard.
bañista *m/f* bather.
baño *m* bath; *Lat Am* shower; dip; bathtub; varnish; coating.
baptista *m/f* Baptist.
bar *m* bar.
baraja *f* pack of cards.
barajar *vt* to shuffle (cards); to jumble up.
baranda *f* rail.
barandilla *f* small balustrade, small railing.
baratijas *fpl* trifles *pl*, toys *pl*; trash, junk.
baratillo *m* secondhand goods *pl*; secondhand shop; bargain sale.
barato/ta *adj* cheap; **de** ~ gratis; * *m* cheapness; bargain sale; money extracted from winning gamblers.
baraúnda *f* noise, hurly-burly.
barba *f* chin; beard; ~ **a** ~ face to face; * *m* actor who impersonates old men.
barbacoa *f* barbecue.
barbaridad *f* barbarity, barbarism; outrage.
barbarie *f* barbarism; savagery.
barbarismo *m* barbarism (form of speech).
bárbaro/ra *adj* barbarous; cruel; rude; rough.
barbecho *m* first plowing, fallow land.
barbería *f* barber shop.
barbero *m* barber.
barbilampiño/ña *adj* clean-shaven; (*fig*) inexperienced.
barbilla *f* (tip of the) chin.
barbo *m* barbel.
barbudo/da *adj* bearded.
barca *f* boat.
barco *m* boat; ship.
barítono *m* (*mus*) baritone.
barman *m* barman.

barniz *m* varnish; glaze.
barnizar *vt* to varnish.
barómetro *m* barometer.
barón *m* baron.
baronesa *f* baroness.
barquero *m* boatman.
barquilla *f* (*mar*) log; basket (of an air balloon).
barquillo *m* wafer; cornet, cone.
barra *m* bar; rod; lever; French loaf; sandbank; **de** ~ **a** ~ from place to place.
barrabasada *f* trick, plot.
barraca *f* hut.
barranco *m* gully, ravine; (*fig*) great difficulty.
barranquismo *m* (*sport*) canyoning.
barrena *f* drill, bit, auger.
barrenar *vt* to drill, to bore; (*fig*) to frustrate.
barrendero *m* sweeper.
barreno *m* large drill; borehole.
barreño *m* tub.
barrer *vt* to sweep; to overwhelm.
barrera *f* barrier; turnpike, claypit.
barriada *f* suburb, area of a city; *Lat Am* shanty town.
barricada *f* barricade.
barrido *m* sweep.
barriga *f* abdomen; belly.
barrigudo/da *adj* pot-bellied.
barril *m* barrel; cask.
barrio *m* area, district.
barrizal *m* claypit.
barro *m* clay, mud.
barroco/ca *adj* baroque.
barrote *m* ironwork (of doors, windows, tables); crosspiece.
barruntar *vt* to guess; to foresee; to conjecture.
barrunto *m* conjecture.
bártulos *mpl* gear, belongings *pl*.
barullo *m* uproar.
basamento *m* base.
basalto *m* basalt.
basar *vt* to base; ~**se** *vr*: ~ **en** to be based on.
basca *f* squeamishness, nausea.
báscula *f* scales *pl*.
base *f* base, basis.
básico/ca *adj* basic.
basílica *f* basilica.
basilisco *m* basilisk.
básquetbol *m* *Lat Am* basketball.
basquetbolista *m/f* *Lat Am* basketball player.
bastante *adj* sufficient, enough; * *adv* quite.

bastar *vi* to be sufficient, to be enough.
bastardo/da *adj, m/f* bastard.
bastidor *m* embroidery frame; ~es *mpl* scenery (on stage).
bastión *m* bastion.
basto/ta *adj* coarse, rude, unpolished.
bastón *m* cane, stick; truncheon; (*fig*) command.
bastonazo *m* beating.
bastos *mpl* clubs *pl* (in cards).
basura *f* garbage, trash, refuse; dung.
basurero *m* garbageman, refuse collector; dunghill.
bata *f* dressing gown; coveralls; laboratory coat.
batacazo *m* noise of a fall.
batalla *f* battle, combat; fight.
batallador/a *adj* battling.
batallar *vi* to battle, to fight; to fence with foils; to waver.
batallón *m* (*mil*) battalion.
batata *f* sweet potato.
bate *m* bat.
batería *m* battery; percussion.
bateristo/sta *m/f Lat Am* drummer.
batida *f* beating (of woodland/moorland); search; chase.
batido/da *adj* shot (of silk); well-trodden (of roads); * *m* batter; ~ **de leche** milk shake.
batidora *f* food mixer; whisk.
batir *vt* to beat; to whisk; to dash; to demolish; to defeat.
batista *f* fine cotton cloth, cambric.
batuta *f* baton.
baúl *m* trunk(of a car), trunk (luggage); (*col*) belly.
bautismal *adj* baptismal.
bautismo *m* baptism.
bautizar *vt* to baptize, to christen.
bautizo *m* baptism.
baya *f* berry.
bayeta *f* cloth.
bayo/ya *adj* bay (color of a horse).
bayoneta *f* bayonet.
bayonetazo *m* thrust with a bayonet.
baza *f* card trick.
bazar *m* bazaar.
bazo *m* spleen.
bazofia *f* refuse; hogwash.
be *m* baa (of sheep).
beatificación *f* beatification.
beatificar *vt* to beatify; to hallow, to sanctify, to make blessed.
beato/ta *adj* happy; blessed; devout; * *m*

lay brother; *m/f* pious person; beatified person.
bebé *m/f* baby.
bebedero *m* drinking trough.
bebedizo *m* (love) potion.
bebedor/ra *m/f* (hard) drinker.
beber *vt* (*vi*) to drink.
bebida *f* drink, beverage.
beca *f* fellowship; grant, bursary, scholarship; sash; hood.
becada *f* woodcock.
becerro *m* yearling calf.
bedel *m* janitor; uniformed employee.
befa *f* jeer, taunt.
befarse *vr:* ~ **de** to mock, to ridicule.
beldad *f* beauty.
belén *m* nativity scene.
bélico/ca *adj* warlike, martial.
belicoso/sa *adj* warlike; aggressive.
beligerante *adj* belligerent.
bellaco/ca *adj* artful; cunning.
belladona *f* (*bot*) deadly nightshade.
belleza *f* beauty.
bello/lla *adj* beautiful; handsome; lovely; fine.
bellota *f* acorn; Adam's apple; pomander.
bemol *m* (*mus*) flat.
bencina *f* benzine.
bendecir *vt* to bless; to consecrate; to praise.
bendición *f* blessing, benediction.
bendito/ta *adj* saintly; blessed; simple; happy.
benedictino/na, benito/ta *adj, m/f* Benedictine.
beneficiado *m* incumbent; beneficiary.
beneficiar *vt* to benefit; to be of benefit to.
beneficiario/ra *m/f* beneficiary.
beneficio *m* benefit, advantage; profit; benefit night.
beneficioso/sa *adj* beneficial.
benéfico/ca *adj* beneficent, kind.
benemérito/ta *adj* worthy, meritorious.
beneplácito *m* consent, approbation.
benevolencia *f* benevolence.
benévolo/la *adj* benevolent, kind-hearted.
benigno/na *adj* benign; kind; mild.
beodo/da *adj* drunk, drunken.
berberecho *m* cockle.
berenjena *f* eggplant.
bergantín *m* (*mar*) brig.
bermejo/ja *adj* red.
berrear *vi* to low, to bellow.
berrido *m* bellowing (of calf).
berrinche *m* anger, rage, tantrum (applied to children).

berro *m* watercress.
berza *f* cabbage.
besamanos *m invar* levee; royal audience.
besamel *f* white sauce.
besar *vt* to kiss; to graze; **~se** *vr* to kiss.
beso *m* kiss; collision of persons/things.
bestia *f* beast, animal; idiot.
bestial *adj* bestial; (*col*) marvelous, great.
bestialidad *f* bestiality.
besugo *m* sea bream.
besuquear *vt* to cover with kisses.
besuqueo *m* repeated kisses *pl*.
betún *m* shoe polish.
bezo *m* thick lip; (*med*) swollen tissue in a wound.
biberón *m* feeding bottle.
Biblia *f* Bible.
bíblico/ca *adj* biblical.
bibliófilo/la *m/f* book-lover, bookworm.
bibliografía *f* bibliography.
bibliográfico/ca *adj* bibliographical.
bibliógrafo/fa *m/f* bibliographer.
biblioteca *f* library.
bibliotecario/ra *m/f* librarian.
bicarbonato *m* bicarbonate.
bicho *m* small animal; bug; **mal ~** villain.
bici *f* (*col*) bike.
bicicleta *f* bicycle; **~ de montaña** mountain bike.
bidé *m* bidet.
bielda *f* pitchfork.
bien *m* good, benefit; profit; **~es** *mpl* goods *pl*, property; wealth; **~es raíces** *mpl* real estate; * *adv* well, right; very; willingly; easily; **~ que** *conj* although; **está ~** he is well.
bienal *adj* biennial.
bienaventuranza *f* blessedness; bliss; happiness; prosperity; **~s** *fpl* the Beatitudes.
bienestar *m* wellbeing.
bienhablado/da *adj* well-spoken.
bienhecho/cha *adj* well-shaped.
bienhechor/ra *m/f* benefactor.
bienio *m* space of two years.
bienvenida *f* welcome.
bifurcación *f* fork.
bigamia *f* bigamy.
bígamo/ma *m/f* bigamist.
bigote *m* mustache; whiskers *pl*.
bigotudo/da *adj* with a big mustache.
bikini *m* bikini.
bilingüe *adj* bilingual.
bilioso/sa *adj* bilious.
bilis *f* bile.
billar *m* billiards *pl*.

billete *m* note, banknote, greenback; ticket; (*rail*) ticket; **~ sencillo** single ticket; **~ de ida y vuelta** return ticket.
billetero *m* billfold, wallet.
billón *m* trillion.
bimensual *adj* twice-monthly.
bimotor *m* twin-engined plane.
binario *m* binary.
binoculares *mpl* binoculars *pl*; opera glasses *pl*.
binóculos *mpl Lat Am* binoculars.
biodegradable *adj* biodegradable.
biodiversity *f* biodiversity.
biografía *f* biography.
biógrafo/fa *m/f* biographer.
biología *f* biology.
biológico/ca *adj* biological.
biólogo/ga *m/f* biologist.
biombo *m* screen.
biopsia *f* biopsy.
bípedo *m* biped.
birlar *vt* to knock down at one blow; (*col*) to pinch.
birreta *f* biretta.
bis *excl* encore.
bisabuela *f* great-grandmother.
bisabuelo *m* great-grandfather.
bisagra *f* hinge.
bisexual *adj* bisexual.
bisexualidad *f* bisexuality.
bisiesto *adj*: **año ~** leap year.
bisnieto/ta *m/f* great-grandson/daughter.
bisoño/na *adj* raw, inexperienced; novice.
bisonte *m* American bison, buffalo.
bistec *m* steak.
bisturí *m* scalpel.
bisutería *f* costume jewelry.
bizarro/rra *adj* brave, gallant; generous.
bizco/ca *adj* cross-eyed.
bizcocho *m* sponge cake; biscuit; ship's biscuit.
bizquear *vi* to squint.
blanco/ca *adj* white; blank; * *m* whiteness; white person; blank, blank space; target (to shoot at).
blancura *f* whiteness.
blandir *vt* to brandish a sword; **~se** *vr* to swing.
blando/da *adj* soft, smooth; mild, gentle; (*col*) cowardly.
blanducho/cha *adj* flabby.
blandura *f* softness; gentleness, mildness.
blanquear *vt* to bleach; to whitewash; to launder (money); * *vi* to show white.
blanquecino/na *adj* whitish.

blanqueo *m* laundering (of money).
blasfemador/ra *m/f* blasphemer.
blasfemar *vi* to blaspheme.
blasfemia *f* blasphemy; verbal insult.
blasfemo/ma *adj* blasphemous; * *m* blasphemer.
blasón *m* heraldry, honor, glory.
blasonar *vt* to emblazon; to praise highly.
bledo *m*: **me importa un** ~ (*col*) I don't give a damn.
blindado/da *adj* armor-plated; bullet-proof.
bloc *m* writing pad.
bloque *m* block.
bloquear *vt* to block; to blockade.
bloqueo *m* blockade.
blusa *f* blouse.
boato *m* ostentation, pompous show.
bobada *f* folly, foolishness.
bobear *vt* to act/talk in a stupid manner.
bobería *f* silliness, foolishness.
bobina *f* bobbin.
bobo/ba *m/f* idiot, fool; clown, funny man; * *adj* stupid, silly.
boca *f* mouth; entrance, opening; mouth of a river; ~ **en** ~ *adv* by word of mouth; **a pedir de** ~ to one's heart's content.
bocacalle *f* entrance to a street.
bocadillo *m* sandwich, roll.
bocado *m* mouthful.
bocal *m* pitcher; mouthpiece of a trumpet.
bocamanga *f* cuff, wristband.
bocanada *f* mouthful (of liquor); gust.
bocazas *m/f invar* loudmouth.
boceto *m* sketch.
bochinche *m Lat Am* (*col*) racket.
bochorno *m* sultry weather, scorching heat; blush.
bochornoso/sa *adj* sultry; shameful.
bocina *f* trumpet; megaphone; car horn.
bocón/ona *m/f Lat Am* (*col*) big mouth.
boda *f* wedding.
bodega *f* wine cellar; warehouse; bar.
bodegón *m* cheap restaurant, diner; still life (in art).
bodoque *m* pellet; lump; (*col*) idiot.
bodorrio *m* quiet wedding.
bofes *mpl* lungs; lights.
bofetada *f* slap (in the face).
bofetón *m* hard slap.
boga *f* fashion; (*rail*) bogie/bogy; rower; rowing; **estar en** ~ to be fashionable.
bogar *vi* to row, to paddle.
bohemio *m/f* Bohemian.
boicot *m* boycott.
boicotear *vt* to boycott.

boina *f* beret.
boj *m* box; boxwood; box tree.
bola *f* ball; marble; globe; slam (in cards); shoe polish; (*col*) lie, fib.
bolazo *m* blow with a ball.
bolchevique *adj* Bolshevik.
bolear *vi* to knock balls about (billiards); * *vt* to throw (a ball).
bolera *f* bowling alley.
bolero *m* bolero jacket; bolero dance.
boleta *f* entrance ticket; pass, permit.
boletería *f Lat Am* ticket office.
boletín *m* bulletin; journal, review.
boleto *m Lat Am* ticket.
boli *m* (*col*) (ballpoint) pen.
boliche *m* jack (at bowls); bowls, bowling alley; dragnet.
bolígrafo *m* (ballpoint) pen.
bolillo *m* bobbin.
bollo *m* bread roll; lump.
bolo *m* ninepin; (large) pill.
bolsa *f* purse, handbag; bag; pocket; sac; stock exchange; ~ **de dormir** *Lat Am* sleeping bag.
bolsillo *m* pocket; purse.
bolsista *m/f* stockbroker.
bolso *m* purse.
bomba *f* pump; bomb; surprise; **dar a la** ~ to pump; ~ **de gasolina** gas pump.
bombardear *vt* to bombard.
bombardeo *m* bombardment.
bombardero *m* bomber.
bombazo *m* explosion; bombshell.
bombero *m* firefighter, fireman
bombilla *f* light bulb.
bombín *m* derby.
bombo *m* large drum.
bombón *m* candy; chocolate.
bonachón/ona *adj* good-natured.
bonanza *f* fair weather (at sea); prosperity; bonanza.
bondad *f* goodness, kindness; courtesy.
bondadoso/sa *adj* good, kind.
bonete *m* clerical hat; college cap.
bonito *adj* pretty, nice-looking; pretty good, passable; * *m* tuna (fish).
bono *m* bond (financial).
boñiga *f* cow pat.
bonsái *m* bonsai.
boqueada *f* act of opening the mouth; **la última** ~ the last gasp.
boquear *vi* to gape;, to gasp; to breathe one's last; * *vt* to pronounce, to utter (a word).
boquerón *m* anchovy; large hole.
boquete *m* gap, narrow entrance.

boquiabierto/ta *adj* open-mouthed; gaping.
boquilla *f* mouthpiece of a musical instrument; nozzle.
borbollón, borbotón *m* bubbling; **salir a borbollones** to gush forth.
borda *f* (*mar*) gunwale/gunnel; hut.
bordado *m* embroidery.
bordadora *f* embroiderer.
bordar *vt* to embroider; to do anything very well.
borde *m* border; margin; (*mar*) board.
bordear *vi* (*mar*) to tack; * *vt* to go along the edge of; to flank.
bordillo *m* curb.
bordo *m* (*mar*) board; **a ~** on board (a ship).
boreal *adj* boreal, northern.
borgoña *m* burgundy wine.
borla *f* tassel; tuft.
borona *f* maize; corn; corn bread.
borrachera *f* drunkenness; hard drinking; spree.
borracho/cha *adj* drunk, intoxicated; blind with passion; * *m/f* drunk, drunkard.
borrador *m* first draft; scribbling pad; eraser.
borraja *f* (*bot*) borage.
borrar *vt* to erase, to rub out; to blur; to obscure.
borrasca *f* storm; violent squall of wind; hazard; danger.
borrascoso/sa *adj* stormy.
borrego/ga *m/f* yearling lamb; simpleton, blockhead.
borrico/ca *m/f* donkey, ass; blockhead.
borrón *m* blot, blur; rough draft of a writing; first sketch of a painting; stain, blemish.
borronear *vt* to sketch.
boscaje *m* grove, small wood; landscape (in painting).
bosque *m* forest; wood.
bosquejar *vt* to make a sketch of (a painting); to make a rough model of (a figure).
bosquejo *m* sketch (of a painting); unfinished work.
bostezar *vi* to yawn; to gape.
bostezo *m* yawn; yawning.
bota *f* leather wine-bag; boot.
botánica *f* botany.
botánico/ca *adj* botanic; * *m/f* botanist.
botanista *m/f* botanist.
botar *vt* to cast, to fling; to launch.
bote *m* bounce; thrust; tin, can; boat.
botella *f* bottle.
botica *f* drugstore.

boticario/ria *m/f* pharmacist.
botijo *m* earthenware jug.
botín *m* high boot, half-boot; gaiter; booty.
botiquín *m* medicine chest.
botón *m* button; knob (of a radio etc); (*bot*) bud.
botonadura *f* set of buttons.
botones *m invar* bellhop, bellboy.
bóveda *f* arch; vault, crypt.
box *m Lat Am* boxing.
boxeador *m* boxer.
boxeo *m* boxing.
boya *f* (*mar*) buoy.
boyante *adj* buoyant, floating; (*fig*) fortunate, successful.
bozal *m* muzzle.
bozo *m* down (on the upper lip/chin); headstall, head collar (of a horse).
braceada *f* violent movement of the arms.
bracear *vi* to swing the arms.
bracero *m* day-laborer; farmhand.
braga *f* sling, rope; diaper; **~s** *fpl* pants *pl*.
bragazas *m invar* henpecked husband.
braguero *m* truss.
bragueta *f* fly, flies *pl* (of trousers).
braille *m* Braille.
bramante *m* twine, string.
bramar *vi* to roar, to bellow; to storm, to bluster.
bramido *m* roar, bellow, howl.
brasa *f* live coal; **estar hecho una ~** to be very flushed.
brasero *m* brazier.
bravamente *adv* bravely, gallantly; fiercely; roughly; extremely well.
bravío/vía *adj* ferocious, savage, wild; coarse; * *m* fierceness, savageness.
bravo/va *adj* brave, valiant; bullying; savage, fierce; rough; sumptuous; excellent, fine; * *excl* well done!
bravura *f* ferocity; courage.
braza *f* fathom.
brazada *f* extension of the arms; armful.
brazado *m* armful.
brazal *m* armband; irrigation channel.
brazalete *m* bracelet.
brazo *m* arm; branch (of a tree); enterprise; courage; **luchar a ~ partido** to fight hand to hand.
brea *f* pitch; tar.
brear *vt* to pitch; to tar; to abuse; to illtreat; to play a joke on.
brebaje *m* potion.
brecha *f* (*mil*) breach; gap, opening; **batir en ~** (*mil*) to make a breach.

bregar *vi* to struggle; to quarrel; to slog away.
breva *f* early fig; early large acorn.
breve *m* papal brief; * *f* (*mus*) breve; * *adj* brief, short; **en ~** shortly.
brevedad *f* brevity, shortness, conciseness.
breviario *m* breviary; (*fig*) daily reading.
brezo *m* (*bot*) heather.
bribón/ona *adj* dishonest, rascally.
bribonear *vi* to be idle; to play dirty tricks.
bricolaje *m* home improvement.
brida *f* bridle; clamp, flange.
bridge *m* bridge (card game).
brigada *f* brigade; squad, gang.
brigadier *m* brigadier.
brillante *adj* brilliant; bright, shining; * *m* diamond.
brillar *vi* to shine; to sparkle, to glisten; to shine, to be outstanding.
brillo *m* brilliance, brightness.
brincar *vi* to skip; to leap, to jump; to gambol; to fly into a passion.
brinco *m* leap, jump; bounce.
brindar *vi*: ~ **a la salud de/~ por** to drink the health of, to toast; * *vt* to offer, to present.
brindis *m invar* toast.
brío *m* spirit, dash.
briosamente *adv* spiritedly, dashingly.
brioso/sa *adj* dashing, full of spirit; lively.
brisa *f* breeze.
brisca *f* card game.
broca *f* reel; drill; shoemaker's tack (nail).
brocado *m* gold/silver brocade; ~/**da** *adj* embroidered; like brocade.
brocal *m* rim, mouth; curb.
brocha *f* large brush; ~ **de afeitar** shaving brush.
brochada *f* brushstroke.
broche *m* clasp; brooch; cufflink.
broma *f* joke.
bromear *vi* to joke.
bromista *m/f* joker.
bronca *f* row.
bronce *m* bronze.
bronceado/da *adj* tanned; * *m* bronzing, suntan.
broncearse *vr* to get a suntan.
bronco/ca *adj* rough, coarse; rude; harsh.
bronquitis *f* bronchitis.
broquel *m* shield.
brotar *vi* (*bot*) to bud, to germinate; to gush, to rush out; (*med*) to break out.
brote *m* (*bot*) shoot; (*med*) outbreak.
bruces *adv*: **de ~** face downward(s).
bruja *f* witch.

brujería *f* witchcraft.
brujo *m* sorcerer, magician, wizard.
brújula *f* compass.
bruma *f* mist; (*mar*) sea mist.
brumoso/sa *adj* misty.
bruñido *m* polish.
bruñir *vt* to polish; to put rouge on.
brusco/ca *adj* rude; sudden; brusque.
brutal *adj* brutal, brutish.
brutalidad *f* brutality; brutal action.
bruto *m* brute, beast; ~/**ta** *adj* stupid; gross; brutish.
buba *f* tumor.
bucal *adj* oral.
bucear *vi* to dive.
buceo *m* diving.
bucle *m* curl.
bucólica *f* pastoral poetry; (*col*) food.
buche *m* craw, maw; (*col*) guts *pl*; mouthful; crease (in clothes).
budismo *m* Buddhism.
buen *adj* (before **m** nouns) good.
buenamente *adv* easily; willingly.
buenaventura *f* fortune, good luck.
bueno/na *adj* good, perfect; fair; fit, proper; good-looking; **¡buenos días!** good morning!; **¡buenas tardes!** good afternoon!; **¡buenas noches!** good night!; **¡~!** right!
buey *m* ox, bullock.
bufa *f* joke, mock.
búfalo *m* buffalo.
bufanda *f* scarf.
bufar *vi* to choke with anger; to snort.
bufete *m* desk, writing-table; lawyer's office.
bufido *m* snorting (of an animal).
bufo/fa *adj* comic; **ópera ~a** *f* comic opera.
bufón *m* buffoon; jester; ~/**ona** *adj* funny, comical.
bufonada *f* buffoonery; joke.
buhardilla *f* attic.
búho *m* owl; unsociable person.
buhonero *m* hawker, peddler.
buitre *m* vulture.
bujía *f* candle; spark plug.
bula *f* papal bull.
bulbo *m* (*bot*) bulb.
bulboso/sa *adj* bulbous.
bulevar *m* boulevard.
bulla *f* confused noise, clatter; crowd; **meter ~** to make a noise.
bullicio *m* bustle; uproar.
bullicioso/sa *adj* lively, restless, noisy, busy; turbulent; boisterous.
bulto *m* bulk; tumor, swelling; bust; baggage.
buñuelo *m* donut/doughnut; fritter.

buque *m* vessel, ship, tonnage, capacity (of a ship); hull (of a ship).
burbuja *f* bubble.
burbujear *vi* to bubble.
burdel *m* brothel.
burdo/da *adj* coarse, rough.
burgués/esa *adj* bourgeois.
burguesía *f* bourgeoisie.
buril *m* engraver's chisel.
burla *f* trick; gibe; joke; **de ~s** in fun.
burlar *vt* to hoax; to defeat; to play tricks on, to deceive; to frustrate; **~se** *vr* to joke, to laugh at.
burlesco/ca *adj* burlesque; comical, funny.
burlón/ona *m/f* joker.
burocracia *f* bureaucracy.
burócrata *m/f* bureaucrat.

burrada *f* drove of asses; stupid action.
burro *m* ass, donkey; idiot; saw-horse.
bursátil *adj* stock exchange *compd*.
bus *m* bus.
busca *f* search, hunt; bleeper.
buscapiés *m invar* jumping jack (fireworks).
buscar *vt* to seek, to search for; to look for; to hunt after; * *vi* to look, to search, to seek
buscavidas *m* prying person, busybody.
buscón *m* petty thief, small-time crook.
búsqueda *f* search.
busto *m* bust.
butaca *f* armchair; seat.
butano *m* butane.
butifarra *f* Catalan sausage.
buzo *m* diver.
buzón *m* mailbox; conduit, canal; cover of a jar.

C

cabal *adj* just, exact; right; complete; accomplished.
cábalas *fpl* intrigue.
cabalgada *f* cavalcade; (*mil*) cavalry raid.
cabalgadura *f* mount, horse; beast of burden.
cabalgar *vi* to ride, to go riding.
cabalgata *f* procession.
cabalístico/ca *adj* cabalistic.
caballa *f* mackerel.
caballar *adj* equine.
caballería *f* mount, steed; cavalry; cavalry horse; chivalry; knighthood.
caballeriza *f* stable; stud; stablemen, stableboys *pl*.
caballerizo *m* groom.
caballero *m* knight; gentleman; rider, horseman; horse soldier; ~ **andante** knight errant.
caballerosidad *f* chivalry.
caballeroso/sa *adj* noble; gentlemanlike.
caballete *m* ridge of a roof; painter's easel; trestle; bridge (of the nose).
caballo *m* horse; ~ **de carreras** racehorse; knight (at chess); queen (in cards); **a** ~ **on** horseback.
cabaña *f* hut, cabin; hovel; livestock; balk (in billiards).
cabaré *m* cabaret.
cabecear *vi* to nod (with sleep); to shake one's head; (*mar*) to pitch.
cabeceo *m* nod; shaking (of the head).
cabecera *f* headboard; head; far end; pillow; headline; vignette.
cabecilla *m* ringleader.
cabellera *f* head of hair; wig; tail of a comet.
cabello *m* hair.
cabelludo/da *adj* hairy, shaggy.
caber *vi* to fit.
cabestrillo *m* sling.
cabestro *m* halter; leading/bell ox.
cabeza *f* head; chief, leader; main town, chief center.
cabezada *f* butt; nod/shake of the head.
cabezal *m* pillow; compress.
cabezón *m* collar (of a shirt); opening in a garment for the head.
cabezudo/da *adj* big-headed; pig-headed.
cabida *f* room, capacity; **tener** ~ **con una persona** to have influence with someone.
cabildo *m* chapter (of a church); meeting of a chapter; corporation of a town.

cabina *f* cabin; telephone booth.
cabizbajo/ja, cabizcaído/da *adj* crestfallen; pensive, thoughtful.
cable *m* cable, lead, wire.
cabo *m* end, extremity; cape, headland; (*mar*) cable, rope.
cabra *f* goat.
cabrero *m* goatherd.
cabrío/a *adj* goatish.
cabriola *f* caper; gambol.
cabritilla *f* kidskin.
cabrito *m* kid.
cabrón *m* cuckold; ¡~! (*col*) bastard!
cacahuete *m* peanut.
cacao *m* (*bot*) cacao tree; cocoa.
cacarear *vi* to crow; to brag, to boast.
cacareo *m* crowing of a cock, cackling of a hen; boast, brag.
cacería *f* hunting-party.
cacerola *f* pan, saucepan; casserole.
cachalote *m* sperm whale.
cacharro *m* pot; piece of junk.
cachear *vt* to frisk.
cachemir *m* cashmere.
cacheo *m* frisking.
cachete *m* cheek; slap in the face.
cachimbo *m Lat Am* pipe.
cachiporra *f* club, truncheon.
cachivache *m* pot; piece of junk.
cacho *m* crumb, bit, small slice, piece; horn (of an animal).
cachondeo *m* (*col*) farce.
cachondo/da *adj* randy; funny.
cachorro/ra *m/f* puppy; cub (of any animal).
cacique *m* chief; local party boss.
caco *m* pickpocket; coward.
cacofonía *f* cacophony.
cacto/cactus *m* cactus.
cada *adj invar* each; every.
cadalso *m* scaffold.
cadáver *m* corpse, cadaver.
cadavérico/ca *adj* cadaverous.
cadena *f* chain; series, link; radio/TV network.
cadencia *f* cadence.
cadente *adj* harmonious.
cadera *f* hip.
cadete *m* (*mil*) cadet.
caducar *vi* to become senile; to expire, to lapse; to deteriorate.

caducidad *f* expiry.
caduco/ca *adj* worn out; decrepit; perishable; expired, lapsed.
caer *vi* to fall; to tumble down; to lapse; to happen; to die; ~se *vr* to fall down.
café *m* coffee; coffee bar/shop.
cafetera *f* coffee pot.
cafetería *f* coffee shop/bar; small restaurant.
cafetero/ra *m/f* coffee merchant; coffee bar/shop owner.
cafre *adj* savage, inhuman; rude.
cagar *vi* (*col*) to have a shit.
caída *f* fall, falling; slope, descent.
caimán *m* cayman/caiman, alligator.
caja *f* box, case; casket; cashbox; cash desk; check-out, till; ~ de ahorros savings bank; ~ de cambios gearbox; ~ negra black box.
cajero/ra *m/f* cashier, teller.
cajero automático *m* cash dispenser, cash machine, cash point, automated teller machine (ATM).
cajetilla *f* packet.
cajón *m* chest of drawers; locker.
cal *f* lime; ~ viva quick lime.
cala *f* creek, small bay; small piece of melon etc; (*mar*) hold; dipstick.
calabacín *m* small marrow, courgette.
calabaza *f* pumpkin, squash.
calabozo *m* prison; cell.
calada *f* soaking; lowering of nets; puff, drag; swoop.
calado *m* openwork in metal/wood/linen.
calafatear *vt* (*mar*) to caulk.
calamar *m* squid.
calambre *m* cramp.
calamidad *f* calamity, disaster.
calamitoso/sa *adj* calamitous.
calaña *f* model; pattern.
calandria *f* lark.
calar *vt* to soak, to drench; to penetrate, to pierce; to see through; to lower; ~se *vr* to stall (of a car).
calavera *f* skull; madcap.
calaverada *f* ridiculous/foolish action.
calcañar *m* heel.
calcar *vt* to trace, to copy.
calcáreo/rea *adj* chalky, calcareous.
calceta *f* (knee-length) stocking.
calcetín *m* sock.
calcio *m* calcium.
calco *m* tracing.
calcomanía *f* transfer.
calculable *adj* calculable.
calculadora *f* calculator.

calcular *vt* to calculate, to reckon; to compute.
cálculo *m* calculation, estimate; calculus; (*med*) gallstone.
caldear *vt* to weld; to warm, to heat up.
caldera *f* kettle, boiler; las ~s de Pero Botero (*col*) hell.
calderada *f* stew.
calderilla *f* holy-water vessel; small change.
caldero *m* small boiler.
caldo *m* stock; broth.
caldoso/sa *adj* having too much broth/gravy.
calefacción *f* heating.
calendario *m* calendar.
calentador *m* heater.
calentamiento global *m* global warming.
calentar *vt* to warm up, to heat up; ~se *vr* to grow hot; to dispute.
calentura *f* fever.
calenturiento/ta *adj* feverish.
calesa *f* buggy, chaise.
calibre *m* calibre; (*fig*) calibre.
calidad *f* grade, quality, condition; kind.
cálido/da *adj* hot; (*fig*) warm.
caliente *adj* hot; fiery; en ~ in the heat of the moment.
califa *m* caliph.
califato *m* caliphate.
calificación *f* qualification; grade.
calificar *vt* to qualify; to assess, to mark; ~se *vr* to register as a voter.
caligrafía *f* calligraphy.
cáliz *m* chalice.
caliza *f* limestone.
calizo/za *adj* limy (of ground).
callado/da *adj* silent, quiet.
callandico *adv* softly, silently.
callar *vi*, ~se *vr* to be silent, to keep quiet.
calle *f* street; road.
calleja *f* lane, narrow passage.
callejear *vi* to loiter about the streets.
callejero/ra *adj* loitering.
callejón *m* alley.
callejuela *f* lane, narrow passage; subterfuge.
callista *m/f* chiropodist, podiatrist.
callo *m* corn; callus; ~s *mpl* tripe.
callosidad *f* hard patch, callosity.
calloso/sa *adj* callous; horny.
calma *f* calm, calmness.
calmante *m* (*med*) sedative.
calmar *vt* to calm, to quiet, to pacify; * *vi* to become calm.
calmoso/sa *adj* calm; tranquil.

calor *m* heat, warmth; ardor, passion.
caloría *f* calorie.
calumnia *f* calumny, slander.
calumniar *vt* to slander.
calumnioso/sa *adj* slanderous.
caluroso/sa *adj* warm; hot; lively.
calva *f* bald patch.
calvario *m* Calvary; (*fig*) debts *pl*.
calvicie *f* baldness.
calvinismo *m* Calvinism.
calvinista *m/f* Calvinist.
calvo/va *adj* bald; bare, barren.
calza *f* wedge.
calzado *m* footwear.
calzador *m* shoehorn.
calzar *vt* to put on (shoes); to wear (shoes); to stop (a wheel); ~se *vr* to put on one's shoes.
calzón *m* shorts *pl*; pants *pl*; panties *pl*.
calzonazos *m invar* stupid guy; **es un** ~ he is a weak-willed guy.
calzoncillos *mpl* underpants *pl*, shorts *pl*.
calzonudo *m Lat Am* stupid guy; **es un** ~ he is a weak-willed guy.
cama *f* bed; **hacer la** ~ to make the bed.
camada *f* litter (of animals); ~ **de ladrones** gang of thieves.
camafeo *m* cameo.
camaleón *m* chameleon.
camalote *m Lat Am* water hyacinth.
camandulero/ra *adj* prudish; hypocritical; sly, tricky.
cámara *f* hall; chamber; room; camera; cine camera.
camarada *m/f* comrade, companion.
camarera *f* waitress; maid; *Lat Am* air stewardess.
camarero *m* waiter; *Lat Am* air steward.
camarilla *f* clique; lobby.
camarín *m* dressing room; elevator car.
camarón *m* shrimp, prawn.
camarote *m* berth, cabin.
cambalache *m* exchange, swap.
cambalachear *vt* to exchange, to swap.
cambiable *adj* changeable, variable; interchangeable.
cambiar *vt* to exchange; to change; * *vi* to change, to alter; ~se *vr* to move house.
cambio *m* change, exchange; rate of exchange; bureau de change.
cambista *m/f* exchange broker.
camelar *vt* to flirt with.
camello *m* camel.
camilla *f* couch; cot; stretcher.
caminante *m/f* traveler; walker.

caminar *vi* to travel; to walk, to go.
caminata *f* long walk; hike.
camino *m* road; trail, way.
camión *m* truck.
camioneta *f* light truck, van.
camisa *f* shirt; chemise.
camiseta *f* T-shirt; undershirt.
camisón *m* nightgown.
camorra *f* quarrel, dispute.
camorrista *m/f* quarrelsome person.
campamento *m* (*mil*) encampment, camp.
campana *f* bell.
campaña *f* countryside; level country, plain; (*mil*) campaign.
campanada *f* peal of a bell; (*fig*) scandal.
campanario *m* belfry.
campaneo *m* bellringing, chime.
campanero *m* bell founder; bellringer.
campanilla *f* handbell; (*med*) uvula.
campante *adj* outstanding; smug.
campánula *f* bellflower.
campear *vi* to go out to pasture; to work in the fields.
campechano/na *adj* open.
campeón/ona *m/f* champion.
campeonato *m* championship.
campesino/na, campestre *adj* rural.
campiña *f* flat tract of cultivated farmland.
camping *m* camping, campsite.
campista *m/f* camper.
campo *m* country; countryside, field; camp; ground; pitch; scope, range; ~ **de refugiados** refugee camp; ~ **abierto** range, open countryside.
campus *m invar* campus.
camuflaje *m* camouflage.
caña *f* cane, reed; stalk; shinbone; glass of beer; ~ **dulce** sugar cane.
canal *m* channel; canal.
canalla *f* mob, rabble.
canalón *m* large gutter.
cáñamo *m* hemp.
cañamón *m* hemp seed.
canana *f* cartridge belt.
canapé *f* couch, sofa.
canario *m* canary.
canas *fpl* gray hair; **peinar** ~ to grow old.
canasta *f* basket, hamper.
canastilla *f* small basket.
canasto *m* large basket.
cañaveral *m* reedbed.
cancel *m* storm door.
cancelación *f* cancellation.
cancelar *vt* to cancel; to write off.
Cáncer *m* Cancer (zodiac sign).

cáncer m cancer.
canceriano/na adj Lat Am Cancerian.
cancerígeno/na adj carcinogenic.
canceroso/sa adj cancerous.
cancha f (sport) court, Lat Am course, Lat Am pitch.
canciller m chancellor; foreign minister.
canción f song.
cancionero m songbook.
candado m padlock.
candela f candle.
candelabro m candlestick.
candente adj red-hot.
candidato/ta m/f candidate.
cándido/da adj simple, naive; white, snowy.
candil m oil lamp.
candilejas fpl footlights pl.
candor m candor; innocence.
canela f cinnamon.
canelón m icicle.
cañería f water conduit, water pipe.
cangrejo m crab, crawfish.
canguro m kangaroo, ˈ f baby-sitter.
caníbal m/f cannibal, man-eater.
canica f marble.
canícula f dog days pl.
canijo/ja adj weak, sickly.
canilla f shinbone; arm-bone; tap of a cask; spool.
canillera f Lat Am(sport) shin pad.
canino/na adj canine; **hambre ~a** f ravenous hunger.
canje m exchange.
canjear vt to exchange.
caño m tube, pipe; sewer.
cano/na adj gray-haired; white-haired.
canoa f canoe.
canon m canon; tax; royalty; rent.
cañón m tube, pipe; barrel; gun; canyon.
cañonazo m gunshot; (fig) bombshell.
cañonear vt to shell, to bombard.
cañoneo m shelling, gunfire.
cañonera f gunboat.
canónico/ca adj canonical.
canónigo m canon, prebendary.
canonización f canonization.
canonizar vt to canonize.
canoso/sa adj gray-haired; white-haired.
cansado/da adj weary, tired; tedious, tiresome.
cansancio m tiredness, fatigue.
cansar vt to tire, to tire out; to bore; **~se** vr to get tired, to grow weary.
cantable adj suitable for singing.
cantante m/f singer.

cantar m song; * vt to sing; to chant; * vi to sing; to chirp.
cántara f large jug, pitcher.
cantarín/ina m/f someone who sings a lot.
cántaro m pitcher; jug; **llover a ~s** to rain heavily, to pour.
cantera f quarry.
cantero m quarryman.
cántico m canticle.
cantidad f quantity, amount; number.
cantimplora f water bottle; hip flask.
cantina f (rail) restaurant car; canteen; wine cellar.
cantinela f ballad, song.
canto m stone; singing; song; edge.
cantón m corner; canton.
cantonear vi to loaf around.
cantor/ra m/f singer.
canuto m (col) joint, marijuana cigarette.
caoba f mahogany.
caos m chaos; confusion.
capa f cloak; cape; layer, stratum; cover; **pretext, ~ de ozono** ozone layer.
capacho m hamper; big basket.
capacidad f capacity; extent; talent.
capar vt to geld; to castrate; (fig) to curtail.
caparazón m caparison.
capataz m foreman, overseer.
capaz adj capable; capacious, spacious, roomy.
capazo m large basket; carrycot.
capcionar vt to seize, to arrest.
capcioso/sa adj wily, deceitful.
capear vt to flourish (one's cloak in front of a bull); * vi (mar) to ride out/weather (a storm).
capellán m chaplain.
capeo m challenging of a bull with a cloak.
caperuza f hood.
capilar adj capillary.
capilla f hood, cowl; chapel.
capirote m hood.
capital m capital; capital sum; * f capital, capital city; * adj capital; principal.
capitalismo m capitalism.
capitalista m/f capitalist.
capitalizar vt to capitalize.
capitán m captain.
capitana f flagship; (sport) female captain.
capitanear vt to captain; to command.
capitanía f captaincy.
capitel m capital (of a column).
capitolio m capitol; imposing building.
capitulación f capitulation; agreement; **~ones** fpl marriage contract.

capitular *vi* to come to terms, to make an agreement.

capítulo *m* chapter (of a cathedral); chapter (of a book).

capó *m* (*auto*) hood.

capón *m* capon.

caporal *m* chief, ringleader.

capota *f* hat, bonnet; (*auto*) hood.

capote *m* greatcoat; bullfighter's cloak.

capricho *m* caprice, whim, fancy.

caprichoso/sa *adj* capricious, whimsical; obstinate.

capricorniano/na *adj Lat Am* Capricornean (zodiac sign).

Capricornio *m* Capricorn (zodiac sign).

cápsula *f* capsule.

captar *vt* to captivate; to understand; (*rad*) to tune in to, to receive.

captura *f* capture, arrest.

capturar *vt* to capture.

capucha *f* circumflex (accent); cap, cowl, hood of a cloak.

capuchino *m* Capuchin monk; (**café**) ~ cappuccino (coffee).

capullo *m* cocoon of a silkworm; rosebud; coarse cloth made of spun silk.

caqui *adj*, *m* khaki.

cara *f* face; appearance; ~ **a** ~ face to face.

carabina *f* carbine, rifle.

carabinero *m* carabineer.

caracol *m* snail; seashell; spiral.

caracola *f* shell.

caracolear *vi* to prance about (of a horse).

carácter *m* character; quality; condition; handwriting.

característico/ca *adj* characteristic.

caracterizar *vt* to characterize.

caradura *m/f*: **es un** ~ he's got a nerve.

caramba *excl* well!

carámbano *m* icicle.

carambola *f* cannon (at billiards); trick.

caramelo *m* caramel (candy).

caramente *adv* dearly.

caramillo *m* small flute; piece of gossip.

carantoña *f* hideous mask; dressed-up old woman; ~**s** *fpl* caresses *pl*.

carátula *f* pasteboard mask; **la** ~ the stage.

caravana *f* group of wagons/camels/pack mules etc traveling in single file ; tailback (of traffic); trailer.

caray *excl* well!

carbón *m* coal; carbon; carbon paper.

carbonada *f* grill; kind of pancake.

carboncillo *m* charcoal.

carbonera *f* coal tip; coal mine.

carbonería *f* coalyard.

carbonero *m* someone who sells coal; (*mar*) coal ship.

carbónico/ca *adj* carbonic.

carbonilla *f* coaldust.

carbonizar *vt* to carbonize.

carbono *m* (*chem*) carbon.

carbunclo, carbunco *m* carbuncle.

carburador *m* carburetor.

carcaj *m* quiver.

carcajada *f* (loud) laugh.

carcamal *m* nickname for an old person.

cárcel *f* prison; jail.

carcelero *m* warder, jailer.

carcoma *f* deathwatch beetle; woodworm; anxious concern.

carcomer *vt* to gnaw, to corrode; ~**se** *vr* to get worm-eaten.

carcomido/da *adj* worm-eaten.

cardar *vt* to card (wool).

cardenal *m* cardinal; cardinal bird; (*med*) bruise, weal.

cardenalicio/cia *adj* belonging to a cardinal.

cárdeno/na *adj* purple; livid.

cardíaco/ca, cardiaco/ca *adj* cardiac; * heart *compd*.

cardinal *adj* cardinal, principal.

cardo *m* thistle.

carear *vt* to bring face to face; to compare; ~**se** *vr* to come face to face.

carecer *vi*: ~ **de** to want, to lack.

carencia *f* lack.

careo *m* confrontation.

carero/ra *adj* pricey.

carestía *f* scarcity, want; famine.

careta *f* pasteboard mask.

carga *f* load; freight, cargo; (*mil*) charge; duty, obligation; tax.

cargadero *m* loading place.

cargado/da *adj* loaded; live (electricity).

cargador *m* loader; carrier; longshoreman.

cargamento *m* cargo.

cargar *vt* to load, to burden; to charge; * *vi* to charge; to load (up); to lean.

cargo *m* burden, loading; employment, post; office; charge, care; obligation; accusation.

carguero *m* freighter.

cariarse *vr* to decay.

caricato *m Lat Am* caricature.

caricatura *f* caricature.

caricia *f* caress.

caridad *f* charity.

caries *f* (*med*) tooth decay, caries.

carilargo/ga *adj* long-faced.

carilla *f* side (of paper); beekeeper's mask.
cariño *m* fondness, tenderness; love.
cariñoso/sa *adj* affectionate; loving.
caritativo/va *adj* charitable.
cariz *m* look.
carmelita *adj*, *m/f* Carmelite.
carmesí *adj*, *m* crimson.
carmín *m* carmine; rouge; lipstick.
carnada *f* bait, lure.
carnal *adj* carnal, of the flesh; **primo ~** first cousin.
carnaval *m* carnival.
carn *f* flesh; meat; pulp (of fruit).
carné, carnet *m* driving license; **~ de identidad** identity card.
carnero *m* sheep; mutton.
carnicería *f* butcher's shop; carnage, slaughter.
carnicero/ra *m/f* butcher; * *adj* carnivorous.
carnívoro/ra *adj* carnivorous.
carnoso/sa, carnudo/da *adj* beefy, fat; fleshy.
caro/ra *adj* dear; affectionate; dear, expensive; * *adv* dearly.
carótida *f* carotid artery.
carpa *f* carp (fish); *Lat Am* tent.
carpeta *f* table cover; folder, file, portfolio.
carpintería *f* carpentry; carpenter's premises.
carpintero *m* carpenter.
carraca *f* carrack (ship); rattle.
carrasca *f* kermes oak tree.
carraspera *f* hoarseness.
carrera *f* career; course; race; run, running; route; journey; **a ~ abierta** at full speed.
carreta *f* long narrow cart.
carrete *m* reel, spool, bobbin.
carretera *f* road; **~ de circunvalación** belt, beltway, ring road.
carretero *m* carter, cartwright.
carretilla *f* carter; truck; trolley; go-cart; squib, cracker; wheelbarrow.
carretón *m* small cart.
carril *m* lane (of highway); furrow; **~ bus** bus lane.
carrillo *m* cheek; pulley.
carro *m* cart; car.
carrocería *f* bodywork, coachwork.
carromato *m* covered wagon, Gypsy caravan.
carroña *f* carrion.
carroza *f* state coach; (*mar*) awning.
carruaje *m* carriage; vehicle.
carrusel *m* merry-go-round.

carta *f* letter; map; document; playing card; menu; **~ blanca** carte blanche; **~ bomba** letter-bomb; **~ credencial/de creencia** credentials *pl*; **~ certificada** registered letter; **~ postal** *Lat Am* postcard; **~ verde** green card.
cartabón *m* square (tool).
cartapacio *m* notebook; folder.
cártel *m* cartel.
cartel *m* placard; poster; wall chart; cartel.
cartera *f* satchel; billfold; handbag; briefcase; postwoman.
carterista *m/f* pickpocket.
cartero *m* postman.
cartilaginoso/sa *adj* cartilaginous.
cartílago *m* cartilage.
cartilla *f* first reading book, primer.
cartón *m* cardboard, pasteboard; cartoon.
cartuchera *f* (*mil*) cartridge belt.
cartucho *m* (*mil*) cartridge.
cartuja *f* Carthusian order.
cartujo *m* Carthusian monk.
cartulina *f* card, pass; thin cardboard.
casa *f* house; home; firm, company; **~ de campo** country house; **~ de moneda** mint; **~ de huéspedes** boarding house.
casaca *f* coat.
casación *f* abrogation.
casadero/ra *adj* marriageable.
casado/da *adj* married.
casamentero/ra *m/f* marriage-maker, matchmaker.
casamiento *m* marriage, wedding.
casar *vt* to marry; to couple; to abrogate; to annul; **~se** *vr* to marry, to get married.
cascabel *m* small bell; rattlesnake.
cascada *f* cascade, waterfall.
cascanueces *m invar* nutcracker.
cascar *vt* to crack, to break into pieces; (*col*) to beat; **~se** *vr* to be broken open.
cáscara *f* rind, peel; husk, shell; bark.
cascarón *m* eggshell.
casco *m* skull; helmet; fragment; shard; hulk (of a ship); crown (of a hat); hoof; empty bottle, returnable bottle; **~s azules** blue berets (soldiers of a UN peacekeeping force).
cascote *m* rubble, fragment of material used in building.
casera *f* landlady.
caserío *m* country house; small village.
casero *m* landlord; janitor; * **~/ra**, *adj* domestic; household *compd*; home-made.
casette, casete *m* cassette; * *f* cassette-player.

casi *adv* almost, nearly; ~ **nada** next to nothing; ~ **nunca** hardly ever, almost never.

casilla *f* hut, cabin; box office; square (on a chess board); pigeonhole, compartment.

casillero *m* pigeonholes (set of) *pl*; baggage locker.

casino *m* club, social club.

caso *m* case; occurrence, event; happening, casualty; occasion; (*gr*) case; **en ese** ~ in that case; **en todo** ~ in any case; ~ **que** in case.

casorio *m* unwise marriage.

caspa *f* dandruff.

casquete *m* helmet.

casquillo *m* bottle top; tip, cap; point.

casta *f* caste; race; lineage; breed; kind, quality.

castaña *f* chestnut; demijohn.

castañar *m* chestnut grove.

castañetear *vi* to play the castanets.

castaño *m* chestnut tree; ~/**ña** *adj* brown, chestnut(-colored).

castañuela *f* castanet.

castellano *m* Castilian, Spanish.

castidad *f* chastity.

castigar *vt* to castigate, to punish; to afflict.

castigo *m* punishment; correction; penalty.

castillo *m* castle.

castizo/za *adj* pure, thoroughbred.

casto/ta *adj* pure, chaste.

castor *m* beaver.

castrar *vt* to geld, to castrate; to prune; to cut the honeycombs out of (beehives).

casual *adj* casual, accidental.

casualidad *f* chance, accident.

casucha *f* hovel; slum.

casulla *f* chasuble.

cata *f* tasting.

catacumbas *fpl* catacombs *pl*.

catador/ra *m/f* wine tester.

catadura *f* looks *pl*, face.

catalejo *m* telescope.

catalizador *m* catalyst; catalytic converter.

catálogo *m* catalog.

catamarán *m* catamaran.

cataplasma *f* poultice.

catapulta *f* catapult.

catar *vt* to taste; to inspect, to examine; to look at; to esteem.

catarata *f* (*med*) cataract; waterfall.

catarro *m* catarrh.

catarroso/sa *adj* catarrhal.

catástrofe *f* catastrophe.

catavino *m* small cup for tasting wine; ~s *m/f invar* wine-taster; tippler.

catecismo *m* catechism.

cátedra *f* professorship, chair (university).

catedral *f* cathedral.

catedrático/ca *m/f* professor (of a university).

categoría *f* category; rank.

categórico/ca *adj* categorical, decisive.

catequismo *m* catechism.

caterva *f* mob.

catolicismo *m* Catholicism.

católico/ca *adj, m/f* catholic.

catorce *adj, m* fourteen.

catre *m* cot.

cauce *m* riverbed; (*fig*) channel.

caucho *m* rubber; tire.

caución *f* caution; (*law*) security, bail.

caucionar *vt* to prevent, to guard against; (*law*) to bail.

caudal *m* volume, flow; property, wealth; plenty.

caudaloso/sa *adj* carrying much water (of rivers); wealthy, rich.

caudillo *m* leader.

causa *f* cause; motive, reason; lawsuit; **a** ~ **de** considering, because of.

causal *adj* causal.

causante *m/f* originator; * *adj* causing, originating.

causar *vt* to cause; to produce; to occasion.

cáustico *m* caustic; ~/**ca** *adj* caustic.

cautela *f* caution, cautiousness.

cauteloso/sa *adj* cautious, wary.

cauterizar *vt* (*med*) to cauterize; to apply a drastic remedy to.

cautivar *vt* to take prisoner in war; to captivate, to charm.

cautiverio *m* captivity.

cautividad *f* captivity.

cautivo/va *adj, m/f* captive.

cauto/ta *adj* cautious, wary.

cava *f* digging and earthing of vines; wine cellar; sparkling wine.

cavar *vt* to dig up, to excavate; * *vi* to dig, to delve; to think profoundly.

caverna *f* cavern, cave.

cavernoso/sa *adj* cavernous.

cavidad *f* cavity, hollow.

cavilación *f* deep thought.

cavilar *vt* to ponder, to consider carefully.

caviloso/sa *adj* obsessed; suspicious.

cayado/da *m/f* shepherd's crook.

caza *f* hunting; shooting; chase; game; * *m* fighter-plane.

cazador/ra m/f hunter; m huntsman; ~ **furtivo** poacher.

cazamoscas m invar flycatcher (bird).

cazar vt to chase, to hunt; to catch.

cazo m saucepan; ladle.

cazuela f casserole; pan.

cazurro/rra adj silent, taciturn.

cebada f barley.

cebar vt to feed (animals), to fatten.

cebo m feed, food; bait, lure; priming.

cebolla f onion; bulb.

cebolleta f spring onion, scallion.

cebollino m onion seed; chive.

cebón m fattened hog/pig.

cebra f zebra.

cecear vt to pronounce s the same as c; to lisp.

cecina f dried meat; salt beef.

cedazo m sieve, strainer.

ceder vt to hand over; to transfer, to make over; to yield, to give up; * vi to submit, to comply, to give in; to diminish, to grow less.

cederrón m CD-ROM.

cedro m cedar.

cédula f certificate; document; slip of paper; bill; ~ **de cambio** bill of exchange; ~ **de identidad** Lat Am identity card.

cegar vi to grow blind; * vt to blind; to block up.

cegato/ta adj short-sighted.

ceguera f blindness.

ceja f eyebrow; edging of clothes; (mus) bridge of a stringed instrument; brow of a hill.

cejar vi to go backward(s); to slacken, to give in.

celada f helmet; ambush; trick.

celador m guard, watchman; maintenance man; linesman.

celda f cell.

celdilla f cell; cavity.

celebración f celebration; praise.

celebrar vt to celebrate; to praise; ~ **misa** to say mass.

célebre adj famous, renowned; witty, funny.

celebridad f celebrity, fame.

celeridad f speed, velocity.

celeste adj heavenly; sky-blue.

celestial adj heavenly; delightful.

celibato m celibacy.

célibe m/f bachelor, spinster.

celo m zeal; rut (in animals); Sellotape™; **~s** mpl jealousy.

celofán m Cellophane™.

celosía f lattice (of a window).

celoso/sa adj zealous; jealous.

célula f cell.

celular adj cellular; * m Lat Am cellular phone, mobile phone.

celulitis f cellulitis.

celuloide m celluloid.

cementerio m graveyard.

cemento m cement; Lat Am glue.

cena f dinner, supper.

cenador m arbor.

cenagoso/sa adj miry, marshy.

cenagal m quagmire.

cenar vt to have for dinner; * vi to have supper, to have dinner.

cencerro m jangle, clatter.

cenicero m ashtray.

ceniciento/ta adj ash-colored.

ceñido/da adj tight-fitting; sparing, frugal.

ceñir vt to surround, to circle; to abbreviate, to abridge; to fit tightly.

cenit m zenith.

ceniza f ashes pl; **miércoles de ~** Ash Wednesday.

ceño m frown.

censo m census; tax; ground rent; ~ **electoral** electoral roll.

censor/ra m/f censor; reviewer, critic.

censura f censorship; review; censure, blame.

censurar vt to review, to criticize; to censure, to blame.

centella f lightning; spark.

centellear vi to sparkle.

centena f hundred.

centenadas adv: **a ~** by hundreds.

centenar m hundred.

centenario/ia adj centenary; * m centenary.

centeno m rye.

centésimo/ma adj hundredth; * m hundredth.

centígrado m centigrade.

centímetro m centimeter.

céntimo m cent.

centinela f sentry, guard; lookout.

central adj central; * f head office, headquarters; (telephone) exchange; ~ **nuclear** nuclear power station.

centralización m centralization.

centralizar vt to centralize.

céntrico adj central.

centrífugo/ga adj centrifugal.

centrista adj centrist.

centro *m* center; ~ comercial shopping center.
centuplicar *vt* to increase a hundredfold.
céntuplo/pla *adj* one hundredfold.
ceñudo/da *adj* frowning, grim.
cepa *f* stock (of a vine); origin (of a family).
cepillar *vt* to brush.
cepillo *m* brush; plane (tool).
cepo *m* branch, bough; trap; snare; poor box.
cera *f* wax; ~s *fpl* honeycomb.
cerámica *f* pottery.
cerca *f* enclosure; fence; ~s *mpl* objects *pl* in the foreground of a painting; * *adv* near, at hand, close by; ~ de close, near.
cercanías *fpl* outskirts.
cercano/na *adj* near, close by; neighboring, adjoining.
cercar *vt* to enclose, to circle; to fence in.
cerciorar *vt* to assure, to ascertain, to affirm; ~se *vr* to find out.
cerco *m* enclosure; *Lat Am* fence; (*mil*) siege.
cerdo *m* pig, hog.
cereal *m* cereal.
cerebelo *m* cerebellum.
cerebro *m* brain.
ceremonia *f* ceremony.
ceremonial *adj*, *m* ceremonial.
ceremonioso/sa *adj* ceremonious.
cereza *f* cherry; *Lat Am* coffee bean.
cerezo *m* cherry tree.
cerilla *f* wax taper; ear wax; match, safety match.
cerner *vt* to sift; * *vi* to bud, to blossom; to drizzle; ~se *vr* to hover; to swagger.
cernido *m* sifting.
cero *m* nothing, zero.
cerquita *adv* close by.
cerrado/da *adj* closed, shut; locked; overcast, cloudy; broad (of accent).
cerradura *f* locking-up; lock.
cerrajería *f* trade of a locksmith; locksmith's (premises).
cerrajero *m* locksmith.
cerrar *vt* to close, to shut; to block up; to lock; ~ una cuenta to close an account; ~se *vr* to close; to heal; to cloud over; *vi* to close, to shut; to lock.
cerril *adj* mountainous; rough, wild, untamed.
cerro *m* hill; neck (of an animal); backbone; combed flax/hemp; en ~ bareback.
cerrojo *m* bolt (of a door).
certamen *m* competition, contest.
certero *adj* accurate; well-aimed.
certeza, certidumbre *f* certainty.

certificación *f* certificate.
certificado *m* certificate; ~/da *adj* registered (of a letter).
certificar *vt* to certify, to affirm.
cervato *m* fawn.
cervecería *f* bar; brewery.
cervecero *m* brewer.
cerveza *m* beer.
cerviz *f* nape of the neck; cervix.
cesación *f* cessation, stoppage.
cesar *vt* to cease, to stop; to fire (*col*); to remove from office; * *vi* to cease, to stop; to retire.
cese *m* suspension; dismissal; ~ del fuego *Lat Am* ceasefire.
cesión *f* cession; transfer.
césped *m* grass; lawn.
cesta *f* basket, pannier.
cestería *f* shop that specializes in baskets; basketwork.
cesto *m* (large) basket.
cetrino/na *adj* greenish-yellow; sallow; jaundiced, melancholic.
cetro *m* scepter.
chabacano/na *adj* coarse, vulgar; shoddy.
chabola *f* shack.
cháchara *f* chitchat, chatter, idle talk.
chacolí *m* light white wine with a sharp taste.
chafar *vt* to crush; to ruin.
chal *m* shawl.
chalado/da *adj* crazy.
chale(t) *m* detached house.
chaleco *m* vest.
chalupa *f* (*mar*) boat, launch.
chamarra *f* sheepskin jacket.
champán *m* champagne.
champiñón *m* mushroom.
champú *m* shampoo.
chamuscar *vt* to singe, to scorch.
chamusquina *f* scorching; (*fig*) row, quarrel.
chance *m/f Lat Am* chance.
chancho *m Lat Am* pig, hog.
chanchullo *m* (*col*) fix, fiddle.
canciller *m* chancellor.
chancleta *f* slipper.
chanclo *m* clog; galosh.
chándal *m* tracksuit.
chanfaina *f* cheap stew.
chantaje *m* blackmail.
chanza *f* joke, jest; ~s *fpl* fun.
chapa *f* metal plate; panel; (*auto*) license plate.
chaparrón *m* heavy rain shower.
chapotear *vt* to wet with a sponge; * *vi* to paddle (in water).

chapucear *vt* to botch, to bungle.

chapucero *m* bungler; **~/ra** *adj* clumsy, crude.

chapurrar *vt* to speak (a language) badly; to mix (drinks).

chapuza *f* badly done job.

chapuzarse *vr* to duck; to dive.

chaqueta *f* jacket, coat; **~ deportiva** sports coat, sports jacket.

charca *f* pool.

charco *m* pool, puddle.

charcutería *f* shop selling pork meat products.

charla *f* chat, talk.

charlar *vi* to chat.

charlatán/ana *m/f* chatterbox.

charlatanería *f* talkativeness.

charol *m* varnish; patent leather.

charrada *f* coarse thing; bad breeding; bad taste.

charretera *f* shoulder pad.

charro *m* coarse individual; **~/rra** *adj* coarse; gaudy.

charter *m* charter flight.

chasco *m* disappointment; joke, jest.

chasis *m invar* (*auto*) chassis.

chasquear *vt* to crack (a whip); to disappoint.

chasquido *m* crack; click.

chatarra *f* scrap.

chato/ta *adj* flat, flattish; snub-nosed.

chaval/la *m/f* lad/lass.

cheque *m* check.

chequeo *m* check-up; service.

chequera *f* checkbook.

chicano/na *adj* Chicano.

chicha *f* corn liquor.

chicharra *f* harvest fly.

chicharrón *m* pork crackling.

chichón *m* lump, bump.

chichonera *f* helmet.

chicle *m* chewing gum.

chico/ca *adj* little, small; * *m/f* boy/girl.

chicote *m Lat Am* whip.

chifla *f* whistle; hiss.

chiflado/da *adj* crazy.

chiflar *vt* to boo.

chile *m* chili pepper.

chillar *vi* to scream, to shriek; to howl; to creak.

chillido *m* squeak; shriek, howl.

chillón/ona *adj* loud, noisy; gaudy; * *m/f* whiner, moaner.

chimenea *f* chimney; fireplace.

china *f* pebble; porcelain, chinaware; China silk.

chinche *f* bug; *Lat Am* thumbtack; * *m* nuisance.

chincheta *f* thumbtack.

chinela *f* slipper.

chinita *f Lat Am* maid.

chino/na *adj*, *m/f* Chinese; * *m* Chinese language.

chiquero *m* pigpen.

chiripa *f* fluke.

chirla *f* mussel.

chirriar *vi* to hiss; to creak; to chirp.

chirrido *m* chirping (of birds); squeaking.

chis *excl* sh!

chisgarabís *m* (*col*) meddler.

chisme *m* tale, thing.

chismear *vi* to tell tales.

chismoso/sa *adj* gossiping; * *m/f* gossip.

chispa *f* spark; sparkle; wit; drop (of rain); drunkenness.

chispazo *m* spark.

chispeante *adj* sparkling.

chispear *vi* to sparkle; to drizzle.

chisporrotear *vi* to crackle; to sparkle; to hiss (of liquids).

chistar *vi* to speak.

chiste *m* funny story, joke.

chistoso/sa *adj* witty, amusing, funny.

chivato *m* kid; child.

chivo/va *m/f* billy/nanny goat.

chocante *adj* startling; odd.

chocar *vi* to strike, to knock; to crash; * *vt* to shock.

chochear *vi* to dodder, to be senile; to dote.

chocho *adj* doddering; doting.

chocolate *m* chocolate.

chocolatero/ra *adj* fond of chocolate.

chófer *m* driver.

chollo *m* bargain.

chopo *m* black poplar tree.

choque *m* shock; crash, collision; clash, conflict.

chorizo *m* pork sausage.

chorlito *m* plover (bird).

chorrear *vi* to spout, to gush; to drip.

chorrera *f* channel; frill.

chorro *m* gush; jet; stream; **a ~s** abundantly.

choto *m* kid; calf.

choza *f* hut, shack.

chubasco *m* squall.

chuchería *f* trinket.

chucho *m* mongrel.

chufleta *f* joke; taunt, jeer.

chulada *f* funny speech/action.

chulear *vi* to brag.

chuleta *f* chop.

chulo *m* rascal; pimp.
chunga *f* fun, joke; **estar de ~** to be in good humor.
chunguearse *vr* to be in good humor.
chupado/da *adj* skinny; easy.
chupaflor *m Lat Am* hummingbird.
chupar *vt* to suck; to absorb.
chupete *m* pacifier.
chupetear *vi* to suck gently.
chupón/ona *m/f (col)* swindler, sponger.
churro *m* fritter.
churruscarse *vr* to scorch.
churrusco *m* burnt toast.
chusco/ca *adj* pleasant; funny.
chusma *f* rabble, mob.
chuzo *m* little spear/spike; **llover a ~s** to pour (with rain) heavily.
cianuro *m* cyanide.
ciática *f* sciatica.
ciático/ca *adj* sciatic.
cibercafé *m* Internet café.
ciberespacio *m* cyberspace.
cicatear *vi* to be mean.
cicatriz *f* scar.
cicatrizar *vt* to heal.
ciclismo *m* cycling.
ciclista *m/f* cyclist.
ciclo *m* cycle.
ciclón *m* cyclone.
cicloturismo *m* bicycle tourism.
cicuta *f (bot)* hemlock.
ciegamente *adv* blindly.
ciego/ga *adj* blind.
cielo *m* sky; heaven; atmosphere; climate.
cien *adj, m* a hundred.
ciénaga *f* swamp.
ciencia *f* science.
cieno *m* mud; mire.
cienpiés *m invar* centipede.
científico/ca *adj* scientific.
ciento *adj, m* a hundred.
cierne *m*: **en ~** in blossom; **estar en ~** to be in its infancy.
cierre *m* zipper.
cierto/ta *adj* certain, sure; right, correct; **por ~** certainly.
cierva *f* hind.
ciervo *m* deer, stag; **~ volante** stag beetle.
cierzo *m* cold northerly wind.
cifra *f* number, numeral; quantity; cipher; abbreviation.
cifrar *vt* to write in code; to abridge.
cigala *f* langoustine.
cigarra *f* cicada.
cigarrera *m* cigar case.

cigarrería *f Lat Am* tobacconist's (shop).
cigarrillo *m* cigarette.
cigarro *m* cigar; cigarette.
cigüeña *f* stork; crank, handle; winch.
cilicio *m* hair shirt; spiked belt.
cilíndrico/ca *adj* cylindrical.
cilindro *m* cylinder.
cima *f* summit; peak; top.
címbalo *m* cymbal.
cimbor(r)io *m* cupola, dome.
cimbr(e)ar *vt* to shake, to swish, to swing; **~ a uno** to give one a clout (with a stick); **~se** *vr* to sway.
cimbronazo *m Lat Am* shock wave.
cimentado *m* refinement of gold.
cimentar *vt* to lay the foundation of (a building); to found; to refine (metals); to strengthen, to cement.
cimiento *m* foundation, groundwork; basis, origin.
cinc *m* zinc.
cincel *m* chisel.
cincelar *vt* to chisel, to engrave.
cincha *f* girth.
cinchar *vt* to fasten a girth (on a horse).
cinco *adj, m* five.
cincuenta *adj, m* fifty.
cine *m* movie theater, movie house.
cineasta *m/f* film maker.
cinematográfico/ca *adj* cinematographic.
cínico/ca *adj* cynical.
cinismo *m* cynicism.
cinta *f* band, ribbon; reel.
cinto *m* belt.
cintura *f* waist.
cinturón *m* belt, girdle; *(fig)* zone; **~ de seguridad** seatbelt.
ciprés *m* cypress tree.
circo *m* circus.
circuito *m* circuit; circumference.
circulación *f* circulation; traffic.
circular *adj* circular; circulatory; * *vt* to circulate; * *vi (auto)* to drive.
círculo *m* circle; *(fig)* scope, compass.
circuncidar *vt* to circumcise.
circuncisión *f* circumcision.
circundar *vt* to surround, to encircle.
circunferencia *f* circumference.
circunflejo/ja *adj*: **acento ~** *m* circumflex.
circunscribir *vt* to circumscribe.
circunscripción *f* division; electoral district.
circunspección *f* circumspection.
circunspecto/ta *adj* circumspect, cautious.
circunstancia *f* circumstance.
circunstante *m/f* bystander.

circunvalación f: **carretera de** ~ beltway, bypass.
cirio m wax candle.
ciruela f plum; ~ **pasa** prune.
ciruelo m plum tree.
cirugía f surgery.
cirujano m surgeon.
cisco m coaldust.
cisma m schism; discord.
cismático/ca adj schismatic.
cisne m swan.
cisterna f cistern.
cisura f incision.
cita f quotation; appointment, meeting.
citación f quotation; (law) summons.
citar vt to make an appointment with; to quote; (law) to summon.
cítrico/ca adj citric; ~s mpl citric fruits pl.
ciudad f city; town.
ciudadanía f citizenship.
ciudadano/na m/f citizen; * adj civic.
ciudadela f citadel.
cívico/ca adj civic.
civil adj civil; **polite, courteous,** * m Civil Guard; civilian.
civilización f civilization.
civilizar vt to civilize.
civismo m public spirit; patriotism.
cizaña f discord.
clamar vt to clamor for.
clamor m clamor, outcry; peal of bells.
clamoroso/sa adj noisy, loud.
clandestino/na adj clandestine, secret, concealed.
clara f egg-white.
claraboya f skylight.
clarear vi to dawn; ~se vr to be transparent.
clarete adj, m claret.
claridad f brightness, clearness.
clarificar vt to brighten; to clarify.
clarín m bugle; bugler.
clarinete m clarinet; * m/f clarinetist.
claro/ra adj clear, bright; evident, manifest; * m opening; clearing (in a wood); skylight.
claroscuro m chiaroscuro (in painting).
clase f class; rank; order.
clásico/ca adj classical.
clasificación f classification.
clasificado m Lat Am classified ad/advertisement.
clasificar vt to classify.
claudicar vi to limp; to act deceitfully; to back down.
claustro m cloister; faculty (of a university); womb, uterus.

cláusula f clause.
clausura f closure, closing.
clavado/da adj tight-fitting; nailed.
clavar vt to nail; to fasten in, to force in; to drive in; (col) to cheat, to deceive; ~se vr to penetrate.
clave f key; (mus) clef; * m harpsichord.
clavel m (bot) carnation.
clavetear vt to decorate with studs.
clavicordio m clavichord.
clavícula f clavicle, collar bone.
clavija f pin, peg.
clavo m nail; corn (on the feet); clove.
claxon m horn.
clemencia f clemency.
clemente adj clement, merciful.
cleptómano/na m/f kleptomaniac.
clerecía f clergy.
clerical adj clerical.
clérigo m priest; clergyman.
clero m clergy.
clic, click m click.
cliché m cliché; negative (of a photo).
cliente m/f client.
clientela f clientele.
clima m climate.
climatizado/da adj air-conditioned.
clínica f clinic; private hospital.
clínico/ca adj clinical.
clip m paperclip.
cloaca f sewer.
cloquear vi to cluck.
clon m clone.
clonación f cloning.
clonar vt to clone.
clónico/ca adj cloned.
clóset m Lat Am fitted cupboard.
club m club.
clueca f broody hen.
coacción f coercion, compulsion.
coactivo/va adj coercive.
coadjutor/ra m/f coadjutor.
coagular vt, ~se vr to coagulate; to curdle.
coágulo m: ~ **sanguíneo** blood clot.
coalición f coalition.
coartada f (law) alibi.
coartar vt to limit, to restrict, to restrain.
cobalto m cobalt.
cobarde adj cowardly, timid.
cobardía f cowardice.
cobayo/ya m/f guinea pig.
cobertizo m small shed; shelter.
cobertura f cover; coverage; bedspread.
cobija f Lat Am blanket.
cobijar vt to cover; to shelter.

cobra *f* cobra.

cobrador/ra *m/f* conductor/conductress; collector.

cobrar *vt* to recover; ~se *vr* (*med*) to come to.

cobre *m* copper; kitchen utensils *pl*; (*mus*) brass.

cobrizo/za *adj* coppery.

cobro *m* payment; recovery.

cocaína *f* cocaine.

cocción *f* cooking.

cocear *vt* to kick; (*fig*) to resist.

cocer *vt* to boil; to bake (bricks); * *vi* to boil; to ferment; ~se *vr* to suffer intense pain.

cochambre *m* dirty, stinking object.

cochambroso/sa *adj* nasty; filthy, stinking.

coche *m* car; coach, carriage; baby carriage; ~ **bomba** car bomb; (*rail*) ~ **cama** sleeping car/carriage; (*rail*) ~ **restaurante** restaurant car/carriage.

cochera *f* garage, carport, depot.

cochero *m* coachman.

cochinilla *f* woodlouse; cochineal.

cochino/na *adj* dirty, filthy; nasty; * *m* hog, pig.

cochiquera *f* pigpen.

cocido/da *adj* boiled; (*fig*) skilled, experienced; * *m* stew.

cocina *f* kitchen; cooker; cookery.

cocinero/ra *m/f* cook.

coco *m* coconut; bogeyman.

cocodrilo *m* crocodile.

codazo *m* blow given with the elbow.

codear *vt*, *vi* to elbow; ~se *vr*: ~se con to rub shoulders with.

códice *m* codex, old manuscript.

codicia *m* covetousness, greediness.

codiciable *adj* covetable.

codiciar *vt* to covet, to desire.

codicilo *m* (*law*) codicil.

codicioso/sa *adj* greedy, covetous.

código *m* law; set of rules; code; ~ **postal** post code.

codillo *m* knee (animal); (*bot*) stump; (*tec*) elbow (joint), bend; angle iron.

codo *m* elbow.

codorniz *f* quail.

coerción *f* coercion; restraint.

coercitivo/va *adj* coercive.

coetáneo/nea *adj* contemporary.

coexistencia *f* coexistence.

coexistente *adj* coexistent.

coexistir *vi* to coexist.

cofia *f* (nurse's) cap.

cofrade *m* member (of a brotherhood).

cofradía *f* brotherhood, fraternity.

cofre *m* chest; case; trunk.

cogedor *m* shovel; dustpan.

coger *vt* to catch, to take hold of; to occupy, to take up; ~se *vr* to catch.

cognitivo/va *adj* cognitive.

cogollo *m* heart of a lettuce/cabbage; shoot of a plant.

cogote *m* back of the neck.

cohabitar *vi* to cohabit, to live together.

cohechar *vt* to bribe, to suborn.

cohecho *m* bribery.

coherencia *f* coherence.

coherente *adj* coherent.

cohete *m* rocket.

cohibido/da *adj* shy.

cohibir *vt* to prohibit; to restrain.

cohorte *m* cohort.

coincidencia *f* coincidence.

coincidente *adj* coincidental.

coincidir *vi* to coincide.

coito *m* intercourse, coitus.

cojear *vi* to limp, to hobble; (*fig*) to go astray.

cojera *f* lameness; limp.

cojín *m* cushion.

cojo/ja *adj* lame, crippled.

col *f* cabbage.

cola[1] *f* tail; queue; last place; *Lat Am* (*col*) bum.

cola[2] *f* glue.

colaborador/ra *m/f* collaborator; contributor.

colaborar *vi* to collaborate.

colación *f* comparison; light meal, snack; buffet meal.

colada *f* wash, washing; (*chem*) bleach; sheep run.

coladera *f* *Lat Am* colander, strainer.

coladero *m* colander, strainer.

colador *m* sieve.

colapso *m* collapse.

colar *vt* to strain, to filter; * *vi* to ooze; ~se *vr*: ~ en to get into without paying.

colateral *adj* collateral.

colcha *f* bedspread, counterpane.

colchón *m* mattress.

colchoneta *f* mattress.

coleada *f* wagging (of an animal's tail).

colear *vi* to wag the tail.

colección *f* collection.

coleccionar *vt* to collect.

coleccionista *m/f* collector.

colecta *f* collection (for charity).

colectar *vt* to collect (taxes).

colectivo/va *adj* collective.
colector *m* collector; sewer.
colega *m/f* colleague.
colegial *m* schoolboy.
colegiala *f* schoolgirl.
colegiata *f* collegiate church.
colegio *m* college; school.
colegir *vt* to collect; to deduce, to infer.
cólera *f* bile; anger; fury, rage.
coléricamente *adv* in a rage.
colérico/ca *adj* angry; furious; bad-tempered.
colesterol *m* cholesterol.
coleta *f* pigtail.
colgadero *m* hook, hanger, peg.
colgadura *f* tapestry; hangings *pl*, drapery.
colgajo *m* tatter, rag.
colgante *adj* hanging; * *m* pendant.
colgar *vt* to hang; to suspend; to decorate with tapestry; * *vi* to be suspended.
colibrí *m* hummingbird.
cólico *m* colic.
coliflor *m* cauliflower.
colilla *f* end/butt of a cigarette.
colina *f* hill.
colindante *adj* neighboring.
colindar *vi* to adjoin.
coliseo *m* coliseum, opera house; theater.
colisión *f* collision; friction.
collar *m* necklace; (dog) collar.
colmar *vt* to heap up; * *vi* to fulfill, to realize.
colmena *f* hive, beehive.
colmenar *m* apiary.
colmillo *m* eyetooth; tusk.
colmo *m* height, summit; extreme; **a ~** plentifully.
colocación *f* employment; placing; situation.
colocar *vt* to arrange; to place; to provide with a job; **~se** *vr* to get a job.
colon *m* (*med*) colon.
colonia *f* colony; silk ribbon.
colonial *adj* colonial.
colonización *f* colonization.
colonizador/a *m/f* settler; * *adj* colonizing.
colonizar *vt* to colonize.
colono *m* colonist; farmer.
coloquio *m* conversation; conference.
color *m* color, hue; dye; rouge; suit (in cards).
coloración *f* coloring, coloration.
colorado/da *adj* ruddy; red.
colorar *vt* to color; to dye.
colorear *vt* to color; to excuse.

colorete *m* rouge.
colorido *m* coloring.
colosal *adj* colossal.
columna *f* column.
columnata *f* colonnade.
columpiar *vt*, **~se** *vr* to swing to and fro.
columpio *m* swing, seesaw.
colusión *f* collusion.
colza *f* (*bot*) rape; rape seed.
coma *f* (*gr*) comma; * *m* (*med*) coma.
comadre *f* midwife; godmother; neighbor.
comadreja *f* weasel.
comadrón/ona *m/f* midwife.
comandancia *f* command.
comandante *m* commander.
comandar *vt* to command.
comarca *f* territory, district.
comba *f* curve, warp (of lumber); skipping rope.
combar *vt* to bend; **~se** *vr* to warp.
combate *m* combat, conflict; fighting.
combatiente *m* combatant.
combatir *vt* to combat, to fight; to attack; * *vi* to fight.
combi *f* *Lat Am* minibus.
combinación *f* combination; (*chem*) compound; cocktail; scheme.
combinar *vi* to combine.
combustible *adj* combustible; * *m* fuel.
combustión *f* combustion.
comedero *m* dining room; trough.
comedia *f* comedy; play, drama.
comediante *m/f* player, actor/actress.
comedido/da *adj* moderate, restrained.
comedirse *vr* to restrain oneself.
comedor/ra *m/f* glutton; * *m* dining room.
comendatorio/ria *adj* introductory (of letters).
comensal *m/f* fellow diner.
comentar *vt* to comment on, to expound.
comentario *m* comment, remark; commentary.
comentarista *m/f* commentator.
comenzar *vi* to commence, to begin.
comer *vt* to eat; to take (a piece at chess); * *vi* to have lunch.
comercial *adj* commercial; * *m* *Lat Am* commercial.
comerciante *m/f* trader, merchant, dealer.
comerciar *vi* to trade, to do business.
comercio *m* trade, commerce; business; **~ electrónico** e-commerce; **~ justo** fair trade.
comestible *adj* eatable; * *mpl* **~s** food, foodstuffs *pl*.
cometa *m* comet; * *f* kite.

cometer *vt* to commit, to charge; to entrust.
cometido *m* task.
comezón *f* itch; itching.
comicios *mpl* elections *pl.*
cómico/ca *adj* comic, comical.
comida *f* food; eating; meal; lunch; ~ **basura** junk food.
comienzo *m* beginning.
comillas *fpl* quotation marks *pl.*
comilón/ona *m/f* great eater, glutton; * *f* blow-out.
comino *m* cumin (plant/seed).
comisaría *f* police station; commissariat.
comisario/-a *m/f* commissioner.
comisión *f* commission; committee.
comisionado/da *m/f* commissioner; committee member.
comisionar *vt* to commission.
comité *m* committee.
comitiva *f* suite, retinue, followers *pl.*
como *adv* as; like; such as.
cómo *adv* how?; why? * *excl* what?
cómoda *f* chest of drawers.
comodidad *f* comfort; convenience; ~**es** *fpl* wealth, comforts *pl.*
comodín *m* joker.
cómodo/da *adj* convenient; comfortable; cozy.
compact disc *m* compact disc.
compacto/ta *adj* compact; close, dense.
compadecer *vt* to pity; ~**se** *vr* to agree with each other.
compadre *m* godfather; friend.
compaginar *vt* to arrange, to put in order; ~**se** *vr* to tally.
compañero/ra *m/f* companion, friend; comrade; partner.
compañia *f* company.
comparación *f* comparison.
comparar *vt* to compare.
comparativo/va *adj* comparative.
comparecer *vi* to appear in court.
comparsa *m/f* extra (in the theater/movies).
compartimento *m* compartment.
compartir *vt* to divide into equal parts.
compás *m* čompass; pair of compasses; (*mus*) measure, beat.
compasión *f* compassion, commiseration.
compasivo/va *adj* compassionate.
compatibilidad *f* compatibility.
compatible *adj*: ~ **con** compatible with, consistent with.
compatriota *m/f* countryman; countrywoman; fellow citizen.
compeler *vt* to compel, to constrain.

compendiar *vt* to abridge.
compendio *m* abridgment; summary.
compensación *f* compensation; recompense.
compensar *vt* to compensate; to recompense.
competencia *f* competition, rivalry; competence.
competente *adj* competent; adequate.
competer *vi* to be one's responsibility.
competición *f* competition.
competidor/ra *m/f* competitor, contestant; rival.
competir *vi* to vie; ~ **con** to compete with, to rival.
compilación *f* compilation.
compilador *m* compiler.
compilar *vt* to compile.
compinche *m* (*col*) pal, buddy.
complacencia *f* pleasure; indulgence.
complacer *vt* to please; ~**se** *vr* to be pleased with.
complaciente *adj* pleasing.
complejo *m* complex; ~/**ja** *adj* complex.
complementario/ria *adj* complementary.
complemento *m* complement.
completar *vt* to complete.
completo/ta *adj* complete; perfect.
complexión *f* constitution, temperament; build.
complicado/da *adj* complicated.
complicar *vt* to complicate.
cómplice *m/f* accomplice.
complicidad *f* complicity.
complot *m* plot.
componer *vt* to compose; to constitute; to mend, to repair; to strengthen, to restore; to adorn; to adjust; to reconcile; to compose, to calm; ~**se** *vr*: ~ **de** to consist of.
comportamiento *m* behavior.
comportarse *vr* to behave.
composición *f* composition; composure, agreement; settlement.
compositor/ra *m/f* composer; compositor.
compostura *f* composition, composure; mending, repairing; discretion; modesty, demureness.
compota *f* sauce.
compra *f* purchase; ~ **a plazos** installment plan.
comprador/ra *m/f* buyer; customer, shopper.
comprar *vt* to buy, to purchase.
comprender *vt* to include, to contain; to comprehend, to understand.
comprensible *adj* comprehensible.

comprensión *f* comprehension, understanding.
comprensivo/va *adj* comprehensive.
compresa *f* sanitary napkin.
compresión *f* compression.
comprimido *m* pill.
comprimir *vt* to compress; to repress, to restrain.
comprobante *m* receipt; voucher.
comprobar *vt* to verify, to confirm; to prove.
comprometer *vt* to compromise; to embarrass; to implicate; to put in danger; ~se *vr* to compromise oneself.
compromiso *m* compromise.
compuerta *f* hatch; sluice.
compuesto *m* compound; ~/ta *adj* composed; made up of.
compulsar *vt* to collate, to compare; to make an authentic copy.
compulsivo/va *adj* compulsive.
compunción *f* compunction, regret.
compungirse *vr* to feel remorseful.
computación *f* Lat Am computing.
computador/dora *m/f* computer.
computar *vt* to calculate; to compute.
cómputo *m* computation; calculation.
comulgar *vt* to administer communion to; * *vi* to receive communion.
común *adj* common, usual, general; * *m* community; public; **en** ~ in common.
comunal *adj* communal.
comunicación *f* communication; report.
comunicado *m* announcement.
comunicar *vt* to communicate; ~se *vr* to communicate (with each other).
comunicativo/va *adj* communicative.
comunidad *f* community; **C**~ **Europea** European Community.
comunión *f* communion.
comunismo *m* communism.
comunista *adj*, *m/f* communist.
comunitario/ria *adj* of the European Union.
con *prep* with; by; ~ **que** so then, providing that.
coñac *m* brandy, cognac.
conato *m* endeavor; effort; attempt.
concavidad *f* concavity.
cóncavo/va *adj* concave.
concebir *vt* to conceive; * *vi* to become pregnant.
conceder *vt* to give; to grant; to concede, to allow.
concejal/la *m/f* member of a council.

concejo *m* council.
concentración *f* concentration.
concentrar *vt*, ~se *vr* to concentrate.
concéntrico/ca *adj* concentric.
concepción *f* conception; idea.
concepto *m* conceit, thought; judgement, opinion.
concerniente *adj*: ~ **a** concerning, relating to.
concernir *v imp* to regard, to concern.
concertar *vt* to coordinate; to settle; to adjust; to agree; to arrange, to fix up; * *vi* (*mus*) to harmonize, to be in tune.
concesión *f* concession.
concesionario *m* agent.
concha *f* shell; tortoiseshell.
conchabar *vt* to mix, to blend; ~se *vr* to plot, to conspire.
conciencia *f* conscience.
concienciar *vt* to make aware; ~se *vr* to become aware.
concientizar *vt* Lat Am to make aware; ~se *vr* to become aware.
concierto *m* concert; agreement; concerto; **de** ~ in agreement, in concert.
conciliación *f* conciliation, reconciliation.
conciliar *vt* to reconcile; * *adj* of a council.
conciliatorio/ria *adj* conciliatory.
concilio *m* council.
concisión *f* conciseness.
conciso/sa *adj* concise, brief.
conciudadanía *f* joint-citizenship.
conciudadano/na *m/f* fellow citizen.
cónclave *m* conclave.
concluir *vt* to conclude, to end, to complete; to infer, to deduce; ~se *vr* to conclude.
conclusión *f* conclusion.
concluyente *adj* conclusive.
concordancia *f* concordance, concord; harmony.
concordar *vt* to reconcile, to make agree; * *vi* to agree, to correspond.
concordato *m* concordat.
concordia *f* conformity, agreement.
concretar *vt* to make concrete; to specify.
concreto/ta *adj* concrete; * *m* Lat Am concrete.
concubina *f* concubine.
concupiscencia *f* lust.
concurrencia *f* concurrence; coincidence; competition; crowd, gathering.
concurrido/da *adj* busy.
concurrir *vi* to meet; to contribute; to coincide; to compete.
concursante *m/f* competitor.

concurso *m* crowd; competition; help, co-operation.
concusión *f* concussion.
condado *m* county.
conde *m* earl, count.
condecoración *f* medal.
condecorar *vt* to adorn; (*mil*) to decorate.
condena *f* condemnation.
condenable *adj* culpable.
condenar *vt* to condemn; to find guilty; ~se *vr* to blame oneself; to confess (one's guilt).
condenatorio/ria *adj* condemnatory.
condensación *f* condensation.
condensar *vt* to condense.
condesa *f* countess.
condescendencia *f* helpfulness, willingness; acquiescence; compliance.
condescender *vi* to acquiesce, to comply.
condición *f* condition, state; quality; status; rank; stipulation.
condicionado/da *adj* conditioned.
condicional *adj* conditional.
condimentar *vt* to flavor, to season.
condimento *m* condiment, seasoning.
condiscípulo/la *m/f* fellow pupil; fellow student.
condolerse *vr* to sympathize.
condón *m* condom.
condominio *m* Lat Am condominium.
condonar *vt* to condone; to forgive.
conducción *f* conveyance; management; (*auto*) driving.
conducente *adj*: ~ a leading to.
conducir *vt* to convey, to conduct; to drive; to manage; * *vi* to drive; ~ (a) to lead (to); ~se *vr* to conduct oneself.
conducta *f* conduct, behavior; management.
conducto *m* conduit, pipe; drain; (*fig*) channel.
conductor/ra *m/f* conductor, guide; (*rail*) guard; driver.
conectado/da *adj* on-line.
conectar *vt* to connect.
conejera *f* warren, burrow.
conejo *m* rabbit.
conexión *f* connection; plug; relationship.
conexo/xa *adj* connected, related.
confabularse *vr* to conspire.
confección *f* preparation; clothing industry.
confeccionar *vt* to make up.
confederación *f* confederacy.
confederado/da *adj* confederate.
confederarse *vr* to confederate.
conferencia *f* conference; telephone call.

conferenciar *vi* to confer; to be in conference.
conferir *vt* to award; to compare.
confesar *vt* to confess; to admit.
confesión *f* confession.
confesionario *m* confessional.
confeso/sa *adj* (*law*) self-confessed.
confesonario *m* confessional.
confesor *m* confessor.
confeti *m* confetti.
confiable *adj* Lat Am reliable.
confiado/da *adj* trusting; confident; arrogant.
confianza *f* trust; confidence; conceit; familiarity; en ~ confidential.
confiar *vt* to confide, to entrust; * *vi* to trust.
confidencia *f* confidence.
confidencial *adj* confidential.
confidente *m/f* confidant/e; informer.
configurar *vt* to shape, to form.
confín *m* limit, boundary.
confinar *vt* to confine; * *vi*: ~ con to border upon.
confirmación *f* confirmation.
confirmar *vt* to confirm; to corroborate.
confiscación *f* confiscation.
confiscar *vt* to confiscate.
confite *m* candy.
confitería *f* , candy; candy store.
confitero/ra *m/f* confectioner.
confitura *f* preserve; jam.
conflagración *f* conflagration.
conflictivo/va *adj* controversial.
conflicto *m* conflict.
confluencia *f* confluence.
confluir *vi* to join (of rivers); to gather (of people).
conformar *vt* to shape; to adjust, to adapt; * *vi* to agree; ~se *vr* to conform; to resign oneself.
conforme *adj* alike, similar; agreed; * *prep* according to.
conformidad *f* similarity; agreement; resignation.
conformista *m/f* conformist.
confortable *adj* comfortable.
confortar *vt* to comfort; to strengthen; to console.
confortativo/va *adj* comforting.
confraternidad *f* fraternity.
confrontación *f* confrontation.
confrontar *vt* to confront.
confundir *vt* to confound, to jumble; to confuse; ~se *vr* to make a mistake.
confusamente *adv* confusedly.

confusión f confusion.
confuso/sa adj confused.
congelación f freezing.
congelado/da adj frozen; * mpl: ~s frozen food.
congelador m freezer.
congelar vt to freeze; ~se vr to congeal.
congeniar vi to get on well.
congestión f congestion.
congestionar vt to congest.
congoja f anguish, distress, grief.
congraciarse vr to ingratiate oneself.
congratulación f congratulation.
congratular vt to congratulate.
congregación f congregation, assembly.
congregar vt, ~se vr to assemble, to meet, to collect.
congresista m/f delegate.
congreso m congress.
cónico/ca adj conical.
conjetura f conjecture, guess.
conjeturar vt to conjecture, to guess.
conjugación f (gr) conjugation.
conjugar vt (gr) to conjugate; to combine.
conjunción f conjunction.
conjuntamente adv together.
conjunto/ta adj united, joint; * m whole; (mus) ensemble, band; team.
conjuración f conspiracy, plot.
conjurado/da m/f conspirator.
conjurar vt to exorcise; * vi to conspire, to plot.
conjuro m incantation, exorcism.
conmemoración f commemoration.
conmemorar vt to commemorate.
conmigo pn with me.
conminación f threat.
conminar vt to threaten.
conminatorio/ria adj threatening.
conmiseración f commiseration, pity, sympathy.
conmoción f shock; upheaval; commotion; (med) concussion.
conmovedor/ra adj touching.
conmover vt to move; to disturb.
conmutación f commutation, exchange.
conmutador m switch; Lat Am switchboard.
conmutar vt (law) to commute; to exchange.
connotar vt to imply.
coño excl (col) hell!, damn!
cono m cone.
conocedor/ra m/f connoisseur.
conocer vt to know, to understand; ~se vr to know one another.

conocido/da m/f acquaintance.
conocimiento m knowledge, understanding; (med) consciousness; acquaintance; (mar) bill of lading.
conque m condition.
conquista f conquest.
conquistador m conqueror; * adj ~/ra conquering.
conquistar vt to conquer.
consabido/da adj well-known; above-mentioned.
consagración f consecration.
consagrar vt to consecrate.
consanguíneo/nea adj related by blood.
consanguinidad f blood relationship.
consecución f acquisition; attainment.
consecuencia f consequence; conclusion; consistency; por ~ therefore.
consecuente adj consistent.
consecutivo/va adj consecutive.
conseguir vt to attain; to get, to obtain.
consejero/ra m/f adviser; councilor/councillor.
consejo m advice; council.
consenso m consensus.
consentido/da adj spoiled (of children).
consentimiento m consent.
consentir vt to consent to; to allow; to admit; to spoil (a child).
conserje m/f doorman, porter; janitor.
conservación f conservation.
conservante m preservative.
conservar vt to conserve; to keep; to preserve (fruit).
conservas fpl canned food.
conservatorio m (mus) conservatoire.
considerable adj considerable.
consideración f consideration; respect.
consideradamente adv considerately.
considerado/da adj respected; considerate.
considerar vt to consider.
consigna f (mil) watchword; order, instruction; (rail) checkroom.
consignación f consignment.
consignar vt to consign, to dispatch; to assign; to record, to register.
consignatario/ria m/f consignee.
consigo pn (m) with him; (f) with her; (vd) with you; (reflexivo) with oneself.
consiguiente adj consequent.
consistencia f consistence, consistency.
consistente adj consistent; firm, solid.
consistir vi: ~ en to consist of; to be due to.
consistorio m town council; town hall.
consocio/cia m/f fellow member; partner.

consola f control panel; console.
consolación f consolation.
consolador/ra adj consoling, comforting.
consolar vt to console, to comfort, to cheer.
consolidar vt to consolidate.
consomé m consommé.
consonancia f consonance.
consonante m rhyme; * f (gr) consonant; * adj consonant, harmonious.
consorcio m partnership.
consorte m/f consort, companion, partner; accomplice.
conspiración f conspiracy, plot.
conspirador/ra m/f conspirator, plotter.
conspirar vi to conspire, to plot.
constancia f constancy; steadiness.
constante adj constant; firm.
constar vi to be evident, to be certain; to be composed of, to consist of.
constatar vt to note; to check.
constelación f constellation.
consternación f consternation.
consternar vt to dismay; to shock.
constipado/da adj: **estar** ~ to have a cold.
constiparse vr to catch a cold.
constitución f constitution.
constitucional adj constitutional.
constituir vt to constitute; to establish; to appoint.
constitutivo/va adj constitutive; essential.
constituyente adj constituent.
constreñimiento m constraint.
constreñir vt to restrict; to force; (med) to constipate; to constrict.
constricción f constriction, contraction.
construcción f construction.
constructor/ra m/f builder.
construir vt to form; to build, to construct; to construe.
consuegro/gra m/f father-in-law/mother-in-law of one's son/daughter.
consuelo m consolation, comfort.
cónsul m consul.
consulado m consulate.
consulta f consultation.
consultar vt to consult, to ask for advice.
consultivo/va adj consultative.
consultor/ra m/f adviser, consultant.
consultorio m (med) surgery.
consumación f consummation, finishing.
consumado/da adj consummate; complete; accomplished; perfect.
consumar vt to consummate, to finish; to carry out.
consumición f consumption; drink.

consumidor/ra m/f consumer.
consumir vt to consume; to burn, to use; to waste, to exhaust; ~**se** vr to waste away, to be consumed.
consumismo m consumerism.
consumo m consumption.
contabilidad f accounting; bookkeeping.
contable m/f accountant.
contacto m contact; (auto) ignition.
contado/da adj: ~**s** scarce, few; * m: **pagar al** ~ to pay (in) cash.
contador m meter; counter in a cafe; ~/a m/f Lat Am accountant.
contaduría f Lat Am accountancy; accountant's office.
contagiar vt to infect; ~**se** vr to get infected.
contagio m contagion.
contagioso/sa adj contagious.
contaminación f contamination; pollution.
contaminar vt to contaminate; to pollute; to corrupt.
contante m cash.
contar vt to count, to reckon; to tell; * vi to count; ~ **con** to rely upon.
contemplación f contemplation.
contemplar vt to look at; to contemplate, to consider; to meditate.
contemplativo/va adj contemplative.
contemporáneo/nea adj contemporary.
contemporizar vi to temporize.
contencioso/sa adj contentious; quarrelsome.
contender vi to contend, to compete.
contendiente m/f competitor.
contenedor m container.
contener vt to contain, to hold; to hold back; to repress; ~**se** vr to control oneself.
contenido/da adj moderate, restrained; * m contents pl.
contentar vt to content, to satisfy; to please; ~**se** vr to be pleased/satisfied.
contento/ta adj glad; pleased; content; * m contentment; (law) release.
contestación f answer, reply.
contestador m: ~ **automático** answering machine.
contestar vt to answer, to reply; to prove, to corroborate.
contexto m context.
contienda f contest, dispute.
contigo pn with you.
contigüidad f contiguity.
contiguo/gua adj contiguous, close.
continencia f continence, abstinence, moderation.

continental *adj* continental.
continente *m* continent, mainland; * *adj* continent.
contingencia *f* risk; contingency.
contingente *adj* contingent, accidental; * *m* contingent.
continuación *f* continuation; sequel.
continuar *vt, vi* to continue.
continuidad *f* continuity.
continuo/nua *adj* continuous.
contonearse *vr* to walk affectedly.
contoneo *m* affected manner of walking.
contorno *m* environs *pl*; contour, outline; en ~ round about.
contorsión *f* contortion.
contra *prep* against; contrary to; opposite.
contraataque *m* counter-attack.
contrabajo *m* (*mus*) double bass; bass guitar; low bass.
contrabandista *m/f* smuggler.
contrabando *m* contraband; smuggling.
contracción *f* contraction.
contrachapado *m* plywood
contradecir *vt* to contradict.
contradicción *f* contradiction.
contradictorio/ria *adj* contradictory.
contraer *vt* to contract, to shrink, to make (a bargain); ~se *vr* to shrink, to contract.
contrafuerte *m* buttress; foothill; heel-pad.
contragolpe *m* backlash.
contrahecho/cha *adj* deformed; hunchbacked; counterfeit, fake, false.
contralto *m* (*mus*) contralto.
contramaestre *m* (*mar*) boatswain; foreman.
contrapartida *f* (*com*) balancing entry.
contrapaso *m* step backwards.
contrapelo *adv*: a ~ against the grain.
contrapesar *vi* to counterbalance.
contrapeso *m* counterpoise; counterweight.
contraponer *vt* to compare, to oppose.
contraposición *f* comparison; contrast.
contraproducente *adj* counterproductive.
contraprogramación *f* competitive scheduling.
contrapunto *m* (*mus*) counterpoint.
contrariar *vt* to contradict, to oppose; to vex.
contrariedad *f* opposition; setback; annoyance.
contrario/ria *m/f* opponent; * *adj* contrary, opposite; por el ~ on the contrary.
contrarreloj *f* time trial.
contrarrestar *vt* to return a ball; (*fig*) to counteract.

contrarrevolución *f* counter-revolution.
contraseña *f* countersign; (*mil*) watchword.
contrasentido *m* contradiction.
contrastar *vt* to resist; to contradict; to assay (metals); to verify (measures and weights); * *vi* to contrast.
contraste *m* contrast.
contrata *f* contract.
contratación *f* signing-up, hiring.
contratar *vt* to contract; to hire, to engage.
contratiempo *m* setback; accident.
contratista *m* contractor.
contrato *m* contract, agreement.
contravención *f* contravention.
contraveneno *m* antidote.
contravenir *vi* to contravene, to transgress; to violate.
contraventana *f* shutter.
contribución *f* contribution; tax.
contribuir *vt, vi* to contribute.
contribuyente *m/f* contributor; taxpayer.
contrincante *m* competitor.
contrito/ta *adj* contrite, penitent.
controlador/ra *m/f* controller.
controlar *vt* to control; to check.
controversia *f* controversy, dispute.
contumacia *f* obstinacy, stubbornness; (*law*) contempt of court.
contumaz *adj* obstinate, stubborn; (*law*) guilty of contempt of court.
contundente *adj* overwhelming; blunt.
contusión *f* bruise.
convalecencia *f* convalescence.
convalecer *vi* to recover from sickness, to convalesce.
convaleciente *m/f, adj* convalescent.
convalidar *vt* to recognize.
convencer *vt* to convince.
convencimiento *m* conviction.
convención *f* convention, pact.
convencional *adj* conventional.
conveniencia *f* suitability, usefulness; agreement; ~s *fpl* property.
conveniente *adj* useful; suitable.
convenio *m* convention, agreement, treaty.
convenir *vi* to agree, to suit.
convento *m* convent, nunnery; monastery.
conventual *adj* monastic.
convergencia *f* convergence.
converger *vi* to converge.
conversa *f Lat Am* conversation, talk.
conversación *f* conversation, talk; communication.
conversar *vi* to talk, to converse.

conversión *f* conversion, change.
converso/sa *m/f* convert.
convertir *vt*, ~se *vr* to convert.
convexo/xa *adj* convex.
convicción *f* conviction.
convicto/ta *adj* convicted (found guilty).
convidado/da *m/f* guest.
convidar *vt* to invite.
convincente *adj* convincing.
convite *m* invitation; banquet.
convivencia *f* living together.
convocar *vt* to convoke, to assemble.
convocatoria *f* summons; notice of a meeting.
convoy *m* convoy.
convulsión *f* convulsion.
convulsivo/va *adj* convulsive.
conyugal *adj* conjugal, married.
cónyuge *m/f* spouse.
cooperar *vi* to cooperate.
cooperativa *f* cooperative.
cooperativo/va *adj* cooperative.
coordinadora *f* coordinating committee.
coordinar *vt* to arrange, to coordinate.
copa *f* cup; glass; top of a tree; crown of a hat; ~s *fpl* hearts *pl* (in cards).
copete *m* quiff; pride.
copia *f* plenty, abundance; copy, duplicate.
copiador/ra *m/f* copyist; copier.
copiar *vt* to copy; to imitate.
copioso/sa *adj* copious, abundant, plentiful.
copla *f* verse; (*mus*) popular song, folk song.
copo *m* small bundle; flake of snow.
copropietario/ria *m/f* joint owner.
cópula *f* copulation; conjunction; (*gr*) copula.
copulativo/va *adj* copulative.
coqueta *f* coquette, flirt.
coquetear *vi* to flirt.
coquetería *f* coquetry, flirtation.
coraje *m* courage; anger; passion.
coral *m* coral; choir; * *adj* choral.
coraza *f* cuirass; armor-plating.
corazón *m* heart; core; **de** ~ willingly.
corazonada *f* feeling; inspiration; quick decision; presentiment.
corbata *f* tie.
corbeta *f* corvette.
corcel *m* steed, charger.
corchea *f* (*mus*) quaver.
corchete *m* clasp; hook and eye.
corcho *m* cork; float (for fishing); cork bark.
cordel *m* cord, rope; (*mar*) line.
cordero *m* lamb; lambskin; meek/gentle person.

cordial *adj* cordial, affectionate; * *m* cordial.
cordialidad *f* cordiality.
cordillera *f* range of mountains.
cordón *m* cord, string; lace; cordon.
cordura *f* prudence, good sense, wisdom.
corista *m/f* chorister.
cornada *f* thrust with a bull's horn.
cornadura *f* horns *pl*.
cornamenta *f* horns *pl* of an animal.
córnea *f* cornea.
cornear *vt* to gore.
córneo/ea *adj* horny, corneous.
corneta *f* bugle.
cornisa *f* cornice.
cornudo/da *adj* horned.
coro *m* choir; chorus.
corona *f* crown; coronet; top of the head; crown (of a tooth); tonsure; halo.
coronación *f* coronation.
coronar *vt* to crown; to complete, to perfect.
coronario/ria *adj* coronary.
coronel *m* (*mil*) colonel.
coronilla *f* crown of the head.
corpiño *m* bodice.
corporación *f* corporation.
corporal *adj* corporal.
corpóreo/rea *adj* corporeal.
corpulencia *f* corpulence.
corpulento/ta *adj* corpulent, bulky.
Corpus *m* Corpus Christi.
corral *m* yard; farmyard; corral; playpen.
correa *f* leather strap, thong; flexibility.
correaje *m* leather straps *pl*.
corrección *f* correction; reprehension; amendment.
correccional *m* reformatory.
correctivo/va *adj* corrective.
correcto/ta *adj* exact, correct.
corrector/ra *m/f* proof-reader.
corredizo/za *adj* sliding; easy to be untied.
corredor/ra *adj* running; * *m/f* broker, runner; *m* corridor.
corregir *vt* to correct, to amend; to reprehend; ~se *vr* to reform.
correlación *f* correlation.
correo *m* post, mail; courier; postman; ~ **electrónico** e-mail; **a vuelta de** ~ by return of post; ~s *mpl* post office.
correoso/sa *adj* flexible, leathery.
correr *vt* to run; to flow; to travel over; to pull (a drape); * *vi* to run, to rush; to flow; to blow (applied to the wind); ~se *vr* to be ashamed; to slide, to move; to run (of colors).

correría f incursion.
correspondencia f correspondence; communication; agreement.
corresponder vi to correspond; to answer; to be suitable; to belong; to concern; ~**se** vr to love one another.
correspondiente adj corresponding, suitable.
corresponsal m/f correspondent.
corretear vi to rush around; to hang about the streets.
corrida f run, dash; bullfight.
corrido/da adj expert; knowing; ashamed.
corriente f current; course, progression; electric current; * adj current; common, ordinary, general; fluent; flowing, running.
corrillo m circle of persons; clique.
corro m circle of people.
corroborar vt to corroborate.
corroer vt to corrode, to erode.
corromper vt to corrupt; to rot; to turn bad; to seduce; to bribe; ~**se** vr to rot; to become corrupted; * vi to stink.
corrosión f corrosion.
corrosivo/va adj corrosive.
corrupción f corruption; rot, decay.
corruptible adj corruptible.
corrupto/ta adj corrupted, corrupt.
corruptor/ra m/f corrupter, perverter.
corrusco m broken bread.
corsé f corset.
cortacésped m lawn mower.
cortada f Lat Am shortcut.
cortado m coffee with a little milk; ~/**da** adj cut; sour; embarrassed.
cortadura f cut; cutting; incision; fissure; ~**s** fpl shreds pl, cuttings pl, parings pl.
cortafuegos m invar fire lane, firebreak.
cortaplumas m invar penknife.
cortar vt to cut; to cut off, to curtail; to intersect; to carve; to chop; to cut (in cards); to interrupt; ~**se** vr to be ashamed/ embarrassed; to curdle.
cortauñas m invar nail clippers pl.
corte[1] m cutting; cut; section; length (of cloth); style.
corte[2] f (royal) court; capital city; Lat Am law court; **C~s** fpl Spanish Parliament.
cortedad f shortness, smallness; stupidity; bashfulness.
cortejar vt to court.
cortejo m entourage; courtship; procession; lover.
cortés/csa adj courteous, polite.
cortesana f courtesan.

cortesía f courtesy, good manners pl.
corteza f bark; peel; crust; (fig) outward appearance.
cortina f drape; ~**s** drapes.
cortinaje m set of drapes.
corto/ta adj short; scanty, small; stupid; bashful; **a la ~a o a la larga** sooner or later.
corvo/va adj bent, crooked.
corzo/za m/f roe deer, fallow deer.
cosa f thing; matter, affair; **¡no hay tal ~!** nothing of the sort!
cosaco m Cossack.
cosecha f harvest; harvest time; **de su ~** of one's own invention.
cosechar vt to harvest, to reap.
coser vt to sew; to join.
cosido m stitching, sewing.
cosmético/a adj, m cosmetic.
cosmopolita adj, m cosmopolitan.
cosquillas fpl tickling; (fig) agitation.
costa f cost, price; charge, expense; coast, shore; **a toda ~** at all events.
costado m side; (mil) flank; side of a ship.
costal m sack, large bag.
costalada f heavy fall.
costar vt to cost; to need.
coste m cost, expense.
costear vt to pay for.
costera f side; slope; coast.
costero/ra adj coastal; (mar) coasting.
costilla f rib; (fig) wife; cutlet; ~**s** fpl back, shoulders pl.
costillar m human ribs pl.
costo m cost, price; expense.
costoso/sa adj costly, dear, expensive.
costra f crust; (med) scab.
costumbre f custom, habit.
costura f sewing; seam; needlework.
costurera f seamstress.
costurero m sewing box.
cotejar vt to compare.
cotejo m comparison, collation.
cotidiano/na adj daily.
cotilla m/f gossip.
cotización f quotation.
cotizar vt to quote; ~**se** vr: **~ a** to sell at; to be quoted at.
coto m enclosure; reserve; boundary stone.
cotorra f magpie; small parrot; (col) chatterbox.
covacha f small cave, grotto.
coyote m coyote.
coyuntura f joint, articulation; juncture.
coz f kick; recoil (of a gun); ebbing (of a flood); (fig) insult.

cráneo *m* skull.
cráter *m* crater.
creación *f* creation.
creador/ra *adj* creative; * *m/f* creator.
crear *vt* to create, to make; to establish.
crecer *vi* to grow, to increase; to rise.
creces *fpl* increase.
crecida *f* swell (of rivers).
crecido/da *adj* full-grown (of a person); large; (*fig*) vain.
creciente *f* crescent (moon); (*mar*) flood tide; * *adj* growing; crescent.
crecimiento *m* increase; growth.
credenciales *fpl* credentials *pl*.
credibilidad *f* credibility.
crédito *m* credit; belief, faith; reputation.
credo *m* creed.
credulidad *f* credulity.
crédulo/la *adj* credulous.
creencia *f* credence, belief.
creer *vt*, *vi* to believe; to think; to consider.
crema *f* cream; custard.
cremallera *f* zipper.
crepúsculo *m* twilight.
crespo/pa *adj* curled; angry, displeased.
crespón *m* crepe.
cresta *f* crest (of birds).
creyente *m/f* believer.
cría *f* breeding; young.
criada *f* servant, maid.
criadero *m* (*bot*) nursery; breeding place.
criadilla *f* testicle; small loaf; truffle.
criado/da *m/f* servant; *adj* reared, brought up, bred.
criador *f* creator; breeder.
crianza *f* breeding, rearing.
criar *vt* to create, to produce; to breed; to nurse; to breast-feed; to bring up, to raise.
criatura *f* creature; child.
criba *f* sieve.
cribar *vt* to sift.
crimen *m* crime.
criminal *adj*, *m/f* criminal.
criminalista *m/f* criminologist; criminal lawyer.
crin *f* mane; horsehair.
crío/a *m/f* (*col*) kid.
criollo/lla *adj*, *m/f* Creole.
cripta *f* crypt.
crisis *f invar* crisis.
crisma *f* holy oil, chrism.
crisol *m* crucible; melting pot.
crispar *vt* to set on edge; to tense up.
cristal *m* crystal; glass; pane; lens.
cristalino/na *adj* crystalline.

cristalización *f* crystallization.
cristalizar *vt* to crystallize.
cristiandad *f* Christianity.
cristianismo *m* Christianity.
cristiano/na *adj*, *m/f* Christian.
Cristo *m* Christ.
criterio *m* criterion.
crítica *m/f* criticism.
criticar *vt* to criticize.
crítico/ca *m/f* critic; * *adj* critical.
croar *vi* to croak.
cromo *m* chrome.
crónica *f* chronicle; news report; feature.
crónico/ca *adj* chronic.
cronista *m/f* chronicler; reporter, columnist.
cronología *f* chronology.
cronológico/ca *adj* chronological.
cronómetro *m* stopwatch.
cruce *m* crossing; crossroads.
crucero *m* cruiser; cruise; transept; crossing; Southern Cross (constellation).
crucificar *vt* to crucify; to torment.
crucifijo *m* crucifix.
crucigrama *m* crossword.
crudeza *f* unripeness; crudeness; undigested food (in the stomach).
crudo/da *adj* raw; green, unripe; crude; cruel; hard to digest.
cruel *adj* cruel.
crueldad *f* cruelty.
cruento/ta *adj* bloody; cruel.
crujido *m* crack; creak; clash; crackling.
crujiente *adj* crunchy.
crujir *vi* to crackle; to rustle.
crustáceo *m* crustacean.
cruz *f* cross; tails (of a coin).
cruzada *f* crusade.
cruzado *m* crusader; ~/da *adj* crossed.
cruzar *vt* to cross; (*mar*) to cruise ~se *vr* to cross; to pass each other.
cuaderna *f* fourth part; rib.
cuaderno *m* notebook; exercise book; logbook.
cuadra *f* block; stable.
cuadrado/da *adj*, *m* square.
cuadragenario/ria *adj* forty-year-old.
cuadragésimo/ma *adj*, *m* fortieth.
cuadrangular *adj* quadrangular, four-cornered; * *m Lat Am* home run.
cuadrángulo *m* quadrangle.
cuadrante *m* quadrant; dial.
cuadrar *vt*, *vi* to square; to fit, to suit, to correspond.
cuadricular *adj* squared.
cuadrilátero/ra *adj*, *m* quadrilateral.

cuadrilla *f* party, group; gang, crew.
cuadro *m* square; picture, painting; window frame; scene; chart; (*sport*) team; executive; *Lat Am* slaughterhouse.
cuadrúpedo/da *adj* quadruped.
cuádruple *adj* quadruple.
cuádruplo/pla *adj* quadruple, fourfold.
cuajada *f* curd.
cuajar *vt* to coagulate; to thicken; to adorn; to set; ~se *vr* to coagulate, to curdle; to set; to fill up.
cuál *pn* which (one).
cual *pn* which; who; whom; * *adv* as; like; * *adj* such as.
cualidad *f* quality.
cualquier *adj* any.
cualquiera *adj* anyone, anybody; someone, somebody; whoever; whichever.
cuándo *adv* when; ¿de ~ acá? since when?.
cuando *adv* when; if; even; * *conj* since; de ~ en ~ from time to time; ~ más/mucho at most/at best; ~ menos at least
cuantía *f* quantity, amount; importance.
cuantioso/sa *adj* numerous; substantial.
cuantitativo/va *adj* quantitative, quantitive.
cuánto *adj* what a lot of; how much?; ¿~s? how many?; * *pn*, *adv* how; how much; how many.
cuanto/ta *adj* as many as; as much as; all; whatever; * *adv* en ~ as soon as; en ~ a as regards; ~ más moreover, the more as.
cuarenta *adj*, *m* forty.
cuarentena *f* space of forty days; Lent; quarantine.
cuaresma *f* Lent.
cuarta *f* fourth; span; (*mar*) point (of the compass).
cuartear *vt* to quarter, to divide up; ~se *vr* to split into pieces.
cuartel *m* quarter, district; barracks *pl*.
cuarteta *f* (*poet*) quatrain.
cuartilla *f* fourth part; sheet of paper.
cuarto *m* fourth part; quarter; room, apartment; span; ~s *mpl* cash, money; ~/ta *adj* fourth.
cuarzo *m* quartz.
cuatrero *m* horse thief.
cuatro *adj*, *m* four.
cuatrocientos/tas *adj* four hundred.
cuba *f* cask; tub; (*fig*) drunkard.
cubeta *f* small cask.
cúbico/ca *adj* cubic.
cubierta *f* cover; deck of a ship; (*auto*) hood; tire; pretext.

cubierto *m* cover; shelter; place at table; meal at a fixed charge; ~s *mpl* cutlery.
cubil *m* lair.
cubilete *m* tumbler; dice box.
cubo *m* cube; bucket.
cubo de la basura *m* ash can, trash can, garbage can.
cubrecama *m* bedspread.
cubrir *vt* to cover; to disguise; to protect; to roof a building; ~se *vr* to become overcast.
cucaña *f* (*col*) soft job; bargain; cinch.
cucaracha *f* cockroach.
cuchara *f* spoon.
cucharada *f* spoonful; ladleful.
cucharadita *f* teaspoonful.
cucharita *f* teaspoon.
cucharón *m* ladle; large spoon.
cuchichear *vi* to whisper.
cuchicheo *m* whispering.
cuchilla *f* large kitchen knife; chopping knife; blade.
cuchillada *f* cut; gash; ~s *fpl* wrangles, quarrels
cuchillo *m* knife.
cuchitril *m* pigpen.
cuclillas *adv*: en ~ squatting.
cuclillo *m* cuckoo; (*fig*) cuckold.
cuco *m* cuckoo; ~/ca *adj* sharp.
cucurucho *m* paper cornet.
cuello *m* neck; collar.
cuenca *m* bowl, deep valley; hollow; socket of the eye.
cuenco *m* earthenware bowl.
cuenta *f* calculation; account; check (in a restaurant); count, counting; bead; importance.
cuentakilómetros *m invar* odometer.
cuentapropista *m/f Lat Am* self-employed person.
cuentarrevoluciones *m invar* tachometer.
cuentista *m/f* storyteller.
cuento *m* tale, story, narrative.
cuerazo *m Lat Am* lash.
cuerda *f* rope; string; spring.
cuerdo/da *adj* sane; prudent, judicious, canny.
cuerear *vt Lat Am* to lash.
cuerno *m* horn.
cuero *m* hide, skin, leather; *Lat Am* whip.
cuerpo *m* body; cadaver, corpse.
cuervo *m* raven.
cuesta *f* slope, hill; incline; ir ~ abajo to go downhill; ~ arriba uphill.
cuestión *f* question, matter; dispute; quarrel; problem.

cuestionable *adj* questionable, problematic.
cuestionar *vt* to question, to dispute.
cuete *m Lat Am* rocket.
cueva *f* cave; cellar.
cuidado *m* care, worry, concern; charge.
cuidadosamente *adv* observantly.
cuidadoso/sa *adj* careful; anxious.
cuidar *vt* to care for; to mind, to look after.
culata *f* butt, breech (of a gun); hindquarters *pl* (of an animal); rear of a horse.
culebra *f* snake.
culinario/ria *adj* culinary.
culminación *f* culmination.
culo *m* backside, bottom; (*col*) ass.
culpa *f* fault, blame; guilt.
culpabilidad *f* guilt.
culpable *adj* culpable; guilty; * *m/f* culprit.
culpar *vt* to accuse, to blame.
cultivación *f* cultivation, culture.
cultivar *vt* to cultivate.
cultivo *m* cultivation; crop.
culto/ta *adj* cultivated, cultured; refined, civilized; * *m* culture; worship.
cultura *f* culture.
cumbre *f* top, summit.
cumpleaños *m invar* birthday.
cumplido/da *adj* large, plentiful; complete, perfect, courteous; * *m* compliment.
cumplidor/ora *adj* reliable.
cumplimentar *vt* to compliment.
cumplimiento *m* fulfillment; accomplishment; completion.
cumplir *vt* to carry out, to fulfill; to serve (a prison sentence); to carry out (death penalty); to attain, to reach (a certain age); ~se *vr* to be fulfilled; to expire, to be up.
cúmulo *m* heap, pile.
comunicado *m* communiqué.
cuna *f* cradle.
cuña *f* wedge.
cuñado/da *m/f* brother/sister-in-law.
cundir *vi* to spread; to grow, to increase.
cuneta *f* ditch.
cuota *f* quota; fee; *Lat Am* installment.
cupé *m* (*auto*) coupé.

cupo *m* share.
cupón *m* coupon.
cúpula *f* cupola, dome.
cura *m* priest; * *f* cure; treatment.
curable *adj* curable.
curación *f* cure; curing; **primera** ~ first aid.
curandero *m* quack (doctor).
curar *vt* to cure; to treat, to dress (a wound); to salt; to dress; to tan.
curativo/va *adj* curative, healing.
curia *f* ecclesiastical court.
curiosear *vt* to glance at; * *vi* to look round.
curiosidad *f* curiosity.
curioso/sa *adj* curious; * *m/f* bystander.
Curita™ *f Lat Am* Band-Aid™.
currante *m/f* (*col*) worker.
currar *vi* (*col*) to work.
currículum *m* curriculum vitae.
cursado/da *adj* skilled; versed.
cursar *vt* to frequent a place; to send, to dispatch; to study.
cursillo *m* short course of lectures (in a university).
cursivo/va *adj* italic (type).
curso *m* course, direction; year (at university); subject.
cursor *m* cursor.
curtidor *m* tanner.
curtidos *mpl* tanned leather.
curtir *vt* to tan leather; ~se *vr* to become sunburned; to become inured.
curva *f* curve, bend.
curvatura *f* curvature.
curvilíneo/nea *adj* curvilinear.
curvo/va *adj* curved, bent.
cuscurro *m* little crust of bread.
cúspide *f* summit, peak; apex.
custodia *f* custody, safekeeping, care; monstrance.
custodio *m* guard, keeper; watchman.
cutáneo/nea *adj* cutaneous.
cutícula *f* cuticle.
cutis *m* skin.
cutre *adj* (*col*) unpleasant, nasty, mean; of poor quality.
cuyo/ya *pn* whose, of which, of whom.

D

dactilógrafo/fa *m/f* typist.
dádiva *f* gift, present; donation.
dadivoso/sa *adj* generous, open-handed.
dado *m* die; ~s dice.
daga *f* dagger.
dale *excl* come on!
daltónico/ca *adj* color-blind.
dama *f* lady, gentlewoman; mistress; queen; actress who performs principal parts.
damasco *m* damask (fabric); damson (plum).
damasquino/na *adj* damask.
damnificar *vt* to hurt, to injure, to damage.
danza *f* dance.
danzar *vi* to dance; to meddle.
danzarín *m* fine dancer; meddler.
dañar *vt* to hurt, to injure; to damage.
dañino/na *adj* harmful; noxious; mischievous.
daño *m* harm, damage; prejudice; loss.
dar *vi* to give, to supply, to administer, to afford; to deliver; to bestow; to strike, to beat, to knock; to communicate; ~se *vr* to conform (to the will of another); to give oneself up; ~se prisa to hurry.
dardo *m* dart.
datar *vt* to date.
dátil *m* (*bot*) date.
dativo *m* (*gr*) dative.
dato *m* fact.
de *prep* of; from; for; by; on; to; with.
deambular *vi* to stroll.
deán *m* dean.
debajo *adv* under, underneath, below.
debate *m* debate, discussion; contest; altercation.
debatir *vt* to debate, to argue, to discuss.
debe *m* (*com*) debit; ~ y haber debit and credit.
deber *m* obligation, duty; debt; * *vt* to owe; to be obliged to; * *vi*: debe (de) it must, it should.
debidamente *adv* justly, duly; exactly, perfectly.
débil *adj* feeble, weak; sickly; frail.
debilidad *f* dimness; weakness.
debilitar *vt* to debilitate, to weaken.
débito *m* debt; duty.
debutar *vi* to make one's debut.
década *f* decade.
decadencia *f* decay, decline.
decaer *vi* to decay, to molder; to decline, to fade.

decaimiento *m* decay, decline.
decálogo *m* Decalogue.
decano *m* senior; dean.
decantar *vt* to decant.
decapitación *f* decapitation, beheading.
decapitar *vt* to behead.
decena *f* ten.
decencia *f* decency.
decente *adj* decent; honest.
decepción *f* disappointment.
dechado *m*: ~ de virtudes model of virtue and perfection.
decidir *vt* to decide, to determine.
decimal *adj* decimal.
décimo/ma *adj*, *m* tenth.
decir *vt* to say; to tell; to speak; to name.
decisión *f* decision; determination, resolution; sentence.
decisivo/va *adj* decisive; final.
declamación *f* declamation, discourse, oration.
declamar *vi* to declaim; to harangue.
declaración *f* declaration; explanation, interpretation; (*law*) deposition.
declarar *vt* to declare; to manifest; to expound; to explain; (*law*) to decide; ~se *vr* to declare one's opinion; * *vi* to testify.
declinación *f* declination, descent; decline.
declinar *vi* to decline; to decay, to degenerate; * *vt* (*gr*) to decline.
declive *m* slope; decline.
decolaje *m* *Lat Am* take-off.
decolar *vi* *Lat Am* to take off.
decolorarse *vr* to become discolored.
decomiso *m* confiscation.
decoración *f* decoration.
decorado *m* scenery.
decorar *vt* to decorate, to adorn; to illustrate.
decorativo/va *adj* decorative.
decoro *m* honor, respect; circumspection; honesty; decency.
decoroso/sa *adj* decorous, decent.
decrecer *vi* to decrease.
decrépito/ta *adj* decrepit, worn out with age.
decrepitud *f* decrepitude.
decretar *vt* to decree, to determine.
decreto *m* decree; decision; judicial decree.
dedal *m* thimble; very small drinking glass.
dedicación *f* dedication; consecration.
dedicar *vt* to dedicate, to devote; to consecrate; ~se *vr* to apply oneself to.

dedicatoria *f* dedication.

dedo *m* finger; toe; small bit; ~ **meñique** little finger; ~ **pulgar** thumb; ~ **índice** index finger; ~ **corazón** middle finger; ~ **anular** ring finger.

deducción *f* deduction, inference; derivation.

deducir *vt* to deduce, to infer; to allege in pleading; to subtract.

defección *f* defection; apostasy.

defectivo/va *adj* defective.

defecto *m* defect; defectiveness.

defectuoso/sa *adj* defective, imperfect, faulty.

defender *vt* to defend, to protect; to justify, to assert, to maintain; to prohibit, to forbid; to resist, to oppose.

defensa *f* defense, justification, apology; guard, shelter, protection, fence.

defensiva *f* defensive.

defensivo *m* defense, safeguard; ~/**va** *adj* defensive.

defensor/ra *m/f* defender, protector; lawyer, defense counsel.

deferente *adj* pliant, docile, yielding.

deferir *vi* to defer; to yield (to another's opinion); * *vt* to communicate.

deficiencia *f* deficiency.

deficiente *adj* defective.

déficit *m* deficit.

definición *f* definition; decision.

definir *vt* to define, to describe, to explain; to decide.

definitivo/va *adj* definitive; positive.

deformar *vt* to deform; ~**se** *vr* to become deformed.

deforme *adj* deformed; ugly.

deformidad *f* deformity; ugliness; gross error.

defraudación *f* fraud; usurpation.

defraudar *vt* to defraud, to cheat; to usurp; to disturb.

defunción *f* death; funeral.

degeneración *f* degeneration; degeneracy.

degenerar *vi* to degenerate.

degollación *f* beheading.

degollar *vt* to behead; to destroy, to ruin.

degradación *f* degradation.

degradar *vt* to degrade; ~**se** *vr* to degrade/ demean oneself.

degustar *vt* to taste.

dehesa *f* pasture, field.

deidad *f* deity, divinity; goddess.

dejadez *f* slovenliness, neglect.

dejado/da *adj* slovenly, idle, indolent; dejected.

dejar *vt* to leave, to quit; to omit; to let; to permit, to allow; to leave, to forsake; to

bequeath; to pardon; ~ **de** to stop; to fail to; ~**se** *vr* to abandon oneself.

dejo *m* accent; aftertaste, tang.

del *adj* of the (contraction of **de** and **el**).

delantal *m* apron.

delante *adv* in front; opposite; ahead; ~ **de** in front of; before.

delantera *f* front, forepart (of something); advantage; forward line.

delantero/ra *adj* front; * *m/f* forward.

delatar *vt* to accuse; to denounce.

delator *m* accuser; informer, denouncer.

delegación *f* delegation; substitution.

delegado/da *m/f* delegate; deputy.

delegar *vt* to delegate; to substitute.

deleitar *vt* to delight.

deletrear *vt* to spell; to examine; to conjecture.

delfín *m* dolphin; dauphin.

delgadez *f* thinness.

delgado/da *adj* thin; delicate, fine; light; slender, lean; acute; ingenious; little, scanty.

deliberación *f* deliberation; resolution.

deliberadamente *adv* deliberately.

deliberar *vi* to consider, to deliberate; * *vt* to debate; to consult.

delicadeza *f* tenderness, softness; delicacy, daintiness; subtlety.

delicado/da *adj* delicate, tender; faint; exquisite; delicious, dainty; slender, subtle.

delicia *f* delight, pleasure.

delicioso/sa *adj* delicious; delightful.

delincuencia *f* delinquency.

delincuente *m* delinquent.

delineante *m/f* draftsman/woman.

delinear *vt* to delineate, to sketch; to describe.

delinquir *vi* to offend.

delirante *adj* delirious.

delirar *vi* to rave; to talk nonsense.

delirio *m* delirium; dotage; nonsense.

delito *m* offense; crime.

demacrado/da *adj* pale and drawn.

demagogia *f* demagogy.

demagogo *m* demagog.

demanda *f* demand, claim; pretension, complaint; challenge; request.

demandado/da *m/f* defendant.

demandante *m/f* claimant.

demandar *vt* to demand; to ask; to claim; to sue.

demarcación *f* demarcation; boundary line.

demarcar *vt* to mark out (limits).

demás *adj* other; remaining; * *pn* **los/las** ~ the others, the rest; **estar** ~ to be over and above; to be useless/superfluous; **por** ~ in vain, to no purpose.

demasía *f* excess; arduous enterprise; rudeness; want of respect; abundance, plenty; **en** ~ excessively.

demasiado/da *adj* too; excessive; * *adv* too, too much.

demencia *f* madness.

demente *adj* mad, insane.

democracia *f* democracy.

demócrata *m/f* democrat.

democrático/ca *adj* democratic.

demoler *vt* to demolish; to destroy.

demolición *f* demolition.

demonio *m* demon.

demora *f* delay; demurrage.

demorar *vt* to delay; ~**se** *vr* to be delayed; * *vi* to linger.

demostrable *adj* demonstrable.

demostración *f* demonstration; manifestation.

demostrar *vt* to prove, to demonstrate; to manifest.

demostrativo/va *adj* demonstrative.

denegación *f* denial; refusal.

denegar *vt* to deny; to refuse.

dengue *m* prudery.

denigración *f* defamation; stigma, disgrace.

denigrar *vt* to blacken; to insult.

denominación *f* denomination.

denominar *vt* to name; to designate.

denotar *vt* to denote; to express.

densidad *f* density; obscurity.

denso/sa *adj* dense, thick; compact.

dentado/da *adj* jagged, toothed; perforated (of stamps).

dentadura *f* set of teeth.

dentellada *f* gnashing of the teeth; nip; pinch with the teeth; **a** ~**s** snappishly, peevishly.

dentera *f* (*fig*) the shivers *pl*.

dentición *f* dentition, teething.

dentífrico *m* toothpaste.

dentista *m/f* dentist.

dentro *adv* within; * *pn*: ~ **de** in, inside.

denuncia *f* denunciation; accusation; report.

denunciar *vt* to advise; to denounce; to report.

deparar *vt* to offer, to present.

departamento *m* department; (*rail*) compartment; apartment.

dependencia *f* dependency; relation, affinity; dependence; office; business, affair.

depender *vi*: ~ **de** to depend on, to be dependent on.

dependienta *f* saleswoman.

dependiente *m* shop/store assistant; * *adj* dependent.

depilar *vt* to depilate, remove hair from.

depilatorio *m* hair remover.

deplorable *adj* deplorable, lamentable.

deplorar *vt* to deplore.

deponer *vt* to depose; to declare; to displace; to deposit.

deportación *f* deportation.

deportar *vt* to deport.

deporte *m* sport.

deportista *m/f* sportsman/woman.

deportivo/va *adj* sports *compd*.

deposición *f* deposition; assertion, affirmation; (*law*) deposition upon oath.

depositar *vt* to deposit; to confide; to put away for safekeeping.

depósito *m* deposit; warehouse; tank.

depravación *f* depravity.

depravar *vt* to deprave, to corrupt.

depreciar *vt* to depreciate.

depredador/ra *adj* predatory; * *m* predator.

depresión *f* depression.

deprimido/da *adj* depressed.

deprimir *vt* to depress; ~**se** *vr* to become depressed.

deprisa *adv* quickly.

depuración *f* purification.

depuradora *f* purifier.

depurar *vt* to cleanse; to purify; to filter.

de quitapón *adj* detachable, removable.

derecha *f* right hand, right side; right.

derecho/cha *adj* right; straight; just; perfect; certain; * *m* right, justice; law; tax, duty; fee; * *adv* straight.

derivación *f* derivation; source; origin.

derivado/da *adj* derivative; * *m* derivative; by-product.

derivar *vt*, *vi* to derive; (*mar*) to drift.

dermatología *f* dermatology.

dermatólogo/ga *m/f* dermatologist.

derogar *vt* to derogate, to abolish; to reform.

derogatorio/ria *adj* derogatory.

derramamiento *m* effusion; waste; dispersion; ~ **de sangre** bloodshed.

derramar *vt* to drain off (water); to spread; to spill, to scatter; to waste, to shed; ~**se** *vr* to pour out.

derrame *m* spelling; overflow; discharge; leakage.

derredor *m* circumference, circuit; **al/en** ~ around, about.

derrengado/da *adj* bent, crooked.
derrengar *vt* to sprain.
derretir *vt* to melt; to consume; to thaw; ~**se** *vr* to melt.
derribar *vt* to demolish; to flatten.
derribo *m* demolition; ruins of a demolished building *pl*.
derrocar *vt* to pull down, to demolish.
derrochador *m* spendthrift.
derrochar *vt* to dissipate; to squander.
derroche *m* waste.
derrota *f* ship's course; road, path; defeat.
derrotar *vt* to destroy; to defeat.
derrotero *m* collection of sea charts; ship's course; (*fig*) course, way.
derruir *vt* to demolish.
derrumbar *vt* to throw down; ~**se** *vr* to collapse.
desabastecer *vt* to cut off supplies from.
desabillé *m* deshabille/dishabille.
desabollar *vt* to take the bulges out of.
desabotonar *vt* to unbutton; ~**se** *vr* to come undone.
desabrido/da *adj* tasteless, insipid; rude; unpleasant.
desabrigado/da *adj* uncovered; unsheltered.
desabrigar *vt* to uncover; to deprive of clothes/shelter.
desabrochar *vt* to undo; ~**se** *vr* to come undone.
desacatar *vt* to treat in a disrespectful manner.
desacato *m* disrespect, incivility.
desacertado/da *adj* mistaken; unwise; inconsiderate.
desacierto *m* error, gross mistake, blunder.
desaconsejado/da *adj* inconsiderate; ill-advised.
desaconsejar *vt* to advise against.
desacorde *adj* discordant.
desacostumbrado/da *adj* unusual.
desacreditar *vt* to discredit.
desacuerdo *m* blunder; disagreement; forgetfulness.
desafiar *vt* to challenge; to defy.
desafilado/da *adj* blunt.
desafinado/da *adj* out of tune.
desafinar *vi* to be out of tune.
desafío *m* challenge; struggle; contest, combat.
desaforado/da *adj* huge; disorderly, lawless; impudent.
desafortunadamente *adv* unfortunately.
desafortunado/da *adj* unfortunate, unlucky.
desafuero *m* outrage; excess.

desagradable *adj* disagreeable, unpleasant.
desagradar *vt* to displease; to pester.
desagradecido/da *adj* ungrateful.
desagradecimiento *m* ingratitude.
desagrado *m* harshness; displeasure.
desagraviar *vt* to make amends for.
desagravio *m* amends *pl*; satisfaction.
desaguar *vt* to drain; * *vi* to drain off.
desagüe *m* channel, drain; drainpipe; drainage.
desaguisado *m* outrage.
desahogado/da *adj* comfortable; roomy.
desahogar *vt* to ease; to vent; ~**se** *vr* to recover; to relax; to let off steam.
desahogo *m* ease, relief; freedom.
desahuciar *vt* to cause to despair; to give up; to evict.
desahucio *m* eviction.
desairado/da *adj* disregarded; slighted.
desairar *vt* to disregard, to take no notice of.
desaire *m* disdain, disrespect; unattractiveness.
desajustar *vt* to make uneven; to unbalance; ~**se** *vr* to get out of order.
desajuste *m* disorder; imbalance.
desalentador/ra *adj* disheartening.
desalentar *vt* to make breathless; to discourage.
desaliento *m* dismay.
desaliño *m* slovenliness; carelessness.
desalinizadora *f* desalination plant.
desalinizar *vt* to desalinate.
desalmado/da *adj* cruel, inhuman.
desalojar *vt* to eject; to move out; * *vi* to move out.
desamarrar *vt* to cast off (a ship); to untie; to remove.
desamor *m* indifference.
desamparado/da *adj* helpless.
desamparar *vt* to forsake, to abandon; to relinquish.
desamparo *m* abandonment; helplessness; dereliction.
desamueblar *vt* to remove the furniture from.
desandar *vt* to retrace; to go back the same road.
desangrar *vt* to bleed; to drain (a pond); (*fig*) to exhaust (one's means); ~**se** *vr* to lose a lot of blood.
desanimado/da *adj* downhearted.
desanimar *vt* to discourage; ~**se** *vr* to lose heart.
desapacible *adj* disagreeable; unpleasant, harsh.
desaparecer *vi* to disappear.

desaparecido/da *adj* missing; * *mpl* ~s missing people.

desaparejar *vt* to unharness, unhitch (beasts); (*mar*) to unrig (a ship).

desaparición *f* disappearance.

desapego *m* coolness; lack of interest.

desapercibido/da *adj* unnoticed.

desaplicado/da *adj* lazy; careless, neglectful.

desapolillar *vt* to free from moths; ~se *vr* (*fig*) to get rid of the cobwebs.

desaprensivo/va *adj* unscrupulous.

desaprobación *f* disapproval.

desaprobar *vt* to disapprove; to condemn; to reject.

desaprovechado/da *adj* useless; unprofitable; backward; slack.

desaprovechar *vt* to waste, to turn to a bad use.

desarmar *vt* to disarm; to disband (troops); to dismantle; (*fig*) to pacify.

desarme *m* disarmament.

desarraigar *vt* to uproot; to root out; to extirpate.

desarraigo *m* eradication.

desarrapado/da *adj* ragged.

desarreglado/da *adj* untidy.

desarreglar *vt* to disorder, to upset.

desarreglo *m* disorder; untidiness.

desarrollar *vt* to develop; to unroll; to unfold; ~se *vr* to develop; to be unfolded; to open.

desarrollo *m* development.

desarropar *vt* to undress.

desarticular *vt* to take apart.

desasir *vt* to loosen, to disentangle; ~se *vr* to extricate oneself.

desasosegar *vt* to disquiet, to disturb.

desasosiego *m* restlessness; anxiety.

desastrado/da *adj* wretched, miserable; ragged.

desastre *m* disaster; misfortune.

desastroso/sa *adj* disastrous.

desatado/da *adj* untied; wild.

desatar *vt* to untie, to loose; to separate; to solve; ~se *vr* to come undone; to break.

desatascar *vt* to unblock; to clear.

desatender *vt* to pay no attention to; to disregard.

desatinado/da *adj* foolish; extravagant; * *m* fool, madman.

desatinar *vi* to talk nonsense; to reel, to stagger.

desatino *m* blunder; nonsense.

desatornillar *vt* to unscrew.

desatrancar *vt* to unbar; to unblock.

desautorizado/da *adj* unauthorized.

desautorizar *vt* to deprive of authority; to deny.

desavenencia *f* discord, disagreement.

desavenido/da *adj* contrary, disagreeing.

desaventajado/da *adj* disadvantageous, unprofitable.

desayunar *vt* to have for breakfast; ~se *vr* to breakfast; * *vi* to have breakfast;

desayuno *m* breakfast.

desazón *f* disgust; uneasiness; annoyance.

desazonado/da *adj* ill-adapted; ill-humored.

desazonar *vt* to annoy; ~se *vr* to be annoyed; to be anxious.

desbancar *vt* to break (the bank in gambling); (*fig*) to supplant.

desbandarse *vr* to disband; to go off in all directions.

desbarajuste *m* confusion.

desbaratar *vt* to destroy.

desbarrar *vi* to talk rubbish.

desbastar *vt* to smooth; to polish; to waste.

desbloquear *vt* to unblock.

desbocado/da *adj* open-mouthed; wild (of a horse); foul-mouthed; indecent.

desbocarse *vr* to bolt (of a horse).

desbordar *vt* to exceed; ~se *vr* to overflow.

descabalgar *vi* to dismount.

descabellado/da *adj* disheveled; disorderly; wild, unrestrained; disproportional; violent.

descabellar *vt* to ruffle.

descafeinado/da *adj* decaffeinated.

descalabrado/da *adj* wounded on the head; imprudent.

descalabrar *vt* to wound on the head; to smash.

descalabro *m* blow; misfortune; considerable loss.

descalificar *vt* to disqualify; to discredit.

descalzar *vt*, ~se *vr* to take off one's shoes.

descalzo/za *adj* barefooted; (*fig*) destitute.

descambiar *vt* to exchange.

descaminado/da *adj* (*fig*) misguided.

descaminar *vt* to misguide, to lead astray.

descamisado/da *adj* shirtless.

descampado/da *adj* disengaged; free; open; * *m* open space, open country.

descansado/da *adj* rested, refreshed; quiet.

descansar *vt* to rest; * *vi* to rest; to lie down.

descansillo *m* landing.

descanso *m* rest, repose; break; interval.

descapotable *m* convertible.

descarado/da *adj* cheeky, barefaced.

descararse *vr* to behave insolently.
descarga *f* unloading; volley, discharge.
descargar *vt* to unload, to discharge; ~se *vr* to unburden oneself.
descargo *m* discharge; evidence; receipt.
descarnado/da *adj* scrawny.
descarnar *vt* to strip the flesh from; to clean away the flesh from; to corrode; ~se *vr* to grow thin.
descarado/da *adj* cheeky.
descaro *m* nerve.
descarriar *vt* to lead astray; to misdirect; ~se *vr* to lose one's way; to stray; to err.
descarrilamiento *m* (*rail*) derailment.
descarrilar *vi* (*rail*) to leave/run off the rails.
descarrío *m* losing of one's way.
descartar *vt* to discard; to dismiss; to rule out; ~se *vr* to excuse oneself.
descascarillado/da *adj* peeling.
descastado *adj* degenerate; ungrateful.
descendencia *f* descent; offspring.
descendente *adj* descending; **tren** ~ *m* (*rail*) down train.
descender *vt* to take down; * *vi* to descend, to walk down; to flow; to fall; ~ **de** to be derived from.
descendiente *adj* descending; * *m/f* descendant.
descenso *m* descent; drop; relegation.
descerrajar *vt* to force the lock (of a door etc); to discharge firearms.
descifrar *vt* to decipher; to unravel.
desclavar *vt* to draw out nails (from).
descocado/da *adj* bold, impudent.
descodificador *m* decoder (for TV).
descolgar *vt* to take down; to pick up; ~se *vr* to let oneself down.
descollar *vi* to excel.
descolorido/da *adj* pale, colorless.
descomedido/da *adj* impudent, insolent; huge.
descompaginar *vt* to disarrange.
descomponer *vt* to discompose, to set at odds; to disconcert; (*chem*) to decompose.
descomposición *f* disagreement; discomposure; decomposition.
descompuesto/ta *adj* decomposed; broken.
descomunal *adj* uncommon; huge.
desconcertado/da *adj* disconcerted; bewildered.
desconcertar *vt* to disturb; to confound; to disconcert; ~se *vr* to be bewildered; to be upset.
desconchado/da *adj* peeling.
desconchar *vt* to peel off.

desconcierto *m* disorder, confusion; uncertainty.
desconectar *vt* to disconnect.
desconfiado/da *adj* mistrustful, distrustful.
desconfianza *f* distrust; jealousy.
desconfiar *vi*: ~ **de** to mistrust, to suspect.
descongelar *vt* to defrost.
descongestionar *vt* to clear.
desconocer *vt* to disown, to disavow; to be totally ignorant of (a thing); not to know (a person); not to acknowledge (a favor received).
desconocido/da *adj* unknown; disguised; * *m/f* stranger.
desconocimiento *m* ignorance.
desconsiderado/da *adj* inconsiderate; imprudent.
desconsolado/da *adj* disconsolate; painful; sad.
desconsolar *vt* to distress.
desconsuelo *m* distress; trouble; despair.
descontado *adj*: **por** ~ of course; **dar por** ~ to take for granted.
descontar *vt* to discount; to deduct.
descontento *m* dissatisfaction; disgust.
descorazonar *vt* to dishearten, to discourage.
descorchar *vt* to uncork.
descorrer *vt* to draw.
descortés/esa *adj* impolite, rude.
descortesía *f* rudeness.
descoser *vt* to undo, take apart; to separate; ~se *vr* to come apart at the seams.
descosido/da *adj* unstitched; disjointed.
descoyuntar *vt* to dislocate; to vex, to annoy.
descrédito *m* discredit.
descreído/da *adj* incredulous.
descremado/da *adj* skimmed.
describir *vt* to describe; to draw, to delineate.
descripción *f* description; delineation; inventory.
descriptivo/va *adj* descriptive.
descuartizar *vt* to quarter; to carve.
descubierto *m* deficit; overdraft; ~/ta *adj* uncovered.
descubrimiento *m* discovery; revelation.
descubrir *vt* to discover, to disclose; to uncover; to reveal; to show; ~se *vr* to reveal oneself; to take off one's hat; to confess.
descuento *m* discount; decrease.
descuida *excl* don't worry!
descuidado/da *adj* careless, negligent.
descuidar *vt* to neglect; * *vi*, ~se *vr* to be careless.

descuido *m* carelessness, negligence; forgetfulness; incivility; improper action.

desde *prep* since; after; from; ~ **luego** of course; ~ **entonces** since then.

desdecirse *vr* to retract one's words.

desdén *m* disdain, scorn.

desdentado/da *adj* toothless.

desdentar *vt* to draw out (teeth).

desdeñable *adj* contemptible, despicable.

desdeñar *vt* to disdain, to scorn; ~**se** *vr* to be disdainful.

desdeñoso/sa *adj* disdainful; contemptuous.

desdicha *f* misfortune, calamity; great poverty.

desdichado/da *adj* unfortunate; wretched, miserable.

desdoblar *vt* to unfold, to spread open.

desear *vt* to desire, to wish; to require, to demand.

desecación *f* desiccation.

desecar *vt* to dry up.

desechar *vt* to depreciate; to reject; to refuse; to throw away.

desecho *m* residue; ~**s** *mpl* rubbish.

desembalar *vt* to unpack.

desembarazado/da *adj* free.

desembarazar *vt* to free; to clear; ~**se** *vr* ~ **de** to get rid of.

desembarcadero *m* landing stage.

desembarcar *vt* to unload, to disembark; * *vi* to disembark, to land; *Lat Am* to get off.

desembarco *m* landing.

desembargo *m* (*law*) raising an embargo.

desembarque *m* landing.

desembocadura *f* mouth.

desembocar *vi*: ~ **en** to flow into.

desembolsar *vt* to pay out.

desembolso *m* expenditure.

desembragar *vi* to declutch.

desembuchar *vt* to disgorge; to tell all.

desempaquetar *vt* to unpack.

desempatar *vi* (*sport*) to hold a play-off.

desempate *m* play-off.

desempeñar *vt* to redeem; to extricate from debt; to fulfill (any duty/promise); to acquit; ~**se** *vr* to get out of debt.

desempeño *m* redeeming a pledge; occupation.

desempleado/da *adj* unemployed; * *m/f* unemployed person.

desempleo *m* unemployment.

desempolvorar *vt* to dust.

desencadenar *vt* to unchain; ~**se** *vr* to break loose; to burst.

desencajar *vt* to disjoint; to dislocate; to disconnect.

desencallar *vt* to refloat.

desencanto *m* disenchantment.

desenchufar *vt* to unplug.

desenfadado/da *adj* free; unembarrassed.

desenfado *m* ease; facility; calmness, relaxation.

desenfocado/da *adj* out of focus.

desenfrenado/da *adj* outrageous; ungovernable.

desenfreno *m* wildness; lack of self-control.

desenganchar *vt* to unhook; to uncouple.

desengañado/da *adj* disillusioned.

desengañar *vt* to disillusion; ~**se** *vr* to become disillusioned.

desengaño *m* disillusionment; disappointment.

desengrasar *vt* to take the grease off.

desenhebrar *vt* to unthread; to unravel.

desenlace *m* climax; outcome.

desenmarañar *vt* to disentangle; to unravel.

desenmascarar *vt* to unmask.

desenredar *vt* to disentangle.

desenrollar *vt* to unroll.

desenroscar *vt* to untwist; to unroll.

desentenderse *vr* to pretend not to understand; to pass by without noticing.

desenterrar *vt* to exhume; to dig up.

desentonar *vi* to be out of tune; to clash.

desentrañar *vt* to unravel.

desentumecer *vt* to stretch; to loosen up.

desenvainar *vt* to unsheathe; to show.

desenvoltura *f* sprightliness; cheerfulness; impudence, boldness.

desenvolver *vt* to unfold; to unroll; to decipher, to unravel; to develop; ~**se** *vr* to develop; to cope.

desenvuelto/ta *adj* forward; natural.

deseo *m* desire, wish.

deseoso/sa *adj* anxious.

desequilibrado/da *adj* unbalanced.

deserción *f* desertion; defection.

desertar *vt* to desert; to abandon (a cause).

desertificación *f* desertification.

desertor *m* deserter; fugitive.

desesperación *f* despair, desperation; anger, fury.

desesperado/da *adj* desperate, hopeless.

desesperar *vi*, ~**se** *vr* to despair; * *vt* to make desperate.

desestabilizar *vt* to destabilize.

desestatizar *vt* *Lat Am* to privatize.

desestatización *f Lat Am* privatization.
desestimar *vt* to disregard, to reject.
desfachatez *f* impudence.
desfalcar *vt* to embezzle.
desfalco *m* embezzlement.
desfallecer *vi* to get weak; to faint.
desfallecimiento *m* fainting.
desfasado/da *adj* old-fashioned.
desfase *m* gap.
desfavorable *adj* unfavorable.
desfigurar *vt* to disfigure, to deform; to disguise.
desfiladero *m* gorge.
desfilar *vi* (*mil*) to parade.
desfogarse *vr* to give vent to one's passion/anger.
desforestación *f* deforestation.
desgajar *vt* to tear off; to break in pieces; ~se *vr* to be separated; to be torn to pieces.
desgana *f* disgust; loss of appetite; aversion, reluctance.
desganado/da *adj* not hungry; half-hearted; **estar** ~ to lose all pleasure in doing a thing; to lose one's appetite.
desgano *m Lat Am* disgust; loss of appetite; aversion, reluctance.
desgañitarse *vr* to scream, to bawl.
desgarrador/a *adj* heartrending.
desgarrar *vt* to tear; to shatter.
desgarro *m* tear; grief; impudence.
desgarrón *m* large tear.
desgastar *vt* to waste; to corrode; ~se *vr* to get worn out.
desgaste *m* wear (and tear).
desglosar *vt* to break down.
desgracia *f* misfortune; disgrace; accident; setback.
desgraciado/da *adj* unfortunate; unhappy, miserable; out of favor; disagreeable.
desgreñado/da *adj* disheveled.
desgreñar *vt* to dishevel (the hair); to disorder.
desguarnecer *vt* to strip down; to dismantle.
deshabitado/da *adj* deserted, uninhabited; desolate.
deshacer *vt* to undo, to destroy; to cancel, to efface; to rout (an army); to solve; to melt; to break up, to divide; to dissolve in a liquid; to violate (a treaty); to diminish; to disband (troops); ~se *vr* to melt; to come apart.
desharrapado/da *adj* shabby; ragged, in tatters.
deshecho/cha *adj* undone, destroyed;

wasted; melted; in pieces; * *m Lat Am* short cut.
deshelar *vt* to thaw; ~se *vr* to thaw, to melt.
desheredar *vt* to disinherit.
deshidratado/da *adj* dehydrated.
deshidratar *vt* to dehydrate.
deshielo *m* thaw.
deshilachar *vt* to unravel.
deshilar *vt* to fray.
deshinchar *vt* to deflate; ~se *vr* to go flat, to go down.
deshojar *vt* to strip the leaves off.
deshollinador *m* chimney sweep.
deshonesto/ta *adj* indecent.
deshonra *f* dishonor; shame.
deshonrar *vt* to affront, to insult, to defame; to dishonor.
deshonroso/sa *adj* dishonorable, indecent.
deshora *f* unseasonable time.
deshuesar *vt* to get rid of bones; to stone.
desidia *f* idleness, indolence.
desierto/ta *adj* deserted; solitary; * *m* desert; wilderness.
designación *f* designation.
designar *vt* to design; to intend; to appoint; to express, to name.
designio *m* design, purpose; road, course.
desigual *adj* unequal, unlike; uneven, craggy.
desigualdad *f* inequality, dissimilitude; inconstancy; roughness, unevenness.
desilusión *f* disappointment.
desilusionar *vt* to disappoint; ~se *vr* to become disillusioned.
desinfección *f* disinfection.
desinfectar *vt* to disinfect.
desinflar *vt* to deflate.
desintegración *f* disintegration.
desinterés *m* unselfishness; disinterestedness.
desinteresado/da *adj* disinterested; unselfish.
desistir *vi* to desist, to cease.
deslave *m Lat Am* landslide.
desleal *adj* disloyal; unfair.
deslealtad *f* disloyalty, breach of faith.
desleír *vt* to dilute; to dissolve.
deslenguado/da *adj* foul-mouthed.
desligar *vt* to separate; to loosen, to unbind; ~se *vr* to extricate oneself.
desliz *m* slip, sliding; lapse, weakness.
deslizadizo/za *adj* slippery, slippy; glib.
deslizar *vt* to slip, to slide; to let slip (a comment); ~se *vr* to slip; to skid; to flow softly; to creep in.
deslucido/da *adj* tarnished; dull; shabby.

deslucir *vt* to tarnish; to damage; to discredit.

deslumbramiento *m* glare; confusion.

deslumbrar *vt* to dazzle; to puzzle.

desmán *m* outrage; disaster; misconduct.

desmandarse *vr* to behave badly.

desmantelar *vt* to dismantle; to abandon,
to forsake.

desmaquillador *m* make-up remover.

desmarañar *vt* to disentangle.

desmayado/da *adj* unconscious; dismayed;
appalled; weak.

desmayar *vi* to be dispirited; to be fainthearted; ~**se** *vr* to faint.

desmayo *m* unconsciousness; faint, swoon;
dismay.

desmedido/da *adj* disproportionate.

desmejorar *vt* to impair; to weaken.

desmembrar *vt* to dismember; to separate.

desmemoriado/da *adj* forgetful.

desmentir *vt* to give the lie to; ~**se** *vr* to
contradict oneself.

desmenuzar *vt* to crumble; to chip at; to
fritter away; to examine minutely.

desmerecer *vt* to be unworthy of; * *vi* to
deteriorate.

desmesurado/da *adj* excessive; huge; immeasurable.

desmontar *vt* to level; to remove (a heap
of rubbish); to dismantle; * *vi* to dismount.

desmoralización *f* demoralization.

desmoralizar *vt* to demoralize.

desmoronar *vt* to destroy little by little;
~**se** *vr* to fall into disrepair.

desnatado/da *adj* skimmed.

desnatar *vt* to skim (milk); to take the
choicest part of.

desnaturalizar *vt* to divest of naturaliza-
tion rights; ~**se** *vr* to forsake one's
country.

desnivel *m* unevenness of the ground.

desnucar *vt* to break (one's neck).

desnudar *vt* to undress; to strip; to discover,
to reveal; ~**se** *vr* to undress.

desnudez *f* nakedness.

desnudo/da *adj* naked; bare, uncovered; ill-
clothed; (*fig*) plain, evident.

desnutrición *f* malnutrition.

desnutrido/da *adj* undernourished.

desobedecer *vt*, *vi* to disobey.

desobediencia *f* disobedience; insubordination.

desobediente *adj* disobedient.

desocupado/da *adj* empty; at leisure.

desocupar *vt* to vacate; to empty; ~**se** *vr* to

retire from a business; to withdraw from
an arrangement.

desodorante *m* deodorant.

desolación *f* destruction; affliction.

desolado/da *adj* desolate, disconsolate.

desolar *vt* to lay waste; to harass.

desollar *vt* to flay, to skin; (*fig*) to extort.

desorden *m* disorder, confusion.

desordenado/da *adj* disorderly; untidy.

desordenar *vt* to disorder; to untidy; ~**se** *vr*
to get out of order.

desorganización *f* disorganization.

desorganizar *vt* to disorganize.

desorientar *vt* to mislead; to confuse; ~**se**
vr to lose one's way.

desovar *vi* to spawn.

despabilado/da *adj* watchful, vigilant; wide-
awake.

despabilar *vt* to snuff (a candle); (*fig*) to
dispatch quickly; to sharpen; ~**se** *vr* to
wake up.

despacio *adv* slowly, leisurely; little by little;
(*Lat Am*) quietly; ¡~! softly!, gently!

despachar *vt* to dispatch; to expedite; to
sell; to send.

despacho *m* dispatch, expedition; cabinet;
office; commission; warrant, patent; expedient; smart answer.

despachurrar *vt* to squash, to crush; to
mangle.

desparejar *vt* to make unequal/uneven.

desparpajo *m* ease; savoir-faire.

desparramar *vt* to disseminate, to spread;
to spill; to squander, to lavish; ~**se** *vr* to be
dissipated.

despavorido/va *adj* frightened.

despectivo/va *adj* pejorative, derogatory.

despecho *m* indignation; displeasure; spite;
dismay, despair; deceit; derision, scorn; **a ~
de** in spite of.

despedazar *vt* to tear into pieces; to mangle.

despedida *f* farewell; sacking.

despedir *vt* to discharge; to dismiss (from
office); to see off; ~**se** *vr*: ~ **de** to say
goodbye to.

despegado/da *adj* cold; detached.

despegar *vt* to unglue; to take off; ~**se** *vr* to
come loose.

despego *m* detachment; coolness.

despegue *m* take-off.

despeinado/da *adj* disheveled.

despeinar *vt* to ruffle.

despejado/da *adj* sprightly, quick; clear.

despejar *vt* to clear away; ~**se** *vr* to cheer
up; to clear; * *vi* to clear.

despellejar vt to skin.

despensa f pantry, larder; provisions pl.

despeñadero m precipice.

despeñar vt to precipitate; ~se vr to throw oneself headlong.

despepitarse vr to bawl.

desperdiciar vt to squander.

desperdicio m waste; ~s mpl rubbish; waste.

desperdigar vt to separate; to scatter.

desperezarse vr to stretch oneself.

desperfecto m slight damage; flaw.

despertador m alarm clock.

despertar vt to wake up, to rouse from sleep; to excite; * vi to wake up; to grow lively/ sprightly; ~se vr to wake up.

despiadado/da adj heartless; merciless.

despido m dismissal.

despierto/ta adj awake; vigilant; fierce; brisk, sprightly.

despilfarrar vt to waste.

despilfarro m slovenliness; waste; mismanagement.

despintar vt to deface (a painting); to obscure (things); to mislead; ~se to lose its color.

despistar vt to mislead; to throw off the track; ~se vr to take the wrong way; to become confused.

desplante m bold statement; wrong stance; insolence.

desplazamiento m displacement.

desplazar vt to move; to scroll; ~se vr to travel.

desplegar vt to unfold, to display; to explain, to elucidate; (mar) to unfurl; ~se vr to open out; to travel.

despliegue m display.

desplomarse vr to fall to the ground; to collapse.

desplumar vt to fleece; to pluck.

despoblado m desert.

despoblar vt to depopulate; to desolate; ~se vr to become depopulated.

despojar vt: ~ (de) to strip (of); to deprive (of); ~se vr to undress.

despojo m plunder; loot; ~s mpl giblets pl; remains pl; offal.

desposado/da adj newlywed.

desposar vt to marry, to betroth; ~se vr to be betrothed/married.

desposeer vt to dispossess.

desposeimiento m dispossession.

déspota m despot.

despótico/ca adj despotic.

despotismo m despotism.

despreciable adj contemptible, despicable.

despreciar vt to offend; to despise.

desprecio m scorn, contempt.

desprender vt to unfasten, to loosen; to separate; ~se vr to give way; to fall down; to extricate oneself.

desprendimiento m alienation, disinterestedness.

despreocupado/da adj careless; unworried.

despreocuparse vr to be carefree.

desprestigiar vt to run down.

desprevenido/da adj unawares, unprepared.

desproporción f disproportion.

desproporcionado/da adj disproportionate.

desproporcionar vt to disproportion.

despropósito m absurdity.

desprovisto/ta adj unprovided.

después adv after, afterwards; next.

despuntar vt to blunt; * vi to sprout; to dawn; **al ~ del día** at break of day.

desquiciar vt to upset; to discompose; to disorder.

desquitar vt to retrieve (a loss); ~se vr to win one's money back again; to return by giving like for like; to take revenge.

desquite m recovery of a loss; revenge, retaliation.

desrizar vt to uncurl.

destacamento m (mil) detachment; **~ de policía** Lat Am police station.

destacar vt to emphasize; (mil) to detach (a body of troops); ~se vr to stand out.

destajo m piecework; **trabajar a ~** to do piecework.

destapar vt to uncover; to open; ~se vr to be uncovered.

destartalado/da adj untidy.

destello m signal light; sparkle.

destemplado/da adj out of tune; badly blended (of paint); intemperate.

desteñir vt to discolor; ~se vr to fade.

desternillarse vr: **~ de risa** to roar with laughter.

desterrar vt to banish; to expel, to drive away.

destetar vt to wean.

destete m weaning.

destierro m exile, banishment.

destilación f distillation.

destilar vt, vi to distill.

destinar vt to assign to; to destine for, to intend for.

destinatario/a m/f addressee.

destino m destiny; fate, doom; destination; office.

destitución f destitution, abandonment.
destituir vt to dismiss.
destornillador m screwdriver.
destornillar vt to unscrew.
destreza f dexterity, cleverness, cunning, expertness, skill.
destripar vt to disembowel; to trample.
destronar vt to dethrone.
destrozar vt to destroy, to break into pieces; (mil) to defeat.
destrozo m destruction; (mil) defeat, massacre.
destrucción f destruction, ruin.
destructivo/va adj destructive.
destruir vt to destroy.
desunir vt to separate, to disunite; to cause discord between.
desuso m disuse.
desvaído/da adj tall and graceless.
desvalido/da adj helpless; destitute.
desvalijar vt to rob; to burgle.
desván m garret.
desvanecer vt to dispel; ~se vr to grow vapid, to become insipid; to vanish; to be affected with giddiness; to faint.
desvanecimiento m pride, haughtiness; giddiness; fainting fit.
desvariar vi to be delirious.
desvarío m delirium; giddiness; inconstancy, caprice; extravagance.
desvelar vt to keep awake; ~se vr to stay awake.
desvelo m want of sleep; watchfulness.
desvencijado/da adj broken-down, rickety.
desvencijar vt to disunite, to divide; to weaken; ~se vr to be ruptured; to come apart.
desventaja f disadvantage; damage.
desventura f misfortune; calamity.
desventurado/da adj unfortunate; calamitous.
desvergonzado/da adj impudent, shameless.
desvergonzarse vr to behave in an impudent manner.
desvergüenza f impudence; shamelessness.
desvestir vt, ~se vr to undress.
desviar vt to divert; to dissuade; to parry (at fencing); ~se vr to go off course.
desvío m turning away, going astray; aversion; disdain; indifference.
desvivirse vr: ~ por to long for.
detallar vt to detail, to relate minutely.
detalle m detail.
detallista m retailer.

detención f detention; delay.
detener vt to stop, to detain; to arrest; to keep back; to reserve; to withhold; ~se vr to stop; to stay.
detenidamente adv carefully.
detenido/da adj detailed; sparing, niggardly; slow, inactive.
detergente m detergent.
deterioración f deterioration; damage.
deteriorar vt to damage.
deterioro m deterioration.
determinación f determination, resolution; boldness.
determinado/da adj determined; resolute.
determinar vt to determine; ~se vr to decide.
detestable adj detestable.
detestar vt to detest, to abhor.
detonación f detonation.
detonar vi to detonate.
detractar vt to denigrate, to defame, to slander.
detrás adv behind; at the back, in the back
detrimento m detriment; damage; loss.
deuda f debt; fault; offense.
deudor/ra m/f debtor.
devaluación f devaluation.
devanar vt to reel; to wrap up.
devastación f devastation, desolation.
devastador/ra adj devastating.
devastar vt to devastate.
devengar vt to accrue.
devoción f devotion, piety; strong affection; ardent love.
devolución f return; (law) devolution.
devolutivo/va adj (law) transferable.
devolver vt to return; to send back; to refund; to throw up; * vi to be sick.
devorar vt to devour, to swallow up.
devoto/ta adj devout, pious; devotional; strongly attached.
día m day.
diablo m devil.
diablura f prank.
diabólico/ca adj diabolical; devilish.
diácono m deacon.
diadema m/f diadem; halo.
diafragma m diaphragm; midriff.
diagnosis f invar diagnosis.
diagnóstico m diagnosis.
diagonal adj diagonal.
diagrama m diagram.
dialecto m dialect.
diálisis f invar dialysis.
diálogo m dialog.

diamante *m* diamond.
diámetro *m* diameter.
diana *f* (*mil*) reveille; bull's-eye.
diapasón *m* (*mus*) diapason, octave.
diapositiva *f* transparency, slide.
diario *m* journal, diary; daily newspaper; daily expenses *pl*; ~/ria *adj* daily.
diarrea *f* diarrhea.
dibujar *vt* to draw, to design.
dibujo *m* drawing; sketch, draft; description.
dicción *f* diction; style; expression.
diccionario *m* dictionary.
diciembre *m* December.
dictado *m* dictation.
dictador *m* dictator.
dictadura *f* dictatorship.
dictamen *m* opinion, notion; suggestion, insinuation; judgement.
dictar *vt* to dictate; *Lat Am* to teach.
dicha *f* happiness, good fortune; **por** ~ by chance.
dicho *m* saying; sentence; declaration; promise of marriage; ~/cha *adj* said.
dichoso/sa *adj* happy, prosperous.
diecinueve *adj*, *m* nineteen.
dieciocho *adj*, *m* eighteen.
dieciséis *adj*, *m* sixteen.
diecisiete *adj*, *m* seventeen.
diente *m* tooth; fang; tusk.
diestro/tra *adj* right; dexterous, skillful, clever; sagacious, prudent; sly, cunning; * *m* skillful fencer; halter; bridle.
diesel, diésel *adj* diesel *compd*.
dieta *f* diet, regimen; diet, assembly.
dietista *m/f Lat Am* dietician.
diez *adj*, *m* ten.
diezmar *vt* to decimate.
diezmo *m* tithe.
difamación *f* defamation.
difamar *vt* to defame, to libel.
difamatorio/ria *adj* defamatory, calumnious.
diferencia *f* difference.
diferencial *adj* differential.
diferenciar *vt* to differentiate, to distinguish; ~se *vr* to differ, to distinguish oneself.
diferente *adj* different, unlike.
diferido/da *adj* recorded.
diferir *vt* to defer, to put off; to differ.
difícil *adj* difficult.
dificultad *f* difficulty.
dificultar *vt* to put difficulties in the way of; to render difficult.
dificultoso/sa *adj* difficult; painful.
difundir *vt* to diffuse, to spread; to divulge; ~se *vr* to spread (out).

difunto/ta *adj* dead, deceased; late.
difusión *f* diffusion.
difuso/sa *adj* diffusive, copious; large; long-winded; circumstantial.
digerir *vt* to digest; to bear with patience; to adjust, to arrange; (*chem*) to digest.
digestión *f* digestion; concoction.
digestivo/va *adj* digestive.
digitador/a *m/f Lat Am* (*comput*) someone who keys in text by means of a keyboard.
digital *adj* digital.
digitalizar *vt* to digitize.
digitar *vt Lat Am* (*comput*) to key in.
dignarse *vr* to condescend, to deign.
dignidad *f* dignity, rank.
digno/na *adj* worthy; suitable.
dije *m* relic; trinket.
dilapidar *vt* to squander, to waste.
dilatación *f* dilation, extension; greatness of mind; calmness.
dilatado/da *adj* large; numerous; prolix; spacious, extensive.
dilatar *vt* to dilate, to expand; to spread out; to defer, to protract.
dilatorio/ria *adj* dilatory.
dilema *m* dilemma.
diligencia *f* diligence; affair, business; call of nature; stage coach.
diligente *adj* diligent, assiduous, prompt, swift.
dilucidar *vt* to elucidate, to explain.
diluir *vt* to dilute.
diluviar *vi* to rain in torrents.
diluvio *m* flood, deluge, inundation; abundance.
dimensión *f* dimension; extent; capacity, bulk.
diminutivo/va *adj* diminutive.
diminuto/ta *adj* defective, faulty; minute, small.
dimisión *f* resignation.
dimitir *vt* to give up, to abdicate; * *vi* to resign.
dinámica *f* dynamics.
dinámico/ca *adj* dynamic.
dinamita *f* dynamite.
dínamo, dinamo *f* dynamo; *m Lat Am* dynamo.
dinastía *f* dynasty.
dineral *m* large sum of money.
dinero *m* money.
diocesano/na *adj* diocesan.
diócesis *f* diocese.
Dios *m* God.
diosa *f* goddess.
diploma *m* diploma, patent.

diplomacia, diplomática *f* diplomacy.
diplomado/da *adj* qualified.
diplomático/ca *adj* diplomatic; * *m/f* diplomat.
diptongo *m* diphthong.
diputación *f* deputation.
diputado *m* deputy.
diputar *vt* to depute.
dique *m* dike, dam.
dirección *f* direction, guidance; administration; steering.
directivo/va *adj* governing.
directo/ta *adj* direct, straight; apparent, evident; live.
director/ra *m/f* director; conductor; president; manager; headmaster (of a private school).
dirigir *vt* to direct; to conduct; to regulate, to govern; ~**se** *vr* to go toward(s); to address oneself to.
discernimiento *m* discernment.
discernir *vt* to discern, to distinguish.
disciplina *f* discipline.
discípulo *m* disciple; scholar.
disco *m* disc; record; discus; light; face (of the sun/moon); lens (of a telescope); ~ **compacto** compact disc.
díscolo/la *adj* ungovernable; peevish.
disconforme *adj* differing.
discordancia *f* disagreement, discord.
discordante *adj* dissonant, discordant.
discordar *vi* to clash, to disagree.
discorde *adj* discordant; (*mus*) dissonant.
discordia *f* discord, disagreement.
discoteca *m* discotheque, disco.
discreción *f* discretion; acuteness of mind.
discrecional *adj* discretionary.
discrepancia *f* discrepancy.
discrepar *vi* to differ.
discreto/ta *adj* discreet; ingenious; witty, eloquent.
discriminación *f* discrimination.
disculpa *f* apology; excuse.
disculpar *vt* to exculpate, to excuse; to acquit, to absolve; ~**se** *vr* to apologize; to excuse oneself.
discurrir *vi* to ramble about; to run to and fro; to discourse (upon a subject); * *vt* to invent, to contrive; to meditate.
discurso *m* speech; conversation; dissertation; space of time.
discusión *f* discussion.
discutir *vt, vi* to discuss.
disecar *vt* to dissect; to stuff.
disección *f* dissection.

diseminar *vt* to scatter; to disseminate, to propagate.
disentería *f* dysentery.
disentir *vi* to dissent, to disagree.
diseñador/ra *m/f* designer.
diseñar *vt* to draw; to design.
diseño *m* design; draft; description; picture.
disfraz *m* disguise; mask.
disfrazar *vt* to disguise, to conceal; to cloak, to dissemble; ~**se** *vr* to disguise oneself as.
disfrutar *vt* to enjoy; ~**se** *vr* to enjoy oneself.
disgustar *vt* to disgust; to offend; ~**se** *vr* to be displeased; to fall out.
disgusto *m* disgust, aversion; quarrel; annoyance; grief, sorrow.
disidente *adj* dissident; * *m/f* dissident, dissenter.
disimular *vt* to hide; to tolerate.
disimulo *m* dissimulation; tolerance.
disipado/da *adj* prodigal, lavish.
disipar *vt* to dissipate, to disperse, to scatter; to lavish.
dislocación *f* dislocation.
dislocarse *vr* to be dislocated/out of joint.
disminución *f* diminution.
disminuir *vt* to diminish; to decrease.
disolución *f* dissolution; liquidation.
disolver *vt* to loosen, to untie; to dissolve; to disunite; to melt, to liquefy; to interrupt.
disonancia *f* dissonance; disagreement, discord.
disparada *f Lat Am* flight; stampede.
disparar *vt* to shoot, to discharge, to fire; to let off; to throw with violence; * *vi* to shoot, to fire.
disparatado/da *adj* inconsistent; absurd, extravagant.
disparate *m* nonsense, absurdity, extravagance.
disparo *m* shot; discharge; explosion.
dispensar *vt* to dispense; to excuse; to dispense with; to distribute.
displicencia *f* displeasure; dislike.
disponer *vt* to arrange, to prepare; to dispose.
disponible *adj* available; disposable.
disposición *f* disposition, order; resolution; command; power, authority.
dispositivo *m* device.
dispuesto/ta *adj* disposed; fit, ready.
disputa *f* dispute, controversy.
disputar *vt* to dispute, to controvert, to question; * *vi* to debate, to argue.
disquera *f Lat Am* record company.

disquete *m* floppy disk.
distancia *f* distance; interval; difference.
distanciarse *vr* to become estranged.
distante *adj* distant, far off.
distinción *f* distinction; difference; prerogative.
distinguido/da *adj* distinguished, conspicuous.
distinguir *vt* to distinguish; to discern; ~**se** *vr* to distinguish oneself.
distintivo *m* distinctive mark; particular attribute.
distinto/ta *adj* distinct, different; clear.
distracción *f* distraction, want of attention.
distraer *vt* to distract; ~**se** *vr* to be absentminded, to be inattentive.
distraído/da *adj* absent-minded, inattentive.
distribución *f* distribution; division, separation; arrangement.
distribuidor *m* distributor.
distribuir *vt* to distribute.
distrito *m* district; territory.
disturbar *vt* to disturb, to interrupt.
disturbio *m* riot; disturbance, interruption.
disuadir *vt* to dissuade.
disuasión *f* dissuasion.
diurno/na *adj* daily.
diva *f* prima donna.
divagar *vt* to digress.
diván *m* divan.
divergencia *f* divergence.
divergente *adj* divergent.
diversidad *f* diversity; variety of things.
diversificar *vt* to diversify; to vary.
diversión *f* diversion; sport; amusement; (*mil*) diversion.
diverso/sa *adj* diverse, different; several, sundry.
divertido/da *adj* amused; amusing.
divertir *vt* to divert (the attention); to amuse, to entertain; (*mil*) to draw off; ~**se** *vr* to amuse oneself.
dividir *vt* to divide; to disunite; to separate; to share out.
divieso *m* (*med*) boil.
divinidad *f* divinity.
divino/na *adj* divine, heavenly; excellent.
divisa *f* emblem.
divisar *vt* to perceive.
divisible *adj* divisible.
división *f* division; partition; separation; difference.
divorciar *vt* to divorce; to separate; ~**se** *vr* to get divorced.

divorcio *m* divorce; separation, disunion.
divulgación *f* publication; dissemination.
divulgar *vt* to publish, to divulge.
dobladillo *m* hem; cuff.
dobladura *f* fold.
doblar *vt* to double; to fold; to bend; * *vi* to turn; to toll (bell); ~**se** *vr* to bend, to bow, to submit.
doble *adj* double; dual; deceitful; **al** ~ doubly; * *m* double.
doblegar *vt* to bend; ~**se** *vr* to yield.
doblez *m* crease; fold; turn-up; * *f* duplicity.
doce *adj*, *m* twelve.
docena *f* dozen.
docente *adj* teaching.
dócil *adj* docile, tractable.
docilidad *f* docility, gentleness; compliance.
doctor/ra *m/f* doctor.
doctorado *m* doctorate.
doctrina *f* doctrine, instruction; science.
doctrinal *m* catechism; * *adj* doctrinal.
documentación *f* documentation.
documento *m* document; record.
dogma *m* dogma.
dólar *m* dollar.
dolencia *f* disease; affliction.
doler *vi* to feel pain; to ache; ~**se** *vr* to feel for the sufferings of others; to complain.
dolor *m* pain; aching, ache; affliction.
doloroso/sa *adj* painful.
domador/ra *m/f* trainer; tamer.
domar *vt* to tame; to subdue, to master.
domesticar *vt* to domesticate.
domiciliarse *vr* to establish oneself in a residence.
domicilio *m* domicile; home, abode.
dominación *f* domination; dominion; authority, power.
dominante *adj* dominant; domineering.
dominar *vt* to dominate; to be fluent in; ~**se** *vr* to moderate one's passions.
domingo *m* Sunday; (Christian) Sabbath.
dominguero/ra *adj* done/worn on Sunday; * *m/f* Sunday driver.
dominical *adj* Sunday.
dominio *m* dominion; domination; power, authority; domain.
donación *f* donation; gift.
donar *vt* to donate; to bestow.
donativo *m* contribution.
doncella *f* virgin, maiden; lady's maid.
donde *adv* where.
dónde *adv* where; ¿**de** ~? from where?; ¿**por** ~? where?
dondequiera *adv* anywhere.

dorado/da adj gilt compd; golden; * m gilding.

dorar vt to gild; (fig) to palliate.

dormilón/ona m/f dull, sleepy person.

dormir vi to sleep; ~se vr to fall asleep.

dormitorio m dormitory.

dorsal adj dorsal.

dos adj, m two.

dosaje m Lat Am dose.

doscientos/tas adj pl two hundred.

dosis f invar dose.

dotado/da adj gifted.

dotar vt to endow.

dote f dowry; ~s fpl gifts of nature pl; endowments pl.

dragón m dragon; (mil) dragoon.

drama m drama.

dramático/ca adj dramatic.

dramatizar vt to dramatize.

dramaturgo/ga m/f dramatist.

droga f drug; stratagem; artifice, deceit.

drogadicción f drug addiction.

drogadicto/ta m/f drug addict.

droguería f hardware store.

dromedario m dromedary.

dubitativo/va adj doubtful, dubious; uncertain.

ducado m duchy; ducat.

ducha f shower; (med) douche.

ducharse vr to have a shower.

ducho/cha adj skilled, experienced.

duda f doubt; suspense; hesitation.

dudar vt to doubt.

dudoso/sa adj doubtful, dubious.

duelo m grief, affliction; mourning.

duende m elf, hobgoblin.

dueño/ña m/f owner; landlord/lady; employer.

dulce adj sweet; mild, gentle, meek; soft; * m candy.

dulcificar vt to sweeten.

dulzura f sweetness; gentleness; softness.

dúo m (mus) duo, duet.

duodécimo/ma adj twelfth.

duplicación f duplication.

duplicado m duplicate.

duplicar vt to duplicate, to double; to repeat.

duplicidad f duplicity; falseness.

duplo m double.

duque m duke.

duquesa f duchess.

duración f duration.

duradero/ra adj lasting, durable.

durante adv during.

durar vi to last, to continue.

duraznero m Lat Am peach tree.

durazno m Lat Am peach; peach tree.

dureza f hardness; harshness; ~ de oído hardness of hearing.

durmiente adj sleeping; * m (rail) sleeping car.

duro/ra adj hard; cruel; harsh, rough; * m five peseta coin; * adv hard.

duunviro m magistrate in ancient Rome.

E

e *conj* and (before words starting with i and hi).
ea *interj* hey!, come on!; ¡~ pues! well then!, let's see!
ebanista *m* cabinet-maker, carpenter.
ébano *m* ebony.
ebrio/ia *adj* drunk.
ebullición *f* boiling.
eccema *m* eczema.
echar *vt* to throw; to add; to fire; to pour out; to mail; to give off; to bud; ~se *vr* to lie down; to rest; to stretch out.
eclesiástico/ca *adj* ecclesiastical.
eclipsar *vt* to eclipse; to outshine.
eclipse *m* eclipse.
eco *m* echo.
ecografía *f* ultrasound scan.
ecología *f* ecology.
ecologismo *m* green movement.
ecologista *m/f* ecologist, environmentalist.
economato *m* cut-rate store.
economía *f* economy.
económico/ca *adj* economic; cheap; thrifty; financial; avaricious.
economista *m/f* economist.
ecosistema *m* ecosystem.
ecotasa *f* ecotax.
ecoturismo *m* ecotourism.
ecuación *f* equation.
ecuador *m* equator.
ecuánime *adj* level-headed.
ecuestre *adj* equestrian.
ecuménico/ca *adj* ecumenical; universal.
edad *f* age.
edecán *m* (*mil*) aide-de-camp.
edición *f* edition; publication.
edicto *m* edict.
edificación *f* construction.
edificante *adj* edifying, instructive.
edificar *vt* to build, to construct; to edify.
edificio *m* building; structure.
editar *vt* to edit; to publish.
editor/ra *m/f* editor; publisher.
educación *f* education; upbringing; (good) manners *pl*.
educador/ra *m/f* teacher, educator.
educando/da *m/f* pupil.
educar *vt* to educate, to instruct; to bring up.
efectivamente *adv* exactly; really; in fact.
efectivo/va *adj* effective; true; certain.

efecto *m* effect; consequence; purpose; ~ invernadero greenhouse effect ~s *mpl* effects *pl*, goods *pl*; en ~ in fact, really.
efectuar *vt* to effect, to carry out.
efeméride *f* event (remembered on its anniversary).
efervescencia *f* effervescence, fizziness.
eficacia *f* effectiveness, efficacy.
eficaz *adj* efficient; effective.
eficiente *adj* efficient.
efigie *f* effigy, image.
efímero/ra *adj* ephemeral.
efluvio *m* outflow.
efusión *f* effusion.
efusivo/va *adj* effusive.
égloga *f* (*poet*) eclogue.
egoísmo *m* selfishness.
egoísta *m/f* self-seeker; * *adj* selfish.
egregio/gia *adj* eminent, remarkable.
egresado/da *m/f Lat Am* graduate.
egresar *vi Lat Am* to graduate.
egreso *m Lat Am* graduation.
eje *m* axle; axis.
ejecución *f* execution.
ejecutar *vt* to execute, to carry out, to perform; to put to death; (*law*) to attach, to seize.
ejecutivo/va *adj* executive; * *m/f* executive.
ejecutor/ra *m/f* executor.
ejecutoria *f* (*law*) writ of execution.
ejecutorio/ria *adj* (*law*) executory.
ejemplar *m* specimen; copy; example; * *adj* exemplary.
ejemplificar *vt* to exemplify.
ejemplo *m* example; por ~ for example, for instance.
ejercer *vt* to exercise.
ejercicio *m* exercise.
ejercitación *f* exercise, practice.
ejercitar *vt* to exercise; ~se *vr* to train.
ejército *m* army.
ejote *m* green bean.
el *art*, *m* the.
él *pn* he, it.
elaboración *f* elaboration.
elaborado/da *adj* elaborate.
elaborar *vt* to elaborate.
elasticidad *f* elasticity.
elástico/ca *adj* elastic.
elección *f* election; choice.
eleccionario/a *adj Lat Am* electoral.

elector/ra m/f elector.
electorado m electorate.
electoral adj electoral.
electricidad f electricity.
electricista m/f electrician.
eléctrico/ca adj electric, electrical.
electrización f electrification.
electrizar vt to electrify.
electrocardiograma m electrocardiogram.
electrocutar vt to electrocute.
electrodoméstico m (electrical) domestic appliance.
electrónico/ca adj electronic.
electrotecnia f electrical engineering.
elefante m elephant.
elegancia f elegance.
elegante adj elegant, fine.
elegía f elegy.
elegir vt to choose, to elect.
elemental adj elemental; elementary.
elemento m element; ~s mpl elements pl, rudiments pl, first principles pl.
elevación f elevation; highness; rise; haughtiness, pride; height; altitude.
elevar vt to raise; to elevate; ~se vr to rise; to be enraptured; to be conceited.
eliminar vt to eliminate, to remove.
eliminatoria f preliminary (round).
elipse f (geom) ellipse.
elipsis f (gr) ellipsis.
elite, élite f elite.
elixir m elixir.
ella pn she; it.
ello pn it.
elocución f elocution.
elocuencia f eloquence.
elocuente adj eloquent.
elogiar vt to praise, to eulogize.
elogio m eulogy, praise.
elote m corn on the cob.
elucidación f elucidation, explanation.
eludir vt to elude, to escape.
emanación f emanation.
emanar vi to emanate.
emancipación f emancipation.
emancipar vt to emancipate, to set free.
embadurnar vt to smear, to bedaub.
embajada f embassy.
embajador/ra m/f ambassador.
embalaje m packing, package.
embalar vt to bale, to pack in bales.
embaldosar vt to pave with tiles.
embalsamador m embalmer.
embalsamar vt to embalm.
embalse m reservoir.

embarazada f pregnant woman; * adj pregnant.
embarazar vt to embarrass; to make pregnant; ~se vr to become intricate.
embarazo m pregnancy; embarrassment; obstacle.
embarazoso/sa adj difficult; intricate, entangled.
embarcación f embarkation; any vessel/ship.
embarcadero m quay, wharf; port; harbor.
embarcar vt to embark; ~se vr to go on board; (fig) to get involved (in a matter).
embargar vt to lay on an embargo; to impede, to restrain.
embargo m embargo; sin ~ still, however.
embarque m embarkation.
embastar vt to stitch, to tack.
embate m breakers pl, surf, surge; sudden attack.
embaucador/ra m/f swindler; impostor.
embaucar vt to deceive; to trick.
embebecer vt to fascinate; ~se vr to be fascinated.
embebecimiento m amazement, astonishment; fascination.
embeber vt to soak; to saturate; * vi to shrink; ~se vr to be enraptured; to be absorbed.
embelesamiento m rapture.
embelesar vt to amaze, to astonish.
embeleso m amazement, enchantment.
embellecer vt to embellish, to beautify.
emberrincharse vr to have a tantrum.
embestida f assault, violent attack.
embestir vt to assault, to attack.
emblanquecer vt to whiten; ~se vr to grow white; to bleach.
emblema m emblem.
embobado/da adj amazed; fascinated.
embobamiento m astonishment; fascination.
embobar vt to amaze; to fascinate; ~se vr to be amazed; to stand gaping.
embobecer vt to make silly; ~se vr to get silly.
embobecimiento m silliness.
émbolo m plunger; piston.
embolsar vt to put money into (a purse); to pocket.
emborrachar vt to intoxicate, to inebriate; ~se vr to get drunk.
emboscada f (mil) ambush.
emboscarse vr (mil) to lie in ambush.
embotar vt to blunt; ~se vr to go numb.
embotellamiento m traffic jam.

embotellar *vt* to bottle (wine).
embozado/da *adj* covered; covert.
embozar *vt* to muffle up (the face); (*fig*) to cloak, to conceal.
embozo *m* part of a cloak, veil, anything with which the face is muffled; covering of one's face.
embrague *m* clutch.
embrear *vt* to cover with tar/pitch.
embriagar *vt* to intoxicate, to inebriate; to transport, to enrapture.
embriaguez *f* intoxication, drunkenness; rapture, delight.
embrión *m* embryo.
embrollador/ra *m/f* troublemaker.
embrollar *vt* to muddle; to entangle, to embroil.
embrollo *m* muddle.
embromar *vt* to tease; to cajole, to wheedle.
embrujar *vt* to bewitch.
embrutecer *vt* to brutalize; ~se *vr* to become depraved.
embudo *m* funnel.
embuste *m* fraud; lie, fib, story (*col*).
embustero/ra *m/f* impostor, cheat; liar; * *adj* deceitful.
embutido *m* sausage; inlay.
embutir *vt* to insert; to stuff; to inlay; to cram.
emergencia *f* emergency.
emerger *vi* to emerge, to appear.
emético/ca *adj* emetic.
emigración *f* emigration; migration.
emigrado/da *adj* emigrated; * *m/f* emigrant.
emigrante *m/f* emigrant.
emigrar *vi* to emigrate.
eminencia *f* eminence.
eminente *adj* eminent, high; excellent, conspicuous.
emisario *m* emissary.
emisión *f* emission; broadcasting; program; issue.
emisora *f* broadcasting station.
emitir *vt* to emit, to send forth; to issue; to broadcast.
emoción *f* emotion; feeling; excitement.
emocionante *adj* exciting.
emocionar *vt* to excite; to move, to touch.
emoliente *adj* emollient, softening.
emolumento *m* emolument.
emotivo/va *adj* emotional.
empacar *vt* to pack; to crate.
empachar *vt* to give indigestion; ~se *vr* to have indigestion.

empacho *m* (*med*) indigestion.
empachoso/sa *adj* indigestible.
empadronamiento *m* register; census.
empadronarse *vr* to register.
empalagar *vt* to sicken; to disgust.
empalago *m* disgust; boredom.
empalagoso/sa *adj* cloying; tiresome.
empalizada *f* (*mil*) palisade.
empalmadura *f* join; weld; splice.
empalmar *vt* to join.
empalme *m* (*rail*) junction; connection.
empanada *f* (meat) pie.
empanar *vt* to cover with breadcrumbs.
empantanarse *vr* to get swamped; to get bogged down.
empañar *vt* to wrap up (baby); to mist; to steam up; ~se *vr* to steam up; to tarnish one's reputation.
empapar *vt* to soak; to soak up; ~se *vr* to soak.
empapelar *vt* to paper.
empaquetar *vt* to pack, to parcel up.
emparedado *m* sandwich.
emparejar *vt* to level; to match, to fit; to equalize.
emparentar *vi* to be related by marriage.
emparrado *m* vine arbor.
empastar *vt* to paste; to fill (a tooth).
empaste *m* filling (of a tooth).
empatar *vi* to draw, tie, have a dead heat.
empate *m* draw, dead heat.
empedernido/da *adj* inveterate; heartless.
empedernir *vt* to harden; ~se *vr* to be inflexible.
empedrado *m* paving.
empedrador *m* paver.
empedrar *vt* to pave.
empeine *m* instep.
empellón *m* push; heavy blow.
empeñado/da *adj* determined; pawned.
empeñar *vt* to pawn, to pledge; ~se *vr* to pledge oneself to pay debts; to get into debt; ~se en algo to insist on something.
empeño *m* obligation; determination; perseverance.
empeorar *vt* to make worse; * *vi*, ~se *vr* to grow worse.
empequeñecer *vt* to dwarf; (*fig*) to belittle.
emperador *m* emperor.
emperatriz *f* empress.
emperifollarse *vr* to dress oneself up.
empero *conj* yet, however.
emperrarse *vr* to get stubborn; to be obstinate.

empezar *vt* to begin, to start.
empinado/da *adj* high; proud.
empinar *vt* to raise; to exalt; * *vi* to drink heavily; ~se *vr* to stand on tiptoe; to soar.
empírico/ca *adj* empirical.
empirismo *m* empiricism.
empizarrado *m* slate roofing.
empizarrar *vt* to slate, to roof with slate.
emplasto *m* plaster.
emplazamiento *m* summons; location.
emplazar *vt* to summon; to locate.
empleado/da *m/f* official; employee.
emplear *vt* to employ; to occupy; to commission.
empleo *m* employ, employment, occupation.
empobrecer *vt* to reduce to poverty; * *vi* to become poor.
empobrecimiento *m* impoverishment.
empollar *vt* to incubate; to hatch; (*col*) to cram.
empolvar *vt* to powder; to sprinkle powder upon.
emponzoñador/ra *m/f* poisoner.
emponzoñamiento *m* poisoning.
emponzoñar *vt* to poison; to taint, to corrupt.
emporio *m* emporium.
empotrado/da *adj* built-in.
empotrar *vt* to embed; to build in.
emprendedor/ra *m/f* entrepreneur.
emprender *vt* to embark on; to tackle; to undertake.
empresa *f* (*com*) company; enterprise, undertaking.
empresario/ria *m/f* manager.
empréstito *m* loan.
empujar *vt* to push; to press forward.
empuje *m* thrust; pressure; (*fig*) drive.
empujón *m* push; impulse; **a** ~**ones** in fits and starts.
empuñadura *f* hilt (of a sword).
empuñar *vt* to clench, to grip with the fist; to clutch.
emulación *f* emulation.
emular *vt* to emulate, to rival.
emulsión *f* emulsion.
en *prep* in; for; on, upon.
enaguas *fpl* petticoat.
enajenación *f* alienation; absentmindedness.
enajenamiento *m* alienation; absent-mindedness.
enajenar *vt* to alienate; ~se *vr* to fall out.
enamoradamente *adv* lovingly.
enamoradizo/za *adj* inclined to fall in love.

enamorado/da *adj* in love, lovesick.
enamoramiento *m* falling in love.
enamorar *vt* to inspire love in; ~se *vr* to fall in love.
enano/na *adj* dwarfish; * *m* dwarf.
enarbolar *vt* to hoist, to raise high.
enardecer *vt* to fire with passion, to inflame.
enarenar *vt* to fill with sand.
encabezamiento *m* heading; foreword.
encabezar *vt* to head; to put a heading to; to lead.
encabritarse *vr* to rear (of horses).
encadenamiento *m* linking together, chaining.
encadenar *vt* to chain, to link together; to connect, to unite.
encajadura *f* insertion; socket; groove.
encajar *vt* to insert; to drive in; to encase; to intrude; ~se *vr* to squeeze; to gatecrash; * *vi* to fit (well).
encaje *m* encasing; joining; socket; groove; inlaid work.
encajera *f* lacemaker.
encajonamiento *m* packing into boxes etc.
encajonar *vt* to pack up in a box.
encalabrinar *vt* to make confused; ~se *vr* to become obstinate.
encaladura *f* whitening, whitewash.
encalar *vt* to whitewash.
encallar *vi* (*mar*) to run aground.
encallecer *vi* to get corns.
encamarse *vr* to take to one's bed.
encaminar *vt* to guide, to show the way; ~se *vr*: ~ **a** to take the road to.
encandilar *vt* to dazzle.
encanecer *vi* to grow gray; to grow old.
encantado/da *adj* bewitched; delighted; pleased.
encantador/ra *adj* charming; *m/f* magician.
encantamiento *m* enchantment.
encantar *vt* to enchant, to charm; (*fig*) to delight.
encanto *m* enchantment; spell, charm.
encañonar *vt* to hold up; to point a gun at; * *vi* to grow feathers.
encapotar *vt* to cover with a cloak; ~se *vr* to be cloudy.
encapricharse *vr* to become stubborn.
encapuchar *vt* to cover with a hood.
encaramar *vt* to raise; to extoll; *Lat Am* to make blush.
encararse *vr*: ~ **a** to come face to face with.
encarcelación *f* incarceration.
encarcelar *vt* to imprison.

encarecer vt to raise the price of; ~se vr to get dearer.

encarecimiento m price increase; con ~ insistently.

encargado/da adj in charge; * m/f representative; person in charge.

encargar vt to charge; to commission.

encargo m charge; commission; job; order.

encariñarse vr: ~ con to grow fond of.

encarnación f incarnation, embodiment.

encarnado/da adj incarnate; flesh-colored; * m flesh color.

encarnar vt to embody, to personify.

encarnizado/da adj bloodshot, inflamed; bloody, fierce.

encarrilar vt to put back on the rails; to put on the right track.

encasillar vt to pigeonhole; to typecast.

encasquetar vt to pull on (a hat).

encastillarse vr to refuse to yield.

encauzar vt to channel.

encebollado m casserole of beef/lamb and onions, seasoned with spice.

encenagado/da adj muddy, mud-stained.

encenagamiento m wallowing in mud.

encenagarse vr to wallow in mud.

encendedor m lighter, cigarette lighter.

encender vt to kindle, to light, to set on fire; to inflame, to incite; to switch on, to turn on; ~se vr to catch fire; to flare up.

encendido/da adj inflamed; high-colored; * m ignition (of car).

encerado m chalkboard; adhesive tape.

encerar vt to wax; to polish.

encerrar vt to shut up, to confine; to contain; ~se vr to withdraw from the world.

encespedar vt to turf.

enchapar vt to veneer.

encharcarse vr to be flooded.

enchufar vt to plug in; to connect.

enchufe m plug; socket; connection; (col) contact, connection.

encía f gum (of the teeth).

encíclica f encyclical.

enciclopedia f encyclopedia.

enciclopédico/ca adj encyclopedic.

encierro m confinement; enclosure; prison; bullpen; penning (of bulls).

encima adv above; over; at the top; besides; ~ de prep above; over; at the top of; besides.

encina f holm oak, evergreen oak.

encinar m holm oak wood/grove.

encinta adj pregnant.

enclaustrado/da adj cloistered; hidden away.

enclenque adj weak, sickly; * m weakling.

encoger vt to contract, to shorten; to shrink; to discourage; ~se vr to shrink; (fig) to cringe.

encogidamente adv shyly, timidly, bashfully.

encogido/da adj shy, timid, bashful.

encogimiento m contraction; shrinkage; shyness; timidness; bashfulness.

encoladura f gluing.

encolar vt to glue.

encolerizar vt to provoke, to irritate; ~se vr to get angry.

encomendar vt to recommend; to entrust; ~se vr: ~ a to entrust oneself to; to put one's trust in.

encomiar vt to praise.

encomienda f commission, charge; message; (mil) command; patronage, protection; Lat Am parcel post.

encomio m eulogy, praise; commendation.

enconar vt to inflame; to irritate.

encono m ill-feeling, rancor.

enconoso/sa adj hurtful, prejudicial; malevolent.

encontrado/da adj conflicting; hostile.

encontrar vt to meet, to encounter; ~se vr: ~se con to run into; * vi to assemble, to come together.

encopetado/da adj presumptuous, boastful.

encorvadura f curvature; crookedness.

encorvar vt to bend, to curve.

encrespar vt to curl, to frizzle (hair); (fig) to anger; ~se vr to get rough (of the sea); (fig) to get cross.

encrucijada f crossroads; junction.

encuadernación f binding.

encuadernador/ra m/f bookbinder.

encuadernar vt to bind (books).

encubiertamente adv secretly; deceitfully.

encubierto/ta adj hidden, concealed.

encubridor/ra m/f concealer, harborer; receiver of stolen goods.

encubrimiento m concealment, hiding; receiving of stolen goods.

encubrir vt to hide, to conceal.

encuentro m meeting; collision, crash; match, game.

encuesta f inquiry; opinion poll.

encumbrado/da adj high; elevated.

encumbramiento m elevation; height.

encumbrar vt to raise, to elevate; ~se vr to be raised; (fig) to become conceited.

encurtir vt to pickle.

endeble adj feeble, weak.

endecasílabo/ba *adj* consisting of eleven syllables.

endecha *f* dirge, lament.

endemoniado/da *adj* possessed with the devil; devilish.

enderezamiento *m* guidance, direction.

enderezar *vt* to straighten out; to set right; ~se *vr* to stand upright.

endeudarse *vr* to get into debt.

endiablado/da *adj* devilish, diabolical; ugly.

endiosar *vt* to deify; ~se *vr* to be high and mighty.

endosar *vt* to endorse.

endoso *m* endorsement.

endrina *f* sloe, fruit of the blackthorn.

endrino *m* blackthorn, sloe.

endulzar *vt* to sweeten; to soften.

endurecer *vt* to harden, to toughen; ~se *vr* to become cruel; to grow hard.

endurecidamente *adv* cruelly.

endurecimiento *m* hardness; obstinacy; hard-heartedness.

enebro *m* (*bot*) juniper.

enemigo/ga *adj* hostile; * *m* enemy.

enemistad *f* enmity.

enemistar *vt* to make an enemy; ~se *vr* to become enemies; to fall out.

energía *f* energy, power, drive; strength of will; ~ **nuclear** nuclear power; ~ **solar** solar energy; ~ **renovables** renewable forms of energy.

enérgico/ca *adj* energetic; forceful.

energúmeno/na *m/f* (*col*) madman/woman.

enero *m* January.

enervar *vt* to enervate.

enfadadizo/za *adj* irritable, crotchety.

enfadar *vt* to anger, to irritate; to trouble; ~se *vr* to become angry.

enfado *m* trouble; anger.

enfadoso/sa *adj* annoying, troublesome.

énfasis *m* emphasis.

enfático/ca *adj* emphatic.

enfermar *vi* to fall ill; * *vt* to make sick; to weaken.

enfermedad *f* illness.

enfermería *f* infirmary; sick bay.

enfermero/ra *m/f* nurse.

enfermizo/za *adj* infirm, sickly.

enfermo/ma *adj* sick, ill; * *m/f* invalid, sick person; patient.

enfervorizar *vt* to arouse; to inflame, to incite.

enflaquecer *vt* to weaken; to make thin.

enflaquecimiento *m* loss of weight; (*fig*) weakening.

enfocar *vt* to focus; to consider (a problem).

enfoque *m* focus.

enfrascarse *vr* to be deeply embroiled.

enfrentar *vt* to confront; to put face to face; ~se *vr* to face each other; to meet (two teams).

enfrente *adv* over against, opposite; in front.

enfriamiento *m* refrigeration; (*med*) cold, chill.

enfriar *vt* to cool; to refrigerate; ~se *vr* to cool down; (*med*) to catch a cold/chill.

enfurecer *vt* to madden, to enrage; ~se *vr* to get rough (of the wind and sea); to become furious/enraged.

enfurruñarse *vr* to get sulky; to frown.

engalanar *vt* to adorn, to deck.

engallarse *vr* to be arrogant.

engañabobos *m invar* trickster; trick, trap.

engañadizo/za *adj* gullible, easily deceived.

engañador/ra *adj* cheating; deceptive; * *m/f* cheat, impostor, deceiver.

engañar *vt* to deceive, to cheat; ~se *vr* to be deceived; to make a mistake.

enganchar *vt* to hook, to hang up; to hitch up; to couple, to connect; to recruit into military service; ~se *vr* (*mil*) to enlist.

engañifa *f* deceit, trick.

engaño *m* mistake; misunderstanding; deceit, fraud.

engañoso/sa *adj* deceitful, artful, false.

engarzar *vt* to thread; to link; to curl.

engastar *vt* to set, to mount.

engaste *m* setting, mount.

engatusamiento *m* deception, coaxing.

engatusar *vt* to coax.

engendrar *vt* to beget, to engender; to produce.

engendro *m* fetus, embryo; (*fig*) monstrosity; brainchild.

englobar *vt* to include.

engolfarse *vr* (*mar*) to sail out to sea; ~ **en** to be deeply involved in.

engolosinar *vt* to entice; ~se *vr* to find delight in.

engomadura *f* gluing.

engomar *vt* to glue.

engordar *vt* to fatten; * *vi* to grow fat; to put on weight.

engorro *m* nuisance, bother.

engorroso/sa *adj* troublesome, cumbersome.

engranaje *m* gear; gears, gearing.

engrandecer *vt* to augment; to magnify; to speak highly of; to exaggerate.

engrandecimiento *m* increase; aggrandizement; exaggeration.

engrapadora *f Lat Am* stapler.

engrapar *vt Lat Am* to staple.

engrasar *vt* to grease, to lubricate.

engreído/da *adj* conceited, vain.

engreimiento *m* presumption, vanity.

engreír *vt* to make proud; ~se *vr* to grow proud.

engrosar *vt* to enlarge; to increase.

engrudo *m* paste.

engullidor/ra *m/f* devourer; guzzler.

engullir *vt* to swallow; to gobble, to devour.

enharinar *vt* to cover/sprinkle with flour.

enhebrar *vt* to thread.

enhilar *vt* to thread.

enhorabuena *f* congratulations *pl*; * *interj* congratulations!

enhoramala *interj* good riddance.

enigma *m* enigma, riddle.

enigmático/ca *adj* enigmatic; dark, obscure.

enjabonar *vt* to soap; (*col*) to soft soap.

enjaezar *vt* to harness (a horse).

enjalbegar *vt* to whitewash.

enjambre *m* swarm (of bees); crowd, multitude.

enjaular *vt* to shut up in a cage; to imprison.

enjoyar *vt* to adorn with jewels.

enjuagar *vt* to rinse out; to wash out.

enjuague *m* (*med*) mouthwash; rinsing, rinse.

enjugar *vt* to dry (the tears); to wipe off.

enjuiciar *vt* to prosecute, to try; to pass judgement on, to judge.

enjuto/ta *adj* dried up; (*fig*) lean.

enlace *m* connection, link; relationship.

enladrillado *m* brick paving.

enladrillador *m* bricklayer.

enladrillar *vt* to pave with bricks.

enlazable *adj* able to be fastened together.

enlazar *vt* to join, to unite; to tie.

enlodar *vt* to cover in mud; (*fig*) to stain.

enloquecer *vt* to madden, to drive crazy; * *vi* to go mad.

enloquecimiento *m* madness.

enlosar *vt* to pave with flagstones.

enlutar *vt* to put into mourning; ~se *vr* to go into mourning.

enmaderar *vt* to roof with lumber.

enmarañar *vt* to entangle; to complicate; to confuse; ~se *vr* to become entangled; to get confused.

enmascarar *vt* to mask; ~se *vr* to go in disguise, to masquerade.

enmendar *vt* to correct; to reform; to repair, to compensate for; to amend; ~se *vr* to mend one's ways.

enmienda *f* correction, amendment.

enmohecer *vt* to make moldy; to rust; ~se *vr* to grow moldy/musty; to rust.

enmohecido/da *adj* moldy.

enmudecer *vt* to silence; ~se *vr* to grow dumb; to be silent.

ennegrecer *vt* to blacken; to darken; to obscure.

ennoblecer *vt* to ennoble.

ennoblecimiento *m* ennoblement.

enojadizo/za *adj* peevish; short-tempered, irritable.

enojar *vt* to irritate, to make angry; to annoy; to upset; to offend; ~se *vr* to get angry.

enojo *m* anger, annoyance.

enojoso/sa *adj* offensive, annoying.

enorgullecerse *vr*: ~ (de) to be proud (of).

enorme *adj* enormous, vast, huge; horrible.

enormidad *f* enormity; monstrousness.

enramar *vt* to cover with the branches of trees.

enranciarse *vr* to grow rancid.

enrarecer *vt* to thin, to rarefy.

enredadera *f* climbing plant; bindweed.

enredador/ra *m/f* gossip; troublemaker; busybody.

enredar *vt* to entangle, to ensnare, to confound, to perplex; to puzzle; to sow discord among; ~se *vr* to get entangled; to get complicated; to get embroiled.

enredo *m* entanglement; mischievous lie; plot of a play.

enredoso/sa *adj* complicated.

enrejado *m* trelliswork.

enrejar *vt* to fix a grating to (a window); to grate, to lattice.

enrevesado/da *adj* complicated.

enriquecer *vt* to enrich; to adorn; ~se *vr* to grow rich.

enristrar *vt* to string (garlic, onions); to straighten out; to go straight to.

enrobustecer *vt* to strengthen.

enrojecer *vt* to redden; * *vi* to blush.

enrolar *vt* to recruit; ~se *vr* (*mil*) to join up.

enrollar *vt* to roll (up).

enronquecer *vt* to make hoarse; * *vi* to grow hoarse.

enroscadura *f* twist.

enroscar *vt* to twist; ~se *vr* to curl/roll up.

ensalada f salad.
ensaladera f salad bowl.
ensaladilla (rusa) f Russian salad.
ensalmar vt to set (dislocated bones); to heal by spells.
ensalmo m enchantment, spell.
ensalzar vt to exalt, to aggrandize; to exaggerate.
ensamblador/ra m/f joiner.
ensamblar vt to assemble.
ensanchar vt to widen; to extend; to enlarge; ~se vr to expand; to assume an air of importance.
ensanche m dilation, augmentation; widening; expansion.
ensangrentar vt to stain with blood.
ensañar vt to irritate, to enrage; ~se con vr to treat brutally.
ensartar vt to string (beads etc).
ensayar vt to test; to rehearse.
ensayo m test, trial; rehearsal of a play; essay.
ensenada f creek.
enseña f colors pl, standard.
enseñanza f teaching, instruction; education.
enseñar vt to teach, to instruct; to show.
enseres mpl belongings pl.
ensillar vt to saddle.
ensimismarse vr to be/become lost in thought.
ensoberbecer vt to make proud; ~se vr to become proud; (mar) to get rough.
ensordecer vt to deafen; * vi to grow deaf.
ensordecimiento m deafness.
ensortijar vt to fix a ring in (the nose); to curl the hair.
ensuciar vt to stain, to soil; to defile; ~se vr to wet oneself; to dirty oneself.
ensueño m fantasy; daydream; illusion.
entablar vt to board (up); to strike up (conversation), * vi Lat Am to draw.
entablillar vt (med) to put in a splint.
entallar vt to tailor (a suit); * vi to fit.
ente m organization; entity, being; (col) odd character.
entendederas fpl understanding; brains pl.
entender vt, vi to understand, to comprehend; to remark, to take notice (of); to reason, to think; a mi ~ in my opinion; ~se vr to understand each other.
entendido/da adj understood; wise; learned, knowing.
entendimiento m understanding; knowledge; judgement.

enteramente adv entirely, completely.
enterar vt to inform; to instruct; ~se vr to find out.
entereza f entireness, integrity; firmness of mind.
enternecer vt to soften; to move (to pity); ~se vr to be moved.
enternecimiento m compassion, pity.
entero/ra adj entire, complete; perfect; honest; resolute; por ~ entirely, completely.
enterrador m gravedigger.
enterrar vt to inter, to bury.
entiblar vt to cool.
entidad f entity; company; body; society.
entierro m burial; funeral.
entoldar vt to cover with an awning.
entomología f entomology.
entonación f intonation, modulation, (fig) presumption, pride.
entonar vt to tune, to intone; to tone; * vi to be in tune; ~se vr to give oneself airs.
entonces adv then, at that time.
entontecer vt to fool; * vi, se vr to get silly.
entontecimiento m silliness.
entornar vt to half close.
entorpecer vt to dull; to make lethargic; to hinder; to delay.
entorpecimiento m numbness; lethargy.
entrada f entrance, entry; (com) receipts pl; entree; ticket (for movies, theater etc).
entrambos/bas pn, pl both.
entrampar vt to trap, to snare; to mess up; to burden with debts; ~se vr get into debt.
entrañable adj intimate; affectionate.
entrañas fpl entrails pl, intestines pl.
entrante adj coming, next.
entrar vi to enter, to go in; to commence.
entre prep between; among(st); in; ~ manos in hand.
entreabrir vt to half open (a door), to leave ajar.
entrecano/na adj gray-black, grayish.
entrecejo m space between the eyebrows; frown.
entrecortado/da adj faltering; difficult.
entredicho m (law) injunction; estar en ~ to be banned; poner en ~ to cast doubt on.
entrega f delivery; installment.
entregar vt to deliver; to hand over; ~se vr to surrender; to devote oneself.
entrelazar vt to interlace.
entremedias adv in the meantime.
entremeses mpl hors d'oeuvres pl.

entremeter *vt* to put (one thing) between (others); ~se *vr* to interfere, to meddle.

entremetido/da *m/f* meddler; * *adj* meddling.

entremetimiento *m* insertion; meddling.

entrenador/ra *m/f* trainer, coach.

entrenar *vt* to train; ~se *vr* to train.

entreoír *vt* to half hear.

entrepaño *m* panel.

entrepierna *f* crotch.

entresaca *f* thinning out (of trees).

entresacar *vt* to thin out; to sift, to separate.

entresuelo *m* mezzanine floor, entresol.

entretanto *adv* meanwhile.

entretejer *vt* to interweave.

entretela *f* interfacing, stiffening, interlining.

entretener *vt* to amuse; to entertain, to divert; to hold up; to maintain; ~se *vr* to amuse oneself; to linger.

entretenido/da *adj* pleasant; amusing; entertaining.

entretenimiento *m* amusement, entertainment.

entrever *vt* to have a glimpse of.

entreverado/da *adj* patchy; streaky.

entrevista *f* interview.

entrevistar *vt* to interview; ~se *vr* to have an interview.

entristecer *vt* to sadden.

entrometer *vt* to put (one thing) between (others); ~se *vr* to interfere, to meddle.

entrometido/da *m/f* meddler; * *adj* meddling.

entroncar *vi* to be related/connected.

entronización *f* enthronement.

entronizar *vt* to enthrone.

entumecer *vt* to swell; to numb; ~se *vr* to become numb.

entumecido/da *adj* numb, stiff.

entumecimiento *m* numbness.

enturbiar *vt* to make cloudy; to obscure, to confound; ~se *vr* to become cloudy; (*fig*) to get confused.

entusiasmar *vt* to excite, to fill with enthusiasm; to delight.

entusiasmo *m* enthusiasm.

entusiasta *m/f* enthusiast.

enumeración *f* enumeration.

enumerar *vt* to enumerate.

enunciación *f*, enunciado *m* enunciation, declaration.

enunciar *vt* to enunciate, to declare.

envainar *vt* to sheath(e).

envalentonar *vt* to give courage to; ~se *vr* to boast.

envanecer *vt* to make vain; to swell with pride; ~se *vr* to become proud.

envaramiento *m* stiffness; numbness.

envarar *vt* to numb.

envasar *vt* to pack; to bottle; to can.

envase *m* packing; bottling; canning; container; package; bottle; can.

envejecer *vt* to make old; * *vi*, ~se *vr* to grow old.

envenenador/ra *m/f* poisoner.

envenenar *vt* to poison; to embitter.

envenenamiento *m* poisoning.

envergadura *f* (*fig*) scope.

envés *m* wrong side (of material).

enviado/da *m/f* envoy, messenger.

enviar *vt* to send, to transmit, to convey, to dispatch.

enviciar *vt* to vitiate, to corrupt; ~se *vr* to get corrupted.

envidia *f* envy; jealousy.

envidiable *adj* enviable.

envidiar *vt* to envy; to grudge; to be jealous of.

envidioso/sa *adj* envious; jealous.

envilecer *vt* to vilify, to debase; ~se *vr* to degrade oneself.

envío *m* (*com*) dispatch, remittance of goods; consignment.

enviudar *vi* to become a widower/widow.

envoltorio *m* bundle of clothes.

envoltura *f* cover; wrapping.

envolver *vt* to involve; to wrap up.

enyesar *vt* to plaster; (*med*) to put in a plaster cast.

enzarzarse *vr* to get involved in a dispute; to get oneself into trouble.

épico/ca *adj* epic.

epicúreo/rea *adj* Epicurean.

epidemia *f* epidemic.

epidémico/ca *adj* epidemic.

epidermis *f* epidermis; cuticle.

Epifanía *f* Epiphany.

epígrafe *f* epigraph, inscription; motto; headline.

epigrama *m* epigram.

epilepsia *f* epilepsy.

epílogo *m* epilog.

episcopado *m* episcopacy; bishopric.

episcopal *adj* Episcopal.

episódico/ca *adj* episodic.

episodio *m* episode, installment.

epístola *f* epistle, letter.

epistolar *adj* epistolary.

epistolario *m* collected letters *pl*.
epitafio *m* epitaph.
epíteto *m* epithet.
epítome *m* epitome; compendium.
época *f* epoch; period, time.
epopeya *f* epic.
equidad *f* equity, honesty; impartiality, justice.
equidistar *vi* to be equidistant.
equilátero/ra *adj* equilateral.
equilibrar *vt* to balance; to poise.
equilibrio *m* balance, equilibrium.
equinoccial *adj* equinoctial.
equinoccio *m* equinox.
equipaje *m* baggage; fixings; equipment.
equipar *vt* to fit out, to equip, to furnish.
equipararse *vr*: ~ **con** to be on a level with.
equipo *m* equipment; team; shift.
equitación *f* horsemanship; riding.
equitativo/va *adj* equitable; just.
equivalencia *f* equivalence.
equivalente *adj* equivalent.
equivaler *vi* to be of equal value.
equivocación *f* mistake, error, misunderstanding.
equivocado/da *adj* mistaken, wrong.
equivocar *vt* to mistake; ~**se** *vr* to make a mistake, to be wrong.
equívoco/ca *adj* equivocal, ambiguous; * *m* equivocation; quibble.
era *f* era, age; threshing floor.
erario *m* treasury, public funds *pl*.
erección *f* foundation, establishment; erection, elevation.
erguir *vt* to erect, to raise up straight; ~**se** *vr* to straighten up.
erial *m* fallow land.
erigir *vt* to erect, to raise, to build; to establish.
erizamiento *m* standing on end (of hair etc).
erizarse *vr* to bristle; to stand on end.
erizo *m* hedgehog; ~ **de mar** sea urchin.
ermita *f* hermitage.
ermitaño *m* hermit.
erosionar *vt* to erode.
erótico/ca *adj* erotic.
erotismo *m* eroticism.
errante *adj* errant; stray; roving.
errar *vi* to be mistaken; to wander.
errata *f* misprint.
erre ~ **que** *adv* obstinately.
erróneo/nea *adj* erroneous.
error *m* error, mistake, fault.
cructar *vi* to belch, to burp.

eructo *m* belch, burp.
erudición *f* erudition, learning.
erudito/ta *adj* learned, erudite.
erupción *f* eruption, outbreak.
esa *f* of ese.
ésa *f* of ése.
esbelto/ta *adj* slim, slender.
esbirro *m* bailiff; henchman; killer.
esbozo *m* outline.
escabechar *vt* to marinate; to pickle.
escabeche *m* pickle; pickled fish.
escabel *m* footstool.
escabrosidad *f* unevenness, roughness; harshness.
escabroso/sa *adj* rough, uneven; craggy; rude, risqué.
escabullirse *vr* to escape, to evade; to slip through one's fingers.
escafandra *f* diving suit; space suit.
escala *f* ladder; (*mus*) scale; port of call; stopover.
escalador/ra *m/f* climber.
escalar *vt* to climb.
escaldado/da *adj* cautious, suspicious, wary.
escaldar *vt* to scald.
escalera *f* staircase; ladder.
escalfar *vt* to poach (eggs)
escalofríos *mpl* shivers *pl*.
escalofriante *adj* chilling.
escalón *m* step of a stair; rung.
escama *f* (fish) scale.
escamado/da *adj* wary, cautious.
escamar *vt* to scale, to take off the scales; ~**se** *vr* to flake off; to become suspicious.
escamoso/sa *adj* scaly.
escamotear *vt* to swipe; to make disappear.
escampar *vi* to stop raining.
escanciador *m* wine waiter; cupbearer.
escanciar *vt* to pour (wine).
escandalizar *vt* to scandalize; ~**se** *vr* to be shocked.
escándalo *m* scandal; uproar.
escandaloso/sa *adj* scandalous; shocking.
escanear *vt* to scan.
escáner *m* scanner.
escaño *m* bench with a back.
escapada *f* escape, flight.
escapar *vi* to escape; ~**se** *vr* to get away; to leak (water etc).
escaparate *m* shop/store front, shop/store window; wardrobe.
escapatoria *f* escape, flight; excuse.
escape *m* escape, flight; leak; exhaust (of motor); **a todo** ~ at full speed.
escapulario *m* scapulary.

escarabajo *m* beetle.
escaramuza *f* skirmish; dispute, quarrel.
escaramuzar *vt* to skirmish.
escarbadura *f* act and effect of scratching.
escarbar *vt* to scratch (the earth as hens do); to inquire into.
escarcha *f* white frost.
escarchar *vi* to be frosty.
escardador *m* weeding hoe.
escardillo *m* small weeding hoe.
escarlata *adj* scarlet.
escarlatina *f* scarlet fever.
escarmentar *vi* to learn one's lesson; * *vt* to punish severely.
escarmiento *m* warning, caution; punishment.
escarnecer *vt* to mock, to ridicule.
escarnio *m* gibe, ridicule.
escarola *f* (*bot*) endive.
escarpa *f* slope; escarpment.
escarpado/da *adj* sloped; craggy.
escarpín *m* sock; pump (shoe).
escasear *vi* to be scarce.
escasez *f* shortage; poverty.
escaso/sa *adj* small, short, little; sparing; scarce; scanty.
escatimar *vt* to curtail, to lessen; to be scanty with.
escena *f* stage; scene.
escenario *m* stage; set.
escepticismo *m* skepticism.
escéptico/ca *adj* skeptical.
esclarecer *vt* to lighten; to illuminate; to illustrate; to shed light on (problem etc).
esclarecido/da *adj* illustrious, noble.
esclarecimiento *m* clarification; enlightenment.
esclavina *f* short cloak/cape.
esclavitud *f* slavery, servitude.
esclavizar *vt* to enslave.
esclavo/va *m/f* slave; captive.
esclusa *f* sluice, floodgate.
escoba *f* broom, brush.
escobazo *m* blow given with a broom.
escobilla *f* brush, small broom; blade.
escobillar *vt Lat Am* to brush.
escocer *vt* to sting; to burn; ~se *vr* to chafe.
escoger *vt* to choose, to select.
escolar *m/f* schoolboy/girl; * *adj* scholastic.
escolástico/ca *adj* scholastic; * *m* scholar.
escollo *m* reef, rock.
escolta *f* escort.
escoltar *vt* to escort.
escombros *mpl* rubbish; debris.

esconder *vt* to hide, to conceal; ~se *vr* to be hidden.
escondidas: a ~ *adv* in a secret manner.
escondite *m* hiding place; juego del ~ hide-and-seek.
escondrijo *m* hiding place.
escopeta *f* shotgun; a tiro de ~ within gunshot.
escopetazo *m* gunshot; gunshot wound.
escopetero *m* gunsmith.
escoplo *m* chisel.
escorbuto *m* scurvy.
escoria *f* dross; scum; dregs *pl*.
Escorpio *m* Scorpio (zodiac sign).
escorpión *m* scorpion.
escotado/da *adj* low-cut.
escotadura *f* low neck(line).
escotar *vt* to cut low in front.
escote *m* low neck (of a dress).
escotilla *f* (*mar*) hatchway.
escozor *m* smart; burning pain; sting(ing).
escriba *m* scribe (of the Hebrews).
escribanía *f* clerk's office; writing desk.
escribano *m* court clerk; lawyer's clerk.
escribiente *m* transcriber; copyist; clerk.
escribir *vt* to write; to spell; * *vi* to write.
escrito *m* document; manuscript, text.
escritor/ra *m/f* writer, author.
escritorio *m* writing desk; office, study.
escritura *f* writing; deed.
escrúpulo *m* doubt, scruple, scrupulousness.
escrupulosidad *f* scrupulousness.
escrupuloso/sa *adj* scrupulous; exact.
escrutar *vt* to examine; to count (ballot papers).
escrutinio *m* scrutiny, inquiry.
escrutiñador *m* scrutinizer, inquirer.
escuadra *f* square; squadron; squad.
escuadrar *vt* to square.
escuadrón *m* squadron.
escuálido/da *adj* skinny; squalid.
escucha *f* listening(-in); * *m* scout.
escuchar *vt* to listen to, to heed.
escudar *vt* to shield; to guard from danger; ~se *vr* to protect oneself.
escudero *m* squire; page.
escudilla *f* bowl.
escudo *m* shield.
escudriñamiento *m* investigation, scrutiny.
escudriñar *vt* to search, to examine; to pry into.
escuela *f* school; ~ primaria grade school; ~ secundaria secondary/high school.
escueto/ta *adj* plain; simple.
esculpir *vt* to sculpt.

escultor/ra *m/f* sculptor.
escultura *f* sculpture.
escupidera *f* cuspidor.
escupidura *f* spit.
escupir *vt* to spit.
escurreplatos *m invar* plate rack.
escurridizo/za *adj* slippery.
escurrir *vt* to drain; to drip; ~**se** *vr* to slip away; to slip, to slide; * *vi* to wring out.
ese/esa *adj* that; **esos/as** *pl* those.
ése/ésa *pn* that (one); **ésos/as** *pl* those (ones).
escencia *f* essence.
esencial *adj* essential; principal.
esfera *f* sphere; globe.
esférico/ca *adj* spherical.
esferoide *f* spheroid.
esfinge *m* sphinx.
esforzado/da *adj* strong, vigorous; valiant.
esforzarse *vr* to exert oneself, to make an effort.
esfuerzo *m* effort.
esfumarse *vr* to fade away.
esgrima *f* fencing.
esgrimidor *m* fencer.
esgrimir *vi* to fence.
esguince *m* (*med*) sprain.
eslabón *m* link of a chain; steel; shackle.
eslabonar *vt* to link; to unite.
esmaltador *m* enameler.
esmaltar *vt* to enamel.
esmalte *m* enamel.
esmerado/da *adj* careful, neat.
esmeralda *m* emerald.
esmerar *vt* to polish; ~**se** *vr* to take great care; to work hard.
esmeril *m* emery.
esmerillar *vt* to polish with emery.
esmero *m* careful attention, great care.
esnob *adj* snobbish; * *m/f* snob.
eso *pn* that.
esófago *m* esophagus; throat.
esos, ésos *pl* of **ese, ése.**
espabilar *vt* to wake up; ~**se** *vr* to wake up; (*fig*) to get a move on.
espacial *adj* space *compd.*
espaciar *vt* to spread out; to space (out).
espacio *m* space; (*rad/TV*) program.
espaciosidad *f* spaciousness, capacity.
espacioso/sa *adj* spacious, roomy.
espada *f* sword; acc of spades.
espadachín *m* bully.
espadaña *f* (*bot*) bulrush.
espadín *m* small short sword.
espaguetis *mpl* spaghetti.

espalda *f* back, back-part; ~**s** *fpl* shoulders *pl.*
espaldilla *f* shoulder blade.
espantadizo/za *adj* timid, easily frightened.
espantajo *m* scarecrow; bogeyman.
espantapájaros *m invar* scarecrow.
espantar *vt* to frighten; to chase/drive away.
espanto *m* fright; menace, threat; astonishment; *Lat Am* ghost.
espantoso/sa *adj* frightful, dreadful; amazing.
español/la *adj* Spanish; * *m/f* Spaniard; * *m* Spanish (language).
esparadrapo *m* adhesive tape.
esparcir *vt* to scatter; to divulge; ~**se** *vr* to amuse oneself.
espárrago *m* asparagus.
esparto *m* (*bot*) esparto.
espasmo *m* spasm.
espátula *f* spatula.
especia *f* spice.
especial *adj* special; particular; **en ~** especially.
especialidad *f* specialty.
especie *f* species; kind, sort; matter.
especificación *f* specification.
especificar *vt* to specify.
específico/ca *adj* specific.
espectáculo *m* spectacle; show.
espectador/ra *m/f* spectator.
espectro *m* specter, phantom, ghost, apparition.
especulación *f* speculation; contemplation; venture.
especulador/ra *m/f* speculator.
especular *vt* to speculate.
especulativo/va *adj* speculative; thoughtful.
espejismo *m* mirage.
espejo *m* mirror.
espeluznante *adj* horrifying.
espera *f* stay, waiting; (*law*) respite, adjournment, delay.
esperanza *f* hope.
esperanzar *vt* to give hope to.
esperar *vt* to hope; to expect, to wait for.
esperma *f* sperm.
espesar *vt* to thicken; to condense; ~**se** *vr* to grow thick; to solidify.
espeso/sa *adj* thick, dense.
espesor *m* thickness.
espesura *f* thickness; density, solidity.
espía *m/f* spy.
espiar *vt* to spy.
espiga *f* ear (of corn).
espigón *m* ear of corn; sting; (*mar*) breakwater.

espina *f* thorn; fishbone.
espinaca *f* (*bot*) spinach.
espinazo *m* spine, backbone.
espinilla *f* shinbone.
espino *m* hawthorn.
espinoso/sa *adj* thorny; dangerous.
espionaje *m* spying, espionage.
espiral *adj*, *f* spiral.
espirar *vt* to exhale.
espíritu *m* spirit, soul; mind; intelligence; el E~ Santo the Holy Ghost; ~s *pl* demons *pl*, hobgoblins *pl*.
espiritual *adj* spiritual; ghostly.
espiritualidad *f* spirituality.
espiritualizar *vt* to spiritualize.
esplendidez *f* splendor.
espléndido/da *adj* splendid.
esplendor *m* splendor.
espliego *m* (*bot*) lavender.
espolear *vt* to spur, to instigate, to incite.
espolón *m* spur (of a cock); spur (of a mountain range); sea wall; jetty; (*mar*) buttress.
espolvorear *vt* to sprinkle.
espondeo *m* (*poet*) spondee.
esponja *f* sponge.
esponjar *vt* to sponge; ~se *vr* to be puffed up with pride.
esponjoso/sa *adj* spongy.
esponsales *mpl* betrothal.
espontaneidad *f* spontaneity.
espontáneo/nea *adj* spontaneous.
esposa *f* wife.
esposar *vt* to handcuff.
esposas *fpl* handcuffs *pl*.
esposo *m* husband.
espuela *f* spur; stimulus; (*bot*) larkspur.
espuerta *f* pannier, basket.
espulgar *vt* to delouse; to examine closely.
espuma *f* froth, foam.
espumadera *f* skimmer.
espumajear *vi* to foam at the mouth.
espumar *vt* to skim, to take the scum off.
espumarajo *m* foam, froth (from the mouth).
espumoso/sa *adj* frothy, foamy; sparkling (wine).
espurio/ria *adj* spurious; adulterated; illegitimate.
esputo *m* spit, saliva.
esqueje *m* cutting (of plant).
esquela *f* note, slip of paper.
esqueleto *m* skeleton.
esquema *m* scheme; diagram; plan.
esquí *m* ski; skiing.
esquiar *vi* to ski.

esquife *m* skiff, small boat.
esquilador *m* sheep-shearer.
esquilar *vt* to shear sheep.
esquina *f* corner, angle.
esquinado/da *adj* cornered, angled.
esquinar *vt* to form a corner with.
esquirol *m* blackleg.
esquivar *vt* to shun, to avoid, to evade.
esquivez *f* disdain; shyness.
esquivo/va *adj* scornful; shy, reserved.
esta: *f* of este.
ésta: *f* of éste.
estabilidad *f* stability.
estable *adj* stable.
establecer *vt* to establish.
establecimiento *m* establishment.
establo *m* stable.
estaca *f* stake; stick; post.
estacada *f* fence; fencing; stockade.
estacazo *m* blow with a stick.
estación *f* season (of the year); station; railroad station, terminus; ~ de autobuses bus station; ~ de servicio service station.
estacional *adj* seasonal.
estacionamiento *m* parking; parking lot; (*mil*) stationing.
estacionar *vt* to park; (*mil*) to station.
estacionario/ria *adj* stationary.
estadía *f* *Lat Am* stay.
estadio *m* phase; stadium.
estadista *m* statesman; statistician.
estadística *f* statistics *pl*.
estadístico/ca *adj* statistical.
estado *m* state, condition.
Estados Unidos *mpl* United States (of America).
estafa *f* trick, fraud.
estafador/ra *m/f* swindler, racketeer.
estafar *vt* to deceive, to defraud.
estafeta *f* post office.
estallar *vi* to crack; to burst; to break out.
estallido *m* explosion; (*fig*) outbreak.
estambre *m* stamen.
estamento *m* estate; body; layer; class.
estameña *f* serge.
estampa *f* print; engraving; appearance.
estampado/da *adj* printed; * *m* printing; print; stamping.
estampar *vt* to print.
estampida *f* stampede.
estampido *m* report (of a gun); crack.
estampilla *f* seal; *Lat Am* stamp.
estancar *vt* to check (a current); to monopolize; to prohibit, to suspend; ~se *vr* to stagnate.

estancia *f* stay; bedroom; ranch; (*poet*) stanza.

estanco *m* tobacconist's (shop); ~/**ca** *adj* watertight.

estándar *adj*, *m* standard.

estandarizar *vt* to standardize.

estandarte *m* banner, standard.

estanque *m* pond, pool; reservoir.

estanquero/ra *m*/*f* tobacconist.

estante *m* shelf (for books).

estantería *f* shelves *pl*, shelving.

estaño *m* tin.

estar *vi* to be; to be (in a place).

estatal *adj* state *compd*.

estática *f* statics *pl*.

estático/ca *adj* static.

estatua *f* statue.

estatura *f* stature.

estatuto *m* statute, law.

este[1] *m* east;

este/ta[2] *adj* this; **estos/tas** *pl* these.

éste *pn m* this (one); **éstos/tas** *pl* these (ones).

estera *f* mat.

estercolar *vt* to manure.

estercolero *m* dunghill.

estéreo *adj invar*, *m* stereo.

estereotipar *vt* to stereotype.

estereotipo *m* stereotype.

estéril *adj* sterile, infertile.

esterilidad *f* sterility, infertility.

esterilla *f* mat; *Lat Am* canework.

esterlina *adj*: **libra** ~ pound sterling.

estético/ca *adj* esthetic; * *f* esthetics.

estiércol *m* dung; manure.

estilar *vi*, ~**se** *vr* to be in fashion; to be used.

estilo *m* style; fashion; stroke (in swimming).

estima *f* esteem.

estimable *adj* estimable, worthy of esteem.

estimación *f* estimation, valuation.

estimar *vt* to estimate, to value; to esteem; to judge; to think.

estimulante *adj* stimulating; * *m* stimulant.

estimular *vt* to stimulate, to excite; to goad.

estímulo *m* stimulus.

estío *m* summer.

estipendiario *m* stipendiary.

estipulación *f* stipulation.

estipular *vt* to stipulate.

estirado/da *adj* stretched tight; (*fig*) pompous.

estirar *vt* to stretch out.

estirón *m* pulling; tugging; **dar un** ~ to grow rapidly.

estirpe *f* race, origin, stock.

estival *adj* summer *compd*.

esto *pn* this.

estocada *f* stab.

estofa *f*: **de baja** ~ poor quality.

estofado *m* stew.

estola *f* stole.

estolidez *f* stupidity.

estólido/da *adj* stupid.

estomacal *adj* stomach *compd*.

estómago *m* stomach.

estopa *f* tow.

estoque *m* rapier, sword.

estorbar *vt* to hinder; (*fig*) to bother; * *vi* to be in the way.

estorbo *m* obstacle, hindrance, impediment.

estornudar *vi* to sneeze.

estornudo *m* sneeze.

estos, éstos *pl* of **este, éste**.

estrada *f* highway; expressway.

estrado *m* drawing room; stage, platform; ~ **de los testigos** witness stand.

estrafalario/ria *adj* slovenly, eccentric.

estrago *m* ruin, destruction; havoc.

estrambótico/ca *adj* eccentric, odd.

estrangulador/ra *m*/*f* strangler.

estrangulamiento *m* bottleneck.

estrangular *vt* to strangle; (*med*) to strangulate.

estraperlo *m* black market.

estratagema *f* stratagem, trick.

estrategia *f* strategy.

estratégico/ca *adj* strategic.

estrato *m* stratum, layer.

estraza *f* rag; **papel de** ~ brown paper.

estrechar *vt* to tighten; to contract, to constrain; to compress; ~ **la mano** to shake hands; ~**se** *vr* to grow narrow; to embrace.

estrechez *f* strictness, narrowness; shortage of money.

estrecho *m* straits *pl*; ~/**cha** *adj* narrow, close; tight; intimate; rigid, austere; short (of money).

estrella *f* star.

estrellado/da *adj* starry; **huevos** ~**s** fried eggs.

estrellar *vt* to dash to pieces; ~**se** *vr* to smash; to crash; to fail.

estremecer *vt* to shake, to make tremble; ~**se** *vr* to shake, to tremble.

estremecimiento *m* trembling, shaking.

estrenar *vt* to wear for the first time; to move into (a house); to show (a film) for the first time; ~**se** *vr* to make one's debut.

estreñido/da *adj* constipated.

estreñimiento *m* constipation.
estrépito *m* noise, racket; fuss.
estrepitoso/sa *adj* noisy.
estribar *vi*: ~ **en** to be supported by; to be based on.
estribillo *m* chorus.
estribo *m* buttress; stirrup; bracket; brace; **perder los ~s** to fly off the handle *(col)*.
estribor *m* (*mar*) starboard.
estrictez *f Lat Am* strictness.
estricto/ta *adj* strict; severe.
estrofa *f* (*poet*) verse, strophe.
estropajo *m* scourer.
estropajoso/sa *adj* tough, leathery; despicable; mean; stammering.
estropear *vt* to spoil; to damage; ~**se** *vr* to get damaged.
estructura *f* structure.
estruendo *m* clamor, noise; confusion, uproar; pomp, ostentation.
estrujar *vt* to press, to squeeze.
estrujón *m* pressing, squeezing.
estuario *m* estuary.
estuche *m* case (for scissors etc); sheath.
estudiante *m/f* student.
estudiantil *adj* student *compd*.
estudiar *vt* to study.
estudio *m* study; studio; ~**s** *mpl* studies *pl*; learning.
estudioso/sa *adj* studious.
estufa *f* heater, fire.
estufilla *f* muff; small stove.
estupefacción *f* stupefaction.
estupefaciente *m* narcotic.
estupefacto *adj* speechless; thunderstruck.
estupendo/da *adj* terrific, marvelous.
estupidez *f* stupidity.
estúpido/da *adj* stupid.
estupor *m* stupor; astonishment.
estupro *m* rape.
etapa *f* stage; stopping place; (*fig*) phase.
etcétera *adv* etcetera, and so on.
éter *m* ether.
etéreo/rea *adj* ethereal.
eternidad *f* eternity.
eternizar *vt* to eternalize, to perpetuate.
eterno/na *adj* eternal.
ética *f* ethics.
ético/ca *adj* ethical, moral.
etimología *f* etymology.
etimológico/ca *adj* etymological.
etiqueta *f* etiquette; label, tag.
Eucaristía *f* Eucharist.
eufemismo *m* euphemism.
euforia *f* euphoria.

euro *m* euro.
eurocámara *f* European Parliament.
eurodiputado/da *m/f* Euro-MP.
euroescéptico/ca *m/f* Euroskeptic.
Europa *f* Europe.
eurotúnel *m* Eurotunnel, Channel tunnel.
evacuación *f* evacuation.
evacuar *vt* to evacuate, to empty.
evadir *vt* to evade, to escape.
evaluar *vt* to evaluate.
evangélico/ca *adj* evangelical.
evangelio *m* gospel.
evangelista *m* evangelist.
evangelizar *vt* to evangelize.
evaporar *vt* to evaporate; ~**se** *vr* to vanish.
evasión *f* evasion, escape.
evasivo/va *adj* evasive; * *f* excuse.
eventual *adj* possible; temporary, casual (worker).
evidencia *f* evidence, proof.
evidente *adj* evident, clear.
evitable *adj* avoidable.
evitar *vt* to avoid.
evocación *f* evocation; invocation.
evocar *vt* to call out; to invoke.
evolución *f* evolution, development; change; (*mil*) maneuver.
evolucionar *vi* to evolve.
ex *adj* ex.
exacción *f* exaction; extortion.
exacerbar *vt* to exacerbate; to irritate.
exactamente *adv* exactly.
exactitud *f* exactness.
exacto/ta *adj* exact; punctual; accurate.
exageración *f* exaggeration.
exagerar *vt* to exaggerate.
exaltación *f* exaltation, elation.
exaltar *vt* to exalt, to elevate; to praise, to extoll; ~**se** *vr* to get excited.
examen *m* exam, examination, test; inquiry.
examinador *m* examiner.
examinar *vt* to examine.
exánime *adj* lifeless, weak.
exasperación *f* exasperation.
exasperar *vt* to exasperate, to irritate.
excavación *f* excavation.
excavadora *f* excavator.
excavar *vt* to excavate, to dig out.
excedente *adj* excessive.
exceder *vt* to exceed, to surpass, to excel, to outdo.
excelencia *f* excellence.
Excelencia *f* Excellency (title).
excelente *adj* excellent.
excelso/sa *adj* elevated, sublime, lofty.

excentricidad *f* eccentricity.
excéntrico/ca *adj* eccentric.
excepción *f* exception.
excepto *adv* excepting, except (for).
exceptuar *vt* to except, to exempt.
excesivo/va *adj* excessive.
exceso *m* excess.
excitación *f* excitement; excitation.
excitar *vt* to excite; ~se *vr* to get excited.
exclamación *f* exclamation.
exclamar *vt* to exclaim, to cry out.
excluir *vt* to exclude.
exclusión *f* exclusion.
exclusiva *f* exclusive; (*com*) sole right.
exclusivamente, exclusive *adv* exclusively.
exclusivo/va *adj* exclusive.
excomulgar *vt* to excommunicate.
excomunión *f* excommunication.
excremento *m* excrement.
excursión *f* excursion, trip.
excusa *f* excuse, apology.
excusable *adj* excusable.
excusado *m* bathroom, lavatory.
excusar *vt* to excuse; to avoid; ~ de to exempt from; ~se *vr* to apologize.
execrable *adj* execrable, abhorrent.
execrar *vt* to execrate, to curse.
exención *f* exemption; immunity, privilege.
exento/ta *adj* exempt, free.
exequias *fpl* funeral rites *pl*, obsequies *pl*.
exhalación *f* exhalation; fumes *pl*, vapor.
exhalar *vt* to exhale; to give off; to heave (a sigh).
exhausto/ta *adj* exhausted.
exhibición *f* exhibition, display.
exhibir *vt* to exhibit.
exhortación *f* exhortation.
exhortar *vt* to exhort.
exhumación *f* exhumation.
exhumar *vt* to disinter, to exhume.
exigencia *f* demand, requirement.
exigir *vt* to demand, to require.
exiguo/gua *adj* meager, small.
exiliado/da *adj* exiled; * *m/f* exile.
exilio *m* exile.
eximir *vt* to exempt, to free; to excuse.
existencia *f* existence, being.
existente *adj* existing, in existence.
existir *vi* to exist, to be.
éxito *m* outcome, success; (*mus*) hit; tener ~ to be successful.
exoneración *f* exoneration.
exonerar *vt* to exonerate.
exorbitante *adj* exorbitant, excessive.

exorcismo *m* exorcism.
exorcista *m* exorcist.
exorcizar *vt* to exorcise.
exótico/ca *adj* exotic.
expandir *vt* to expand.
expansión *f* expansion; extension.
expansivo/va *adj* expansive.
expatriarse *vr* to emigrate; to go into exile.
expectativa *f* expectation; prospect.
expectoración *f* expectoration.
expectorar *vt* to expectorate.
expedición *f* expedition.
expedicionario/ria *adj* expeditionary.
expediente *m* expedient; means; (*law*) proceedings *pl*; dossier, file.
expedir *vt* to send, to forward, to dispatch.
expeditivo/va *adj* expeditious.
expedito/ta *adj* speedy; clear, free.
expeler *vt* to expel.
expendio *m Lat Am* shop.
expensas *fpl*: a ~ de at the expense of.
experiencia *f* experience; trial.
experimentado/da *adj* experienced; expert.
experimental *adj* experimental.
experimentar *vt* to experience; * *vi*: ~ con to experiment with.
experimento *m* experiment, trial.
experto/ta *adj* expert; experienced.
expiación *f* expiation; purification.
expiar *vt* to atone for; to purify.
expiatorio/ria *adj* expiatory.
expirar *vi* to expire.
explanada *f* esplanade.
explayarse *vr* to speak at length.
explicación *f* explanation.
explicar *vt* to explain, to expound; ~se *vr* to explain oneself.
explícito/ta *adj* explicit.
exploración *f* exploration.
explorador/ra *m/f* explorer.
explorar *vt* to explore.
explosión *f* explosion.
explotación *f* exploitation; running.
explotar *vt* to exploit; to run; * *vi* to explode.
exponente *m* (*math*) exponent.
exponer *vt* to expose; to explain.
exportación *f* export; exports *pl*.
exportar *vt* to export.
exposición *f* exposure; exhibition; explanation; account.
expresar *vt* to express.
expresión *f* expression.
expresivo/va *adj* expressive; energetic.
expreso/sa *adj* express, clear, specific; fast (train).

express *m* (*rail*) express train.
exprimidor *m* squeezer.
exprimir *vt* to squeeze out.
ex profeso *adv* on purpose.
expropriar *vt* to expropriate.
expuesto/ta *adj* exposed; on display.
expulsar *vt* to expel, to drive out.
expulsión *f* expulsion.
exquisito/ta *adj* exquisite; excellent.
éxtasis *m* ecstasy, enthusiasm.
extático/ca *adj* ecstatic.
extender *vt* to extend, to stretch out; ~se *vr* to extend; to spread.
extensión *f* extension; extent.
extensivo/va *adj* extensive.
extenso/sa *adj* extensive.
extenuación *f* emaciation; debility, exhaustion.
extenuar *vt* to exhaust, to debilitate.
exterior *adj* exterior, external; * *m* exterior, outward appearance.
exteriormente *adv* externally.
exterminador *m* exterminator.
exterminar *vt* to exterminate.
exterminio *m* extermination.
externo/na *adj* external, outer; * *m/f* day pupil/student.
extinción *f* extinction.
extinguidor *m* *Lat Am* (fire) extinguisher.
extinguir *vt* to wipe out; to extinguish.
extintor *m* (fire) extinguisher.
extirpación *f* extirpation, extermination.
extirpar *vt* to extirpate, to root out.

extorsión *f* extortion.
extra *adj* *invar* extra; good quality; * *m/f* extra; * *m* bonus.
extracción *f* extraction.
extracto *m* extract.
extradición *f* extradition.
extraditar *vt* to extradite.
extraer *vt* to extract.
extranjero/ra *m/f* stranger; foreigner; * *adj* foreign, alien.
extrañar *vt* to find strange; to miss; ~se *vr* to be surprised; to grow apart.
extrañeza *f* strangeness; surprise.
extraño/ña *adj* foreign; rare; singular, strange, odd.
extraordinario/ria *adj* extraordinary, uncommon, odd.
extravagancia *f* extravagance.
extravagante *adj* extravagant.
extraviado/da *adj* lost, missing.
extraviar *vt* to mislead; ~se *vr* to lose one's way.
extravío *m* deviation; loss.
extremado/da *adj* extreme; accomplished.
extremaunción *f* extreme unction.
extremidad *f* extremity; brim; tip; ~es *fpl* extremities *pl*.
extremo/ma *adj* extreme, last; * *m* extreme, highest degree; **en** ~ extremely.
extrínseco/ca *adj* extrinsic, external.
extrovertido/da *adj*, *m/f* extrovert.
exuberancia *f* exuberance; luxuriance.

F

fábrica *f* factory.
fabricación *f* manufacture, production.
fabricante *m/f* producer, manufacturer.
fabricar *vt* to build, to construct; to manufacture; (*fig*) to fabricate.
fabril *adj* manufacturing *compd*, industrial.
fábula *f* fable; fiction; rumor, common talk.
fabulista *m/f* writer of fables.
fabuloso/sa *adj* fabulous, fictitious.
facción *f* (political) faction; feature.
faccioso/sa *adj* factious, turbulent.
facha *f* appearance, look; face.
fachada *f* facade, face, front.
fácil *adj* facile, easy.
facilidad *f* facility, easiness; con ~ *adv* cozily, easily.
facilitar *vt* to facilitate.
fácilmente *adv* easily
facineroso *adj* wicked, criminal.
facsímil *m* facsimile, fax.
factible *adj* feasible, practicable.
factor *m* (*math*) factor; (*com*) factor, agent.
factoría *f* agency; factory.
factura *f* invoice.
facultad *f* faculty; *Lat Am* college.
facultativo/va *adj* optional; * *m/f* doctor, practitioner.
faena *f* task, job; hard work.
faisán *m* pheasant.
faja *f* band, sash; strip (of land); corset.
fajo *m* bundle; wad.
falacia *f* fallacy; fraud.
falange *f* phalanx.
falaz *adj* deceitful, fraudulent; fallacious.
falda *f* skirt; lap; flap; train; slope, hillside.
faldero/ra *adj*: hombre ~ ladies' man; perrito ~ lap-dog.
faldón *m* coat-tails *pl*; skirt.
falencia *f* *Lat Am* bankruptcy.
falible *adj* fallible.
falla *f* *Lat Am* mistake.
fallar *vt* (*law*) to pronounce sentence on, to judge; * *vi* to fail.
fallecer *vi* to die.
fallecimiento *m* decease, death.
fallido/da *adj* unsuccessful, frustrated.
fallo *m* judgement, sentence; failure.
falsamente *adv* falsely.
falsario/ria *adj* falsifying, forging.
falsear *vt* to falsify, to counterfeit.

falsedad *f* falsehood; untruth, lie; hypocrisy.
falsete *m* (*tec*) plug; bung; (*mus*) falsetto.
falsificación *f* falsification.
falsificador/ora *m/f* forger, counterfeiter.
falsificar *vt* to falsify, to forge, to counterfeit.
falso/sa *adj* false, untrue; deceitful; fake.
falta *f* fault; defect; want; flaw, mistake; (*sport*) foul.
faltante *m* *Lat Am* deficit.
faltar *vi* to be wanting; to fail; not to fulfill one's promise; to need; to be missing.
falto/ta *adj* wanting, deficient, lacking; miserable, wretched.
faltriquera *f* pocket.
fama *f* fame; reputation, name.
famélico/ca *adj* starving.
familia *f* family.
familiar *adj* familiar; homely, domestic; * *m/f* relative, relation.
familiaridad *f* familiarity.
familiarizarse *vr*: ~ con to familiarize oneself with.
famoso/sa *adj* famous.
fan *m/f* fan.
fanático/ca *adj* fanatical; enthusiastic; * *m/f* fanatic; fan.
fandango *m* fandango.
fanfarrón/ona *m/f* bully, braggart.
fanfarronada *f* boast, brag.
fanfarronear *vi* to bully, to brag.
fanfarronería *f* boast, brag.
fango *m* mire, mud.
fangoso/sa *adj* muddy, miry.
fantasía *f* fancy; fantasy; caprice; presumption.
fantasma *f* phantom, ghost.
fantástico/ca *adj* fantastic, whimsical; presumptuous.
fardo *m* bale, parcel.
farfullar *vi* to talk with a stammer.
farisaico/ca *adj* pharisaical; hypocritical.
fariseo *m* Pharisee; hypocrite.
farmacéutico/ca *adj* pharmaceutical; * *m/f* druggist.
farmacia *f* drugstore.
faro *m* (*mar*) lighthouse; (*auto*) headlamp/light; floodlight.
farol *m* lantern.
farola *f* street light.

farsa *f* farce.
farsante *m/f* fraud, fake.
fascículo *m* part, installment.
fascinación *f* fascination.
fascinar *vt* to fascinate; to enchant.
fascismo *m* fascism.
fascista *adj, m/f* fascist.
fase *f* phase.
fastidiar *vt* to annoy; to offend; to spoil.
fastidio *m* annoyance; boredom; disgust.
fastidioso/sa *adj* annoying; tedious.
fatal *adj* fatal; mortal; awful.
fatalidad *f* fatality; mischance, ill-luck.
fatalismo *m* fatalism.
fatalista *m/f* fatalist.
fatiga *f* weariness, fatigue.
fatigar *vt* to fatigue, to tire; to harass.
fatigoso/sa *adj* tiresome, troublesome.
fatuidad *f* fatuity, foolishness, silliness.
fatuo/tua *adj* fatuous, stupid, foolish; conceited.
fauces *fpl* jaws *pl*; gullet.
fausto/ta *adj* happy, fortunate; * *m* splendor, pomp.
favor *m* favor; protection; good turn.
favorable *adj* favorable.
favorecer *vt* to favor, to protect.
favorecido/da *m/f Lat Am* prizewinner.
favorito/ta *adj* favorite.
fax *m* fax.
faz *f* face.
fe *f* faith, belief.
fealdad *f* ugliness.
febrero *m* February.
febril *adj* feverish.
fecha *f* date (of a letter etc).
fechar *vt* to date.
fechoría *f* misdeed; exploit.
fecundar *vt* to fertilize.
fecundidad *f* fecundity, fertility.
fecundo/da *adj* fruitful, fertile.
federación *f* federation.
felicidad *f* happiness.
felicitaciones *interj Lat Am* congratulations!
felicitar *vt* to congratulate.
feligrés/esa *m/f* parishioner.
feliz *adj* happy, fortunate.
felpa *f* plush; toweling.
felpudo *m* doormat.
femenil *adj* feminine, womanly.
femenino/na *adj* feminine; female.
feminismo *m* feminism.
feminista *adj, m/f* feminist.
fenómeno *m* phenomenon; (*fig*) freak, accident; * *adj* (*col*) great, marvelous.

feo/ea *adj* ugly; bad, nasty.
feracidad *f* productivity, fertility.
feraz *adj* fertile, fruitful.
féretro *m* bier, casket.
feria *f* fair, rest day; village market.
feriado *m Lat Am* public holiday.
fermentación *f* fermentation.
fermentar *vi* to ferment.
fermento *m* ferment; leaven.
ferocidad *f* ferocity, wildness; cruelty.
feroz *adj* ferocious, savage; cruel.
ferretería *f* hardware store.
ferrocarril *m* railroad.
ferroviario/ria *adj* rail *compd*.
ferry *m* ferry.
fértil *adj* fertile, fruitful.
fertilidad *f* fertility, fruitfulness.
fertilización *f* fertilization.
fertilizar *vt* to fertilize.
férula *f* ferule; (*med*) splint.
ferviente *adj* fervent; ardent.
fervor *m* fervor, zeal; ardor.
fervoroso/sa *adj* fervent, ardent, passionate.
festejar *vt* to feast; to court, to woo.
festejo *m* courtship; feast.
festín *m* feast.
festividad *f* festivity.
festivo/va *adj* festive, merry; witty; **día ~** holiday.
festón *m* garland; festoon.
festonear *vt* to decorate with garlands.
fétido/da *adj* fetid, stinking.
feto *m* fetus.
feudal *adj* feudal.
fiable *adj* trustworthy; reliable.
fiador/ra *m/f* guarantor; (*com*) backer.
fiambre *m* cold meat.
fiambrera *f* dinner pail; lunch basket.
fianza *f* (*law*) surety.
fiar *vt* to entrust, to confide; to bail; to sell on credit; to buy on credit; * *vi* to trust.
fibra *f* fiber.
fibroso/sa *adj* fibrous.
ficción *f* fiction.
ficha *f* token, counter (at games); (index) card.
ficticio/cia *adj* fictitious.
fidedigno/na *adj* reliable, trustworthy.
fideicomisario/ria *m/f* trustee.
fideicomiso *f* trust.
fidelidad *f* fidelity; loyalty.
fideos *mpl* vermicelli *pl*.
fiebre *f* fever.
fiel *adj* faithful, loyal; * *mpl* **los ~es** the faithful *pl*.

fieltro m felt.
fiera f wild beast.
fiereza f fierceness, ferocity; cruelty.
fiero/ra adj fierce, ferocious; cruel; rough, harsh.
fierrero/ra m/f Lat Am weightlifter.
fierro m Lat Am iron.
fiesta f party; festivity; ~s fpl feast days; holidays pl.
figura f figure, shape.
figurado/da adj figurative.
figurar vt to figure; ~se vr to fancy, to imagine.
figurilla f ridiculous little figure.
fijador m fixative; gel (for the hair).
fijar vt to fix, to fasten; ~se vr to become fixed; to establish oneself; ~se en to notice.
fijo/ja adj fixed, firm; settled, permanent.
fila f row, line; (mil) rank; en ~ in a line, in a row.
filamento m filament.
filantropía f philanthropy.
filántropo/pa m/f philanthropist.
fildeador/ra m/f Lat Am fielder.
fildear vi Lat Am to field.
fildeo m Lat Am fielding.
filete m fillet; fillet steak.
filiación f lineage; personal description, personal particulars pl.
filial adj filial; * f (com) subsidiary.
filibustero m pirate.
filigrana f filigree.
filmar vt to film.
filo m edge, blade.
filología f philology.
filológico/ca adj philological.
filólogo/ga m/f philologist.
filoso/sa adj Lat Am sharp.
filosofar vt to philosophize.
filosofía f philosophy.
filosófico/ca adj philosophical.
filósofo/fa m/f philosopher.
filtración f filtration.
filtrar vt to filter, to strain.
filtro m filter.
fin m end; termination, conclusion; aim, purpose; al ~ at last; en ~ (fig) well then; por ~ finally, lastly.
final adj final; * m end; termination, conclusion; * f (sport) final.
finalizar vt to finish, to conclude; * vi to be finished.
finalmente adv finally, at last.
financiar vt to finance.

financista m/f Lat Am financier.
finca f land, property, real estate; country house; farm; Lat Am plantation.
fineza f fineness, perfection; elegance; courtesy; small gift.
fingido/da adj feigned, fake, sham.
fingimiento m simulation, pretense.
fingir vt to feign, to fake; to invent; to imitate; ~se vr to pretend to be; * vi to pretend.
finito/ta adj finite.
fino/na adj fine, pure; slender; polite; acute; dry (of sherry).
finura f fineness.
firma f signature; (com) company.
firmamento m firmament, sky, heaven.
firmar vt to sign.
firme adj firm, stable, strong, secure; constant; resolute; * m road surface.
firmeza f firmness, stability, constancy.
fiscal adj fiscal; * m/f district attorney.
fiscalía f office and business of the district attorney.
fiscalizar vt to inspect; to criticize.
fisco m treasury.
fisgar vt to pry into.
fisgón/ona m/f prying person, snooper.
física f physics.
físico/ca adj physical; * m/f physicist; * m physique.
fisonomía f physiognomy.
fisonomista m/f: ser buen ~ to have a good memory for faces.
flaco/ca adj lean, skinny; feeble.
flagelación f flagellation.
flagrante adj flagrant.
flamante adj flaming, bright; brand-new.
flan m crème caramel.
flanco m flank.
flanquear vt (mil) to flank.
flaquear vi to flag; to weaken.
flaqueza f thinness, leanness; feebleness, weakness.
flash m flash.
flato m (med) flatulence; depression.
flatulento/ta adj flatulent.
flauta f (mus) flute.
flautista m/f flute player, flautist.
flecha f arrow.
fleco m hair cut straight across the forehead, fringe.
flema f phlegm.
flemático/ca adj phlegmatic.
flemón m ulcer in the gums.
flequillo m hair cut straight across the forehead, fringe.

fletar vt to freight (a ship).
flete m (mar) freight; charter.
flexibilidad f flexibility.
flexible adj flexible; compliant; docile.
flojedad f feebleness; laxity, laziness; negligence.
flojera f: me da ~ I can't be bothered.
flojo/ja adj loose; flexible; lax, slack; lazy.
flor f flower.
florecer vi to blossom.
florero m vase.
floresta f wood, grove; beauty spot.
florete m fencing foil.
florido/da adj full of flowers; in bloom; choice.
florista m/f florist.
flota f fleet.
flotador m float.
flotante adj floating.
flotar vi to float.
flote m: a ~ afloat.
flotilla f small fleet, flotilla.
fluctuación f fluctuation; uncertainty.
fluctuar vi to fluctuate; to waver.
fluidez f fluidity; fluency.
fluido/da adj fluid; (fig) fluent; * m fluid.
fluir vi to flow.
flujo m flux; flow; ~ **de sangre** (med) loss of blood.
fluvial adj fluvial, river compd.
foca f seal.
foco m focus; center; source; floodlight; (light)bulb; Lat Am street light; Lat Am car headlight.
fofo/fa adj spongy; soft; bland.
fogata f blaze; bonfire.
fogón m stove; hearth.
fogonazo m flash; explosion.
fogosidad f dash, verve; fieriness.
fogoso/sa adj fiery; ardent, fervent; impetuous, boisterous.
folk m folk music.
follaje m foliage.
folletista m/f pamphleteer.
folleto m pamphlet; folder, brochure.
follón m (col) mess; fuss.
fomentar vt to encourage; to promote.
fomento m promotion.
fonda f hotel; inn; boarding house.
fondeadero m anchorage.
fondeado/da adj Lat Am wealthy.
fondear vi to drop anchor.
fondista m/f innkeeper.
fondo m bottom; back; background; space; ~s mpl stock, funds pl, capital; **a** ~ perfectly, completely.

fontanería f plumbing.
fontanero/ra m/f plumber.
footing m jogging.
forajido m outlaw.
foral adj belonging to the statute law of a country.
forastero/ra adj strange, exotic; * m/f stranger.
forcejear vi to struggle.
forense adj forensic; * m/f forensic scientist.
forjador/ra m/f framer; forger.
forjadura f forging.
forjar vt to forge; to frame; to invent.
forma f form, shape; pattern; (med) fitness; (sport) form; means, method; **de ~ que** in such a manner that.
formación f formation; form, figure; education; training.
formal adj formal; proper, genuine; serious, grave.
formalidad f formality; gravity.
formalizar vt (law) to formalize; to regularize; ~**se** vr to be regularized.
formar vt to form, to shape.
formidable adj formidable, dreadful; (col) terrific.
fórmula f formula.
formulario m formulary.
fornicación f fornication.
fornicador m fornicator.
fornicar vi to commit fornication, to fornicate.
fornido/da adj well-built.
foro m court of justice; forum.
forraje m forage.
forrajear vt to forage.
forrar vt to line; to face; to cover.
forro m lining; book jacket.
fortalecer vt to fortify, to strengthen.
fortaleza f courage; strength, vigor; (mil) fortress, stronghold.
fortificación f fortification.
fortificar vt to strengthen; to fortify (a place).
fortín m (mil) small fort.
fortuito/ta adj fortuitous.
fortuna f fortune; wealth.
forzar vt to force.
forzoso/sa adj indispensable, necessary.
forzudo/da adj strong, vigorous.
fosa f grave; pit.
fósforo m phosphorus; ~s mpl matches pl.
fósil adj, m fossil.
foso vt pit; moat, ditch, fosse.

foto f photo.
fotocopia f photocopy.
fotocopiar vt to photocopy.
fotografía f photography; photograph.
fotógrafo/fa m/f photographer.
frac m tails, dress coat.
fracasar vi to fail.
fracaso m failure.
fracción f fraction.
fractura f fracture.
fracturar vt to break (a bone).
fragancia f fragrance, sweetness of smell; odor.
fragante adj fragrant, scented.
fragata f (mar) frigate.
frágil adj fragile, frail.
fragilidad f fragility, brittleness; frailty.
fragmento m fragment.
fragosidad f roughness; denseness.
fragoso/sa adj craggy, rough, uneven.
fragua f forge.
fraguar vt to forge; to contrive; * vi to solidify, to harden.
fraile m friar, monk.
frambuesa f raspberry.
francés/sa adj French; * m French (language); * m/f Frenchman/woman.
franco/ca adj frank; candid; free, gratis.
franela f flannel; undershirt.
franja f strip, band, fringe.
franquear vt to clear; to overcome; to stamp (letters); ~se to unbosom oneself.
franqueo m postage.
franqueza f frankness.
franquicia f immunity from taxes.
frasco m flask.
frase f phrase.
fraternal adj fraternal, brotherly.
fraternidad f fraternity, brotherhood.
fratricida m/f fratricide (person).
fratricidio m fratricide (act).
fraude m fraud, deceit; cheat.
fraudulento/ta adj fraudulent, deceitful.
frazada f Lat Am blanket.
frecuencia f frequency.
frecuentar vt to frequent.
frecuente adj frequent.
freezer m Lat Am freezer.
fregadero m (kitchen) sink.
fregado m scouring, scrubbing; (fig) intrigue; underhand work.
fregar vt to scrub; to wash up.
fregona f kitchen maid, someone who washes dishes.
freír vt to fry.

frenar vt to brake; (fig) to check.
frenesí m frenzy.
frenético/ca adj frantic; frenzied, wild.
frenillo m speech impediment.
freno m bit (horse's); brake; (fig) check.
frente f front; (mil) front; face; ~ a ~ face to face; en ~ opposite; * m forehead.
fresa f strawberry.
fresal m strawberry plant; ground bearing strawberry plants.
fresco/ca adj fresh; cool; new; ruddy; * m fresh air; * m/f (col) shameless/impudent person.
frescura f freshness; frankness; cheek, nerve.
fresno m ash tree.
frialdad f coldness; indifference.
fricción f friction.
friega f rubbing; nuisance.
frígido/da adj frigid.
frigorífico m refrigerator.
frijol m bean.
frío/fría adj cold, indifferent; * m cold; indifference.
friolento/ta adj Lat Am chilly.
friolera f trifle.
friso m frieze; wainscot.
fritada f dish of fried meat/fish.
fritar vt Lat Am to fry.
frito/ta adj fried.
frivolidad f frivolity.
frívolo/la adj frivolous.
frondosidad f foliage.
frondoso/sa adj leafy.
frontera f frontier.
fronterizo/za adj frontier compd; bordering.
frontón m (sport) pelota court; pelota.
frotación, frotadura f friction, rubbing.
frotar vt to rub.
fructífero/ra adj fruit-bearing, fruitful.
fructificar vi to bear fruit; to come to fruition.
fructuoso/sa adj fruitful.
frugal adj frugal, sparing.
frugalidad f frugality, parsimony.
fruncir vt to pleat; to knit; to contract; ~ las cejas to knit the eyebrows.
frustrar vt to frustrate.
fruta f fruit; ~ del tiempo seasonal fruit.
frutal m fruit tree.
frutera f fruit dish.
frutería f fruit shop.
frutero/ra m/f fruiterer, fruit seller; * m fruit basket.

frutilla *f* strawberry.
fruto *m* fruit; benefit, profit.
fuego *m* fire.
fuelle *m* bellows *pl*.
fuente *f* fountain; spring; source; large dish.
fuera *adv* out(side); away; ~ **de** *prep* outside; ¡~! out of the way!
fueraborda *m* outboard motor.
fuero *m* statute law of a country; jurisdiction.
fuerte *m* (*mil*) fortification, fort; forte; * *adj* vigorous, tough; strong; loud; heavy; * *adv* strongly; hard.
fuerza *f* force, strength; (electric) power; violence; **a** ~ **de** by dint of; ~**s** *mpl* troops *pl*.
fuga *f* flight, escape; leak (of gas).
fugarse *vr* to escape, to flee.
fugaz *adj* fleeting.
fugitivo/va *adj*, *m/f* fugitive.
fulano/na *m/f* so-and-so, what's-his-name/ what's-her-name.
fulgurar *vi* to flash.
fullería *f* cheating.
fullero *m* cardsharp, cheat.
fulminar *vt* to fulminate; * *vi* to explode.
fumador/ra *m/f* smoker.
fumar *vt*, *vi* to smoke.
fumigación *f* fumigation.
funambulista *m/f* tightrope walker.
función *f* function; duties *pl*; show, performance.
funcionar *vi* to function; to work (of a machine).
funcionario/ria *m/f* official; civil servant.
funda *f* case, sheath; ~ **de almohada** pillowcase.
fundación *f* foundation.

fundador/ra *m/f* founder.
fundamental *adj* fundamental.
fundamentalismo *m* fundamentalism.
fundamentalista *adj*, *m/f* fundamentalist.
fundamento *m* foundation; groundwork; reason, cause.
fundar *vt* to found; to establish; to ground.
fundición *f* fusion; foundry.
fundir *vt* to fuse; to melt; to smelt; ~**se** *vr* (*com*) to merge; to bankrupt; to blow (of a fuse).
fúnebre *adj* mournful, sad; funereal.
funeral *m* funeral; ~**es** *mpl* funeral, funeral rites *pl*, obsequies *pl*.
funerario/ria *adj* funeral *compd*, funereal.
funesto/ta *adj* ill-fated, unfortunate; fatal.
furgón *m* wagon.
furgoneta *f* pick-up truck; station wagon.
furia *f* fury, rage.
furibundo/da *adj* furious; frenzied.
furioso/sa *adj* furious.
furor *m* fury, rage.
furtivamente *adv* furtively.
furtivo/va *adj* furtive.
furúnculo *m* (*med*) boil.
fusible *m* fuse.
fusil *m* rifle.
fusilar *vt* to shoot.
fusilero *m* rifleman.
fusión *f* fusion; (*com*) merger.
fusta *f* riding crop.
fútbol *m* football; ~ **americano** American football.
futbolista *m/f* football player, footballer.
fútil *adj* futile; trifling.
futilidad *f* futility.
futuro/ra *adj*, *m* future.

G

gabán *m* overcoat.
gabardina *f* raincoat.
gabarra *f* (*mar*) lighter.
gabinete *m* cabinet (in politics), study; office (of lawyers etc).
gaceta *f* gazette.
gachas *fpl* any soft/semi-liquid food; porridge.
gacho/cha *adj* curved, bent downward.
gafas *fpl* glasses *pl*, spectacles *pl*.
gafe *m* jinx.
gaita *f* bagpipe; flageolet.
gaitero/ra *m/f* bagpiper, bagpipe player.
gaje *m*: ~**s del oficio** occupational hazards *pl*.
gajo *m* segment (of orange).
gala *f* full dress; (*fig*) cream, flower; ~**s** *fpl* finery; **hacer ~ de** to display, to show off.
galán *m* lover; handsome young man; (*theat*) male lead.
galante *adj* gallant.
galanteador *m* lover, suitor.
galantear *vt* to court, to woo.
galanteo *m* gallantry, courtship.
galantería *f* gallantry; politeness; compliment.
galápago *m* tortoise.
galardón *m* reward, prize.
galardonar *vt* to reward, to recompense.
galaxia *f* galaxy.
galbana *f* laziness, idleness.
galeón *m* (*mar*) galleon.
galera *f* (*mar*) galley; wagon.
galería *f* gallery.
galgo *m* greyhound.
gallardete *m* (*mar*) pennant, streamer.
gallardía *f* fineness, elegance, gracefulness; dash.
gallardo/da *adj* graceful, elegant; brave, daring.
gallería *f Lat Am* cockpit.
galleta *f* cookie.
gallina *f* hen; * *m/f* (*fig*) coward; ~ **ciega** blindman's buff.
gallinero *m* henhouse, coop; poulterer; (*theat*) top gallery; hubbub.
gallineta *f* woodcock (bird).
gallo *m* cock.
galón *m* (*mil*) stripe; braid; galloon.
galopar *vi* to gallop.
galope *m* gallop.

galvánico/ca *adj* galvanic.
galvanismo *m* galvanism.
gallardete *m* (*mar*) pennant, streamer.
gallardía *f* fineness, elegance, gracefulness; dash.
gallardo/da *adj* graceful, elegant; brave, daring.
galleta *f* biscuit.
gallina *f* hen; * *m/f* (*fig*) coward; ~ **ciega** blindman's buff.
gallinazo *m Lat Am* turkey vulture/buzzard.
gallinero *m* henhouse, coop; poulterer; (*theat*) top gallery; hubbub.
gallineta *f Lat Am* woodcock (bird).
gallo *m* cock.
gama[1] *f* (*mus*) scale; (*fig*) range, gamut.
gama[2] *f* doe (of the fallow deer).
gamba *f* shrimp; prawn.
gamberro/rra *m/f* hooligan.
gamo *m* buck (of the fallow deer).
gamuza *f* chamois (goat antelope); chamois leather.
gana *f* desire, wish; appetite; will; longing; **de buena ~** with pleasure, voluntarily; **de mala ~** unwillingly, with reluctance.
ganadería *f* cattle raising; cattle; livestock.
ganadero *m* rancher; cattle dealer.
ganado *m* livestock, cattle *pl*; ~ **mayor** horses and mules *pl*; ~ **menor** sheep, goats and pigs *pl*.
ganancia *f* gain, profit; increase.
ganancial *adj* lucrative.
ganar *vt* to gain; to win; to earn; * *vi* to win.
gancho *m* hook; crook.
gandul *adj*, *m/f* layabout, lazy person.
ganga *f* bargain.
gangoso/sa *adj* nasal.
gangrena *f* gangrene.
gangrenarse *vr* to become gangrenous.
gangrenoso/sa *adj* gangrenous.
ganso/sa *m/f* gander; goose; (*col*) idiot.
garabatear *vi*, *vt* to scrawl, to scribble.
garabatos *mpl* scrawling letters/characters *pl*.
garaje *m* garage.
garage *m Lat am* garage.
garante *m/f* guarantor; * *adj* responsible.
garantía *f* warranty, guarantee.
garañón *m* jackass, male donkey.
garapatear *vi*, *vt* to scrawl, to scribble.
garapiñar *vt* to freeze; to ice.

97

garbanzo *m* chickpea.
garbo *m* gracefulness, elegance; stylishness; generosity.
garboso/sa *adj* graceful; elegant, stylish; generous.
garduña *f* marten (animal).
gargajo *m* phlegm, spit.
garganta *f* throat, gullet; instep; neck (of a bottle); narrow pass between mountains; river gorge.
gargantilla *f* necklace.
gárgara *f* noise made by gargling.
gargarismo *m* gargling, gargle.
gargarizar *vi* to gargle.
garita *f* (*mil*) sentry box; (*rail*) signal box.
garra *f* claw; talon; paw.
garrafa *f* carafe; (gas) cylinder.
garrafal *adj* great, vast, huge.
garrapata *f* tick (insect).
garrocha *f* *Lat Am* vaulting pole.
garrotazo *m* blow with a stick/club.
garrote *m* stick, club, cudgel; (*med*) tourniquet; (*law*) garrote.
garrotillo *m* (*med*) croup.
garrucha *f* pulley.
garza *f* heron.
garzo/za *adj* blue-eyed.
gas *m* gas; petrol, gas.
gasa *f* gauze.
gaseoso/sa *adj* fizzy; * *f* lemonade.
gasfitero/ra *m/f* plumber.
gasoil *m* diesel (oil).
gasolina *f* gasoline.
gasolinera *f* service station.
gasómetro *m* gasometer.
gastador/ra *m/f* spendthrift.
gastar *vt* to spend; to expend; to waste; to wear away; to use up; ~se *vr* to wear out; to waste.
gasto *m* expense, expenditure; use.
gastronomía *f* gastronomy.
gata *f* she-cat; a ~s on all fours.
gatear *vi* to go on all fours.
gatera *f* catlover; (*mar*) cat hole.
gatillazo *m* click of the trigger in firing.
gatillo *m* trigger of a gun; (*med*) dental forceps.
gato *m* tomcat; jack, clamp, vice.
gatuno/na *adj* catlike, feline.
gaveta *f* drawer of a desk, locker.
gavilán *m* sparrow hawk.
gavilla *f* sheaf of corn.
gaviota *f* seagull.
gay *adj invar*, *m* (*col*) gay; homosexual.
gazapo *m* young rabbit; liar; lie.

gazmoñada, gazmoñería *f* prudery; hypocrisy.
gazmoñero/ra, gazmoño/ña *adj* hypocritical.
gaznate *m* gullet, wind pipe.
gazpacho *m* Spanish cold tomato soup.
gazuza *f* ravenous hunger.
gelatina *f* jelly; gelatin.
gemelo/la *m/f* twin.
gemido *m* groan, moan, howl.
geminiano/na *adj* *Lat Am* Geminian (zodiac sign).
Géminis *m* Gemini (zodiac sign).
gemir *vi* to groan, to moan.
genciana *f* (*bot*) gentian.
gendarme *m* policeman.
gendarmería *f* police.
genealogía *f* genealogy.
genealógico/ca *adj* genealogical.
generación *f* generation; progeny, race.
general *m* general; * *adj* general; en ~ generally, in general.
generalidad *f* generality.
generalizar *vt* to generalize.
generalmente *adv* generally.
genérico/ca *adj* generic.
género *m* genus; kind, type; gender; (*com*) cloth, material; ~s *mpl* goods *pl*, commodities *pl*.
generosidad *f* generosity.
generoso/sa *adj* noble, generous.
Génesis *f* Genesis.
genial *adj* inspired, brilliant; genial.
genio *m* nature, character; genius.
genital *adj* genital; * *mpl* ~es genitals *pl*.
genitivo *m* (*gr*) genitive case.
gente *f* people; nation; family.
gentil *m/f* pagan, heathen; * *adj* elegant; graceful; charming.
gentileza *f* grace; charm; politeness.
gentilhombre *m* gentleman.
gentío *m* crowd, throng.
genuflexión *f* genuflection.
genuino/na *adj* genuine; pure.
geografía *f* geography.
geográfico/ca *adj* geographical.
geógrafo/fa *m/f* geographer.
geología *f* geology.
geólogo/ga *m/f* geologist.
geometría *f* geometry.
geométrico/ca *adj* geometrical, geometric.
geranio *m* (*bot*) geranium.
gerenciar *vt* *Lat Am* to manage.
gerente *m/f* manager; director.
geriatría *f* (*med*) geriatrics.

germen *m* germ, bud; source, origin.
germinar *vi* to germinate, to bud.
gerundio *m* (*gr*) gerund.
gesticular *vi* to gesticulate.
gestión *f* management; negotiation.
gesto *m* face; grimace; gesture.
giganta *f* giantess.
gigante *m* giant; * *adj* gigantic.
gigantesco/ca *adj* gigantic, giant.
gilipollas *adj invar* (*col*) stupid; * *m/f invar* wimp.
gimnasia *f* gymnastics.
gimnasio *m* gymnasium.
gimnasta *m/f* gymnast.
gimnástico/ca *adj* gymnastic.
ginebra *f* gin.
ginecólogo/ga *m/f* gynecologist.
gira *f* trip, tour.
girar *vt* to turn around; to swivel; (*com*) to draw, to issue; * *vi* to go round, to revolve; (*com*) to do business; to draw.
giratorio/ria *adj* revolving.
girasol *m* sunflower.
giro *m* turning round; tendency; change; (*com*) draft.
gitano/na *m/f* Gypsy.
glacial *adj* icy.
glaciar *m* glacier.
glándula *f* gland.
glandular *adj* glandular.
globalización *f* globalization.
globo *m* globe; sphere; orb; balloon; ~ aerostático air balloon.
glóbulo *m* globule; corpuscle.
gloria *f* glory.
gloriarse *vr*: ~ **en** to glory in, to take pride in; to take delight in.
glorieta *f* bower, arbor; traffic circle.
glorificación *f* glorification; praise.
glorificar *vt* to glorify.
glorioso/sa *adj* glorious.
glosa *f* gloss; comment.
glosar *vt* to gloss; to comment on.
glotón/ona *m/f* glutton.
glotonería *f* gluttony.
gobernación *f* government.
gobernador/ra *m/f* governor.
gobernar *vt* to govern; to regulate; to direct.
gobierno *m* government.
goce *m* enjoyment.
gol *m* goal.
goleta *f* schooner.
golf *m* golf.
golfa *f* (*col*) slut.
golfito *m Lat Am* mini-golf.

golfo¹ *m* gulf, bay.
golfo² (*col*) urchin; lout.
golondrina *f* swallow.
golosina *f* delicacy, tidbit; bauble, trifle; sweet tooth.
goloso/sa *adj* sweet-toothed.
golpe *m* blow, stroke, hit; knock; clash; coup; **de ~** suddenly.
golpear *vt* to beat, to knock; to punch.
golpiza *f Lat Am* beating.
goma *f* gum; rubber; elastic.
gomosidad *f* stickiness, viscosity.
gomoso/sa *adj* gummy, viscous.
góndola *f* gondola; (*rail*) freight car.
gondolero *m* gondolier.
gordinflón/ona *m/f* very fat person.
gordo/da *adj* fat, plump, big-bellied; first, main; (*col*) enormous.
gordura *f* grease; fatness, corpulence, obesity.
gorgojo *m* grub, weevil.
gorgorito *m* trill, warble.
gorila *m* gorilla.
gorjear *vi* to twitter, to chirp.
gorjeo *m* chirping.
gorra *f* cap; bonnet; (*mil*) bearskin.
gorrión *m* sparrow.
gorro *m* cap; bonnet.
gorrón/ona *m/f* scrounger.
gota *f* drop; (*med*) gout.
gotear *vt* to drip; to drizzle.
gotera *f* leak.
gótico/ca *adj* Gothic.
gotoso/sa *adj* gouty.
gozar *vt* to enjoy, to have, to possess; ~**se** *vr* to enjoy oneself, to rejoice.
gozne *m* hinge.
gozo *m* joy, pleasure.
gozoso/sa *adj* joyful, cheerful; content, glad, pleased.
grabación *f* recording.
grabado *m* engraving.
grabador *m* engraver.
grabadora *f* tape recorder.
grabar *vt* to engrave; to record.
gracejo *m* wit;, charm; gracefulness.
gracia *f* grace, gracefulness; wit; ¡(muchas) ~s! thanks (very much); **tener ~** to be funny.
gracioso/sa *adj* graceful; beautiful; funny; pleasing; * *m* comic character.
grada *f* step of a staircase; tier, row; ~s *fpl* seats *pl* of a stadium/theater.
gradería *f* (flight of) steps *pl*; row of seats; *Lat Am* terraces.

grado *m* step; degree; **de buen** ~ willingly.
graduación *f* graduation; (*mil*) rank.
gradual *adj* gradual.
graduar *vt* to graduate.
gráfico/ca *adj* graphic; * *m* diagram; * *f* graph.
grajo/ja *m/f* rook.
grama *f* grass; *Lat Am* lawn.
gramática *f* grammar.
gramatical *adj* grammatical.
gramático/ca *m/f* grammarian.
gramo *m* gram.
gran *adj* = **grande**.
grana *f* grain; scarlet.
granada *f* (*mil*) grenade; pomegranate.
granadero *m* (*mil*) grenadier.
granadilla *f* passionflower; passion fruit.
granado *m* pomegranate tree.
granate *m* garnet (precious stone).
grande *adj* great; big; tall; grand; * *m/f* adult.
grandeza *f* greatness; grandeur; size.
grandiosidad *f* greatness; grandeur, magnificence.
grandioso/sa *adj* grand, magnificent.
granel *adv*: **a** ~ in bulk.
granero *m* granary.
granito *m* granite.
granizada *f* hail; hailstorm; shower, volley.
granizado *m* iced drink.
granizar *vi* to hail (weather).
granizo *m* hail (weather).
granja *f* farm.
granjero/ra *m/f* farmer.
grano *m* grain.
granuja *m* rogue; urchin.
grapa *f* staple; clamp.
grasa *f* suet, fat; grease.
grasiento/ta *adj* greasy; rusty; filthy.
grasoso/sa *adj* Lat Am greasy; rusty; filthy.
gratificación *f* gratification; recompense.
gratificar *vt* to gratify; to reward, to recompense.
gratis *adj* free; *adv* freely.
gratitud *f* gratitude, gratefulness.
grato/ta *adj* pleasant, agreeable.
gratuito/ta *adj* gratuitous; free.
gravamen *m* charge, obligation; nuisance; tax.
gravar *vt* to burden; (*com*) to tax.
grave *adj* weighty, heavy; grave, important; serious.
gravedad *f* gravity; graveness.
gravemente *adv* gravely, seriously.
gravilla *f* gravel.
gravitación *f* gravitation.
gravitar *vt* to gravitate; to weigh down on.

gravoso/sa *adj* onerous, burdensome; costly.
graznar *vi* to croak; to cackle; to quack.
graznido *m* croak; cackle; quack.
greda *f* clay.
gremial *f Lat Am* (labor) union.
gremialista *m/f Lat Am* union member.
gremio *m* union, guild; society; company, corporation.
greña *f* tangle; shock of hair.
greñudo/da *adj* disheveled.
gresca *f* clatter; outcry; confusion; wrangle, quarrel.
grieta *f* crevice, crack, chink.
grifo *m* faucet; gas station.
grilletes *mpl* shackles *pl*; fetters *pl*.
grillo *m* cricket; bud, shoot; ~s *mpl* fetters *pl*, irons *pl*.
grima *f* disgust; annoyance.
gripe *f* flu, influenza.
gris *adj* gray.
gritar *vi* to cry out, to shout, to yell.
gritería *f* shouting, clamor, uproar.
grito *m* shout, cry, scream.
grosella *f* redcurrant; ~ **negra** blackcurrant.
grosellero *m* currant bush.
grosería *f* coarseness, rudeness; vulgar comment.
grosero/ra *adj* coarse; rude, bad-mannered.
grosor *m* thickness.
grotesco/ca *adj* grotesque.
grúa *f* crane (machine); derrick.
grueso/sa *adj* thick; bulky; large; coarse; * *m* bulk.
grulla *f* crane (bird).
grumo *m* clot; curd.
grumoso/sa *adj* clotted.
gruñido *m* grunt; growl.
gruñidor/ra *m/f* grunter, mumbler; (*fig*) grumbler.
gruñir *vi* to grunt; to grumble; to creak (of hinges etc).
grupa *f* rump.
grupo *m* group.
gruta *f* grotto.
guachimán *m Lat Am* night watchman.
guadaña *f* scythe.
guagua *f* trifle, small thing.
gualdrapa *f* trappings *pl* (of a horse); tatter, rag.
guantada *f* slap.
guante *m* glove.
guapo/pa *adj* good-looking; handsome; smart.
guarda *m/f* guard, keeper; * *f* custody, keeping.
guardaagujas *m invar* (*rail*) switchman.

guardabosque *m* ranger, gamekeeper, forester.

guardacostas *m invar* coastguard vessel.

guardaespaldas *m/f invar* bodyguard.

guardafuegos *m invar* firescreen.

guardameta *m/f* goalkeeper.

guardapolvo *m* dust cover; coveralls *pl*.

guardar *vt* to keep, to preserve; to save (money); to guard; ~se *vr* to be on one's guard; ~se de to avoid, to abstain from.

guardarropa *f* wardrobe; cloakroom.

guardavallas *m/f invar Lat Am* goalkeeper.

guardia *f* guard; (*mar*) watch; care, custody; * *m/f* guard; policeman/woman; * *m* (*mil*) guardsman.

guardián/ana *m/f* keeper; guardian.

guardilla *f* garret, attic.

guarecer *vt* to protect; to shelter; ~se *vr* to take refuge.

guarida *f* den, lair; shelter; hiding place.

guarismo *m* figure, numeral.

guarnecer *vt* to provide, to equip; to reinforce; to garnish, to set (in gold etc); to adorn

guarnición *f* trimming; gold setting; sword guard; garnish; (*mil*) garrison.

guasa *f* joke.

guasón/ona *m/f* joker, jester.

gubernativo/va *adj* governmental.

guedeja *f* lock of hair.

guerra *f* war; hostility.

guerrear *vi* to fight, to wage war.

guerrero/ra *m/f* warrior; * *adj* martial, warlike.

guerrilla *f* guerrilla warfare; guerrilla group.

gueto *m* ghetto.

guía *m/f* guide; * *f* guidebook.

guiar *vt* to guide; (*auto*) to steer.

guijarral *m* stony place.

guijarro *m* pebble.

guillotina *f* guillotine.

guillotinar *vt* to guillotine.

guinda *f* cherry.

guindal *m* cherry tree.

guindilla *f* chili pepper.

guiñapo *m* tatter, rag; rogue.

guiñar *vt* to wink.

guión *m* hyphen (in writing); script (of film).

guirigay *m* gibberish, confused language.

guirnalda *f* garland, wreath.

güiro *m Lat Am* gourd.

guisado *m* stew.

guisante *m* (*bot*) pea.

guisar *vt* to cook.

guiso *m* cooked dish; stew; seasoning.

guisote *m* hash; (*col*) grub

guitarra *f* guitar.

guitarrista *m/f* guitar player.

gula *f* gluttony.

gusano *m* maggot, worm.

gustar *vt* to taste; to sample; * *vi* to please, to be pleasing; me gusta... I like....

gusto *m* taste; pleasure, delight; liking.

gustosamente *adv* gladly, with pleasure.

gustoso/sa *adj* pleasant; tasty.

gutural *adj* guttural.

H

haba *f* broad bean.

haber *vt* to get, to lay hands on; to occur; * *v imp*: **hay** there is, there are; * *v aux* to have; ~**se** *vr*: **habérselas con uno** to have it out with somebody; * *m* income, salary; assets *pl*; (*com*) credit.

habichuela *f* bean.

hábil *adj* able, clever, skillful, dexterous, apt.

habilidad *f* ability, ableness, dexterity, aptitude.

habilitación *f* entitlement, qualification.

habilitar *vt* to qualify, to enable; to finance.

habitable *adj* habitable.

habitación *f* habitation, abode, lodging, dwelling, residence; room.

habitante *m/f* inhabitant, occupant.

habitar *vt* to inhabit, to live in.

hábito *m* dress; habit, custom.

habitual *adj* habitual, customary.

habituar *vt* to accustom; ~**se** *vr* to become accustomed to.

habla *f* speech; language; dialect.

hablador/ra *m/f* talkative person.

habladuría *f* rumor; ~**s** *fpl* gossip.

hablante *adj* speaking; * *m/f* speaker.

hablar *vt* (*vi*) to speak; to talk.

hacedor/ra *m/f* maker; author.

hacendado *m* property owner; landowner; rancher.

hacendoso/sa *adj* industrious.

hacer *vt* to make; to do; to put into practice; to perform; to effect; to prepare; to imagine; to force; (*math*) to amount to, to make; * *vi* to act, to behave; ~**se** *vr* to become.

hacha *f* torch; ax, hatchet.

hachazo *m* blow with an ax.

hacia *adv* toward(s); about; ~ **arriba/abajo** up(wards)/down(wards).

hacienda *f* property; large farm; ranch; **H~** Treasury.

hacinar *vt* to stack/pile up; to hoard.

hada *f* fairy.

hado *m* fate, destiny.

halagar *vt* to cajole, to flatter.

halago *m* cajolery; pleasure.

halagüeño *adj* attractive, flattering.

halcón *m* falcon.

halconero *m* falconer.

hálito *m* breath; gentle breeze.

hall *m* hall; (*theat*) foyer.

hallar *vt* to find; to meet with; to discover; ~**se** *vr* to find oneself; to be.

hallazgo *m* finding, discovery.

hamaca *f* hammock.

hambre *f* hunger; famine; longing.

hambreado/da *adj Lat Am* hungry; starved.

hambriento/ta *adj* hungry; starved.

hamburguesa *f* hamburger.

haragán/ana *m/f* idler, good-for-nothing.

haraganear *vi* to idle, to loiter.

haraganería *f* idleness, laziness.

harapo *m* rag, tatter.

haraposo *adj* ragged.

hardware *m* (*comput*) hardware.

harina *f* flour; ~ **de maíz** cornstarch.

harinoso/sa *adj* floury.

hartar *vt* to satiate; to glut; to tire, to sicken; ~**se** *vr* to gorge oneself (with food); to get fed up.

harto/ta *adj* full; fed up; * *adv* enough.

hartura *f* surfeit; plenty, abundance.

hasta *prep* up to; down to; until, as far as; * *adv* even.

hastío *m* loathing; disgust; boredom.

hatajo *m* lot, collection.

hato *m* clothes *pl*; herd of cattle, flock of sheep; provisions *pl*; crowd, gang, collection.

haya *f* beech tree.

haz *m* bunch, bundle; beam (of light).

hazaña *f* exploit, achievement.

hazmerreír *m invar* ridiculous person, laughing stock.

hebilla *f* buckle.

hebra *f* thread; vein of minerals/metals; grain of wood.

hebraico/ca *adj* belonging to the Hebrews.

hebreo/ea *m/f* Hebrew; Israeli; * *m* Hebrew language; * *adj* Hebrew; Israeli.

hechicería *f* witchcraft; charm.

hechicero/ra *adj* charming, bewitching; * *m/f* sorcerer/ sorceress.

hechizar *vt* to bewitch, to enchant; to charm.

hechizo *m* bewitchment, enchantment.

hecho/cha *adj* made; done; mature; ready-to-wear; cooked; * *m* action; act; fact; matter; event.

hechura *f* form, shape; fashion; making; workmanship; creature.

hectárea f hectare.
heder vi to stink, to smell bad.
hediondez f strong stench.
hediondo/da adj fetid, stinking.
hedor m stench, stink.
helada f frost; freeze-up.
helado/da adj frozen; glacial, icy; astonished; astounded; * m ice cream.
helar vt to freeze; to congeal; to astonish, to amaze; ~se vr to be frozen; to turn into ice; to congeal; * vi to freeze; to congeal.
helecho m fern.
hélice f spiral, helix; propeller.
helicóptero m helicopter.
hembra f female.
hemisferio m hemisphere.
hemorragia f hemorrhage.
hemorroides fpl hemorrhoids pl, piles pl.
henchir vt to fill up; ~se vr to fill/stuff oneself.
hendedura f fissure, chink, crevice.
hender vt to crack, to split; to go through; to open a passage.
hendidura f = hendedura.
heno m hay.
heraldo m herald.
herborizar vi to pick herbs; to collect plants.
heredad f inherited property; country estate, ranch, large farm.
heredar vt to inherit.
heredera f heiress.
heredero m heir.
hereditario/ria adj hereditary.
hereje m/f heretic.
herejía f heresy.
herencia f inheritance, heritage, heredity.
herida f wound, injury.
herido/da adj wounded, hurt.
herir vt to wound, to hurt; to beat, to strike; to affect, to touch, to move; to offend.
hermafrodita m hermaphrodite.
hermana f sister.
hermanar vt to match, to suit, to harmonize.
hermanastra f step-sister, half-sister.
hermanastro m step-brother, half-brother.
hermandad f fraternity; brotherhood.
hermano m brother; ~/na adj matched; resembling.
hermético/ca adj hermetic, watertight.
hermoso/sa adj beautiful, handsome, lovely; large, robust.
hermosura f beauty.
hernia f hernia, rupture.
héroe m hero.

heroicidad f heroism; heroic deed.
heroico/ca adj heroic.
heroína[1] f heroine.
heroína[2] f heroin (drug).
heroísmo m heroism.
herpes m herpes; * fpl (med) shingles.
herrador m farrier, blacksmith.
herradura f horseshoe.
herramienta f tool.
herrar vt to shoe (horses).
herrería f ironworks; forge.
herrero m smith, blacksmith.
hervidero m boiling; unrest; swarm.
hervir vt to boil; to cook; * vi to boil; to bubble; to seethe.
hervor m boiling; fervor, passion.
heterogeneidad f heterogeneousness.
heterogéneo/nea adj heterogeneous.
heterosexual adj, m/f heterosexual.
heterosexualidad f heterosexuality.
hexámetro m hexameter.
hez f sediment, dregs pl.
hidalgo m nobleman.
hidalguía f nobility.
hidra f hydra.
hidráulica f hydraulics.
hidráulico/ca adj hydraulic.
hidroavión m hydroplane, seaplane.
hidrofobia f hydrophobia.
hidrógeno m (chem) hydrogen.
hidromasaje m whirlpool bath.
hidrovía f Lat Am waterway.
hiedra f ivy.
hiel f gall, bile.
hielo m frost; ice.
hiena f hyena.
hierba f grass; herb.
hierro m iron.
hígado m liver; (fig) courage, pluck.
higiene f hygiene.
higiénico/ca adj hygienic.
higo m fig.
higuera f fig tree.
hijastro/tra m/f stepson/stepdaughter.
hijo/ja m/f son/daughter; child; offspring.
hilandero/ra m/f spinner.
hilar vt to spin.
hilera f row, line, file.
hilo m thread; wire.
hilván m tacking.
hilvanar vt to tack; to perform in a hurry.
himno m hymn.
hincada f Lat Am genuflection.
hincapié m: hacer ~ en to emphasize.
hincar vt to thrust in, to drive in.

hincha *m/f* (*col*) fan, supporter.
hinchado/da *adj* swollen; vain, arrogant.
hinchar *vt* to swell; to inflate; (*fig*) to exaggerate; ~se *vr* to swell; to become vain.
hinchazón *f* swelling, lump.
hinojo *m* (*bot*) fennel.
hipar *vi* to hiccup.
hipérbola *f* hyperbola, section of a cone.
hipérbole *f* hyperbole, exaggeration.
hiperbólico/ca *adj* hyperbolic, hyperbolical.
hipermercado, híper *m* hypermarket, superstore.
hípica *f* horseracing; showjumping.
hipnotismo *m* hypnotism.
hipo *m* hiccups *pl*.
hipocondria *f* hypochondria.
hipocondríaco/ca *adj* hypochondriac.
hipocresía *f* hypocrisy.
hipócrita *adj* hypocritical; * *m/f* hypocrite.
hipódromo *m* racetrack.
hipopótamo *m* hippopotamus.
hipoteca *f* mortgage.
hipotecar *vt* to mortgage.
hipotecario/ria *adj* belonging to a mortgage.
hipótesis *f* hypothesis.
hipotético/ca *adj* hypothetical.
hisopo *m* (*bot*) hyssop; water sprinkler; paintbrush.
hispano/na *adj* Hispanic.
Hispanoamérica *f* Spanish America.
hispanoamericano/na *adj,m/f* Spanish American.
histeria *f* hysteria.
histérico/ca *adj* hysterical.
historia *f* history; tale, story.
historiador/ra *m/f* historian.
histórico/ca *adj* historical; historic.
historieta *f* short story; short novel; comic strip.
hito *m* landmark; boundary post; target.
hocico *m* snout; **meter el ~ en todo** to meddle in everything.
hogar *m* hearth, fireplace; (*fig*) house, home; family life.
hogaza *f* large loaf of bread.
hoguera *f* bonfire; blaze.
hoja *f* leaf; petal; sheet of paper; blade.
hojalata *f* tin plate.
hojaldre *f* puff pastry.
hojarasca *f* dead leaves *pl*; rubbish.
hojear *vt* to turn the pages of.
hola *excl* hello!
holgado/da *adj* loose, wide, baggy; at leisure; idle, unoccupied, well-to-do; well-off.

holgar *vi* to rest; to be out of work; to be superfluous.
holgazán/ana *m/f* idler, loafer.
holgazanear *vt* to idle, to loaf around, to lounge around.
holgazanería *f* idleness, laziness.
holgura *f* looseness, bagginess; leisure; comfort; enjoyment.
hollín *m* soot.
holocausto *m* holocaust.
hombre *m* man; human being.
hombrera *f* shoulder pad.
hombro *m* shoulder.
hombruno/na *adj* manlike; virile, manly.
homenaje *m* homage.
homicida *m/f* murderer; * *adj* murderous, homicidal.
homicidio *m* murder.
homilía *f* homily.
homogeneidad *f* homogeneity.
homogéneo/nea *adj* homogeneous.
homólogo/ga *adj* homologous; synonymous.
homosexual *adj*, *m/f* homosexual.
honda *f* sling, catapult.
hondazo *m* throw with a sling.
hondo/da *adj* deep; profound; intense.
hondonada *f* dale, hollow; ravine.
hondura *f* depth, profundity.
honestidad *f* honesty; modesty; decency.
honesto/ta *adj* honest; modest.
hongo *m* mushroom; fungus; derby (hat).
honor *m* honor.
honorable *adj* honorable.
honorario/ria *adj* honorary; ~s *mpl* fees *pl*.
honorífico/ca *adj* creditable, honorable.
honra *f* honor, reverence; self-esteem; reputation; integrity; ~s **funebres** *pl* funeral honors *pl*.
honradez *f* honesty, integrity.
honrado/da *adj* honest; honorable; reputable.
honrar *vt* to honor.
honroso/sa *adj* honorable; respectable; honest.
hora *f* hour; time.
horadar *vt* to drill, to bore.
horario/ria *adj* hourly, hour *compd*; * *m* timetable.
horca *f* gallows; pitchfork; string (of garlic/onions etc).
horcajadas *adv*: **a ~** astride.
horchata *f* a drink made from almonds/barley and orange flower water.

horero *m Lat Am* hour hand.
horizontal *adj* horizontal.
horizonte *m* horizon.
horma *f* mold, form.
hormiga *f* ant.
hormigón *m* concrete.
hormiguear *vi* to itch; to swarm, to team.
hormiguero *m* anthill; place swarming with people.
hormona *f* hormone.
hornada *f* batch.
horno *m* oven; furnace.
horóscopo *m* horoscope.
horqueta *f Lat Am* fork.
horquilla *f* pitchfork; hairpin.
horrendo/da *adj* horrible; frightful.
hórreo *m* granary.
horrible *adj* horrid, horrible.
horripilante *adj* hair-raising.
horror *m* horror, fright; atrocity.
horrorizar *vt* to horrify; ~se *vr* to be terrified.
horroroso/sa *adj* horrid, hideous, frightful.
hortaliza *f* vegetable.
hortelano/na *m/f* gardener; truck farmer.
hortera *m* shop/store assistant; (*fig*) coarse person.
hosco/ca *adj* sullen, gloomy.
hospedaje *m* board and lodging.
hospedar *vt* to put up, to lodge; to entertain.
hospedería *f* inn; guest room; hospice.
hospedero/ra *m/f* landlord/lady; host/hostess.
hospicio *m* orphanage; hospice.
hospital *m* hospital.
hospitalario/ria *adj* hospitable.
hospitalidad *f* hospitality.
hostal *m* small hotel.
hostelería *f* hotel business/trade.
hostería *f* inn, tavern, hostelry.
hostia *f* host; wafer; (*col*) whack, punch.
hostigar *vt* to lash, to whip; to trouble, to pester, to bore.
hostil *adj* hostile; adverse.
hostilidad *f* hostility.
hostilizar *vt* (*mil*) to harry, to harass.
hotel *m* hotel.
hoy *adv* today; now, nowadays; de ~ en adelante as from today.
hoya *f* hole, pit; *Lat Am* river basin.
hoyito *m Lat Am* dimple.
hoyo *m* hole, pit; excavation.

hoz *f* sickle; gorge.
hozar *vi* to grub (of pigs).
hucha *f* money-box.
hueco/ca *adj* hollow, concave; empty; vain, ostentatious; * *m* interval; gap, hole; vacancy.
huelga *f* strike.
huella *f* track, footstep.
huérfano/na *adj*, *m/f* orphan.
huero/ra *adj* empty; addled.
huerta *f* truck farm; irrigated region.
huerto *m* orchard; kitchen garden; ~ de hortalizas truck farm.
hueso *m* bone; stone, core.
huésped/da *m/f* guest, lodger; innkeeper.
hueste *f* army; crowd.
huesudo/da *adj* bony.
huevera *f* eggcup.
huevo *m* egg.
huida *f* flight, escape.
huir *vi* to flee, to escape.
hule *m* oilcloth.
humanidad *f* humanity; corpulence; ~es *fpl* humanities *pl*.
humano/na *adj* human; humane, kind.
humareda *f* cloud of smoke.
humeante *adj* smoking; steaming.
humear *vi* to smoke; * *vt Lat Am* to fumigate.
humedad *f* humidity, moisture; wetness.
humedecer *vt* to moisten; to wet; to soak.
húmedo/da *adj* humid; wet; moist, damp.
humildad *f* humility, humbleness; submission.
humilde *adj* humble.
humillación *f* humiliation, submission.
humillar *vt* to humble; to subdue; ~se *vr* to humble oneself.
humo *m* smoke; fumes *pl*.
humor *m* mood, temper; humor.
hundir *vt* to submerge; to sink; to ruin; ~se *vr* to sink, to go to the bottom; to collapse; to be ruined.
huracán *m* hurricane.
huraño/ña *adj* shy; unsociable.
hurgar *vt* to stir; to poke.
hurón *m* ferret; (*fig*) shy person; busybody.
huronear *vt* to ferret out.
hurtadillas *adv*: a ~ by stealth.
hurtar *vt* to steal, to rob.
hurto *m* theft, robbery.
húsar *m* hussar.
husmear *vt* to scent; to pry into.
huso *m* spindle.

I

ictericia f jaundice.
ida f departure, going; (**viaje de**) ~ outward journey; ~ **y vuelta** round trip; ~**s y venidas** comings and goings pl.
idea f idea; scheme.
ideal adj ideal.
idealmente adv ideally.
idear vt to conceive; to think, to contrive.
ídem pn ditto.
idéntico/ca adj identical.
identidad f identity.
identificar vt to identify.
ideología f ideology.
idilio m idyll.
idioma m language.
idiosincrasia f idiosyncrasy.
idiota m/f idiot.
idiotez f idiocy.
idólatra m/f idolater.
idolatrar vt to idolize; to worship.
idolatría f idolatry.
ídolo m idol.
idoneidad f aptitude, fitness.
idóneo/nea adj suitable, fit.
iglesia f church.
ignominia f ignominy; infamy.
ignominioso/sa adj ignominious.
ignorancia f ignorance.
ignorante adj ignorant, uninformed.
ignorar vt to be ignorant of, not to know.
igual adj equal; similar; the same; **al** ~ equally.
igualar vt to equalize, to equal; to match; to level off; ~**se** vr to be equal; to agree.
igualdad f equality.
igualmente adv equally.
ijar m flank.
ilegal adj illegal, unlawful.
ilegalidad f illegality.
ilegitimidad f illegitimacy.
ilegítimo/ma adj illegal; illegitimate.
ileso/sa adj unhurt.
ilícito/ta adj illicit, unlawful; * m Lat Am crime.
ilimitado/da adj unlimited.
illustrar vt to illustrate; to instruct.
iluminación f illumination.
iluminar vt to illumine, to illuminate, to enlighten.
ilusión f illusion; hope; **hacerse** ~**ones** to build up one's hopes.

ilusionista m/f conjurer.
iluso/sa adj easily deceived.
ilusorio/ria adj illusory.
ilustración f illustration; enlightenment.
ilustre adj illustrious, famous.
imagen f image.
imaginable adj imaginable.
imaginación f imagination; fancy.
imaginar vt to imagine; to think up; * vi, ~**se** vr to imagine.
imán m magnet.
imbécil m/f imbecile, idiot.
imbecilidad f imbecility.
imbuir vt to imbue; to infuse.
imitable adj imitable.
imitación f imitation; **a** ~ **de** in imitation of.
imitador/ra m/f imitator.
imitar vt to imitate, to copy; to counterfeit.
impaciencia f impatience.
impacientar vt to make impatient; to irritate.
impaciente adj impatient.
impacto m impact.
impago/ga adj Lat Am unpaid.
impar adj odd.
imparcial adj impartial.
imparcialidad f impartiality.
impasibilidad f impassivity.
impasible adj impassive.
impavidez f intrepidity; cheek(iness).
impávido/da adj dauntless, intrepid; cheeky.
impecable adj impeccable.
impedimento m impediment, obstacle.
impedir vt to impede, to hinder; to prevent.
impeler vt to drive, to propel; to impel; to incite, to stimulate.
impenetrable adj impenetrable, impervious; incomprehensible.
impenitente adj impenitent.
impensado/da adj impenitent.
imperativo/va adj, m imperative.
imperceptible adj imperceptible.
imperdible m safety pin.
imperdonable adj unforgivable.
imperfección f imperfection.
imperfecto/ta adj imperfect.
imperial adj imperial.
impericia f lack of experience.
imperio m empire.
imperioso/sa adj imperious; arrogant, haughty; urgent.

impermeable *adj* waterproof; * *m* raincoat.
impermutable *adj* immutable.
impersonal *adj* impersonal.
impertérrito/ta *adj* intrepid, fearless.
impertinencia *f* impertinence; irrelevance.
impertinente *adj* not pertinent; touchy; impertinent.
imperturbable *adj* imperturbable; unruffled.
ímpetu *m* impetus; impetuosity.
impetuoso/sa *adj* impetuous.
implacable *adj* implacable, inexorable.
implicación *f* implication.
implicar *vt* to implicate, to involve.
implícito/ta *adj* implicit.
implorar *vt* to beg, to implore.
imponderable *adj* imponderable; (*fig*) priceless.
imponer *vt* to impose; to command; ~se *vr* to assert oneself; to prevail.
impopular *adj* unpopular.
importación *f* importing; imports *pl*.
importancia *f* importance; significance, weight; size.
importante *adj* important, considerable.
importar *vi* to be important, to matter; * *vt* to import; to be worth.
importe *m* amount, cost.
importunar *vt* to bother, to pester.
importunidad *f* pestering; annoyance.
importuno/na *adj* annoying; unreasonable.
imposibilidad *f* impossibility.
imposibilitar *vt* to make impossible.
imposible *adj* impossible; extremely difficult; slovenly.
imposición *f* imposition; tax; deposit.
impostor/ra *m/f* impostor, fraud.
impostura *f* imposture, deceit, cheat.
impotencia *f* impotence.
impotente *adj* impotent.
impracticable *adj* impracticable, unworkable.
imprecación *f* curse.
imprecar *vt* to curse.
imprecatorio/ria *adj* containing curses, full of evil wishes.
impreciso/sa *adj* imprecise, vague.
impregnarse *vr* to be impregnated.
imprenta *f* printing; press; printing office.
imprescindible *adj* essential.
impresión *f* impression; stamp; print; edition.
impresionante *adj* impressive; marvelous; tremendous.

impresionar *vt* to move; to impress; ~se *vr* to be impressed; to be moved.
impreso *m* printed paper; printed book.
impresor *m* printer.
impresora *f* printer; ~ láser laser printer.
imprevisto/ta *adj* unforeseen, unexpected.
imprimir *vt* to print; to imprint; to stamp.
improbable *adj* improbable, unlikely.
improperio *m* insult, taunt.
impropio/pia *adj* improper; unfit; unbecoming.
improvisar *vt* to extemporize; to improvize.
improviso/sa *adj*: de ~ unexpectedly.
imprudencia *f* imprudence; indiscretion; carelessness.
imprudente *adj* imprudent; indiscreet; unwise.
impudencia *f* shamelessness.
impudente *adj* shameless.
impúdico/ca *adj* shameless; lecherous.
impuesto/ta *adj* imposed; * *m* tax, duty.
impugnación *f* opposition, contradiction.
impugnar *vt* to oppose; challenge; impugn.
impulsivo/va *adj* impulsive.
impulso *m* impulse; thrust; (*fig*) impulse.
impune *adj* unpunished.
impunidad *f* impunity.
impureza *f* impurity.
impuro/ra *adj* impure;, foul.
imputable *adj* attributable, chargeable.
imputar *vt* to impute, to attribute.
inaccesible *adj* inaccessible.
inacción *f* inaction, inactivity.
inadmisible *adj* inadmissible.
inadvertencia *f* carelessness, inadvertence.
inadvertido/da *adj* unnoticed.
inagotable *adj* inexhaustible.
inaguantable *adj* unbearable, intolerable.
inalterable *adj* unalterable.
inapelable *adj* without appeal.
inapreciable *adj* imperceptible; invaluable.
inaudito/ta *adj* unheard-of.
inauguración *f* inauguration, opening.
inaugurar *vt* to inaugurate.
incalculable *adj* incalculable.
incandescente *adj* incandescent.
incansable *adj* untiring, tireless.
incapacidad *f* incapacity, inability.
incapaz *adj* incapable, unable.
incauto/ta *adj* incautious, unwary.
incendiar *vt* to kindle, to set on fire.
incendiario/ria *adj* incendiary; * *m/f* arsonist.
incendio *m* fire.
incentivo *m* incentive.

incertidumbre *f* doubt, uncertainty.
incesante *adj* incessant, continual.
incesto *m* incest.
incestuoso/sa *adj* incestuous.
incidencia *f* incidence; incident.
incidente *m* incident.
incidir *vi*: ~ en to fall upon; to influence, to affect.
incienso *m* incense.
incierto/ta *adj* uncertain, doubtful.
incineración *f* incineration; cremation.
incipiente *adj* incipient.
incisión *f* incision, cut.
incisivo/va *adj* incisive.
inciso *m* (*gr*) comma.
incitación *f* incitement.
incitar *vt* to incite; to excite.
incivil *adj* uncivil, rude.
inclemencia *f* inclemency, severity; inclemency (of the weather).
inclinación *f* inclination.
inclinar *vt* to incline; to nod, to bow (the head); ~se *vr* to bow; to stoop.
incluir *vt* to include, to comprise; to incorporate; to enclose.
inclusión *f* inclusion.
inclusive *adv* inclusive.
incluso/sa *adj* included; * *adv* inclusively; even.
incógnito/ta *adj* unknown; de ~ incognito.
incoherencia *f* incoherence.
incoherente *adj* incoherent.
incombustible *adj* incombustible, fireproof.
incomodar *vt* to inconvenience; to bother, to annoy.
incomodidad *f* inconvenience; annoyance; discomfort.
incómodo/da *adj* uncomfortable; annoying; inconvenient.
incomparable *adj* incomparable, matchless.
incompatibilidad *f* incompatibility.
incompatible *adj* incompatible.
incompetencia *f* incompetence.
incompetente *adj* incompetent.
incompleto/ta *adj* incomplete.
incomprehensible *adj* incomprehensible.
incomunicación *f* isolation; lack of communication.
incomunicado/da *adj* isolated, cut off; in solitary confinement.
inconcebible *adj* inconceivable.
incondicional *adj* unconditional; wholehearted; staunch.
inconexo/xa *adj* unconnected, disconnected.

inconfundible *adj* unmistakable.
incongruencia *f* incongruity, incongruence.
incongruo/grua *adj* incongruous.
inconmensurable *adj* immeasurable.
inconsciencia *f* unconsciousness; thoughtlessness.
inconsciente *adj* unconscious; thoughtless.
inconsecuencia *f* inconsequence.
inconsiderado/da *adj* inconsiderate, thoughtless.
inconsolable *adj* inconsolable.
inconstancia *f* inconstancy, unsteadiness.
inconstante *adj* inconstant, variable, fickle.
incontestable *adj* indisputable, incontrovertible, undeniable.
incontinencia *f* incontinence.
incontinente *adj* incontinent.
inconveniencia *f* inconvenience; impoliteness; unsuitability.
inconveniente *adj* inconvenient, unsuitable; impolite.
incorporación *f* incorporation, involvement.
incorporar *vt* to incorporate; ~se *vr* to sit up; to join (an organization), to become incorporated.
incorrecto/ta *adj* incorrect.
incorregible *adj* incorrigible.
incorruptible *adj* incorruptible.
incredulidad *f* incredulity.
incrédulo/la *adj* incredulous.
increíble *adj* incredible.
incremento *m* increment, increase; growth; rise.
increpar *vt* to reprehend, to reprimand.
incruento/ta *adj* bloodless.
inculcar *vt* to inculcate.
inculpar *vt* to accuse, to blame.
inculto/ta *adj* uncultivated; uneducated; uncouth.
incumbencia *f* obligation; duty.
incumbir *vi*: ~ a uno to be incumbent upon one.
incurable *adj* incurable; irremediable.
incurrir *vt*: ~ en to incur; to commit (a crime).
incursión *f* incursion, raid.
indagación *f* search, inquiry.
indagar *vt* to inquire into.
indebido/da *adj* undue; illegal, unlawful.
indecencia *f* indecency.
indecente *adj* indecent.
indecible *adj* unspeakable, unutterable.
indecisión *f* hesitation; indecision.
indeciso/sa *adj* hesitant; undecided.

indecoroso/sa *adj* unseemly, unbecoming.
indefectible *adj* infallible.
indefenso/sa *adj* defenseless.
indefinible *adj* indefinable.
indefinido/da *adj* indefinite.
indeleble *adj* indelible.
indemnización *f* indemnification, compensation.
indemnizar *vt* to indemnify, to compensate.
independencia *f* independence.
independiente *adj* independent.
indestructible *adj* indestructible.
indeterminado/da *adj* indeterminate; indefinite.
indicación *f* indication.
indicador *m* indicator; gage.
indicar *vt* to indicate.
indicativo/va *adj*, *m* indicative.
índice *m* ratio, rate; hand (of a watch/clock); index, table of contents; catalog; forefinger, index finger.
indicio *m* indication, mark, sign, token; clue.
indiferencia *f* indifference, apathy.
indiferente *adj* indifferent.
indígena *adj* indigenous, native; * *m/f* native.
indigencia *f* indigence, poverty, need.
indigente *adj* indigent, poor, destitute.
indigestión *f* indigestion.
indigesto/ta *adj* undigested; indigestible.
indignación *f* indignation, anger.
indignar *vt* to irritate; to provoke, to tease; ~se *vr*: ~ por to get indignant about.
indigno/na *adj* unworthy, contemptible, low.
indirecta *f* innuendo, hint.
indirecto/ta *adj* indirect.
indisciplinado/da *adj* undisciplined.
indiscreción *f* indiscretion, tactlessness; gaffe.
indiscreto/ta *adj* indiscreet, tactless.
indisoluble *adj* indissoluble.
indispensable *adj* indispensable.
indisponer *vt* to spoil, to upset; to make ill; ~se *vr* to fall ill.
indisposición *f* indisposition, slight illness.
indispuesto/ta *adj* indisposed.
indisputable *adj* indisputable, incontrovertible.
indistinto/ta *adj* indistinct.
individual *adj* individual; single (of a room); * *m* (*sport*) singles.
individualidad *f* individuality.
individualizar *vt* to specify individually.

individuo *m* individual.
indivisible *adj* indivisible.
indocilidad *f* disobedience.
índole *f* disposition, nature, character; class, kind.
indolencia *f* indolence, laziness.
indolente *adj* indolent, lazy.
indómito/ta *adj* untamed, ungoverned.
inducción *f* induction, persuasion.
inducir *vt* to induce, to persuade.
inductivo/va *adj* inductive.
indudable *adj* undoubted; unquestionable.
indulgencia *f* indulgence.
indulgente *adj* indulgent.
indultar *vt* to pardon; to exempt.
indulto *m* pardon; exemption.
industria *f* industry; skill.
industrial *adj* industrial.
industrialización *f* industrialization.
inédito/ta *adj* unpublished; (*fig*) new.
inefable *adj* ineffable, indescribable.
ineficacia *f* inefficacy.
ineficaz *adj* ineffective, inefficient.
ineptitud *f* inability; unfitness, ineptitude.
inepto/ta *adj* inept, unfit, useless.
inercia *f* inertia, inactivity.
inerme *adj* unarmed; defenseless.
inerte *adj* inert; dull; sluggish, motionless.
inescrutable *adj* inscrutable.
inesperado/da *adj* unexpected, unforeseen.
inestable *adj* unstable.
inestimable *adj* inestimable.
inevitable *adj* unavoidable.
inexactitud *f* inaccuracy.
inexacto/ta *adj* inaccurate, untrue.
inexorable *adj* inexorable.
inexperto/ta *adj* inexperienced.
infalibilidad *f* infallibility.
infalible *adj* infallible.
infame *adj* infamous.
infancia *f* infancy, childhood.
infanta *f* infanta, princess.
infante *m* infante, prince; (*mil*) infantryman.
infantería *f* infantry.
infanticida *m/f* infanticide (person).
infanticidio *m* infanticide (act).
infantil *adj* infantile; childlike; children's.
infarto *m* heart attack; ~ de miocardio heart attack.
infatigable *adj* tireless, untiring.
infección *f* infection.
infectar *vt* to infect.
infeliz *adj* unhappy, unfortunate.
inferior *adj* inferior.

inferioridad *f* inferiority.
inferir *vt* to infer.
infernal *adj* infernal, hellish.
infestar *vt* to harass; to infest.
infidelidad *f* infidelity, unfaithfulness.
infiel *adj* unfaithful; disloyal; inaccurate.
infierno *m* hell.
infiltración *f* infiltration.
infiltrarse *vr* to infiltrate.
ínfimo/ma *adj* lowest; of very poor quality.
infinidad *f* infinity; immensity.
infinitivo *m* (*gr*) infinitive.
infinito/ta *adj* infinite; immense.
inflación *f* inflation.
inflamable *adj* flammable.
inflamación *f* ignition; inflammation.
inflamar *vt* to inflame; to excite, to arouse; ~se *vr* to catch fire.
inflamatorio/ria *adj* inflammatory.
inflar *vt* to inflate, to blow up; (*fig*) to exaggerate.
inflexibilidad *f* inflexibility.
inflexible *adj* inflexible.
influencia *f* influence.
influir *vt* to influence.
influjo *m* influence.
infografía *f* computer graphics.
información *f* information; news; (*mil*) intelligence; investigation, judicial inquiry.
informal *adj* irregular, incorrect; untrustworthy; informal.
informalidad *f* irregularity; untrustworthiness; informality.
informar *vt* to inform; to reveal, to make known; ~se *vr* to find out; * *vi* to report; (*law*) to plead; to inform.
informática *f* computer science, information technology.
informe *m* report, statement; piece of information, account; * *adj* shapeless, formless.
infortunio *m* misfortune, ill luck.
infracción *f* infraction; breach, infringement.
infraccionar *vt Lat Am* to fine.
infractor/ra *m/f* offender.
infructuoso/sa *adj* fruitless, unproductive, unprofitable.
infundado/da *adj* groundless.
infundir *vt* to infuse, to instil.
infusión *f* infusion.
infuso/sa *adj* infused; introduced.
ingeniar *vt* to devise; ~se *vr*: ~ **para** to manage to.
ingeniería *f* engineering; ~ **genética** genetic engineering.

ingeniero/ra *m/f* engineer.
ingenio *m* talent; wit; ingenuity; engine; ~ **de azúcar** sugar mill.
ingenioso/sa *adj* ingenious, clever; witty.
ingenuidad *f* ingenuousness; candor, frankness.
ingenuo/nua *adj* ingenuous.
ingerir *vt* to ingest; to swallow; to consume.
ingle *f* groin.
inglés/esa *adj* English; * *m* English (language); * *m/f* Englishman/woman.
ingratitud *f* ingratitude, unthankfulness.
ingrato/ta *adj* ungrateful, thankless; disagreeable.
ingrediente *m* ingredient.
ingresar *vt* to deposit; * *vi* to come in.
ingreso *m* entry; admission; ~s *mpl* income; takings *pl*.
inhabilitar *vt* to disqualify, to disable.
inhabitable *adj* uninhabitable.
inherente *adj* inherent.
inhibición *f* inhibition.
inhibir *vt* to inhibit; to restrain.
inhumano/na *adj* inhuman.
inicial *adj*, *f* initial.
iniciar *vt* to initiate; to begin.
iniciativa *f* initiative.
inimaginable *adj* unimaginable, inconceivable.
inimitable *adj* inimitable.
ininteligible *adj* unintelligible.
iniquidad *f* iniquity, injustice.
injertar *vt* to graft.
injerto *m* graft.
injuria *f* offense; insult.
injuriar *vt* to insult, to wrong.
injurioso/sa *adj* insulting; offensive.
injusticia *f* injustice.
injusto/ta *adj* unjust.
inmaculado/da *adj* immaculate.
inmadurez *f* immaturity.
inmediaciones *fpl* neighborhood; surrounding area.
inmediatamente *adv* immediately, at once.
inmediato/ta *adj* immediate.
inmemorial *adj* immemorial.
inmensidad *f* immensity.
inmenso/sa *adj* immense.
inmensurable *adj* immeasurable.
inmigración *f* immigration.
inmigrante *m/f* immigrant.
inmigrar *vi* to immigrate.
inminente *adj* imminent.

inmobiliario/ria *adj* real-estate *compd*;
* *f* estate agency.
inmoral *adj* immoral.
inmortal *adj* immortal.
inmortalidad *f* immortality.
inmortalizar *vt* to immortalize.
inmóvil *adj* immovable.
inmovilidad *f* immobility.
inmueble *m* property; * *adj*: **bienes ~s**
real estate.
inmundicia *f* nastiness, filth.
inmundo/da *adj* filthy, dirty; nasty.
inmune *adj* (*med*) immune; free, exempt.
inmunidad *f* immunity; exemption.
inmutabilidad *f* immutability.
inmutable *adj* immutable.
inmutarse *vr* to turn pale.
innato/ta *adj* inborn, innate.
innecesario/ria *adj* unnecessary.
innegable *adj* undeniable.
innovación *f* innovation.
innovador/ra *m/f* innovator.
innovar *vt* to innovate.
innumerable *adj* innumerable, countless.
inocencia *f* innocence.
inocentada *f* practical joke.
inocente *adj* innocent.
inoculación *f* inoculation.
inocular *vt* to inoculate.
inodoro *m* lavatory.
inofensivo/va *adj* harmless.
inolvidable *adj* unforgettable.
inopinado/da *adj* unexpected.
inoxidable *adj*: **acero ~** stainless steel.
inquietar *vt* to worry, to disturb; **~se** *vr* to
worry, to get worried.
inquieto/ta *adj* anxious, worried.
inquietud *f* uneasiness, anxiety.
inquilino/na *m/f* tenant; lodger.
inquirir *vt* to inquire into, to investigate.
insaciable *adj* insatiable.
insalubre *adj* unhealthy.
insalubridad *f* unhealthiness.
insano/na *adj* insane, mad.
inscribir *vt* to inscribe; to list, to register.
inscripción *f* inscription; enrollment, registration.
insecticida *m* insecticide.
insecto *m* insect.
inseguridad *f* insecurity.
inseminación *f* insemination; **~ artificial**
artificial insemination.
insensatez *f* stupidity, folly.
insensato/ta *adj* senseless, stupid; mad.
insensibilidad *f* insensitivity; callousness.

insensible *adj* insensitive; imperceptible;
numb.
insensiblemente *adv* insensitively; imperceptibly.
inseparable *adj* inseparable.
inserción *f* insertion.
insertar *vt* to insert.
inservible *adj* useless.
insidioso/sa *adj* insidious.
insigne *adj* notable.
insignificante *adj* insignificant.
insignia *f* badge; **~s** *fpl* insignia *pl*.
insinuación *f* insinuation.
insinuar *vt* to insinuate; **~se** *vr*: to make
advances; **~ en** to worm one's way into.
insipidez *f* insipidness.
insípido/da *adj* insipid.
insistencia *f* persistence; insistence.
insistir *vi* to insist.
insolación *f* (*med*) sunstroke.
insolencia *f* insolence, rudeness, effrontery.
insolente *adj* insolent, rude.
insólito/ta *adj* unusual.
insolvencia *f* insolvency.
insolvente *adj* insolvent.
insomnio *m* insomnia.
insondable *adj* unfathomable; inscrutable.
insoportable *adj* unbearable.
inspección *f* inspection, survey; check.
inspeccionar *vt* to inspect; to supervise.
inspector/ra *m/f* inspector; superintendent.
inspiración *f* inspiration.
inspirar *vt* to inspire; (*med*) to inhale.
instalación *f* installation.
instalar *vt* to install; *Lat Am* to set up.
instancia *f* instance.
instantáneo/nea *adj* instantaneous; * *f*
snap(shot); **café ~** instant coffee.
instante *m* instant; **al ~** immediately, instantly.
instar *vt* to press, to urge.
instigación *f* instigation.
instigar *vt* to instigate.
instinto *m* instinct.
institución *f* institution.
instituir *vt* to institute.
instituto *m* institute.
institutriz *f* governess.
instrucción *f* instruction.
instructivo/va *adj* instructive; educational.
instructor/ra *m/f* instructor, teacher.
instruir *vt* to instruct, to teach.
instrumento *m* instrument; tool, implement.
insuficiencia *f* lack, inadequacy.

insuficiente *adj* insufficient, inadequate.
insufrible *adj* insufferable, insupportable.
insulina *f* insulin.
insulso/sa *adj* insipid; dull.
insultar *vt* to insult.
insulto *m* insult.
insumos *mpl Lat Am* supplies *pl*; raw materials *pl*.
insuperable *adj* insuperable, insurmountable.
insurgente *m/f* insurgent.
insurrección *f* insurrection.
intacto/ta *adj* untouched; entire; intact.
integral *adj* integral, whole; pan ~ wholewheat bread.
integrar *vt* to make up; to integrate.
integridad *f* integrity; completeness.
íntegro/gra *adj* integral, entire.
intelectual *adj*, *m/f* intellectual.
inteligencia *f* intelligence; understanding.
inteligente *adj* intelligent.
inteligible *adj* intelligible.
intemperie *f*: a la ~ out in the open.
intempestivo/va *adj* untimely.
intención *f* intention, purpose; plan.
intencionado/da *adj* meaningful; deliberate.
intendencia *f* administration, management.
intendente *m* manager.
intensidad *f* intensity; strength.
intenso/sa *adj* intense, strong; deep.
intentar *vt* to try, to attempt.
intento *m* intent, purpose; attempt.
intercalación *f* insertion.
intercalar *vt* to insert.
intercambio *m* exchange, swap.
interceder *vi* to intercede.
interceptar *vt* to intercept.
intercesión *f* intercession, mediation.
intercesor/ra *m/f* intercessor, mediator.
interés *m* interest; share, part; concern, advantage; profit.
interesado/da *adj* interested; prejudiced; mercenary.
interesante *adj* interesting; useful, conveniente.
interesar *vt* to be of interest to, to interest; ~se *vr*: ~se en/por to take an interest in; * *vi* to be of interest.
interfaz, interface *f* interface.
interferir *vt* to interfere with; to jam (a telephone); * *vi* to interfere.
interfono *m* intercom.
interinato *m Lat Am* temporary post.
interinidad *f* temporary holding of office.
interino/na *adj* provisional, temporary; * *m/f* temporary holder of a post; stand-in.

interior *adj* interior, internal; * *m* interior, inside.
interioridad *f* inwardness.
interiorismo *m* interior design.
interiorista *m/f* interior designer.
interjección *f* (*gr*) interjection.
interlocutor/ra *m/f* speaker.
intermediar *vt* to interpose.
intermedio/dia *adj* intermediate; * *m* interval.
interminable *adj* interminable, endless.
intermitente *adj* intermittent; *m* (*auto*) indicator.
internacional *adj* international.
internado *m* boarding school.
internar *vt* to intern; to commit; ~se *vr* to penetrate.
interno/na *adj* interior, internal; * *m/f* boarder.
interpelación *f* interpellation, appeal, plea.
interpelar *vt* to appeal to.
interpolar *vt* to interpolate; to interrupt.
interponer *vt* to interpose, to put in.
interposición *f* insertion; interjection.
interpretación *f* interpretation.
interpretar *vt* to interpret, to explain; (*theat*) to perform; to translate.
intérprete *m/f* interpreter; translator; (*theat*) performer.
interracial *adj* interracial.
interrogación *f* interrogation; question mark.
interrogante *adj* questioning.
interrogar *vt* to interrogate.
interrogatorio *m* questioning; (*law*) examination; questionnaire.
interrumpir *vt* to interrupt.
interrupción *f* interruption.
interruptor *m* switch.
intertanto *adv Lat Am* meanwhile.
intervalo *m* interval.
intervención *f* supervision, control; (*com*) auditing; (*med*) operation; intervention.
intervenir *vt* to control, to supervise; (*com*) to audit; (*med*) to operate on; * *vi* to participate; to intervene.
interventor/ra *m/f* inspector; (*com*) auditor; *Lat Am* administrator.
interviú *f* interview.
intestino/na *adj* internal, interior; * *m* intestine.
intimar *vt* to intimate; * *vi* to become friendly.
intimidad *f* intimacy; private life.
intimidar *vt* intimidate.
íntimo/ma *adj* internal, innermost; intimate, private.

intolerable *adj* intolerable, insufferable.
intolerancia *f* intolerance.
intolerante *adj* intolerant.
intranquilizarse *vr* to get anxious/worried.
intranquilo/la *adj* worried.
intransigente *adj* intransigent.
intransitable *adj* impassable.
intransitivo/va *adj* (*gr*) intransitive.
intratable *adj* intractable, difficult.
intrepidez *f* intrepidity; fearlessness.
intrépido/da *adj* intrepid, daring.
intriga *f* intrigue.
intrigante *m/f* intriguer.
intrigar *vt, vi* to intrigue.
intrínseco/ca *adj* intrinsic.
introducción *f* introduction.
introducir *vt* to introduce; to insert.
introductor *m* introducer.
introvertido/da *adj, m/f* introvert.
intrusión *f* intrusion.
intruso/sa *adj* intrusive; * *m/f* intruder.
intuición *f* intuition.
intuitivo/va *adj* intuitive.
inundación *f* inundation, flood(ing).
inundar *vt* to inundate, to overflow; to flood.
inusitado/da *adj* unusual.
inútil *adj* useless.
inutilidad *f* uselessness.
inutilizar *vt* to render useless.
invadir *vt* (*mil*) to invade; to overrun.
invalidar *vt* to invalidate, to render null and void.
inválido/da *adj* invalid, null and void; * *m/f* invalid.
invariable *adj* invariable.
invasión *f* invasion.
invasor/ra *adj* invading; * *m/f* invader.
invencible *adj* invincible.
invención *f* invention.
inventar *vt* to invent.
inventario *m* inventory.
invento *m* invention.
inventor/ra *m/f* inventor.
invernadero *m* greenhouse.
invernar *vi* to pass the winter.
inverosímil *adj* unlikely, improbable.
inverosimilitud *f* unlikeliness, improbability.
inversión *f* (*com*) investment; inversion.
inverso/sa *adj* inverse; inverted; contrary.
invertir *vt* (*com*) to invest; to invert.
investidura *f* investiture.
investigación *f* investigation, research.
investigar *vt* to investigate; to do research into.

investir *vt* to confer.
invicto/ta *adj* unconquerable.
invierno *m* winter.
inviolabilidad *f* inviolability.
inviolable *adj* inviolable.
invisible *adj* invisible.
invitado/da *m/f* guest.
invitar *vt* to invite; to entice; to pay for.
invocación *f* invocation.
invocar *vt* to invoke.
involucrar *vt Lat Am* to involve.
involuntario/ria *adj* involuntary.
invulnerable *adj* invulnerable.
inyección *f* injection.
ir *vi* to go; to walk; to travel; ~se *vr* to go away, to depart.
ira *f* anger, wrath.
iracundo/da *adj* irate; irascible.
iris *m* iris (eye); arco ~ rainbow.
ironía *f* irony.
irónico/ca *adj* ironic(al).
irracional *adj* irrational.
irradiación *f* irradiation.
irrazonable *adj* unreasonable.
irreal *adj* unreal.
irreconciliable *adj* irreconcilable.
irreflexión *f* rashness, thoughtlessness.
irregular *adj* irregular; abnormal.
irregularidad *f* irregularity; abnormality.
irremediable *adj* irremediable; incurable.
irremisible *adj* irretrievable; unpardonable.
irreparable *adj* irreparable.
irresistible *adj* irresistible.
irresoluto/ta *adj* irresolute; hesitant.
irreverencia *f* irreverence; disrespect.
irreverente *adj* irreverent; disrespectful.
irrevocable *adj* irrevocable.
irrisorio/ria *adj* derisory, ridiculous.
irritación *f* irritation.
irritar *vt* to irritate, to exasperate; to stir up; to inflame.
irrupción *f* irruption; invasion.
isla *f* island, isle.
Islam *m* Islam.
islámico/ca *adj* Islamic.
islote *m* small island.
istmo *m* isthmus.
italiano/na *adj* Italian; * *m* Italian (language); * *m/f* Italian man/woman.
ítem *m* item.
itemizar *vt Lat Am* to itemize.
itinerario *m* itinerary.
izar *vt* (*mar*) to hoist.
izquierda *f* left; left-hand side.
izquierdo/da *adj* left; left-handed.

J

jabalí *m* wild boar.
jabalina *f* wild sow; (*sport*) javelin.
jabón *m* soap.
jabonar *vt* to soap.
jaca *f* pony; *Lat Am* fighting cock.
jacinto *m* hyacinth.
jacuzzi *m* jacuzzi.
jactancia *f* boasting.
jactancioso/sa *adj* boastful.
jactarse *vr* to boast.
jadear *vi* to pant.
jaguar *m* jaguar.
jalea *f* jelly.
jaleo *m* racket, uproar.
jalón *m* pull, tug.
jamás *adv* never; **para siempre** ~ for ever and ever.
jamón *m* ham; ~ **de York** (cooked) ham; ~ **serrano** cured ham.
jaque *m* check (at game of chess); ~ **mate** checkmate.
jaqueca *f* migraine.
jarabe *m* syrup.
jarcia *f* (*mar*) ropes *pl*, rigging.
jardín *m* garden.
jardinería *f* gardening.
jardinero/ra *m/f* gardener; *Lat Am* outfielder.
jarra *f* jug, jar, pitcher; **en ~s, de ~s** with arms akimbo; with hands to the sides.
jarro *m* jug.
jarrón *m* vase.
jaspe *m* jasper.
jaspear *vt* to marble; to speckle.
jaula *f* cage; cell for mad people.
jauría *f* pack of hounds.
jazmín *m* jasmin.
jazz *m* jazz.
jean *m* *Lat Am* jeans.
jefatura *f*: ~ **de policía** police headquarters.
jefe *m* chief, head, leader; (*rail*) ~ **de tren** guard, conductor.
jején *m* *Lat Am* gnat.
jengibre *m* ginger.
jerarquía *f* hierarchy.
jerárquico/ca *adj* hierarchical.
jerga *f* coarse cloth; jargon.
jergón *m* coarse mattress.
jerigonza *f* jargon, gibberish.
jeringa *f* syringe.
jeroglífico/ca *adj* hieroglyphic; * *m* hieroglyph, hieroglyphic.

jersey *m* sweater, pullover.
Jesucristo *m* Jesus Christ.
jesuita *m* Jesuit.
jesuítico/ca *adj* Jesuitical.
jibia *f* cuttlefish.
jícara *f* small cup (for chocolate).
jilguero *m* goldfinch.
jinete/ta *m/f* horseman/woman, rider.
jipijapa *m* straw hat.
jirafa *f* giraffe.
jirón *m* rag, shred.
jocosidad *f* humor, jocularity.
jocoso/sa *adj* good-humored.
jol *m* *Lat Am* hall.
jonrón *m* *Lat Am* home run.
jonronear *vi* *Lat Am* to hit a home run.
jornada *f* journey; day's journey; working day.
jornal *m* day's wage.
jornalero *m* (day) laborer.
joroba *f* hump; * *m/f* hunchback.
jorobado/da *adj* hunchbacked.
jorobar *vt* to pester, to annoy.
jota *f* jot, iota; Spanish dance.
joven *adj* young; * *m/f* youth; young woman.
jovial *adj* jovial, cheerful.
jovialidad *f* joviality, cheerfulness.
joya *f* jewel; ~**s** *fpl* jewelry.
joyería *f* jewelry; jeweler's place of business.
joyero/ra *m/f* jeweler.
juanete *m* (*med*) bunion.
jubilación *f* retirement.
jubilado/da *adj* retired; * *m/f* senior citizen.
jubilar *vt* to pension off; to superannuate; to discard; ~**se** *vr* to retire.
jubileo *m* jubilee.
júbilo *m* joy, rejoicing.
judaico/ca *adj* Judaic, Jewish.
judaísmo *m* Judaism.
judía *f* bean; ~ **verde** green bean, French bean.
judicatura *f* judicature; office of a judge.
judicial *adj* judicial.
judío/día *adj* Jewish; * *m/f* Jewish man/ woman.
juego *m* play; amusement; sport; game; *Lat Am* match; gambling; ~**s Olímpicos** Olympic Games.
juerga *f* binge; party.
jueves *m* *invar* Thursday.

juez *m/f* judge.
jugada *f* playing of a card; stroke, shot.
jugador/ra *m/f* player; gambler.
jugar *vt*, *vi* to play, to sport, to gamble.
jugarreta *f* bad play, unskillful play.
jugo *m* sap, juice.
jugoso/sa *adj* juicy, succulent.
juguete *m* toy, plaything.
juguetear *vi* to play.
juguetón/ona *adj* playful.
juicio *m* judgement, reason; sanity; opinion.
juicioso/sa *adj* judicious, prudent.
julio *m* July.
junco *m* (*bot*) rush; junk (small Chinese ship).
jungla *f* jungle.
junio *m* June.
junta *f* meeting; assembly; congress; council.
juntamente *adv* jointly; at the same time.
juntar *vt* to join; to unite; ~se *vr* to meet, to assemble; to draw closer.
junto/ta *adj* joined; united; near; adjacent; ~s together; * *adv*: **todo** ~ all at once.

juntura *f* junction; joint.
Júpiter *m* Jupiter (planet).
jurado *m* jury; juror; member of a panel.
juramento *m* oath; curse.
jurar *vt*, *vi* to swear.
jurídico/ca *adj* lawful, legal; juridical.
jurisdicción *f* jurisdiction; district.
jurisprudencia *f* jurisprudence.
jurista *m/f* jurist.
justa *f* joust, tournament.
justamente *adv* justly; just.
justicia *f* justice; equity.
justificación *f* justification.
justificante *m* voucher; receipt.
justificar *vt* to justify.
justo/ta *adj* just; fair, right; exact, correct; tight; * *adv* exactly, precisely; just in time.
juvenil *adj* youthful.
juventud *f* youthfulness, youth; young people *pl*.
juzgado *m* tribunal; court.
juzgar *vt*, *vi* to judge.

K

karaoke *m* karaoke.
ketchup *m* ketchup.
kilogramo *m* kilogram.
kilometraje *m* distance in kilometers.

kilómetro *m* kilometer.
kilovatio *m* kilowatt.
kiosco *m* kiosk.

L

la *art f* the; * *pn* her; you; it.
laberinto *m* labyrinth.
labia *f* fluency; (*col*) the gift of the gab.
labio *m* lip; edge.
labor *f* labor, task; needlework; farmwork; plowing.
laboratorio *m* laboratory.
laboriosidad *f* laboriousness.
laborioso/sa *adj* laborious; hard-working.
labrado/da *adj* worked; carved; wrought; * *m* cultivated land.
labrador/ra *m/f* farmer; peasant.
labranza *f* farming; cultivation; farmland.
labrar *vt* to work; to carve; to farm; (*fig*) to bring about.
labriego/ga *m/f* peasant.
laca *f* lacquer; hairspray.
lacayo *m* lackey, footman.
lacerar *vt* to tear to pieces, to lacerate.
lacio/cia *adj* faded, withered; languid; lank (hair).
lacónico/ca *adj* laconic.
laconismo *m* laconic style, terseness.
lacra *f* scar; blot, blemish; *Lat Am* scab.
lacrar *vt* to seal (with sealing wax).
lacre *m* sealing wax.
lactancia *f* lactation; breast-feeding.
lácteo/tea *adj*: productos ~s dairy products.
ladear *vt* to move to one side; to incline; ~se *vr* to lean; to tilt.
ladera *f* slope.
ladino/na *adj* cunning, crafty.
lado *m* side; faction, party; favor, protection; (*mil*) flank; al ~ de beside; poner a un ~ to put aside; por todos ~s on all sides.
ladrar *vt* to bark.
ladrido *m* bark, barking.
ladrillo *m* brick.
ladrón/ona *m/f* thief, robber, burglar.
lagar *m* wine press.
lagartija *f* (small) lizard.
lagarto *m* lizard.
lago *m* lake.
lágrima *f* tear.
lagrimal *m* corner of the eye.
lagrimoso/sa *adj* weeping, shedding tears.
laguna *f* lake; lagoon; gap.
laico/ca *adj* lay; * *m* layman.
lama *f Lat Am* slime; moss.
lamedura *f* licking.

lamentable *adj* lamentable, deplorable; pitiable.
lamentación *f* lamentation.
lamentar *vt* to be sorry about; to lament, to regret; * *vi*, ~se *vr* to lament, to complain; to mourn.
lamento *m* lament.
lamer *vt* to lick, to lap.
lámina *f* plate, sheet of metal; engraving.
lámpara *f* lamp.
lamparilla *f* nightlight.
lamparón *m* grease spot.
lampiño/ña *adj* beardless.
lamprea *f* lamprey (fish).
lana *f* wool.
lance *m* cast, throw; move, play (in a game); event, incident.
lancero *m* (*mil*) lancer.
lancha *f* barge, lighter; launch.
langosta *f* locust; lobster.
langostino *m* king prawn.
languidez *f* languor.
lánguido/da *adj* languid, faint, weak.
lanudo/da *adj* wooly, fleecy.
lanza *f* lance, spear.
lanzada *f* stroke with a lance.
lanzadera *f* shuttle.
lanzamiento *m* throwing; (*mar, com*) launch, launching.
lanzar *vt* to throw; (*sport*) to bowl, to pitch; to launch, to fling; (*law*) to evict.
lapicero *m* pencil, ballpoint pen; *Lat Am* propelling pencil.
lápida *f* flat stone, tablet.
lapidario/ria *adj*, *m* lapidary.
lápiz *m* pencil; propelling pencil.
lapso *m* interval; error.
lapsus *m* error, mistake.
largamente *adv* for a long time.
largar *vt* to loosen, to slacken; to let go; to launch; to throw out; ~se *vr* (*col*) to beat it.
largo/ga *adj* long; lengthy, generous; copious; a la ~a in the end, eventually.
largueza *f* liberality, generosity.
largura *f* length.
laringe *f* larynx.
laringitis *f* laryngitis.
las *art fpl* the; * *pn* them; you.
lascivia *f* lasciviousness; lewdness.
lascivo/va *adj* lascivious; lewd.
láser *m* laser.

lasitud *f* lassitude, weariness.
lástima *f* compassion, pity; shame.
lastimadura *f Lat Am* graze.
lastimar *vt* to hurt; to wound; to feel pity for; ~**se** *vr* to hurt oneself.
lastimero/ra *adj* pitiful, pathetic.
lastimoso/sa *adj* pathetic, mournful.
lastrar *vt* to ballast (a ship).
lastre *m* ballast; good sense.
lata *f* tin; can; (*col*) nuisance.
lateral *adj* lateral.
latero/ra *m/f Lat Am* tinsmith.
latido *m* (heart)beat.
latifundio *m* large estate.
latigazo *m* lash, crack (of a whip).
látigo *m* whip.
latín *m* Latin.
latinizar *vt* to Latinize.
latino/na *adj* Latin.
Latinoamérica *f* Latin America.
latinoamericano/na *adj*, *m/f* Latin American.
latir *vi* to beat, to palpitate
latitud *f* latitude.
latón *m* brass.
latoso/sa *adj* annoying; boring.
latrocinio *m* theft, robbery.
laúd *f* lute (musical instrument).
laudable *adj* laudable, praiseworthy.
láudano *m* laudanum.
laureado/da *adj* honored; * *m* laureate.
laurel *m* (*bot*) laurel; reward.
lava *f* lava.
lavabo *m* washbasin; washroom.
lavadero *m* washing place; laundry.
lavado *m* washing; laundry.
lavadora *f* washing machine.
lavanda *f* lavender.
lavandera *f* laundress.
lavandería *f* laundry; ~ **automática** Laundromat™.
lavaparabrisas *m invar* windshield washer.
lavaplatos *m invar* dishwasher.
lavar *vt* to wash; to wipe away; ~**se** *vr* to wash oneself.
lavativa *f* (*med*) enema; (*fig*) nuisance.
laxante *m* (*med*) laxative.
laxitud *f* laxity, slackness, laxness.
laxo/xa *adj* lax, slack.
lazada *f* bow, knot.
lazarillo *m*: **perro** ~ guide dog.
lazo *m* knot; bow; snare, trap; tie; bond.
le *pn* him; you; (*dative*) to him; to her; to it; to you.
leal *adj* loyal; faithful.

lealtad *f* loyalty.
lebrel *m* greyhound.
lebrillo *m* glazed earthenware dish.
lección *f* reading; lesson; lecture; class.
leche *f* milk.
lechera *f* milkmaid, dairymaid; milk can, milk churn.
lechería *f* dairy.
lecho *m* bed; layer.
lechón *m* sucking pig.
lechuga *f* lettuce.
lechuza *f* owl.
lector/ra *m/f* reader.
lectura *f* reading.
leer *vt*, *vi* to read.
legado *m* bequest, legacy; legate.
legajo *m* file.
legal *adj* legal; trustworthy.
legalidad *f* legality.
legalización *f* legalization.
legalizar *vt* to legalize.
legaña *f* sleep (in eyes).
legar *vt* to leave, to bequeath
legible *adj* legible.
legión *f* legion.
legionario/ria *m/f* legionary.
legislación *f* legislation.
legislador/ra *m/f* legislator, lawmaker.
legislar *vt* to legislate.
legislativo/va *adj* legislative.
legislatura *f* legislature.
legitimar *vt* to legitimize.
legitimidad *f* legitimacy.
legítimo/ma *adj* legitimate, lawful; authentic.
legua *f* league.
legumbres *fpl* pulses *pl*.
leído/da *adj* well-read.
lejano/na *adj* distant, remote; far.
lejía *f* bleach.
lejos *adv* at a great distance, far off.
lelo/la *adj* stupid, ignorant; * *m/f* idiot.
lema *m* motto; slogan.
lencería *f* linen, drapery.
lengua *f* tongue; language.
lenguado *m* sole.
lenguaje *m* language.
lente *m/f* lens; ~ **de contacto** contact lense; ~**s** *mpl Lat Am* glasses.
lenteja *f* lentil.
lentilla *f* contact lens.
lentitud *f* slowness.
lento/ta *adj* slow.
leña *f* wood, lumber.
leñador *m* woodsman, woodcutter.

leño *m* block, log; trunk of a tree.
leñoso/sa *adj* woody.
Leo *m* Leo (zodiac sign).
león *m* lion; *Lat Am* puma.
leona *f* lioness.
leonado/da *adj* lion-colored, tawny.
leonino/na *adj Lat Am* Leonian (zodiac sign).
leopardo *m* leopard.
leotardos *mpl* tights.
lepra *f* leprosy.
leproso/sa *adj* leprous; * *m/f* leper.
lerdo/da *adj* slow, heavy; dull; slow-witted.
les *pn* them; you; (*dativo*) to them; to you.
lesbiana *adj, f* lesbian.
lesión *f* wound; injury; damage.
letal *adj* mortal, deadly.
letanía *f* litany.
letárgico/ca *adj* lethargic.
letargo *m* lethargy.
letra *f* letter; handwriting; printing type; draft of a song; draft; ~s *fpl* letters *pl*, learning.
letrado/da *adj* learned, lettered; * *m/f* lawyer; counsel.
letrero *m* sign; label.
letrina *f* latrine.
leucemia *f* leukemia.
leva *m* (*mar*) weighing anchor; (*mil*) levy.
levadizo/za *adj* that can be lifted/raised; puente ~ drawbridge.
levadura *f* yeast; brewer's yeast.
levantamiento *m* raising; insurrection.
levantar *vt* to raise, to lift up; to build; to elevate; to hearten, to cheer up; ~se *vr* to get up; to stand up.
levante *m* Levant; east; east wind.
leve *adj* light; trivial.
levita *f* a heavy overcoat; greatcoat, frock coat.
léxico *m* vocabulary.
ley *f* law; standard (for metal).
leyenda *f* legend.
liar *vt* to tie, to bind; to confuse.
libelo *m* petition; satire, lampoon.
libélula *f* dragonfly.
liberación *f* liberation; release.
liberal *adj* liberal, generous; * *m/f* liberal.
liberalidad *f* liberality, generosity.
libertad *f* liberty, freedom.
libertador/ra *m/f* liberator.
libertar *vt* to free, to set at liberty; to exempt, to clear from an obligation/debt.
libertinaje *m* licentiousness.
libertino/na *m/f* permissive person.

libra *f* pound; ~ esterlina pound sterling.
Libra *f* Libra (zodiac sign).
librano/na *adj Lat Am* Libran (zodiac sign).
librar *vt* to free, to deliver; (*com*) to draw; to make out (a check); (*law*) to exempt; to fight (a battle); ~se *vr* to escape.
libre *adj* free; exempt; vacant.
libremente *adv* freely.
librería *f* bookshop.
librero/ra *m/f* bookseller.
libreta *f* notebook; ~ de ahorros savings book.
libretista *m/f Lat Am* screenwriter.
libreto *m Lat Am* script.
libro *m* book.
licencia *f* license; licentiousness; *Lat Am* leave.
licenciado/da *adj* licensed; * *m/f* graduate.
licenciar *vt* to permit, to allow; to license; to discharge; to confer a degree upon; ~se *vr* to graduate.
licencioso/sa *adj* licentious, dissolute.
liceo *m* lyceum; secondary school.
lícitamente *adv* lawfully.
lícito/ta *adj* lawful, fair; permissible.
licor *m* liquor.
licuadora *f* blender, liquidizer.
lid *m* contest, fight; dispute.
líder *m/f* leader.
liderazgo *m* leadership.
liebre *f* hare.
lienzo *m* linen; canvas; face/front of a building.
liga *f* garter; birdlime; league; coalition; alloy.
ligadura *f* (*med, mus*) ligature; binding; bond, tie.
ligamento *m* ligament; tie; bond.
ligar *vt* to tie, to bind, to fasten; ~se *vr* to commit oneself; * *vi* to mix, blend; (*col*) to pick up.
ligazón *f* union, connection.
ligereza *f* lightness; swiftness; agility; superficiality.
ligero/ra *adj* light, swift; agile; superficial.
liguero *m* garter belt.
lija *f* dogfish; sandpaper.
lijar *vt* to smooth, to sandpaper.
lila *f* lilac.
lima *f* file.
limadura *f* filing.
limar *vt* to file; to polish.
limitación *f* limitation, restriction.
limitado/da *adj* limited.
limitar *vt* to limit; to restrict; to cut down.
límite *m* limit, boundary.

limítrofe *adj* neighboring, bordering.
limón *m* lemon.
limonada *f* lemonade.
limonar *m* plantation/orchard of lemon trees.
limosna *f* alms *pl*, charity.
limpiabotas *m/f invar* shoeshine boy/girl.
limpiaparabrisas *m invar* windshield wiper.
limpiar *vt* to clean; to cleanse; to purify; to polish; (*fig*) to clean up.
limpieza *f* cleanliness; cleaning; cleansing; polishing; purity.
limpio/pia *adj* clean; neat; pure.
linaje *m* lineage, family, descent.
linaza *f* linseed.
lince *m* lynx.
linchar *vt* to lynch.
lindar *vi* to be adjacent.
linde *m* boundary.
lindero *m* edge; boundary.
lindo/da *adj* pretty; lovely.
lindura *f Lat Am* prettiness.
línea *f* line; cable; outline.
lineal *adj* linear.
lingote *m* ingot.
lingüista *m/f* linguist.
lino *m* flax.
linterna *f* flashlight; lantern, lamp; torch.
lío *m* bundle, parcel; (*col*) muddle, mess.
liposucción *f* liposuction.
liquidación *f* liquidation.
liquidar *vt* to liquidate; to settle (accounts).
líquido/da *adj* liquid.
lira *f* (*mus*) lyre.
lirio *m* (*bot*) iris.
lirón *m* dormouse; (*fig*) sleepyhead.
lisiado/da *adj* injured; * *m/f* physically disabled person.
lisiar *vt* to injure; to hurt.
liso/sa *adj* plain, even, flat, smooth.
lisonja *f* adulation, flattery.
lisonjear *vt* to flatter.
lisonjero/ra *m/f* flatterer; * *adj* flattering; pleasing.
lista *f* list; school register; catalog; menu.
lista de correos *f* general delivery.
listo/ta *adj* ready; smart, clever.
listón *m* ribbon; strip (of wood/metal).
litera *f* berth; bunk, bunk bed.
literal *adj* literal.
literario/ria *adj* literary.
literato/ta *adj* literary; * *m/f* writer, literary person; ~s *mpl* literati *pl*.
literatura *f* literature.
litigar *vt* to fight; * *vi* (*law*) to go to law; (*fig*) to dispute.

litigio *m* lawsuit.
litografía *f* lithography.
litográfico/ca *adj* lithographic.
litoral *adj* coastal; * *m* coast.
litro *m* liter.
liturgia *f* liturgy.
litúrgico/ca *adj* liturgical.
liviandad *f* fickleness; triviality; lightness.
liviano/na *adj* light; fickle; trivial.
lívido/da *adj* livid.
llaga *f* wound; sore.
llama *f* flame; llama (animal).
llamada *f* call.
llamado *m Lat Am* call.
llamador *m* door-knocker.
llamamiento *m* call.
llamar *vt* to call; to name; to summon; to ring up, to telephone; * *vi* to knock at the door; to ring up, to telephone; ~se *vr* to be named.
llamarada *f* blaze; outburst.
llamativo/va *adj* showy; loud (color).
llano/na *adj* plain; even, level, smooth; clear, evident; * *m* plain.
llanta *f* (wheel) rim; tire; inner (tube); *Lat Am* tire.
llanto *m* flood of tears, crying.
llanura *f* evenness, flatness; plain, prairie.
llave *f* faucet; key; ~ **maestra** master key.
llavero *m* key ring.
llegada *f* arrival, coming.
llegar *vi* to arrive; ~ **a** to reach; ~se *vr* to come near, to approach.
llenar *vt* to fill; to cover; to fill out (a form); to satisfy, to fulfill; ~se *vr* to gorge oneself.
lleno/na *adj* full, full up; complete.
llevadero/ra *adj* tolerable.
llevar *vt* to take; to wear; to carry; to convey, to transport; to drive; to lead; to bear; ~se *vr* to carry off, to take away.
llorar *vt, vi* to weep, to cry.
lloriquear *vt* to whine.
lloro *m* weeping, crying.
llorón/ona *m/f* tearful person; crybaby.
lloroso/sa *adj* mournful, full of tears.
llover *vi* to rain.
lloviznar *vi* to drizzle.
lluvia *f* rain; ~ **ácida** acid rain.
lluvioso/sa *adj* rainy.
lo *pn* it; him; you; * *art* the.
loable *adj* laudable.
loar *vt* to praise.
lobato *m* young wolf.
lobo *m* wolf.
lóbrego/ga *adj* murky, dark, gloomy.

lóbulo *m* lobe.
local *adj* local; * *m* place, site.
localidad *f* locality; location.
localizar *vt* to localize.
loción *f* lotion.
loco/ca *adj* mad; * *m/f* mad person.
locomoción *f Lat Am* public transport.
locomotora *f* locomotive.
locuacidad *f* loquacity.
locuaz *adj* loquacious, talkative.
locución *f* expression.
locura *f* madness, folly.
locutor/ra *m/f* (*rad*) announcer; (*TV*) newsreader.
locutorio *m* telephone booth.
lodazal *m* muddy place.
lodo *m* mud, mire.
logaritmo *m* logarithm.
lógica *f* logic.
lógico/ca *adj* logical.
lograr *vt* to achieve; to gain, to obtain.
logro *m* achievement; success.
loma *f* small hill, hillock.
lombarda *f* red cabbage.
lombriz *f* worm.
lomo *m* loin; back (of an animal); spine (of a book); **llevar/traer a** ~ to carry on the back.
lona *f* canvas.
loncha *f* slice; rasher.
longaniza *f* pork sausage.
longitud *f* length; longitude.
lonja¹ *f* slice; rasher.
lonja² *f* market, exchange; ~ **de pescado** fish market.
loro *m* parrot.
los *art mpl* the; * *pn* them; you.
losa *f* flagstone.
lote *m* lot; portion; *Lat Am* plot of land.
lotería *f* lottery.
loza *f* crockery.
lozanía *f* luxuriance, lushness; vigor; self-assurance.
lozano/na *adj* luxuriant, lush; sprightly.

lubricante *m* lubricant.
lucero *m* bright star; ~ **del alba** morning star.
lucha *f* struggle, fight.
luchador/ra *m/f* fighter; * *m* wrestler.
luchar *vi* to struggle; to wrestle.
lúcido/da *adj* lucid.
luciérnaga *f* glowworm.
lucimiento *m* splendor, luster; brightness.
lución *m* slowworm.
lucir *vt* to light (up); to show off; * *vi* to shine; *Lat Am* to look; ~**se** *vr* to make a fool of oneself.
lucrativo/va *adj* lucrative.
lucro *m* gain, profit.
luego *adv* next; afterward(s); **desde** ~ of course.
lugar *m* place, spot; village; reason; **en** ~ **de** instead of, in lieu of.
lugareño/ña *adj* belonging to a village; * *m/f* inhabitant of a village.
lugarteniente *m* deputy.
lúgubre *adj* lugubrious; sad, gloomy.
lujo *m* luxury; abundance.
lujoso/sa *adj* luxurious; showy; profuse, lavish.
lujuria *f* lust.
lujurioso/sa *adj* lustful, lewd.
lumbre *f* fire; light.
lumbrera *f* luminary; skylight.
luminaria *f* illumination.
luminoso/sa *adj* luminous, shining.
luna *f* moon; glass plate for mirrors; lens.
lunar *m* mole, spot; * *adj* lunar.
lunático/ca *adj, m/f* lunatic.
lunes *m invar* Monday.
lupa *f* magnifying glass, magnifier.
lupanar *m* brothel.
lustre *m* gloss, luster; splendor.
lustro *m* lustrum, space of five years.
lustroso/sa *adj* bright, brilliant.
luteranismo *m* Lutheranism.
luterano/na *adj, m/f* Lutheran.
luto *m* mourning (dress); grief.
luz *f* light.

M

macarrones *mpl* macaroni.
macedonia *f*: ~ de frutas fruit salad.
macerar *vt* to macerate, to soften.
maceta *f* flowerpot.
machacar *vt* to pound, to crush; * *vi* to insist, to go on.
machacón/ona *adj* wearisome, tedious.
machete *m* machete, cutlass.
machista *adj*, *m* sexist.
macho *adj* male; (*fig*) virile; * *m* male; (*fig*) he-man.
machucar *vt* to pound, to bruise.
macilento/ta *adj* lean; haggard, withered.
macizo/za *adj* massive; solid; * *m* mass, chunk.
madeja *f* skein of thread; mop of hair.
madera *f* lumber, timber, wood.
madero *m* lumber beam, timber beam.
madrastra *f* stepmother.
madraza *f* loving mother.
madre *f* mother; womb.
madreperla *f* mother-of-pearl.
madreselva *f* honeysuckle.
madrigal *m* madrigal.
madriguera *f* burrow; den.
madrina *f* godmother.
madroño *m* strawberry plant.
madrugada *f* dawn; de ~ at day break.
madrugador/ra *m/f* early riser.
madrugar *vi* to get up early; to get ahead.
madurar *vt* to ripen; * *vi* to ripen, to grow ripe; to mature.
madurez *f* maturity; ripeness; wisdom.
maduro/ra *adj* ripe, mature.
maestra *f* mistress; schoolmistress; teacher.
maestría *f* mastery, skill; *Lat Am* master's degree.
maestro *m* master; teacher; ~/tra *adj* masterly, skilled; principal.
magia *f* magic.
mágico/ca *adj* magical.
magisterio *m* teaching; teaching profession; teachers *pl*.
magistrado/da *m/f* magistrate.
magistral *adj* magisterial; masterly.
magistratura *f* magistracy.
magnanimidad *f* magnanimity.
magnánimo/ma *adj* magnanimous.
magnate *m* magnate.
magnético/ca *adj* magnetic.
magnetismo *m* magnetism.

magnetizar *vt* to magnetize.
magnetofón, magnetófono *m* tape recorder.
magnetofónico/ca *adj*: cinta magnetofónica recording tape.
magnificencia *f* magnificence, splendor.
magnífico/ca *adj* magnificent, splendid.
magnitud *f* magnitude.
mago/ga *m/f* magician.
magro/gra *adj* thin, lean; meager.
magulladura *f* bruise.
magullar *vt* to bruise; to damage; (*col*) to bash.
magullón *m Lat Am* bruise.
mahometano/na *m/f*, *adj* Muslim.
mahometanismo *m* Islam.
mahonesa *f* mayonnaise.
maíz *m* corn; maize.
maizal *m* corn field.
majada *f* sheepfold.
majadería *f* absurdity; silliness.
majadero/ra *adj* dull; silly, stupid; * *m* idiot.
majestad *f* majesty.
majestuoso/sa *adj* majestic.
majo/ja *adj* nice; attractive; smart.
majuelo *m* vine (newly planted); hawthorn.
mal *m* evil; hurt; harm, damage; misfortune; illness; * *adj* (before masculine nouns) bad.
malamente *adv* badly.
malaria *f* malaria.
malcriado/da *adj* rude, ill-behaved; naughty; spoiled.
maldad *f* wickedness.
maldecir *vt* to curse.
maldición *f* curse.
maldito/ta *adj* wicked; damned, cursed.
malear *vt* to damage; to corrupt.
malecón *m* pier.
maledicencia *f* slander; scandal.
maleducado/da *adj* bad-mannered, rude.
maleficio *m* curse; spell; witchcraft.
maléfico/ca *adj* harmful, damaging, evil.
malestar *m* discomfort; (*fig*) uneasiness; unrest.
maleta *f* suitcase; (*auto*) trunk.
maletero *f* (*auto*) trunk.
malevolencia *f* malevolence.
malévolo/la *adj* malevolent.
maleza *f* weeds *pl*; thicket.
malgastar *vt* to waste, to ruin.

malhablado/da *adj* foul-mouthed.
malhechor/ra *m/f* malefactor; criminal.
malhumorado/da *adj* cross, bad-tempered.
malicia *f* malice, wickedness; suspicion; cunning.
malicioso/sa *adj* malicious, wicked, evil; sly, crafty; spiteful.
malignidad *f* (*med*) malignancy; evil nature; malice.
maligno/na *adj* malignant; malicious.
malinformar *vt Lat Am* to misinform.
malla *f* mesh, network; ~s *fpl* leotard.
malo/la *adj* bad; ill; wicked; * *m/f* villain.
malograr *vt* to spoil; to upset (a plan); to waste; ~se *vr* to fail; to die early.
malparado/da *adj*: salir ~ to come off badly.
malparida *f* woman who has had a miscarriage.
malparir *vi* to miscarry, to have a miscarriage.
malsano/na *adj* unhealthy.
malteada *f Lat Am* milk shake.
maltratamiento *m* ill-treatment.
maltratar *vt* to ill-treat, to abuse, to mistreat.
malva *f* (*bot*) mallow.
malvado/da *adj* wicked, villainous.
malversación *f* embezzlement.
malversador/ra *m/f* embezzler.
malversar *vt* to embezzle.
mama *f* teat; breast.
mamá *f* (*col*) mom, mommy.
mamar *vt, vi* to suck.
mamarrachada *f* ridiculous sight.
mamarracho *m* mess, botch-up.
mamífero *m* mammal.
mamita *f* (*col*) *Lat Am* mom, mommy.
mamón/ona *m/f* small baby; scrounger.
mampara *f* partition; screen.
mampostería *f* masonry; stonemasonry.
maná *m* manna.
manada *f* flock, herd; pack; crowd.
manantial *m* source, spring; origin.
manar *vt* to run with, to flow; * *vi* to spring from; to flow; to abound.
mancha *f* stain, spot.
manchado/da *adj* spotted.
manchar *vt* to stain, to soil.
mancilla *f* spot, blemish.
manco/ca *adj* one-armed; one-handed; maimed; faulty.
mancomunar *vt* to associate, to unite; to make jointly responsible.
mancomunidad *f* union, fellowship; community; (*law*) joint responsibility.

mandado *m* command; errand, message.
mandamiento *m* order, command; commandment.
mandar *vt* to command, to order; to bequeath; to send.
mandarín *m* mandarin.
mandarina *f* tangerine; mandarin orange.
mandatario/ria *m/f* agent; leader.
mandato *m* mandate, order; term of office.
mandíbula *f* jaw.
mandil *m* apron.
mando *m* command, authority, power; term of office; ~ a distancia remote control.
mandón/ona *adj* bossy, domineering.
manecilla *f* small hand (of a watch/meter); book-clasp.
manejable *adj* manageable.
manejar *vt* to manage; to operate; to handle; *Lat Am* (*auto*) to drive; ~se *vr* to manage; to behave; *Lat Am* to drive.
manejo *m* management; handling; *Lat Am* driving; confidence.
manera *f* manner, way; fashion; kind.
manga *f* sleeve; hose, hosepipe.
mango[1] *m* handle.
mango[2] *m* mango.
mangonear *vi* to interfere; * *vt* to boss about.
manguera *f* hose; hosepipe.
manguito *m* muff.
maní *m* peanut.
manía *f* mania; craze; dislike; spite.
maniatar *vt* to tie the hands of; to handcuff.
maniático/ca *adj* maniac, mad, frantic; * *m/f* maniac.
manicomio *m* mental home, lunatic asylum.
manicura *f* manicure.
manifestación *f* manifestation; show; demonstration; mass meeting.
manifestar *vt* to manifest, to declare.
manifiesto/ta *adj* manifest, open, clear; * *m* manifesto.
manija *f Lat Am* handle.
maniobra *f* maneuvering; handling; (*mil*) maneuver.
maniobrar *vt* to maneuver; to handle.
manipulación *f* manipulation.
manipular *vt* to manipulate.
maniquí *m* dummy; * *m/f* model.
manirroto/ta *adj* lavish, extravagant.
manivela *f* crank.
manjar *m* (tasty) dish.
mano *f* hand; hand (of a clock or watch);

foot, paw (of an animal); coat (of paint); lot, series; hand (at game); *Lat Am* bunch (of bananas); **a ~ by hand; a ~s llenas** liberally, generously.

manojo *m* handful, bunch.

manopla *f* gauntlet; glove; washcloth.

manosear *vt* to handle; to finger, to mess up.

manoseo *m* handling; fingering.

manotazo *m* slap, smack.

manoteo *m* gesticulation.

mansalva *f*: **a ~** *adv* indiscriminately.

mansedumbre *f* meekness, gentleness.

mansión *f* mansion.

manso/sa *adj* tame; gentle, soft.

manta *f* blanket.

manteca *f* fat; **~ de cerdo** lard.

mantecado *m* cake eaten at Christmas; ice cream.

mantecoso/sa *adj* greasy.

mantel *m* tablecloth.

mantelería *f* table linen.

mantener *vt* to maintain, to support; to nourish; to keep; **~se** *vr* to hold one's ground; to support oneself.

mantenimiento *m* maintenance; subsistence.

mantequilla *f* butter.

mantilla *f* mantilla (head covering for women); **~s** *fpl* baby clothes *pl*.

manto *m* mantle; cloak, robe.

mantón *m* shawl.

manual *adj* manual; * *m* manual, handbook.

manubrio *m* *Lat Am* handlebars *pl*.

manufactura *f* manufacture.

manufacturar *vt* to manufacture.

manuscrito *m* manuscript; * *adj* handwritten.

manutención *f* support, maintenance.

manzana *f* apple.

manzanilla *f* chamomile; chamomile tea; manzanilla sherry.

manzano *m* apple tree.

maña *f* handiness, dexterity, cleverness, cunning; habit, custom; trick.

mañana *f* morning; * *adv* tomorrow.

mañoso/sa *adj* skillful, handy; cunning.

mapa *m* map.

mapamundi *f* map of the world.

maquillaje *m* make-up; making up.

maquillar *vt* to make up; **~se** *vr* to put on make-up.

máquina *f* machine; (*rail*) engine; camera; (*fig*) machinery; plan, project.

maquinación *f* machination.

maquinador/ra *m/f* schemer, plotter.

maquinalmente *adv* mechanically.

maquinar *vt*, *vi* to machinate; to conspire.

maquinaria *f* machinery; mechanism.

maquinilla *f*: **~ de afeitar** razor.

maquinista *m* (*rail*) train driver; operator; (*mar*) engineer.

mar *m/f* sea.

maraña *f* shrub, thicket; tangle.

maravilla *f* wonder.

maravillar *vt* to astonish, to amaze; **~se** *vr* to be amazed, to be astonished.

maravilloso/sa *adj* wonderful, marvelous.

marca *f* mark; stamp; (*com*) make, brand.

marcado/da *adj* strong, marked.

marcador *m* scoreboard; scorer; *Lat Am* felt-tip pen.

marcar *vt* to mark; to dial; to score; to record; to set (hair); * *vi* to score; to dial.

marcha *f* march; running; gear; speed; (*fig*) progress.

marchar *vi* to go; to work; **~se** *vr* to go away.

marchitar *vt* to wither; to fade.

marchito/ta *adj* faded; withered.

marcial *adj* martial, warlike.

marciano/na *adj* Martian.

marco *m* frame; framework; (*sport*) goalposts *pl*.

marea *f* tide; **~ negra** oil slick.

marear *vt* (*mar*) to sail, to navigate; to annoy, to upset; **~se** *vr* to feel sick; to feel faint; to feel dizzy.

marejada *f* swell, heavy sea, surge.

mareo *m* sick feeling; dizziness; nuisance.

marfil *m* ivory.

margarina *f* margarine.

margarita *f* daisy.

margen *m* margin; border; * *f* bank (of river).

marginal *adj* marginal.

marginar *vt* to exclude; to leave margins on (a page); to make notes in the margin of.

marica *m* (*col*) sissy.

maricón *m* (*col*) queer.

marido *m* husband.

mariguana, marihuana *f* cannabis.

marimacho *f* (*col*) mannish woman.

marina *f* navy.

marinero/ra *adj* sea *compd*; seaworthy; * *m* sailor.

marino/na *adj* marine; * *m* sailor, seaman.

marioneta *f* puppet.

mariposa *f* butterfly.

mariquita *f* ladybug.

mariscal *m* marshal.

marisco *m* shellfish.
marital *adj* marital.
maritimo/ma *adj* maritime, marine.
marmita *f* pot.
mármol *m* marble.
marmóreo/rea *adj* marbled, marble *compd*.
marmota *f* marmot.
maroma *f* rope.
marqués *m* marquis.
marquesa *f* marchioness.
marrano *m* hog, boar; pig.
marrón *adj* brown.
marrullería *f* plausibility; plausible excuse; **~s** *fpl* cajolery.
marrullero/ra *adj* crafty, cunning.
marta *f* marten, sable.
Marte *m* Mars (planet).
martes *m invar* Tuesday.
martillar *vt* to hammer.
martillo *m* hammer.
mártir *m/f* martyr.
martirio *m* martyrdom.
martirizar *vt* to martyr.
marxismo *m* Marxism.
marxista *adj*, *m/f* Marxist.
marzo *m* March.
mas *adv* but, yet.
más *adv* more; most; besides, moreover; **a ~ tardar** at latest; **sin ~ ni ~** without more ado.
masa *f* dough, paste; mortar; mass.
masacre *m* massacre.
masaje *m* massage.
mascar *vt* to chew.
máscara *m/f* masked person; * *f* mask.
mascarada *f* masquerade.
mascarilla *f* (*med*) mask.
masculino/na *adj* masculine, male.
mascullar *vt* to mumble, to mutter.
masivo/va *adj* massive, en masse.
masoquista *m/f* masochist.
masticación *f* mastication.
masticar *vt* to masticate, to chew.
mástil *m* (*mar*) mast.
mastín *m* mastiff.
masturbación *f* masturbation.
masturbarse *vr* to masturbate.
mata *f* shrub; sprig, blade; grove, group of trees; mop of hair.
matadero *m* slaughterhouse.
matador/ra *adj* killing; * *m/f* killer; * *m* bullfighter.
matanza *f* slaughtering; massacre.
matar *vt* to kill; to execute; to murder; **~se** *vr* to kill oneself, to commit suicide.

matasanos *m invar* quack (doctor).
matasellos *m invar* postmark.
mate[1] *m* checkmate.
mate[2] *adj* matte.
matemáticas *fpl* mathematics; math.
matemático/ca *adj* mathematical; * *m/f* mathematician.
materia *m* matter, materials *pl*; subject.
material *adj* material, physical; * *m* equipment, materials *pl*.
materialidad *f* outward appearance.
materialismo *m* materialism.
materialista *m/f* materialist.
maternal *adj* maternal, motherly.
maternidad *f* motherhood.
materno/na *adj* maternal.
matinal *adj* morning *compd*.
matiz *m* shade of color; shading.
matizar *vt* to mix colors; to tinge, to tint.
matón *m* bully.
matorral *m* shrub, thicket.
matraca *f* rattle.
matricida *m/f* matricide (person).
matricidio *m* matricide (act).
matrícula *f* register, list; (*auto*) registration number; license plate.
matricular *vt* to register, to enroll.
matrimonial *adj* matrimonial.
matrimonio *m* marriage, matrimony.
matriz *f* matrix; womb; mold, form.
matrona *f* matron.
matutino/na *adj* morning.
maullar *vi* to mew.
maullido *m* mew (of a cat).
mausoleo *m* mausoleum.
máxima *f* maxim.
máxime *adv* principally.
máximo/ma *adj* maximum; top; highest.
mayo *m* May.
mayonesa *f* mayonnaise.
mayor *adj* main, chief; (*mus*) major; biggest; eldest; greater, larger; elderly; * *m* chief, boss; adult; **al por ~** wholesale; **~es** *mpl* forefathers.
mayoral *m* foreman.
mayordomo *m* steward.
mayoreo *m Lat Am* wholesale.
mayoría *f* majority, greater part; **~ de edad** coming of age.
mayorista *m/f* wholesaler.
mayormente *adv* principally, chiefly.
mayúsculo/la *adj* (*fig*) tremendous; * *f* capital letter.
maza *f* club; mace.
mazada *f* blow with a club.

mazapán *m* marzipan.
mazmorra *f* dungeon.
mazo *m* bunch, handful; club, mallet; bat.
mazorca *f* cob; corncob; ear.
me *pn* me; to me.
mear *vi* (*col*) to pee, to piss.
mecánica *f* mechanics.
mecánico/ca *adj* mechanical; * *m/f* mechanic.
mecanismo *m* mechanism.
mecanografía *f* typing.
mecanógrafo/fa *m/f* typist.
mecate *m* rope.
mecedora *f* rocking chair.
mecer *vt* to rock; to dandle (a child).
mecha *f* wick; fuse.
mechar *vt* to lard; to stuff.
mechero *m* (cigarette) lighter.
mechón *m* lock of hair; large bundle of threads/fibers.
medalla *f* medal.
medallón *m* medallion.
media *f* stocking, sock, average.
mediación *f* mediation, intervention.
mediado/da *adj* half-full; half-complete; a ~s de in the middle of.
mediador/ra *m/f* mediator; go-between.
medialuna *f Lat Am* croissant.
mediana *f* median strip.
medianero/ra *adj* dividing; adjacent.
mediano/na *adj* medium; middling; mediocre.
medianoche *f* midnight.
mediante *prep* by means of.
mediar *vi* to intervene; to mediate.
medias *fpl* pantyhose *pl.*
medicación *f* medication.
medicamento *m* medicine.
medicina *f* medicine.
medicinal *adj* medicinal.
médico/ca *adj* medical; * *m/f* doctor.
medida *f* measure.
medidor *m Lat Am* meter.
medio/dia *adj* half; a medias partly; * *m* middle; average; way, means; medium.
mediocre *adj* middling; moderate; mediocre.
mediocridad *f* mediocrity.
mediodía *m* noon, midday.
medir *vt* to measure; ~se *vr* to be moderate.
meditación *f* meditation.
meditar *vt* to meditate.
mediterráneo/nea *adj* Mediterranean; * *m*: el M~ the Mediterranean.
medrar *vi* to grow, to thrive, to prosper; to improve.

medroso/sa *adj* fearful, timid.
médula *f* marrow; essence, substance; pith.
medusa *f* jellyfish.
megafonía *f* public-address system.
megáfono *m* megaphone.
mejilla *f* cheek.
mejillón *m* mussel.
mejor *adj*, *adv* better; best.
mejora *f* improvement.
mejorar *vt* to improve, to ameliorate; to enhance; * *vi* to improve; (*med*) to recover, to get better; ~se *vr* to improve, to get better.
mejoría *f* improvement; recovery.
melancolía *f* melancholy.
melancólico/ca *adj* melancholy, sad, gloomy.
melena *f* long hair, loose hair; mane.
melenudo/da *adj* long-haired.
melindroso/sa *adj* prudish, finicky.
mella *f* notch in edged tools; gap.
mellado/da *adj* jagged; gap-toothed.
mellar *vt* to notch.
mellizo/za *adj*, *m/f* twin.
melocotón *m* peach.
melodía *f* melody.
melodioso/sa *adj* melodious.
melodrama *f* melodrama.
melón *m* melon.
melosidad *f* sweetness.
meloso/sa *adj* honeyed; mellow.
membrana *f* membrane.
membranoso/sa *adj* membranous.
membresía *f Lat Am* membership.
membrete *m* letterhead.
membrillo *m* quince; quince tree.
membrudo/da *adj* strong, robust; burly.
memorable *adj* memorable.
memorándum *m* notebook; memorandum.
memoria *f* memory; report; record; ~s *fpl* memoirs *pl.*
memorial *m* memorial; petition.
mención *f* mention.
mencionar *vt* to mention.
mendigar *vt* to beg.
mendigo/ga *m/f* beggar.
mendrugo *m* crust.
menear *vt* to move from place to place; (*fig*) to handle; ~se *vr* to move; to shake; to sway.
meneo *m* movement; shake; swaying.
menester *m* necessity; need; want; ~es *mpl* duties *pl.*
menesteroso/sa *adj* needy.
menestra *f* vegetable soup/stew.
menguante *f* decreasing.

menguar *vi* to diminish; to discredit.
menopausia *f* menopause.
menor *m/f* young person, juvenile; * *adj* less; smaller; minor; al por ~ retail.
menoría *f*: a ~ retail.
menos *adv* less; least; a lo ~/por lo ~ at least; * *prep* except; minus.
menoscabar *vt* to damage; to harm; to lessen; to discredit.
menoscabo *m* damage; harm; loss.
menospreciar *vt* to undervalue; to despise, to scorn.
menosprecio *m* contempt, scorn; undervaluation.
mensaje *m* message.
mensajero/ra *m/f* messenger; courier.
menstruación *f* menstruation.
mensual *adj* monthly.
menta *f* mint.
mental *adj* mental; intellectual.
mentar *vt* to mention.
mente *f* mind; understanding.
mentecato/ta *adj* silly, stupid; * *m/f* idiot.
mentir *vt* to feign; to pretend; * *vi* to lie.
mentira *f* lie, falsehood.
mentiroso/sa *adj* lying; * *m/f* liar.
menú *m* menu; set meal.
menudencia *f* trifle, small thing; minuteness; ~s *fpl* odds and ends *pl*.
menudillos *mpl* giblets *pl*.
menudo/da *adj* small; minute; petty, insignificant; a ~ frequently, often.
meñique *m* little finger.
meollo *m* marrow; (*fig*) core.
mequetrefe *m* good-for-nothing; busybody.
meramente *adv* merely, solely.
mercader *m* dealer, trader.
mercadería *f* commodity; trade; ~s *fpl* *Lat Am* merchandise.
mercadería *f* commodity; trade; ~s *fpl* merchandise.
mercado *m* market; marketplace.
mercancía *f* commodity; ~s *fpl* goods *pl*, merchandise.
mercantil *adj* commercial, mercantile.
mercenario/ria *adj* mercenary; * *m* mercenary; laborer.
mercería *f* dry goods store.
mercurio *m* mercury.
Mercurio *m* Mercury (planet).
merecedor/ra *adj* deserving.
merecer *vt* to deserve, to merit.
merecido/da *adj* deserved.
merendar *vi* to have tea; to have a picnic.
merengue *m* meringue.

meridiano *m* meridian.
meridional *adj* southern.
merienda *f* (light) tea; afternoon snack; picnic.
mérito *m* merit; worth, value.
meritorio/ria *adj* meritorious.
merluza *f* hake.
merma *f* waste, leakage.
mermar *vi* to waste, to diminish.
mermelada *f* jelly, jam.
mero *m* pollack (fish); ~/ra *adj* mere, pure.
merodeador *m* (*mil*) marauder.
merodear *vi* to pillage, to go marauding.
mes *m* month.
mesa *f* table; desk; plateau; ~ redonda round table.
mesada *f* *Lat Am* monthly installment.
meseta *f* meseta, tableland, plateau.
mesón *m* inn.
mestizo/za *adj* of mixed race; crossbred; * *m/f* half-caste.
mesura *f* gravity; politeness; moderation.
mesurado/da *adj* moderate; dignified; courteous.
meta *f* goal; finish.
metabolismo *m* metabolism.
metafísica *f* metaphysics.
metafísico/ca *adj* metaphysical.
metáfora *f* metaphor.
metafórico/ca *adj* metaphorical.
metal *m* metal; (*mus*) brass; timbre/timber (of the voice).
metálico/ca *adj* metallic.
metalurgia *f* metallurgy.
metamorfosis *f* *invar* metamorphosis; transformation.
meteoro *m* meteor.
meteorología *f* meteorology.
meter *vt* to place, to put; to insert, to put in; to involve; to make, to cause; ~se *vr* to meddle, to interfere.
metódico/ca *adj* methodical.
método *m* method.
metralla *f* (*mil*) shrapnel.
metralleta *f* submachine-gun.
métrico/ca *adj* metric.
metro[1] *m* meter.
metro[2] *m* subway.
metrópoli *f* metropolis; mother country.
mezcla *f* mixture; medley.
mezclar *vt* to mix; ~se *vr* to mix; to mingle.
mezquindad *f* meanness; pettiness; wretchedness.
mezquino/na *adj* mean; small-minded, petty; wretched.

mezquita *f* mosque.
mi *adj* my.
mí *pn* me; myself.
microbio *m* microbe.
microbús *m* minibus.
microchip *m* microchip.
micrófono *m* microphone.
microondas *m inv* microwave oven.
microplaqueta *f* microchip.
microscópico/ca *adj* microscopic.
microscopio *m* microscope.
miedo *m* fear, dread.
miel *f* honey.
miembro *m* member.
mientras *adv* meanwhile; * *conj* while; as long as.
miércoles *m invar* Wednesday.
mierda *f* (*col*) shit.
mies *f* harvest.
miga *f* crumb; ~s *fpl* fried breadcrumbs *pl*.
migaja *f* scrap, crumb.
migración *f* migration.
mijo *m* (*bot*) millet.
mil *m* one thousand.
milagro *m* miracle, wonder.
milagroso/sa *adj* miraculous.
milano *m* kite (bird).
milésimo/ma *adj*, *m* thousandth.
mili *f*: **hacer la** ~ (*col*) to do one's military service.
milicia *f* militia; military service.
miliciano *m* militiaman.
milímetro *m* millimeter.
militante *adj* militant.
militar *adj* military; * *m* soldier; * *vi* to serve in the army; (*fig*) to be a member of a party.
milla *f* mile.
millar *m* thousand.
millón *m* million.
millonario/ria *m/f* millionaire.
mimar *vt* to spoil, pamper.
mimbre *m* wicker.
mímica *f* sign language; mimicry.
mimo *m* caress; spoiling; mime.
mimoso/sa *adj* spoilt, pampered; delicate.
mina *f* mine; underground passage.
minar *vt* to undermine; to mine.
mineral *m* mineral; * *adj* mineral.
mineralogía *f* mineralogy.
minero/ra *m/f* miner.
miniatura *f* miniature.
minicadena *f* midi system.
minifalda *f* miniskirt.
mínimo/ma *adj* minimum.

ministerio *m* ministry.
ministro/ra *m/f* minister.
minoría *f* minority.
minucioso/sa *adj* meticulous; very detailed.
minúsculo/la *adj* minute; * *f* small letter.
minusválido/da *adj* (physically) handicapped; * *m/f* (physically) handicapped person.
minuta *f* minute, first draft; menu.
minutero *m* minute hand (of a watch/clock).
minuto *m* minute.
mío/mía *adj* mine.
miope *adj* short-sighted.
mira *f* sight of a gun; (*fig*) aim.
mirada *f* glance; gaze.
mirador *m* viewpoint, vantage point.
miramiento *m* consideration; circumspection.
mirar *vt* to look at; to observe; to consider; * *vi* to look; ~se *vr* to look at oneself; to look at one another.
mirilla *f* peephole.
mirlo *m* blackbird.
mirón/ona *m/f* spectator, onlooker, bystander; voyeur.
misa *f* mass; ~ del gallo midnight mass.
misal *m* missal.
misantropía *f* misanthropy.
misántropo/pa *m/f* misanthropist.
miserable *adj* miserable; mean; squalid (place); (*col*) despicable; * *m/f* rotter.
miseria *f* misery; poverty; meanness; squalor.
misericordia *f* mercy.
misil *m* missile.
misión *f* mission.
misionero/ra *m/f* missionary.
mismo/ma *adj* same; very.
misterio *m* mystery.
misterioso/sa *adj* mysterious.
mística *f* mysticism.
místico/ca *adj* mystic(al); * *m/f* mystic.
mitad *f* half; middle.
mitigación *f* mitigation.
mitigar *vt* to mitigate.
mitin *m* (political) rally.
mito *m* myth.
mitología *f* mythology.
mitológico/ca *adj* mythological.
mitones *mpl* mittens *pl*.
mixto/ta *adj* mixed.
mobiliario *m* furniture.
mochila *f* backpack.
mochuelo *m* red owl.

moción f motion.
moco m mucus; (col) snot.
moda f fashion, style.
modales mpl manners pl.
modalidad f kind, variety.
modelaje m Lat Am modeling.
modelar vt to model, to form.
modelo m model, pattern.
módem m modem.
moderación f moderation.
moderado/da adj moderate.
moderar vt to moderate.
moderno/na adj modern.
modestia f modesty, decency.
modesto/ta adj modest.
módico/ca adj moderate.
modificación f modification.
modificar vt to modify.
modisto/ta m/f dressmaker.
modo m mode, method, manner.
modorra f drowsiness.
modulación f modulation.
modular vt to modulate.
mofa f mockery.
mofarse vr: ~ de to mock, to scoff at.
moflete m fat cheek.
moho m rust; mold, mildew.
mohoso/sa adj moldy, musty.
mojar vt to wet, to moisten; ~se vr to get wet.
mojigato adj hypocritical.
mojón m landmark.
molde m mold; Lat Am pattern; model.
moldura f molding.
mole f bulk; pile.
molécula f molecule.
moler vt to grind, to pound; to tire out; to annoy, to bore.
molestar vt to annoy, to bother; to trouble; * vi to be a nuisance.
molestia f trouble; inconvenience; (med) discomfort.
molesto/ta adj annoying; inconvenient; uncomfortable; annoyed.
molinero m miller.
molinillo m: ~ de café coffee grinder.
molino m mill.
molusco m mollusk.
momentáneo/nea adj momentary.
momento m moment.
momia f mummy (as in Egyptian).
monacal adj monastic.
monaguillo m acolyte.
monarca m/f monarch.
monarquía f monarchy.

monárquico/ca adj monarchical; * m/f royalist, monarchist.
monasterio m monastery, convent.
monástico/ca adj monastic.
mondadientes m invar toothpick.
mondar vt to clean; to cleanse; to peel; ~se vr: ~ de risa (col) to split one's sides laughing.
mondo/da adj clean; pure; ~ y lirondo bare, plain; pure and simple.
moneda f money; currency; coin.
monedero m purse; Lat Am phone booth.
monería f funny face; mimicry; prank; trifle.
monetario/ra adj monetary, financial.
monitor m monitor.
monja f nun.
monje f monk.
mono[1] m monkey; ape.
mono[2] m coveralls pl, overalls pl.
mono/na[3] adj lovely; pretty; nice.
monólogo m monolog.
monopolio m monopoly.
monopolista m monopolist.
monosílabo/ba adj monosyllabic.
monotonía f monotony.
monótono/na adj monotonous.
monovolumen m people mover.
monstruo m monster.
monstruosidad f monstrosity.
monstruoso/sa adj monstrous.
monta f amount, sum total.
montaje m assembly; decor (of theater); montage.
montaña f mountain.
montañes/esa adj mountain compd; * m/f highlander.
montañoso/sa adj mountainous.
montar vt to mount, to get on (a bicycle, horse etc); to assemble, to put together; to overlap; to set up (a business); to beat, to whip (in cooking); * vi to mount; to ride; ~ a to amount to.
montaraz adj mountainous; wild, untamed.
monte m mountain; woodland; ~ alto forest; ~ bajo scrub.
montería f hunting, chase.
montés/esa adj wild, untamed.
montón m heap, pile; mass; a ~ones, abundantly, by the score.
montura f mount; saddle.
monumento m monument.
monzón m monsoon.
moño m bun; Lat Am bow.
moquillo m distemper (disease in dogs).
mora f blackberry.

morada *f* home, abode, residence.
morado/da *adj* violet, purple.
morador/ra *m/f* inhabitant.
moral[1] *m* mulberry tree.
moral[2] *f* morals *pl*, ethics *pl*; * *adj* moral.
moraleja *f* moral.
moralidad *f* morality.
moralista *m/f* moralist.
moralizar *vi* to moralize.
moralmente *adv* morally.
morar *vi* to inhabit, to dwell.
moratoria *f* moratorium.
mórbido/da *adj* morbid, diseased.
morboso/sa *adj* diseased, morbid.
morcilla *f* blood sausage, black pudding.
mordacidad *f* sharpness, pungency.
mordaz *adj* biting, scathing; pungent.
mordaza *f* gag; clamp.
mordedura *f* bite.
morder *vt* to bite; to nibble; to corrode, to eat away.
mordisco *m* bite.
moreno/na *adj* brown; swarthy; dark-skinned.
moribundo/da *adj* dying.
morigeración *f* temperance.
morir *vi* to die; to expire; to die down; ~se *vr* to die; (*fig*) to be dying.
morisco/ca *adj* Moorish.
moro/ra *adj* Moorish.
morosidad *f* slowness, sluggishness.
moroso/sa *adj* slow, sluggish; (*com*) slow to pay up.
morral *m* haversack.
morriña *f* depression; sadness.
morro *m* snout; nose (of plane etc).
morsa *f* walrus.
mortaja *f* shroud; cigarette paper.
mortal *adj* mortal; fatal, deadly.
mortalidad *f* mortality.
mortandad *f* death toll.
mortero *m* mortar (cannon).
mortífero/ra *adj* deadly, fatal.
mortificación *f* mortification.
mortificar *vt* to mortify.
mortuorio *m* mortuary.
moruno/na *adj* Moorish.
mosca *f* fly.
moscardón *m* botfly, hornet; (*col*) pest, bore.
moscatel *adj, m* muscatel.
moscón *m* (*col*) pest, bore.
mosquearse *vr* (*col*) to get cross; (*col*) to take offense.
mosquetero *m* musketeer.
mosquitero *m* mosquito net.

mosquito *m* gnat, mosquito.
mostaza *f* mustard.
mosto *m* must, new wine.
mostrador *m* counter, bar.
mostrar *vt* to show, to exhibit; to explain; ~se *vr* to appear, to show oneself.
mota *f* speck, tiny piece; dot; defect, fault.
mote *m* nickname.
motejar *vt* to nickname.
motín *m* revolt; mutiny.
motivar *vt* to motivate; to explain, to justify.
motivo *m* motive, cause, reason.
moto *f* (*col*) motor scooter, motorbike.
motocicleta *f* motorcycle.
motor *m* engine, motor.
movedizo/za *adj* movable; variable; changeable; fickle.
mover *vt* to move; to shake; to drive; (*fig*) to cause; ~se *vr* to move; (*fig*) to get a move on.
móvil *adj* mobile, movable; moving; * *m* motive; cellular phone.
movilidad *f* mobility.
movimiento *m* movement, motion.
mozo/za *adj* young; * *m/f* youth, young man/girl; waiter/waitress.
muchacho/a *m/f* boy/girl; * *f* maid(servant).
muchedumbre *f* crowd.
mucho/cha *adj* a lot of, much; * *adv* much, a lot; long.
muda *f* change of clothes.
mudable *adj* changeable, variable; mutable.
mudanza *f* change; move.
mudar *vt* to change; to shed, to molt; ~se *vr* to change one's clothes; to change house; * *vi* to change;
mudo/da *adj* dumb; silent, mute.
mueble *m* piece of furniture; ~s *mpl* furniture.
mueca *f* grimace, funny face.
muela *f* tooth, molar.
muelle *m* spring; regulator; quay, wharf.
muérdago *m* (*bot*) mistletoe.
muerte *f* death.
muerto *m* corpse; ~/ta *adj* dead.
muesca *f* notch, groove.
muestra *f* pattern; indication; demonstration; proof; sample; token; model.
mugido *m* lowing (of cattle).
mugir *vi* to low, to bellow.
mugre *m* dirt, filth.
mugriento/ta *adj* greasy; dirty, filthy.
mujer *f* woman.
mulato/ta *adj* mulatto.
muleta *f* crutch.

mullido/da adj soft; springy.
mulo/la m/f mule.
multa f fine, penalty.
multar vt to fine.
multimedia adj multimedia.
múltiple adj multiple; ~s many, numerous.
multiplicación f multiplication.
multiplicado m (math) multiplicand.
multiplicar vt to multiply.
multiplicidad f multiplicity.
multitud f multitude.
mundano/na adj worldly; mundane.
mundial adj worldwide; world compd.
mundo m world.
munición f ammunition.
municipio m town council; municipality.
municipal adj municipal.
muñeca f wrist; child's doll.
muñeco m scarecrow, puppet.
muñón m stump.
muralla f rampart, wall.
murciélago m bat (animal).
murmullo m murmur, mutter.
murmuración f backbiting, gossip.

murmurador/ra m/f detractor, backbiter.
murmurar vi to murmur; to gossip, to backbite.
muro m wall.
muscular adj muscular.
músculo m muscle.
muselina f muslin.
museo m museum.
musgo m moss.
música f music.
musical adj musical.
músico/ca m/f musician; * adj musical.
muslo m thigh.
mustio/tia adj parched, withered; sad, sorrowful.
musulmán/ana adj, m/f Muslim.
mutabilidad f mutability.
mutación f mutation, change.
mutilación f mutilation.
mutilar vt to mutilate, to maim.
mutuo/tua adj mutual, reciprocal.
mutuamente adv mutually.
muy adv very; too; greatly; ~ **ilustre** most illustrious.

N

nabo *m* turnip.

nácar *m* mother-of-pearl, nacre.

nacarado/da *adj* mother-of-pearl *compd*; pearl-colored.

nacer *vi* to be born; to bud, to shoot (of plants); to rise; to grow.

nacido/da *adj* born; recién ~ newborn.

nacimiento *m* birth; nativity.

nación *f* nation.

nacional *adj* national.

nacionalidad *f* nationality.

nacionalizar *vt* to nationalize; ~se to become naturalized.

nada *f* nothing; * *adv* no way, not at all, by no means.

nadador/ra *m/f* swimmer.

nadar *vi* to swim.

nadie *pn* nobody, no one.

nado *adv*: a ~ afloat.

naipe *m* (playing) card.

nalgas *fpl* buttocks *pl*.

naranja *f* orange.

naranjada *f* orangeade.

naranjal *m* orange grove.

naranjo *m* orange tree.

narciso *m* (*bot*) daffodil; narcissus (flower); fop.

narcótico/ca *adj* narcotic; * *m* drug, narcotic.

narcotraficante *m/f* drug trafficker.

nardo *m* (*bot*) spikenard, nard.

narigón/ona, narigudo/da *adj* big-nosed.

nariz *f* nose; sense of smell.

narración *f* narration.

narrar *vt* to narrate, to tell.

narrativa *f* narrative; story.

nata *f* cream.

natación *f* swimming.

natal *adj* natal, native.

natalicio *m* birthday.

natillas *fpl* custard.

natividad *f* nativity.

nativo/va *adj*, *m/f* native.

natural *m* temperament, natural disposition; native; inhabitant; * *adj* natural; native; common, usual; al ~ unaffectedly.

naturaleza *f* nature.

naturalidad *f* naturalness.

naturalista *m* naturalist.

naturalizar *vi* to naturalize; ~se *vr* to become naturalized; to become acclimatized.

naturalmente *adv* in a natural way; ¡~! of course!

naturópata *m/f* naturopath.

naufragar *vi* to be shipwrecked; to suffer ruin in one's affairs.

naufragio *m* shipwreck.

náufrago/ga *adj* shipwrecked.

nauseabundo/da *adj* nauseating.

náuseas *fpl* nauseousness, nausea.

náutica *f* navigation.

navaja *f* pocketknife, penknife; razor.

naval *adj* naval.

nave *f* ship; nave.

navegable *adj* navigable.

navegación *f* navigation; sea journey.

navegador *m* (*comput*) browser.

navegante *m* navigator.

navegar *vt*, *vi* to navigate; to sail; to fly.

navidad *f* Christmas.

navideño/ña *adj* Christmas *compd*.

navío *m* ship.

nazi *adj*, *m/f* Nazi.

neblina *f* mist; fine rain, drizzle.

nebuloso/sa *adj* misty; cloudy; nebulous; foggy; hazy; drizzling; * *f* nebula.

necedad *f* gross ignorance, stupidity; imprudence.

necesario/ria *adj* necessary.

neceser *m* toilet bag; carryall.

necesidad *f* necessity, need, want.

necesitado/da *adj* necessitous, very needy.

necesitar *vt* to need; * *vi* to want, to need.

necio/cia *adj* ignorant; stupid, foolish; imprudent; *Lat Am* stubborn.

necrología *f* obituary.

nectarina *f* nectarine.

néctar *m* nectar.

nefando/da *adj* base, nefarious, abominable.

nefasto/ta *adj* unlucky.

negación *f* negation; denial.

negado/da *adj* incapable, unfit.

negar *vt* to deny; to refuse; ~se *vr*: ~ a hacer to refuse to do.

negativo/va *adj*, *m* negative; * *f* negative; refusal.

negligencia *f* negligence.

negligente *adj* negligent; careless, heedless.

negociación *f* negotiation; commerce.

negociante *m/f* trader, dealer.

negociar *vt*, *vi* to negotiate.

negocio *m* business, affair; transaction; firm; place of business.

negro/gra *adj* black; dark; * *m* black; * *m/f* black person, Negro/Negress.

negrura *f* blackness.

negruzco/ca *adj* blackish.

nene *m*, **nena** *f* baby.

nenúfar *m* water lily.

neófito *m* neophyte.

Neptuno *m* Neptune (planet).

nervio *m* nerve.

nervioso/sa *adj* nervous.

neto/ta *adj* neat, pure; net.

neumático/ca *adj* pneumatic; * *m* tire.

neurona *f* neuron.

neutral *adj* neutral; neuter.

neutralidad *f* neutrality.

neutralizar *vt* to neutralize; to counter-act.

neutro/tra *adj* neutral; neuter; * *m Lat Am* neutral.

neutrón *m* neutron.

nevada *f* heavy fall of snow.

nevar *vi* to snow.

nevera *f* icebox.

nevería *f* ice-cream parlor.

nexo *m* link.

ni *conj* neither, nor.

nica *m/f Lat Am* (*col*) Nicaraguan.

nicho *m* niche.

nido *m* nest; hiding place.

niebla *f* fog; mist.

nieta *f* granddaughter.

nieto *m* grandson.

nieve *f* snow.

nigromancia *f* necromancy.

nimiedad *f* small-mindedness; triviality.

nimio/mia *adj* trivial.

ninfa *f* nymph.

ningún, ninguno/na *adj* no; * *pn* nobody; none; not one; neither.

niña *f* little girl; pupil (of eye).

niñera *f* nursemaid.

niñería *f* childishness; childish act.

niñero/ra *adj* fond of children.

niñez *f* childhood.

niño/ña *adj* childish; * *m/f* child; infant; **desde ~** from infancy, from a child; * *m* boy.

níspero *m* medlar.

nitidez *f* clarity; brightness; sharpness.

nitrato *m* (*chem*) nitrate.

nitrógeno *m* nitrogen.

nivel *m* level; standard; height; **a ~** perfectly level.

niveladora *f* bulldozer.

nivelar *vt* to level; to even up; to balance.

no *adv* no; not; * *excl* no!

noble *adj* noble, illustrious; generous.

nobleza *f* nobleness, nobility.

nocaut *m Lat Am* knockout.

noción *f* notion, idea.

nocivo/va *adj* harmful.

nocturno/na *adj* nocturnal, nightly; * *m* nocturne.

noche *f* night; evening; darkness; **¡buenas ~s!** good night!

Nochebuena *f* Christmas Eve.

Nochevieja *f* New Year's Eve.

nodriza *f* nurse.

nogal *m* walnut tree.

nómada *adj* nomadic; * *m/f* nomad.

nomás *adv Lat Am* just.

nombramiento *m* nomination; appointment.

nombrar *vt* to name; to nominate; to appoint.

nombre *m* name; title; reputation.

nomenclatura *f* nomenclature.

nómina *f* list; (*com*) payroll.

nominador *m* nominator.

nominal *adj* nominal.

nominativo *m* (*gr*) nominative.

non *adj* odd, uneven; * *m* odd number.

nonagenario/ria *adj* ninety-year-old; * *m/f* nonagenarian.

no obstante *adv* nevertheless, notwithstanding.

noquear *vt Lat Am* to thrash.

nor(d)este *adj* northeast, northeastern; * *m* northeast.

nórdico/ca *adj* northern; Nordic.

noria *f* water wheel; big wheel.

normal *adj* normal; usual.

normalizar *vt* to normalize; to standardize; **~se** *vr* to return to normal.

normar *vt Lat Am* to regulate.

noroeste *adj* northwest, northwestern; * *m* northwest.

norte *adj* north, northern; * *m* north; (*fig*) rule, guide.

nos *pn* us; to us; for us; from us; to ourselves.

nosocomio *m Lat Am* hospital.

nosotros/tras *pn* we; us.

nostalgia *f* homesickness.

nota *f* note; notice, remark; mark.

notable *adj* notable, remarkable.

notar *vt* to note; to mark; to remark; **~se** *vr* to be obvious.

notaría *f* notary profession; notary's office.

notario *m* notary.

noticia *f* notice; knowledge, information; note; **~s** *fpl* news.

noticiario *m* newsreel; news bulletin.
noticiero *m* news bulletin.
notificación *f* notification.
notificar *vt* to notify, to inform.
notoriedad *f* notoriety.
notorio/ria *adj* notorious.
novato/ta *adj* inexperienced; * *m/f* beginner; freshman.
novecientos/tas *adj* nine hundred.
novedad *f* novelty; modernness; newness; piece of news; change.
novela *f* novel.
novelero/ra *adj* highly imaginative.
novelesco/ca *adj* fictional; romantic; fantastic.
noveno/na *adj* ninth.
noventa *adj*, *m* ninety.
novia *f* bride; girlfriend; fiancée.
noviazgo *m* engagement.
novicio *m* novice.
noviembre *m* November.
novilla *f* heifer.
novillada *f* drove of young bulls; bullfight with young bulls and novice bullfighters.
novillo *m* young bull/ox.
novio *m* bridegroom; boyfriend; fiancé.
nubarrón *m* large cloud.
nube *f* cloud.
nublado/da *adj* cloudy; * *m* storm cloud.
nublarse *vr* to grow dark.
nublazón *m* Lat Am storm cloud.
nuca *f* nape (of the neck); scruff of the neck.

nuclear *adj* nuclear; * *vt* Lat Am to bring together.
núcleo *m* core; nucleus.
nudillo *m* knuckle.
nudo *m* knot.
nuera *f* daughter-in-law.
nuestro/tra *adj* our; * *pn* ours.
nuevamente *adv* again; anew.
nueve *adj*, *m* nine.
nuevo/va *adj* new; modern; fresh; * *f* piece of news; ¿qué hay de ~? is there any news?, what's new?
nuez *f* nut; walnut; Adam's apple; ~ moscada nutmeg.
nulidad *f* incompetence; (*law*) nullity; nonentity.
nulo/la *adj* useless; drawn; null.
numeración *f* numeration.
numerador *m* numerator.
numeral *m* numeral.
numerar *vt* to number.
numérico/ca *adj* numerical.
número *m* number; cipher.
numeroso/sa *adj* numerous.
nunca *adv* never.
nuncio *m* nuncio.
nupcial *adj* nuptial.
nupcias *fpl* nuptials *pl*, wedding.
nutria *f* otter.
nutrición *f* nutrition.
nutrir *vt* to nourish; to feed.
nutritivo/va *adj* nutritious, nourishing.
nylon *m* nylon.

#

ñato/ta *adj* snub-nosed.
ñoñería *f* insipidness.

ñoño/ña *adj* insipid; spineless; silly.

O

obcecación *f* obduracy.
obcecar *vt* to blind; to darken.
obedecer *vt* to obey.
obediencia *f* obedience.
obediente *adj* obedient.
o *conj* or; either.
oasis *m invar* oasis.
obelisco *m* obelisk.
obertura *f (mus)* overture.
obesidad *f* obesity.
obeso/sa *adj* obese, fat.
obispado *m* bishopric, episcopate.
obispo *m* bishop.
objeción *f* objection, opposition, exception.
objetar *vi* to object.
objetor *m* ~ de conciencia conscientious objector.
objetivo/va *adj, m* objective.
objeto *m* object; aim.
oblea *f* wafer.
oblicuo/cua *adj* oblique.
obligación *f* obligation; *(com)* bond.
obligar *vt* to force; ~se *vr* to bind oneself.
obligatorio/ria *adj* obligatory.
oblongo/ga *adj* oblong.
oboe *m* oboe.
obra *f* work; building, construction; play; por ~ de thanks to.
obrar *vt* to work, to operate; to put into practice; * *vi* to behave, to act; to have an effect.
obrero/ra *adj* working; labor *compd*; * *m/f* workman; laborer.
obscenidad *f* obscenity.
obsceno/na *adj* obscene.
obsequiar *vt* to lavish attention on; ~ con to present with.
obsequio *m* gift; courtesy.
obsequioso/sa *adj* obsequious, compliant; officious.
observación *f* observation; remark.
observador/ra *m/f* observer.
observancia *f* observance.
observar *vt* to observe; to notice.
observatorio *m* observatory.
obsesión *f* obsession.
obsesionar *vt* to obsess.
obstáculo *m* obstacle, impediment, hindrance.
obstar *vi*: ~ a, ~ para to oppose, to obstruct, to hinder.

obstetricia *f* obstetrics.
obstinación *f* obstinacy, stubbornness.
obstinado/da *adj* obstinate.
obstinarse *vr* to be obstinate; ~ en to persist in.
obstrucción *f* obstruction.
obstruir *vt* to obstruct; ~se *vr* to be blocked up, to be obstructed.
obtener *vt* to obtain; to gain.
obtuso/sa *adj* obtuse, blunt.
obús *m (mil)* shell.
obviar *vt* to obviate, to remove.
obvio/via *adj* obvious, evident.
ocasión *f* occasion, opportunity.
ocasional *adj* occasional.
ocasionar *vt* to cause, to occasion.
ocaso *m (fig)* decline.
occidental *adj* occidental, western.
occidente *m* occident, west.
océano *m* ocean.
ochenta *adj, m* eighty.
ocho *adj, m* eight.
ochocientos *m, adj* eight hundred.
ocio *m* leisure; pastime.
ociosidad *f* idleness, leisure.
ocioso/sa *adj* idle; useless.
ocre *m* ocher.
octavilla *f* pamphlet.
octavo/va *adj* eighth.
octogenario/ria *adj, m/f* octogenarian.
octubre *m* October.
ocular *adj* ocular; eye *compd*.
oculista *m/f* oculist.
ocultar *vt* to hide, to conceal.
oculto/ta *adj* hidden, concealed; secret.
ocupación *f* occupation; business; employment.
ocupado/da *adj* busy; occupied; engaged.
ocupar *vt* to occupy; to hold (an office); ~se *vr*: ~ de/~ en to concern oneself with; to look after.
ocurrencia *f* event; bright idea.
ocurrir *vi* to occur, to happen.
oda *f* ode.
odiar *vt* to hate; ~se *vr* to hate one another.
odio *m* hatred.
odioso/sa *adj* odious, hateful.
odontólogo/ga *m/f* dentist.
odorífero/ra *adj* odoriferous, odorous.
oeste *adj* west, western; * *m* west.
ofender *vt* to offend; to injure ~se *vr* to be vexed; to take offense.

ofensa *f* offense; injury.
ofensivo/va *adj* offensive, injurious.
ofensor *m* offender.
oferta *f* offer; offering.
oficial *adj* official; * *m* officer; official.
oficialismo *m Lat Am*: el ~ the Government.
oficialista *adj Lat Am* pro-government.
oficiar *vi* to officiate, to minister (of clergymen etc).
oficina *f* office.
oficio *m* office; employment, occupation; ministry; function; trade, business; ~s *mpl* divine service.
oficiosidad *f* diligence; officiousness; importunity.
oficioso/sa *adj* officious; diligent; unofficial, informal.
ofrecer *vt* to offer; to present; to exhibit; ~se *vr* to offer oneself; to occur, to present itself.
ofrecimiento *m* offer, promise.
ofrenda *f* offering, oblation.
ofrendar *vt* to offer, to contribute.
oftalmólogo/ga *m/f* ophthalmologist.
ofuscación *f* dimness of sight; obfuscation.
ofuscar *vt* to darken, to render obscure; to bewilder.
oídas *fpl*: de ~ by hearsay.
oído *m* hearing; ear.
oír *vt, vi* to hear; to listen (to).
ojal *m* buttonhole.
¡ojalá! *conj* if only!, would that!
ojeada *f* glance.
ojear *vt* to eye, to view; to glance.
ojera *f* bag under the eyes.
ojeriza *f* spite, grudge, ill-will.
okey *interj Lat Am* OK.
okupa *m/f (col)* squatter.
ojo *m* eye; sight; eye of a needle; arch of a bridge.
ola *f* wave.
oleada *f* surge; violent emotion.
oleaje *m* succession of waves, sea swell.
óleo *m* oil.
oler *vt* to smell, to scent; * *vi* to smell; ~ a to smack of.
olfatear *vt* to smell; (*fig*) to sniff out.
olfato *m* sense of smell.
oligarquía *f* oligarchy.
oligárquico/ca *adj* oligarchical.
olimpíada *f* Olympiad; las O~s the Olympics.
olímpico/ca *adj* Olympic.
oliva *f* olive.
olivar *m* olive grove.

olivo *m* olive tree.
olla *f* pan; stew; ~ podrida dish composed of different boiled meats and vegetables; ~ exprés/~ a presión pressure cooker.
olmo *m* elm tree.
olor *m* smell, odor; scent.
oloroso/sa *adj* fragrant; odorous.
olvidadizo/za *adj* forgetful.
olvidar *vt* to forget.
olvido *m* forgetfulness.
ombligo *m* navel.
omelet *f Lat Am* omelet.
omisión *f* omission.
omitir *vt* to omit.
omnipotencia *f* omnipotence.
omnipotente *adj* omnipotent, almighty.
once *adj, m* eleven.
onda *f* wave.
ondear *vi* to undulate; to fluctuate.
ondulado/da *adj* wavy.
oneroso/sa *adj* burdensome.
onomástico *m Lat Am* birthday.
opa *f* takeover bid.
opacidad *f* opacity; gloom, darkness.
opaco/ca *adj* opaque; dark.
opción *f* option, choice.
ópera *f* opera.
operación *f* operation; ~ de cesárea *f* cesarean section/operation.
operador/ra *m/f* operator; projectionist; cameraman/woman.
operar *vi* to operate; to act.
operativo *m Lat Am* operation.
opinar *vt* to think; * *vi* to give one's opinion.
opinión *f* opinion.
opio *m* opium.
oponente *m/f* opponent.
oponer *vt* to oppose; ~se *vr* to be opposed, ~ a to oppose.
oportunidad *f* opportunity.
oportunismo *m* opportunism.
oportuno/na *adj* seasonable, opportune.
oposición *f* opposition; ~ones *fpl* public examinations *pl*.
opositor/ra *m/f* opponent; candidate (in public examination).
opresión *f* oppression.
opresivo/va *adj* oppressive.
opresor *m* oppressor.
oprimir *vt* to oppress; to crush; to press; to squeeze.
optar *vt* to choose, to elect.
optativo/va *adj* optional.
óptica *f* optics.
óptico/ca *adj* optical; * *m/f* optician.

optimista *m/f* optimist.
óptimo/ma *adj* best.
opuesto/ta *adj* opposite; contrary; adverse.
opulencia *f* wealth, riches *pl*.
opulento/ta *adj* opulent, wealthy.
oración *f* oration, speech; prayer.
orador/ra *m/f* orator.
oral *adj* oral.
orangután *m* orang-utan.
orar *vi* to pray.
oratoria *f* oratory, rhetorical skill.
órbita *f* orbit.
orden *m/f* order; ~ **del día** order of the day.
ordenación *f* arrangement; ordination; edict, ordinance.
ordenado/da *adj* methodical; orderly.
ordenador *m* computer.
ordenanza *f* order; statute, ordinance; ordination.
ordenar *vt* to arrange; to order; to ordain; ~**se** *vr* to take holy orders.
ordeña *f Lat Am* milking.
ordeñar *vt* to milk.
órdenes sagradas *fpl* holy orders *pl*.
ordinal *adj* ordinal.
ordinario/ria *adj* ordinary, common; **de** ~ regularly, commonly, ordinarily.
orégano *m* oregano.
oreja *f* ear.
orejera *f* earflap.
orfanato *m* orphanage.
orfandad *f* orphanhood.
orgánico/ca *adj* organic; harmonious.
organigrama *m* flowchart.
organismo *m* organism; organization.
organista *m/f* organist.
organización *f* organization; arrangement.
organizar *vt* to organize.
órgano *m* organ.
orgasmo *m* orgasm.
orgía *f* orgy.
orgullo *m* pride, haughtiness.
orgulloso/sa *adj* proud, haughty.
orientación *f* position; direction.
oriental *adj* oriental, eastern; *Lat Am* Uruguayan.
orientar *vt* to orient; to point; to direct; to guide; ~**se** *vr* to get one's bearings; to decide on a course of action.
oriente *m* orient.
orificio *m* orifice; mouth; aperture.
origen *m* origin, source; native country; family, extraction.
original *adj* original, primitive; * *m* original, first copy.

originalidad *f* originality.
originar *vt, vi* to originate.
originario/ria *adj* original.
orilla *f* limit, border, margin; edge (of cloth); shore.
orín *m* rust.
orina *f* urine.
orinal *m* chamber pot.
orinar *vi* to pass water, urinate.
oriundo/da *adj*: ~ **de** native of.
ornamento *m* ornament, embellishment.
ornitología *f* ornithology.
oro *m* gold.
oros *mpl* diamonds *pl* (in cards).
orquesta *f* orchestra.
orquídea *f* orchid.
ortiga *f* (*bot*) nettle.
ortodoxia *f* orthodoxy.
ortodoxo/xa *adj* orthodox.
ortografía *f* orthography.
ortográfico/ca *adj* orthographic(al).
oruga *f* (*bot*) caterpillar.
orza *f* jar.
orzuelo *m* (*med*) stye,sty.
os *pn* you; to you.
osa *f* she-bear; **O**~ **Mayor/Menor** Great/ Little Bear.
osadamente *adv* boldly, daringly.
osadía *f* boldness, intrepidity; zeal, fervor.
osamenta *f* skeleton.
osar *vi* to dare, to venture.
óscar *m* Oscar.
oscilación *f* oscillation.
oscilar *vi* to oscillate.
oscurecer *vt* to obscure; to darken; * *vi* to grow dark; ~**se** *vr* to disappear.
oscuridad *f* obscurity; darkness.
oscuro/ra *adj* obscure; dark.
osificarse *vr* to ossify.
oso *m* bear; ~ **blanco** polar bear.
ostensible *adj* ostensible, apparent.
ostentación *f* ostentation, ambitious display, show.
ostentar *vt* to show; * *vi* to boast, to brag.
ostentoso/sa *adj* sumptuous, ostentatious.
ostra *f* oyster.
otitis *f* earache.
otoñal *adj* fall.
otoño *m* fall.
otorgamiento *m* granting; execution.
otorgar *vt* to concede; to grant.
otorrino/na, otorrinolaringólogo/ga *m/f* ear, nose and throat specialist.
otro/tra *adj* another; other.
ovación *f* ovation.

ovalado/da *adj* oval.
óvalo *m* oval.
ovario *m* ovary.
oveja *f* sheep.
overol *m Lat Am* coveralls *pl*.
ovillo *m* ball of wool.
ovíparo/ra *adj* oviparous, egg-bearing.

ovulación *f* ovulation.
óvulo *m* ovum.
oxidación *f* rusting.
oxidar *vt* to rust; ~se *vr* to go rusty.
óxido *f* (*chem*) oxide.
oxígeno *m* (*chem*) oxygen.
oyente *m/f* listener, hearer.

P

pabellón *m* pavilion; summer house; block, section.
pábilo *m* wick.
pacer *vt* to pasture, to graze.
paciencia *f* patience.
paciente *adj*, *m/f* patient.
pacificación *f* pacification.
pacificar *vt* to pacify, to appease.
pacífico/ca *adj* pacific, peaceful; * *m*: el P~ the Pacific.
pacotilla *f*: de ~ third-rate; cheap.
pactar *vt* to covenant; to contract; to stipulate.
pacto *m* contract, pact.
padecer *vt* to suffer; to sustain (an injury); to put up with.
padecimiento *m* suffering, sufferance.
padrastro *m* stepfather.
padrazo *m* loving, over-indulgent father.
padre *m* father; ~s *mpl* parents *pl*.
padrino *m* godfather.
padrón *m* census; register; pattern; model.
paella *f* paella (dish of rice with shellfish, meat etc).
paga *f* payment, fee.
pagadero/ra *adj* payable.
paganismo *m* paganism, heathenism.
pagano/na *adj*, *m/f* heathen, pagan.
pagar *vt* to pay; to pay for; (*fig*) to repay; * *vi* to pay.
pagaré *m* bond, note of hand, promissory note, IOU (I owe you).
página *f* page.
pago *m* payment; reward.
país *m* country; region.
paisaje *m* landscape.
paisano/na *adj* of the same country; * *m/f* fellow countryman/woman.
paja *f* straw; (*fig*) trash.
pajar *m* straw loft.
pajarita *f* bow tie.
pájaro *m* bird; sly, acute fellow.
pajarraco *m* large bird; cunning fellow.
paje *m* page.
pajita *f* (drinking) straw.
pajizo/za *adj* straw-colored.
pala *f* spade, shovel.
palabra *f* word; de ~ by word of mouth.
palabrota *f* swearword.
palaciego/ga *adj* pertaining/relating to the palace; * *m* courtier.

palacio *m* palace.
paladar *m* palate; taste, relish.
paladear *vt* to taste.
palanca *f* lever; tener ~ *Lat Am* to have connections.
palanca de cambios *f* gear shift.
palangana *f* basin; *Lat Am* wooden platter.
palco *m* box (in a theater).
paleta *f* bat; palette; trowel.
paleto/ta *m/f* rustic.
paliar *vt* to mitigate.
paliativo/va *adj*, *m* palliative.
palidecer *vi* to turn pale.
palidez *f* paleness, wanness.
pálido/da *adj* pallid, pale.
palillo *m* small stick; toothpick; ~s *mpl* chopsticks *pl*.
paliza *f* beating, thrashing.
palma *f* palm tree; palm of the hand; palm leaf.
palmada *f* slap, clap; ~s *fpl* clapping of hands, applause.
palmatoria *f* candlestick; cane.
palmear *vi* to slap; to clap.
palmera *f* palm tree.
palmeta *f* cane.
palmo *m* palm; small amount.
palmotear *vi* to slap; to applaud.
palmoteo *m* clapping of hands.
palo *m* stick; cudgel; blow given with a stick; post; mast; bat; suit (in cards); *Lat Am* tree.
paloma *f* pigeon, dove; ~ torcaz ring dove/wood pigeon; ~ mensajera carrier pigeon, homing pigeon.
palomar *m* pigeon house/loft.
palomilla *f* moth; wing nut; angle iron.
palomino *m* young pigeon.
palomitas *fpl* popcorn.
palpable *adj* palpable, evident.
palpar *vt* to feel, to touch.
palpitación *f* palpitation; panting.
palpitante *adj* palpitating; (*fig*) burning.
palta *f* avocado (pear).
paludismo *m* malaria.
palpitar *vi* to palpitate.
palurdo/da *adj* rustic, clownish, rude.
pampa *f* pampa(s), prairie.
pámpano *m* vine branch.
pamplina *f* trifle.
pan *m* bread; loaf.

pana *f* corduroy.
panacea *f* panacea, universal medicine.
panadería *f* baker's (shop).
panadero/ra *m/f* baker.
panal *m* honeycomb; sweet rusk.
pancarta *f* placard.
pancito *m Lat Am* bread roll.
panda *m* panda (bcar).
pandereta *f* tambourine.
pandilla *f* group; gang; clique.
panecito *m Lat Am* bread roll.
panegírico/ca *adj* panegyrical; * *m* eulogy.
panel *m* panel.
panfleto *m* pamphlet.
pánico *m* panic.
panorama *m* panorama.
panqueque *m Lat Am* pancake.
pantalla *f* screen; lampshade.
pantalón *m*, **pantalones** *mpl* pants *pl*, women's slacks *pl*.
pantano *m* swamp; marsh; reservoir; obstacle, difficulty.
pantanoso/sa *adj* swampy, marshy.
panteísta *f* pantheist.
panteón *m*: ~ **familiar** family tomb.
pantera *f* panther.
pantomima *f* pantomime.
pantorrilla *f* calf (of the leg).
pantufla *m* slipper.
panza *f* belly, paunch.
panzada *f* bellyful of food.
panzón/ona *adj Lat Am* big-bellied.
panzudo/da *adj* big-bellied.
pañal *m* diaper; ~ **desechable** disposable diaper.
paño *m* cloth; piece of cloth; duster, rag.
pañuelo *m* handkerchief.
papa *f* potato; * *m*: **el P~** the Pope.
papá *m* (*col*) pop, dad.
papada *f* double chin.
papagayo *m* parrot.
papal *adj* papal.
papanatas *m invar* (*col*) simpleton.
Papanicolau *m Lat Am* smear test.
paparrucha *f* piece of nonsense.
papaya *f* papaya, pawpaw.
papel *m* paper; writing; part, role (acted in a play); ~ **de estraza** brown paper; ~ **sellado** stamped paper.
papeleo *m* red tape.
papelera *f* writing desk; wastepaper basket.
papelería *f* stationer's (shop).
papeleta *f* slip of paper; ballot paper; report.
paperas *fpl* mumps.

papilla *f* baby food.
papista *m* papist.
paquete *m* packet; parcel; package tour.
par *adj* equal; alike; even; * *m* pair; couple; peer; **sin** ~ matchless.
para *prep* for; to, in order to; toward(s).
parabién *m* congratulations *pl*; felicitations *pl*.
parábola *f* parable; parabola.
parabólico/ca *adj* parabolic(al).
parabrisas *m invar* windshield.
paracaídas *m invar* parachute.
paracaidista *m/f* parachutist; (*mil*) paratrooper.
parachoques *m invar* fender; shock absorber.
parada *f* halt; suspension; pause; stop; shutdown; stopping place; ~ **a petición** flag stop; ~ **de autobús** bus stop.
paradero *m* halting place; term, end.
parado/da *adj* motionless; at a standstill; stopped; *Lat Am* standing (up); unemployed; * *m/f* unemployed person.
paradoja *f* paradox.
parador *m* parador, state-owned hotel.
parafrasear *vt* to paraphrase.
paráfrasis *f invar* paraphrase.
parágrafo *m Lat Am* paragraph.
paraguas *m invar* umbrella.
paraíso *m* paradise.
paraje *m* place, spot.
paralelo/la *adj*, *m* parallel.
paralítico/ca *adj* paralytic, palsied.
paralizar *vt* to paralyze; ~**se** *vr* to become paralyzed; (*fig*) to come to a standstill.
páramo *m* desert; wilderness.
parangón *m* paragon, model; comparison.
paranoico/ca *m/f* paranoiac.
parapente *m* paragliding.
parapeto *m* parapet.
parar *vi* to stop, to halt; * *vt* to stop, to detain; *Lat Am* to raise; **sin** ~ instantly, without delay; ~**se** *vr* to stop, to halt; *Lat Am* to stand up.
pararrayos *m invar* lightning conductor/rod.
parásito *m* parasite; (*fig*) sponger.
parasol *m* parasol.
parcela *f* piece of ground.
parche *m* patch.
parcial *adj* partial.
parcialidad *f* prejudice; bias.
parco/ca *adj* sober, moderate.
pardo/da *adj* gray.
parear *vt* to match, to pair, to couple.
parecer *m* opinion, advice, counsel; coun-

tenance, air, mien; * *vi* to appear; to seem; ~se *vr*: ~ a to resemble.

parecido/da *adj* resembling, like.

pared *f* wall; (*law*) ~ **medianera** party-wall.

pareja *f* pair, couple; a lumber/timber beam that serves as a support, brace.

parejo/ja *adj* equal; even.

parentela *f* parentage, kindred.

parentesco *m* relationship.

paréntesis *m invar* parenthesis.

parida *f* woman who has recently given birth.

paridad *f* parity, equality.

pariente/ta *m/f* relative, relation.

parir *vt* to give birth to; * *vi* to give birth.

parking *m* parking lot.

parlamentar *vi* to parley.

parlamentario/ria *m/f* member of parliament; * *adj* parliamentary.

parlamento *m* parliament.

parlanchín/ina *adj*, *m/f* chatterer, jabberer.

parlante *m Lat Am* speaker.

parlotear *vi* to prattle, to chatter, to gossip.

paro *m* unemployment; *Lat Am* strike.

parodia *f* parody.

parpadear *vi* to blink; to flicker.

párpado *m* eyelid.

parque *m* park; ~ **eólico** wind farm.

parque de bomberos *m* fire station, fire house.

parquímetro *m* parking meter.

parra *f* vine raised on stakes/nailed to a wall.

párrafo *m* paragraph.

parricida *m/f* parricide (person).

parricidio *m* parricide (act).

parrilla *f* grill; grille; *Lat Am* roof rack.

párroco *m* parish priest.

parroquia *f* parish; customers *pl*.

parroquial *adj* parochial.

parroquiano *m* parishioner; customer; ~/na *adj* parochial.

parsimonia *f* parsimony.

parte *m* message; report; * *f* part; side; party; **de ocho días a esta** ~ within these last eight days; **de ~ a** ~ from side to side, through and through.

partera *f* midwife.

partición *f* partition, division.

participación *f* participation.

participante *m/f* participant.

participar *vi* to participate, to partake.

partícipe *m/f* participant.

participio *m* participle.

partícula *f* particle.

particular *adj* particular, special; * *m* private individual; particular matter/subject.

particularidad *f* particularity.

particularizar(se) *vt* (*vr*) to particularize; to distinguish; to specify.

partida *f* departure; party; item in an account; parcel; game.

partidario/ria *adj* partisan; * *m/f* supporter.

partido *m* party; match; team.

Partido Democrático *m* Democratic Party.

Partido Republicano *m* Republican Party.

partidor *m* apportioner, divider.

partir *vt* to part; to divide, to separate; to cut; to break; * *vi* to depart; ~se *vr* to break (in two etc).

parto *m* birth.

parvulario *m* kindergarten.

pasa *f* raisin.

pasada *f* passage, passing; **de** ~ on the way, in passing.

pasadizo *m* narrow passage; narrow, covered way.

pasado/da *adj* past; bad; overdone; out of date; ~ **mañana** the day after tomorrow; **la semana pasada** last week; * *m* past.

pasador *m* bolt; hair slide; grip.

pasaje *m* passage; fare; passengers *pl*.

pasajero/ra *adj* transient; transitory; fugitive; * *m/f* traveler; passenger.

pasamanos *m invar* (hand)rail; banister.

pasamontañas *m invar* balaclava helmet.

pasaporte *m* passport.

pasar *vt* to pass; to surpass; to suffer; to strain; to dissemble; * *vi* to pass; to happen; ~se *vr* to go over (to another party); to go bad/off.

pasarela *f* footbridge; gangway.

pasatiempo *m* pastime, amusement.

Pascua *f* Passover; Easter.

pase *m* pass; showing; permit.

paseante *m* walker.

pasear *vt* to walk; *vi*, ~se *vr* to walk; to walk about.

paseo *m* walk; *Lat Am* trip; shopping mall.

pasillo *m* passage.

pasión *f* passion.

pasionaria *f* passionflower, granadilla.

pasivo/va *adj* passive.

pasmar *vt* to amaze; to numb; to chill; ~se *vr* to be astonished.

pasmo *m* astonishment, amazement.

pasmoso/sa *adj* marvelous, wonderful.

paso *m* pace, step; passage; manner of walking; flight of steps; accident; (*rail*) ~ **a nivel** grade crossing; **al** ~ on the way, in passing.

paso de peatones *m* crosswalk.
pasota *adj, m/f (col)* dropout; **ser un** ~ not to care about anything.
pasta *f* paste; dough; pastry; *(col)* dough, money; ~**s** *fpl* pastries *pl*; pasta; ~ **de dientes** toothpaste.
pastar *vt* to pasture, to graze.
pastel *m* cake; pie; pastel drawing; crayon.
pastelería *f* shop that sells cakes and pastries.
pasteurizado/da *adj* pasteurized.
pastilla *f* bar (of soap); tablet, pill.
pasto *m* pasture; *Lat Am* lawn, grass; **a** ~ abundantly.
pastor *m* shepherd; pastor.
pastoso/sa *adj* mellow,pleasant (voice); soft, doughy.
pata *f* leg (of animal/furniture); foot; **a la** ~ **coja** hopscotch (children's game); **a** ~ *(col)* on foot; **meter la** ~ to put one's foot in it.
patada *f* kick; *Lat Am* electric shock.
patalear *vi* to kick violently.
pataleo *m* act of stamping one's foot.
pataleta *f* fit, convulsion; swoon.
patán *m* clown; churl, surly person.
patata *f* potato.
patatús *m* dizzy spell, fainting fit.
paté *m* pâté.
patear *vt* to kick; to stamp on.
patente *adj* patent, manifest, evident; * *f* patent; warrant.
paternal *adj* paternal, fatherly.
paternidad *f* paternity, fatherhood.
paterno/na *adj* paternal, fatherly.
patético/ca *adj* pathetic.
patíbulo *m* scaffold; gallows.
patillas *fpl* sideburns *pl*.
patín *m* skate; runner.
patinaje *m* skating.
patinar *vi* to skate; to skid; *(col)* to blunder.
patinete *m* scooter (child's).
patio *m* courtyard; playground (in schools).
patizambo/ba *adj* knock-kneed.
pato *m* duck.
patochada *f* blunder, folly; nonsense.
patología *f* pathology.
patológico/ca *adj* pathological.
patón/ona *adj Lat Am (col)* clumsy.
patoso/sa *adj (col)* clumsy.
patraña *f* lie.
patria *f* native country.
patriarca *m* patriarch.
patriarcado *m* patriarchy.
patriarcal *adj* patriarchal.
patrimonial *adj* patrimonial.

patrimonio *m* patrimony.
patrio/tria *adj* native; paternal.
patriota *m/f* patriot.
patriótico/ca *adj* patriotic.
patriotismo *m* patriotism.
patrocinar *vt* to sponsor; to back, to support.
patrocinio *m* sponsorship; backing, support.
patrón/ona *m/f* boss, master/mistress; landlord/lady; patron saint; * *m* pattern.
patronal *adj*: **la clase** ~ management.
patronato *m* patronage, sponsorship; trust, foundation.
patronímico *m* patronymic.
patrulla *f* patrol.
patrullar *vi* to patrol.
patudo/da *adj Lat Am (col)* clumsy.
paulatino/na *adj* gradual, slow.
pausa *f* pause; repose.
pausado/da *adj* slow, deliberate; calm, quiet.
pausar *vi* to pause.
pauta *f* guideline.
pavesa *f* embers *pl*, hot cinders *pl*.
pavimento *m* sidewalk; paving.
pavo *m* turkey; ~ **real** peacock.
pavonearse *vr* to strut, to walk with affected dignity.
pavor *m* dread, terror.
pavoroso/sa *adj* awful, formidable.
payaso/sa *m/f* clown.
payo/ya *m/f* non-Gypsy (for a Gypsy).
paz *f* peace; tranquility, ease.
peaje *m* toll.
peal *m Lat Am* lasso.
peana *f* pedestal; footstool.
peatón *m* pedestrian.
peca *f* freckle; spot.
pecado *m* sin.
pecador/ra *m/f* sinner.
pecaminoso/sa *adj* sinful.
pecar *vi* to sin.
pecho *m* chest; breast(s) *(pl)*; teat; bosom; *Lat Am* breaststroke; *(fig)* courage, valor; **dar el** ~ **a** to breast-feed; **tomar a** ~ to take to heart.
pechuga *f* breast (of a fowl); *(col)* bosom.
pecoso/sa *adj* freckled.
peculiar *adj* peculiar; special.
pecuniario/ria *adj* pecuniary.
pedagogía *f* pedagogy.
pedagógico/ca *adj* pedagogic.
pedagogo/ga *m/f* pedagog.
pedal *m* pedal.
pedalear *vi* to pedal.
pedante *adj* pedantic; * *m/f* pedant.

pedantería *f* pedantry.
pedazo *m* piece, tidbit.
pedernal *m* flint.
pedestal *m* pedestal, foot.
pediatra *m/f* pediatrician.
pediatría *f.* pediatrics *pl.*
pedicurista *m/f Lat Am* podiatrist.
pedicuro/ra *m/f* podiatrist, chiropodist.
pedido *m* (*com*) order; *Lat Am* request.
pedir *vt* to ask for; to petition; to beg; to order; to need; to solicit; * *vi* to ask.
pedo *m* (*col*) fart; **tirarse un** ~ to fart.
pedrada *f* throw (of a stone).
pedregal *m* stony place.
pedregoso/sa *adj* stony.
pedrería *f* (collection of) precious stones *pl.*
pedrisco *m* hailstone.
pedrusco *m* rough piece of stone.
pegadizo/za *adj* clammy, sticky; catchy; contagious.
pegajoso/sa *adj* sticky, viscous; contagious; attractive.
pegamento *m* glue.
pegar *vt* to cement; to join, to unite; to beat; ~ **fuego a** to set fire to; * *vi* to stick; to match; ~**se** *vr* to intrude; to steal in.
pegatina *f* sticker.
pegote *m* adhesive tape, sticking plaster; intruder; hanger-on, (*col*) sponger.
peinado *m* hairstyle.
peinador/ra *m/f Lat Am* hairdresser.
peinar *vt* to comb; to style.
peine *m* comb.
peineta *f* convex comb for women.
peladilla *f* sugared almond, burnt almond; small pebble.
pelado/da *adj* peeled; shorn; bare; broke; * *m* (*col*) haircut.
peladura *f* peeling; plucking.
pelaje *m* fur coat; (*fig*) appearance.
pelapapas *m inv Lat Am* potato peeler.
pelar *vt* to cut (hair); to pluck (feathers); to peel; ~**se** *vr* to peel off; to have one's hair cut.
peldaño *m* step (of a flight of stairs).
pelea *f* battle, fight; quarrel.
pelear *vt* to fight, to combat; ~**se** *vr* to scuffle.
pelele *m* dummy; man of straw.
peletería *f* fur shop.
peletero *m* furrier.
peliagudo/da *adj* tricky; arduous, difficult.
pelícano *m* pelican.
película *f* film; pellicle.
peligrar *vi* to be in danger; ~ **de** to risk.

peligro *m* danger, peril; risk.
peligroso/sa *adj* dangerous, perilous.
pelirrojo/ja *m/f* redhead; * *adj* red-haired.
pellejo *m* skin; hide, pelt; peel; wine skin, leather bag for wine; oilskin; drunkard.
pelliza *f* fur jacket.
pellizcar *vt* to pinch.
pellizco *m* pinch; nip; small bit; (*fig*) remorse.
pelmo/ma, pelmazo/za *m/f* (*col*) pain (in the neck).
pelo *m* hair; pile; flaw (in precious stones).
pelón/ona *adj* hairless, bald.
pelota *f* ball.
pelotazo *m* blow with a ball.
pelotera *f* quarrel.
pelotero/ra *m/f Lat Am* baseball player.
pelotón *m* large ball; crowd; posse; (*mil*) platoon.
peluca *f* wig.
peluche *m*: **muñeco de** ~ soft toy.
peludo/da *adj* hairy.
peluquería *f* hairdresser's (premises); barber shop.
peluquero/ra *m/f* hairdresser; barber.
pelusa *f* bloom (on fruit); fluff.
pena *f* punishment, pain; **a duras** ~**s** with great difficulty/trouble.
penacho *m* tuft on the heads of some birds; crest.
penal *adj* penal; * *m Lat Am* penalty (kick).
penalidad *f* suffering, trouble; hardship; penalty.
penar *vi* to suffer pain; * *vt* to chastise.
pendencia *f* quarrel, dispute.
pendenciero/ra *adj* quarrelsome.
pender *vi* to hang; to be pending; to depend.
pendiente *f* slope, declivity; * *m* earring; * *adj* pending; unsettled.
pendón *m* standard; banner.
péndulo *m* pendulum.
pene *m* penis.
penetración *f* penetration; perception.
penetrante *adj* deep; sharp; piercing; searching; biting.
penetrar *vt* to penetrate.
penicilina *f* penicillin.
península *f* peninsula.
penique *m* penny.
penitencia *f* penitence; penalty, fine.
penitenciaría *f* penitentiary.
penitente *adj* penitent, repentant; * *m* penitent.
penoso/sa *adj* painful.
pensador/ra *m/f* thinker.

pensamiento *m* thought, thinking.
pensar *vi* to think.
pensativo/va *adj* pensive, thoughtful.
pensión *f* pension; guest-house; worry; regret.
pensionista *m/f* pensioner; lodger.
Pentecostés *m* Pentecost, Whitsuntide.
penúltimo/ma *adj* penultimate, last but one.
penumbra *f* half-light.
penuria *f* penury, poverty, neediness, extreme want.
peña *f* rock, large stone.
peñasco *m* large rock.
peñón *m* rocky mountain.
peón *m* (day)laborer; foot soldier; pawn (at chess).
peonía *f* (*bot*) peony.
peonza *f* spinning top.
peor *adj, adv* worse; **cada vez ~** worse and worse.
pepinillo *m* gherkin.
pepino *m* cucumber.
pepita *f* kernel; pip.
pepitoria *f* fricassee.
pequeñez *f* smallness, childhood, infancy; triviality.
pequeño/ña *adj* little, small; young.
pera *f* pear.
peral *m* pear tree.
percance *m* perquisite (perk); bad luck, setback.
percatarse *vr*: **~ de** to notice.
percepción *f* perception; notion.
perceptible *adj* perceptible, perceivable.
percha *f* coat hook; coat hanger; perch.
percibir *vt* to receive; to perceive, to comprehend.
percusión *f* percussion.
perder *vt* to lose; to waste; to miss; **~se** *vr* to go astray; to be lost; to be spoiled.
perdición *f* loss, losing; perdition, ruin.
pérdida *f* loss, damage; lost object.
perdido/da *adj* lost; stray.
perdigón *m* young partridge; **~ones** *mpl* buckshot, pellets.
perdiz *f* partridge.
perdón *m* pardon; mercy; ¡~! sorry!; excuse me!
perdonable *adj* pardonable.
perdonar *vt* to pardon, to forgive; to excuse.
perdurable *adj* perpetual, everlasting.
perdurar *vi* to last; to still exist.
perecedero/ra *adj* perishable.
perecer *vi* to perish, to die; to shatter (an object).
peregrinación *f* pilgrimage.

peregrinar *vi* to go on a pilgrimage.
peregrino/na *adj* (*fig*) strange; * *m/f* pilgrim.
perejil *m* parsley.
perenne *adj* perennial; perpetual.
perentorio/ria *adj* peremptory; urgent.
pereza *f* laziness, idleness.
perezoso/sa *adj* lazy, idle.
perfección *f* perfection.
perfeccionar *vt* to perfect; to complete, to finish.
perfecto/ta *adj* perfect; complete.
perfidia *f* perfidy.
pérfido/da *adj* perfidious.
perfil *m* profile.
perfilado/da *adj* well-formed, delicate (of features).
perfilar *vt* to outline; **~se** *vr*: **~ en** to show up against.
perforar *vt* to perforate; to drill; to punch a hole in; * *vi* to drill.
performance *m Lat Am* performance.
perfumador *m* perfumer.
perfumar *vt* to perfume.
perfume *m* perfume.
perfumería *f* perfumery.
pergamino *m* parchment.
pericia *f* skill, knowledge; expertise.
periferia *f* periphery; outskirts *pl*.
periférico *m* beltway, bypass, ring road.
perífrasis *f invar* periphrasis, circumlocution.
perímetro *m* perimeter; circumference.
periódico/ca *adj* periodical; * *m* newspaper.
periodista *m/f* journalist.
período, periodo *m* period; sentence; (*med*) menstrual period.
peripecia *f* vicissitude; sudden change.
peripuesto/ta *adj* dressed up, very spruce.
periquito *m* budgie, budgerigar.
perito/ta *adj* skillful, experienced; * *m/f* expert; skilled worker; technician.
perjudicar *vt* to prejudice, to damage; to injure, to hurt.
perjudicial *adj* prejudicial, damaging.
perjuicio *m* damage, harm.
perjurar *vi* to perjure, to swear falsely; to swear.
perjurio *m* perjury; false oath.
perjuro/ra *adj* perjured; * *m/f* perjurer.
perla *f* pearl; **de ~s** fine.
permanecer *vi* to stay; to continue to be.
permanencia *f* permanence; stay.
permanente *adj* permanent.
permiso *m* permission, leave, license.
permitir *vt* to permit, to allow.
permuta *f* permutation, exchange.

permutar *vt* to exchange, to permute.
pernera *f* trouser leg.
pernicioso/sa *adj* pernicious, destructive; wicked.
pernio *m* hinge.
perno *m* bolt.
pernoctar *vi* to spend the night.
pero *m* kind of apple; * *conj* but, yet.
perogrullada *f* truism, platitude.
perol *m* large metal pan.
perorata *f* harangue, speech.
perpendicular *adj* perpendicular.
perpetrar *vt* to perpetrate, to commit (a crime).
perpetuar *vt* to perpetuate.
perpetuidad *f* perpetuity.
perpetuo/tua *adj* perpetual.
perplejidad *f* perplexity.
perplejo/ja *adj* perplexed.
perra *f* bitch; (*col*) money.
perrera *f* kennel.
perro *m* dog.
persecución *f* persecution; toil, trouble; fatigue.
perseguidor *m* persecutor.
perseguir *vt* to pursue; to persecute; to chase after.
perseverancia *f* perseverance, constancy.
perseverante *adj* persistent.
perseverar *vi* to persevere, to persist.
persiana *f* (Venetian) blind.
persignarse *vr* to make the sign of the cross.
persistencia *f* persistence; steadiness.
persistir *vi* to persist.
persona *f* person; **de ~ a ~** from person to person.
personaje *m* celebrity; character.
personal *adj* personal; single; * *m* personnel.
personalidad *f* personality.
personarse *vr* to appear in person.
personero/ra *m/f Lat Am* spokesperson.
personificar *vt* to personify.
perspectiva *f* perspective; view; outlook.
perspicacia *f* perspicacity, clear-sightedness.
perspicaz *adj* perspicacious, clear-sighted.
persuadir *vt* to persuade; **~se** *vr* to be persuaded.
persuasión *f* persuasion.
persuasivo/va *adj* persuasive.
pertenecer *vi*: **~ a** to belong to; to appertain, to concern.
pertenencia *f* ownership; **~s** *fpl* possessions *pl*.

perteneciente *adj*: **~ a** belonging to.
pértiga *f* long pole/rod.
pertinacia *f* pertinacity; obstinacy, stubbornness.
pertinaz *adj* pertinacious; obstinate.
pertinente *adj* relevant; appropriate.
pertrechar *vt* to supply with ammunition and other warlike stores; to dispose; to arrange, to prepare; **~se** *vr* to be provided with the necessary defensive stores and arms.
pertrechos *mpl* tools *pl*, instruments *pl*; ammunition, fixings *pl*.
perturbación *f* perturbation; disturbance.
perturbado/da *adj* mentally unbalanced.
perturbador *m* disturber (of the peace).
perturbar *vt* to perturb, to disturb.
perversidad *f* perversity.
perversión *f* perversion; depravation, corruption.
perverso/sa *adj* perverse; extremely wicked.
pervertido/da *adj* perverted; * *m/f* pervert.
pervertir *vt* to pervert; to corrupt.
pesa *f* weight.
pesadez *f* heaviness, weight; gravity; slowness; peevishness, fretfulness; trouble; fatigue.
pesadilla *f* nightmare.
pesado/da *adj* peevish; troublesome; cumbersome; tedious; heavy, weighty.
pesadumbre *f* weightiness; gravity; quarrel, dispute; grief; trouble.
pésame *m* message of condolence.
pesar *m* sorrow, grief; repentance; **a ~ de** in spite of, notwithstanding; * *vi* to weigh; to repent; * *vt* to weigh.
pesario *m* pessary.
pesaroso/sa *adj* sorrowful, full of repentance; restless, uneasy.
pesca *f* fishing.
pescadería *f* fish market; shop that sells only fish.
pescado *m* fish (in general).
pescador *m* fisher, fisherman.
pescar *vt* to fish for, to catch (fish); * *vi* to fish.
pescuezo *m* neck.
pesebre *m* crib, manger.
peseta *f* peseta.
pesimista *m* pessimist.
pésimo/ma *adj* very bad.
peso *m* weight, heaviness; balance scales *pl*.
pespunte *m* back-stitching.
pesquero/ra *adj* fishing *compd*.
pesquisa *f* inquiry, examination.
pestaña *f* eyelash.
pestañear *vi* to blink.

pestañeo *m* blink.
peste *f* pest, plague, pestilence.
pesticida *m* pesticide.
pestífero/ra *adj* pestilential.
pestilencia *f* pestilence.
pestillo *m* bolt.
petaca *f* covered hamper; tobacco pouch.
pétalo *m* petal.
petardo *m* petard; cheat, fraud; imposition.
petate *m* straw bed; sleeping mat of the Indians; (*mar*) sailors' bedding on board ship; (*mar*) passengers' baggage; poor fellow.
petición *f* petition, demand.
peticionante *m/f Lat Am* petitioner.
peticionar *vt Lat Am* to petition.
peto *m* breastplate; bodice.
petrificar(se) *vt* (*vr*) to petrify.
petróleo *m* oil, petroleum.
petrolero/ra *adj* petroleum *compd*; * *m* (oil) tanker; (*com*) oil man.
petulancia *f* petulance; insolence.
petulante *adj* petulant; insolent.
peyorativo/va *adj* pejorative.
pez[1] *m* fish.
pez[2] *f* pitch.
pezón *m* nipple.
pezuña *f* hoof.
piadoso/sa *adj* pious; mild; merciful; moderate.
pial *m Lat Am* lasso.
pianista *m/f* pianist.
piano *m* piano.
piar *vi* to squeak; to chirp.
piara *f* herd (of cattle); flock (of sheep).
pibe/ba *m/f* boy/girl.
pica *f* pike.
picacho *m* sharp point.
picadero *m* riding school.
picadillo *m* minced meat.
picado/da *adj* pricked; minced, chopped; bad (tooth); cross.
picador *m* riding master; picador.
picadura *f* prick; puncture.
picaflor *m Lat Am* hummingbird.
picana *f Lat Am* goad.
picanear *vt Lat Am* to goad.
picante *adj* hot, spicy; racy.
picapedrero *m* stonecutter.
picaporte *m* door handle; latch.
picar *vt* to prick; to sting; to mince; to nibble; * *vi* to prick; to sting; to itch; ~se *vr* to be piqued; to take offense; to be moth-eaten; to begin to rot.
picardía *f* roguery; deceit; malice; lewdness.
picaresco/ca *adj* roguish; picaresque.

pícaro/ra *adj* roguish; mischievous, malicious; sly; * *m/f* rogue, knave.
picazón *f* itching; stinging; displeasure.
pichón *m* young pigeon.
pico *m* beak; bill, nib; peak; pick-ax.
picotazo *m* peck (of a bird).
picotear *vt* to peck (of birds).
picudo/da *adj* with a beak; sharp-pointed.
pie *m* foot; leg; basis; trunk (tree); foundation; occasion; **a ~** on foot.
piedad *f* piety; mercy, pity.
piedra *f* stone.
piel *f* skin; hide; peel.
pienso *m* fodder.
pierna *f* leg.
pieza *f* piece; room.
pigmeo/mea *m/f*, *adj* pigmy.
pijama *m* pajamas *pl*.
pila *f* battery; trough; font; sink; pile, heap; **nombre de ~** first name.
pilar[1] *m* basin.
pilar[2] *m* pillar, column; mainstay.
píldora *f* pill.
pileta *f* basin; swimming pool.
pillaje *m* pillage, plunder.
pillar *vt* to pillage, to plunder, to foray, to seize; to catch onto; to catch.
pillo/lla *adj*, *m* rascal, scoundrel.
pilotaje *m* pilotage.
piloto *m/f* pilot.
piltrafa *f* piece of meat that is nearly all skin.
pimentón *m* paprika.
pimienta *f* allspice; pepper, pimento.
pimiento *m* sweet pepper, pimiento.
pinacoteca *f* art gallery.
pináculo *m* pinnacle.
pinar *m* grove of pine trees.
pincel *m* paintbrush.
pincelada *f* dash with a paintbrush.
pinchar *vt* to prick; to puncture.
pinchazo *m* prick; puncture; (*fig*) prod.
pinchito *m* small snack.
pincho *m* thorn; snack.
pingajo *m* rag, tatter.
ping-pong *m* table tennis.
pingüe *adj* fat, greasy; fertile.
pingüino *m* penguin.
pino *m* pine tree.
pinta *f* spot, blemish; scar; mark (on playing cards); pint.
pintado/da *adj* painted, mottled; **venir ~** to fit exactly.
pintar *vt* to paint; to picture; to describe; to exaggerate; * *vi* to paint; (*col*) to count, to be important; ~se *vr* to put on make-up.

pintarrajear *vt* to daub.
pintarrajo *m* daub.
pintor/ra *m/f* painter.
pintoresco/ca *adj* picturesque.
pintura *f* painting.
pinza *f* claw; clothes peg; pincers *pl*; ~s *fpl* tweezers *pl.*
piña *f* pineapple; fir cone; group.
piñal *m Lat Am* pineapple plantation.
piñón *m* pine nut; pinion.
pío/pía *adj* pious, devout; merciful.
piojo *m* louse; troublesome hanger-on.
piojoso/sa *adj* lousy; miserable, stingy.
piola *f Lat Am* cord.
pionero/ra *adj* pioneering; * *m/f* pioneer.
pipa *f* pipe (for smoking); seed; sunflower seed.
pipí *m* (*col*): **hacer** ~ to have to go (urinate).
pique *m* pique, offense taken; rivalry; **echar a** ~ to sink a ship; **a** ~ in danger; **a** ~ **de** on the point of.
piquete *m* slight prick/sting; picket.
pira *f* funeral pyre.
piragua *f* canoe.
piragüismo *m* canoeing.
piramidal *adj* pyramidal.
pirámide *f* pyramid.
pirata *m* pirate.
piropo *m* compliment; flattery.
pirotecnia *f* fireworks *pl.*
pirueta *f* pirouette.
pisada *f* footstep; footprint.
pisar *vt* to tread, to trample; to stamp on (the ground); to hammer down; * *vi* to tread, to walk.
pisciano/na *adj Lat Am* Piscean (zodiac sign).
piscina *f* swimming pool; ~ **para niños** paddling pool.
Piscis *m* Pisces (zodiac sign).
piso *m* flat, apartment; tread, trampling; floor, pavement; floor, story.
pisotear *vt* to trample, to tread under foot.
pista *f* trace, footprint; clue.
pisto *m* thick soup/broth.
pistola *f* pistol.
pistolera *f* pistol holster.
pistolero/ra *m/f* gunman/woman, gangster.
pistoletazo *m* pistol shot.
pistón *m* piston; (musical) key.
pita *f* (*bot*) any plant of the family Agavaceae, with tall flowers and thick, fleshy leaves.
pitada *f Lat Am* (*col*) puff.
pitar *vt* to blow; to whistle at; * *vi* to whistle; to toot one's horn; to smoke.
pitillo *m* cigarette.

pito *m* whistle; horn.
pitón *m* python.
pitonisa *f* sorceress, enchantress.
pitorreo *m* joke; **estar de** ~ to be joking.
piyama *m/f Lat Am* pajamas.
pizarra *f* slate.
pizarral *m* slate quarry, slate pit.
pizarrón *m Lat Am* chalkboard.
pizca *f* mite; pinch.
placa *f* plate; badge; ~ **de matrícula** license plate.
placentero/ra *adj* joyful, merry.
placer *m* pleasure; delight; * *vt* to please.
plácido/da *adj* placid.
plaga *f* plague.
plagar *vt* to plague, to torment.
plagio *m* plagiarism.
plan *m* plan; design; plot.
plana *f* trowel; page (of a book); level; ~ **mayor** (*mil*) staff.
plancha *f* plate; iron; gangway; press-up.
planchar *vt* to iron.
planchuela *n* doorplate *f.*
planeador *m* glider.
planear *vt* to plan; * *vi* to glide.
planeta *m* planet.
planetario/ria *adj* planetary.
planicie *f* plain.
planificación *f* planning; ~ **familiar** family planning, birth control.
planilla *f Lat Am* form.
plano/na *adj* plain, level, flat; * *m* plan; ground plot; ~ **inclinado** (*rail*) dead level.
planta *f* plant; plantation.
plantación *f* plantation.
plantar *vt* to plant; to fix upright; to strike/ hit (a blow); to found; to establish; ~**se** *vr* to stand upright.
plantear *vt* to plan; to implant.
plantel *m Lat Am* team.
plantilla *f* personnel; insole of a shoe.
plantón *m* long wait; (*mil*) sentry.
plañir *vi* to lament, to grieve, to bewail.
plasmar *vt* to mold; to represent.
plasta *f* paste, soft clay; mess.
plástico/ca *adj* plastic; * *m* plastic; * *f* sculpture (the art of).
plata *f* silver; plate (wrought silver); cash; *Lat Am* money; **en** ~ briefly.
plataforma *f* platform; ~ **giratoria** (*rail*) turntable.
plátano *m* banana tree; plane tree.
plateado/da *adj* silvered; silver-plated.
platería *f* silversmith's (premises); trade of silversmithing.

plática f discourse, conversation.
platicar vi to converse.
platillo m saucer; ~s mpl cymbals pl; ~ volador/~ volante flying saucer.
platino m platinum; ~s mpl contact points pl.
plato m dish; plate.
platónico/ca adj platonic.
plausible adj plausible.
playa f beach.
playera f T-shirt; ~s fpl sneakers pl, tennis shoes pl.
plaza f square; place; office, employment; room; seat.
plazo m term; installment; expiry date.
pleamar f (mar) high water.
plebe f common people pl, populace.
plebeyo/ya adj plebeian; * m commoner.
plebiscito m plebiscite.
plegable adj pliable; folding.
plegar vt to fold; to plait.
plegaria f prayer.
pleitear vt to plead, to litigate.
pleito m contract, bargain; dispute, controversy, Lat Am debate; lawsuit.
plenamente adv fully; completely.
plenario/ria adj complete; full.
plenilunio m full moon.
plenipotenciario m plenipotentiary.
plenitud f fullness; abundance.
pleno/na adj full; complete; * m plenum.
pliego m sheet of paper.
pliegue m fold; plait.
plisado/da adj pleated; * m pleating.
plomero m plumber.
plomizo/za adj leaden.
plomo m lead; a ~ perpendicularly.
pluma f feather, plume.
plumaje m plumage; plume.
plumero m bunch of feathers; feather duster.
plumón m felt-tip pen; marker; down (feathers).
plural adj (gr) plural.
pluralidad f plurality.
Plutón m Pluto (planet).
población f population; town.
poblado m town; village; inhabited place.
poblador/ra m/f populator, founder.
poblar vt to populate, to people; to fill, to occupy.
pobre adj poor.
pobreza f poverty, poorness.
pocilga f pigpen.
pocillo m coffee cup.

pócima, poción f potion.
poco/ca adj little, scanty; few pl; * adv little; ~ a ~ gently; little by little; * m small part; little.
poda f pruning (of trees).
podadera f pruning knife.
podadora f Lat Am pruning knife.
podar vt to prune.
podenco m hound.
poder m power, authority; command; force; * vi to be able to; to possess the power of doing/performing.
poderío m power, authority; wealth, riches pl.
poderoso/sa adj powerful; eminent, excellent.
podiatra m/f Lat Am podiatrist.
podredumbre f putrid matter; grief.
podrido/da adj rotten, bad; (fig) rotten.
podrir vt to rot, to putrefy; ~se vr to rot, to decay.
poema m poem.
poesía f poetry.
poeta m poet.
poético/ca adj poetical.
poetisa f poetess.
poetizar vt to poetize.
polar adj polar.
polea f pulley; (mar) tackle-block.
polémica f polemic.
polémico/ca adj polemical.
polen m pollen.
policía f police; * m/f police officer.
polideportivo m sports center.
poligamia f polygamy.
polígamo m polygamist.
polígono m polygon.
polilla f moth.
polio f polio.
pólipo m polypus.
politécnico/ca adj polytechnic.
politeísmo m polytheism.
política f politics; policy.
político/ca adj political; * m/f politician.
póliza f written order; policy.
polizón m stowaway.
pollera f skirt.
pollería f poulterer's (shop).
pollo m chicken.
polo m pole; Popsicle™; polo; polo neck.
polución f pollution.
polvareda f cloud of dust.
polvera f powder compact.
polvo m powder, dust.
pólvora f gunpowder.

polvoriento/ta *adj* dusty.
polvorín *m* powder reduced to the finest dust; powder flask.
pomada *f* cream, ointment.
pomelo *m* grapefruit.
pómez *f*: **piedra ~** pumice stone.
pompa *f* pomp; bubble.
pomposo/sa *adj* pompous.
pómulo *m* cheekbone.
ponchar *vt Lat Am* to strike out.
ponche *m* punch.
poncho/cha *adj* soft, mild; * *m* poncho.
ponderación *f* pondering, considering; exaggeration.
ponderar *vt* to ponder, to weigh; to exaggerate.
ponedero/ra *adj* egg-laying; capable of being laid/placed; * *m* nest; nest egg.
poner *vt* to put, to place; to put on; to impose; to lay (eggs); **~se** *vr* to oppose; to set (of stars); to become.
poniente *m* west; west wind.
pontificado *m* pontificate.
pontífice *m* Pope, pontiff.
pontificio/cia *adj* pontifical.
pontón *m* pontoon.
ponzoña *f* poison.
ponzoñoso/sa *adj* poisonous.
popa *f (mar)* poop, stern.
populacho *m* populace, mob.
popular *adj* popular.
popularidad *f* popularity.
popularizarse *vr* to become popular.
populoso/sa *adj* populous.
poquedad *f* paucity, smallness; cowardice.
por *prep* for; by; about; by means of; through; on account of.
porcelana *f* porcelain, china.
porcentaje *m* percentage.
porción *f* part, portion; lot.
porcuno/na *adj* hoggish, piggish; porcine.
pordiosero/ra *m/f* beggar.
porfiar *vt* to dispute obstinately; to persist in a pursuit.
pormenor *f* detail.
pornografía *f* pornography.
poro *m* pore.
porosidad *f* porosity.
poroso/sa *adj* porous.
porque *conj* because; since; so that.
porqué *m* cause, reason.
porquería *f* nastiness, foulness; brutishness, rudeness; trifle; dirty action.
porqueriza *f* pigpen.
porra *f* cudgel.

porrillo: a ~ *adv* copiously, abundantly.
porrón *m* spouted wine jar.
portada *f* portal, porch; frontispiece.
portador/ra *m/f* carrier, porter.
portaequipajes *m invar* trunk (in car); baggage rack.
portal *m* porch; portal.
portaligas *m inv Lat Am* garter belt.
portamonedas *m invar* purse.
portarse *vr* to behave.
portátil *adj* portable; * *m* laptop.
portaaviones *m invar* aircraft carrier.
portavoz *m/f* spokesman/woman.
portazo *m* bang of a door; the act of banging a door in someone's face.
porte *m* transportation charges *pl*; deportment, demeanor, conduct.
portento *m* prodigy, portent.
portentoso/sa *adj* prodigious, marvelous, strange.
portería *f* porter's office; goal (sport).
portero/ra *m/f* porter; janitor; gatekeeper; goalkeeper.
portezuela *f* little door.
pórtico *m* portico, porch, lobby.
portilla *f*, **portillo** *m* aperture in a wall; gate; gap, breach.
portón *m* main door (of a house).
porvenir *m* future.
pos *prep*: **en ~ de** after, behind; in pursuit of.
posada *f* shelter; inn, hotel.
posaderas *fpl* buttocks *pl*.
posadero *m* innkeeper.
posar *vi* to sit, to pose; * *vt* to lay down (a burden); **~se** *vr* to settle; to perch; to land.
posdata *f* postcript.
pose *f* pose.
poseedor/ra *m/f* owner, possessor; holder.
poseer *vt* to hold, to possess.
poseído/da *adj* possessed by the devil.
posesión *f* possession.
posesivo/va *adj* possessive.
posesor/ra *m/f* possessor.
posibilidad *f* possibility.
posibilitar *vt* to make possible; to make feasible.
posible *adj* possible.
posición *f* position; posture; situation.
positivo/va *adj* positive.
poso *m* sediment, dregs *pl*.
posponer *vt* to postpone.
posta *f*: **a ~** on purpose.
postal *adj* postal; * *f* postal card, postcard.
poste *m* pole, post, pillar.
póster *m* poster.

postergación *f* missing out, passing over; putting over.

postergar *vt* to leave behind; to postpone.

posteridad *f* posterity.

posterior *adj* posterior.

posterioridad *f*: **con ~** subsequently, later.

postigo *m* postern; small door; shutter (of a window).

postizo/za *adj* artificial (not natural); * *m* wig.

postor *m* bidder at a public sale; better.

postración *f* prostration.

postrar *vt* to humble, to humiliate; **~se** *vr* to prostrate oneself.

postre *m* dessert.

postrer(o)/ra *adj* last, hindmost.

postrimerías *fpl* dying moments; final stages.

póstumo/ma *adj* posthumous.

postulante *m/f Lat Am* candidate.

postura *f* posture, position; attitude; bet, wager; agreement, convention.

potable *adj* drinkable.

potaje *m* pottage; drink made up of several ingredients; medley of various useless things.

pote *m* pot, jar; flower pot.

potencia *f* power; mightiness.

potencial *m* potential.

potentado *m* potentate; prince.

potente *adj* potent, powerful, mighty.

potestad *f* power; dominion; jurisdiction.

potrero *m Lat Am* pasture.

potro/ra *m/f* colt; foal.

poyo *m* stone seat/bench.

pozo *m* well.

práctica *f* practice.

practicable *adj* practicable, feasible.

practicante *adj* practicing; * *m/f* practitioner.

practicar *vt* to practice.

práctico/ca *adj* practical; skillful, experienced.

pradera *f* meadow.

prado *m* lawn; meadow.

pragmático/ca *adj* pragmatic.

preámbulo *m* preamble; circumlocution.

prebenda *f* prebend.

precampaña *f* run-up to an election campaign.

precario/ria *adj* precarious.

precaución *f* precaution.

precaver *vt* to prevent; to guard against.

precedencia *f* precedence; preference; superiority.

precedente *adj* preceding, foregoing.

preceder *vt* to precede, to go before.

precepto *m* precept, order.

preceptor/ra *m/f* master, teacher, preceptor.

preciado/da *adj* esteemed, valued.

preciarse *vr* to boast; **~ de** to take pride in.

precinto *m* seal.

precio *m* price; value.

preciosidad *f* excellence; preciousness.

precioso/sa *adj* precious; (*col*) beautiful.

precipicio *m* precipice; violent, sudden fall; ruin, destruction.

precipitación *f* precipitation, rush.

precipitado/da *adj* precipitate, headlong, hasty.

precipitar *vt* to precipitate; **~se** *vr* to act hastily; to rush.

precisamente *adv* precisely; exactly.

precisar *vt* to compel, to oblige; to need.

precisión *f* necessity, compulsion; preciseness.

preciso/sa *adj* necessary, requisite; precise, exact; abstracted.

precocidad *f* precocity.

preconizar *vt* to proclaim; to recommend.

precoz *adj* precocious.

precursor/ra *m/f* harbinger, forerunner.

predecesor/ra *m/f* predecessor.

predecir *vt* to foretell.

predestinación *f* predestination.

predestinar *vt* to predestine.

predicación *f* preaching; sermon.

predicado *m* predicate.

predicador *m* preacher.

predicar *vt* to preach.

predicción *f* prediction.

predilección *f* predilection.

predilecto/ta *adj* darling, favorite.

predio *m Lat Am* building.

predisponer *vt* to predispose; to prejudice.

predisposición *f* inclination; prejudice.

predominar *vi* to predominate, to prevail.

predominio *m* predominant power, superiority.

preeminencia *f* pre-eminence; superiority.

preeminente *adj* pre-eminent; superior.

preescolar *adj* pre-school.

preestreno *m* prevue.

preexistencia *f* pre-existence.

preexistente *adj* pre-existent.

preexistir *vt* to pre-exist, to exist before.

prefabricado/da *adj* prefabricated.

prefacio *m* preface.

prefecto *m* prefect.

prefectura *f* prefecture.

preferencia *f* preference.

preferible *adj* preferable.
preferir *vt* to prefer.
prefijar *vt* (*gr*) to prefix; to fix beforehand.
prefijo *m* dial code.
pregón *m* proclamation; hue and cry.
pregonar *vt* to proclaim.
pregonero *m* town crier.
pregunta *f* question; inquiry.
preguntar *vt* to ask; to question; to demand; to inquire.
preguntón/ona *m/f* inquisitive person.
prehistórico/ca *adj* prehistoric.
prejuicio *m* prejudgement; preconception; prejudice.
prelado *m* prelate.
preliminar *adj*, *m* preliminary.
preludio *m* prelude.
prematuro/ra *adj* premature.
premeditación *f* premeditation, forethought.
premeditar *vt* to premeditate, to think out.
premiar *vt* to reward, to remunerate.
premio *m* reward, recompense; premium.
premisa *f* premise.
premura *f* pressure, haste, hurry.
prenatal *adj* pre-natal.
prenda *f* pledge; garment; sweetheart; person/thing dearly loved; ~s *fpl* accomplishments *pl*, talents *pl*.
prendar *vt* to enchant; ~se *vr*: ~ de to fall in love with.
prendedor *m* brooch.
prender *vt* to seize, to catch, to lay hold of; to imprison; *Lat Am* to switch on; ~se *vr* to catch fire; * *vi* to take root.
prendimiento *m* seizure; capture.
prensa *f* press.
prensar *vt* to press.
preñado/da *adj* pregnant.
preñez *f* pregnancy.
preocupación *f* worry, preoccupation.
preocupado/da *adj* worried, anxious.
preocupar(se) *vt* (*vr*) to worry.
preparación *f* preparation.
preparador/ra *m/f* trainer.
preparar *vt* to prepare; ~se *vr* to be prepared.
preparativo/va *adj* preparatory; preliminary; qualifying; * *m* preparation.
preparatorio/ria *adj* preparatory.
preponderancia *f* preponderance.
preponderar *vi* to preponderate, to prevail.
preposición *f* (*gr*) preposition.
prepucio *m* foreskin.
prerrogativa *f* prerogative, privilege.
presa *f* capture, seizure; dike, dam.

presagiar *vt* to presage, to forebode.
presagio *m* omen.
presbítero *m* priest, clergyman.
presciencia *f* prescience, foreknowledge.
prescindir *vi*: ~ de to do without; to dispense with.
prescribir *vt* to prescribe.
prescripción *f* prescription.
presencia *f* presence.
presenciar *vt* to attend; to be present at; to witness.
presentación *f* presentation.
presentador/ra *m/f* (*rad*, *TV*) presenter; compere.
presentar *vt* to present; to introduce; to offer; to show; ~se *vr* to present oneself; to appear; to run (as candidate); to apply.
presente *m* present, gift; * *adj* present.
presentemente *adv* presently, now.
presentimiento *m* presentiment.
presentir *vt* to have a premonition of.
preservación *f* preservation.
preservar *vt* to preserve; to defend.
preservativo *m* condom, sheath; *Lat Am* preservative.
presidencia *f* presidency.
presidente/ta *m/f* president.
presidiario/ria *m/f* convict.
presidio *m* penitentiary, prison.
presidir *vt* to preside at.
presilla *f* clip; loop (in clothes).
presión *f* pressure, pressing; ~ de los neumáticos tire pressure.
presionar *vt* to press; (*fig*) to put pressure on.
preso/sa *m/f* prisoner.
prestado/da *adj* on loan; **pedir** ~ to borrow.
prestamista *m* borrower, lender.
préstamo *m* loan.
prestar *vt* to lend.
presteza *f* quickness; haste, speed.
prestigio *m* prestige.
presto/ta *adj* quick; prompt; ready; * *adv* soon; quickly.
presumible *adj* presumable.
presumido/da *adj* presumptuous, arrogant.
presumir *vt* to presume, to conjecture; * *vi* to be conceited.
presunción *f* presumption, conjecture; conceit.
presunto/ta *adj* supposed; so-called.
presuntuoso/sa *adj* presumptuous.
presuponer *vt* to presuppose.
presupuesto *m* estimate; budget.
presuroso/sa *adj* hasty, quick; prompt; nimble.

pretencioso/sa *adj* pretentious.
pretender *vt* to pretend, to claim; to try, to attempt.
pretendiente *m* pretender; suitor.
pretensión *f* pretension.
pretérito/ta *adj* past.
pretextar *vt* to plead, use as an excuse.
pretexto *m* pretext; pretense; plea, excuse.
prevalacer *vi* to prevail; to triumph; to take root.
prevención *f* disposition, preparation; supply of provisions; foresight; prevention; (*mil*) guardroom, guardhouse.
prevenido/da *adj* prepared; careful, cautious; foreseeing.
prevenir *vt* to prepare; to foresee, to know in advance; to prevent; to warn; ~se *vr* to be prepared; to be predisposed.
preventivo/va *adj* preventive.
prever *vt* to foresee, to forecast.
previo/via *adj* previous.
previsión *f* foresight, prevision; forecast.
previsor/ra *adj* far sighted.
previsivo/va *adj Lat Am* far-sighted.
prima *f* bonus; (female) cousin.
primacía *f* priority; primacy.
primado *m* primate.
primario/ria *adj* primary.
primavera *f* spring (the season).
primeramente *adv* in the first place, mainly.
primer(o)/ra *adj* first; prior; former; * *adv* first; rather, sooner.
primicias *fpl* first fruits *pl*.
primitivo/va *adj* primitive; original.
primo/ma *m* cousin.
primogénito/ta *adj, m/f* first-born.
primogenitura *f* primogeniture.
primor *m* beauty; dexterity, ability.
primordial *adj* basic, fundamental.
primoroso/sa *adj* neat, elegant; fine, excellent; handsome.
princesa *f* princess.
principal *adj, m* principal, chief.
príncipe *m* prince.
principiante *m* beginner, learner.
principiar *vt, vi* to commence, to begin.
principio *m* beginning, commencement; principle.
pringoso/sa *adj* greasy; sticky.
pringue *m/f* grease; lard, fat.
prioridad *f* priority.
prisa *f* speed; hurry; urgency; promptness.
prisión *f* prison; imprisonment.
prisionero *m* prisoner.
prisma *m* prism.

prismáticos *mpl* binoculars *pl*.
privación *f* deprivation, want.
privado/da *adj* private; particular.
privar *vt* to deprive; to prohibit; ~se *vr* to deprive oneself.
privativo/va *adj* private, one's own; particular, peculiar.
privilegiado/da *adj* privileged; very good.
privilegiar *vt* to privilege.
privilegio *m* privilege.
pro *m/f* profit; benefit; advantage.
proa *f* (*mar*) prow.
probabilidad *f* probability, likelihood.
probable *adj* probable, likely.
probado/da *adj* proved, tried.
probador *m* fitting room.
probar *vt* to try; to prove; to taste; * *vi* to try.
probeta *f* test tube.
problema *m* problem.
problemático/ca *adj* problematic.
procedencia *m* derivation.
procedente *adj* reasonable; proper; ~ de coming from.
proceder *m* procedure; * *vi* to proceed, to go on; to act.
procedimiento *m* proceeding; legal procedure.
procesado/da *m/f* accused.
procesador *m*: ~ de textos word processor.
procesar *vt* to put on trial.
procesión *f* procession.
proceso *m* process; lawsuit.
proclama *f* proclamation, publication.
proclamación *f* proclamation; acclamation.
proclamar *vt* to proclaim.
procreación *f* procreation, generation.
procrear *vt* to procreate, to generate.
procura *f Lat Am* search.
procurador/ra *m/f* procurer; attorney; solicitor.
procurar *vt* to try; to obtain; to produce.
prodigalidad *f* plenty, abundance.
prodigar *vt* to waste, to lavish.
prodigio *m* prodigy; monster.
prodigioso/sa *adj* prodigious, monstrous; exquisite; excellent.
pródigo/ga *adj* prodigal.
producción *f* production.
producir *vt* to produce; (*law*) to produce as evidence; ~se *vr* to come about; to arise; to be made; to break out.
productividad *f* productivity.
productivo/va *adj* productive.
producto *m* product.

productor/ra adj productive; * m/f producer.
proeza f prowess, valor, bravery.
profanación f desecration.
profanar vt to profane, to desecrate.
profano/na adj profane.
profecía f prophecy.
profesar vt to profess, to practice.
profesión f profession.
profesional adj, m/f professional.
profeso/sa adj professed.
profesor/ra m/f teacher; lecturer.
profesorado m teaching profession.
profeta m prophet.
profético/ca adj prophetic.
profetizar vt to prophesy.
prófugo/ga m/f fugitive.
profundidad f profundity, profoundness; depth; grandeur.
profundizar vt to go deeply into; to deepen; to penetrate.
profundo/da adj profound.
profusamente adv profusely.
profusión f profusion; prodigality.
progenie f progeny, offspring; race; generation.
progenitor m progenitor, ancestor, forefather.
programa m program.
programación f computer programing.
programador/ra m/f programer.
programar vt to program.
progresar vi to progress.
progresión f progression.
progresista adj, m/f progressive.
progreso m progress.
progresivo/va adj progressive.
prohibición f prohibition, ban.
prohibir vt to prohibit, to forbid; to hinder.
prójimo m fellow creature; neighbor.
prole f offspring, progeny; race.
proletariado m proletariat.
proletario/ria adj proletarian.
proliferación f proliferation.
proliferar vi to proliferate.
prolífico/ca adj prolific.
prolijidad f prolixity; minute attention to detail.
prolijo/ja adj long-winded; tedious.
prólogo m prolog.
prolongación f prolongation.
prolongar vt to prolong.
promedio m average; middle.
promesa f promise.
prometer vt to promise; to assure; ~se vr to become engaged.

prometido/da adj promised; engaged; * m/f fiancé/fiancée.
prominencia f protuberance.
prominente adj prominent, jutting out.
promiscuo/cua adj promiscuous; confusedly mingled; ambiguous.
promoción f promotion.
promontorio m promontory, cape.
promotor m promoter.
promover vt to promote, to advance; to stir up.
promulgación f promulgation.
promulgar vt to promulgate, to publish.
pronombre m (gr) pronoun.
pronosticar vt to predict, to foretell; to conjecture.
pronóstico m prediction; forecast.
prontitud f promptness.
pronto/ta adj prompt; ready; * adv promptly.
pronunciación f pronunciation.
pronunciamiento m (law) publication; insurrection, sedition.
pronunciar vt to pronounce; to deliver; ~se vr to rebel.
propagación f propagation; extension.
propagador/ra m/f propagator.
propaganda f propaganda; advertising.
propagar vt to propagate.
propasar vt to go beyond, to exceed.
propender vi to incline.
propensión f propensity, inclination.
propenso/sa adj prone, inclined.
propiamente adv properly; really.
propiciar vt to favor; to cause.
propiciatorio/ria adj propitiatory.
propicio/cia adj propitious.
propiedad f property, possessions pl; right of property; propriety.
propietario/ria adj proprietary; * m/f proprietor.
propina f tip.
propinar vt to hit; to give.
propio/pia adj proper; own; typical; very.
proponer vt to propose.
proporción f proportion; symmetry.
proporcionado/da adj proportionate; fit; **bien** ~ well-proportioned.
proporcional adj proportional.
proporcionar vt to provide; to adjust, to adapt.
proposición f proposition.
propósito m aim, purpose; **a** ~ on purpose.
propuesta f proposal, offer; representation.
propulsar vt to propel; (fig) to promote.

prórroga *f* prolongation; extension; extra time.
prorrogable *adj* extendable.
prorrogar *vt* to extend; to postpone.
prorrumpir *vi* to break forth, to burst forth.
prosa *f* prose.
prosaico/ca *adj* prosaic.
proscribir *vt* to proscribe, to outlaw.
proscripción *f* proscription.
proscrito/ta *adj* banned.
prosecución *f* continuation.
proseguir *vt* to continue; * *vi* to continue, to go on.
prospección *f* exploration; prospecting.
prospecto *m* prospectus.
prosperar *vi* to prosper, to thrive.
prosperidad *f* prosperity.
próspero/ra *adj* prosperous.
prostíbulo *m* brothel.
prostitución *f* prostitution.
prostituir *vt* to prostitute.
prostituta *f* prostitute.
protagonista *m/f* protagonist.
protagonizar *vt* to take the chief role in.
protección *f* protection.
protector *m* to protect.
proteger *vt* protector.
proteína *f* protein.
protesta *f* protest.
protestante *m/f* Protestant.
protestar *vt* to protest; to make a public declaration (of faith); * *vi* to protest.
protocolo *m* protocol.
prototipo *m* prototype.
provecho *m* profit; advantage.
provechoso/sa *adj* profitable; advantageous.
proveedor/ra *m/f* purveyor.
proveer *vt* to provide; to provision; to decree.
provenir *vi* to arise, to originate; to issue.
proverbial *adj* proverbial.
proverbio *m* proverb; ~s *mpl* Book of Proverbs.
providencia *f* providence; foresight; divine providence.
providencial *adj* providential.
provincia *f* province.
provincial *adj, m* provincial.
provinciano/na *adj* provincial; country *compd*.
provisión *f* provision; store.
provisional *adj* provisional.
provisionalmente *adv* provisionally.
provisorio/ria *adj Lat Am* provisional.

provocación *f* provocation.
provocador/ra *adj* provocative.
provocar *vt* to provoke; to lead to; to excite.
provocativo/va *adj* provocative.
próximamente *adv* soon.
proximidad *f* proximity, closeness.
próximo/ma *adj* next; neighboring; close, nearby.
proyección *f* projection; showing; influence.
proyectar *vt* to throw; to cast; to screen; to plan.
proyectil *m* projectile, missile.
proyecto *m* plan; project.
proyector *m* projector.
prudencia *f* prudence, wisdom.
prudente *adj* prudent.
prueba *f* proof; reason; argument; token; experiment; essay; attempt; relish, taste.
prurito *m* itching.
psicoanálisis *m* psychoanalysis.
psicoanalista *m/f* psychoanalyst.
psicología *f* psychology.
psicólogo/ga *m/f* psychologist.
psiquiatra *m/f* psychiatrist.
psiquiátrico/ca *adj* psychiatric.
psíquico/ca *adj* psychic(al).
púa *f* sharp point, prickle; shoot; pick.
pubertad *f* puberty.
publicación *f* publication.
publicar *vt* to publish; to make public.
publicidad *f* publicity.
público/ca *adj* public; * *m* public; audience; crowd.
puchero *m* pot; stew.
púdico/ca *adj* chaste, pure.
pudiente *adj* rich, opulent.
pudor *m* bashfulness.
pudrir *vt* to rot, to putrefy; ~se *vr* to decay, to rot.
pueblo *m* people *pl*; town, village; population; populace.
puente *m* bridge.
puenting *m* bungee-jumping.
puerco/ca *adj* nasty; filthy, dirty; rude, coarse; * *m* hog, pig; ~ espín porcupine.
pueril *adj* childish; puerile.
puerilidad *f* puerility.
puerro *m* leek.
puerta *f* door; doorway; gateway; ~ trasera back door.
puerto *m* port, harbor; haven; pass; narrow pass.
pues *adv* then; therefore; well; ¡~! well, then!
puesto *m* place; particular spot; post, employment; barracks *pl*; stand.

púgil *m* boxer.
pugilato *m* boxing.
pugna *f* combat, battle.
pugnar *vi* to fight, to combat; to struggle.
pujante *adj* powerful, strong; robust; stout, strapping.
pujanza *f* power, strength.
pujar *vt* to outbid; to strain.
pulcritud *f* beauty.
pulcro/cra *adj* beautiful; affected.
pulga *f* flea; **tener malas ~s** to be easily piqued; to be ill-tempered.
pulgada *f* inch.
pulgar *m* thumb.
pulir *vt* to polish; to put the last touches to.
pulla *f* smart repartee; obscene expression.
pulmón *m* lung.
pulmonía *f* pneumonia.
pulpa *f* pulp; soft part (of fruit).
pulpería *f* small grocery shop.
púlpito *m* pulpit.
pulpo *m* octopus.
pulsación *f* pulsation.
pulsador *m* push button.
pulsar *vt* to touch; to play; to press.
pulsera *f* bracelet.
pulso *m* pulse; wrist; firmness/steadiness of the hand.
pulular *vi* to swarm.
pulverización *f* pulverization.
pulverizador *m* spray gun.
pulverizar *vt* to pulverize.
puna *f* (*med*) mountain sickness.
pungir *vt* to punch, to prick.
punición *f* punishment, chastisement.
punitivo/va *adj* punitive.
punta *f* point; end; trace.
puntada *f* stitch.
puntaje *m* Lat Am grade.
puntal *m* prop, stay; buttress.
puntapié *m* kick.
puntear *vt* to tick; to pluck (the guitar); to stitch.
puntería *f* aiming.
puntero *m* pointer; **~/ra** *adj* leading.
puntiagudo/da *adj* sharp-pointed.

puntilla *f* narrow lace edging; **de ~s** on tiptoe.
punto *m* point; end; spot; stitch.
puntuación *f* punctuation.
puntual *adj* punctual; exact; reliable.
puntualidad *f* punctuality.
puntualizar *vt* to fix; to specify.
puntuar *vt* to punctuate; to evaluate.
punzada *f* prick; sting; pain; compunction.
punzante *adj* sharp.
punzar *vt* to punch; to prick; to sting.
punzón *m* punch.
puñado *m* handful.
puñal *m* dagger.
puñalada *f* stab.
puñetazo *m* punch.
puño *m* fist; handful; wrist-band; cuff; handle.
pupila *f* pupil (of eye).
pupitre *m* desk.
puré *m* puree; (thick) soup; **~ de patatas** mashed potatoes *pl*.
pureza *f* purity, chastity.
purga *f* purge.
purgante *m* purgative.
purgar *vt* to purge; to purify; to atone, to expiate.
purgativo/va *adj* purgative, purging.
purgatorio *m* purgatory.
purificación *f* purification.
purificador/ra *m/f* purifier; * *adj* purifying.
purificar *vt* to purify.
purismo *m* purism.
purista *m* purist.
puritano/na *adj* puritanical; * *m/f* Puritan.
puro/ra *adj* pure; mere; clear; genuine.
púrpura *f* purple.
purpúreo/rea *adj* purple.
purulento/ta *adj* purulent.
pus *m* pus.
pusilánime *adj* pusillanimous, fainthearted.
pusilanimidad *f* pusillanimity.
pústula *f* pustule, pimple.
puta *f* whore.
putrefacción *f* putrefaction.
pútrido/da *adj* putrid, rotten.

Q

que *pn* that; who; which; what; * *conj* that; than.

qué *adj* what, which, * *pn* what; which.

quebrada *f* broken, uneven ground; *Lat Am* stream.

quebradero *m* breaker; ~ de cabeza worry.

quebradizo/za *adj* brittle; flexible.

quebrado *m* (*math*) fraction.

quebradura *f* fracture; rupture, hernia.

quebrantamiento *m* fracture; rupture; breaking; weariness, fatigue; violation (of the law).

quebrantar *vt* to break; to crack; to burst; to pound, to grind; to violate; to fatigue; to weaken.

quebranto *m* weakness; great loss, severe damage.

quebrar *vt* to break; to transgress; to violate (a law); * *vi* to go bankrupt; ~se *vr* to break into pieces; to be ruptured.

queda *f* resting time; (*mil*) tattoo.

quedar *vi* to stay; ~se *vr* to remain.

quedo/da *adj* quiet, still; * *adv* softly, gently.

quehacer *m* task.

queja *f* complaint.

quejarse *vr* to complain of.

quejido *m* complaint.

quejoso/sa *adj* complaining, querulous.

quejumbroso/sa *adj* complaining, plaintive.

quema *f* burning, combustion; fire.

quemador *m* burner.

quemadura *f* burn.

quemar *vt* to burn; to kindle; ~se *vr* to be parched with heat; to burn oneself; * *vi* to be too hot.

quemarropa *f*: a ~ *adv* point-blank.

quemazón *f* burn; itch.

querella *f* charge; dispute; complaint.

querellarse *vr* to complain; to file a complaint.

querendón/ona *adj Lat Am* affectionate.

querer *vt* to want; to desire; to will; to love; * *m* will, desire.

querido/da *adj* dear, beloved; * *m/f* darling; lover; ~do mío/~da mía my dear, my love, my darling.

querosén *m Lat Am* kerosene/kerosine.

queroseno *m* kerosene/kerosine.

querubín *m* cherub.

quesería *f* shop that specializes in cheese.

queso *m* cheese.

quicio *m* hook, hinge (of a door).

quiebra *f* break, fracture; bankruptcy; slump.

quien *pn* who; whom.

quién *pn* who; whom.

quienquiera *adj* whoever.

quieto/ta *adj* still, peaceable.

quietud *f* quietness, peace, tranquility, calmness.

quijada *f* jaw; jawbone.

quijotada *f* quixotic action.

quijote *m* quixotic person.

quijotesco/ca *adj* quixotic.

quilate *m* carat.

quilla *f* keel.

quimera *f* chimera.

quimérico/ca *adj* chimerical, fantastic.

química *f* chemistry.

químico/ca *m/f* chemist, * *adj* chemical.

quimioterapia *f* chemotherapy.

quina *f* Peruvian bark, quinine.

quincalla *f* hardware.

quince *adj, m* fifteen; fifteenth.

quincena *f* fortnight.

quinientos/tas *adj* five hundred.

quinina *f* quinine.

quinquenal *adj* quinquennial.

quinquenio *m* space of five years.

quinqui *m* delinquent.

quinta *f* country house; levy, drafting of soldiers.

quintaesencia *f* quintessence.

quintilla *f* (*poet*) metrical composition of five verses.

quinto *adj* fifth; * *m* fifth; drafted soldier.

quíntuplo/pla *adj* quintuple, fivefold.

quiosco *m* bandstand; newsstand.

quirófano *m* operating theater.

quiromancia *f* palmistry.

quirúrgico/ca *adj* surgical.

quisquilloso/sa *adj* difficult, touchy; peevish, irritable.

quiste *m* cyst.

quitaesmalte *m* nail-polish remover.

quitamanchas *m invar* stain remover.

quitanieves *m invar* snowplow.

quitar *vt* to take away, to remove; to take off; to relieve; to annul; ~se *vr* to take off (clothes etc); to withdraw.

quitasol *m* parasol.

quizá, quizás *adv* perhaps.

R

rabadilla *f* coccyx; rump, croup (of a horse/other four-legged animal).
rábano *m* radish.
rabí *m* rabbi.
rabia *f* rage, fury.
rabiar *vt* to be furious, to rage.
rabieta *f* touchiness, petulance; fit of bad temper.
rabino *m* rabbi.
rabioso/sa *adj* rabid; furious.
rabo *m* tail.
racha *f* gust of wind; **buena/mala** ~ spell of good/bad luck.
racial *adj* racial, race *compd*.
racimo *m* bunch of grapes.
raciocinio *m* reasoning; argument.
ración *f* ration.
racional *adj* rational; reasonable.
racionalidad *f* rationality.
racionar *vt* to ration (out).
racismo *m* racialism.
racista *adj*, *m/f* racist.
radar *m* radar.
radiación *f* radiation.
radiactivo/va, radioactivo/va *adj* radioactive.
radiador *m* radiator.
radiante *adj* radiant.
radiar *vt* to radiate.
radicación *f* taking root; becoming rooted (of a habit).
radical *adj* radical.
radicar *vt* to take root; ~se *vr* to establish oneself.
radio *f* radio; radio (set); * *m* radius; ray.
radiografía *f* radiography; X-ray.
radioso/sa *adj Lat Am* radiant.
radioterapia *f* radiotherapy.
raer *vt* to scrape; to grate; to erase.
ráfaga *f* gust; flash; burst.
rafting *m* rafting.
raído/da *adj* scraped; worn-out; impudent.
raíz *f* root; base, basis; origin.
raja *f* splinter, chip (of wood); chink, fissure.
rajar *vt* to split; to chop, to cleave.
rajatabla *f*: **a** ~ *adv* strictly.
ralea *f* race; breed, species.
rallador *m* grater.
rallar *vt* to grate.
ralo/la *adj* thin, rare.

rama *f* branch (of a tree, of a family).
ramadán *m* Ramadan.
ramaje *m* branches *pl*.
rambla *f* avenue.
ramera *f* whore, prostitute.
ramificación *f* ramification.
ramificarse *vr* to ramify.
ramillete *m* bunch.
ramo *m* branch (of a tree).
rampa *f* ramp.
rampante *adj* rampant.
rana *f* frog.
ranchera *f* station wagon.
ranchero *m* rancher;farmer.
rancho *m* grub; ranch; farm; settlement, camp.
rancio/cia *adj* rank; rancid.
rango *m* rank, standing.
ranúnculo *m* (*bot*) buttercup.
ranura *f* groove; slot.
rapacidad *f* rapacity.
rapadura *f* shaving; baldness.
rapar *vt* to shave; to plunder.
rapaz/za *adj* rapacious; * *m/f* young boy/girl.
rape *m* quick shave; monkfish.
rapé *m* snuff.
rapidez *f* speed, rapidity.
rápido/da *adj* quick, rapid, swift.
rapiña *f* robbery.
rappel *m* abseiling.
raptar *vt* to kidnap.
rapto *m* kidnaping; (*fig*) ecstasy, rapture.
raqueta *f* racket.
raquítico/ca *adj* stunted; (*fig*) inadequate.
rareza *f* rarity, rareness.
raro/ra *adj* rare, scarce; extraordinary.
ras *m*: **a** ~ **de** level with; **a** ~ **de tierra** at ground level.
rasar *vt* to level.
rascacielos *m invar* skyscraper.
rascar *vt* to scratch, to scrape.
rasgar *vt* to tear, to rip.
rasgo *m* dash, stroke; grand/magnanimous action; ~s *mpl* features *pl*.
rasguear *vi* to form bold strokes with a pen; (*mus*) to strum.
rasguñar *vt* to scratch, to scrape.
rasguño *m* scratch.
rasguñón *m Lat Am* scratch.
raso/sa *adj* plain; flat; * *m* satin; **al raso** in the open air.

raspa *f* beard (of an ear of corn); backbone (of fish); stalk (of grapes); rasp.

raspadura *f* filing, scraping; filings *pl.*

raspar *vt* to scrape, to rasp.

rastra *f* rake; **a ~s** by dragging.

rastreador *m* tracker.

rastrear *vt* to trace; to inquire into; * *vi* to skim along close to the ground (of birds).

rastrero/ra *adj* creeping; low, humble, cringing.

rastrillar *vt* to rake.

rastrillo *m* rake.

rastro *m* track; rake; trace.

rastrojera *f* stubble field.

rastrojo *m* stubble.

rasurador/ra *m/f* electric shaver.

rasurarse *vr* to shave.

rata *f* rat.

ratería *f* larceny, petty theft.

ratero/ra *adj* creeping, mean, vile; * *m/f* pickpocket; burglar.

ratificación *f* ratification.

ratificar *vt* to ratify; to approve of.

rato *m* moment; **a ~s perdidos** in leisure time.

ratón *m* mouse.

ratonera *f* mousetrap.

raudal *m* torrent.

raya *f* stroke; line; part; frontier; ray (fish); roach (fish).

rayado/da *adj* ruled; crossed; striped.

rayar *vt* to draw lines on; to cross out; to underline; to cross; to rifle.

rayo *m* ray, beam (of light).

rayón *m* rayon.

raza *f* race, lineage; quality.

razón *f* reason; right; reasonableness; account; calculation.

razonable *adj* reasonable.

razonado/da *adj* rational; prudent.

razonamiento *m* reasoning; discourse.

razonar *vi* to reason; to discourse, to talk.

reacción *f* reaction.

reaccionar *vi* to react.

reaccionario/ria *adj* reactionary.

reacio/cia *adj* stubborn.

reactor *m* reactor.

reajuste *m* readjustment.

real *adj* real, actual; royal; * *m* (*mil*) camp.

realce *m* embossment; flash; luster, splendor.

realidad *f* reality; sincerity.

realista *m* realist; royalist.

realizador/ra *m/f* producer (in TV etc).

realizar *vt* to realize; to achieve; to undertake.

realmente *adv* really, actually.

realzar *vt* to raise, to elevate; to emboss; to heighten.

reanimar *vt* to cheer, to encourage; to reanimate.

reanudar *vt* to renew; to resume.

reaparición *f* reappearance.

reasumir *vt* to retake, to resume.

reata *f* collar, leash; string (of horses).

rebaja *f* abatement; deduction; **~s** *fpl* sale.

rebajar *vt* to abate, to lessen, to diminish; to lower.

rebanada *f* slice.

rebaño *m* flock (of sheep), herd (of cattle).

rebasar *vt* to exceed.

rebatir *vt* to resist; to parry, to ward off; to refute; to repress.

rebeca *f* cardigan.

rebelarse *vr* to revolt; to rebel; to resist.

rebelde *m/f* rebel; * *adj* rebellious.

rebeldía *f* rebelliousness, disobedience; (*law*) contumacy; **en ~** by default.

rebelión *f* rebellion, revolt.

rebosar *vi* to run over, to overflow; to abound.

rebotar *vt* to bounce; to clinch; to repel; * *vi* to rebound.

rebote *m* rebound; **de ~** on the rebound.

rebozado/da *adj* fried in batter/breadcrumbs.

rebozar *vt* to wrap up; to fry in batter/breadcrumbs.

rebozo *m Lat Am* shawl.

rebullir *vi* to stir, to begin to move.

rebuscado/da *adj* affected; recherché; far-fetched.

rebuznar *vi* to bray.

rebuzno *m* braying (of an ass).

recabar *vt* to obtain by entreaty.

recado *m* message; gift.

recaer *vi* to fall back.

recaída *f* relapse.

recalcar *vt* to stress, to emphasize.

recalcitrante *adj* recalcitrant.

recalentamiento *m* overheating.

recalentar *vt* to heat again; to overheat.

recámara *f* bedroom.

recambio *m* spare; refill.

recapacitar *vt* to reflect.

recapitulación *f* recapitulation.

recapitular *vt* to recapitulate.

recargado/da *adj* overloaded.

recargar *vt* to overload; to recharge; to charge again.

recargo *m* extra load; new charge/accusation.

recatado/da *adj* prudent; circumspect; modest.

recato *m* prudence; circumspection; modesty; bashfulness.

recaudación *f* take, income; recovery of debts; tax collector's office.

recaudador *m* tax collector.

recaudar *vt* to gather; to obtain; to recover.

recelar *vt* to fear; to suspect, to doubt.

recelo *m* dread; suspicion, mistrust.

receloso/sa *adj* mistrustful; shy.

recepción *f* reception.

recepcionar *vt Lat Am* to receive.

recepcionista *m/f* receptionist.

receptáculo *m* receptacle.

receptor *m* receiver; investigating official.

recesión *f* (*com*) recession.

receta *f* recipe; prescription.

recetar *vt* to prescribe.

rechazar *vt* to refuse; to repulse; to contradict.

rechazo *m* rebound; denial; recoil.

rechifla *f* booing; (*fig*) derision.

rechiflar *vt* to boo.

rechinar *vi* to gnash (teeth).

rechistar *vi*: **sin** ~ without a murmur.

rechoncho/cha *adj* chubby.

recibidor *m* entrance hall.

recibimiento *m* reception.

recibir *vt* to receive, to accept; to let in; to go to meet; ~**se** *vr*: ~ **de** *Lat Am* to qualify as.

recibo *m* receipt.

reciclado/da *adj* recycled.

reciclar *vt* to recycle.

recién *adv* recently, lately; *Lat Am* only.

reciente *adj* recent; new, fresh; modern.

recinto *m* district, precinct.

recio/cia *adj* stout; strong, robust; coarse, thick; rude; arduous, rigid; * *adv* strongly, stoutly; **hablar** ~ to talk loud.

recipiente *m* container.

reciprocidad *f* reciprocity.

recíproco/ca *adj* reciprocal, mutual.

recitación *f* recitation.

recital *m* recital; reading.

recitar *vt* to recite.

recitativo/va *adj* recitative.

reclamación *f* claim; reclamation; protest.

reclamar *vt* to claim.

reclame *m Lat Am* advertisement.

reclamo *m* claim; advertisement; attraction; decoy bird; catchword (in printing); *Lat Am* complaint.

reclinar *vt* to recline; ~**se** *vr* to lean back.

recluir *vt* to shut up.

reclusión *f* seclusion; prison.

recluta *f* recruitment; * *m/f* recruit.

reclutador *m* recruitment officer.

reclutar *vt* to recruit.

recobrar *vt* to recover; ~**se** *vr* to recover (from sickness).

recodo *m* corner/angle jutting out.

recogedor *m* scraper (instrument).

recoger *vt* to collect; to retake, to take back; to get; to gather; to shelter; to compile; ~**se** *vr* to take shelter/refuge; to retire; to withdraw from the world.

recogido/da *adj* retired, secluded; quiet.

recogimiento *m* collection; retreat; shelter; abstraction from all worldly concerns.

recolección *f* summary; recollection.

recomendación *f* recommendation.

recomendado/da *adj Lat Am* registered.

recomendar *vt* to recommend.

recompensa *f* compensation; recompense, reward.

recompensar *vt* to recompense, to reward.

recomponer *vt* to recompose; to mend.

reconcentrar *vt* to concentrate on.

reconciliación *f* reconciliation.

reconciliar *vt* to reconcile; ~**se** *vr* to make one's peace.

recóndito/ta *adj* recondite, secret, concealed.

reconfortar *vt* to comfort.

reconocer *vt* to recognize; to examine closely; to acknowledge; to consider; (*mil*) to reconnoiter.

reconocido/da *adj* recognized; grateful.

reconocimiento *m* recognition; acknowledgement; gratitude; confession; search; submission; inquiry; (*mil*) reconnaissance.

reconquista *f* reconquest.

reconquistar *vt* to reconquer.

reconstituyente *m* tonic.

reconstruir *vt* to reconstruct.

reconvenir *vt* to return the accusations of.

reconversión *f*: ~ **industrial** industrial rationalization.

recopilación *f* summary, abridgement.

recopilador *m* compiler.

recopilar *vt* to compile.

récord *adj invar* record; * *m* record.

recordar *vt* to remember; to remind; * *vi* to remember.

recorrer *vt* to run over, to peruse; to cover.

recorrida *f Lat Am* journey.

recortar *vt* to cut out.

recorte *m* cutting; trimming.

recostar *vt* to lean, to recline; ~**se** *vr* to lie down.
recoveco *m* cubbyhole; bend.
recrear *vt* to amuse, to entertain; to delight.
recreativo/va *adj* recreational.
recreo *m* recreation; playtime (at school).
recriminación *f* recrimination.
recriminar *vt* to recriminate.
recrudecer *vt*, *vi*, ~**se** *vr* to worsen.
recrudecimiento *m* upsurge.
recta *f* straight line.
rectángulo/la *adj* rectangular; * *m* rectangle.
rectificación *f* rectification.
rectificar *vt* to rectify.
rectilíneo/nea *adj* rectilinear.
rectitud *f* straightness; rectitude; justness, honesty; exactitude.
recto/ta *adj* straight; right; just, honest; * *m* rectum.
rector/ra *m/f* superior of a community or establishment; vice-chancellor (of a university); presiding judge; curate, rector; * *adj* governing.
rectorado *m* rectorship; vice-chancellorship.
rectoría *f* rectory; rectorship.
recua *f* train (of mules, pack animals).
recuadro *m* box; inset.
recuento *m* inventory.
recuerdo *m* souvenir; memory.
recular *vi* to fall back, to recoil.
recuperable *adj* recoverable.
recuperación *f* recovery.
recuperar *vt* to recover; ~**se** *vr* to recover (from sickness).
recurrir *vi*: ~ **a** to resort to.
recurso *m* recourse.
recusación *f* refusal.
recusar *vt* to refuse; to refuse to admit.
red *f* net; network; snare.
redacción *f* editing; editor's office.
redactar *vt* to draft; to edit.
redactor/ra *m/f* editor.
redada *f*: ~ **policial** police raid.
redecilla *f* hairnet.
rededor *m* environs *pl*; **al** ~ round about.
redención *f* redemption.
redentor/ra *m/f* redeemer.
redescubrir *vt* to rediscover.
redicho/cha *adj* affected.
redil *m* enclosure for sheep.
redimible *adj* redeemable.
redimir *vt* to redeem; to ransom.
rédito *m* revenue, rent.
redoblado/da *adj* redoubled; stout and thick; reinforced.

redoblar *vt* to redouble; to rivet.
redoble *m* doubling, repetition; (*mil*) roll of a drum.
redomado/da *adj* sly; out-and-out.
redondear *vt* to round.
redondel *m* circle; traffic circle.
redondez *f* roundness, circular form.
redondo/da *adj* round; complete.
reducción *f* reduction.
reducible *adj* reducible; convertible.
reducido/da *adj* reduced; limited; small.
reducir *adj* to reduce; to limit; ~**se** *vr* to diminish.
reducto *m* (*mil*) redoubt.
redundancia *f* superfluity, redundancy, excess.
redundar *vi* to contribute.
reelegir *vt* to re-elect, to elect again.
reembolsar *vt* to refund; to reimburse.
reembolso *m* reimbursement; refund; **contra** ~ C.O.D.
reemplazar *vt* to replace; to restore.
reemplazo *m* replacement; reserve.
reenganchar *vt* (*mil*) to re-enlist; ~**se** *vr* to enlist again.
referencia *f* reference.
referéndum *m* referendum.
referí *m Lat Am* referee.
referir *vt* to refer, to relate, to report; ~**se** *vr* to refer/relate to.
refilón *m*: **de** ~ *adv* obliquely.
refinado/da *adj* refined; subtle, artful.
refinar *vt* to refine.
refinería *f* refinery.
reflejar *vt* to reflect.
reflejo *m* reflex; reflection.
reflexión *f* meditation, reflection.
reflexionar *vt* to reflect on; * *vi* to reflect, to meditate.
reflexivo/va *adj* reflexive; thoughtful.
reflujo *m* reflux, ebb; **flujo y** ~ the tides *pl*.
reforma *f* reform; correction; repair.
reformar *vt* to reform; to correct; to restore; ~**se** *vr* to mend.
reformatorio *m* reformatory.
reforzar *vt* to strengthen, to fortify; to encourage.
refracción *f* refraction.
refractario/ria *adj* refractory.
refrán *m* proverb.
refregar *vt* to scrub.
refrenar *vt* to refrain; to check.
refrendar *vt* to countersign; to approve.
refrescante *adj* refreshing.
refrescar *vt* to refresh; ~**se** *vr* to get cooler;

to go out for a breath of fresh air; * *vi* to cool down.

refresco *m* refreshment.

refriega *f* affray, skirmish, fray.

refrigerador/ra *m/f* refrigerator, fridge.

refrigerar *vt* to cool; to refresh; to refrigerate; to comfort.

refrigerio *m* refrigeration; refreshment; consolation, comfort.

refuerzo *m* reinforcement.

refugiado/da *m/f* refugee.

refugiar *vt* to shelter; ~se *vr* to take refuge.

refugio *m* refuge, asylum.

refulgir *vi* to shine.

refunfuñar *vi* to snarl; to growl; to grumble.

refutación *f* refutation.

refutar *vt* to refute.

regadera *f* watering can.

regadío *m* irrigated land.

regalar *vt* to give (as present); to give away; to pamper; to caress.

regalía *f* regalia; bonus; royalty; privilege.

regaliz *m* licorice.

regalo *m* present, gift; pleasure; comfort.

regañadientes: a ~ *adv* reluctantly.

regañar *vt* to scold; * *vi* to growl; to grumble; to quarrel.

regañón/ona *adj* snarling, growling; grumbling; troublesome.

regar *vt* to water, to irrigate.

regata *f* irrigation ditch; regatta.

regatear *vt* (*com*) to bargain over; to be mean with; * *vi* to haggle; to dribble (in sport).

regateo *m* haggling; bartering; dribbling.

regazo *m* lap.

regencia *f* regency.

regeneración *f* regeneration.

regenerar *vt* to regenerate.

regentar *vt* to rule; to govern.

regente *m* regent; manager.

régimen *m* regime, management; diet; (*gr*) rules of verbs *pl*.

regimiento *m* regime; (*mil*) regiment.

regio/gia *adj* royal, regal.

región *f* region.

regir *vt* to rule, to govern; to direct; * *vi* to apply.

registrador/ra *m/f* registrar; controller.

registradora *f Lat Am* cash register.

registrar *vt* to survey; to inspect, to examine; to record, to enter in a register; ~se *vr* to register; to happen.

registro *m* examining; enrolling office; register; registration.

regla *f* rule, ruler; period.

reglamentar *vt* to regulate.

reglamentario/ria *adj* statutory.

reglamento *m* regulation; bylaw/bye-law.

regocijar *vt* to gladden; ~se *vr* to rejoice.

regocijo *m* joy, pleasure; merriment, rejoicing.

regodearse *vr* to be delighted; to trifle, to play the fool; to joke, to jest.

regodeo *m* joy, merriment.

regordete *adj* chubby, plump.

regresar *vi* to return, to go back.

regreso *m* return, regression.

reguero *m* small rivulet; trickle of spilt liquid; drain, gutter.

regulación *f* regulation.

regulador/ra *m/f* regulator; knob, control.

regular *vt* to regulate, to adjust; * *adj* regular; ordinary.

regularidad *f* regularity.

regularizar *vt* to regularize.

rehabilitación *f* rehabilitation.

rehabilitar *vt* to rehabilitate.

rehacer *vt* to repair, to make again; to redo; ~se *vr* to recover; (*mil*) to rally.

rehén *m* hostage.

rehuir *vt* to avoid.

rehusar *vt* to refuse, to decline.

reimpresión *f* reprint.

reimprimir *vt* to reprint.

reina *f* queen.

reinado *m* reign.

reinante *adj* (*fig*) prevailing.

reinar *vi* to reign; to govern.

reincidencia *f* relapse.

reincidir *vi*: ~ **en** to relapse into, to fall back into.

reino *m* kingdom, reign.

reintegración *f* reintegration, restoration.

reintegrar *vt* to reintegrate, to restore; ~se *vr* to be reinstated/restored.

reintegro *m* reintegration.

reír(se) *vi* (*vr*) to laugh.

reiteración *f* repetition, reiteration.

reiterar *vt* to reiterate, to repeat.

reivindicación *f* claim; vindication.

reivindicar *vt* to claim.

reja *f* plowshare; lattice, grating.

rejilla *f* grating, grille; vent; rack (for baggage).

rejoneador *m* mounted bullfighter.

rejonear *vt* to spear (bulls).

rejuvenecer *vt*, *vi* to rejuvenate.

relación *f* relation; relationship; report; account.

relacionar *vt* to relate.
relajación *f* relaxation; remission; laxity.
relajar *vt* to relax, to slacken; ~**se** *vr* to relax.
relajo *m* Lat Am (*col*) mess; racket.
relamerse *vr* to lick one's lips; to relish.
relamido/da *adj* affected; overdressed.
relámpago *m* flash of lightning.
relampaguear *vi* to flash.
relatar *vt* to relate, to tell.
relativo/va *adj* relative.
relato *m* story; recital.
relax *m* relaxation.
releer *vt* to reread.
relegación *f* relegation; exile.
relegar *vt* to relegate; to banish, to exile.
relente *m* evening dew.
relevante *adj* excellent, great; eminent.
relevar *vt* to emboss, to work in relief; to exonerate; to relieve; to assist.
relevo *m* (*mil*) relief.
relicario *m* reliquary.
relieve *m* relief; (*fig*) prominence.
religión *f* religion.
religiosidad *f* religiousness.
religioso/sa *adj* religious.
relinchar *vi* to neigh.
relincho *m* neigh, neighing.
reliquia *f* residue, remains *pl*; (saintly) relic.
rellano *m* landing (of stairs).
rellenar *vt* to fill up; to stuff.
relleno/na *adj* satiated, full up; stuffed; * *m* stuffing.
reloj *m* clock; watch.
relojero *m* watchmaker.
relucir *vi* to shine, to glitter; to excel, to be brilliant.
relumbrar *vi* to sparkle, to shine.
remachar *vt* to rivet; (*fig*) to drive home.
remanente *m* remainder; (*com*) balance; surplus.
remangar *vt* to roll up.
remansarse *vr* to form a pool.
remanso *m* stagnant water; quiet place.
remar *vi* to row.
rematadamente *adv* entirely, totally.
rematado/da *adj* utter, complete.
rematar *vt* to terminate, to finish; to sell off cheaply; * *vi* to end.
remate *m* end, conclusion; shot; tip; last/ best bid.
remedar *vt* to copy, to imitate; to mimic.
remediable *adj* remediable.
remediar *vt* to remedy; to assist, to help; to free from danger; to avoid.

remedio *m* amendment, correction; recourse; refuge.
remedo *m* imitation, copy.
remendar *vt* to patch, to mend; to correct.
remero *m* rower, oarsman.
remesa *f* shipment; remittance.
remiendo *m* patch; mend.
remilgado/da *adj* prim; affected.
remilgo *m* primness, affectation.
reminiscencia *f* reminiscence, recollection.
remiso/sa *adj* remiss, careless; indolent.
remitente *m* sender.
remitir *vt* to remit, to send; to pardon (a fault); to suspend, to put off; * *vi*, ~**se** *vr* to slacken.
remo *m* oar; rowing.
remojar *vt* to steep; to dunk.
remojo *m* steeping, soaking.
remolacha *f* beet (crop).
remolcar *vt* to tow.
remolino *m* whirlwind; whirlpool; crowd.
remolón/ona *adj* stubborn; lazy.
remolque *m* tow, towing; tow rope.
remontar *vt* to mend; ~**se** *vr* to tower, to soar.
remorder *vt* to disturb.
remordimiento *m* remorse.
remoto/ta *adj* remote, distant; far.
remover *vt* to stir; to move around; Lat Am to dismiss.
remozar *vt* to rejuvenate; to renovate.
remuneración *f* remuneration, recompense.
remunerador/ra *m/f* remunerator.
remunerar *vt* to reward, to remunerate.
renacer *vi* to be born again; to revive.
renacimiento *m* regeneration; rebirth.
renacuajo *m* tadpole.
renal *adj* renal, kidney *compd*.
rencilla *f* quarrel.
rencor *m* rancor, grudge.
rencoroso/sa *adj* rancorous.
rendición *f* surrender; profit.
rendido/da *adj* submissive; exhausted.
rendija *f* crevice, crack, cleft.
rendimiento *m* output; efficiency.
rendir *vt* to subject, to subdue; ~**se** *vr* to yield; to surrender; to be tired out.
renegado *m* apostate; wicked person.
renegar *vt* to deny; to disown; to detest, to abhor; * *vi* to apostatize; to blaspheme, to curse.
renglón *m* line; item.
reno *m* caribou, reindeer.
renombrado/da *adj* renowned.
renombre *m* renown.

renovación *f* renovation; renewal.
renovar *vt* to renew; to renovate; to reform.
renquear *vi* to limp.
renta *f* income; rent; profit.
renuncia *f* renunciation; resignation.
renunciar *vt* to renounce; * *vi* to resign.
reñido/da *adj* at variance, at odds; hard-fought.
reñir *vt, vi* to wrangle, to quarrel; to scold, to chide.
reo *m* offender, criminal.
reojo *m*: **mirar de** ~ to look at furtively.
reparación *f* repair; reparation.
reparar *vt* to repair; to consider, to observe; to parry; * *vi*: ~ **en** to notice; to pass (in cards).
reparo *m* repair, reparation; consideration; difficulty.
repartición *f* distribution.
repartidor *m/f* distributor; assessor of taxes.
repartir *vt* to distribute; to deliver.
reparto *m* distribution; delivery; cost; property development.
repasar *vt* to pass again; to revise; to check; to mend.
repaso *m* revision; check-up.
repatriar *vt* to repatriate.
repecho *m* slope.
repelente *adj* repellent, repulsive.
repeler *vt* to repel; to refute, to reject.
repente: **de** ~ *adv* suddenly.
repentino/na *adj* sudden, unforeseen.
repercusión *f* reverberation.
repercutir *vi* to reverberate; to rebound.
repertorio *m* repertory; index; list.
repetición *f* repetition; (*mus*) encore.
repetidor/ra *m/f* repeater.
repetir *vt, vi* to repeat.
repicar *vt* to ring.
repique *m* chime.
repiquetear *vt* to ring merrily.
repisa *f* pedestal, stand; shelf; windowsill.
replegar *vt* to redouble; to fold over; ~**se** *vr* (*mil*) to fall back.
repleto/ta *adj* replete, very full.
réplica *f* reply, answer; repartee.
replicar *vi* to reply.
repoblación *f* repopulation; restocking; ~ **forestal** reforestation.
repoblar *vt* to repopulate; to reforest.
repollo *m* cabbage.
reponer *vt* to replace; to restore; ~**se** *vr* to recover lost health/property.
reportaje *m* report, article; *Lat Am* interview.

reportero/ra *m/f* reporter.
reposado/da *adj* quiet, peaceful; settled (wine).
reposar *vi* to rest, to repose.
reposición *f* replacement; remake.
reposo *m* rest, repose.
repostería *f* confectioner's (shop).
repostero *m* confectioner.
reprender *vt* to reprimand.
represa *f* dam; lake.
represalia *f* reprisal.
representación *f* representation; authority.
representante *m/f* representative; understudy (theater).
representar *vt* to represent; to play on the stage; to look (age).
representativo/va *adj* representative.
represión *f* repression.
reprimenda *f* reprimand.
reprimir *vt* to repress; to check; to contain.
reprobable *adj* reprehensible.
reprobación *f* reprobation, reproof.
reprobar *vt* to reject; to condemn, to upbraid; *Lat Am* to fail.
réprobo *m* reprobate.
reprochar *vt* to reproach.
reproche *m* reproach.
reproducción *f* reproduction.
reproducir *vt* to reproduce.
reptil *m* reptile.
república *f* republic.
republicano/na *adj, m/f* republican.
repudiar *vt* to repudiate.
repudio *m* repudiation.
repuesto *m* supply; spare part.
repugnancia *f* reluctance; repugnance.
repugnante *adj* repugnant.
repugnar *vt* to disgust.
repulsa *f* refusal.
repulsar *vt* to reject; to decline, to refuse.
repulsión *f* repulsion.
repulsivo/va *adj* repulsive.
repuntar *vi* *Lat Am* to improve.
reputación *f* reputation, renown.
reputar *vt* to consider.
requebrar *vt* to woo, to court.
requerimiento *m* request; requisition; intimation; summons.
requerir *vt* to intimate, to notify; to request; to require, to need; to summon.
requesón *m* cottage cheese.
requiebro *m* endearing expression.
réquiem *m* requiem.
requisa *f* inspection; (*mil*) requisition.
requisito *m* requisite.

res *f* animal; head of cattle; ~**es** *Lat Am* cattle.

resabio *m* (unpleasant) aftertaste; vicious habit, bad custom.

resaca *f* surge, surf; (*fig*) backlash; (*col*) hangover.

resaltar *vi* to rebound; to jut out; to be evident; to stand out.

resarcimiento *m* compensation, reparation.

resarcir *vt* to compensate, to make amends for.

resbalada *f Lat Am* slip, slide.

resbaladizo/za *adj* slippery.

resbalar(se) *vi* (*vr*) to slip, to slide.

resbalón *m* slip, slide.

rescatar *vt* to ransom, to redeem.

rescate *m* ransom.

rescindir *vt* to rescind, to annul.

rescisión *f* rescindment, revocation.

rescoldo *m* embers *pl*, cinders *pl*.

resecarse *vr* to dry up.

reseco/on *adj* very dry.

resentido/da *adj* resentful.

resentimiento *m* resentment.

resentirse *vr*: ~ **de** to suffer; ~ **con** to resent.

reseña *f* review; account.

reseñar *vt* to describe; to review.

reserva *f* reserve; reservation.

reservado/da *adj* reserved, cautious, circumspect.

reservar *vt* to keep; to reserve; ~**se** *vr* to preserve oneself; to keep to oneself.

resfriado *m* cold.

resfriarse *vr* to catch cold.

resguardar *vt* to preserve, to defend; ~**se** *vr* to be on one's guard.

resguardo *m* guard; security, safety; voucher; receipt.

residencia *f* residence.

residente *adj* residing, resident; * *m/f* resident.

residir *vi* to reside, to dwell.

residuo *m* residue, remainder.

resignación *f* resignation.

resignadamente *adv* resignedly.

resignarse *vr* to resign oneself.

resina *f* resin.

resinoso/sa *adj* resinous.

resistencia *f* resistance, opposition.

resistente *adj* strong; resistant.

resistir *vt* to resist, to oppose; to put up with; * *vi* to resist; to hold out.

resma *f* ream (of paper).

resol *m* glare (of the sun).

resollar *vi* to wheeze; to breath with difficulty.

resolución *f* resolution, boldness; decision.

resolver *vt* to resolve, to decide; to analyze; ~**se** *vr* to resolve, to determine.

resonar *vi* to resound.

resoplar *vi* to snore; to snort.

resoplido *m* heavy breathing.

resorte *m* spring.

respaldar *vt* to endorse; ~**se** *vr* to lean back.

respaldo *m* backing; endorsement; back of a seat.

respectivo/va *adj* respective.

respecto *m* respect; relation; **al** ~ on this matter.

respetable *adj* respectable.

respetar *vt* to respect; to revere.

respeto *m* respect, regard, consideration; homage.

respetuoso/sa *adj* respectful.

respingar *vi* to shy.

respingo *m* start; jump.

respiración *f* respiration, breathing.

respiradero *m* vent, breathing hole; rest, repose.

respirar *vi* to breathe.

respiratorio/ria *adj* respiratory.

respiro *m* breathing; (*fig*) respite.

resplandecer *vi* to shine; to glisten.

resplandeciente *adj* resplendent.

resplandor *m* splendor, brilliance.

responder *vt* to answer; * *vi* to answer; to correspond; ~ **de** to be responsible for.

respondón/ona *adj* ever ready to reply; cheeky.

responsable *adj* responsible; accountable, answerable.

responsabilidad *f* responsibility.

responsabilizarse *vr* to take charge.

responso *m* prayer for the dead.

respuesta *f* answer, reply.

resquemor *m* resentment.

resquicio *m* crack, cleft; (*fig*) chance.

restablecer *vt* to re-establish; ~**se** *vr* to recover.

restablecimiento *m* re-establishment.

restallar *vi* to crack; to click.

restante *adj* remaining.

restar *vt* to subtract, to take away; * *vi* to be left.

restauración *f* restoration.

restaurant *m Lat Am* diner.

restaurante *m* diner.

restaurar *vt* to restore.

restitución *f* restitution.

restituir *vt* to restore; to return.
resto *m* remainder, rest.
restregar *vt* to scrub, to rub.
restricción *f* restriction, limitation.
restringir *vt* to restrict, to limit; to restrain.
resucitar *vt* to resuscitate, to revive; to renew.
resuello *m* breath, breathing.
resuelto/ta *adj* resolute, determined; prompt.
resultado *m* result, consequence.
resultar *vi* to be; to turn out; to amount to.
resumen *m* summary.
resumidamente *adv* summarily.
resumir *vt* to abridge; to sum up; to summarize.
resurrección *f* resurrection, revival.
retablo *m* picture drawn on a board; splendid altarpiece.
retaguardia *f* rearguard.
retahíla *f* range, series.
retal *m* remnant.
retar *vt* to challenge.
retardar *vt* to retard; to delay.
retardo *m* delay.
retazo *m* remnant; cutting.
retén *m* *Lat Am* reformatory.
retención *f* retention.
retener *vt* to retain, to keep back.
retentiva *f* memory.
reticencia *f* reticence.
retina *f* retina.
retintín *m* tinkling sound; affected tone of voice.
retirada *f* (*mil*) retreat, withdrawal; recall.
retirar *vt* to withdraw, to retire; to remove; ~se *vr* to retire, to retreat; to go to bed.
retiro *m* retreat, retirement; pension.
reto *m* challenge; threat, menace.
retocar *vt* to retouch; to mend; to finish off (work).
retoñar *vi* to sprout.
retoño *m* shoot; offspring.
retoque *m* finishing stroke; retouching.
retorcer *vt* to twist; to wring.
retorcimiento *m* twisting, contortion.
retórica *f* rhetoric.
retórico/ca *adj* rhetorical; * *f* rhetoric; affectedness.
retornar *vt, vi* to return.
retorno *m* return; barter, exchange.
retortero: andar al ~ to bustle about.
retortijón *m* twisting; ~ de tripas stomach cramp.
retozar *vi* to frisk, to skip.
retozo *m* romp.
retozón/ona *adj* wanton; romping.

retracción *f* retraction.
retractar *vt* to retract.
retraer *vt* to draw back; to dissuade; ~se *vr* to take refuge; to flee.
retraído/da *adj* shy.
retransmisión *f* broadcast.
retransmitir *vt* to broadcast; to relay; to retransmit.
retrasado/da *adj* late; (*med*) mentally handicapped; backward.
retraso *m* delay; slowness; backwardness; lateness; (*rail*): el tren ha tenido ~ the train is overdue/late.
retratar *vt* to portray; to photograph; to describe.
retrato *m* portrait, effigy.
retreta *f* (*mil*) retreat.
retrete *m* bathroom, lavatory.
retribución *f* retribution.
retribuir *vt* to repay.
retroacción *f* retroaction.
retroactivo/va *adj* retroactive.
retroceder *vi* to go backward(s), to fly back; to back down.
retrógrado/da *adj* retrograde; reactionary.
retrospectivo/va *adj* retrospective.
retrovisor *m* rear-view mirror.
retumbar *vi* to resound, to jingle.
reuma *f* rheumatism.
reumático/ca *adj* rheumatic.
reumatismo *m* rheumatism.
reunión *f* reunion, meeting.
reunir *vt* to reunite; to unite; ~se *vr* to gather, to meet.
revalidación *f* confirmation, ratification.
revalidar *vt* to ratify, to confirm.
revancha *f* revenge.
revelación *f* revelation.
revelado *m* developing.
revelar *vt* to reveal; to develop (photographs).
reventar *vi* to burst, to explode; to toil, to overwork.
reventón *m* (*auto*) blow-out.
reverberación *f* reverberation.
reverberar *vi* to reverberate.
reverdecer *vi* to grow green again; to revive.
reverencia *f* reverence, veneration; respect.
reverenciar *vt* to venerate, to revere.
reverendo/da *adj* reverend.
reverente *adj* respectful, reverent.
reverso *m* reverse.
revés *m* back; wrong side; disappointment, setback.
revestir *vt* to put on; to coat, to cover.

revisar *vt* to revise, to review; *Lat Am* to search.
revisión *f* revision.
revisor/ra *m/f* inspector; ticket collector.
revista *f* magazine; review, revision.
revivir *vi* to revive.
revocación *f* revocation.
revocar *vt* to revoke.
revolcarse *vr* to wallow.
revolotear *vi* to flutter.
revoloteo *m* fluttering.
revoltijo *m* confusion, disorder.
revoltoso/sa *adj* rebellious, unruly.
revolución *f* revolution.
revolucionario/ria *adj*, *m/f* revolutionary.
revolver *vt* to move about; to turn around; to mess up; to revolve; ~**se** *vr* to turn round; to change (of the weather).
revólver *m* revolver.
revuelo *m* fluttering; (*fig*) commotion.
revuelta *f* turn; disturbance, revolt.
rey *m* king; king (in cards/chess).
reyerta *f* quarrel, brawl.
rezagar *vt* to leave behind; to defer; ~**se** *vr* to remain behind.
rezar *vi* to pray, to say one's prayers.
rezo *m* prayer.
rezongar *vi* to grumble.
rezumar *vt* to ooze, to leak.
ría *f* estuary.
riada *f* flood.
ribera *f* shore, bank.
ribereño/ña *adj* coastal; riverside.
ribete *m* trimming; seam, border.
ribetear *vt* to hem, to border.
ricino *m*: **aceite de** ~ castor oil.
rico/ca *adj* rich; delicious; lovely; cute.
ridiculez *f* absurdity.
ridiculizar *vt* to ridicule.
ridículo/la *adj* ridiculous.
riego *m* irrigation.
riel *m* (*rail*) rail.
rienda *f* rein of a bridle; **dar ~ suelta** to give free rein to.
riesgo *m* risk, danger.
riesgoso/sa *adj Lat Am* risky.
rifa *f* raffle, lottery.
rifar *vt* to raffle.
rifle *m* rifle.
rigidez *f* rigidity.
rígido/da *adj* rigid, inflexible; severe.
rigor *m* rigor.
riguroso/sa *adj* rigorous.
rima *f* rhyme.
rimar *vi* to rhyme.
rimbombante *adj* pompous.

rímel, rimmel *m* mascara.
rincón *m* (inside) corner.
rinoceronte *m* rhinoceros.
riña *f* quarrel, dispute.
riñón *m* kidney.
río *m* river, stream.
rioja *m* rioja (wine).
riqueza *f* riches *pl*, wealth.
risa *f* laugh, laughter.
risco *m* steep rock.
risible *adj* risible, laughable.
risotada *f* loud laugh.
ristra *f* string.
risueño/ña *adj* smiling.
rítmico/ca *adj* rhythmic.
ritmo *m* rhythm.
rito *m* rite, ceremony.
ritual *adj*, *m* ritual.
rival *adj*, *m/f* rival.
rivalidad *f* rivalry.
rivalizar *vi*: ~ **con** to rival, to vie with.
rizado/da *adj* curly.
rizar *vt* to curl (hair)
rizo *m* curl; ripple (on water).
robar *vt* to rob; to steal; to break into.
roble *m* oak tree.
robledal *m* oakwood.
robo *m* robbery; theft.
robot *m* robot.
robustez *f* robustness.
robusto/ta *adj* robust, strong.
roca *f* rock.
rocalla *f* pebbles *pl*.
roce *m* rub; brush; friction.
rociada *f* sprinkling; spray, shower.
rociar *vt* to sprinkle; to spray.
rocín *m* nag; hack; stupid person.
rocío *m* dew.
rocoso/sa *adj* rocky.
rodada *f* rut, track of a wheel.
rodador *m Lat Am* gnat.
rodadura *f* act of rolling.
rodaja *f* slice.
rodaje *m* filming; **en** ~ (*auto*) running in.
rodar *vi* to roll.
rodear *vi* to make a detour; * *vt* to surround, to enclose; *Lat Am* to round up.
rodeo *m* detour; subterfuge; evasion; rodeo.
rodilla *f* knee; **de** ~**s** on one's knees.
rodillo *m* roller.
roedor/ra *adj* gnawing; * *m* rodent.
roedura *f* gnawing.
roer *vt* to gnaw; to corrode.
rogar *vt*, *vi* to ask for; to beg, to entreat; to pray.

rogativa *f* supplication, prayer.
rojez *f* redness.
rojizo/za *adj* reddish.
rojo/ja *adj* red; ruddy.
rol *m* list, roll, catalog; role.
rollizo/za *adj* round; plump, chubby.
rollo *m* roll; coil.
romance *m* Romance language; romance.
romancero *m* collection of romances/ballads.
romanticismo *m* romanticism.
romántico/ca *adj* romantic.
rombo *m* rhombus.
romboide *m* rhomboid.
romería *f* pilgrimage.
romero *m* (*bot*) rosemary.
romo/ma *adj* blunt; snub-nosed.
rompecabezas *m invar* riddle; jigsaw.
romper *vt* to break; to tear up; to wear out; to break up (land); * *vi* to break (of waves); to break through.
rompimiento *m Lat Am* tearing, breaking; crack.
ron *m* rum.
roncar *vi* to snore; to roar.
roncha *f* weal, bruise.
ronco/ca *adj* hoarse; husky; raucous.
ronda *f* night patrol; round (of drinks, cards etc).
rondar *vt, vi* to patrol; to prowl around.
ronquera *f* hoarseness.
ronquido *m* snore; roar.
ronzal *m* halter.
ronronear *vi* to purr.
roña *f* scab, mange; grime; rust.
roñoso/sa *adj* filthy; mean.
ropa *f* clothes *pl*; clothing; dress.
ropaje *m* gown, robes *pl*; drapery.
ropero *m* linen cupboard; closet.
rosa *f* rose; birthmark.
rosado/da *adj* pink; rosy.
rosal *m* rosebush.
rosario *m* rosary.
rosca *f* thread (of a screw); coil, spiral.
rosedal *m Lat Am* rose garden.
rosetón *m* rosette; rose window, wheel window.
rosquilla *f* doughnut, donut.
rostro *m* face.
rotación *f* rotation.
roto/ta *adj* broken, destroyed; debauched.
rótula *f* kneecap; ball-and-socket joint.
rotulador *m* felt-tip pen, fiber-tip pen.
rotular *vt* to inscribe, to label.
rótulo *m* inscription; label, ticket; placard, poster.
rotundo/da *adj* round; emphatic.
rotura *f* breaking; crack; tear.

roturar *vt* to plow.
rozadura *f* graze, scratch.
rozar *vt* to rub; to chafe; to nibble (the grass); to scrape; to touch lightly.
rubí *m* ruby.
rubicundo/da *adj* reddish.
rubio/bia *adj* fair-haired, blond/blonde; * *m/f* blond/blonde.
rubor *m* blush; bashfulness.
rúbrica *f* red mark; flourish at the end of a signature; title, heading, rubric.
rubricar *vt* to sign with a flourish; to sign and seal.
rubro *m Lat Am* heading; item.
rudeza *f* roughness, rudeness; stupidity.
rudimento *m* principle; beginning; ~s *mpl* rudiments *pl*.
rudo/da *adj* rough, coarse; plain, simple; stupid.
rueca *f* distaff.
rueda *f* wheel; circle; slice, round.
ruedo *m* rotation; border, selvage; arena, bullring.
ruego *m* request, entreaty.
rufián *m* pimp, pander; lout.
rugby *m* rugby.
rugido *m* roar.
rugir *vi* to roar, to bellow.
rugoso/sa *adj* wrinkled.
ruibarbo *m* rhubarb.
ruido *m* noise, sound; din, row; fuss.
ruidoso/sa *adj* noisy, loud.
ruin *adj* mean, despicable; mean, stingy.
ruina *f* ruin, collapse; downfall, destruction; ~s *fpl* ruins *pl*.
ruindad *f* meanness, lowness; mean act.
ruinoso/sa *adj* ruinous, disastrous.
ruiseñor *m* nightingale.
ruleta *f* roulette.
rulo *m* rolling pin; hair curler.
rumba *f* rumba.
rumbo *m* (*mar*) course, bearing; road, route, way; course of events, pomp, ostentation.
rumboso/sa *adj* generous, lavish.
rumiante *m* ruminant.
rumiar *vt* to chew; * *vi* to ruminate.
rumor *m* rumor; murmur.
runrún *m* rumor; sound of voices, whirr.
ruptura *f* rupture.
rural *adj* rural.
rusticidad *f* rusticity; coarseness.
rústico/ca *adj* rustic; * *m/f* peasant.
ruta *f* route, itinerary.
rutina *f* routine; habit.

S

sábado *m* Saturday; (Jewish) Sabbath.
sábana *f* sheet; altar cloth.
sabandija *f* bug, insect.
sabañón *m* chilblain.
sabelotodo *m/f invar* know-all.
saber *vt* to know; to be able to; to find out, to learn; to experience; * *vi*: ~ a to taste of; * *m* learning, knowledge.
sabiduría *f* learning, knowledge; wisdom.
sabiendas *adv*: a ~ knowingly.
sabihondo/da *adj* know-all; pedantic.
sabio/bia *adj* sage, wise; * *m/f* sage, wise person.
sablazo *m* sword wound; (*col*) sponging, scrounging.
sable *m* saber, cutlass.
sabor *m* taste, savor, flavor.
saborear *vt* to savor, to taste; to enjoy.
sabotaje *m* sabotage.
saboteador/ora *m/f* saboteur.
sabotear *vt* to sabotage.
sabroso/sa *adj* tasty, delicious; pleasant; salted.
sabueso *m* bloodhound.
sacacorchos *m invar* corkscrew.
sacapuntas *m invar* pencil sharpener.
sacar *vt* to take out, to extract; to get out; to bring out (a book etc); to take off (clothes); to receive, to get; (*sport*) to serve.
sacarina *f* saccharin.
sacerdotal *adj* priestly.
sacerdote *m* priest.
sacerdotisa *f* priestess.
saciar *vt* to satiate.
saciedad *f* satiety.
saco *m* bag, sack; *Lat Am* jacket; *Lat Am* coat; ~ de dormir sleeping bag.
sacramental *adj* sacramental.
sacramento *m* sacrament.
sacrificar *vt* to sacrifice.
sacrificio *m* sacrifice.
sacrilegio *m* sacrilege.
sacrílego/ga *adj* sacrilegious.
sacristán *m* sacristan, sexton.
sacristía *f* sacristy, vestry.
sacro/cra *adj* holy, sacred.
sacrosanto/ta *adj* sacrosanct.
sacudida *f* shake, jerk.
sacudir *vt* to shake, to jerk; to beat, to hit.
sacudón *m Lat Am* shake, jerk.
sádico/ca *adj* sadistic; * *m/f* sadist.

sadismo *m* sadism.
saeta *f* arrow, dart.
sagacidad *f* shrewdness, cleverness, sagacity.
sagaz *adj* shrewd, clever, sagacious.
sagitariano/na *adj Lat Am* Sagittarian (zodiac sign).
Sagitario *m* Sagittarius (zodiac sign).
sagrado/da *adj* sacred, holy.
sagrario *m* shrine; tabernacle.
sainete *m* (*theat*) farce; flavor, relish; seasoning.
saíno *m Lat Am* peccary.
sal *f* salt.
sala *f* large room; (*theat*) house, auditorium; public hall; (*law*) court; (*med*) ward.
salado/da *adj* salted; witty, amusing.
salamandra *f* salamander.
salar *vt* to salt.
salarial *adj* wage *compd*, salary *compd*.
salario *m* salary.
salazón *f* salting.
salchicha *f* sausage.
salchichón *m* salami-type sausage.
saldar *vt* to pay; to sell off; (*fig*) to settle.
saldo *m* settlement; balance; remainder; ~s *mpl* sale.
saledizo/za *adj* projecting, salient.
salero *m* salt cellar.
saleroso *adj* witty, amusing.
salida *f* exit, way out; leaving, departure; production, output; (*com*) sale; sales outlet.
saliente *adj* projecting; rising; (*fig*) outstanding.
salina *f* saltworks, salt mine.
salino/na *adj* saline.
salir *vi* to go out, to leave; to depart, to set out; to appear; to turn out, to prove; ~se *vr* to escape, to leak.
salitre *m* saltpeter.
saliva *f* saliva.
salmo *m* psalm.
salmón *m* salmon.
salmonete *m* red mullet.
salmuera *f* brine.
salobre *adj* brackish, salty.
salón *m* living room, lounge; public hall.
salpicadero *m* dashboard.
salpicar *vt* to sprinkle, to splash, to spatter.
salpimentar *vt* to season with pepper and salt.

salsa f sauce.
salsera f sauce boat; gravy boat.
saltamontes m invar grasshopper.
saltar vt to jump, to leap; to skip, to miss out; * vi to leap, to jump; to bounce; (fig) to explode, to blow up.
salteador m highwayman.
saltear vt to rob in a stick-up; to assault; to sauté (in cooking).
saltimbanqui m/f acrobat.
salto m leap, jump.
saltón/ona adj bulging; protruding.
salubre adj healthy.
salubridad f healthiness.
salud f health.
saludable adj healthy.
saludar vt to greet; (mil) to salute.
saludo m greeting.
salutación f salutation, greeting.
salva f (mil) salute, salvo.
salvación f salvation; rescue.
salvado m bran.
salvaguardar vt to safeguard.
salvaguardia m safeguard.
salvaje adj savage.
salvajismo m savagery.
salvar vt to save; to rescue; to overcome; to cross, to jump across; to cover, to travel; to exclude; ~se vr to escape from danger.
salvavidas adj invar: **bote** ~ lifeboat; **chaleco** ~ life preserver.
salvia f (bot) sage.
salvo/va adj safe; * adv save, except (for).
salvoconducto m safe-conduct.
san adj saint (as title).
sanamente adv healthily.
sanar vt, vi to heal.
sanatorio m sanitarium; nursing home.
sanción f sanction.
sancionar vt to sanction.
sandalia f sandal.
sándalo m sandal, sandalwood.
sandez f folly, stupidity.
sandía f watermelon.
sánduche m Lat Am sandwich.
sandwich m sandwich.
saneamiento m sanitation.
sanear vt to drain.
sangrar vt, vi to bleed.
sangre f blood; **a** ~ **fría** in cold blood; **a** ~ **y fuego** without mercy.
sangría f sangria (drink); bleeding.
sangriento/ta adj bloody, blood-stained, gory; cruel.
sanguijuela f leech.

sanguinario/ria adj bloodthirsty, cruel.
sanguíneo/nea adj blood compd.
sanidad f sanitation; health.
sanitario/ria adj sanitary; health; ~s mpl bathroom facilities pl.
sano/na adj healthy, fit; intact, sound.
santiamén m: **en un** ~ in no time at all.
santidad f sanctity.
santificar vt to sanctify; to make holy.
santiguarse vr to make the sign of the cross.
santo/ta adj holy; sacred; * m/f saint; ~ y **seña** password, watchword.
santuario m sanctuary.
saña f anger, passion.
sañudo/da adj furious, enraged.
sapo m toad.
saque m (sport) serve, service, throw-in.
saqueador/ra m/f ransacker, looter.
saquear vt to ransack, to plunder.
saqueo m looting, sacking.
sarampión m measles.
sarao m evening party, soiree.
sarcasmo m sarcasm.
sarcástico/ca adj sarcastic.
sarcófago m sarcophagus.
sardina f sardine.
sardónico/ca adj sardonic; ironic(al).
sargento m sergeant.
sarmiento m vine shoot.
sarna f itch; mange; (med) scabies.
sarnoso/sa adj itchy, scabby, mangy.
sarpullido m (med) rash.
sarro m (med) tartar.
sarta f string of beads etc; string, row.
sartén f frying pan.
sastre m tailor.
sastrería f tailor's premises.
Satanás m Satan.
satélite m satellite.
sátira f satire.
satírico/ca adj satirical.
satirizar vt to satirize.
sátiro m satyr.
satisfacción f satisfaction; apology.
satisfacer vt to satisfy; to pay (a debt); ~se vr to satisfy oneself; to take revenge.
satisfactorio/ria adj satisfactory.
satisfecho/cha adj satisfied.
saturación f (chem) saturation.
Saturno m Saturn (planet).
sauce m willow tree.
saúco m elder tree.
sauna f sauna.
savia f sap.
saxofón m saxophone.

sazonado/da *adj* flavored, seasoned.
sazonar *vt* to ripen; to season.
se *pn reflexivo*: himself; herself; itself; yourself; themselves; yourselves; each other; one another; oneself.
sebo *m* fat, grease.
seboso/sa *adj* fat, greasy.
secador *m*: ~ de pelo hairdryer.
secadora *f* tumble dryer.
secamente *adv* drily/dryly, curtly.
secano *m* dry, arable land which is not irrigated.
secar *vt* to dry; ~se *vr* to dry up; to dry oneself.
sección *f* section.
seco/ca *adj* dry; dried up; skinny; cold (of character); brusque, sharp; bare.
secretaría *f* secretariat.
secretario/ria *m/f* secretary.
secreto/ta *adj* secret; hidden; * *m* secret; secrecy.
secta *f* sect.
sectario/ria *adj*, *m/f* sectarian.
sector *m* sector.
secuela *f* sequel; consequence.
secuencia *f* sequence.
secuestrador/ra *m/f* kidnaper.
secuestrar *vt* to kidnap; to confiscate.
secuestro *m* kidnaping; confiscation.
secular *adj* secular.
secularización *f* secularization.
secularizar *vt* to secularize.
secundar *vt* to second.
secundario/ria *adj* secondary.
sed *f* thirst; **tener** ~ to be thirsty.
seda *f* silk.
sedal *m* fishing line.
sedante *m* sedative.
sede *f* see; seat; headquarters.
sedentario/ria *adj* sedentary.
sedición *f* sedition.
sedicioso/sa *adj* seditious, mutinous.
sediento/ta *adj* thirsty; eager.
sedoso/sa *adj* silky.
seducción *f* seduction.
seducir *vt* to seduce; to bribe; to charm, to attract.
seductor/ra *adj* seductive; charming; attractive; * *m/f* seducer.
segador/ra *m/f* reaper, harvester.
segadora-trilladora *f* combine (harvester).
segar *vt* to reap, to harvest; to mow.
seglar *adj* secular, lay.
segmento *m* segment.
segregación *f* segregation, separation.

segregar *vt* to segregate, to separate.
seguido/da *adj* continuous; successive; long-lasting; * *adv* straight (on); after; *Lat Am* often.
seguidor/ra *m/f* follower; supporter.
seguimiento *m* pursuit; continuation.
seguir *vt* to follow, to pursue; to continue; * *vi* to follow; to carry on; ~se *vr* to follow, to ensue.
según *prep* according to.
segundo/da *adj* second; * *m* second (of time).
seguramente *adv* surely; for sure.
seguridad *f* security; certainty; safety; confidence; stability.
seguro/ra *adj* safe, secure; sure, certain; firm, constant; * *adv* for sure; * *m* safety device; insurance; safety, certainty.
seis *adj*, *m* six; sixth.
seiscientos/tas *adj* six hundred.
seísmo *m* earthquake.
selección *f* selection, choice.
seleccionar *vt* to select, to choose.
selecto/ta *adj* select, choice.
sellar *vt* to seal; to stamp (a document).
sello *m* seal; stamp.
selva *f* forest.
semáforo *m* traffic lights *pl*; signal.
semana *f* week.
semanada *f Lat Am* weekly pocket money.
semanal *adj* weekly.
semanario/ria *m* weekly (magazine).
semblante *m* face; (*fig*) look; appearance.
sembrado *m* sown field.
sembrar *vt* to sow; to sprinkle, to scatter.
semejante *adj* similar, like; * *m* fellow man.
semejanza *f* resemblance, likeness.
semejar *vi* to resemble; ~se *vr* to look alike.
semen *m* semen.
semental *m* stud.
sementera *f* sowing time; land sown with seed.
semestral *adj* half yearly.
semicircular *adj* semicircular.
semicírculo *m* semicircle.
semifinal *f* semifinal.
semilla *f* seed, bean.
semilla de soja *f* soybean.
semillero *m* seed plot.
seminario *m* seedbed; seminary.
seminarista *m* seminarist.
semitono *m* (*mus*) half step, semitone.
sémola *f* semolina.
sempiterno/na *adj* everlasting.
senado *m* senate.
senador/ra *m/f* senator.

sencillez *f* plainness; simplicity; naturalness.
sencillo/lla *adj* simple; natural; unaffected; single.
senda *f m* path, footpath.
senderismo *m* hillwalking.
senderista *m/f* hillwalker.
sendero *m* path, footpath.
senil *adj* senile.
seno *m* bosom; lap; womb; hole, cavity; sinus; ~s *mpl* breasts *pl*.
sensación *f* sensation, feeling; sense.
sensacional *adj* sensational.
sensato/ta *adj* sensible.
sensibilidad *f* sensibility, sensitivity.
sensible *adj* sensitive; perceptible, appreciable; regrettable.
sensitivo/va *adj* sense *compd*, sensitive.
sensorial *adj* sensorial, sensory.
sensual *adj* sensuous, sensual.
sensualidad *f* sensuousness; sensuality; sexiness.
sentado/da *adj* sitting, seated; sedate; settled.
sentar *vt* to seat; (*fig*) to establish; * *vi* to suit; ~se *vr* to sit down.
sentencia *f* (*law*) sentence; opinion; saying.
sentenciar *vt* (*law*) to sentence, to pass judgement on; * *vi* to give one's opinion.
sentencioso/sa *adj* sententious.
sentido *m* sense; feeling; meaning; ~/da *adj* regrettable; sensitive.
sentimental *adj* sentimental.
sentimiento *m* feeling, emotion, sentiment; sympathy; regret, grief.
sentir *vt* to feel; to hear; to perceive; to sense; to suffer from; to regret, to be sorry for; ~se *vr* to feel; to feel pain; to crack (of walls etc); * *m* opinion, judgement.
seña *f* sign, mark, token; signal; (*mil*) password; ~s *fpl* address.
señal *f* sign, token; symptom; signal; landmark; (*com*) deposit.
señalado/da *adj* distinct; special; distinguished, notable.
señalar *vt* to stamp, to mark; to signpost; to point out; to fix, to settle; ~se *vr* to distinguish oneself, to excel.
señor *m* man; gentleman; master; Mr; sir.
señora *f* lady; Mrs; madam; wife.
señorita *f* Miss; young lady.
señorito *m* Master; young gentleman; rich kid.
señuelo *m* decoy; bait, lure.
separable *adj* separable.
separación *f* separation.

separar *vt* to separate; ~se *vr* to separate; to come away, to come apart; to withdraw.
septentrional *adj* north, northern.
séptico *adj* septic.
septiembre *m* September.
séptimo/ma *adj* seventh.
sepulcral *adj* sepulchral.
sepulcro *m* sepulcher, grave, tomb.
sepultar *vt* to bury, to inter.
sepultura *f* burial, interment; grave, tomb.
sepulturero *m* gravedigger, sexton.
sequedad *f* dryness; brusqueness.
sequía *f* dryness; thirst; drought.
séquito *m* retinue, suite; group of supporters; aftermath.
ser *vi* to be; to exist; ~ de to come from; to be made of; to belong to; * *m* being.
serenarse *vr* to calm down.
serenata *f* (*mus*) serenade.
serenidad *f* serenity.
sereno *m* night watchman; ~/na *adj* serene, calm, quiet.
serial *m* serial.
serie *f* series; sequence.
seriedad *f* seriousness, gravity; reliability; sincerity.
serio/ria *adj* serious; grave; reliable.
sermón *m* sermon.
sermonear *vt* to lecture; * *vi* to sermonize.
seronegativo/va *adj* HIV-negative.
seropositivo/va *adj* HIV-positive.
serpentear *vi* to wriggle; to wind, to snake.
serpentina *f* streamer.
serpiente *f* snake.
serranía *f* range of mountains; mountainous country.
serrano/na *m/f* highlander.
serrar *vt* to saw.
serrín *m* sawdust.
serruchar *vt* Lat Am to saw up.
serrucho *m* handsaw.
servible *adj* serviceable.
servicial *adj* helpful, obliging.
servicio *m* service; service charge; service, set of dishes; ~s *mpl* bathroom facilities *pl*.
servidor/ra *m/f* servant.
servidumbre *f* servitude; servants *pl*, staff.
servil *adj* servile.
servilleta *f* napkin, serviette.
servir *vt* to serve; to wait on; * *vi* to serve; to be of use; to be in service; ~se *vr* to serve oneself, to help oneself; to deign, to please; to make use of.
sesenta *adj, m* sixty; sixtieth.

sesentón/ona *m/f* person of about sixty years of age.

sesgar *vt* to slope, to slant.

sesgo *m* slope.

sesión *f* session; sitting; performance; showing

seso *m* brain.

sestear *vi* to take a nap.

sesudo/da *adj* sensible, prudent.

seta *f* mushroom.

setecientos/tas *adj* seven hundred.

setenta *adj*, *m* seventy.

setiembre *m* September.

seto *m* fence; enclosure; hedge.

seudo- *pref* pseudo-.

seudónimo *m* pseudonym.

severidad *f* severity.

severo/ra *adj* severe, strict; grave, serious.

sexagenario/ria *adj* sixty years old.

sexagésimo/ma *adj* sixtieth.

sexenio *m* space of six years.

sexo *m* sex.

sexto/ta *adj*, *m* sixth.

sexual *adj* sexual.

short *m Lat Am* shorts.

si *conj* whether; if.

sí *adv* yes; certainly; indeed; * *pn* oneself; himself; herself; itself; yourself; themselves; yourselves; each other; one another.

siderúrgico/ca *adj* iron and steel *compd*.

sidra *f* cider.

siega *f* harvest, mowing.

siembra *f* sowing time.

siempre *adv* always; all the time; ever; *Lat Am* still; ~ **jamás** for ever and ever.

sien *f* temple (of the head).

sierra *f* saw; range of mountains.

siervo/va *m/f* slave.

siesta *f* siesta, afternoon nap.

siete *adj*, *m* seven.

sietemesino/na *adj* born seven months after conception; premature; (*fig*) half-witted.

sífilis *f* syphilis.

sifón *m* siphon; soda.

sigilo *m* secrecy.

sigiloso/sa *adj* reserved; silent.

sigla *f* acronym; abbreviation.

siglo *m* century.

significación *f* significance, meaning.

significado *m* significance, meaning.

significar *vt* to signify, to mean; to make known, to express.

significativo/va *adj* significant.

signo *m* sign, mark.

siguiente *adj* following, successive, next.

sílaba *f* syllable.

silbar *vt*, *vi* to hiss; to whistle.

silbato *m* whistle.

silbido, silbo *m* hiss; whistling.

silencio *m* silence; ¡~! silence!, quiet!

silencioso/sa *adj* silent.

silla *f* chair; saddle; seat; ~ **de ruedas** wheelchair.

sillón *m* armchair, easy chair; rocking chair.

silo *m* silo.

silogismo *m* syllogism.

silueta *f* silhouette; outline; figure.

silvestre *adj* wild, uncultivated; rustic.

sima *f* abyss; pothole, cavern.

simbólico/ca *adj* symbolic.

simbolizar *vt* to symbolize.

símbolo *m* symbol.

simetría *f* symmetry.

simétrico/ca *adj* symmetrical.

simiente *f* seed.

similar *adj* similar.

similitud *f* similarity, similitude.

simio *m* ape.

simpatía *f* liking; kindness; solidarity; affection.

simpático/ca *adj* pleasant; kind.

simpatizante *m/f* sympathizer.

simpatizar *vi*: ~ **con** to get on well with.

simple *adj* single; simple, easy; mere; sheer; silly; * *m/f* simpleton.

simpleza *f* simpleness, gullibility; silliness.

simplicidad *f* simplicity.

simplificar *vt* to simplify.

simulación *f* simulation.

simulacro *m* simulacrum, idol.

simuladamente *adv* deceptively, hypocritically.

simular *vt* to simulate.

simultaneidad *f* simultaneousness.

simultáneo/nea *adj* simultaneous.

sin *prep* without.

sinagoga *f* synagogue.

sinceridad *f* sincerity.

sincero/ra *adj* sincere.

síncope *f* (*med*) syncope, fainting fit.

sincronizar *vt* to synchronize.

sindical *adj* union *compd*.

sindicato *m* labor union; syndicate.

sinfín *m*: **un** ~ **de** a great many.

sinfonía *f* symphony.

singular *adj* singular; exceptional; peculiar, odd.

singularidad *f* singularity.

singularizar *vt* to distinguish; to singularize; ~se vr to distinguish oneself; to stand out.

siniestro/tra adj left; (fig) sinister; * m accident.

sinnúmero m = **sinfín**.

sino conj but; except; save; only; * m fate.

sinónimo/ma adj synonymous; * m synonym.

sinsabor m unpleasantness; disgust.

sintaxis f syntax.

síntesis f synthesis.

sintético/ca adj synthetic.

sintetizar vt synthesize.

síntoma m symptom.

sinuosidad f sinuosity; curve, wave.

sinuoso/sa adj sinuous; wavy.

sinvergüenza m/f rogue.

siquiera conj even if, even though; * adv at least.

sirena f siren; mermaid; car horn.

sirviente/ta m/f servant.

sisa f petty theft; cut, percentage.

sisear vt, vi to hiss.

sistema m system.

sistemático/ca adj systematic.

sitiar vt to besiege.

sitio m place; spot; site, location; room, space; job, post; (mil) siege, blockade.

situación f situation, position; standing.

situar vt to place, to situate; to invest; ~se vr to be established in place/business.

slip m underpants pl, briefs pl.

smoking m tuxedo.

sobaco m armpit, armhole.

sobar vt to handle, to soften; to knead; to massage, to rub hard; to rumple (clothes); to fondle.

soberanía f sovereignty.

soberano/na adj, m/f sovereign.

soberbia f pride, haughtiness; magnificence.

soberbio/bia adj proud, haughty; magnificent.

sobornar vt to suborn, to bribe.

soborno m subornation, bribery; bribe.

sobra f surplus, excess; **de** ~ spare, surplus, extra.

sobradamente adv too; amply.

sobrante adj remaining; * m surplus, remainder.

sobrar vt to exceed, to surpass; * vi to be more than enough; to remain, to be left.

sobrasada f pork sausage spread.

sobre prep on; on top of; above, over; more than; besides; * m envelope; Lat Am purse, handbag.

sobreabundancia f superabundance.

sobreabundar vi to superabound.

sobrecarga f extra load; (com) surcharge.

sobrecargar vt to overload; (com) to surcharge.

sobrecoger vt to surprise.

sobredosis f invar overdose.

sobreentender vt to deduce; ~se vr: se **sobreentiende que** . . . it is implied that . . . .

sobrehumano/na adj superhuman.

sobrellevar vt to carry; to tolerate.

sobremanera adv excessively.

sobremesa f: **de** ~ immediately after dinner.

sobrenatural adj supernatural.

sobrenaturalmente adv supernaturally.

sobrenombre m nickname.

sobrepasar vt to surpass.

sobreponer vt to put (something) over/on top of; ~se vr to pull through.

sobresaliente adj projecting; (fig) outstanding.

sobresalir vi to project; (fig) to stand out.

sobresaltar vt to frighten.

sobresalto m start, scare; sudden shock.

sobreseer vt: ~ **una causa** (law) to stay a case; * vi: ~ **de** to desist from.

sobreseimiento m dismissal, suspension.

sobrevenir vi to happen, to come unexpectedly; to supervene.

sobrevida f Lat Am survival.

sobreviviente adj surviving; * m/f survivor.

sobrevivir vi to survive.

sobrevolar vt to fly over.

sobriedad f sobriety.

sobrino/na m/f nephew/niece.

sobrio/ria adj sober, frugal.

socarrón/ona adj sarcastic; ironic(al).

socarronería f sarcasm; irony.

socavar vt to undermine.

socavón m hole.

sociabilidad f sociability.

sociable adj sociable.

social adj social.

socialdemócrata adj, m/f social democrat.

socialista adj, m/f socialist.

sociedad f society.

socio/cia m/f associate, member.

sociología f sociology.

sociólogo/ga m/f sociologist.

socorrer vt to help.

socorrido/da adj well-stocked/supplied.

socorrista m/f first aider; lifeguard.

socorro m help, aid, assistance, relief.

soda f soda; soda water.

sodomía *f* sodomy.
sodomita *m* sodomite.
soez *adj* dirty, obscene.
sofá *m* sofa.
sofisma *m* sophism.
sofista *m/f* sophist.
sofisticación *f* sophistication.
sofocar *vt* to suffocate.
software *m* (*comput*) software.
soga *f* rope.
sojuzgar *vt* to conquer, to subdue.
sol *m* sun; sunshine, sunlight.
solamente *adv* only, solely.
solapa *f* lapel.
solapado/da *adj* cunning, crafty, artful.
solar *m* building site; piece of land; ancestral home of a family; * *adj* solar.
solariego/ga *adj* belonging to the ancestral home of a family.
solaz *m* recreation, relaxation; solace, consolation.
solazar *vt* to provide relaxation for; to comfort
soldada *f* wages *pl*.
soldadesca *f* military profession.
soldado *m/f* soldier; ~ raso private.
soldador *m* welder; soldering iron.
soldadura *f* soldering; solder.
soldar *vt* to solder; to weld; to unite.
soleado/da *adj* sunny.
soledad *f* solitude; loneliness.
solemne *adj* solemn; impressive, grand.
solemnidad *f* solemnity.
solemnizar *vt* to solemnize; to praise.
soler *vi* to be accustomed to, to be in the habit of.
solfeo *m* (*mus*) solfa.
solicitar *vt* to ask for, to seek; to apply for (a job); to canvass for; to chase after, to pursue.
solícito/ta *adj* diligent; solicitous.
solicitud *f* care, solicitude; request, petition.
solidaridad *f* solidarity.
solidario/ria *adj* joint; mutually binding.
solidez *f* solidity.
sólido/da *adj* solid.
soliloquio *m* soliloquy, monolog.
solista *m/f* soloist.
solitario/ria *adj* lonesome, solitary; * *m* solitaire; * *m/f* hermit.
sollozar *vi* to sob.
sollozo *m* sob.
solo *m* (*mus*) solo; ~/la *adj* alone, single; **a solas** alone, unaided.
sólo *adv* only.

solomillo *m* sirloin.
solsticio *m* solstice.
soltar *vt* to untie, to loosen; to set free, to let out; ~se *vr* to get loose; to come undone.
soltero/ra *m/f* bachelor/single woman; * *adj* single, unmarried.
soltura *f* looseness, slackness; agility, activity; fluency.
soluble *adj* soluble; solvable.
solución *f* solution; denouement.
solucionar *vt* to solve; to resolve.
solvente *adj*, *m* solvent.
sombra *f* shade; shadow.
sombrear *vt* to shade.
sombrero *m* hat.
sombrilla *f* parasol.
sombrío/bría *adj* shady, gloomy; sad.
somero/ra *adj* superficial.
someter *vt* to conquer (a country); to subject to one's will; to submit; to subdue; ~se *vr* to give in, to submit.
sometimiento *m* submission.
somnífero *m* sleeping pill.
somnolencia *f* sleepiness, drowsiness.
son *m* sound; rumor.
sonado/da *adj* celebrated; famous; generally reported.
sonaja *f* (*mus*) timbrel.
sonajero *m* (*mus*) small timbrel.
sonámbulo/la *m/f* sleepwalker; somnambulist.
sonar *vt* to ring; * *vi* to sound; to make a noise; to be pronounced; to be talked of; to sound familiar; ~se *vr* to blow one's nose.
sonata *f* (*mus*) sonata.
sonda *f* sounding; (*med*) probe.
sondear *vt* (*mar*) to sound; to probe; to bore.
sondeo *m* sounding; boring; (*fig*) poll.
soneto *m* sonnet.
sónico/ca *adj* sonic.
sonido *m* sound.
sonoro/ra *adj* sonorous.
sonreír(se) *vi* (*vr*) to smile.
sonrisa *f* smile.
sonrojarse *vr* to blush.
sonrojo *m* blush.
sonsacar *vt* to wheedle, cajole; to obtain by cunning.
sonsear *vi Lat Am* to fool around.
sonsera *f Lat Am* nonsense.
sonso/sa *m/f Lat Am* fool.
sonsonete *m* tapping noise; monotonous voice.

soñador/ra *m/f* dreamer.
soñar *vt, vi* to dream.
soñoliento/ta *adj* sleepy, drowsy.
sopa *f* soup; sop.
sopapo *m* punch, thump.
sopera *f* soup dish.
sopero *m* soup plate.
sopetón *m*: de ~ suddenly.
soplar *vt* to blow away, to blow off; to blow up, to inflate; * *vi* to blow, to puff.
soplete *m* blowlamp.
soplo *m* blowing; puff of wind; (*col*) tip-off.
soplón/ona *m/f* telltale.
sopor *m* drowsiness, sleepiness.
soporífero/ra *adj* soporific; * *m* sleeping pill.
soportable *adj* tolerable, bearable.
soportal *m* portico.
soportar *vt* to suffer, to tolerate; to support.
sorber *vt* to sip; to inhale; to swallow; to absorb.
sorbete *m* sherbet; sorbet.
sorbo *m* sip; gulp, swallow.
sordera *f* deafness.
sordidez *f* sordidness; dirtiness; meanness.
sórdido/da *adj* sordid; dirty; mean.
sorda/da *adj* deaf; silent, quiet; * *m/f* deaf person.
sordomudo/da *adj* deaf and dumb.
sorna *f* slyness; sarcasm; slowness.
soroche *m* mountain sickness.
sorprender *vt* to surprise.
sorpresa *f* surprise.
sortear *vt* to draw/cast (lots); to raffle; to avoid.
sorteo *m* draw; raffle.
sortija *f* ring; ringlet, curl.
sortilegio *m* sorcery.
sosegado/da *adj* quiet, peaceful.
sosegar *vt* to appease, to calm; * *vi* to rest.
sosería *f* insipidness; dullness.
sosiego *m* tranquility, calmness.
soslayar *vt* to do/place (something) obliquely.
soslayo *adv*: al/de ~ obliquely, sideways.
soso/sa *adj* insipid, tasteless; dull.
sospecha *f* suspicion.
sospechar *vt* to suspect.
sospechoso/sa *adj* suspicious; suspect; * *m/f* suspect.
sostén *m* support; bra; sustenance.
sostener *vt* to sustain, to maintain; ~se *vr* to support/maintain oneself; to contrive, to remain.

sostenimiento *m* support; maintenance; sustenance.
sota *f* jack, knave (in cards).
sotana *f* cassock.
sótano *m* basement, cellar.
sotavento *m* (*mar*) leeward, lee.
soto *m* grove, thicket.
squash *m* squash.
status *m invar* status.
su *pn* his, her, its, one's; their; your.
suave *adj* smooth, soft; delicate; gentle; mild, meek.
suavidad *f* softness, sweetness; suavity.
suavizar *vt* to soften.
subalterno/na *adj* secondary; auxiliary.
subasta *f* auction.
subastar *vt* to sell by auction.
subcampeón/ona *m/f* runner-up.
subconsciente *adj, m* subconscious.
subdesarrollado/da *adj* underdeveloped.
subdesarrollo *m* underdevelopment.
subdirector/ora *m/f* assistant director.
súbdito/ta *adj, m/f* subject.
subdividir *vt* to subdivide.
subdivisión *f* subdivision.
subestimar *vt* to underestimate.
subida *f* climb, ascent, rise in value/price.
subido/da *adj* deep-colored; high (price).
subir *vt, vi* to raise, to lift up; to go up; to climb, to ascend; to increase, to swell; to get in, to get on, to board; to rise (in price).
súbito/ta *adj* sudden, hasty; unforeseen.
subjetivo/va *adj* subjective.
subjuntivo *m* (*gr*) subjunctive.
sublevación *f* sedition, revolt.
sublevar *vt* to excite (a rebellion); to incite (a revolt); ~se *vr* to revolt.
sublime *adj* sublime.
sublimidad *f* sublimity.
submarino/na *adj* underwater; * *m* submarine.
subnormal *adj* subnormal; * *m/f* person of low intelligence.
subordinación *f* subordination.
subrayar *vt* to underline.
subrepticio/cia *adj* surreptitious.
subsanar *vt* to excuse; to mend, to repair; to overcome.
subsidio *m* subsidy, aid; benefit, allowance.
subsistencia *f* subsistence.
subsistir *vi* to subsist.
su(b)stancia *f* substance.
su(b)stancial *adj* substantial.
su(b)stancioso/sa *adj* substantial; nutritious.

su(b)stracción f removal; (*math*) subtraction.

su(b)straer vt to remove; (*math*) to subtract; ~**se** vr to avoid; to withdraw.

subterfugio f subterfuge.

subterráneo/nea adj subterranean, underground; * m underground passage; (*rail*) subway.

suburbio m slum quarter; suburbs pl.

subvencionar vt to subsidize.

subversión f subversion, overthrow.

subversivo/va adj subversive.

subvertir vt to subvert, to overthrow.

subyugar vt to subdue, to subjugate.

sucedáneo/nea adj substitute; * m substitute (food).

suceder vt to succeed, to inherit; * vi to happen.

sucesión f succession; issue, offspring; inheritance.

sucesivamente adv: **y así** ~ and so on.

sucesivo/va adj successive.

suceso m event; incident.

sucesor/ra m/f successor; heir.

suciedad f dirtiness, filthiness; dirt.

sucinto/ta adj succinct, concise.

sucio/cia adj dirty, filthy; obscene; dishonest.

suculento/ta adj succulent, juicy.

sucumbir vt to succumb.

sucursal f branch (office).

sudar vt, vi to sweat.

sudeste adj southeast, southeastern; * m southeast.

sudoeste adj southwest, southwestern; * m southwest.

sudor m sweat.

sudorífico/ca adj sweaty.

suegra f mother-in-law.

suegro m father-in-law.

suela f sole (shoe).

sueldo m wages pl, salary.

suelo m ground; floor; soil, surface.

suelto/ta adj loose; free; detached; swift; * m loose change.

sueño m sleep; dream.

suero m (*med*) serum; whey.

suerte f fate, destiny, chance, lot, fortune, good luck; kind, sort.

suéter m sweater.

suficiencia f sufficiency, competence, fitness.

suficiente adj enough, sufficient; fit, capable.

sufragar vt to aid, to assist; * vi *Lat Am*) to vote.

sufragio m vote, suffrage; aid, assistance.

sufrible adj bearable.

sufrido/da adj long-suffering, patient; hardwearing.

sufrimiento m suffering; patience.

sufrir vt to suffer; to bear, to put up with; to support.

sugerencia f suggestion.

sugerir vt to suggest.

sugestión f suggestion.

suicida adj suicidal; * m/f suicide; suicidal person.

suicidio m suicide.

sujeción f subjection.

sujetacorbata m *Lat Am* tie-pin.

sujetador m fastener; bra.

sujetar vt to fasten, to hold down; to subdue; to subject; ~**se** vr to subject oneself.

sujeto/ta adj fastened, secure; subject, liable; * m subject; individual.

sulfúrico adj sulfuric.

sultán m sultan.

sultana f sultana.

suma f total, sum; adding up; summary.

sumamente adv extremely.

sumar vt to add, to add up; to collect, to gather; * vi to add up.

sumario/ria adj brief, concise; * m summary.

sumergir vt to submerge, to sink; to immerse.

sumidero m sewer, drain.

suministrador/ra m/f provider, supplier.

suministrar vt to supply, to furnish.

sumir vt to sink, to submerge; (*fig*) to plunge.

sumisión f submission.

sumiso/sa adj submissive, docile.

sumo/ma adj great, extreme; highest, greatest; **a lo** ~ at most.

suntuosidad f sumptuousness.

suntuoso/sa adj sumptuous.

súper f four-star (gas).

superable adj surmountable.

superabundancia f superabundance.

superabundar vi to superabound.

superar vt to surpass; to overcome; to exceed, to go beyond.

superficial adj superficial; shallow.

superficie f surface; area.

superfluo/lua adj superfluous.

superintendencia f supervision.

superintendente m/f superintendent, supervisor; floorwalker.

superior adj superior; upper; higher; better; * m/f superior.

superioridad *f* superiority.
superlativo/va *adj*, *m* (*gr*) superlative.
supermercado *m* supermarket.
superstición *f* superstition.
supersticioso/sa *adj* superstitious.
supervisor/ra *m/f* supervisor.
supervivencia *f* survival.
superviviente *m/f* survivor; * *adj* surviving.
suplantación *f* supplanting.
suplantar *vt* to supplant.
suplemento *m* supplement.
suplente *m/f* substitute.
supletorio/ria *adj* supplementary.
súplica *f* petition, request; supplication.
suplicante *adj*, *m/f* applicant; supplicant.
suplicar *vt* to beg (for), to plead (for); to beg; to plead with.
suplicio *m* torture.
suplir *vt* to supply; to make good, to make up for; to replace.
suponer *vt* to suppose; * *vi* to have authority.
suposición *f* supposition; authority.
supremo/ma *adj* supreme.
supresión *f* suppression; abolition; removal.
suprimir *vt* to suppress; to abolish; to remove; to delete.
supuesto *m* assumption; ~/ta *adj* supposed; ~ que *conj* since, granted that.
supuración *f* suppuration.
supurar *vt* to suppurate.
sur *adj* south, southern; * *m* south; south wind.
surcar *vt* to furrow; to cut, to score.
surco *m* furrow; groove.
surgir *vi* to emerge; to crop up.
surtido *m* assortment, supply.
surtir *vt* to supply, to furnish, to provide; * *vi* to spout, to spurt.

susceptible *adj* susceptible; impressionable.
suscitar *vt* to excite, to stir up.
suscribir *vt* to sign; to subscribe to.
suscripción *f* subscription.
suscriptor/ra *m/f* subscriber.
susodicho/cha *adj* above-mentioned.
suspender *vt* to suspend, to hang up; to stop; to fail (an exam etc).
suspensión *f* suspension; stoppage.
suspenso/sa *adj* hanging; suspended, failed; * *m Lat Am* suspense.
suspicacia *f* suspicion, mistrust.
suspicaz *adj* suspicious, mistrustful.
suspirar *vi* to sigh.
suspiro *m* sigh.
sustancia *f* = **substancia**.
sustancial *adj* = **substancial**.
sustancioso *adj* = **substancioso**.
sustantivo/va *adj*, *m* (*gr*) substantive, noun.
sustentar *vt* to sustain; to support, to nourish.
sustento *m* food, sustenance; support.
sustitución *f* substitution.
sustituir *vt* to substitute.
sustituto/ta *adj*, *m/f* substitute.
susto *m* fright, scare.
sustracción *f* subtraction.
sustraer *vt* to take away; to subtract.
susurrar *vi* to whisper; to murmur; to rustle; ~se *vr* to be whispered about.
susurro *m* whisper; murmur.
sutil *adj* subtle; thin; delicate; very soft; keen, observant.
sutileza *f* subtlety; thinness; keenness.
suyo/ya *adj* his; hers; theirs; one's; his; her; its own; one's own; their own; de ~ per se; los ~s *mpl* his own, near friends, relations, family, supporters.

T

tabaco *m* tobacco; (*col*) cigarettes *pl*.

tábano *m* horsefly.

tabaquería *f Lat Am* cigar store.

taberna *f* bar, tavern.

tabernero/ra *m/f* barman/barmaid, bartender.

tabicar *vt* to wall up.

tabique *m* thin wall; partition wall.

tabla *f* board; shelf; plank; slab; index of a book; bed of earth in a garden.

tablado *m* scaffold; platform; stage.

tablero *m* plank, board; chessboard; checkerboard; (*auto*) dashboard; bulletin board; gambling den.

tableta *f* tablet; (chocolate) bar.

tablilla *f* small board; (*med*) splint.

tablón *m* plank; beam; ~ de anuncios bulletin board.

tabú *m* taboo.

taburete *m* stool.

tacañería *f* meanness; craftiness.

tacaño/ña *adj* mean, stingy; crafty.

tacha *f* fault, defect; small nail.

tachar *vt* to find fault with; to cross out, to erase.

tachuela *f* tack, nail.

tácito/ta *adj* tacit, silent; implied.

taciturno/na *adj* tacit, silent; sulky.

taco *m* stopper, plug; heel (of a shoe); wad; book of coupons; billiard cue.

tacón *m* heel.

taconear *vi* to stamp with one's heels; to walk on one's heels.

taconeo *m* stamping of the heels in dancing.

táctica *f* tactics *pl*.

tacto *m* touch, feeling; tact.

tafetán *m* taffeta.

tafilete *m* morocco leather.

tahona *f* bakery.

tahúr *m* gambler; cheat.

taimado/da *adj* sly, cunning, crafty.

tajada *f* slice; (*med*) hoarseness.

tajante *adj* sharp.

tajar *vt* to cut; to chop; to slice.

tajo *m* cut, incision; cleft, sheer drop; working area; chopping block.

tal *adj* such; con ~ que provided that; no hay ~ no such thing.

tala *f* felling of trees.

taladrar *vt* to bore; to pierce.

taladro *m* drill; borer.

talante *m* mood; appearance; aspect; will.

talar *vt* to fell (trees); to desolate.

talco *m* talc.

talego/ga *m/f* bag; bagful.

talento *m* talent.

talismán *m* talisman.

talla *f* raised work; sculpture; stature, size; measure (of anything); hand, draw, turn (in cards).

tallado/da *adj* cut; carved; engraved.

tallador *m* engraver.

tallar *vt* to cut, to chop; to carve in wood; to engrave; to measure.

tallarines *mpl* noodles.

talle *m* shape; size; proportion; waist.

taller *m* workshop, laboratory.

tallo *m* shoot, sprout.

talón *m* heel; receipt; check.

talonario *m* check book; receipt book.

talonear *vt Lat Am* to spur.

talvez *adv Lat Am* perhaps.

tamaño *m* size, shape, bulk.

tamarindo *m* tamarind tree.

tambalearse *vr* to stagger, to waver.

tambaleo *m* staggering, reeling.

también *adv* also, as well; likewise; besides.

tambor *m* drum; drummer; eardrum.

tamborilear *vi* to drum.

tamborilero *m* drummer.

tamiz *m* fine sieve.

tampoco *adv* neither, nor.

tampón *m* tampon.

tan *adv* so.

tanda *f* turn; rotation; task; gang; number of persons employed in a workforce.

tangente *f* tangent.

tangible *adj* tangible.

tanque *m* tank; tanker.

tantear *vt* to reckon (up); to measure, to proportion; to consider; to examine.

tanteo *m* computation, calculation; valuation; test; scoring.

tanto *m* certain sum/quantity; point; goal; ~/ta *adj* so much, as much, very great; * *adv* so much, as much; so long, as long.

tañido *m* tune; sound; clink.

tapa *f* lid, cover; snack; (*col*) ~ de los sesos skull.

tapadera *f* lid (of a pot), cover.

tapar vt to stop up, to cover; to conceal, to hide.

taparrabo m loincloth.

tapete m tablecloth; Lat Am carpet.

tapia f wall.

tapiar vt to brick up; to stop up (a passage).

tapicería f tapestry; upholstery; upholsterer's place of business.

tapicero m tapestry-maker; upholsterer.

tapiz m tapestry; carpet.

tapizar vt to upholster.

tapón m cork, plug, bung; Lat Am fuse.

taquigrafía f stenography, shorthand.

taquígrafo/fa m/f stenographer.

taquilla f booking office; takings pl.

taquillero/ra m/f ticket clerk.

tara f (com) tare.

tarántula f tarantula.

tardanza f slowness, delay.

tardar vi to delay; to take a long time; to be late.

tarde f afternoon; evening; * adv late.

tardío/dia adj late; slow, tardy.

tardo/da adj sluggish, tardy.

tarea f task.

tarifa f tariff; price list.

tarima f platform; step.

tarjeta f card; visiting card; ~ **postal** postcard; ~ **de crédito** credit card.

tarro m pot.

tarta f tart; cake.

tartamudear vi to stutter, to stammer.

tartamudo/da adj stammering.

tarugo m wooden peg/pin.

tasa f rate; measure, rule; valuation; ~**s de aeropuerto** airport tax.

tasación f valuation, appraisal.

tasador m appraiser.

tasar vt to appraise, to value.

tasca f (col) joint, barroom, saloon.

tata m Lat Am (col) pop, dad.

tatarabuelo/la m/f great-great-grandfather/mother.

tataranieto/ta m/f great-great-grandson/daughter.

tatuaje m tattoo; tattooing.

tatuar vt to tattoo.

taurino/na adj bullfighting compd; Lat Am Taurean (zodiac sign).

Tauro m Taurus (zodiac sign).

taxi m taxi.

taxista m/f taxi driver.

taza f cup; basin of a fountain.

té m (bot) tea.

te pn you.

tea f torch.

teatral adj theatrical.

teatro m theater, playhouse.

tebeo m comic.

techo m roof; ceiling.

techumbre f upper roof, ceiling.

tecla f key (of an organ, piano etc).

teclado m keyboard.

técnico/ca adj technical.

tecnología f technology.

tedio m boredom; dislike, abhorrence.

teja f tile.

tejado m roof covered with tiles.

tejanos mpl jeans pl.

tejar vt to tile.

tejedor m weaver.

tejemaneje m artfulness, cleverness; restlessness.

tejer vt to weave.

tejido m texture; web.

tejo m quoit (a ring of iron, plastic etc used in the game of quoits); hopscotch; yew tree.

tejón m badger.

tela f cloth; material.

telar m loom.

telaraña f cobweb.

telebanca f telephone banking.

telecomedia f sitcom.

telediario m television news.

telefax m invar fax; fax (machine).

telefonear vt to telephone.

telefonema m Lat Am telephone call.

telefónico/ca adj telephone compd.

teléfono m (tele)phone.

teléfono público m payphone.

telegráfico/ca adj telegraphic.

telégrafo m telegraph.

telegrama m telegram.

telescopio m telescope.

teletienda f home shopping program.

teletrabajador/ra m/f teleworker.

teletrabajo m teleworking.

televidente m/f viewer.

televisar vt to televise.

televisión f television; ~ **por cable** cable television.

televisor m television set.

télex m telex.

telón m drape.

tema m theme.

temblar vi to tremble.

temblón/ona adj trembling.

temblor m trembling; earthquake.

temer vt to fear, to doubt; * vi to be afraid.

temerario/ria adj rash.

temeridad *f* temerity, imprudence.
temeroso/sa *adj* timid; frightful.
temible *adj* dreadful, terrible.
temor *m* dread, fear.
témpano *m* ice-floe.
temperamento *m* temperament.
temperatura *f* temperature.
tempested *f* tempest, storm; violent commotion.
tempestuoso/sa *adj* tempestuous, stormy.
templado/da *adj* temperate, tempered.
templanza *f* temperance, moderation.
templar *vt* to temper, to moderate, to cool; to tune; ~se *vr* to be moderate.
temple *m* temperature; tempera; temperament; tuning; al ~ painted in distemper.
templo *m* temple.
temporada *f* time, season; epoch, period.
temporal *adj* temporary, temporal; * *m* tempest, storm.
temporariamente *adv Lat Am* temporarily.
temporario/ria *adj Lat Am* temporary.
temprano/na *adj* early, anticipated; * *adv* early; very early, prematurely.
tenacidad *f* tenacity; obstinacy.
tenacillas *fpl* small tongs *pl*.
tenaz *adj* tenacious; stubborn.
tenaza(s) *f(pl)* tongs *pl*, pincers *pl*.
tenazmente *adv* tenaciously; obstinately.
tendedero *m* clothes line.
tendencia *f* tendency.
tender *vt* to stretch out; to expand; to extend; to hang out; to lay; *Lat Am* to lay, to set; ~se *vr* to stretch oneself out.
tenderete *m* stall; display of goods.
tendero/ra *m/f* shopkeeper.
tendido/da *adj* lying down; hanging; * *m* row of seats for the spectators at a bullfight.
tendón *m* tendon, sinew.
tenebroso/sa *adj* dark, obscure.
tenedor *m* holder, keeper, tenant; fork.
tenencia *f* possession; tenancy; tenure.
tener *vt* to have; to take; to hold; to possess; ~se *vr* to stand upright; to stop, to halt; to resist; to adhere.
tenia *f* tapeworm.
teniente *m* lieutenant.
tenis *m* tennis.
tenista *m/f* tennis player.
tenor *m* meaning; (*mus*) tenor.
tensar *vt* to tauten; to draw.
tensión *f* tension.
tenso/sa *adj* tense.
tentación *f* temptation.

tentador/ra *m/f* tempter.
tentar *vt* to touch; to try; to tempt; to attempt.
tentativa *f* attempt.
tentempié *m* (*col*) snack.
tenue *adj* thin; tenuous, slender.
tenuidad *f* slenderness; weakness; trifle.
teñir *vt* to tinge, to dye.
teología *f* theology, divinity.
teológico/ca *adj* theological.
teólogo *m* theologian, divine.
teorema *f* theorem.
teoría, teórica *f* theory.
teórico/ca *adj* theoretical.
terapéutico/ca *adj* therapeutic.
terapia *f* therapy.
tercermundista *adj* Third World *compd*.
tercer(o)/ra *adj* third; * *m* (*law*) third party.
tercerización *f Lat Am* outsourcing.
tercerizar *vt Lat Am* to outsource.
terceto *m* (*mus*) trio.
terciar *vt* to put on sideways; to divide into three parts; * *vi* to mediate; to take part.
terciarización *f Lat Am* outsourcing.
terciarizar *vt Lat Am* to outsource.
tercio/cia *adj* third; * *m* third part.
terciopelo *m* velvet.
terco/ca *adj* obstinate.
tergiversación *f* distortion; evasion.
tergiversar *vt* to distort.
termal *adj* thermal.
termas *fpl* thermal waters *pl*.
terminación *f* termination; conclusion; last syllable of a word.
terminal *adj*, *m/f* terminal.
terminante *adj* decisive; categorical.
terminar *vt* to finish; to end; to terminate; * *vi* to end; to stop.
término *m* term; end; boundary; limit; terminus.
terminología *f* terminology.
termodinámico/ca *adj* thermodynamic.
termómetro *m* thermometer.
termo *m* flask.
termostato *m* thermostat.
ternero/ra *m/f* calf; veal; heifer.
ternilla *f* gristle.
ternilloso/sa *adj* gristly.
terno *m* three-piece suit.
ternura *f* tenderness.
terquedad *f* stubbornness, obstinacy.
terrado *m* terrace.
terraplén *m* terrace; platform.

terrateniente *m/f* landowner.
terraza *f* balcony; (flat) roof; terrace (in fields).
terremoto *m* earthquake.
terrenal *adj* terrestrial, earthly.
terreno/na *adj* earthly, terrestrial; * *m* land, ground, field.
terrestre *adj* terrestrial.
terrible *adj* terrible, dreadful; ferocious.
territorial *adj* territorial.
territorio *m* territory.
terrón *m* clod of earth; lump; ~ones *mpl* real estate.
terror *m* terror, dread.
terrorismo *m* terrorism.
terrorista *m/f* terrorist.
terso/sa *adj* smooth, glossy.
tersura *f* smoothness; shine.
tertulia *f* club, assembly, circle.
tesis *f invar* thesis.
tesón *m* tenacity, firmness.
tesorero *m* treasurer.
tesoro *m* treasure; exchequer.
testamentaría *f* testamentary execution.
testamentario *m* executor of a will; ~/ria *adj* testamentary.
testamento *m* will, testament.
testar *vt, vi* to make one's will.
testarudo/da *adj* obstinate.
testículo *m* testicle.
testificación *f* attestation.
testificar *vt* to attest, to witness.
testigo *m* witness, deponent.
testimoniar *vt* to attest, to bear witness to.
testimonio *m* testimony.
teta *f* teat.
tétanos *m* tetanus.
tetera *f* teapot.
tetilla *f* nipple; teat (of a bottle).
tétrico/ca *adj* gloomy, sullen, surly.
textil *adj* textile *compd.*
texto *m* text.
textual *adj* textual.
textura *f* texture.
tez *f* complexion, hue.
ti *pn* you; yourself.
tía *f* aunt; (*col*) dame.
tiara *f* tiara.
tibieza *f* lukewarmness.
tibio/bia *adj* lukewarm.
tiburón *m* shark.
tico/ca *m/f Lat Am* (*col*) Costa Rican.
tiempo *m* time; term; weather; (*gr*) tense; occasion, opportunity; season.
tienda *f* tent; awning; tilt; store.

tiento *m* touch; circumspection; **a** ~/**a tientas** gropingly.
tierno/na *adj* tender; * *m Lat Am* baby.
tierra *f* earth; land, ground; native country.
tieso/sa *adj* stiff, hard, firm; robust; valiant; stubborn.
tiesto *m* large earthenware pot.
tifón *m* typhoon.
tifus *m* typhus.
tigre *m* tiger; *Lat Am* jaguar.
tijeras *fpl* scissors *pl.*
tijeretada *f* cut (with scissors), clip.
tijereta *f* earwig.
tijeretear *vt* to cut (with scissors).
tildar *vt* to brand, to stigmatize.
tilde *f* tilde (ñ).
tilo *m* lime tree.
timar *vt* to steal; to swindle.
timbrar *vt* to stamp.
timbre *m* stamp; bell; timbre; stamp duty.
timidez *f* timidity.
tímido/da *adj* timid; cowardly.
timo *m* swindle.
timón *m* helm, rudder.
tímpano *m* eardrum; small drum.
tina *f* tub; bath(tub).
tinaja *f* large earthenware jar.
tinglado *m* shed; trick; intrigue.
tinieblas *fpl* darkness; shadows *pl.*
tino *m* skill; judgement, prudence.
tinta *f* ink; tint, dye; color.
tinte *m* tint, dye; dry cleaner's (premises).
tintero *m* inkwell.
tinto/ta *adj* dyed; * *m* red wine.
tintorería *f* dry cleaner's (place of business).
tintura *f* tincture; dyeing.
tiña *f* scab.
tiñoso/sa *adj* scabby, scurvy; niggardly.
tío *m* uncle; (*col*) guy.
tiovivo *m* merry-go-round.
tipear *vt Lat Am* to type.
típico/ca *adj* typical.
tiple *m* (*mus*) treble; * *f* soprano.
tipo *m* type; norm; pattern; guy.
tipografía *f* typography.
tipográfico/ca *adj* typographical.
tipógrafo *m* printer, typographer.
tiquet *m* ticket; cash slip.
tiquismiquis *m invar* fussy person.
tira *f* abundance; strip.
tirabuzón *m* curl.
tirachinas *m invar* catapult.
tirado/da *adj* dirt-cheap; (*col*) very easy; * *f* cast; distance; series; edition.
tirador *m* handle.

tiraje *m Lat Am* print run.
tiranía *f* tyranny.
tiránico/ca *adj* tyrannical.
tiranizar *vt* to tyrannize.
tirano/na *m/f* tyrant.
tirante *m* joist; stay; strap; brace; * *adj* taut, extended, drawn.
tirantez *f* tension; tautness.
tirar *vt* to throw; to pull; to draw; to drop; to tend, to aim at; * *vi* to shoot; to pull; to go; to tend to.
Tirita™ *f* Band-Aid™, adhesive tape, sticking plaster.
tiritar *vi* to shiver.
tiritona *f* shiver; shaking with cold.
tiro *m* throw, shot; prank; set of coach horses; **errar el ~** to miss (at shooting).
tirón *m* pull, haul, tug.
tirotear *vt* to shoot at.
tiroteo *m* shooting; sharpshooting.
tirria *f* antipathy.
tísico/ca *adj* consumptive.
tisis *f* tuberculosis.
titere *m* puppet; ridiculous little fellow.
titiritero/ra *m/f* puppeteer.
titubear *vi* to stammer; to stagger; to hesitate.
titubeo *m* staggering; hesitation.
titular *adj* titular; * *m/f* occupant; * *m* headline; * *vt* to title; **~se** *vr* to obtain a title.
título *m* title; name; **a ~** on pretense, under pretext.
tiza *f* chalk.
tiznar *vt* to stain; to tarnish.
tizne *m* soot; smut.
tiznón *m* spot, stain.
tizón *m* half-burnt wood.
toalla *f* towel; **~ higiénica** *Lat Am* sanitary napkin.
tobillo *m* ankle.
tobogán *m* toboggan, sled; roller-coaster; slide.
toca *f* headdress.
tocadiscos *m invar* record player.
tocado *m* headdress, headgear.
tocador *m* dressing table; dressing room.
tocante *prep:* **~ a** concerning, relating to.
tocar *vt* to touch; to strike; (*mus*) to play; to ring (a bell); * *vi* to belong; to concern; to knock; to call; to be a duty/obligation.
tocayo/ya *m/f* namesake.
tocino *m* bacon.
todavía *adv* even; yet, still.
todo/da *adj* all, entire; every; * *pn* everything, all; * *m* whole.

todopoderoso/sa *adj* almighty.
todoterreno *m* all-terrain vehicle.
toga *f* toga; gown.
toldo *m* awning; parasol.
tolerable *adj* tolerable.
tolerancia *f* tolerance, indulgence.
tolerante *adj* tolerant.
tolerar *vt* to tolerate, to suffer.
toma *f* taking (as in the taking of vows); (*med*) dose; plug, socket.
tomacorriente *f Lat Am* socket.
tomar *vt* to take; to seize, to grasp; to understand; to interpret, to perceive; to drink; to acquire; * *vi Lat Am* to drink; to take.
tomate *m* tomato.
tomillo *m* thyme.
tomo *m* bulk; tome; volume.
ton *m:* **sin ~ ni son** without rhyme or reason.
tonada *f* tune, melody.
tonadilla *f* interlude of music; short tune.
tonalidad *f* tone.
tonel *m* cask, barrel.
tonelada *f* ton; (*mar*) tonnage duty.
tónico/ca *adj* tonic, strengthening; * *m* tonic; * *f* tonic (water); (*mus*) tonic; (*fig*) keynote.
tonificar *vt* to tone up.
tono *m* tone.
tono de marcar *m* dial tone.
tontada *f* nonsense.
tontear *vi* to talk nonsense; to act foolishly.
tontera *f Lat Am* foolery, nonsense.
tontería *f* foolery, nonsense.
tonto/ta *adj* stupid, foolish.
topacio *m* topaz.
topar *vt* to run into; to find.
tope *m* butt; scuffle; **~s** *mpl* (*rail*) buffers *pl*.
topera *f* molehill.
tópico/ca *adj* topical.
topo *m* mole; stumbler.
topografía *f* topography.
topográfico/ca *adj* topographical.
toque *m* touch; bell-ringing; crisis.
toquilla *f* headscarf; shawl.
tórax *m* thorax.
torbellino *m* whirlwind.
torcedura *f* twisting.
torcer *vt* to twist, to curve; to turn; to sprain; **~se** *vr* to bend; to go wrong; * *vi* to turn off.
torcido/da *adj* oblique; crooked.
torcimiento *m* bending; deflection; circumlocution.

tordo m thrush; ~/**da** adj speckled black and white.
torear vt to avoid; to tease; * vi to fight bulls.
toreo m bullfighting.
torero m bullfighter.
toril m bull pen (at bullfight).
tormenta f storm, tempest.
tormento m torment, pain, anguish; torture.
tornar vt to return; to restore; ~**se** vr to become; * vi to return; ~ **a hacer** to do again.
tornasolado adj iridescent; shimmering.
torneo m tournament.
tornillo m screw.
torniquete m turnstile; (med) tourniquet.
torno m winch; revolution.
toro m bull.
toronja f grapefruit.
torpe adj dull, heavy; stupid.
torpedo m torpedo.
torpeza f heaviness, dullness; torpor; stupidity.
torre f tower; turret; steeple of a church.
torrefacto/ta adj roasted.
torreja f Lat Am French toast.
torrente m torrent.
tórrido/da adj torrid, parched, hot.
torrija f French toast.
torso m torso.
torta f cake; (col) slap.
tortícolis f invar stiff neck.
tortilla f omelet; pancake; Lat Am tortilla.
tórtola f turtledove.
tortuga f tortoise.
tortuoso/sa adj tortuous, circuitous.
tortura f torture.
torvo/va adj stern, grim.
tos f cough.
toscamente adv coarsely, grossly.
tosco/ca adj coarse, ill-bred, clumsy.
toser vi to cough.
tostada f slice of toast.
tostado/da adj parched; sunburnt; light-yellow; light-brown.
tostador m toaster.
tostar vt to toast, to roast.
total m whole, totality; * adj total, entire; * adv in short.
totalidad f totality.
totalitario/ria adj totalitarian.
totuma f Lat Am calabash.
tóxico/ca adj toxic; * m poison.
toxicómano/na m/f drug addict.

tozudo/da adj obstinate.
traba f obstacle, impediment; trammel, fetter.
trabajador/ra adj working; * m/f worker.
trabajar vt to work, to labor; to persuade; to push; * vi to strive.
trabajo m work, labor, toil; difficulty; ~s mpl troubles pl.
trabajoso/sa adj laborious; painful.
trabalenguas m invar tongue twister.
trabar vt to join, to unite; to take hold of; to fetter, to shackle.
trabucarse vr to mistake.
tracción f traction; ~ **delantera/trasera** front-wheel/rear-wheel drive.
tractor m tractor.
tradición f tradition.
traducción f translation.
traducir vt to translate.
traductor,ra m/f translator.
traer vt to bring, to carry; to attract; to persuade; to wear; to cause.
traficante m merchant, dealer.
traficar vi to trade, to do business, to deal.
tráfico m traffic, trade.
tragaldabas m/f invar glutton.
tragaluz m skylight.
tragamonedas f invar Lat Am slot machine.
tragaperras f invar slot machine.
tragar vt to swallow; to swallow up.
tragedia f tragedy.
trágico/ca adj tragic.
trago m drink; gulp; adversity, misfortune.
tragón/ona adj gluttonous.
traición f treason.
traicionar vt to betray.
traicionero/ra adj treacherous.
traidor/ra m/f traitor; * adj treacherous.
traje m dress, costume; suit.
trajín m haulage; (col) bustle.
trajinar vt to carry; * vi to bustle about; to travel around.
trama f weft, woof; (fig) plot; intrigue.
tramar vt to weave; to plot.
tramitar vt to transact; to negotiate; to handle.
trámite m path; (law) procedure.
tramo m section; piece of ground; flight of stairs.
tramoya f scene, theatrical decoration; trick.
tramoyista m scene-painter; swindler.
trampa f trap, snare; trapdoor; fraud.
trampear vt to swindle, to deceive; * vi to cheat.
trampolín m trampoline; diving board.

tramposo/sa *adj* deceitful, swindling.
tranca *f* bar, crossbeam.
trance *m* danger; last stage of life; trance.
tranco *m* long step/stride.
tranquilidad *f* tranquility; repose, heart's ease.
tranquilizar *vt* to calm; to reassure.
tranquilo/la *adj* tranquil, calm, quiet.
transacción *f* transaction.
transbordador *m* ferry.
transbordar *vt* to transfer.
transbordo *m* transfer; **hacer** ~ to change (trains).
transcribir *vt* to transcribe; to copy.
transcurrir *vi* to pass; to turn out.
transcurso *m*: ~ **del tiempo** course of time.
transeúnte *adj* transitory; * *m* passerby.
transferencia *f* transference; (*com*) transfer.
transferir *vt* to transfer; to defer.
transfiguración *f* transformation, transfiguration.
transformación *f* transformation
transformador *m* transformer.
transformar *vt* to transform; ~se *vr* to change one's sentiments/manners.
tránsfuga, tránsfugo *m* deserter, fugitive; defector.
transfusión *f* transfusion.
transgresión *f* transgression.
transgresor *m* transgressor.
transición *f* transition.
transido/da *adj* worn out with anguish; overcome.
transigir *vi* to compromise.
transistor *m* transistor.
transitar *vi* to travel, to pass through a place.
transitivo/va *adj* transitive.
tránsito *m* passage; transition; road, way; change; removal; death of holy/virtuous persons.
transitorio/ria *adj* transitory.
transmisión *f* transmission; transfer; broadcast.
transmitir *vt* to transmit; to broadcast.
transmutación *f* transmutation.
transmutar *vt* to transmute.
transparencia *f* transparency; clearness; slide.
transparentarse *vr* to be transparent; to shine through.
transparente *adj* transparent.
transpiración *f* perspiration; transpiration.
transpirar *vt* to perspire; to transpire.

transportar *vt* to transport, to convey.
transporte *m* transportation.
transposición *f* transposition, transposal.
transversal *adj* transverse; collateral.
tranvía *m* streetcar, trolley car.
trapacería *f* fraud, deceit.
trapacero/ra *adj* deceitful.
trapecio *m* trapeze.
trapecista *m/f* trapeze artist.
trapero/ra *m/f* ragpicker; dealer in rags.
trapicheo *m* (*col*) fiddle.
trapo *m* rag, tatter.
tráquea *f* windpipe.
traqueteo *m* rattling.
tras *prep* after, behind.
trascendencia *f* transcendency; penetration.
trascendental *adj* transcendental.
trascender *vi* to smell; to come out; ~ **de** to go beyond.
trasegar *vt* to move about; to decant.
trasero/ra *adj* back; * *m* bottom.
trasfondo *m* background.
trasgredir *vt* to contravene.
trashumante *adj* migrating.
trasiego *m* removal; decanting (of drinks).
trasladar *vt* to transport; to transfer; to postpone; to transcribe, to copy; ~se *vr* to move.
traslado *m* move; removal.
traslucirse *vr* to be transparent; to conjecture.
trasluz *m* reflected light.
trasnochar *vi* to watch, to sit up the whole night.
traspapelarse *vr* to get mislaid among other papers.
traspasar *vt* to remove, to transport; to transfix, to pierce; to return; to exceed (the proper bounds); to transfer.
traspaso *m* transfer, sale.
traspié *m* trip; slip, stumble.
trasplantar *vt* to transplant
trasplante *m* transplant.
trasquilar *vt* to shear (sheep); to clip.
trasquilón *m* cut (of the shears); badly cut hair.
traste *m* fret (of a guitar); **dar al** ~ **con algo** to ruin something.
trastear *vt* to move (furniture).
trastera *f* lumber.
trastero *m* lumber room.
trastienda *f* back room behind a shop/store.
trasto *m* piece of junk; useless person.
trastornado/da *adj* crazy.
trastornar *vt* to overthrow, to overturn; to confuse; ~se *vr* to go crazy.

trastorno *m* overturning; confusion.
trastrocar *vt* to invert (the order of things).
tratable *adj* friendly.
tratado *m* treaty, convention; treatise.
tratamiento *m* treatment; style of address.
tratante *m* dealer.
tratar *vt* to traffic, to trade; to use; to treat; to handle; to address; ~**se** *vr* to treat each other.
trato *m* treatment; manner, address; trade, traffic; conversation; (*com*) agreement.
trauma *m* trauma.
través *m* (*fig*) reverse; **de/al** ~ across, crossways; **a** ~ **de** *prep* across; over; through.
travesaño *m* crossbeam; transom.
travesía *f* crossing; crossroad; side street; trajectory; (*mar*) crosswind.
travesura *f* wit; wickedness.
travieso/sa *adj* restless, uneasy, fidgety; turbulent; lively; naughty.
trayecto *m* road; journey, stretch; course.
trayectoria *f* trajectory; path.
traza *f* first sketch; trace, outline; project; manner; means; appearance.
trazar *vt* to plan out; to project; to trace.
trazo *m* sketch, plan, design.
trébedes *fpl* trivet, tripod.
trébol *m* trefoil, clover.
trece *adj*, *m* thirteen; thirteenth.
trecho *m* space, distance of time/place; **a** ~**s** at intervals.
tregua *f* truce, cessation of hostilities.
treinta *adj*, *m* thirty.
tremendo/da *adj* terrible, formidable; awful, grand.
tremolar *vt* to hoist (the colors); to wave.
trémulo/la *adj* tremulous, trembling.
tren *m* train, retinue; baggage; (*rail*) train; ~ **de alta velocidad** high-speed train; ~ **de mercancías** freight train.
trenza *f* plait (in hair); braid.
trenzar *vt* to braid, to plait.
trepar *vi* to climb; to crawl.
tres *adj*, *m* three.
tresillo *m* three-piece suite; (*mus*) triplet.
treta *f* thrust (fencing); trick.
triangular *adj* triangular.
triángulo *m* triangle.
tribu *f* tribe.
tribulación *f* tribulation, affliction.
tribuna *f* tribune.
tribunal *m* tribunal, court of justice.
tributar *vt* to pay; to contribute to; to pay (homage, respect).
tributario/ria *adj* tributary.

tributo *m* tribute.
tricolor *adj* tricolored.
tricotar *vi* to knit.
tridente *m* trident.
trienal *adj* triennial.
trienio *m* period of three years.
trigal *m* wheat field.
trigésimo/ma *adj* thirtieth.
trigo *m* wheat.
trigueño/ña *adj* corn-colored; olive-skinned.
trillado/da *adj* beaten; trite, stale, hackneyed; **camino** ~ common routine.
trilladora *f* threshing machine.
trillar *vt* to thresh.
trimestral *adj* quarterly, three-monthly.
trimestre *m* period of three months.
trinar *vi* to trill, to quaver; to be angry.
trincar *vt* to tie up; to pinion.
trinchante *m* carver; carving knife.
trinchar *vt* to carve, to cut up (meat).
trinchera *f* trench, entrenchment.
trineo *m* sled, sleigh.
Trinidad *f* Trinity.
trino *m* trill.
trío *m* (*mus*) trio.
tripa *f* gut, intestine; ~**s** *fpl* guts; tripe.
triple *adj* triple, treble.
triplicar *vt* to treble.
trípode *m* tripod, trivet.
tripulación *f* crew.
tripulante *m/f* crewman/woman.
tripular *vt* to man; to drive.
triquiñuela *f* trick.
triquitraque *m* clack, clatter; clashing.
tris *m* *invar*: **estar en un** ~ **de** to be on the point of.
triste *adj* sad, mournful, melancholy.
tristeza *f* sadness, mourning.
trituración *f* pulverization.
triturar *vt* to reduce to powder; to grind, to pound.
triunfal *adj* triumphal.
triunfar *vi* to triumph; to trump (in cards).
triunfo *m* triumph; trump (in cards).
trivial *adj* trivial.
trivialidad *f* triviality.
triza *f*: **hacer** ~**s** to smash to bits; to tear to shreds.
trocar *vt* to exchange.
trocha *f* short cut.
troche: **a** ~ **y moche** *adv* helter-skelter.
trofeo *m* trophy.
tromba *f* whirlwind.
trombón *m* trombone.
trombosis *f* *invar* thrombosis.

trompa *f* trumpet; proboscis; spinning top.

trompazo *m* heavy blow; accident; *Lat Am* punch.

trompear *vt Lat Am* to punch.

trompeta *f* trumpet; * *m* trumpeter.

trompetilla *f* small trumpet; speaking-trumpet.

trompicón *m* stumble.

trompo *m* spinning top.

tronar *vi* to thunder; to rage.

troncar *vt* to truncate, to mutilate.

troncha *f Lat Am* chunk.

tronchar *vt* to cut off; to shatter; to tire out.

troncho *m* sprig, stem/stalk.

tronco *m* trunk (of the body, tree); log; stock.

tronera *m* loophole; small window; pocket (of a billiard table).

trono *m* throne.

tropa *f* troop.

tropel *m* confused noise; hurry; bustle, confusion, heap of things; crowd; **en ~ in a** tumultuous and confused manner.

tropelía *f* outrage.

tropezar *vi* to stumble; * *vt* to meet accidentally.

tropezón/ona *adj* stumbling; * *m* trip; a **~ones** by fits and starts.

tropical *adj* tropical.

trópico *m* tropic.

tropiezo *m* stumble, trip; obstacle; slip, fault; quarrel; dispute.

trotamundos *m invar* globetrotter.

trotar *vi* to trot.

trote *m* trot; traveling.

trovador/ra *m/f* troubadour.

trozar *vt Lat Am* to cut up.

trozo *m* piece.

trucha *f* trout.

truco *m* knack; trick.

trueno *m* thunderclap.

trueque *m* exchange.

trufa *f* truffle.

truhán *adj* rogue.

truncado/da *adj* truncated.

truncamiento *m* truncation.

truncar *vt* to truncate, to maim.

trunco/ca *adj Lat Am* incomplete.

tu *adj* your.

tú *pn* you.

tubérculo *m* tuber.

tuberculosis *f* tuberculosis.

tubería *f* pipe; pipeline.

tubo *m* tube.

tuerca *f* screw.

tuerto/ta *adj* one-eyed; squint-eyed; * *m/f* one-eyed person.

tuétano *m* marrow.

tufarada *f* strong scent/smell.

tufo *m* warm vapor arising from the earth; offensive smell.

tugurio *m* slum.

tul *m* tulle.

tulipán *m* tulip.

tullido/da *adj* disabled, maimed.

tumba *f* tomb.

tumbar *vt* to knock down; * *vi* to tumble (to fall down); **~se** *vr* to lie down to sleep.

tumbo *m* fall; jolt.

tumbona *f* easy chair; beach chair.

tumor *m* tumor, growth.

túmulo *m* tomb; sepulchral monument.

tumulto *m* tumult, uproar.

tumultuoso/sa *adj* tumultuous.

tuna *f* student music group; *Lat Am* prickly pear.

tunda *f* beating.

túnel *m* tunnel.

túnica *f* tunic.

tuno *m* rogue.

tupé *m* toupee, wig/hairpiece.

tupido/da *adj* dense.

tupir *vt* to press close; **~se** *vr* to stuff oneself.

turbación *f* perturbation, confusion; trouble, disorder.

turbado/da *adj* disturbed.

turbante *m* turban.

turbar *vt* to disturb, to trouble; **~se** *vr* to be disturbed.

turbina *f* turbine.

turbio/bia *adj* muddy; troubled.

turbulencia *f* turbulence; disturbance.

turbulento/ta *adj* muddy; turbulent.

turismo *m* tourism; -- **rural** rural tourism.

turista *m/f* tourist, vacationer.

turístico/ca *adj* tourist *compd*.

turnar *vi* to alternate.

turno *m* turn; shift; opportunity.

turquesa *f* turquoise.

turrón *m* nougat (almond cake).

tutear *vt* to address as **tu**.

tutela *f* guardianship, tutelage.

tutelar *adj* tutelar, tutelary.

tutor *m* guardian, tutor.

tutora *f* tutoress.

tutoría *f* tutelage.

tuyo/ya *adj* yours; **~s** *pl* friends and relations of the party addressed.

U

u *conj* o (instead of o before o and ho).
ubicar *vt* to place; *Lat Am* to locate; *Lat Am* to find; ~se *vr* to be located.
ubre *f* udder.
ufanarse *vr* to boast.
ufano/na *adj* haughty, arrogant.
ujier *m* usher.
úlcera *f* ulcer.
ulcerar *vi* to ulcerate.
ulterior *adj* ulterior; farther, further.
últimamente *adv* lately.
ultimar *vt* to finalize; to finish; *Lat Am* to kill.
ultimátum *m* ultimatum.
último/ma *adj* last; latest; bottom; top.
ultrajar *vt* to outrage; to despise; to abuse.
ultraje *m* outrage.
ultramar *adj*, *m* overseas.
ultramarinos *mpl* foodstuffs, groceries.
ultrasónico/ca *adj* ultrasonic.
umbilical *adj* umbilical.
umbral *m* threshold.
un/una *art* a, an; * *adj*, *m* one (for uno).
unánime *adj* unanimous.
unanimidad *f* unanimity.
unción *f* unction; extreme/last unction.
ungir *vt* to anoint.
ungüento *m* ointment.
únicamente *adv* only, simply.
único/ca *adj* only; singular, unique.
unicornio *m* unicorn.
unidad *f* unity; unit; conformity; union.
unificar *vt* to unite.
uniformar *vt* to make uniform.
uniforme *adj* uniform; * *m* (*mil*) uniform, regimentals *pl*.
uniformidad *f* uniformity.
unilateral *adj* unilateral.
unión *f* union; U~ Europea European Union.
unir *vt* to join, to unite; to mingle; to bind, to tie; ~se *vr* to associate.
unísono/na *adj* unison.
universal *adj* universal.
universalidad *f* universality.
universidad *f* university.

universitario/ria *adj* university *compd*; * *m/f* student.
universo *m* universe.
uno *m* one; ~/una *adj* one; sole, only; ~ a otro one another; ~ a ~ one by one; a una jointly together.
untar *vt* to anoint; to grease; (*col*) to bribe.
uña *f* nail; hoof; claw, talon.
¡upa! up! up!
urbanidad *f* urbanity, politeness.
uranio *m* uranium.
Urano *m* Uranus (planet).
urbanismo *m* town planning.
urbanización *f* urban development.
urbano/na *adj* urban; urbane, polite.
urdimbre *f* warp; intrigue.
urdir *vt* to warp; to contrive.
urgencia *f* urgency; emergency; need, necessity.
urgente *adj* urgent.
urgentemente *adv* urgently.
urgir *vi* to be urgent.
urinario/ria *adj* urinary; * *m* urinal.
urna *f* urn; ballot box.
urraca *f* magpie.
usado/da *adj* used; experienced; worn.
usanza *f* usage, use, custom.
usar *vt* to use, to make use of; to wear; ~se *vr* to be used.
uso *m* use, service; custom; mode.
usted *pn* you.
usuario *m* user.
usufructo *m* (*law*) usufruct, use.
usura *f* usury.
usurario/ria *adj* usurious.
usurero *m* usurer.
usurpación *f* usurpation.
usurpar *vt* to usurp.
utensilio *m* utensil.
uterino/na *adj* uterine.
útero *m* uterus, womb.
util *adj* useful, profitable; * *m* utility.
utilidad *f* utility; ~es *Lat Am* profits *pl*.
utilizar *vt* to use; to make useful.
utopía *f* Utopia.
utópico/ca *adj* Utopian.
uva *f* grape.

V

vaca *f* cow; beef.
vacaciones *fpl* vacation; holidays *pl*.
vacante *adj* vacant; * *f* vacancy.
vaciar *vt* to empty, to clear; to mold; * *vi* to fall, to decrease (of waters); ~se *vr* to empty.
vacilación *f* hesitation; irresolution.
vacilar *vi* to hesitate; to falter; to fail.
vacío/cía *adj* void, empty; unoccupied; concave; vain; presumptuous; * *m* vacuum; emptiness.
vacuna *f* vaccine.
vacunar *vt* to vaccinate.
vacuno/na *adj* bovine, cow *compd*.
vadear *vt* to wade, to ford.
vagabundo/da *adj* wandering; * *m* vagrant, bum, hobo.
vagancia *f* vagrancy.
vagar *vi* to rove/loiter about; to wander.
vagido *m* cry of a child; convulsive sob.
vagina *f* vagina.
vago/ga *adj* vagrant; restless; vague.
vagón *m* (*rail*) wagon; car, carriage; ~ de mercancías goods wagon.
vaguear *vi* to rove, to loiter; to wander.
vahído *m* vertigo, giddiness.
vaho *m* steam, vapor.
vaina *f* scabbard (of a sword); pod, husk.
vainilla *f* (*bot*) vanilla; *Lat Am* hemstitch.
vaivén *m* fluctuation, instability; giddiness.
vajilla *f* crockery.
vale *m* farewell; promissory note, IOU.
valedero/ra *adj* valid; efficacious; binding.
valentía *f* valor, courage.
valentón *m* braggart.
valentonada *f* brag, boast.
valer *vi* to be valuable; to be deserving; to cost; to be valid; to be worth; to produce; to be current; * *vt* to protect, to favor; to be worth; to be equivalent to; ~se *vr* to employ, to make use of; to have recourse to.
valeroso/sa *adj* valiant, brave; strong, powerful.
valía *f* valuation; worth.
validar *vt* to validate.
validez *f* validity; stability.
válido/da *adj* valid.
valiente *adj* robust, vigorous; valiant, brave; boasting.
valija *f* suitcase.

valioso/sa *adj* valuable.
valla *f* fence; hurdle; barricade.
vallar *vt* to fence in.
valle *m* valley.
valor *m* value; price; validity; force; power; courage, valor.
valoración *f* valuation.
valorar *vt* to value; to evaluate.
valuación *f* valuation.
vals *m* *invar* waltz.
válvula *f* valve.
vampiro *m* vampire.
vanagloriarse *vr* to boast.
vandalismo *m* vandalism.
vándalo/la *adj*, *m* vandal.
vanguardia *f* vanguard.
vanidad *f* vanity; ostentation.
vanidoso/sa *adj* vain, showy; haughty; conceited.
vano/na *adj* vain; useless, frivolous; arrogant; futile; en ~ in vain.
vapor *m* vapor, steam; breath; steamer, steamboat, steamship.
vaporizador *m* atomizer.
vaporizar *vt* to vaporize.
vaporoso/sa *adj* vaporous.
vapular *vt* to whip, to flog.
vaquerizo/za *adj* cattle *compd*; * *m* cowboy, cowhand; cowman.
vaquero *m* cowboy, cowhand; cowman; ~/ra *adj* belonging to a cowboy/cowgirl; ~s *mpl* jeans *pl*.
vara *f* rod; pole, staff; stick.
varejón *m* *Lat Am* thin pole.
variable *adj* variable, changeable.
variación *f* variation.
variado/da *adj* varied; variegated.
variar *vt* to vary; to modify; to change; * *vi* to vary.
várice *f* *Lat Am* varicose vein.
varices *fpl* varicose veins *pl*.
variedad *f* variety; inconstancy.
varilla *f* small rod; curtain rod; spindle, pivot.
vario/ria *adj* varied, different; vague; variegated; ~s *pl* some; several.
varón *m* man, male.
varonil *adj* male, masculine; manly.
vasco/ca *adj*, *m/f* Basque.
vascuence *m* Basque.
Vaselina™ *f* Vaseline™.
vasija *f* vessel.

vaso *m* glass; vessel; vase.
vástago *m* bud, shoot; offspring.
vasto/ta *adj* vast, huge.
vaticinar *vt* to divine, to foretell.
vaticinio *m* prophecy.
vatio *m* watt.
vecindad *f* inhabitants of a place; neighborhood.
vecindario *m* number of inhabitants of a place; neighborhood.
vecino/na *adj* neighboring; near; * *m* neighbor, inhabitant.
veda *f* prohibition.
vedar *vt* to prohibit, to forbid; to impede.
vegetación *f* vegetation.
vegetal *adj* vegetable.
vegetar *vi* to vegetate.
vegetariano/na *adj, m/f* vegetarian.
vehemencia *f* vehemence, force.
vehemente *adj* vehement, violent.
vehículo *m* vehicle.
veinte *adj, m* twenty.
veintena *f* twentieth part; score.
vejación *f* vexation; embarrassment.
vejar *vt* to vex; to humiliate.
vejestorio *m* old man.
vejez *f* old age.
vejiga *f* bladder.
vela *f* wakefulness; vigil; night work; candle; sail; **hacerse a la** ~ to set sail.
velado/da *adj* veiled; blurred; * *f* soiree.
velador *m* night watchman, guard; observer; candlestick; pedestal table.
velar *vi* to stay awake; to be attentive; * *vt* to guard, to watch.
veleidad *f* feeble will; inconstancy.
velero/ra *adj* swift-sailing.
veleta *f* weather cock, weather vane.
vello *m* down; gossamer; short downy hair.
vellón *m* fleece.
velludo/da *adj* shaggy, woolly.
velo *m* veil; pretext.
velocidad *f* speed; velocity.
velocímetro *m* speedometer.
veloz(mente) *adj (adv)* swift(ly), fast.
vena *f* vein.
venado *m* deer; venison.
vencedor/ra *m/f* conqueror, victor, winner.
vencer *vt* to defeat; to conquer, to vanquish; * *vi* to win; to expire.
vencido/da *adj* defeated; due.
vencimiento *m* victory; maturity.
vendaje *m* bandage, dressing for wounds.
vendal *f* bandage.
vendar *vt* to bandage; to hoodwink.

vendaval *m* gale.
vendedor/ra *m/f* seller; ~ **de periódicos** newsdealer; ~ **ambulante** peddler.
vender *vt* to sell.
vendimia *f* grape harvest; vintage.
vendimiador/ra *m/f* grape harvester, vintager.
vendimiar *vt* to harvest; to pick (grapes); (*col*) to make a killing with.
veneno *m* poison, venom.
venenoso/sa *adj* venomous, poisonous.
venerable *adj* venerable.
veneración *f* veneration, worship.
venerar *vt* to venerate, to worship.
venéreo/rea *adj* venereal.
venganza *f* revenge, vengeance.
vengar *vt* to revenge, to avenge; ~**se** *vr* to take revenge.
vengativo/va *adj* revengeful.
venia *f* pardon; leave, permission; bow.
venial *adj* venial.
venida *f* arrival; return; overflow of a river.
venidero/ra *adj* future; ~**s** *mpl* posterity.
venir *vi* to come, to arrive; to follow, to succeed; to happen; to spring from; ~**se** *vr* to ferment.
venta *f* sale.
ventaja *f* advantage.
ventajoso/sa *adj* advantageous.
ventana *f* window; window shutter; nostril.
ventanilla *f* window.
venta por correo *f* mail order.
ventarrón *m* violent wind.
ventilación *f* ventilation; draft.
ventilar *vt* to ventilate; to fan; to discuss.
ventisco/sca *m/f* snowstorm.
ventiscar *vi* to drift, to lie in drifts (snow).
ventisquero *m* snowdrift; ~**s** *mpl* glaciers *pl*.
ventolera *f* gust; pride, loftiness.
ventosidad *f* flatulence.
ventoso/sa *adj* windy; flatulent.
ventrículo *m* ventricle.
ventrílocuo *m* ventriloquist.
ventura *f* happiness; luck, chance, fortune; **por** ~ by chance.
venturoso/sa *adj* lucky, fortunate, happy.
Venus *f* Venus (planet).
ver *vt* to see, to look at; to observe; to visit; * *vi* to understand; to see; ~**se** *vr* to be seen; to be conspicuous; to find oneself; ~**se con uno** to have a bone to pick with someone; * *m* sense of sight; appearance.
vera *f* edge; bank.
veracidad *f* truth; veracity.
veranear *vi* to spend the summer holiday, to vacation.

veraneo *m* summer vacation.
veraniego/ga *adj* summer.
verano *m* summer.
veras *fpl* truth, sincerity; **de ~** in truth, really.
veraz *adj* truthful.
verbal *adj* verbal.
verbena *f* fair; dance.
verbo *m* word, term; (*gr*) verb.
verbosidad *f* verbosity.
verdad *f* truth, veracity; reality; reliability.
verdaderamente *adv* truly, in fact.
verdadero/ra *adj* true; real; sincere.
verde *adj*, *m* green.
verdear, verdecer *vi* to turn green.
verdín *m* bright green; verdure.
verdor *m* greenness; verdure; youth.
verdoso/sa *adj* greenish, greeny.
verdugo *m* hangman; very cruel person.
verdulero/ra *m/f* produce dealer.
verdura *f* verdure; vegetables *pl*, greens *pl*.
vereda *f* path; sidewalk.
veredicto *m* verdict.
vergel *m* orchard.
vergonzoso/sa *adj* bashful; shamefaced.
vergüenza *f* shame; bashfulness; confusion.
verídico/ca *adj* truthful.
verificación *f* verification.
verificar *vt* to check, to verify; **~se** *vr* to happen.
verisímil *adj* probable.
verja *f* grate, lattice.
vermut *m* vermouth.
verosímil *adj* likely; credible.
verosimilitud *f* likeliness; credibility.
verraco *m* boar.
verruga *f* wart, pimple.
versado/da *adj* versed.
versátil *adj* versatile.
versículo *m* versicle; short verse.
versificar *vt* to versify.
versión *f* translation, version.
verso *m* verse.
vértebra *f* vertebra.
vertedero *m* sewer, drain; tip.
verter *vt* to pour; to spill; to empty; * *vi* to flow.
vertical *adj* vertical.
vértice *m* vertex, zenith; crown of the head.
vertiente *f* slope; waterfall, cascade.
vertiginoso/sa *adj* giddy.
vértigo *m* giddiness, vertigo.
vesícula *f* blister.
vespertino/na *adj* evening *compd*.
vestíbulo *m* vestibule, lobby; foyer.

vestido *m* dress; clothes *pl*.
vestidura *f* dress; clothing.
vestigio *m* vestige; footstep; trace.
vestimenta *f* clothing.
vestir *vt* to put on; to wear; to dress; to adorn; to cloak, to disguise; * *vi* to dress; **~se** *vr* to get dressed.
vestuario *m* clothes *pl*; uniform; vestry; changing room.
veta *f* vein (in mines, wood etc); streak; grain.
vetado/da *adj* striped, veined.
vetar *vt* to veto.
veterano/na *adj* experienced, practiced; * *m* veteran, old soldier.
veterinario/ria *adj* veterinary; * *m/f* veterinarian; * *f* veterinary science.
veto *m* veto.
vez *f* time; turn; return; **cada ~** each time; **una ~** once; **a veces** sometimes, by turns.
vía *f* way; road, route; mode, manner, method; (*rail*) railway line.
viajante *m* sales representative.
viajar *vi* to travel.
viaje *m* journey; voyage; travel.
viajero/ra *m/f* traveler.
vial *adj* road *compd*.
viático *m* viaticum; travel allowance.
víbora *f* viper.
vibración *f* vibration.
vibrador *m* vibrator.
vibrante *adj* vibrant.
vibrar *vt*, *vi* to vibrate.
vicaría *f* vicarship; vicarage.
vice- *pref* vice- (deputy etc).
vicealmirante *m* vice-admiral.
viceconsulado *m* vice-consulate.
vicepresidente/ta *m/f* vice-president.
viciar *vt* to vitiate, to corrupt; to invalidate.
vicio *m* vice.
vicioso/sa *adj* vicious; depraved.
vicisitud *f* vicissitude.
víctima *f* victim; sacrifice.
victimar *vt* *Lat Am* to kill.
victimario/ria *m/f* *Lat Am* killer.
victoria *f* victory.
victorioso/sa *adj* victorious.
vicuña *m* vicuna.
vid *f* (*bot*) vine.
vida *f* life.
vidriado *m* glazed earthenware, crockery.
video *m* *Lat Am* video.
vídeo *m* video.
videocámara *f* video camera, camcorder.
videocasete *m* video cassette.
videoclip *m* pop video.

videojuego *m* video game.
vidriar *vt* to glaze.
vidriera *f* stained-glass window; *Lat Am* shop/store window.
vidriero *m* glazier.
vidrio *m* glass; *Lat Am* window; *Lat Am* lense.
vidrioso/sa *adj* glassy; brittle; slippery; very delicate.
vieira *f* scallop.
viejo/ja *adj* old; ancient, antiquated.
viento *m* wind; air.
vientre *m* belly.
viernes *m invar* Friday; **V~ Santo** Good Friday.
viga *f* beam; girder.
vigencia *f* validity.
vigente *adj* in force.
vigésimo/ma *adj, m* twentieth.
vigía *f* (*mar*) lookout; * *m* watchman, guard.
vigilancia *f* vigilance, watchfulness.
vigilante *adj* watchful, vigilant.
vigilar *vt* to watch over; * *vi* to keep watch.
vigilia *f* vigil; watch.
vigor *m* vigor, strength.
vigoroso/sa *adj* vigorous.
vil *adj* mean, sordid, low; worthless; infamous; ungrateful.
vileza *f* meanness, lowness; abjectness.
vilipendiar *vt* to despise, to revile.
villa *f* villa; small town.
villancico *m* Christmas carol.
villano/na *adj* rustic, clownish; villainous; * *m* villain; rustic.
villorio *m* one-horse town; (*col*) dump; shanty town.
vilo: en ~ *adv* in the air; in suspense.
vinagre *m* vinegar.
vinagrera *f* vinegar bottle; **~s** cruet set/ stand; *Lat Am* heartburn.
vinagreta *f* vinaigrette sauce/dressing.
vinculación *f* link; linking.
vincular *vt* to link.
vínculo *m* tie, link, chain; entail.
vindicación *f* revenge.
vindicar *vt* to avenge.
vindicativo/va *adj* vindictive.
vinicultura *f* wine growing.
vino *m* wine; **~ tinto** red wine.
viña *f* vineyard.
viñedo *m* vineyard.
viñeta *f* vignette.
viola[1] *f* (*bot*) viola.
viola[2] *f* (*mus*) viola.
violación *f* violation; rape.

violado/da *adj* violet-colored; violated.
violador/ra *m/f* rapist; violator; profaner.
violar *vt* to rape; to violate; to profane.
violencia *f* violence.
violentar *vt* to force.
violento/ta *adj* violent; forced; absurd; embarrassing.
violeta *f* violet.
violín *m* violin, fiddle.
violinista *m* violinist.
violón *m* double bass.
violoncelo, violonchelo *m* violoncello, cello.
vip *m/f* VIP.
viperino/na *adj* viperish.
viraje *m* turn; bend.
virar *vi* to swerve.
virgen *m/f* virgin.
virgiano/na *adj Lat Am* Virgoan (zodiac sign).
virginidad *f* virginity.
Virgo *f* Virgo (zodiac sign).
viril *adj* virile, manly.
virilidad *f* virility, manhood.
virrey *m* viceroy.
virtual *adj* virtual.
virtud *f* virtue.
virtuoso/sa *adj* virtuous.
viruela *f* smallpox.
virulencia *f* virulence.
virulento/ta *adj* virulent.
virus *m invar* virus.
visa *f*, **visado** *m* visa.
viscosidad *f* viscosity.
viscoso/sa *adj* viscous, glutinous.
visera *f* visor.
visibilidad *f* visibility.
visible *adj* visible; apparent.
visillos *mpl* lace curtains *pl*.
visión *f* sight, vision; fantasy.
visionario/ria *adj* visionary.
visita *f* visit; visitor.
visitar *vt* to visit.
vislumbrar *vt* to catch a glimpse of; to perceive indistinctly.
visón *m* mink.
víspera *f* eve; evening before; **~s** *pl* vespers.
vista *f* sight, view; vision; eyesight; appearance; looks *pl*; prospect; intention; (*law*) trial; * *m* customs officer.
vistazo *m* glance.
visto: ~ que *conj* considering that.
vistoso/sa *adj* colorful, attractive, lively.
visual *adj* visual.
vital *adj* life *compd*; vital.
vitalicio/cia *adj* for life.

vitalidad f vitality.
vitamina f vitamin.
viticultor/ra m/f wine grower.
viticultura f wine growing.
vitorear vt to shout, to applaud.
vítreo/trea adj vitreous.
vitriolo m vitriol.
vitrina f showcase; Lat Am shop/store window.
vituperación f condemnation, censure.
vituperar vt to condemn, to censure.
vituperio m condemnation, censure; insult.
viuda f widow.
viudedad f widowhood; widow's pension.
viudez f widowhood.
viudo m widower.
vivacidad f vivacity, liveliness.
vivamente adv in lively fashion.
vivaracho/cha adj lively, sprightly; bright.
vivaz adj lively.
víveres mpl provisions.
vivero m plant nursery; fish farm.
viveza f liveliness; sharpness.
vividor/ra adj (perj) sharp, clever; unscrupulous.
vivienda f housing; apartment.
viviente adj living.
vivificar vt to vivify, to enliven.
vivíparo/ra adj viviparous.
vivir vt to live through; to go through; * vi to live; to last.
vivo/va adj living; lively; al ~ to the life; very realistically.
vizconde m viscount.
vocablo m word, term.
vocabulario m vocabulary.
vocación f vocation.
vocacional adj vocational.
vocal f vowel; * m/f member (of a committee); * adj vocal, oral.
vocativo m (gr) vocative.
vocear vt to cry; to shout; to cheer; to shriek; * vi to yell.
vocerío/ría m/f shouting.
vocero/ra m/f Lat Am spokesperson.
vociferar vt to shout; to proclaim in a loud voice; * vi to yell.
vodka m/f vodka.
volador/ra adj flying; fast.
volandas: en ~ adv in the air; (fig) swiftly.
volante adj flying; * m (auto) steering wheel; note; pamphlet; shuttlecock.
volar vi to fly; to pass swiftly (of time); to rush, to hurry; * vt to blow up, to explode.

volatería f falconry; fowling; birds pl.
volátil adj volatile; changeable.
volatilizar vt to volatilize, to vaporize.
volcán m volcano.
volcánico adj volcanic.
volcar vt to upset, to overturn; to make giddy; to empty out; to exasperate; ~se vr to tip over.
voleibol m volleyball.
vóleibol m Lat Am volleyball.
voleo m volley.
volquete m tipper truck; dump truck.
voltaje m voltage.
voltear vt to turn over; to overturn; Lat Am to knock over; * vi to roll over, to tumble.
voltereta f tumble; somersault.
voltio m volt.
voluble adj unpredictable; fickle.
volumen m volume; size.
voluminoso/sa adj voluminous.
voluntad f will, willpower; wish, desire.
voluntario/ria adj voluntary; * m/f volunteer.
voluptuoso/sa adj voluptuous.
volver vt to turn (over); to turn upside down; to turn inside out; * vi to return, to go back; ~se vr to turn around.
vomitar vt, vi to vomit.
vómito m vomiting; vomit.
vomitona f violent vomiting.
voracidad f voracity.
voraz(mente) adj, (adv) voracious(ly).
vórtice m whirlpool.
vos pn Lat Am you.
vosotros/tras pn pl you.
votación f voting; vote.
votar vi to vow; to vote.
voto m vow; vote; opinion, advice; swearword; curse; ~s mpl good wishes pl.
voz f voice; shout; rumor; word, term.
vuelco m overturning.
vuelo m flight; wing; projection of a building; ruffle, frill; cazar al ~ to catch in flight; ~ chárter charter flight.
vuelta f turn; circuit; return; row of stitches; cuff; change; bend, curve; reverse, other side; return journey.
vuelto m Lat Am change.
vuestro/tra adj your; * pn yours.
vulgar adj vulgar, common.
vulgaridad f vulgar, common.
vulgaridad f vulgarity, commonness.
vulgo m common people pl.
vulnerable adj vulnerable.

WXYZ

wáter *m* toilet.
whisky *m* whisky.
windsurf *m* windsurfing.
windsurfista *m/f* windsurfer.

xenofobia *f* xenophobia.
xilófono *m* xylophone.
xilógrafo *m* xylographer; wood engraver.

y *conj* and.
ya *adv* already; now; immediately; at once; soon; * *conj*: ~ **que** since, seeing that; ¡~! of course!, sure!
yacer *vi* to lie, to lie down.
yacimiento *m* deposit.
yaguré *m Lat Am* skunk.
yanqui *m/f* Yankee.
yate *m* yacht, sailing boat.
yedra *f* ivy.
yegua *f* mare.
yema *f* bud; leaf; egg yolk; ~ **del dedo** tip of the finger.
yermo *m* wasteland, wilderness; ~/**ma** *adj* waste; (*fig*) barren.
yerno *m* son-in-law.
yerro *m* error, mistake, fault.
yerto/ta *adj* stiff, inflexible; rigid.
yesca *f* tinder.
yeso *m* gypsum; plaster; ~ **mate** plaster of Paris.
yo *pn* I; ~ **mismo** I myself.
yodo *m* iodine.
yogur *m* yogurt.
yugo *m* yoke.
yugular *adj* jugular.
yunque *m* anvil.
yunta *f* yoke; ~**s** *fpl* couple, pair.
yute *m* jute.
yuxtaponer *vt* to juxtapose.
yuxtaposición *f* juxtaposition.

zafado/da *adj Lat Am* crazy, mad.
zafar *vt* to loosen, to untie; to lighten (a ship); ~**se** *vr* to escape; ~**se de** to avoid; to free oneself from (trouble).
zafio/fia *adj* uncouth, coarse.
zafiro *m* sapphire.
zafra *f Lat Am* sugar cane harvest.
zaga *f* rear; **a la** ~ behind.
zagal/la *m/f* boy/girl.

zaguán *m* porch, entrance hall.
zaherir *vt* to criticize; to upbraid.
zahorí *m* clairvoyant.
zalamería *f* flattery.
zalamero/ra *adj* flattering; * *m/f* wheedler, flatterer.
zamarra *f* sheepskin; sheepskin jacket.
zambo/ba *adj* knock-kneed.
zambomba *f* rural drum.
zambullida *f* plunge, dive; dipping, submersion.
zambullirse *vr* to plunge/dive into water.
zampar *vt* to gobble down; to put away hurriedly; ~**se** *vr* to thrust oneself suddenly into any place; to crash, to hurtle.
zanahoria *f* carrot.
zancada *f* stride.
zancadilla *f* trip; trick.
zanco *m* stilt.
zancudo/da *adj* long-legged; * *m Lat Am* mosquito.
zángano *m* drone; idler, slacker.
zanja *f* ditch, trench.
zanjar *vt* to dig (ditches); (*fig*) to surmount; to resolve.
zapador *m* (*mil*) sapper.
zapata *f* boot; ~ **de freno** (*auto*) brake shoe.
zapatazo *m* stamp (dancing).
zapatear *vt* to tap with the shoe; to beat time with the sole of the shoe.
zapatería *f* shoemaking; shoe shop; shoe factory.
zapatero/ra *m/f* shoemaker; ~ **de viejo** cobbler.
zapatilla *f* slipper; pump (shoe); (*sport*) ~**s de lona** *fpl* sneakers *pl*.
zapato *m* shoe.
zapping *m* channel-hopping.
zar *m* czar.
zarandear *vt* to shake vigorously.
zarcillo *m* earring; tendril.
zarpa *f* mud splash, dirt on clothes; claw, paw.
zarpar *vi* to weigh anchor.
zarpazo *m* thud.
zarrapastroso/sa *adj* shabby, rough-looking.

zarza f bramble.
zarzal m bramble patch.
zarzamora f blackberry.
zarzuela f Spanish light opera.
zigzag adj zigzag.
zigzaguear vi to zigzag.
zinc m zinc.
zócalo m plinth, base; base-board.
zocato/ta adj Lat Am stale.
zodiaco m zodiac.
zona f zone; area, belt.
zoncear vi Lat Am to fool around.
zoncera f Lat Am nonsense.
zonzo/sa m/f Lat Am fool.
zoo m zoo.
zoología f zoology.
zoológico/ca adj zoological; * m zoo.
zoólogo/ga m/f zoologist.
zopenco/ca adj dull, very stupid.
zoquete m block; crust of bread, (col) blockhead.
zorra f fox; vixen; (col) whore, tart.

zorro m male fox; cunning person.
zozobra f (mar) capsizing; uneasiness, anxiety.
zozobrar vi (mar) to founder, to capsize; (fig) to fail; to be anxious.
zueco m wooden shoe; clog.
zumba f banter, teasing; beating.
zumbar vt to hit; ~se vr to hit each other; * vi to buzz.
zumbido m humming, buzzing sound.
zumbón/ona adj waggish, funny, teasing.
zumo m juice.
zurcir vt to darn; (fig) to join, to unite; to hatch (lies).
zurdo/da adj left; left-handed.
zurra f flogging; drudgery.
zurrar vt (col) to flog, to lay into; (fig) to criticize harshly.
zurrón m pouch.
zutano/na m/f so-and-so; ~ y fulano such and such a one, so-and-so.

English–Spanish Dictionary

A

a *art* un, uno, una; * *prep* a, al, en.
aback *adv* detrás, atrás; to be taken ~ *vi* quedar consternado/da.
abacus *n* ábaco *m*.
abandon *vt* abandonar, dejar.
abandonment *n* abandono *m*; desamparo *m*.
abase *vt* abatir, humillar.
abasement *n* abatimiento *m*; humillación *f*.
abash *vt* avergonzar, causar confusión.
abate *vt* disminuir, rebajar; * *vi* disminuirse.
abatement *n* rebaja, disminución *f*.
abbess *n* abadesa *f*.
abbey *n* abadía *f*.
abbot *n* abad *m*.
abbreviate *vt* abreviar, acortar.
abbreviation *n* abreviatura *f*.
abdicate *vt* abdicar; renunciar.
abdication *n* abdicación *f*; renuncia *f*.
abdomen *n* abdomen *m*.
abdominal *adj* abdominal.
abduct *vt* secuestrar.
abductor *n* músculo abductor *m*.
abed *adv* en (la) cama.
aberrant *adj* anormal.
aberration *n* error *m*; aberración *f*.
abet *vt*: to aid and ~ ser cómplice de.
abeyance *n* desuso *m*.
abhor *vt* aborrecer, detestar.
abhorrence *n* aborrecimiento, odio *m*.
abhorrent *adj* repugnante.
abide *vt* soportar, sufrir.
ability *n* habilidad, capacidad, aptitud *f*; ~ies *pl* talento *m*.
abject *adj* vil, despreciable, bajo/ja; ~ly *adv* vilmente, bajamente.
abjure *vt* abjurar; renunciar.
ablative *n* (*gr*) ablativo *m*.
ablaze *adj* en llamas.
able *adj* capaz, hábil; to be ~ poder.
able-bodied *adj* robusto/ta, vigoroso/sa.
ablution *n* ablución *f*.
ably *adv* con habilidad.
abnegation *n* abnegación, resignación *f*.
abnormal *adj* anormal.

abnormality *n* anormalidad *f*.
aboard *adv* a bordo.
abode *n* domicilio *m*.
abolish *vt* abolir, anular, revocar.
abolition *n* abolición, anulación *f*.
abominable *adj* abominable, detestable; ~bly *adv* abominablemente.
abomination *n* abominación *f*.
aboriginal *adj* aborigen.
aborigines *npl* aborígenes *mpl*.
abort *vi* abortar.
abortion *n* aborto *m*.
abortive *adj* fracasado/da.
abound *vi* abundar; to ~ with abundar en.
about *prep* acerca de, acerca; I carry no money ~ me no traigo dinero; * *adv* aquí y allá; to be ~ to estar a punto de; to go ~ andar acá y acullá; to go ~ a thing emprender alguna cosa; all ~ en todo lugar.
above *prep* encima; * *adv* arriba, *Lat Am* arriba de; ~ all sobre todo, principalmente; ~ mentioned ya mencionado.
aboveboard *adj* legítimo/ma.
abrasion *n* abrasión *f*.
abrasive *adj* abrasivo/va.
abreast *adv* de costado.
abridge *vt* abreviar, compendiar; acortar.
abridgement *n* compendio *m*, recopilación *f*.
abroad *adv* en el extranjero; to go ~ salir del país.
abrogate *vt* abrogar, anular.
abrogation *n* abrogación, anulación *f*.
abrupt *adj* brusco/ca; ~ly *adv* precipitadamente; bruscamente.
abscess *n* absceso *m*.
abscond *vi* esconderse; huir.
abseiling *n* rappel *m*.
absence *n* ausencia *f*.
absent *adj* ausente; * *vi* ausentarse.
absentee *n* ausente *m*.
absenteeism *n* absentismo *m*.
absent-minded *adj* distraído/da.
absolute *adj* absoluto/ta; categórico/ca; ~ly *adv* totalmente.

absolution *n* absolución *f.*
absolutism *n* absolutismo *m.*
absolve *vt* absolver.
absorb *vt* absorber.
absorbent *adj* absorbente.
absorbent cotton *n* algodón hidrófilo *m.*
absorption *n* absorción *f.*
abstain *vi* abstenerse, privarse.
abstemious *adj* abstemio/mia, sobrio/ria; ~ly *adv* moderadamente.
abstemiousness *n* sobriedad, abstinencia *f.*
abstinence *n* abstinencia *f*; templanza *f.*
abstinent *adj* abstinente, sobrio/ria.
abstract *adj* abstracto/ta; * *n* extracto *m*; sumario *m*; in the ~ de modo abstracto.
abstraction *n* abstracción *f.*
abstractly *adv* en abstracto.
abstruse *adj* oscuro/ra; ~ly *adv* oscuramente.
absurd *adj* absurdo/da; ~ly *adv* absurdamente.
absurdity *n* absurdidad *f.*
abundance *n* abundancia *f.*
abundant *adj* abundante; ~ly *adv* abundantemente.
abuse *vt* abusar; maltratar; * *n* abuso *m*; injurias *fpl.*
abusive *adj* abusivo/va, ofensivo/va; ~ly *adv* abusivamente.
abut *vi* confinar.
abysmal *adj* abismal; insondable.
abyss *n* abismo *m.*
acacia *n* acacia *f.*
academic *adj* académico/ca.
academician *n* académico *m.*
academy *n* academia *f.*
accede *vi* acceder.
accelerate *vt* acelerar.
accelerator *n* acelerador *m.*
acceleration *n* aceleración *f.*
accent *n* acento *m*; tono *m*; * *vt* acentuar.
accentuate *vt* acentuar.
accentuation *n* acentuación *f.*
accept *vt* aceptar; admitir.
acceptable *adj* aceptable.
acceptability *n* aceptabilidad *f.*
acceptance *n* aceptación *f.*
access *n* acceso *m*; entrada *f.*
accessible *adj* accesible.
accession *n* acceso *m.*
accessory *n* accesorio *m*; (*law*) cómplice *m.*
accident *n* accidente *m*; casualidad *f.*
accidental *adj* casual; ~ly *adv* por casualidad.
acclaim *vt* aclamar, aplaudir.
acclamation *n* aclamación *f*; aplauso *m.*
acclimatize *vt* aclimatar.

accommodate *vt* alojar; complacer.
accommodating *adj* servicial.
accommodations *npl* alojamiento *m.*
accompaniment *n* (*mus*) acompañamiento *m.*
accompanist *n* (*mus*) acompañante *m.*
accompany *vt* acompañar.
accomplice *n* cómplice *m.*
accomplish *vt* efectuar, completar.
accomplished *adj* elegante, consumado/da.
accomplishment *n* cumplimiento *m*; ~s *pl* talentos, conocimientos *mpl.*
accord *n* acuerdo, convenio *m*; with one ~ unánimemente; of one's own ~ espontáneamente.
accordance *n*: in ~ with de acuerdo con.
according *prep* según, conforme; ~ to según; ~ly *adv* por consiguiente.
accordion *n* (*mus*) acordeón *m.*
accost *vt* trabar conversación con.
account *n* cuenta *f*; on no ~ de ninguna manera; bajo ningún concepto; on ~ of por motivo de; to call to ~ pedir cuenta; to turn to ~ hacer provechoso; * *vt* to ~ for explicar.
accountability *n* responsabilidad *f.*
accountable *adj* responsable.
accountancy *n* contabilidad *f*, *Lat Am* contaduría *f.*
accountant *n* contable *m*, *Lat Am* contador *m.*
account book *n* libro *m* de cuentas.
account number *n* número *m* de cuenta.
accrue *vi* resultar, provenir.
accumulate *vt* acumular; amontonar; * *vi* crecer.
accumulation *n* acumulación *f*; amontonamiento *m.*
accuracy *n* exactitud *f.*
accurate *adj* exacto/ta; ~ly *adv* exactamente.
accursed *adj* maldito/ta.
accusation *n* acusación *f.*
accusative *n* (*gr*) acusativo *m.*
accusatory *adj* acusatorio/ria.
accuse *vt* acusar; culpar.
accused *n* acusado *m.*
accuser *n* acusador/a *m/f.*
accustom *vt* acostumbrar.
accustomed *adj* acostumbrado/da, habitual.
ace *n* as *m*; within an ~ of... casi, por poco no....
acerbic *adj* mordaz.
acetate *n* (*chem*) acetato *m.*
ache *n* dolor *m*; * *vi* doler.

achieve *vt* realizar; obtener.
achievement *n* realización *f*; hazaña *f*.
acid *adj* ácido/da; agrio/ria; * *n* ácido *m*.
acid rain *n* lluvia ácida *f*.
acidity *n* acidez *f*.
acknowledge *vt* reconocer, confesar.
acknowledgement *n* reconocimiento *m*;
gratitud *f*.
acme *n* apogeo *m*.
acne *n* acne *m*.
acorn *n* bellota *f*.
acoustics *n* acústica *f*.
acquaint *vt* informar, avisar.
acquaintance *n* conocimiento *m*; conocido *m*.
acquiesce *vi* someterse, consentir, asentir.
acquiescence *n* consentimiento *m*.
acquiescent *adj* deferente.
acquire *vt* adquirir.
acquisition *n* adquisición, obtención *f*.
acquit *vt* absolver.
acquittal *n* absolución *f*.
acre *n* acre *m*.
acrid *adj* acre.
acrimonious *adj* mordaz.
acrimony *n* acrimonia, acritud *f*.
across *adv* de una parte a otra; * *prep* a
través de; to come ~ toparse con.
act *vt* representar; * *vi* hacer; * *n* acto, hecho
m; acción *f*; ~s of the apostles Hechos
mpl de los Apóstoles.
acting *adj* interino/na.
action *n* acción *f*; batalla *f*.
action replay *n* repetición *f*.
activate *vt* activar.
active *adj* activo/va; ~ly *adv* activamente.
activity *n* actividad *f*.
actor *n* actor *m*.
actress *n* actriz *f*.
actual *adj* real; efectivo/va; ~ly *adv* en
efecto, realmente.
actuary *n* actuario *m* de seguros.
acumen *n* agudeza, perspicacia *f*.
acupuncture *n* acupuntura *f*.
acute *adj* agudo/da; ingenioso/sa; ~ accent
n acento agudo *m*; ~ angle *n* ángulo agudo
m; ~ly *adv* con agudeza.
acuteness *n* perspicacia, sagacidad *f*.
adage *n* proverbio *m*.
adamant *adj* inflexible.
adapt *vt* adaptar, acomodar; ajustar.
adaptability *n* facilidad de adaptarse *f*.
adaptable *adj* adaptable.
adaptation *n* adaptación *f*.
adapter *n* adaptador *m*.

add *vt* añadir, agregar; to ~ up sumar.
addendum *n* suplemento *m*.
adder *n* culebra *f*; víbora *f*.
addict *n* drogadicto *m*.
addiction *n* dependencia *f*.
additive *adj* que crea dependencia.
addition *n* adición *f*.
additional *adj* adicional; ~ly *adv* en/por
adición.
additive *n* aditivo *m*.
address *vt* dirigir; * *n* dirección *f*; discurso *m*.
adduce *vt* alegar, aducir.
adenoids *npl* vegetaciones adenoideas
fpl.
adept *adj* hábil.
adequacy *n* suficiencia *f*.
adequate *adj* adecuado/da; suficiente; ~ly
adv adecuadamente.
adhere *vi* adherir.
adherence *n* adherencia *f*.
adherent *n* adherente, partidario *m*.
adhesion *n* adhesión *f*.
adhesive *adj* pegajoso/sa.
adhesiveness *n* adhesividad *f*.
adhesive tape *n* esparadrapo *m*.
adieu *adv* adiós; * *n* despedida *f*.
adipose *adj* adiposo/sa.
adjacent *adj* adyacente, contiguo/gua.
adjectival *adj* adjetivado/da; ~ly *adv* como
adjetivo.
adjective *n* adjetivo *m*.
adjoin *vi* estar contiguo/gua.
adjoining *adj* contiguo/gua.
adjourn *vt* aplazar.
adjournment *n* prórroga *f*.
adjudicate *vt* adjudicar.
adjunct *n* adjunto *m*.
adjust *vt* ajustar, acomodar.
adjustable *adj* ajustable.
adjustment *n* ajustamiento, arreglo *m*.
adjutant *n* (*mil*) ayudante *m*.
ad lib *vi* improvisar.
administer *vt* administrar; gobernar; to ~
an oath prestar juramento.
administration *n* administración *f*;
gobierno *m*.
administrative *adj* administrativo/va.
administrator *n* administrador/a *m/f*.
admirable *adj* admirable; ~bly *adv* admirablemente.
admiral *n* almirante *m*.
admiralship *n* almirante *f*.
admiralty *n* almirantazgo *m*.
admiration *n* admiración *f*.
admire *vt* admirar.

admirer *n* admira/a *m/f*.
admiringly *adv* con admiración.
admissible *adj* admisible.
admission *adj* entrada *f*.
admit *vt* admitir; to ~ to confesarse culpable de.
admittance *n* entrada *f*.
admittedly *adj* de acuerdo que.
admixture *n* mixtura, mezcla *f*.
admonish *vt* amonestar, reprender.
admonition *n* amonestación *f*; consejo, aviso *m*.
admonitory *adj* exhortatorio/ria.
ad nauseam *adv* hasta el cansancio.
adolescence *n* adolescencia *f*.
adopt *vt* adoptar.
adopted *adj* adoptivo/va.
adoption *n* adopción *f*.
adoptive *adj* adoptivo/va.
adorable *adj* adorable.
adorably *adv* de modo adorable.
adoration *n* adoración *f*.
adore *vt* adorar.
adorn *vt* adornar.
adornment *n* adorno *m*.
adrift *adv* a la deriva.
adroit *adj* diestro/tra, hábil.
adroitness *n* destreza *f*.
adulation *n* adulación, zalamería *f*.
adulatory *adj* lisonjero/ra.
adult *adj* adulto/ta; * *n* adulto *m*; adulta *f*.
adulterate *vt* adulterar, corromper; * *adj* adulterado/da, falsificado/da.
adulteration *n* adulteración, corrupción *f*.
adulterer *n* adúltero *m*.
adulteress *n* adúltera *f*.
adulterous *adj* adúltero/ra.
adultery *n* adulterio *m*.
advance *vt* avanzar; promover; pagar por adelantado; * *vi* hacer progresos; to make ~s insinuarse; * *n* avance *m*; paga adelantada *f*.
advanced *adj* avanzado/da.
advancement *n* adelantamiento *m*; progreso *m*; promoción *f*.
advantage *n* ventaja *f*; to take ~ of sacar provecho de.
advantageous *adj* ventajoso/sa; ~ly *adv* ventajosamente.
advantageousness *n* ventaja, utilidad *f*.
advent *n* venida *f*.
Advent *n* Adviento *m*.
adventitious *adj* adventicio/cia.
adventure *n* aventura *f*.
adventurer *n* aventurero *m*.

adventurous *adj* intrépido/da; valeroso/sa; ~ly *adv* arriesgadamente.
adverb *n* adverbio *m*.
adverbial *adj* adverbial; ~ly *adv* como adverbio.
adversary *n* adversario, enemigo *m*.
adverse *adj* adverso/sa, contrario/ria.
adversity *n* calamidad *f*; infortunio *m*.
advertise/advertize *vt* anunciar.
advertisement/advertizement *n* anuncio *m*; Lat Am aviso *m*, Lat Am reclame *m*.
advertising *n* publicidad *f*.
advice *n* consejo *m*; aviso *m*.
advisability *n* prudencia, conveniencia *f*.
advisable *adj* prudente, conveniente.
advise *vt* aconsejar; avisar.
advisedly *adv* prudentemente, avisadamente.
advisory *adj* consultivo/va.
advocacy *n* defensa *f*.
advocate *n* abogado *m*; protector *m*; * *vt* abogar por.
advocateship *n* abogacía *f*.
aerial *n* antena *f*.
aerobics *npl* aerobic *m*, Lat Am aerobismo *m*.
aerometer *n* areómetro *m*.
aerosol *n* aerosol *m*.
aerostat *n* globo aerostático *m*.
afar *adv* lejos, distante; from ~ desde lejos.
affability *n* afabilidad, urbanidad *f*.
affable *adj* afable, complaciente; ~bly *adv* afablemente.
affair *n* asunto *m*; negocio *m*.
affect *vt* conmover; afectar.
affectation *n* afectación *f*.
affected *adj* afectado/da, lleno/na de afectación; ~ly *adv* con afectación.
affectingly *adv* con afecto.
affection *n* cariño *m*.
affectionate *adj* afectuoso/sa, Lat Am querendón/ona; ~ly *adv* cariñosamente.
affidavit *n* declaración jurada *f*.
affiliate *vt* afiliar.
affiliation *n* afiliación *f*.
affinity *n* afinidad *f*.
affirm *vt* afirmar, declarar.
affirmation *n* afirmación *f*.
affirmative *adj* afirmativo/va; ~ly *adv* afirmativamente.
affix *vt* pegar; * *n* (gr) afijo *m*.
afflict *vt* afligir.
affliction *n* aflicción *f*; dolor *m*.
affluence *n* abundancia *f*.
affluent *adj* opulento/ta.

afflux n confluencia, afluencia f.
afford vt dar; proveer.
affray n asalto m; tumulto m.
affront n afrenta, injuria f; * vt afrentar, insultar, ultrajar.
aflame adv en llamas.
afloat adv flotante, a flote.
afraid adj espantado/da, tímido/da; **I am ~** temo.
afresh adv de nuevo, otra vez.
African-American adj, n afroamericano/na m/f.
aft adv (mar) a popa.
after prep después; detrás; según; * adv después; **~ all** después de todo.
afterbirth n secundinas fpl.
after-effects npl consecuencias fpl.
afterlife n vida venidera f.
aftermath n consecuencias fpl.
afternoon n tarde f.
aftershave n aftershave m.
aftertaste n resabio m.
afterwards adv después.
again adv otra vez; **~ and ~** muchas veces; **as much ~** otra vez tanto.
against prep contra; **~ the grain** a contrapelo; de mala gana.
agate n ágata f.
age n edad f; **under ~** menor; * vt envejecer.
aged adj viejo/ja, anciano/na.
agency n agencia f.
agenda n orden del día m.
agent n agente m.
agglomerate vt aglomerar.
agglomeration n aglomeración f.
aggrandizement n engrandecimiento m.
aggravate vt agravar, exagerar.
aggravation n agravación f.
aggregate n agregado m.
aggregation n agregación f.
aggression n agresión f.
aggressive adj ofensivo/va.
aggressor n agresor m.
aggrieved adj ofendido/da.
aghast adj horrorizado/da.
agile adj ágil; diestro/tra.
agility n agilidad f; destreza f.
agitate vt agitar.
agitation n agitación f; perturbación f.
agitator n agitador, incitador m.
ago adv pasado, largo tiempo; después; **how long ~?** ¿cuánto hace?
agog adj emocionado/da.
agonizing adj atroz.
agony n agonía f.

agree vt convenir; * vi estar de acuerdo/da.
agreeable adj agradable; amable; **~bly** adv agradablemente; **~ with** según, conforme a.
agreeableness n amabilidad, gracia f.
agreed adj establecido/da, convenido/da; **~!** adv ¡de acuerdo!
agreement n acuerdo m.
agricultural adj agrario/ria.
agriculture n agricultura f.
agriculturist n agricultor m.
agronomy n agronomía f.
aground adv (mar) encallado.
ah! excl ¡ah!, ¡ay!
ahead adv más allá, delante de otro; (mar) por la proa.
ahoy! excl (mar) ¡ohe!
aid vt ayudar, socorrer; **to ~ and abet** ser cómplice de; * n ayuda f; auxilio, socorro m.
aide-de-camp n (mil) ayudante de campo m.
AIDS n SIDA m.
ail vt afligir, molestar.
ailing adj doliente.
ailment n dolencia, indisposición f.
aim vt apuntar aspirar a; intentar; * n designio m; puntería f.
aimless adj sin designio, sin objeto; **~ly** a la deriva.
air n aire m; * vt airear; ventilar.
airbag n airbag m.
air balloon n globo aerostático m.
airborne adj aerotransportado/da.
air-conditioned adj climatizado/da.
air conditioning n aire acondicionado m.
aircraft n avión m.
air cushion n cojinete rellenado de aire m.
air force n fuerzas aéreas fpl.
air freshener n ambientador m.
air gun n escopeta de aire comprimido f.
air hole n respirador m.
airless adj falto de ventilación, sofocado/da.
airlift n puente aéreo m.
airline n línea aérea f.
airmail n: **by ~** por avión.
airplane n avión m.
airport n aeropuerto m.
airport tax n tasas de aeropuerto f.
air pump n bomba de aire f.
airsick adj mareado/da.
airstrip n pista de aterrizaje f.
air terminal n terminal f.
airtight adj herméticamente cerrado/da.
airy adj bien ventilado/da.
aisle n nave de una iglesia f.
ajar adj entreabierto/ta.

akimbo adj corvo/va.
akin adj parecido/da.
alabaster n alabastro m; * adj alabastrino/na.
alacrity n presteza f.
alarm n alarma f; * vt alarmar; inquietar.
alarm bell n timbre de alarma m.
alarmist n alarmista m.
alas adv desgraciadamente.
albeit conj aunque.
album n álbum m.
alchemist n alquimista m.
alchemy n alquimia f.
alcohol n alcohol m.
alcoholic adj alcohólico/ca; * n alcoholizado m.
alcove n nicho m.
alder n aliso m.
ale n cerveza f.
alert adj vigilante; alerto/ta; * n alerta f.
alertness n cuidado m; vigilancia f.
algae npl alga f.
algebra n álgebra f.
algebraic adj algebraico/ca.
alias adj alias.
alibi n (law) coartada f.
alien adj ajeno/na; * n forastero m.
alienate vt enajenar.
alienation n enajenación f.
alight vi apearse; * adj encendido/da.
align vt alinear.
alike adj semejante, igual; * adv igualmente.
alimentation n alimentación f.
alimony n alimentos mpl.
alive adj vivo/va, viviente; activo/va.
alkali n álcali m.
alkaline adj alcalino/na.
all adj todo/da; * adv totalmente; ~ at once, ~ of a sudden de repente; ~ the same sin embargo; ~ the better tanto mejor; not at ~! ¡no hay de qué!; once for ~ una vez por todas; * n todo m.
allay vt aliviar.
all clear n luz verde f.
allegation n alegación f.
allege vt alegar; declarar.
allegiance n lealtad, fidelidad f.
allegorical adj alegórico/ca; ~ly adv alegóricamente.
allegory n alegoría f.
allegro n (mus) alegro m.
allergy n alergia f.
alleviate vt aliviar, aligerar.
alleviation n alivio m; mitigación f.
alley n callejuela f.

alliance n alianza f.
allied adj aliado/da.
alligator n caimán m.
alliteration n aliteración f.
all-night adj abierto/ta toda la noche.
allocate vt repartir.
allocation n cuota f.
allot vt asignar.
allow vt conceder; permitir; dar, pagar; to ~ for tener en cuenta.
allowable adj admisible, permitido/da.
allowance n concesión f.
alloy n liga, mezcla, aleación f.
all right adv bien.
all-round adj completo/ta.
allspice n pimienta de Jamaica f.
allude vt aludir.
allure n fascinación f.
alluring adj seductor/a; ~ly adv seductoramente.
allurement n aliciente, atractivo m.
allusion n alusión f.
allusive adj alusivo/va; ~ly adv de modo alusivo.
alluvial adj aluvial.
ally n aliado m; * vt aliar.
almanac n almanaque m.
almighty adj omnipotente, todopoderoso/sa.
almond n almendra f.
almond tree n almendro m.
almost adv casi; cerca de.
alms n limosna f.
aloft prep arriba.
alone adj solo; * adv solamente, sólo; to leave ~ dejar en paz.
along adv a lo largo; ~ side al lado.
aloof adv lejos.
aloud adv en voz alta.
alphabet n alfabeto m.
alphabetical adj alfabético/ca; ~ly adv por orden alfabético.
alpine adj alpino/na.
already adv ya.
also adv también, además.
altar n altar m.
altarpiece n retablo m.
alter vt modificar.
alteration n alteración f.
altercation n altercado m.
alternate adj alterno/na; * vt alternar, variar; ~ly adv alternativamente.
alternating adj alterno/na.
alternation n alternación f.
alternator n alternador m.

alternative n alternativa f; * adj alternative; ~ly adv si no.
although conj aunque, no obstante.
altitude n altitud, altura f.
altogether adv del todo.
alum n alumbre m.
aluminous adj aluminoso/sa.
aluminum n aluminio m.
always adv siempre, constantemente.
a.m. adv de la mañana.
amalgam n amalgama f.
amalgamate vt,vi amalgamar(se).
amalgamation n amalgamación f.
amanuensis n amanuense, secretario m.
amaryllis n (bot) amarillas f.
amass vt acumular, amontonar.
amateur n aficionado m, amateur m/f.
amateurish adj torpe.
amatory adj amatorio/ria; erótico/ca.
amaze vt asombrar.
amazement n asombro m.
amazing adj pasmoso/sa; ~ly adv extraordinariamente.
amazon n amazona f.
ambassador n embajador m.
ambassadress n embajadora f.
amber n ámbar m; * adj ambarino/na.
ambidextrous adj ambidextro/tra, ambidiestro/tra.
ambient adj ambiente.
ambiguity n ambigüedad, duda f.
ambiguous adj ambiguo; ~ly adv ambiguamente.
ambition n ambición f.
ambitious adj ambicioso/sa; ~ly adv ambiciosamente.
amble vi andar sin prisa.
ambulance n ambulancia f.
ambush n emboscada f; to lie in ~ estar emboscado/da; * vt tender una emboscada a.
ameliorate vt mejorar.
amelioration n mejoramiento m.
amenable adj sensible.
amend vt enmendar.
amendable adj reparable, corregible.
amendment n enmienda f.
amends npl compensación f.
amenities npl comodidades fpl.
America n América f.
American adj americano/na
amethyst n amatista f.
amiability n amabilidad f.
amiable adj amable.
amiableness n amabilidad f.
amiably adv amablemente.

amicable adj amigable, amistoso/sa; ~bly adv amistosamente.
amid(st) prep entre, en medio de.
amiss adv: something's ~ algo pasa.
ammonia n amoniaco m.
ammunition n municiones fpl.
amnesia n amnesia f.
amnesty n amnistía f.
among(st) prep entre, en medio de.
amoral adj amoral.
amorous adj amoroso/sa; ~ly adv amorosamente.
amorphous adj informe.
amount n importe m; cantidad f; * vi sumar.
amp(ere) n amperio m.
amphibian n anfibio m.
amphibious adj anfibio/bia.
amphitheater n anfiteatro m.
ample adj amplio/lia.
ampleness n amplitud, abundancia f.
amplification n amplificación f; extensión f.
amplifier n amplificador m.
amplify vt ampliar, extender.
amplitude n amplitud, extensión f.
amply adv ampliamente.
amputate vt amputar.
amputation n amputación f.
amulet n amuleto m.
amuse vt entretener, divertir.
amusement n diversión f, pasatiempo, entretenimiento m.
amusing adj divertido/da; ~ly adv entretenidamente.
an art un, uno, una.
anachronism n anacronismo m.
analog adj (comput) analógico/ca.
analogous adj análogo.
analogy n analogía f.
analyze vt analizar.
analysis n análisis m invar.
analyst n analizador/a m/f.
analytical adj analítico/ca; ~ly adv analíticamente.
anarchic adj anárquico/ca.
anarchist adj anarquista.
anarchy n anarquía f.
anatomical adj anatómico/ca; ~ly adv anatómicamente.
anatomize vt anatomizar.
anatomy n anatomía f.
ancestor n: ~s pl antepasados mpl.
ancestral adj hereditario/ria.
ancestry n raza, alcurnia f.
anchor n ancla f; * vi anclar; to weigh ~ zarpar.

anchorage *n* fondeadero *m.*
anchovy *n* anchoa *f.*
ancient *adj* antiguo.
ancillary *adj* auxiliar.
and *conj* y, e.
anecdotal *adj* anecdótico/ca.
anecdote *n* anécdota *f.*
anemia *n* anemia *f.*
anemic *adj* (*med*) anémico/ca.
anemone *n* (*bot*) anémona *f.*
anesthetic *n* anestesia *f.*
anew *adv* de nuevo, nuevamente.
angel *n* ángel *m.*
angelic *adj* angélico/ca.
anger *n* cólera *f*; * *vt* enojar, irritar.
angle *n* ángulo *m*; * *vt* pescar con caña.
angled *adj* anguloso/sa.
angler *n* pescador/a de caña *m/f.*
Anglicanism *n* anglicismo *m.*
angling *n* pesca con caña *f.*
angrily *adv* enojado.
angry *adj* enojado/da.
anguish *n* ansia, angustia *f.*
angular *adj* angular.
angularity *n* forma angular *f.*
animal *n adj* animal *m.*
animate *vt* animar; * *adj* viviente.
animated *adj* vivo/va.
animation *n* animación *f.*
animosity *n* rencor *m.*
animus *n* odio *m.*
anise *n* anís *m.*
aniseed *n* anís *m.*
ankle *n* tobillo *m*; ~ bone hueso del tobillo *m.*
annals *n* anales *mpl.*
annex *vt* anejar; * *n* anejo *m.*
annexation *n* anexión *f.*
annihilate *vt* aniquilar.
annihilation *n* aniquilación *f.*
anniversary *n* aniversario *m.*
annotate *vi* anotar.
annotation *n* anotación *f.*
announce *vt* anunciar, publicar.
announcement *n* anuncio *m.*
announcer *n* locutor/a *m/f.*
annoy *vt* molestar.
annoyance *n* molestia *f.*
annoying *adj* molesto/ta; fastidioso/sa.
annual *adj* anual; ~ly *adv* anualmente, cada año.
annuity *n* renta vitalicia *f.*
annul *vt* anular.
annulment *n* anulación *f.*
annunciation *n* anunciación *f.*
anodyne *adj* anodino/na.

anoint *vt* untar, ungir.
anomalous *adj* anómalo.
anomaly *n* anomalía, irregularidad *f.*
anon *adv* más tarde.
anonymity *n* anonimato *m.*
anonymous *adj* anónimo/ma; ~ly *adj* anónimamente.
anorexia *n* anorexia *f.*
another *adj* otro/tra, diferente; one ~ uno a otro.
answer *vt* responder, replicar; corresponder; to ~ for responder de/por; to ~ to corresponder a; * *n* respuesta, réplica *f.*
answerable *adj* responsable.
answering machine *n* contestador automático *m.*
ant *n* hormiga *f.*
antagonism *n* antagonismo *m*; rivalidad *f.*
antagonist *n* antagonista *m.*
antagonize *vt* provocar.
Antarctic *adj* antártico/ca.
anteater *n* oso hormiguero *m.*
antecedent *n*: ~s *pl* antecedentes *mpl.*
antechamber *n* antecámara *f.*
antedate *vt* antedatar.
antelope *n* antílope *m.*
antenna *npl* antena *f.*
anterior *adj* anterior, precedente.
anthem *n* himno *m.*
ant hill *n* hormiguero *m.*
anthology *n* antología *f.*
anthracite *n* antracita *f.*
anthropologist *n* antropólogo/ga *m/f.*
anthropology *n* antropología *f.*
anti-aircraft *adj* antiaéreo/rea.
antibiotic *n* antibiótico *m.*
antibody *n* anticuerpo *m.*
Antichrist *n* Anticristo *m.*
anticipate *vt* anticipar, prevenir.
anticipation *n* anticipación *f.*
anticlockwise *adv* en sentido contrario al de las agujas del reloj.
antidote *n* antídoto *m.*
antifreeze *n* anticongelante *m.*
antimony *n* antimonio *m.*
antipathy *n* antipatía *f.*
antipodes *npl* antípodas *fpl.*
antiquarian *n* anticuario *m.*
antiquated *adj* antiguo/gua; * *n* antigüedad *f.*
antiquity *n* antigüedad *f.*
antiseptic *adj* antiséptico/ca.
antisocial *adj* antisocial.
antithesis *n* antítesis *f.*
antler *n* cuerna *f.*
anvil *n* yunque *m.*

anxiety *n* ansiedad *f*, ansia *f*; afán *m*, zozobra *f*.
anxious *adj* ansioso/sa; ~**ly** *adv* ansiosamente; **to be** ~ *vi* zozobrar.
any *adj pn* cualquier, cualquiera; alguno, alguna; todo; ~**body** alguien, nadie, cualquiera; ~**how** de cualquier manera; ~**more** más; ~**place** en ninguna parte; ~**thing** algo, nada, cualquier cosa.
apace *adv* rápidamente.
apart *adv* aparte, separadamente.
apartment *n* apartamento, departamento *m*.
apartment house *n* casa de apartamentos *f*.
apathetic *adj* apático/ca.
apathy *n* apatía *f*.
ape *n* mono *m*; * *vt* remedar.
aperture *n* abertura *f*.
apex *n* ápice *m*.
aphorism *n* aforismo *m*; máxima *f*.
apiary *n* colmenar *m*, *Lat Am* apiario *m*.
apiece *adv* por cabeza, por persona.
aplomb *n* aplomo *m*.
Apocalypse *n* Apocalipsis *m*.
apocrypha *npl* libros apócrifos *mpl*.
apocryphal *adj* apócrifo/fa, no canónico/ca.
apologetic *adj* de disculpa.
apologist *n* apologista *m*.
apologize *vt* disculpar.
apology *n* apología, defensa *f*.
apoplexy *n* apoplejía *f*.
apostle *n* apóstol *m*.
apostolic *adj* apostólico/ca.
apostrophe *n* apóstrofe *m*.
apotheosis *n* apoteosis *f*.
appall *vt* espantar, aterrar.
appalling *adj* espantoso/sa.
apparatus *n* aparato *m*.
apparel *n* traje, vestido *m*.
apparent *adj* evidente, aparente; ~**ly** *adv* por lo visto.
apparition *n* aparición, visión *f*.
appeal *vi* apelar, recurrir a un tribunal superior; * *n* (*law*) apelación *f*.
appealing *adj* atractivo/va.
appear *vi* aparecer.
appearance *n* apariencia *f*.
appease *vt* aplacar.
appellant *n* (*law*) apelante *m*.
append *vt* anejar.
appendage *n* cosa accesoria *f*.
appendicitis *n* apendicitis *f*.
appendix *n* apéndice *m*.
appertain *vi* tocar a.
appetite *n* apetito *m*.
appetizing *adj* apetitivo/va.

applaud *vi* aplaudir.
applause *n* aplausos *mpl*.
apple *n* manzana *f*.
apple pie *n* pastelillo de manzanas *m*; **in** ~ **order** en sumo orden.
apple tree *n* manzano *m*.
appliance *n* aparato *m*.
applicability *n* aplicabilidad *f*.
applicable *adj* aplicable.
applicant *n* aspirante, candidato *m*.
application *n* aplicación *f*; solicitud *f*.
applied *adj* aplicado/da.
apply *vt* aplicar; * *vi* dirigirse a, recurrir a.
appoint *vt* nombrar.
appointee *n* persona nombrada *f*.
appointment *n* cita *f*; nombramiento *m*.
apportion *vt* repartir.
apportionment *n* repartición *f*.
apposite *adj* adaptado/da.
apposition *n* aposición *f*.
appraisal *n* estimación *f*.
appraise *vt* tasar; estimar.
appreciable *adj* sensible.
appreciably *adv* sensiblemente.
appreciate *vt* apreciar; agradecer.
appreciation *n* aprecio *m*.
appreciative *adj* agradecido/da.
apprehend *vt* arrestar.
apprehension *n* aprensión *f*.
apprehensive *adj* aprensivo/va, tímido/da.
apprentice *n* aprendiz *m*; * *vt* poner de aprendiz.
apprenticeship *n* aprendizaje *m*.
apprise *vt* informar.
approach *vt* (*vi*) aproximar(se); * *n* acceso *m*.
approachable *adj* accesible.
approbation *n* aprobación *f*.
appropriate *vt* apropiarse de; * *adj* apropiado/da.
approval *n* aprobación *f*.
approve (of) *vt* aprobar.
approximate *vi* acercarse; * *adj* aproximativo/va; ~**ly** *adv* aproximadamente.
approximation *n* aproximación *f*.
apricot *n* damasco, albaricoque *m*.
April *n* abril *m*.
apron *n* delantal *m*.
apse *n* ábside *m*.
apt *adj* apto/ta, idóneo/nea; ~**ly** *adv* oportunamente.
aptitude *n* aptitud *f*.
aqualung *n* escafandra autónoma *f*.
aquarium *n* acuario *m*.
Aquarius *n* Acuario *m*.

aquatic *adj* acuático/ca.
aqueduct *n* acueducto *m*.
aquiline *adj* aguileño/ña.
arabesque *n* arabesco *m*.
arable *adj* labrantío/tía.
arbiter *n* árbitro *m*.
arbitrariness *n* arbitrariedad *f*.
arbitrary *adj* arbitrario/ria.
arbitrate *vt* arbitrar, juzgar como árbitro.
arbitration *n* arbitrio *m*.
arbitrator *n* árbitro *m*.
arbor *n* emparrado *m*; enramada *f*.
arcade *n* galería *f*.
arch *n* arco *m*; * *adj* malicioso/sa.
archaic *adj* arcaico/ca.
archangel *n* arcángel *m*.
archbishop *n* arzobispo *m*.
archbishopric *n* arzobispado *m*.
archeological *adj* arqueológico/ca.
archeologist *n* arqueólogo/ga *m/f*.
archeology *n* arqueología *f*.
archer *n* arquero *m*.
archery *n* tiro con arco *m*.
architect *n* arquitecto/ta *m/f*.
architectural *adj* arquitectónico/ca.
architecture *n* arquitectura *f*.
archives *npl* archivos *mpl*.
archivist *n* archivero/ra *m/f*.
archly *adv* maliciosamente.
archway *n* arcada, bóveda *f*.
arctic *adj* ártico/ca.
ardent *adj* apasionado/da; ~ly *adv* con pasión.
ardor *n* ardor *m*; vehemencia *f*; pasión *f*.
arduous *adj* arduo, difícil.
area *n* área *f*; espacio *m*, zona *f*.
arena *n* arena *f*.
arguably *adv* posiblemente.
argue *vi* discutir; * *vt* sostener.
argument *n* argumento *m*, controversia *f*.
argumentation *n* argumentación *f*.
argumentative *adj* discutidor/a.
aria *n* (*mus*) aria *f*.
arid *adj* árido/da, estéril.
aridity *n* sequedad *f*.
Aries *n* Aries *m*.
aright *adv* bien; to set ~ rectificar.
arise *vi* levantarse; nacer.
aristocracy *n* aristocracia *f*.
aristocrat *n* aristócrata *m/f*.
aristocratic *adj* aristocrático/ca; ~ally *adv* aristocráticamente.
arithmetic *n* aritmética *f*.
arithmetical *adj* aritmético/ca; ~ly *adv* aritméticamente.

ark *n* arca *f*.
arm *n* brazo *m*; arma *f*; * *vt* (*vi*) armar(se).
armament *n* armamento *m*.
armchair *n* sillón *m*.
armed *adj* armado/da.
armful *n* brazada *f*.
armhole *n* sobaco *m*.
armistice *n* armisticio *m*.
armor *n* armadura *f*.
armored car *n* carro blindado *m*.
armory *n* arsenal *m*.
armpit *n* sobaco *m*.
armrest *n* apoyabrazos *m invar*.
army *n* ejército *m*; tropas *fpl*.
aroma *n* aroma *m*.
aromatherapy *n* aromaterapia *f*.
aromatic *adj* aromático/ca.
around *prep* alrededor de; * *adv* alrededor.
arouse *vt* despertar; excitar.
arraign *vt* acusar.
arraignment *n* acusación *f*; proceso criminal *m*.
arrange *vt* organizar.
arrangement *n* colocación *f*; arreglo.
arrant *adj* consumado/da.
array *n* serie *f*.
arrears *npl* resto de una deuda *m*; atraso *m*.
arrest *n* arresto *m*; * *vt* detener, arrestar.
arrival *n* llegada *f*.
arrive *vi* llegar.
arrogance *n* arrogancia, presunción *f*.
arrogant *adj* arrogante, presuntuoso/sa; ~ly *adv* arrogantemente.
arrogate *vt* arrogarse.
arrogation *n* arrogación *f*.
arrow *n* flecha *f*.
arsenal *n* (*mil*) arsenal *m*; (*mar*) atarazana, armería *f*.
arsenic *n* arsénico *m*.
arson *n* fuego incendiario *m*.
art *n* arte *m*.
arterial *adj* arterial.
artesian well *n* pozo artesiano *m*.
artery *n* arteria *f*.
artful *adj* ingenioso/sa.
artfulness *n* astucia, habilidad *f*.
art gallery *n* pinacoteca *f*.
arthritis *n* artritis *f*.
artichoke *n* alcachofa *f*.
article *n* artículo *m*.
articulate *vt* articular, pronunciar distintamente.
articulated *adj* articulado/da.
articulation *n* articulación *f*.

artifice *n* artificio, fraude *m*.
artificial *adj* artificial; artificioso/sa; ~ly *adv* artificialmente; artificiosamente.
artificial insemination *n* inseminación artificial *f*.
artificiality *n* artificialidad *f*.
artillery *n* artillería *f*.
artisan *n* artesano/na *m/f*.
artist *n* artista *m*.
artistic *adj* artístico/ca.
artistry *n* habilidad *f*.
artless *adj* sencillo, simple; ~ly *adv* sencillamente, naturalmente.
artlessness *n* sencillez *f*.
as *conj* como; mientras; también; visto que, puesto que; ~ for, ~ to en cuanto a.
asbestos *n* asbesto, amianto *m*.
ascend *vi* ascender, subir.
ascendancy *n* dominio *m*.
ascension *n* ascensión *f*.
ascent *n* subida *f*.
ascertain *vt* establecer.
ascetic *adj* ascético/ca; * *n* asceta *m*.
ascribe *vt* atribuir.
ash *n* (*bot*) fresno *m*; ceniza *f*.
ashcan *n* cubo de la basura *m*.
ashamed *adj* avergonzado/da.
ashore *adv* en tierra, a tierra; **to go ~** desembarcar.
ashtray *n* cenicero *m*.
Ash Wednesday *n* miércoles de ceniza *m*.
aside *adv* a un lado.
ask *vt* pedir, rogar; **to ~ after** preguntar por; **to ~ for** pedir; **to ~ out** invitar.
askance *adv* desconfiado/da.
askew *adv* de lado.
asleep *adj* dormido/da; **to fall ~** dormirse.
asparagus *n* espárrago *m*.
aspect *n* aspecto *m*.
aspen *n* álamo temblón *m*.
aspersion *n* calumnia *f*.
asphalt *n* asfalto *m*.
asphyxia *n* (*med*) asfixia *f*.
asphyxiate *vt* asfixiar.
asphyxiation *n* asfixia *f*.
aspirant *n* aspirante *m*.
aspirate *vt* aspirar, pronunciar con aspiración; * *n* sonido aspirado *m*.
aspiration *n* aspiración *f*.
aspire *vi* aspirar, desear.
aspirin *n* aspirina *f*.
ass *n* asno *m*; **she ~** burra *f*.
assail *vt* asaltar, atacar.
assailant *n* asaltante *m/f*, agresor/a *m/f*.
assassin *n* asesino/na *m/f*.

assassinate *vt* asesinar.
assassination *n* asesinato *m*.
assault *n* asalto *m*; * *vt* acometer, asaltar.
assemblage *n* multitud *f*.
assemble *vt* reunir, convocar; * *vi* juntarse.
assembly *n* asamblea, junta *f*; congreso *m*.
assembly line *n* cadena de montaje *f*.
assent *n* asentimiento *m*; * *vi* asentir.
assert *vt* sostener, mantener; afirmar.
assertion *n* aserción *f*.
assertive *adj* perentorio/ria.
assess *vt* valorar.
assessment *n* valoración *f*.
assessor *n* asesor/a *m/f*.
assets *npl* bienes *mpl*.
assiduous *adj* diligente, aplicado/da; ~ly *adv* diligentemente.
assign *vt* asignar.
assignation *n* cita *f*.
assignment *n* asignación *f*; tarea *f*.
assimilate *vt* asimilar.
assimilation *n* asimilación *f*.
assist *vt* asistir, ayudar, socorrer.
assistance *n* asistencia *f*; socorro *m*.
assistant *n* asistente, ayudante *m*.
associate *vt* asociar; * *adj* asociado/da; * *n* socio *m*.
association *n* asociación, sociedad *f*.
assonance *n* asonancia *f*.
assorted *adj* surtido/da.
assortment *n* surtido *m*.
assuage *vt* mitigar, suavizar.
assume *vt* asumir; suponer.
assumption *n* supuesto *m*.
Assumption *n* Asunción *f*.
assurance *n* seguro *m*.
assure *vt* asegurar.
assuredly *adv* sin duda.
asterisk *n* asterisco *m*.
astern *adv* (*mar*) a popa.
asthma *n* asma *f*.
asthmatic *adj* asmático/ca.
astonish *vt* pasmar, sorprender.
astonishing *adj* asombroso/sa; ~ly *adv* asombrosamente.
astonishment *n* asombro *m*.
astound *vt* pasmar.
astray *adv*: **to go ~** extraviarse; **to lead ~** llevar por mal camino.
astride *adv* a horcajadas.
astringent *adj* astringente.
astrologer *n* astrólogo/ga *m/f*.
astrological *adj* astrológico/ca.
astrology *n* astrología *f*.
astronaut *n* astronauta *m/f*.

astronomer *n* astrónomo *m*.
astronomical *adj* astronómico/ca.
astronomy *n* astronomía *f*.
astute *adj* astuto/ta.
asylum *n* asilo, refugio *m*.
at *prep* a; en; ~ **once** en seguida; ya; ~ **all** en absoluto; ~ **all events** en todo caso; ~ **first** al principio; ~ **last** por fin.
atheism *n* ateísmo *m*.
atheist *n* ateo *m*, atea *f*.
athlete *n* atleta *m/f*.
athletic *adj* atlético/ca.
atlas *n* atlas *m invar*.
atmosphere *n* atmósfera *f*.
atmospheric *adj* atmosférico/ca.
atom *n* átomo *m*.
atom bomb *n* bomba atómica *f*.
atomic *adj* atómico/ca.
atone *vt* expiar.
atonement *n* expiación *f*.
atop *adv* encima.
atrocious *adj* atroz; ~ly *adv* atrozmente.
atrocity *n* atrocidad, enormidad *f*.
atrophy *n* (*med*) atrofia *f*.
attach *vt* adjuntar.
attaché *n* agregado *m*.
attachment *n* afecto *m*.
attack *vt* atacar; acometer; * *n* ataque *m*.
attacker *n* asaltante *m*.
attain *vt* conseguir, obtener.
attainable *adj* asequible.
attempt *vt* intentar; probar, experimentar; * *n* intento *m*, tentativa *f*.
attend *vt* servir; asistir; **to** ~ **to** ocuparse de; * *vi* prestar atención.
attendance *n* presencia *f*.
attendant *n* sirviente *m*.
attention *n* atención *f*; cuidado *m*.
attentive *adj* atento/ta; cuidadoso/sa; ~ly *adv* con atención.
attenuate *vt* atenuar, disminuir.
attest *vt* atestiguar.
attic *n* desván *m*; guardilla *f*.
attire *n* atavío *m*.
attitude *n* actitud, postura *f*.
attorney-at-law *n* abogado/da *m/f*.
attract *vt* atraer.
attraction *n* atracción *f*; atractivo *m*.
attractive *adj* atractivo/va.
attribute *vt* atribuir; * *n* atributo *m*.
attrition *n* agotamiento *m*.
auburn *adj* moreno/na, castaño/ña.
auction *n* subasta *f*.
auctioneer *n* subastador/a, rematador/a *m/f*.

audacious *adj* audaz, temerario/ria; ~ly *adv* atrevidamente.
audacity *n* audacia, osadía *f*.
audible *adj* perceptible al oído; ~ly *adv* de manera audible.
audience *n* audiencia *f*; auditorio *m*.
audit *n* auditoría *f*; * *vt* auditar.
auditor *n* censor/a de cuentas *m/f*.
auditory *adj* auditivo/va.
augment *vt* aumentar, acrecentar; * *vi* crecer.
augmentation *n* aumentación *f*; aumento *m*.
August *n* agosto *m*.
august *adj* majestuoso/sa.
aunt *n* tía *f*.
au pair *n* au pair *f*.
aura *n* aura *f*.
auspices *npl* auspicios *mpl*.
auspicious *adj* propicio/cia; ~ly *adv* favorablemente.
austere *adj* austero/ra, severo/ra; ~ly *adv* austeramente.
austerity *n* austeridad *f*.
authentic *adj* auténtico/ca; ~ly *adv* auténticamente.
authenticate *vt* autenticar.
authenticity *n* autenticidad *f*.
author *n* autor/a *m/f*; escritor/a *m/f*.
authoress *n* autora; escritora *f*.
authoritarian *adj* autoritario/ria.
authoritative *adj* autoritativo/va; ~ly *adv* autoritativamente, con autoridad.
authority *n* autoridad *f*.
authorization *n* autorización *f*.
authorize *vt* autorizar.
authorship *n* autoría *f*.
auto, automobile *n* carro, coche, auto *m*.
autocrat *n* autócrata *m*.
autocratic *adj* autocrático/ca.
autograph *n* autógrafo *m*.
automated *adj* automatizado/da.
automatic *adj* automático/ca.
automaton *n* autómata *m*.
autonomy *n* autonomía *f*.
autopsy *n* autopsia *f*.
autumn *n* otoño *m*.
autumnal *adj* otoñal.
auxiliary *adj* auxiliar, asistente.
avail *vt*: **to** ~ **oneself of** aprovecharse de; * *n*: **to no** ~ en vano.
available *adj* disponible.
avalanche *n* alud *m*.
avarice *n* avaricia *f*.
avaricious *adj* avaro/ra.
avenge *vt* vengarse, castigar.
avenue *n* avenida *f*.

aver vt afirmar, declarar.

average vt tomar un término medio; * n término medio m.

aversion n aversión f, disgusto m.

avert vt desviar, apartar.

aviary n pajarera f.

avoid vt evitar, escapar, huir; * vr zafarse de.

avoidable adj evitable.

await vt aguardar.

awake vt despertar; * vi despertarse; * adj despierto/ta.

awakening n despertar.

award vt otorgar; Lat Am acordar; * n premio m; sentencia, decisión f.

aware adj consciente; vigilante.

awareness n conciencia f.

away adv ausente, fuera; ~! ¡fuera! , ¡quita de ahí!, ¡marcha! far and ~ de mucho, con mucho.

away game n partido fuera de casa m.

awe n miedo, temor m.

awe-inspiring, awesome adj imponente.

awful adj tremendo/da; horroroso/sa; ~ly adv terriblemente.

awhile adv un rato, algún tiempo.

awkward adj torpe, rudo/da, poco diestro/tra; ~ly adv groseramente, toscamente.

awkwardness n tosquedad, grosería, poca habilidad f.

awl n lezna f.

awning n (mar) toldo m.

awry adv oblicuamente, torcidamente, al través.

ax n hacha f; * vt despedir; cortar.

axiom n axioma m.

axis n eje m.

axle n eje m.

ay(e) excl sí.

B

baa *n* balido *m*; * *vi* balar.

babble *vi* charlar, parlotear; ~ , babbling *n* charla, cháchara *f*.

babbler *n* charlador/a, charlatán/ana *m/f*.

babe, baby *n* niño/a, pequeño/a, nene/a, *Lat Am* tierno/na *m/f*; small ~ mamón/ona *m/f*.

baboon *n* babuino *m*.

babyhood *n* niñez *f*.

babyish *adj* niñero/ra; pueril.

baby carriage *n* cochecito *m*.

baby linen *n* ropita de niño *f*.

bachelor *n* soltero *m*; bachiller *m*.

bachelorship *n* soltería *f*; bachillerato *m*.

back *n* dorso *m*; revés de la mano *m*; * *adv* atrás, detrás; a few years ~ hace algunos años; * *vt* sostener, apoyar, favorecer.

backbite *vt* hablar mal del que está ausente; difamar.

backbiter *n* detractor/a *m/f*.

backbone *n* hueso dorsal, espinazo *m*.

backdate *vt* antedatar.

backdoor *n* puerta trasera *f*.

backer *n* partidario/ria *m/f*.

backgammon *n* backgammon *m*.

background *n* fondo *m*.

backlash *n* reacción *f*.

backlog *n* trabajo acumulado *m*.

back number *n* número atrasado *m*.

backpack *n* mochila *f*.

back payment *n* paga atrasada *f*.

backside *n* trasero *m*.

back-up lights *npl* (*auto*) luces de marcha atrás *fpl*.

backward *adj* tardo/da, lento/ta; * *adv* hacia atrás.

bacon *n* tocino *m*.

bad *adj* mal/malo; perverso/sa; infeliz; dañoso/sa; indispuesto/ta; ~ly *adv* malamente.

badge *n* señal *f*; símbolo *m*; divisa *f*.

badger *n* tejón *m*; * *vt* fatigar; cansar, atormentar.

badminton *n* bádminton *m*.

badness *n* maldad, mala calidad *f*.

baffle *vt* confundir, hundir; acosar.

bag *n* saco *m*; bolsa *f*.

baggage *n* bagaje, equipaje *m*.

bagpipe *n* gaita *f*.

bail *n* fianza, caución (juratoria) *f*; fiador *m*; * *vt* caucionar, fiar.

bailiff *n* alguacil *m*; mayordomo *m*.

bait *vt* cebar; atraer; * *n* cebo *m*; anzuelo *m*.

baize *n* bayeta *f*.

bake *vt* cocer en horno.

bakery *n* panadería *f*.

baker *n* hornero/ra, panadero/ra *m/f*; ~'s dozen trece piezas.

baking *n* cocción *f*.

baking powder *n* levadura *f*.

balance *n* balanza *f*; equilibrio *m*; saldo de una cuenta *m*; to lose one's ~ caerse, dar en tierra; * *vt* pesar en balanza; contrapesar; saldar; considerar, examinar.

balance sheet *n* balance *m*.

balcony *n* balcón *m*.

bald *adj* calvo/va.

baldness *n* calvicie *f*.

bale *n* bala *f*; * *vt* embalar; tirar el agua del bote.

baleful *adj* triste, funesto/ta; ~ly *adv* tristemente; míseramente.

ball *n* bola *f*; pelota *f*; baile *m*, balón *m*.

ballad *n* balada *f*.

ballast *n* lastre, *m* * *vt* lastrar.

ballerina *n* bailarina *f*.

ballet *n* ballet *m*.

ballistic *adj* balístico/ca.

balloon *n* globo *m*.

ballot *n* voto *m*; escrutinio *m*; * *vi* votar.

ballpoint (pen) *n* bolígrafo *m*.

ballroom *n* salón de baile *m*.

balm, balsam *n* bálsamo *m*; * *vt* untar con bálsamo.

balmy *adj* balsámico/ca; fragante.

balustrade *n* balaustrada *f*.

bamboo *n* bambú *m*.

bamboozle *vt* (*col*) engañar.

ban *n* prohibición *f*; * *vt* prohibir.

banal *adj* vulgar.

banana *n* plátano *m*.

band *n* faja *f*; cuadrilla *f*; banda (de soldados) *f*; orquesta *f*.

bandage *n* venda *f*, vendaje *m*; * *vt* vendar.

Band-Aid™ *n* Tirita™ *f*, *Lat Am* Curita™ *f*.

bandit *n* bandido/da *m/f*.

bandstand *n* quiosco *m*.

bandy *vt* pelotear; discutir.

bandy-legged *adj* patizambo/ba.

bang *n* golpe *m*; * *vt* golpear; cerrar con violencia.

bangle *n* brazalete *m*.

bangs *npl* flequillo *m*.

banish vt desterrar, echar fuera, proscribir, expatriar.
banishment n destierro m.
banister(s) n(pl) pasamanos m.
banjo n banjo m.
bank n orilla (de río) f; montón de tierra m; banco m; dique m; escollo m; * vt poner dinero en un banco; to ~ on contar con.
bank account n cuenta de banco f.
bank card n tarjeta bancaria f.
banker n banquero/ra m/f.
banking n banca f; electronic ~ banca electrónica.
banknote n billete de banco m.
bankrupt adj insolvente; * n fallido/da, quebrado/da m.
bankruptcy n bancarrota, quiebra f, Lat Am valencia f.
bank statement n detalle de cuenta m.
banner n bandera f; estandarte m.
banquet n banquete m.
banter n zumba f.
baptism n bautismo m.
baptismal adj bautismal.
baptistery n bautisterio m.
baptize vt bautizar.
bar n bar m; barra f; tranca f; obstáculo m; (law) abogacía f; * vt impedir; prohibir; excluir.
barbarian n bárbaro/ra m/f; * adj bárbaro/ra, cruel.
barbaric adj bárbaro/ra.
barbarism n (gr) barbarismo m; crueldad f.
barbarity n barbaridad, inhumanidad f.
barbarous adj bárbaro/ra, cruel.
barbecue n barbacoa f.
barber n peluquero m.
barber shop n peluquería f.
bar code n código de barras m.
bard n bardo m; poeta m.
bare adj desnudo/da, descubierto/ta; simple; puro/ra; * vt desnudar, descubrir.
barefaced adj desvergonzado/da, impudente.
barefoot(ed) adj descalzo, sin zapatos.
bareheaded adj descubierto/ta.
barelegged adj con las piernas desnudas.
barely adv apenas, solamente.
bareness n desnudez f.
bargain n ganga f; contrato, pacto m; * vi pactar; negociar; to ~ for esperar.
barge n barcaza f.
baritone n (mus) barítono m.
bark n corteza f; ladrido m (del perro); * vi ladrar.

barley n cebada f.
barmaid n camarera f.
barman n barman m.
barn n granero, pajar m.
barnacles npl percebe m.
barometer n barómetro m.
baron n barón m.
baroness n baronesa f.
baronial adj de barón.
barracks npl cuartel m.
barrage n descarga f; (fig) lluvia f.
barrel n barril m; cañón de escopeta m.
barrel organ n organillo de cilindro m.
barren adj estéril, infructuoso/sa; (fig) yermo/ma.
barricade n barricada f; estacada f; barrera f; * vt cerrar con barreras, empalizar.
barrier n barrera f; obstáculo m.
barring adv excepto, fuera de.
barrow n carretilla f.
bartender n barman m.
barter vi baratar; * vt cambiar, trocar.
base n fondo m; base f; basa f; pedestal m; zócalo m; * vt apoyar; * adj bajo/ja, vil.
baseball n béisbol m.
base-board n zócalo m.
baseless adj sin fondo/base.
basement n sótano m.
baseness n bajeza, vileza f.
bash vt golpear.
bashful adj vergonzoso/sa, modesto/ta, tímido/da; ~ly adv vergonzosamente.
basic adj básico/ca; ~ally adv básicamente.
basilisk n basilisco m.
basin n jofaina, bacía f.
basis n base f; fundamento m.
bask vi ponerse a tomar el sol.
basket n cesta, canasta f.
basketball n baloncesto m, Lat Am básquetbol m.
bass n (mus) contrabajo m.
bassoon n bajón m.
bass viol n viola f.
bass voice n bajo cantante m.
bastard n, adj bastardo/da m/f.
bastardy n bastardía f.
baste vt pringar; hilvanar.
basting n hilván m; apaleamiento m; paliza f.
bastion n (mil) bastión m.
bat n murciélago m.
batch n serie f.
bath n baño m.
bathe vt (vt) bañar(se).
bathing suit n traje de baño m.
bathos n estilo bajo en la poesía m.

bathroom *n* (cuarto de) baño *m.*

baths *npl* piscina *f.*

bathtub *n* baño *m*, bañera *f.*

baton *n* batuta *f.*

battalion *n* (*mil*) batallón *m.*

batter *vt* apalear; batir, cañonear; * *n* batido *m.*

battering ram *n* (*mil*) ariete *m.*

battery *n* batería *f.*

battle *n* combate *m*; batalla *f*; * *vi* batallar, combatir.

battle array *n* orden de batalla *f.*

battlefield *n* campo de batalla *m.*

battlement *n* muralla almenada *f.*

battleship *n* acorazado *m.*

bawdy *adj* indecente.

bawl *vi* gritar, vocear.

bay *n* bahía *f*; laurel, lauro *m*; * *vi* balar; * *adj* bayo.

bayonet *n* bayoneta *f.*

bay window *n* ventana salediza *f.*

bazaar *n* bazar *m.*

be *vi* ser; estar.

beach *n* playa, orilla *f.*

beacon *n* almenara *f.*

bead *n* cuenta *f*; ~s *npl* rosario *m.*

beagle *n* sabueso *m.*

beak *n* pico *m.*

beaker *n* taza con pico *f.*

beam *n* rayo de luz *m*; travesaño *m*; pareja *f*; * *vi* brillar.

bean *n* alubia *f*, frijol *m*, judía *f*; green ~, French ~ judía verde *f.*

beansprouts *npl* brotes de soja *mpl.*

bear *vt* llevar; sostener; soportar; producir; parir; * *vi* sufrir (algún dolor).

bear *n* oso *m*; she ~ osa *f.*

bearable *adj* soportable.

beard *n* barba *f.*

bearded *adj* barbado/da.

bearer *n* portador/a *m/f*; árbol fructífero *m.*

bearing *n* relación *f.*

beast *n* bestia *f*; hombre brutal *m*; ~ of burden acémila *f.*

beastliness *n* bestialidad, brutalidad *f.*

beastly *adj* bestial, brutal; * *adv* brutalmente.

beat *vt* golpear; tocar (un tambor); to ~ time (with the sole of the shoe) zapatear; * *vi* pulsar, palpitar; * *n* golpe *m*; pulsación *f.*

beatific *adj* beatífico/ca.

beatify *vt* beatificar, santificar.

beating *n* paliza, zurra *f*, *Lat Am* golpiza *f*; pulsación *f*, zumba *f.*

beatitude *n* beatitud, felicidad *f.*

beautiful *adj* hermoso/sa, bello; ~ly *adv* con belleza/perfección.

beautify *vt* hermosear; embellecer; adornar.

beauty *n* hermosura, belleza *f*; ~ salon *n* salón de belleza *m*; ~ spot *n* lunar *m.*

beaver *n* castor *m.*

because *conj* porque, a causa de.

beckon *vi* hacer seña con la cabeza/la mano.

become *vt* convenir; estar bien; * *vi* hacerse, convertirse, venir a parar.

becoming *adj* decente, conveniente.

bed *n* cama *f.*

bedclothes *npl* cobertores *npl*, mantas/ colchas *fpl.*

bedding *n* ropa de cama *f.*

bedecked *adj* adornado/da.

bedlam *n* manicomio *m.*

bedpost *n* pilar de cama *m.*

bedridden *adj* postrado/da en cama, encamado/da.

bedroom *n* dormitorio *m.*

bedspread *n* colcha *f.*

bedtime *n* hora de irse a la cama *f.*

bee *n* abeja *f.*

beech *n* haya *f.*

beef *n* carne de vaca *f.*

beefburger *n* hamburguesa *f.*

beefsteak *n* bistec *m.*

beehive *n* colmena *f.*

beeline *n* línea recta *f.*

beer *n* cerveza *f.*

beeswax *n* cera *f.*

beet *n* remolacha *f.*

beetle *n* escarabajo *m.*

befall *vi* suceder, acontecer, sobrevenir.

befit *vt* convenir, acomodarse a.

before *adv*, *prep* antes de; delante, enfrente; ante.

beforehand *adv* de antemano, anticipadamente.

befriend *vt* proteger, amparar.

beg *vt* mendigar, rogar; suplicar; suponer; * *vi* vivir de limosna.

beget *vt* engendrar.

beggar *n* mendigo/ga *m/f.*

begin *vt*, *vi* comenzar, empezar.

beginner *n* principiante *m*; novicio/cia *m/f.*

beginning *n* principio, origen *m.*

begrudge *vt* envidiar.

behalf *n* on ~ of de parte de.

behave *vi* comportarse, portarse, conducirse.

behavior n conducta f; modo de portarse m.

behead vt decapitar, cortar la cabeza.

behind prep detrás; atrás; a la, en zaga; * adv atrasadamente.

behold vt ver, contemplar, observar.

behoove vi importar, ser útil; incumbir.

beige adj color beige.

being n existencia f; estado m; ser m.

belated adj atrasado/da.

belch vi eructar, vomitar; * n eructo m.

belfry n campanario m.

belie vt desmentir, calumniar.

belief n fe, creencia f; opinión f; credo m.

believable adj creíble.

believe vt creer; * vi pensar, imaginar.

believer n creyente, fiel, cristiano/na m/f.

belittle vt minimizar.

bell n campana f.

bellicose adj belicoso/sa.

belligerent adj beligerante.

bellow vi bramar; rugir; vociferar; * n bramido m.

bellows npl fuelle m.

belly n vientre m; panza f.

bellyful n panzada f; hartura f.

belong vi pertenecer.

belongings npl pertenencias fpl.

beloved adj querido/da, amado/da.

below adv, prep debajo, inferior; abajo.

belt n cinturón, cinto m; zona f.

beltway n periférico m; carretera de circunvalación f.

bemoan vt deplorar, lamentar.

bemused adj confundido/da.

bench n banco m, banquillo m.

bend vt encorvar, inclinar, plegar; hacer una reverencia; * vi encorvarse, inclinarse; * n curva f.

beneath adv, prep debajo, abajo.

benediction n bendición f.

benefactor n bienhechor m.

benefice n beneficio m; beneficio eclesiástico m.

beneficent adj benéfico/ca.

beneficial adj beneficioso/sa, provechoso/sa, útil.

beneficiary n beneficiario/ria m.

benefit n beneficio m; utilidad f; provecho m; * vt beneficiar; * vi utilizarse; prevalerse.

benefit night n representación dramática a beneficio de un actor/de una actriz f.

benevolence n benevolencia f; donativo gratuito m.

benevolent adj benévolo/la.

benign adj benigno/na; afable; liberal.

bent n inclinación f.

benzene n (chem) bencina f.

bequeath vt legar en testamento.

bequest n legado m.

bereave vt privar.

bereavement n pérdida f.

beret n boina f.

berm n arcén m.

berry n baya f.

berserk adj loco/ca.

berth n (mar) amarradero m, camarote m.

beseech vt suplicar, implorar, conjurar, rogar.

beset vt acosar.

beside(s) prep al lado de; excepto; sobre; fuera de; * adv por otra parte.

besiege vt sitiar, bloquear.

best adj mejor; * adv (lo) mejor; * n lo mejor m.

bestial adj bestial, brutal; ~ly adv bestialmente.

bestiality n bestialidad, brutalidad f.

bestow vt dar, conferir; otorgar.

bestseller n bestseller m

bet n apuesta f; * vt apostar.

betray vt traicionar; divulgar algún secreto.

betrayal n traición f.

betroth vt contraer esponsales.

betrothal n esponsales mpl.

better adj, adv mejor; so much the ~ tanto mejor; * vt mejorar, reformar.

betting n juego m.

between prep entre, en medio de.

bevel n cartabón m.

beverage n bebida f; trago m.

bevy n bandada (de aves) f.

beware vi guardarse.

bewilder vt pasmar.

bewilderment n perplejidad f.

bewitch vt encantar, hechizar.

beyond prep más allá, más adelante, fuera de.

bias n propensión, inclinación f; sesgo m; prejuicio m

bib n babador m.

Bible n Biblia f.

biblical adj bíblico/ca.

bibliography n bibliografía f.

bicarbonate of soda n bicarbonato de soda m.

bicker vi escaramucear, reñir, disputar.

bicycle n bicicleta f.

bid vt mandar, ordenar; ofrecer; * n oferta f; tentativa f.

bidding n orden f; mandato m; ofrecimiento m.

bide vt sufrir, aguantar.

biennial adj bienal.

bifocals *npl* gafas bifocales *fpl*.
bifurcated *adj* bifurcado/da.
big *adj* grande, lleno/na; inflado/da.
bigamist *n* bígamo/ma *m/f*.
bigamy *n* bigamia *f*.
big dipper *n* montaña rusa *f*.
bigheaded *adj* engreído/da.
bigness *n* grandeza *f*.
bigot *n* fanático/ca *m/f*.
bigoted *adj* fanático/ca.
bike *n* bici *f*; bicicleta *f*; **mountain ~** bicicleta de montaña.
bikini *n* bikini *m*.
bilberry *n* arándano *m*.
bile *n* bilis *f*.
bilingual *adj* bilingüe.
bilious *adj* bilioso/sa.
bill *n* pico de ave *m*; billete *m*; cuenta *f*.
billboard *n* cartelera *f*.
billet *n* alojamiento *m*.
billfold *n* cartera *f*.
billiards *npl* billar *m*.
billiard-table *n* mesa de billar *f*.
billion *n* mil millones *mpl*, millardo *m*.
billy *n* porra *f*.
bin *n* cubo de la basura *m*.
bind *vt* atar; unir; encuadernar.
binder *n* encuadernador/a *m/f*.
binding *n* venda, faja *f*.
binge *n* juerga *f*.
bingo *n* bingo *m*.
biochemistry *n* bioquímica *f*.
biodegradable *adj* biodegradable.
biodiversity *n* biodiversity *f*.
binoculars *npl* prismáticos *mpl*, *Lat Am* binóculos *mpl*.
biographer *n* biógrafo/fa *m/f*.
biographical *adj* biográfico/ca.
biography *n* biografía *f*.
biological *adj* biológico/ca.
biology *n* biología *f*.
biped *n* bípedo *m*.
birch *n* abedul *m*.
bird *n* ave *f*; pájaro *m*.
bird's-eye view *n* vista de pájaro *f*.
bird-watcher *n* ornitólogo/ga *m/f*.
birth *n* nacimiento *m*; origen *m*; parto *m*.
birth certificate *n* partida de nacimiento *f*.
birth control *n* control de natalidad *m*.
birthday *n* cumpleaños *m invar*, *Lat Am* onomástica *f*.
birthplace *n* lugar de nacimiento *m*.
birthright *n* derechos de nacimiento *mpl*; primogenitura *f*.
biscuit *n* bizcocho *m*.

bisect *vt* bisecar.
bishop *n* obispo *m*.
bison *n* bisonte *m*.
bit *n* bocado *m*; pedacito *m*.
bitch *n* perra *f*; (*fig*) zorra *f*.
bite *vt* morder; picar; **~ the dust** (*col*) morder la tierra, morir; * *n* mordedura *f*.
bitter *adj* amargo/ga, áspero/ra; mordaz, satírico/ca; penoso/sa; **~ly** *adv* amargamente; con pena; severamente.
bitterness *n* amargor *m*; rencor *m*; pena *f*; dolor *m*.
bitumen *n* betún *m*.
bizarre *adj* raro/ra, extravagante.
blab *vi* chismear.
black *adj* negro/gra, oscuro/ra; funesto/ta; * *n* color negro *m*.
blackberry *n* zarzamora *f*.
blackbird *n* mirlo *m*.
black box *n* caja negra *f*.
blacken *vt* teñir de negro; ennegrecer.
black ice *n* hielo invisible *m*.
blackjack *n* veintiuna *f*.
blackleg *n* esquirol *m*.
blacklist *n* lista negra *f*.
blackmail *n* chantaje *m*; * *vt* chantajear.
black market *n* mercado negro *m*.
blackness *n* negrura *f*.
black pudding *n* morcilla *f*.
black sheep *n* oveja negra *f*.
blacksmith *n* herrero *m*.
blackthorn *n* endrino *m*.
bladder *n* vejiga *f*.
blade *n* hoja *f*; filo *m*; escobilla *f*.
blame *vt* culpar; * *n* culpa *f*.
blameless *adj* inocente, irreprensible, puro/ra; **~ly** *adv* inocentemente.
blanch *vt* blanquear.
bland *adj* blando/da, suave, dulce, apacible.
blank *adj* blanco/ca; pálido/da; * *n* blanco *m*.
blank check *n* cheque en blanco *m*.
blanket *n* manta *f*, *Lat Am* cobija *f*, *Lat Am* frazada *f*.
blare *vi* resonar.
blasé *adj* indiferente.
blaspheme *vt* blasfemar, jurar, decir blasfemias.
blasphemous *adj* blasfemo/ma.
blasphemy *n* blasfemia *f*.
blast *n* soplo de aire *m*; carga explosiva *f*; * *vt* volar.
blast-off *n* lanzamiento *m*.
blatant *adj* obvio.
blaze *n* llama *f*; * *vi* encenderse en llamas; brillar, resplandecer.

bleach vt blanquear al sol; * vi blanquear;
* n lejía f.

bleached adj teñido/da de rubio; des-
colorado/da.

bleachers npl gradas al sol fpl.

bleak adj pálido/da, descolorido/da; frío,
helado/da.

bleakness n frialdad f; palidez f.

bleary(-eyed) adj legañoso/sa.

bleat n balido m; * vi balar.

bleed vi, vt sangrar.

bleeding n sangría f.

bleeper n busca m.

blemish vt manchar, ensuciar; infamar; * n
tacha f; deshonra, infamia f.

blend vt mezclar.

bless vt bendecir.

blessing n bendición f; beneficio m;
ventaja f.

blight vt arruinar.

blind adj ciego/ga; ~ alley n callejón sin
salida m; * vt cegar; deslumbrar; * n velo
m; (**Venetian**) ~ persiana f.

blinders npl anteojeras fpl.

blindfold vt vendar los ojos; ~ed adj con
los ojos vendados.

blindly adv ciegamente, a ciegas.

blindness n ceguera f.

blind side n punto ciego m.

blind spot n punto ciego m.

blink vi parpadear.

blinkers npl anteojeras fpl.

bliss n felicidad (eterna) f.

blissful adj feliz en sumo grado; beato/ta,
bienaventurado/da; ~ly adv felizmente.

blissfulness n suprema felicidad f.

blister n ampolla f; * vi ampollarse.

blitz n bombardeo aéreo m.

blizzard n ventisca f.

bloated adj hinchado/da.

blob n gota f.

bloc n bloque m.

block n bloque m; obstáculo m; zoquete m;
manzana f, Lat Am cuadra f; ~ (**up**) vt
bloquear.

blockade n bloqueo m; * vt bloquear.

blockage n obstrucción f.

blockbuster n éxito de público m.

blockhead n bruto, necio, zopenco m; (col)
zoquete m.

blond adj rubio/bia; * n rubio/bia m/f.

blood n sangre f.

blood donor n donante de sangre m/f.

blood group n grupo sanguíneo m.

bloodhound n sabueso m.

bloodily adv sangrientamente, inhumanamente.

bloodiness n (fig) crueldad f.

bloodless adj exangüe; sin efusión de sangre.

blood poisoning n septicemia f.

blood pressure n presión sanguínea f.

blood sausage n morcilla f.

bloodshed n efusión de sangre f; matanza f,
derramamiento de sangre m.

bloodshot adj ensangrentado/da.

bloodstream n corriente sanguínea f.

bloodsucker n sanguijuela f; (fig) desol-
lador/ra m/f.

blood test n análisis de sangre m invar.

bloodthirsty adj sanguinario/ria.

blood transfusion n transfusión sanguínea f.

blood vessel n vena f; vaso sanguíneo m.

bloody adj sangriento/ta, ensangrentado/da;
cruel; ~ minded adj sanguinario/ria.

bloom n flor f; (also fig); * vi florecer.

blossom n flor f.

blot vt manchar (lo escrito); cancelar;
denigrar; * n mancha f.

blotchy adj muy manchado/da.

blotting paper n papel secante m.

blouse n blusa f.

blow vi soplar; sonar; * vt soplar; inflar; **to** ~
up volar; * n golpe m.

blowout n pinchazo m.

blowpipe n soplete m.

blubber n grasa de ballena f; * vi lloriquear.

bludgeon n cachiporra f; palocorto m.

blue adj azul.

bluebell, harebell n (bot) campanilla f.

blue berets npl cascos azules mpl.

bluebottle n moscarda f.

blueness n color azul m.

blueprint n (fig) anteproyecto m.

bluff n farol m; * vt farolear.

bluish adj azulado/da.

blunder n metedura de pata f; error craso
m; * vi meter la pata.

blunt adj obtuso/sa; grosero/ra; * vt embotar.

bluntly adv sin artificio; claramente;
obtusamente.

bluntness n embotadura, franqueza f.

blur n contorno borroso m; * vt hacer
borroso.

blurt out vt descolgarse con.

blush n rubor m; sonrojo m; * vi ponerse
colorado/da, sonrojarse.

blustery adj tempestuoso/sa.

boa n boa f (serpiente).

boar n verraco m; **wild** ~ jabalí m.

board *n* tabla *f*; mesa *f*; consejo *m*; * *vt* embarcarse en; subir a.
boarder *n* pensionista *m/f*.
boarding card *n* tarjeta de embarque *f*.
boarding house *n* pensión *f*, casa de huéspedes *f*.
boarding school *n* internado *m*.
boast *vi* jactarse; * *n* jactancia *f*; ostentación *f*.
boastful *adj* jactancioso/sa.
boat *n* barco *m*; bote *m*; barca *f*.
boating *n* canotaje *m*; paseo en barquilla *m*; regata *f*.
bobsleigh *n* bob *m*.
bode *vt* presagiar, pronosticar.
bodice *n* corsé *m*.
bodily *adj*, *adv* corpóreo/rea; corporalmente.
body *n* cuerpo *m*; individuo *m*; gremio *m*; any ~ cualquier; every ~ cada uno.
body-building *n* culturismo *m*.
bodyguard *n* guardaespaldas *m/f invar*.
bodywork *n* (*auto*) carrocería *f*.
bog *n* pantano *m*.
boggy *adj* pantanoso/sa, palustre.
bogus *adj* postizo.
boil *vi* hervir; bullir; hervirle a uno la sangre; * *vt* cocer; * *n* furúnculo *m*.
boiled egg *n* huevo duro *m*, huevo pasado por agua *m*.
boiled potatoes *npl* patatas hervidas *fpl*.
boiler *n* marmita *f*; caldero *m*.
boiling point *n* punto de ebullición *m*.
boisterous *adj* borrascoso/sa, tempestuoso/sa; violento/ta; ~ly *adv* tumultuosamente, furiosamente.
bold *adj* ardiente, valiente; audaz; temerario/ria; impudente; ~ly *adv* descaradamente.
boldness *n* intrepidez *f*; valentía *f*; osadía *f*.
bolster *n* travesero *m*; cabezal *m*; * *vt* reforzar.
bolt *n* cerrojo *m*; * *vt* cerrar con cerrojo.
bomb *n* bomba *f*; ~ disposal desactivación de explosivos *f*.
bombard *vt* bombardear.
bombardier *n* bombardero *m*.
bombardment *n* bombardeo *m*.
bombshell *n* (*fig*) bomba *f*.
bond *n* ligadura *f*; vínculo *m*; vale *m*; obligación *f*.
bondage *n* esclavitud, servidumbre *f*.
bond holder *n* titular de bonos *m/f*.
bone *n* hueso *m*; * *vt* desosar.
boneless *adj* sin huesos; desosado/da.
bonfire *n* hoguera *f*.

bonnet *n* gorra *f*; bonete *m*.
bonny *adj* bonito/ta.
bonsai *n* bonsái *m*.
bonus *n* cuota, prima *f*.
bony *adj* osudo/da.
boo *vt* abuchear.
booby trap *n* trampa explosiva *f*.
book *n* libro *m*; **to bring to** ~ *vt* pedir cuentas a alguien.
bookbinder *n* encuadernador/a *m/f*.
bookcase *n* estantería *f*.
bookkeeper *n* tenedor/a de libros *m/f*.
bookkeeping *n* teneduría de libros *f*.
bookmaker *n* corredor de apuestas *m*.
bookmarker *n* registro de un libro *m*.
bookseller *n* librero/ra *m/f*.
bookstore *n* librería *f*.
bookworm *n* polilla *f*; ratón de biblioteca *m*.
boom *n* trueno *m*; boom *m*; * *vi* retumbar.
boon *n* presente, regalo *m*; favor *m*.
boor *n* patán, villano/na *m/f*.
boorish *adj* rústico/ca, agreste.
boost *n* estímulo *m*; *vt* estimular.
booster *n* reinyección *f*.
boot *n* bota *f*; zapata *f*; **to** ~ *adv* además.
booth *n* barraca, cabaña *f*.
booty *n* botín *m*; presa *f*; saqueo *m*.
booze *vi* emborracharse; * *n* bebida *f*.
border *n* orilla *f*; borde *m*; margen *f*; frontera *f*; * *vt* lindar con.
borderline *n* frontera *f*.
bore *vt* taladrar; barrenar; fastidiar; * *n* taladro *m*; calibre *m*; pelmazo/za *m/f*.
boredom *n* aburrimiento *m*.
borehole *n* barreno *m*.
boring *adj* aburrido/da, *Lat Am* aburrdor/ra.
born *adj* nacido/da; destinado/da.
borrow *vt* pedir prestado/da.
borrower *n* prestamista *m*.
bosom *n* seno, pecho *m*.
bosom friend *n* amigo/ga íntimo/ma *m/f*.
boss *n* jefe *m*; patrón/ona *m/f*.
botanic(al) *adj* botánico/ca.
botanist *n* botánico *m*.
botany *n* botánica *f*.
botch *vt* chapuzar.
botch-up *n* mamarracho *m*.
both *adj* ambos, entrambos; ambas, entrambas; * *conj* tanto como.
bother *vt* preocupar; fastidiar; * *n* molestia *f*.
bottle *n* botella *f*; * *vt* embotellar.
bottleneck *n* embotellamiento *m*.
bottle-opener *n* abrebotellas *m invar*.

bottom *n* fondo *m*; fundamento *m*; * *adj* más bajo/ja; último/ma.

bottomless *adj* insondable; excesivo/va; impenetrable.

bough *n* brazo del árbol *m*; ramo *m*.

boulder *n* canto rodado *m*.

bounce *vi* rebotar; *ser* rechazado/da, * *n* rebote *m*.

bound *n* límite *m*; salto *m*; repercusión *f*; * *vi* resaltar; * *adj* destinado/da.

boundary *n* límite *m*; frontera *f*.

boundless *adj* ilimitado/da, infinito/ta.

bounteous, bountiful *adj* liberal, generoso/sa, bienhechor.

bounty *n* liberalidad, bondad *f*.

bouquet *n* ramillete de flores *m*.

bourgeois *adj* burgués/esa.

bout *n* ataque *m*; encuentro *m*.

bovine *adj* bovino/na.

bow[1] *vt* encorvar, doblar; * *vi* encorvarse; hacer una reverencia; * *n* reverencia, inclinación *f*.

bow[2] *n* arco *m*; arco de violín; corbata *f*, *Lat Am* bow *m*; nudo *m*.

bowels *npl* intestinos *mpl*; entrañas *fpl*.

bowl *n* taza; bola *f*; * *vi* jugar a las bochas.

bowling *n* bolos *mpl*.

bowling alley *n* bolera *f*.

bowling-green *n* campo *m* para jugar a las bochas.

bowstring *n* cuerda del arco *f*.

bow tie *n* pajarita *f*.

box *n* caja, cajita *f*; palco de teatro *m*; ~ **on the ear** bofetada *f*; * *vt* encajonar; * *vi* boxear.

boxer *n* boxeador *m*.

boxing *n* boxeo *m*, *Lat Am* box *m*.

boxing gloves *npl* guantes de boxeo *mpl*.

boxing ring *n* cuadrilátero *m*.

box office *n* taquilla *f*.

box-seat *n* asiento de palco *m*.

boy *n* muchacho *m*; niño *m*; zagal *m*.

boycott *vt* boicotear; * *n* boicot *m*.

boyfriend *n* novio *m*.

boyish *adj* pueril; frívolo.

bra *n* sujetador *m*.

brace *n* abrazadera *f*; corrector *m*.

bracelet *n* brazalete *m*.

bracing *adj* vigorizante.

bracken *n* (*bot*) helecho *m*.

bracket *n* puntal *m*; paréntesis *m*; corchete *m*; * **to ~ with** *vt* unir, ligar.

bracing *adj* vigorizante.

brag *n* jactancia *f*; * *vi* jactarse, fanfarronear.

braid *n* trenza *f*; * *vt* trenzar.

brain *n* cerebro *m*; seso, juicio *m*; * *vt* descerebrar, matar a uno.

brainchild *n* parto del ingenio *m*.

brainwash *vt* lavar el cerebro.

brainwave *n* idea luminosa *f*.

brainy *adj* inteligente.

brainless *adj* tonto/ta, insensato/ta.

brake *n* freno *m*; * *vt*, *vi* frenar.

brake fluid *n* líquido de frenos *m*.

brake light *n* luz de frenado *f*.

brake shoe *n* (*auto*) zapata de freno *f*.

bramble *n* zarza, espina *f*.

bramble patch *n* zarzal *m*.

bran *n* salvado *m*.

branch *n* ramo *m*; rama *f*; * *vt* (*vi*) ramificar(se).

branch line *n* (*rail*) empalme, ramal *m*.

brand *n* marca *f*; hierro *m*; * *vt* marcar (con un hierro incandescente).

brandish *vt* blandir, ondear.

brand-new *adj* flamante.

brandy *n* coñac *m*.

brash *adj* tosco/ca; descarado/da.

brass *n* bronce *m*.

brassiere *n* sujetador *m*.

brat *n* crío *m*.

bravado *n* baladronada *f*.

brave *adj* bravo/va, valiente, atrevido/da; * *vt* desafiar; * *n* bravo *m*; ~**ly** *adv* bravamente.

bravery *n* valor *m*; magnificencia *f*.

brawl *n* pelea, camorra *f*; * *vi* pelearse.

brawn *n* fuerza muscular *f*; carne de verraco *f*.

bray *vi* rebuznar; * *n* rebuzno (del asno) *m*.

braze *vt* soldar con latón; broncear.

brazen *adj* de latón; desvergonzado/da; impudente; * *vi* hacerse descarado/da.

brazier *n* brasero *m*.

breach *n* rotura *f*; brecha *f*; violación *f*.

bread *n* pan *m*; (*fig*) sustento *m*; **brown ~** pan moreno *m*.

breadbox *n* panera *f*.

breadcrumbs *npl* migajas *fpl*.

breadth *n* anchura *f*.

breadwinner *n* sostén de la familia *m*.

break *vt* romper; quebrantar; violar; arruinar; interrumpir; * *vi* romperse; **to ~ into** forzar; **to ~ out** abrirse salida; * *n* rotura, abertura *f*; interrupción *f*; ~ **of day** despuntar del día *m*, aurora *f*.

breakage *n* rotura *f*.

breakdown *n* avería *f*; descalabro *m*.

breakfast *n* desayuno *m*; * *vi* desayunar.

breaking *n* rompimiento *m*; principio de las vacaciones en las escuelas *m*; fractura *f*.

breakthrough *n* avance *m.*

breakwater *n* rompeolas *m* invar.

breast *n* pecho, seno *m*; pechuga *f* corazón *m.*

breastbone *n* esternón *m.*

breastplate *n* peto *m*; pectoral *m*; coraza *f.*

breaststroke *n* braza *f, Lat Am* pecho *m.*

breath *n* aliento *m*, respiración *f*; soplo de aire *m.*

breathe *vt, vi* respirar; exhalar.

breathing *n* respiración *f*; aliento *m.*

breathing space *n* descanso, reposo *m.*

breathless *adj* falto/ta de aliento; desalentado/da.

breathtaking *adj* pasmoso/sa.

breed *n* casta, raza *f*; * *vt* procrear, engendrar; producir; educar; * *vi* multiplicarse.

breeder *n* criador/a *m/f.*

breeding *n* crianza *f*; buena educación *f.*

breeze *n* brisa *f.*

breezy *adj* refrescado/da con brisas.

brethren *n pl* de **brother** hermanos *mpl* (en estilo grave).

breviary *n* breviario *m.*

brevity *n* brevedad, concisión *f.*

brew *vt* hacer; tramar, mezclar; * *vi* hacerse; tramarse; * *n* brebaje *m.*

brewer *n* cervecero *m.*

brewery *n* cervecería *f.*

briar, brier *n* zarza *f*, espino *m.*

bribe *n* cohecho, soborno *m*; * *vt* cohechar, corromper, sobornar.

bribery *n* cohecho, soborno *m.*

bric-a-brac *n* baratijas *fpl.*

brick *n* ladrillo *m*; * *vt* enladrillar.

bricklayer *n* albañil *m.*

bricklaying *n* albañilería *f.*

bridal *adj* nupcial.

bride *n* novia *f.*

bridegroom *n* novio *m.*

bridesmaid *n* madrina de boda *f.*

bridge *n* puente *m/f*; caballete de la nariz *m*; puente de violín *m*; **to build a ~ (over)** *vt* construir un puente (sobre).

bridle *n* brida *f* freno *m*; * *vt* embridar; reprimir, refrenar.

brief *adj* breve, conciso/sa, sucinto/ta; * *n* compendio *m*; breve *m.*

briefcase *n* cartera *f.*

briefly *adv* brevemente, en pocas palabras.

brier *n* = **briar.**

brigade *n* (*mil*) brigada *f.*

brigadier *n* (*mil*) general de brigada *m.*

brigand *n* bandido *m.*

bright *adj* claro/ra, luciente, brillante; ~ly *adv* espléndidamente.

brighten *vt* pulir, dar lustre; ilustrar; * *vi* aclararse.

brightness *n* esplendor *m*, brillantez *f*; agudeza *f*; claridad *f.*

brilliance *n* brillo *m.*

brilliant *adj* brillante; ~ly *adv* espléndidamente.

brim *n* borde extremo *m*; orilla *f.*

brimful(l) *adj* lleno/na hasta el borde.

bring *vt* llevar, traer; conducir; inducir, persuadir; **to ~ about** efectuar; **to ~ forth** producir; parir; **to ~ up** educar.

brink *n* orilla *f*; margen *m/f*, borde *m.*

brisk *adj* vivo/va, alegre, jovial; fresco/ca.

brisket *n* pecho (de un animal) *m.*

briskly *adv* vigorosamente; alegremente; vivamente.

bristle *n* cerda, seta *f*; * *vi* erizarse.

bristly *adj* cerdoso/sa, lleno/na de cerdas.

brittle *adj* quebradizo, frágil.

broach *vt* comenzar a hablar de.

broad *adj* ancho.

broad bean *n* (*bot*) haba *f*; ~s haba gruesa *fpl.*

broadcast *n* emisión *f*; * *vt, vi* emitir; transmitir.

broadcasting *n* radiodifusión *f.*

broaden *vt* (*vi*) ensanchar(se).

broadly *adv* anchamente.

broad-minded *adj* tolerante.

broadness *n* ancho *m*; anchura *f.*

broadside *n* costado de navío *m*; andanada *f.*

broadways *adv* a lo ancho, por lo ancho.

brocade *n* brocado *m.*

broccoli *n* brécol *m.*

brochure *n* folleto *m.*

brogue *n* abarca *f*; acento irlandés *m.*

broil *vt* asar a la parrilla.

broken *adj* roto/ta, interrumpido/da; ~ **English** inglés mal articulado *m.*

broker *n* corredor/a *m/f.*

brokerage *n* corretaje *m.*

bronchial *adj* bronquial.

bronchitis *n* bronquitis *f.*

bronze *n* bronce *m*; * *vt* broncear.

brooch *n* broche *m.*

brood *vi* empollar; meditar; * *n* raza *f*; nidada *f.*

brood-hen *n* empolladora *f.*

brook *n* arroyo *m.*

broom *n* retama *f*; escoba *f.*

broomstick *n* palo de escoba *m.*

broth *n* caldo *m*.
brothel *n* burdel *m*.
brother *n* hermano *m*.
brotherhood *n* hermandad *f*; fraternidad *f*.
brother-in-law *n* cuñado *m*.
brotherly *adj*, *adv* fraternal; fraternalmente.
brow *n* caja *f*; frente *f*; cima *f*.
browbeat *vt* intimidar.
brown *adj* moreno/na; castaño/ña; ~ **paper** *n* papel de estraza *m*; ~ **bread** *n* pan moreno *m*; ~ **sugar** *n* azúcar terciado *m*; * *n* color moreno *m*; * *vt* volver moreno/na.
browse *vt* ramonear; * *vi* pacer la hierba.
browser *n* navegador *m*.
bruise *vt* magullar; * *n* magulladura, *Lat Am* magullón *m*, contusión *f*; roncha *f*.
brunch *n* desayuno-almuerzo *m*.
brunette *n* morena *f*.
brunt *n* choque *m*.
brush *n* cepillo *m*; escobilla *f*; combate *m*; * *vt* cepillar, *Lat Am* escobillar.
brushwood *n* breñal, zarzal *m*.
brusque *adj* brusco/ca.
Brussels sprout *n* col de Bruselas *f*.
brutal *adj* brutal; ~**ly** *adv* brutalmente.
brutality *n* brutalidad *f*.
brutalize *vt* (*vi*) embrutecer(se).
brute *n* bruto *m*; * *adj* feroz, bestial; irracional.
brutish *adj* brutal, bestial; feroz; ~**ly** *adv* brutalmente.
bubble *n* burbuja *f*; * *vi* burbujear, bullir.
bubblegum *n* chicle *m*.
bucket *n* cubo, pozal *m*.
buckle *n* hebilla *f*; * *vt* hebillar; abrochar; * *vi* encorvarse.
buckshot *n* perdigones *mpl*.
bucolic *adj* bucólico/ca.
bud *n* pimpollo, botón, capullo *m*; yema *f*; * *vi* brotar.
Buddhism *n* Budismo *m*.
budding *adj* en ciernes.
buddy *n* compañero *m*.
budge *vi* moverse, menearse.
budgerigar *n* periquito *m*.
budget *n* presupuesto *m*.
buff *n* entusiasta *m*.
buffalo *n* búfalo *m*.
buffers *npl* (*rail*) parachoques *m invar*, topes *mpl*.
buffet *n* buffet *m*; * *vt* abofetear.
buffoon *n* bufón, chocarrero *m*.
bug *n* chinche *m*.
bugbear *n* espantajo, coco *m*.

bugle(horn) *n* trompa de caza *f*.
build *vt* edificar; construir.
builder *n* constructor/a *m/f*; maestro/tra de obras *m/f*.
building *n* edificio *m*, *Lat Am* predio *m*; construcción *f*.
bulb *n* bulbo *m*; cebolla *f*.
bulbous *adj* bulboso/sa.
bulge *vi* combarse; * *n* bombeo *m*.
bulk *n* masa *f*; volumen *m*; grosura *f*; mayor parte *f*; capacidad de un buque *f*; **in** ~ **a** granel.
bulky *adj* grueso/sa, grande.
bull *n* toro *m*.
bulldog *n* dogo *m*.
bulldozer *n* aplanadora *f*.
bullet *n* bala *f*.
bulletin board *n* tablón de anuncios *m*.
bulletproof *adj* a prueba de balas.
bullfight *n* corrida de toros *f*.
bullfighter *n* torero *m*.
bullfighting *n* toreo *m*.
bullion *n* oro/plata en barras *m/f*.
bullock *n* novillo capado *m*.
bullring *n* plaza de toros *f*.
bull's-eye *n* centro del blanco *m*.
bully *n* valentón *m*; * *vt* tiranizar.
bulwark *n* baluarte *m*.
bum *n* vagabundo/da *m/f*.
bumblebee *n* abejorro, zángano *m*.
bump *n* hinchazón *f*; jiba *f*; bollo *m*; barriga *f*; * *vt* chocar contra.
bumpkin *n* patán *m*; villano/na *m/f*.
bumpy *adj* bacheado/da.
bun *n* bollo *m*; mono *m*.
bunch *n* ramo *m*; grupo *m*.
bundle *n* fardo *m*, haz *m* (de leña etc); paquete *m*; rollo *m*; * *vt* atar, hacer un lío.
bung *n* tapón *m*; * *vt* atarugar.
bungalow *n* bungalow *m*.
bungee-jumping *n* puenting *m*.
bungle *vt* chapucear; * *vi* hacer algo chabacanamente.
bunion *n* juanete *m*.
bunk *n* litera *f*.
bunker *n* refugio *m*; búnker *m*.
buoy *n* (*mar*) boya *f*.
buoyancy *n* capacidad para flotar *f*.
buoyant *adj* boyante.
burden *n* carga *f*; * *vt* cargar.
bureau *n* armario *m*; escritorio *m*.
bureaucracy *n* burocracia *f*.
bureaucrat *n* burócrata *m/f*.
burglar *n* ladrón/ona *m/f*.
burglar alarm *n* alarma antirrobo *f*.

burglary n robo en una casa m.
burial n enterramiento m; exequias fpl;
sepultura f.
burial place n cementerio m.
burlesque n, adj lengua burlesca f; burlesco/
ca m/f.
burly adj fornido/da.
burn vt quemar, abrasar, incendiar; * vi arder;
* n quema dura f.
burner n quemador m; mechero m.
burning adj ardiente.
burrow n madriguera f; * vi esconderse en la
madriguera.
bursar n tesorero/ra m/f.
burse n bolsa, lonja f.
burst vi reventar; abrirse; to ~ into tears
prorrumpir en lágrimas; to ~ out laughing estallarse de risa; * vt to ~ into irrumpir
en; * n reventón m; rebosadura f.
bury vt enterrar, sepultar; esconder.
bus n autobús m.
bush n arbusto, espinal m; cola de zorro f.
bushy adj espeso/sa, lleno/na de arbustos.
busily adv diligentemente, apresura-
damente.
business n asunto m; negocios mpl; empleo
m; ocupación f.
businesslike adj serio/ria.
businessman n hombre de negocios m.
business trip n viaje de negocios m.
businesswoman n mujer de negocios f.
bus lane n carril bus m.
bust n busto m.
bus stop n parada de autobuses f.
bustle vi hacer ruido; menearse; andar al
retortero; * n baraúnda f; ruido m.
bustling adj animado/da.
busy adj ocupado/da; entrometido/da.

busybody n entrometido m.
but conj pero; mas; excepto, menos;
solamente.
butcher n carnicero/ra m/f; * vt matar
atrozmente.
butcher's (shop/store) n carnicería f.
butchery n matadero m.
butler n mayordomo m.
butt n colilla f; cabo, extremo m; * vt
topar.
butter n mantequilla f; * vt untar con
mantequilla.
buttercup n (bot) ranúnculo m.
butterfly n mariposa f.
buttermilk n suero de manteca m.
buttocks npl posaderas fpl.
button n botón m; * vt abotonar.
buttonhole n ojal m.
buttress n estribo m; apoyo m; * vt estribar.
buxom adj frescachona, rolliza.
buy vt comprar.
buyer n comprador/a m/f.
buzz, buzzing n susurro, zumbido m; * vi
zumbar.
buzzard n ratonero m común.
buzzer n timbre m.
by prep por; a, en; de; cerca, al lado de; ~
and ~ de aquí a poco, ahora; ~ the ~ de
paso; ~ much con mucho; ~ all means
por supuesto.
bygone adj pasado/da.
by-law n ordenanza municipal f.
bypass n carretera de circunvalación f.
by-product n derivado m.
by-road n camino secundario m.
bystander n mirador m.
byte n (comput) byte m.
byword n proverbio, refrán m.

C

cab *n* taxi *m*.
cabbage *n* berza, col *f*.
cabin *n* cabaña, cámara de navío *f*.
cabinet *n* consejo de ministros *m*; gabinete *m*; escritorio *m*.
cabinet-maker *n* ebanista *m*.
cable *n* cable *m*.
cable car *n* teleférico *m*.
cable television *n* televisión por cable *f*.
caboose *n* (*mar*) cocina *f*.
cache *n* alijo *m*.
cackle *vi* cacarear, graznar; * *n* cacareo *m*; charla *f*.
cactus *n* cacto *m*, cactus *m invar*.
cadence *n* (*mus*) cadencia *f*.
cadet *n* cadete *m*.
cadge *vt* mangar.
café *n* café *m*.
cafeteria *n* café *m*.
caffeine *n* cafeína *f*.
cage *n* jaula *f*; prisión *f*; * *vt* enjaular.
cagey *adj* cauteloso/sa.
cajole *vt* lisonjear, adular; sonsacar.
cake *n* bollo *m*; tortita *f*.
calamitous *adj* calamitoso/sa.
calamity *n* calamidad, miseria *f*.
calculable *adj* calculable.
calculate *vt* calcular, contar.
calculation *n* cálculo *m*.
calculator *n* calculadora *f*.
calculus *n* cálculo *m*.
calendar *n* calendario *m*.
calf *n* ternero *m*; ternera *f*; carne de ternero *f*.
caliber *n* calibre *m*.
calisthenics *n* calistenia *f*.
call *vt* llamar, nombrar; llamar por teléfono; convocar, citar; apelar; to ~ for preguntar por, ir a buscar; to ~ on visitar; to ~ attention llamar la atención; to ~ names insultar; * *n* llamada *f*, *Lat Am* llamado *m*; instancia *f*; invitación *f*; urgencia *f*; vocación *f*; profesión *f*.
caller *n* visitador/a *m/f*.
calligraphy *n* caligrafía *f*.
calling *n* profesión, vocación *f*.
callous *adj* calloso/sa, endurecido/da; insensible.
calm *n* calma, tranquilidad *f*; * *adj* quieto/ta, tranquilo/la; * *vt* calmar; aplacar, aquietar; ~ly *adv* tranquilamente.
calmness *n* tranquilidad, calma *f*.

calorie *n* caloría *f*.
calumny *n* calumnia *f*.
Calvary *n* calvario *m*.
calve *vi* parir.
Calvinist *n* calvinista *m/f*.
camcorder *n* videocámara *f*.
camel *n* camello *m*.
cameo *n* camafeo *m*.
camera *n* máquina fotográfica *f*; cámara *f*.
cameraman *n* cámara *m*.
chamomile *n* manzanilla *f*.
camouflage *n* camuflaje *m*.
camp *n* campo *m*; * *vi* acampar; refugee ~ campo de refugiados.
campaign *n* campana *f*; run-up-to-the-election ~ precampaña *f*; * *vi* hacer campana.
campaigner *n* defensor/a *m/f*.
camper *n* campista *m/f*.
camping *n* camping *m*.
camphor *n* alcanfor *m*.
campsite *n* camping *m*.
campus *n* ciudad universitaria *f*, campus *m invar*.
can *vi* poder; * *n* lata *f*.
canal *n* estanque *m*; canal *m*.
cancel *vt* cancelar; anular, invalidar.
cancellation *n* cancelación *f*.
cancer *n* cáncer *m*.
Cancer *n* Cáncer *m* (signo del zodiaco).
cancerous *adj* canceroso/sa.
candid *adj* cándido/da, sencillo/lla, sincero/ra; ~ly *adv* cándidamente, francamente.
candidate *n* candidato/ta *m/f*, *Lat Am* postulante *m/f*.
candied *adj* azucarado/da.
candle *n* candela *f*; vela *f*.
candlelight *n* luz de candela *f*.
candlestick *n* candelero *m*.
candor *n* candor *m*; sinceridad *f*.
candy *n* confitería *f*.
cane *n* cana *f*; bastón *m*.
canine *adj* canino/na, perruno/na.
canister *n* bote *m*.
cannabis *n* cannabis *m*.
cannibal *n* caníbal *m/f*, antropófago/ga *m/f*.
cannibalism *n* canibalismo *m*.
cannon *n* cañón *m*.
cannonball *n* bala de artillería *f*.
canny *adj* cuerdo/da, discreto/ta.
canoe *n* canoa *f*.

canon *n* canon *m*; regla *f*; ~law derecho
canónico *m*.
canonization *n* canonización *f*.
canonize *vt* canonizar.
can opener *n* abrelatas *m invar*.
canopy *n* dosel, pabellón *m*.
cantankerous *adj* áspero/ra, fastidioso/sa.
canteen *n* cantina *f*.
canter *n* medio galope *m*.
canvas *n* cañamazo *m*.
canvass *vt* escudriñar, examinar; controvertir; * *vi* solicitar votos; pretender.
canvasser *n* solicitador/a *m/f*.
canyon *n* cañón *m*.
canyoning *n* barranquismo *m*.
cap *n* gorra *f*.
capability *n* capacidad, aptitud, inteligencia *f*.
capable *adj* capaz.
capacitate *vt* hacer capaz.
capacity *n* capacidad *f*; inteligencia, habilidad *f*.
cape *n* cabo, promontorio *m*.
caper *n* cabriola *f*; alcaparra *f*; * *vi* hacer cabriolas.
capillary *adj* capilar.
capital *adj* capital; principal; * *n* capital *f* (la ciudad principal); capital, fondo *m*; mayúscula *f*.
capitalism *n* capitalismo *m*.
capitalist *n* capitalista *m*.
capitalize *vt* capitalizar; to ~ on aprovechar.
capital punishment *n* pena de muerte *f*.
Capitol *n* Capitolio *m*.
capitulate *vi* capitular.
capitulation *n* capitulación *f*.
caprice *n* capricho *m*; extravagancia *f*.
capricious *adj* caprichoso/sa; ~ly *adv* caprichosamente.
Capricorn *n* Capricornio *m* (signo del zodiaco).
capsize *vt* (*mar*) volcar, zozobrar.
capsizing *n* (*mar*) zozobra *f*.
capsule *n* cápsula *f*.
captain *n* capitán/ana *m/f*.
captaincy, captainship *n* capitanía *f*.
captivate *vt* cautivar.
captivation *n* atractivo *m*.
captive *n* cautivo/va, esclavo/va *m/f*.
captivity *n* cautividad, esclavitud *f*, cautiverio *m*.
capture *n* captura *f*; presa *f*; * *vt* apresar, capturar.
car *n* coche, carro *m*; vagón *m*.
carafe *n* garrafa *f*.

caramel *n* caramelo *m*.
carat *n* quilate *m*.
caravan *n* caravana *f*.
caraway *n* (*bot*) alcaravea *f*.
carbohydrates *npl* hidratos de carbono *mpl*.
car bomb *n* coche bomba *m*.
carbon *n* carbono *m*, carbón *m*.
carbon copy *n* copia al carbón *f*.
carbonize *vt* carbonizar.
carbon paper *n* papel carbón *m*.
carbuncle *n* carbúnculo, rubí *m*; carbunco, tumor maligno *m*.
carburetor *n* carburador *m*.
carcass *n* cadáver *m*.
carcinogenic *adj* cancerígeno/na.
card *n* naipe *m*; carta *f*; pack of ~s baraja *f*.
cardboard *n* cartón *m*.
card game *n* juego de naipes *m*.
cardiac *adj* cardíaco/ca, cardiaco/ca.
cardinal *adj* cardinal, principal; * *n* cardenal *m*.
card table *n* mesa para jugar *f*.
care *n* cuidado *m*; solicitud *f*; * *vi* cuidar, tener cuidado/pena, inquietarse; what do I ~? ¿a mí que me importa?; to ~ for *vt* cuidar a; querer.
career *n* carrera *f*; curso *m*; * *vi* correr a carrera tendida.
carefree *n* despreocupado/da.
careful *adj* cuidadoso/sa, diligente, prudente; ~ly *adv* cuidadosamente.
careless *adj* descuidado/da, negligente; indolente; ~ly *adv* descuidadamente.
carelessness *n* negligencia, indiferencia *f*.
caress *n* caricia *f*; * *vt* acariciar, halagar.
caretaker *n* portero *m*, conserje *m/f*.
car-ferry *n* transbordador para coches *m*.
cargo *n* cargamento *m*.
car hire *n* alquiler de coches *m*.
caribou *n* reno *m*.
caricature *n* caricatura *f*, Lat Am caricato *m*; * *vt* hacer caricaturas, ridiculizar.
caries *n* caries *f*.
caring *adj* humanitario/ria.
Carmelite *n* carmelita *m*.
carnage *n* carnicería, matanza *f*.
carnal *adj* carnal; sensual; ~ly *adv* carnalmente.
carnation *n* clavel *m*.
carnival *n* carnaval *m*.
carnivorous *adj* carnívoro/ra.
carol *n* villancico *m*, canción de alegría/ piedad *f*.
carpenter *n* carpintero *m*; ~'s bench banco de carpintero *m*.

carpentry *n* carpintería *f*.
carpet *n* alfombra *f*, *Lat Am* tapete *m*; * *vt* cubrir con alfombras.
carpeting *n* alfombrado *m*.
car radio *n* autorradio *m*.
carriage *n* porte *m*; coche *m*; vehículo *m*.
carriage-free *adj* franco de porte.
carrier *n* portador, carretero *m*.
carrier pigeon *n* paloma correo/mensajera *f*.
carrion *n* carroña *f*.
carrot *n* zanahoria *f*.
carry *vt* llevar, conducir; **to ~ out** ejecutar; * *vi* oírse; **to ~ the day** quedar victorioso/sa; **to ~ on** seguir.
cart *n* carro *m*; carreta *f*; * *vt* llevar (en carro).
cartel *n* cartel *m*.
carthorse *n* caballo de tiro *m*.
Carthusian *n* cartujo (monje) *m*.
cartilage *n* cartílago *m*.
cartload *n* carretada *f*.
carton *n* caja *f*.
cartoon *n* dibujo animado *m*; tira cómica *f*.
cartridge *n* cartucho *m*.
carve *vt* cincelar; trinchar; grabar.
carving *n* escultura *f*.
carving knife *n* cuchillo de trinchar *m*.
car wash *n* lavado de coches *m*.
case *n* caja *f*; maleta *f*; caso *m*; estuche *m*; vaina *f*; **in ~** por si acaso.
cash *n* dinero contante *m*; * *vt* cobrar.
cash card *n* tarjeta de cajero automático *f*.
cash dispenser, cash machine *n* cajero automático *m*.
cashier *n* cajero *m*.
cashmere *n* cachemira *f*.
casing *n* forro *m*; cubierta *f*.
casino *n* casino *m*.
cask *n* barril, tonel *m*.
casket *n* ataúd *m*.
casserole *n* cazuela *f*.
cassette *n* casette *m*.
cassette player, recorder *n* casette *m*.
cassock *n* sotana *f*.
cast *vt* tirar, lanzar; modelar; * *n* reparto *m*; forma *f*.
castanets *npl* castañuelas *fpl*.
castaway *n* réprobo *m*.
caste *n* casta *f*.
castigate *vt* castigar.
casting vote *n* voto de calidad *m*.
cast iron *n* hierro colado *m*.
castle *n* castillo *m*; fortaleza *f*.
castor oil *n* aceite de ricino *m*.

castrate *vt* castrar.
castration *n* capadura *f*.
cast steel *n* acero fundido *m*.
casual *adj* casual, fortuito/ta; **~ly** *adv* casualmente, fortuitamente.
casualty *n* víctima *f*; baja *f*.
cat *n* gato *m*; gata *f*.
catalog *n* catálogo *m*.
catalyst *n* catalizador *m*.
catalytic converter *n* catalizador *m*.
catamaran *n* catamarán *m*.
catapult *n* catapulta, honda *f*.
cataract *n* cascada *f*; catarata *f*.
catarrh *n* catarro *m*; reuma *f*.
catastrophe *n* catástrofe *f*.
catcall *n* silbido *m*; reclamo *m*.
catch *vt* coger, agarrar, asir; atrapar; pillar; sorprender; **to ~ cold** resfriarse; **to ~ fire** encenderse; * *n* presa *f*; captura *f*; (*mus*) canon *m*; trampa *f*.
catching *adj* contagioso/sa.
catch phrase *n* lema *m*.
catchword *n* reclamo *m*.
catchy *adj* pegadizo/za.
catechism *n* catecismo *m*.
catechize *vt* catequizar, examinar.
categorical *adj* categórico/ca; **~ly** *adv* categóricamente.
categorize *vt* clasificar.
category *n* categoría *f*.
cater *vi* abastecer, proveer.
caterer *n* proveedor/a, abastecedor/a *m/f*.
catering *n* alimentación *f*.
caterpillar *n* oruga *f*.
catgut *n* cuerda de violón *f*.
cathedral *n* catedral *f*.
catholic *adj*, *n* católico/ca *m/f*.
Catholicism *n* catolicismo *m*.
cattle *n* ganado *m*.
cattle show *n* feria de ganado *f*.
caucus *n* junta electoral *f*.
cauliflower *n* coliflor *f*.
cause *n* causa *f*; razón *f*; motivo *m*; proceso *m*; * *vt* causar.
causeway *n* arrecife *m*.
caustic *adj*, *n* cáustico *m*.
cauterize *vt* cauterizar.
caution *n* prudencia, precaución *f*; aviso *m*; * *vt* avisar; amonestar; advertir.
cautionary *adj* de escarmiento.
cautious *adj* prudente, circunspecto/ta, cauto/ta.
cavalier *adj* arrogante.
cavalry *n* caballería *f*.
cave *n* caverna *f*; bodega *f*.

caveat *n* aviso *m*; advertencia *f*; (*law*) notificación *f*.
cavern *n* caverna *f*; bodega *f*.
cavernous *adj* cavernoso/sa.
caviar *n* caviar *m*.
cavity *n* hueco *m*; caries *f invar*.
CD-ROM *n* cederrón *m*.
cease *vt* parar, suspender; * *vi* desistir.
cease-fire *n* alto el fuego *m*, *Lat Am* cese del fuego *m*.
ceaseless *adj* incesante, continuo/nua; ~ly *adv* perpetuamente.
cedar *n* cedro *m*.
cede *vt* ceder, transferir.
ceiling *n* techo *m*.
celebrate *vt* celebrar.
celebration *n* celebración *f*.
celebrity *n* celebridad, fama *f*.
celery *n* apio *m*.
celestial *adj* celeste, divino/na.
celibacy *n* celibato *m*, soltería *f*.
celibate *adj* soltero; soltera.
cell *n* celdilla *f*; célula *f*; cueva *f*.
cellar *n* sótano *m*; bodega *f*.
cello *n* violoncelo *m*.
Cellophane™ *n* celofán *m*.
cellular *adj* celular; ~ phone móvil *m*, *Lat Am* celular *m*.
cellulitis *n* celulitis *f*.
cellulose *n* (*chem*) celulosa *f*.
cement *n* cemento; (*fig*) vínculo *m*; * *vt* pegar con cemento.
cemetery *n* cementerio *m*.
cenotaph *n* cenotafio *m*.
censor *n* censor/a *m/f*; crítico/ca *m/f*.
censorious *adj* severo/ra, crítico/ca.
censorship *n* censura *f*.
censure *n* censura, reprensión *f*; * *vt* censurar, reprender; criticar.
census *n* censo *m*.
cent *n* centavo *m*.
centenarian *n* centenario *m*; centenaria *f*.
centenary *n* centena *f*; * *adj* centenario/ria.
centennial *adj* centenario/ria.
center *n* centro *m*; * *vt* centrar; concentrar; * *vi* concentrarse.
centigrade *adj* centígrado *m*.
centiliter *n* centilitro *m*.
centimeter *n* centímetro *m*.
centipede *n* escolopendra *f*.
central *adj* central; ~ly *adv* centralmente, en el centro.
centralize *vt* centralizar.
centrifugal *adj* centrífugo/ga.
century *n* siglo *m*.

ceramic *adj* cerámico/ca.
cereals *npl* cereales *fpl*.
cerebral *adj* cerebral.
ceremonial *adj*, *n* ceremonial *m*; rito externo *m*.
ceremonious *adj* ceremonioso/sa; ~ly *adv* ceremoniosamente.
ceremony *n* ceremonia *f*.
certain *adj* cierto/ta, evidente; seguro/ra; ~ly *adv* ciertamente, sin duda.
certainty, certitude *n* certeza *f*; seguridad *f*.
certificate *n* certificado, testimonio *m*.
certification *n* certificado *m*.
certified mail *n* correo certificado *m*.
certify *vt* certificar, afirmar.
cervical *adj* cervical.
cesarean section/operation *n* (*med*) (operación de) cesárea *f*.
cessation *n* cesación *f*.
cesspool *n* cloaca *f*; sumidero *m*.
chafe *vt* frotar; enojar, irritar.
chaff *n* paja menuda *f*.
chaffinch *n* pinzón *m*.
chagrin *n* disgusto *m*.
chain *n* cadena *f*; serie, sucesión *f*; * *vt* encadenar, atar con cadena.
chain reaction *n* reacción en cadena *f*.
chain store *n* gran almacén *m*.
chair *n* silla *f*; * *vt* presidir.
chairman *n* presidente *m*.
chalice *n* cáliz *m*.
chalk *n* creta *f*; tiza *f*.
chalkboard *n* pizarra *f*, *Lat Am* pizarrón *m*.
challenge *n* desafío *m*; * *vt* desafiar, impugnar.
challenger *n* desafiador/a *m/f*.
challenging *adj* desafiante.
chamber *n* cámara *f*; aposento *m*.
chambermaid *n* moza de cámara *f*.
chameleon *n* camaleón *m*.
chamois leather *n* gamuza *f*.
champagne *n* champaña *m*.
champion *n* campeón *m*; * *vt* defender.
championship *n* campeonato *m*.
chance *n* ventura, suerte *f*; oportunidad *f*, *Lat Am* chance *m*; by ~ por acaso; * *vt* arriesgar.
chancellor *n* canciller *m*.
chancery *n* chancillería *f*.
chandelier *n* araña de luces *f*; candelero *m*.
change *vt* cambiar; * *vi* variar, alterarse; * *n* mudanza, variedad *f*; vicisitud *f*; cambio *m*, *Lat Am* vuelto *m*.
changeable *adj* variable, inconstante; mudable.

changeless *adj* constante, inmutable.
changing *adj* cambiante.
channel *n* canal *m*; estrecho *m*; * *vt* encauzar.
channel-hopping *n* zapping *m*.
chant *n* canto (llano) *m*; * *vt* cantar.
chaos *n* caos *m*; confusión *f*.
chaotic *adj* confuso/sa.
chapel *n* capilla *f*.
chaplain *n* capellán *m*.
chapter *n* capítulo *m*.
char *vt* chamuscar.
character *n* carácter *m*; personaje *m*.
characteristic *adj* característico/ca; ~**ally** *adv* característicamente.
characterize *vt* caracterizar.
characterless *adj* sin carácter.
charade *n* charada *f*.
charcoal *n* carbón de leña *m*.
chard *n* (*bot*) acelga *f*.
charge *vt* cargar; acusar, imputar; * *n* cargo *m*; acusación *f*; (*mil*) ataque *m*; depósito *m*; carga *f*.
chargeable *adj* imputable.
charge card *n* tarjeta de compra *f*.
charitable *adj* caritativo/va; benigno/na, clemente; ~**bly** *adv* caritativamente.
charity *n* caridad, benevolencia *f*; limosna *f*.
charlatan *n* charlatán/tana *m/f*.
charm *n* encanto *m*; atractivo *m*; * *vt* encantar, embelesar, atraer.
charming *adj* encantado/da.
chart *n* carta de navegar *f*.
charter *n* carta *f*; privilegio *m*; * *vt* fletar un buque; alquilar.
charter flight *n* vuelo chárter *m*, charter *m*.
chase *vt* cazar; perseguir; * *n* caza *f*.
chasm *n* vacío *m*.
chaste *adj* casto/ta; puro/ra; honesto/ta.
chasten *vt* corregir, castigar.
chastise *vt* castigar, reformar, corregir.
chastisement *n* castigo *m*.
chastity *n* castidad, pureza *f*.
chat *vi* charlar; * *n* charla, cháchara *f*.
chatter *vi* cotorrear; rechinar; charlar; * *n* chirrido *m*; charla *f*.
chatterbox *n* parlero/ra, hablador/a, gárrulo/la *m/f*.
chatty *adj* locuaz, parlanchín/china.
chauffeur *n* chófer *m*.
chauvinist *n* machista *m*.
cheap *adj* barato/ta; ~**ly** *adv* a bajo precio.
cheapen *vt* regatear; abaratar.

cheaper *adj* más barato/ta.
cheat *vt* engañar, defraudar; * *n* trampa *f*; fraude, engaño *m*; tramposo/sa *m/f*.
check[1] *vt* comprobar; contar; reprimir, refrenar; regañar; registrar; * *n* restricción *f*; freno *m*.
check[2] *n* cheque *m*.
check account *n* cuenta corriente *f*.
checkerboard *n* tablero de damas *m*.
checkered *adj* accidentado/da.
checkers *npl* juego de damas *m*.
checkmate *n* mate *m*.
checkout *n* caja *f*.
checkpoint *n* control *m*.
checkroom *n* consigna *f*.
check-up *n* reconocimiento médico *m*.
cheek *n* mejilla *f*; (*col*) desvergüenza *f*; atrevimiento *m*.
cheekbone *n* hueso del carrillo *m*.
cheeky *adj* descarado/da.
cheer *n* alegría *f*; aplauso *m*; buen humor *m*; * *vt* animar, alentar.
cheerful *adj* alegre, vivo/va, jovial; ~**ly** *adv* alegremente.
cheerfulness, cheeriness *n* alegría *f*; buen humor *m*.
cheese *n* queso *m*.
cheese shop *n* quesería *f*.
chef *n* jefe de cocina *m*.
chemical *adj* químico/ca.
chemist *n* químico *m*.
chemistry *n* química *f*.
chemotherapy *n* quimioterapia *f*.
cherish *vt* fomentar, proteger.
cheroot *n* puro *m*.
cherry *n* cereza *f*; * *adj* bermejo/ja.
cherry tree *n* cerezo *m*.
cherub *n* querubín *m*.
chess *n* ajedrez *m*.
chessboard *n* tablero de ajedrez *m*.
chessman *n* pieza de ajedrez *f*.
chest *n* pecho *m*; arca *f*; ~ **of drawers** cómoda *f*.
chestnut *n* castaña *f*; color de castaña *m*.
chestnut tree *n* castaño *m*.
chew *vt* mascar, masticar.
chewing gum *n* chicle *m*.
chic *adj* elegante.
chicanery *n* quisquilla *f*.
chick *n* polluelo *m*; (*col*) chica *f*.
chicken *n* pollo *m*.
chickenpox *n* varicela *f*.
chickpea *n* garbanzo *m*.
chicory *n* achicoria *f*.
chide *vt* reprobar, regañar.

chief *adj* principal, capital; ~ly *adv* principalmente; * *n* jefe, principal *m*.
chief executive *n* director/a general *m/f*.
chieftain *n* jefe, comandante *m*.
chiffon *n* gasa *f*.
chilblain *n* sabañón *m*.
child *n* niño *m*; niña *f*; hijo *m*; hija *f*; from a ~ desde niño/ña; with ~ preñada, embarazada.
childbirth *n* parto *m*.
childhood *n* infancia, niñez *f*; pequeñez *f*.
childish *adj* frívolo/la, pueril; ~ly *adv* puerilmente.
childishness *n* puerilidad *f*.
childless *adj* sin hijos.
childlike *adj* pueril.
children *npl de* child niños *mpl*.
chill *adj* frío/ría, friolero/ra; * *n* frío *m*; * *vt* enfriar; helar.
chilly *adj* friolero/ra, *Lat Am* friolento/ta.
chime *n* armonía *f*; clave *m*; * *vi* sonar con armonía; concordar.
chimney *n* chimenea *f*.
chimpanzee *n* chimpancé *m*.
chin *n* barbilla *f*.
china(ware) *n* porcelana *f*.
chink *n* grieta, hendedura *f*; * *vi* resonar.
chip *vt* astillar; * *vi* picarse; * *n* astilla *f*; chip *m*; patata/papa frita *f*.
chirp *vi* chirriar, gorjear; * *n* gorjeo, chirrido *m*.
chirping *n* canto de las aves *m*.
chisel *n* cincel *m*; * *vt* cincelar, grabar.
chitchat *n* charla *f*.
chivalrous *adj* caballeresco/ca.
chivalry *n* caballería *f*.
chives *npl* cebollinos *f*.
chlorine *n* cloro *m*.
chloroform *n* cloroformo *m*.
chock-full *adj* de bote en bote, completamente lleno/na.
chocolate *n* chocolate *m*.
choice *n* elección, preferencia *f*; selecto *m*; * *adj* selecto/ta, exquisito/ta, excelente.
choir *n* coro *m*.
choke *vt* sofocar; oprimir; tapar.
cholera *n* cólera *m*.
choose *vt* escoger, elegir.
chop *vt* tajar, cortar; * *n* chuleta *f*; ~s *pl* (*col*) quijadas *fpl*.
chopper *n* helicóptero *m*.
chopping block *n* tajo de cocina *m*.
chopsticks *npl* palillos *mpl*.
chore *n* faena *f*.
choral *adj* coral.

chord *n* cuerda *f*.
chorist, chorister *n* corista *m*.
chorus *n* coro *m*.
Christ *n* Cristo *m*.
christen *vt* bautizar.
Christendom *n* cristianismo *m*; cristiandad *f*.
christening *n* bautismo *m*.
Christian *adj*, *n* cristiano/na *m/f*; ~ name nombre de pila *m*.
Christianity *n* cristianismo *m*; cristiandad *f*.
Christmas *n* Navidad *f*.
Christmas card *n* tarjeta de Navidad *f*.
Christmas Eve *n* Nochebuena *f*.
chrome *n* cromo *m*.
chronic *adj* crónico/ca.
chronicle *n* crónica *f*.
chronicler *n* cronista *m*.
chronological *adj* cronológico/ca; ~ly *adv* cronológicamente.
chronology *n* cronología *f*.
chronometer *n* cronómetro *m*.
chubby *adj* gordo/da.
chuck *vt* lanzar.
chuckle *vi* reírse a carcajadas.
chug *vi* resoplar.
chum *n* compañero/ra, compinche *m/f*.
chunk *n* trozo *m*.
church *n* iglesia *f*.
churchyard *n* cementerio *m*.
churlish *adj* hosco/ca, grosero/ra; tacaño/ña.
churn *n* mantequera *f*; * *vt* batir la leche para hacer manteca.
cider *n* sidra *f*.
cigar *n* cigarro *m*.
cigarette *n* cigarrillo *m*.
cigarette case *n* pitillera *f*.
cigarette end *n* colilla *f*.
cigarette holder *n* boquilla *f*.
cinder *n* carbonilla *f*.
cinnamon *n* canela *f*.
cipher *n* cifra *f*.
circle *n* círculo *m*; corrillo *m*; asamblea *f*; * *vt* circundar; cercar; * *vi* circular.
circuit *n* circuito *m*; recinto *m*.
circuitous *adj* circular, tortuoso/sa.
circular *adj* circular, redondo/da; * *n* carta circular *f*.
circulate *vi* circular; moverse alrededor.
circulation *n* circulación *f*.
circumcise *vt* circuncidar.
circumcision *n* circuncisión *f*.
circumference *n* circunferencia *f*; circuito *m*.

circumflex n acento circunflejo m.
circumlocution n circunlocución f.
circumnavigate vt circunnavegar.
circumnavigation n circunnavegación f.
circumscribe vt circunscribir.
circumspect adj circunspecto/ta, prudente, reservado/da.
circumspection n circunspección, prudencia f.
circumstance n circunstancia, condición f; incidente m.
circumstantial adj accidental; accesorio/ria.
circumstantiate vt circunstanciar, detallar.
circumvent vt burlar.
circumvention n evasión f.
circus n circo m.
cistern n cisterna f.
citadel n ciudadela, fortaleza f.
citation n citación, cita f.
cite vt citar (a juicio); alegar; referirse a.
citizen n ciudadano/na m/f.
citizenship n ciudadanía f.
city n ciudad f.
civic adj cívico/ca.
civil adj civil, cortés; ~ly adv civilmente.
civil defense n protección civil f.
civil engineer n ingeniero/ra civil m/f.
civilian n paisano m.
civility n civilidad, urbanidad, cortesía f.
civilization n civilización f.
civilize vt civilizar.
civil law n derecho civil m.
civil war n guerra civil f.
clad adj vestido/da, cubierto/ta.
claim vt pedir en juicio, reclamar; * n demanda f; derecho m.
claimant n reclamante m; demandador/a m/f.
clairvoyant n clarividente m/f; zahorí m.
clam n almeja f.
clamber vi gatear, trepar.
clammy adj viscoso/sa.
clamor n clamor, grito m; * vi vociferar, gritar.
clamp n abrazadera f; * vt afianzar; **to ~ down on** reforzar la lucha contra.
clan n familia, tribu, raza f.
clandestine adj clandestino/na, oculto/ta.
clang n rechino, sonido desapacible m; * vi rechinar.
clap vt aplaudir.
clapping n palmada f; aplauso, palmoteo m.
claret n clarete m.
clarification n clarificación f.
clarify vt clarificar, aclarar.

clarinet n clarinete m.
clarity n claridad f.
clash vi chocar; * n estruendo m; choque m.
clasp n broche m; hebilla f; abrazo m; * vt abrochar; abrazar.
class n clase f; orden f; * vt clasificar, coordinar.
classic(al) adj clásico/ca; * n autor clásico m.
classification n clasificación f.
classified advertisement n anuncio por palabras m, Lat Am clasificado m.
classify vt clasificar.
classmate n compañero/ra de clase m/f.
classroom n aula f.
clatter vi resonar; hacer ruido; * n ruido m.
clause n cláusula f; artículo m; estipulación f.
claw n garra f; zarpa f; * vt desgarrar, arañar.
clay n arcilla f.
clean adj limpio/pia; casto/ta; * vt limpiar.
cleaning n limpieza f.
cleanliness n limpieza f.
cleanly adj limpio/pia; * adv limpiamente, aseadamente.
cleanness n limpieza f; pureza f.
cleanse vt limpiar, purificar; purgar.
clear adj claro/ra; neto/ta; diáfano/na; evidente; * adv claramente; * vt clarificar, aclarar; justificar, absolver; * vi aclararse.
clearance n despeje m; acreditación f.
clear-cut adj bien definido/da.
clearly adv claramente, evidentemente.
cleaver n cuchillo de carnicero m.
clef n clave f.
cleft n hendedura, abertura f.
clemency n clemencia f.
clement adj clemente, benigno/na.
clenched adj cerrado/da.
clergy n clero m.
clergyman n eclesiástico m.
clerical adj clerical, eclesiástico/ca.
clerk n dependiente m; oficinista m.
clever adj listo/ta; hábil, mañoso/sa; ~ly adv diestramente, hábilmente.
click vt chasquear; * vi taconear.
client n cliente m/f.
cliff n acantilado m.
climate n clima m; temperatura f.
climatic adj climático/ca
climax n clímax m.
climb vt escalar, trepar; * vi subir.
climber n alpinista m/f.
climbing n alpinismo m.
clinch vt cerrar; remachar.

cling vi colgar, adherirse, pegarse.
clinic n clínica f.
clink vt hacer resonar; * vi resonar; * n
retintín m.
clip vt cortar; * n clip m; horquilla f.
clipping n recorte m.
clique n camarilla f.
cloak n capa f; pretexto m; * vi encapotar.
cloakroom n guardarropa m.
clock n reloj m.
clockwork n mecanismo de un reloj m;
* adj sumamente exacto y puntual.
clod n terrón m.
clog n zueco m; * vi atascarse.
cloister n claustro, monasterio m.
clone n clon m.
clone vt clonar.
cloned adj clónico/ca.
cloning n clonación f.
close vt cerrar; concluir, terminar; * vi
cerrarse; * n fin m; conclusión f; * adj
cercano/na; estrecho/cha; ajustado/da;
denso/sa; reservado/da; * adv de cerca; ~
by muy cerca; junto.
closed adj cerrado/da.
closely adv estrechamente; de cerca.
closeness n proximidad f; estrechez;
reclusión f.
closet n armario m.
close-up n primer plano m.
closure n cierre m; conclusión f.
clot n grumo m; embolia f.
cloth n paño m; mantel m; vestido m;
lienzo m.
clothe vt vestir, cubrir.
clothes npl ropa f; ropaje m; ropa de cama
f; bed ~ cobertores mpl.
clothes basket n cesta grande f.
clotheshorse n tendedero m.
clothesline n cuerda (de tendedero) f.
clothespin n pinza f.
clothing n vestidos mpl.
cloud n nube f; nublado m; (fig) adversidad f;
* vt anublar; oscurecer; * vi anublarse;
oscurecerse.
cloudiness n nubosidad f; oscuridad f.
cloudy adj nublado/da; oscuro/ra; sombrío/
ría, melancólico/ca.
clout n tortazo m.
clove n clavo m.
clover n trébol m.
clown n payaso m.
club n cachiporra f.
club car n coche restaurante m.
clue n pista f, indicios m; idea f.

clump n grupo m.
clumsily adv torpemente.
clumsiness n torpeza f.
clumsy adj torpe, pesado/da, Lat Am patón/
ona; sin arte.
cluster n racimo m; manada f; pelotón m;
* vt agrupar; * vi arracimarse.
clutch n embrague m; apretón m; * vt
empuñar.
clutter vt atestar.
coach n autocar, autobús m; vagón m;
entrenador/a m/f; * vt entrenar; enseñar.
coach trip n excursión en autocar f.
coagulate vt coagular, cuajar; * vi coagularse,
cuajarse, espesarse.
coal n carbón m.
coalesce vi juntarse, incorporarse.
coalfield n yacimiento de carbón m.
coalition n coalición, confederación f.
coalman n carbonero m.
coalmine n mina de carbón, carbonería f.
coarse adj basto/ta; grosero/ra; zafio/fia; ~ly
adv groseramente.
coast n costa f.
coastal adj costero/ra; ribereño/ña.
coastguard n guardacostas m invar.
coastline n litoral m.
coat n chaqueta f; abrigo m, Lat Am saco m;
capa f; * vt cubrir.
coat hanger n percha f.
coat hook n percha f.
coating n revestimiento m.
coax vt lisonjear.
cob n mazorca de maíz f.
cobbler n zapatero/ra m/f.
cobbles, cobblestones npl adoquines mpl.
cobweb n telaraña f.
cocaine n cocaína f.
coccyx n rabadilla f.
cock n gallo m; macho m; * vt armar el
sombrero; amartillar, montar una escopeta.
cock-a-doodle-doo n quiquiriquí m.
cockcrow n canto del gallo m.
cockerel n gallito m.
cockfight(ing) n pelea de gallos f.
cockle n berberecho m.
cockpit n cabina f.
cockroach n cucaracha f.
cocktail n cóctel m.
cocoa n coco m; cacao m.
coconut n coco m.
cocoon n capullo (del gusano de seda) m.
cod n bacalao m.
code n código m; prefijo m.
cod-liver oil n aceite de hígado de bacalao m.

coefficient *n* coeficiente *m*.
coercion *n* coerción *f*.
coexistence *n* coexistencia *f*.
coffee *n* café *m*.
coffee break *n* descanso *m*.
coffee house *n* café *m*.
coffee-pot *n* cafetera *f*.
coffee table *n* mesita *f*.
coffer *n* cofre *m*; caja *f*.
coffin *n* ataúd *m*.
cog *n* diente (de rueda) *m*.
cogency *n* fuerza, urgencia *f*.
cogent *adj* convincente, urgente; ~**ly** *adv* de modo convincente.
cognac *n* coñac *m*.
cognate *adj* cognado/da.
cognition *n* conocimiento *m*; convicción *f*.
cognizance *n* conocimiento *m*; competencia *f*.
cognizant *adj* informado/da; (*law*) competente.
cogwheel *n* rueda dentada *f*.
cohabit *vi* cohabitar.
cohabitation *n* cohabitación *f*.
cohere *vi* pegarse; unirse.
coherence *n* coherencia, conexión *f*.
coherent *adj* coherente; consiguiente.
cohesion *n* coherencia *f*.
cohesive *adj* cohesivo/va.
coil *n* rollo *m*; bobina *f*; * *vt* enrollar.
coin *n* moneda *f*; * *vt* acuñar.
coincide *vi* coincidir, concurrir, convenir.
coincidence *n* coincidencia *f*.
coke[1] *n* coque *m*.
Coke[2] *n* Coca-Cola™ *f*.
colander *n* colador *m*, *Lat Am* coladera *f*, pasador *m*.
cold *adj* frío/ría; indiferente, insensible; reservado/da; ~**ly** *adv* fríamente; indiferentemente; * *n* frío *m*; frialdad *f*; resfriado *m*.
cold-blooded *adj* impasible.
coldness *n* frialdad *f*; indiferencia, insensibilidad, apatía *f*.
cold sore *n* herpes labial *m*.
coleslaw *n* ensalada de col *f*.
colic *n* cólico *m*.
collaborate *vt* cooperar.
collaboration *n* cooperación *f*.
collapse *vi* hundirse; * *n* hundimiento; (*med*) colapso *m*.
collapsible *adj* plegable.
collar *n* cuello *m*.
collarbone *n* clavícula *f*.
collate *vt* comparar, confrontar.

collateral *adj* colateral; * *n* garantía subsidiaria *f*.
collation *n* colación *f*.
colleague *n* colega, compañero/ra *m/f*.
collect *vt* recoger; coleccionar.
collection *n* colección *f*; compilación *f*.
collective *adj* colectivo/va, congregado/da; ~**ly** colectivamente.
collector *n* coleccionista *m/f*.
college *n* colegio *m*, *Lat Am* facultad *f*.
collide *vi* chocar.
collision *n* choque *m*, colisión *f*.
colloquial *adj* familiar; coloquial; ~**ly** *adv* familiarmente.
colloquialism *n* lengua usual *f*.
collusion *n* colusión *f*.
colon *n* dos puntos *mpl*; (*med*) colon *m*.
colonel *n* (*mil*) coronel *m*.
colonial *adj* colonial.
colonist *n* colono *m*.
colonize *vt* colonizar.
colony *n* colonia *f*.
color *n* color *m*; ~**s** *pl* bandera *f*; * *vt* colorar; pintar; * *vi* ponerse colorado/da.
color-blind *adj* daltónico/ca.
colorful *adj* lleno de color.
coloring *n* colorido *m*.
colorless *adj* descolorido/da, sin color.
color television *n* televisión en color *f*.
colossal *adj* colosal.
colossus *n* coloso *m*.
colt *n* potro *m*.
column *n* columna *f*.
columnist *n* columnista *m*.
coma *n* coma *f*.
comatose *adj* comatoso/sa.
comb *n* peine *m*; * *vt* peinar.
combat *n* combate *m*; batalla *f*; **single ~** duelo *m*; * *vt* combatir.
combatant *n* combatiente *m*.
combative *adj* combativo/va.
combination *n* combinación, coordinación *f*.
combine *vt* combinar; * *vi* unirse.
combustion *n* combustión *f*.
come *vi* venir; **to ~ across/upon** *vt* topar con; dar con; **to ~ by** *vt* conseguir; **to ~ down** *vi* bajar; ser derribado/da; **to ~ from** *vt* ser de; **to ~ in for** *vt* merecer; **to ~ into** *vt* heredar; **to ~ round/to** *vi* volver en sí; **to ~ up with** *vt* sugerir.
comedian *n* comediante, cómico *m*.
comedienne *n* cómica *f*.
comedy *n* comedia *f*.
comet *n* cometa *m*.

comfort *n* confort *m*; ayuda *f*; consuelo *m*; comodidad *f*; * *vt* confortar; alentar, consolar.

comfortable *adj* cómodo/da.

comfortably *adv* agradablemente; cómodamente.

comforter *n* chupete *m*.

comic(al) *adj* cómico/ca, burlesco/ca; ~ly *adv* cómicamente.

coming *n* venida, llegada *f*; * *adj* venidero/ra.

comma *n* (*gr*) coma *f*.

command *vt* comandar, ordenar; * *n* orden *f*.

commander *n* comandante *m*.

commandment *n* mandamiento, precepto *m*.

commando *n* comando *m*.

commemorate *vt* conmemorar; celebrar.

commemoration *n* conmemoración *f*.

commence *vt*, *vi* comenzar.

commencement *n* principio *m*.

commend *vt* encomendar; alabar; enviar.

commendable *adj* recomendable.

commendably *adv* loablemente.

commendation *n* recomendación *f*.

commensurate *adj* proporcionado/da.

comment *n* comentario *m*; * *vt* comentar; glosar.

commentary *n* comentario *m*; interpretación *f*.

commentator *n* comentarista *m/f*.

commerce *n* comercio, tráfico, trato, negocio *m*.

commercial *adj* comercial.

commiserate *vt* compadecer, tener compasión.

commiseration *n* conmiseración, piedad *f*.

commissariat *n* comisaría *f*.

commission *n* comisión *f*; * *vt* comisionar; encargar.

commissioner *n* comisionado/da, delegado/da *m/f*.

commit *vt* cometer; depositar; encargar.

commitment *n* compromiso *m*.

committee *n* comité *m*.

commodity *n* comodidad *f*.

common *adj* común; bajo/ja; in ~ comúnmente; * *n* pastos comunales *mpl*.

commoner *n* plebeyo *m*.

common law *n* derecho consuetudinario *m*.

commonly *adv* comúnmente, frecuentemente.

commonplace *n* lugar común *m*; * *adj* trivial.

common sense *n* sentido común *m*.

commonwealth *n* república *f*.

commotion *n* tumulto *m*; perturbación del ánimo *f*.

commune *vt* conversar, conferir.

communicable *adj* comunicable, impartible.

communicate *vt* comunicar, participar; *. vi* comunicarse.

communication *n* comunicación *f*.

communicative *adj* comunicativo/va.

communion *n* comunión *f*.

communiqué *n* comunicado *m*.

communism *n* comunismo *m*.

communist *n* comunista *m/f*.

community *n* comunidad *f*; colectividad *f*.

community center *n* centro social *m*.

community chest *n* arca comunitaria *f*.

commutable *adj* conmutable, cambiable.

commutation ticket *n* billete de abono *m*.

commute *vt* conmutar.

compact *adj* compacto/ta, sólido/da, denso/sa; * *n* pacto, convenio *m*; ~ly *adv* estrechamente; en pocas palabras.

compact disc, CD *n* compact disc *m*, disco compacto *m*.

companion *n* compañero/ra, socio/cia, compinche *m/f*.

companionship *n* sociedad, compañía *f*.

company *n* compañía, sociedad *f*; compañía de comercio *f*.

comparable *adj* comparable.

comparative *adj* comparativo/va; ~ly *adv* comparativamente.

compare *vt* comparar.

comparison *n* comparación *f*.

compartment *n* compartimento *m*.

compass *n* brújula *f*.

compassion *n* compasión, piedad *f*.

compassionate *adj* compasivo/va.

compatibility *n* compatibilidad *f*.

compatible *adj* compatible.

compatriot *n* compatriota *m/f*.

compel *vt* compeler, obligar, constreñir.

compelling *adj* convicente.

compensate *vt* compensar.

compensation *n* compensación *f*; resarcimiento *m*.

compere *n* (*rad*, *TV*) presentador/a *m/f*.

compete *vi* concurrir, competir.

competence *n* competencia *f*; suficiencia *f*.

competent *adj* competente, adecuado/da; ~ly *adv* competentemente.

competition *n* competencia *f*; concurrencia *f*.

competitive *adj* competitivo/va.

competitive scheduling *n* contraprogramación *f*.
competitor *n* competidor/a *m/f*, rival *m*.
compilation *n* compilación *f*.
compile *vt* compilar.
complacency *n* autocomplacencia *f*.
complacent *adj* complaciente.
complain *vi* quejarse, lamentarse, lastimarse, dolerse.
complaint *n* queja *f*; reclamación *f*, *Lat Am* reclamo *m*.
complement *n* complemento *m*.
complementary *adj* complementario/ria.
complete *adj* completo/ta, perfecto/ta; ~ly *adv* completamente; * *vt* completar, acabar.
completion *n* terminación *f*.
complex *adj* complejo/ja.
complexion *n* tez *f*; aspecto *m*.
complexity *n* complejidad *f*.
compliance *n* complacencia, sumisión *f*.
compliant *adj* complaciente, oficioso/sa.
complicate *vt* complicar.
complication *n* complicación *f*.
complicity *n* complicidad *f*.
compliment *n* cumplido *m*; * *vt* cumplimentar; hacer cumplidos.
complimentary *adj* elogioso/sa, ceremonioso/sa.
comply *vi* cumplir; condescender, conformarse.
component *adj* componente.
compose *vt* componer; sosegar.
composed *adj* compuesto/ta, moderado/da.
composer *n* compositor/a *m/f*.
composite *adj* compuesto/ta.
composition *n* composición *f*.
compositor *n* cajista *m*.
compost *n* abono, estiércol *m*.
composure *n* composición *f*; tranquilidad, sangre fría *f*.
compound *vt* componer, combinar; * *adj*, *n* compuesto *m*.
comprehend *vt* comprender, contener; entender.
comprehensible *adj* comprensible; ~ly *adv* comprensiblemente.
comprehension *n* comprensión *f*; inteligencia *f*.
comprehensive *adj* comprensivo/va; ~ly *adv* comprensivamente.
compress *vt* comprimir, estrechar; * *n* cabezal *m*.
comprise *vt* comprender, incluir.
compromise *n* compromiso *m*; * *vt* comprometer.

compulsion *n* compulsión *f*; apremio *m*.
compulsive *adj* compulsivo/va; ~ly *adv* compulsivamente.
compulsory *adj* obligatorio/ria.
compunction *n* compunción, contrición *f*.
computable *adj* computable, calculable.
computation *n* computación *f*, cómputo *m*.
compute *vt* computar, calcular.
computer *n* ordenador *m*.
computer graphics *n* infografía *f*.
computerize *vt* computerizar, informatizar.
computer programing *n* programación *f*.
computer science *n* informática *f*.
computing *n* informática *f*, *Lat Am* computación *f*.
comrade *n* camarada, compañero/ra *m/f*.
comradeship *n* compañerismo *m*.
con *vt* estafar; * *n* estafa *f*.
concave *adj* cóncavo/va.
concavity *n* concavidad *f*.
conceal *vt* ocultar, esconder.
concealment *n* ocultación *f*; encubrimiento *m*.
concede *vt* conceder, asentir.
conceit *n* concepto *m*; capricho *m*; pensamiento *m*; presunción *f*.
conceited *adj* afectado/da, vano/na, presumido/da.
conceivable *adj* concebible, inteligible.
conceive *vt* concebir, comprender; * *vi* concebir.
concentrate *vt* concentrar.
concentration *n* concentración *f*.
concentration camp *n* campo de concentración *m*.
concentric *adj* concéntrico/ca.
concept *n* concepto *m*.
conception *n* concepción *f*; sentimiento *m*.
concern *vt* concernir, importar; * *n* negocio *m*; asunto *m*; preocupación *f*.
concerning *prep* tocante a.
concert *n* concierto *m*.
concerto *n* concierto *m*.
concession *n* concesión *f*; privilegio *m*.
conciliate *vt* conciliar.
conciliation *n* conciliación *f*.
conciliatory *adj* conciliador/a.
concise *adj* conciso/sa, sucinto/ta; ~ly *adv* concisamente.
conclude *vt* concluir; decidir; determinar.
conclusion *n* conclusión, determinación *f*; fin *m*.
conclusive *adj* decisivo/va, conclusivo/va; ~ly *adv* concluyentemente.
concoct *vt* cocer, digerir; (*fig*) zurcir.

concoction *n* confección *f;* cocción *f.*
concomitant *adj* concomitante.
concord *n* concordia, armonía *f.*
concordance *n* concordancia *f.*
concordant *adj* concordante, conforme.
concourse *n* concurso *m;* multitud *f;* gentío *m.*
concrete *n* hormigón *m, Lat Am* concreto *m;* * *vt* concretar.
concubine *n* concubina *f.*
concur *vi* concurrir; juntarse.
concurrence *n* concurrencia *f;* unión *f;* asistencia *f.*
concurrently *adv* al mismo tiempo.
concussion *n* conmoción cerebral *f.*
condemn *vt* condenar; desaprobar; vituperar.
condemnation *n* condena *f.*
condensation *n* condensación *f.*
condense *vt* condensar.
condescend *vi* condescender; consentir.
condescending *adj* condescendiente.
condescension *n* condescendencia *f.*
condiment *n* condimento *m;* salsa *f.*
condition *vt* condicionar; *n* situación, condición, calidad *f;* estado *m.*
conditional *adj* condicional, hipotético/ca; ~ly *adv* condicionalmente.
conditioned *adj* condicionado/da.
conditioner *n* acondicionador *m.*
condolences *npl* pésame *m.*
condom *n* condón *m.*
condominium *n* condominio *m.*
condone *vt* perdonar.
conducive *adj* conducente, oportuno/na.
conduct *n* conducta *f;* manejo, proceder *m;* * *vt* conducir, guiar.
conductor *n* conductor *m;* guía, director *m;* conductor de electricidad *m.*
conduit *n* conducto *m;* cano *m.*
cone *n* cono *m.*
confection *n* confitura *f;* confección *f.*
confectioner *n* confitero/ra *m/f.*
confectioner's (shop/store) *n* pastelería *f;* confitería *f.*
confederacy *n* confederación *f.*
confederate *vi* confederarse; * *adj, n* confederado/da *m/f.*
confer *vi* conferenciar; * *vt* conferir, comparar.
conference *n* conferencia *f.*
confess *vt* (*vi*) confesar(se).
confession *n* confesión *f.*
confessional *n* confesionario *m.*
confessor *n* confesor *m.*
confetti *n* confeti *m.*

confidant *n* confidente, amigo/ga íntimo/ma *m/f.*
confide *vt, vi* confiar; fiarse.
confidence *n* confianza, seguridad *f.*
confidence trick *n* timo *m.*
confident *adj* cierto/ta, seguro/ra; confiado/da.
confidential *adj* confidencial.
configuration *n* configuración *f.*
confine *vt* limitar; aprisionar.
confinement *n* prisión *f;* confinación *f.*
confirm *vt* confirmar; ratificar.
confirmation *n* confirmación *f;* ratificación *f;* prueba *f.*
confirmed *adj* empedernido/da.
confiscate *vt* confiscar.
confiscation *n* confiscación *f.*
conflagration *n* conflagración *f;* incendio *m.*
conflict *n* conflicto *m;* combate *m;* pelea *f.*
conflicting *adj* contradictorio/ria.
confluence *n* confluencia *f;* concurso *m.*
conform *vt* (*vi*) conformar(se).
conformity *n* conformidad, conveniencia *f.*
confound *vt* turbar, confundir.
confront *vt* afrontar; confrontar; comparar.
confrontation *n* enfrentamiento *m.*
confuse *vt* confundir; desordenar.
confusing *adj* confuso/sa.
confusion *n* confusión *f;* perturbación *f;* desorden *m.*
congeal *vt, vi* helar, congelar(se).
congenial *adj* congenial.
congenital *adj* congénito/ta.
congested *adj* atestado/da.
congestion *n* congestión *f;* acumulación *f.*
conglomerate *vt* conglomerar, aglomerar; * *adj* aglomerado/da; * *n* (*com*) conglomerado *m.*
conglomeration *n* aglomeración *f.*
congratulate *vt* congratular, felicitar.
congratulations *npl* felicidades *fpl;* * *interj* enhorabuena, *Lat Am* felicitaciones.
congratulatory *adj* congratulatorio/ria.
congregate *vt* congregar, reunir.
congregation *n* congregación, reunión *f.*
congress *n* congreso *m;* conferencia *f.*
congressman *n* miembro del Congreso *m.*
congruity *n* congruencia *f.*
congruous *adj* idóneo/nea, congruo/rua, apto/ta.
conic(al) *adj* cónico/ca.
conifer *n* conífera *f.*
coniferous *adj* (*bot*) conífero/ra.
conjecture *n* conjetura, apariencia *f;* * *vt* conjeturar; pronosticar.

conjugal *adj* conyugal, matrimonial.
conjugate *vt* (*gr*) conjugar.
conjugation *n* conjugación *f*.
conjunction *n* conjunción *f*; unión *f*.
conjuncture *n* coyuntura *f*; ocasión *f*; tiempo crítico *m*.
conjure *vi* conjurar, suplicar.
conjurer *n* conjurador/a, encantador/a *m/f*.
con man *n* timador *m*.
connect *vt* juntar, unir, enlazar.
connection *n* conexión *f*.
connivance *n* connivencia *f*.
connive *vi* tolerar.
connoisseur *n* conocedor/a *m/f*.
conquer *vt* conquistar; vencer.
conqueror *n* vencedor/a, conquistador/a *m/f*.
conquest *n* conquista *f*.
conscience *n* conciencia *f*; escrúpulo *m*.
conscientious *adj* concienzudo/da, escrupuloso/sa; ~ly *adv* concienzudamente.
conscientious objector *n* objetor de conciencia *m*.
conscious *adj* sabedor, consciente; ~ly *adv* a sabiendas.
consciousness *n* conciencia *f*.
conscript *n* conscripto *m*.
conscription *n* reclutamiento *m*.
consecrate *vt* consagrar; dedicar.
consecration *n* consagración *f*.
consecutive *adj* consecutivo/va; ~ly *adv* consecutivamente.
consensus *n* consenso *m*.
consent *n* consentimiento *m*; aprobación *f*; * *vi* consentir; aprobar.
consequence *n* consecuencia *f*; importancia *f*.
consequent *adj* consecutivo/va, concluyente; ~ly *adv* consiguientemente.
conservation *n* conservación *f*.
conservative *adj* conservador/a *m/f*.
conservatory *n* conservatorio *m*.
conserve *vt* conservar; * *n* conserva *f*.
consider *vt* considerar, examinar; * *vi* pensar, deliberar.
considerable *adj* considerable; importante; ~bly *adv* considerablemente.
considerate *adj* considerado/da, prudente, discreto/ta; ~ly *adv* juiciosamente; prudentemente.
consideration *n* consideración *f*; deliberación *f*; importancia *f*; valor, mérito *m*.
considering *conj* en vista de; ~ that a causa de; visto que, en razón a.
consign *vt* consignar.

consignment *n* consignación *f*.
consist *vi* consistir.
consistency *n* consistencia *f*.
consistent *adj* consistente; conveniente, conforme; solido/da, estable; ~ly *adv* conformemente.
console *n* consola *f*.
consolable *adj* consolable.
consolation *n* consolación *f*; consuelo *m*.
consolatory *adj* consolatorio/ria.
console *vt* consolar.
consolidate *vt*, *vi* consolidar(se).
consolidation *n* consolidación *f*.
consonant *adj* consonante, conforme; * *n* (*gr*) consonante *f*.
consort *n* consorte, socio *m*.
conspicuous *adj* conspicuo/cua, aparente; notable; ~ly *adv* claramente.
conspiracy *n* conspiración *f*.
conspirator *n* conspirador/a *m/f*.
conspire *vi* conspirar, maquinar.
constancy *n* constancia, perseverancia, persistencia *f*.
constant *adj* constante; perseverante; ~ly *adv* constantemente.
constellation *n* constelación *f*.
consternation *n* consternación *f*; terror *m*.
constipated *adj* estreñido/da.
constituency *n* circunscripción electoral *f*.
constituent *n* constitutivo *m*; * *adj* constituyente.
constitute *vt* constituir; establecer.
constitution *n* constitución *f*; estado *m*; temperamento *m*.
constitutional *adj* constitucional.
constrain *vt* constreñir, forzar; restringir.
constraint *n* constreñimiento *m*; fuerza, violencia *f*.
constrict *vt* constreñir, estrechar.
construct *vt* construir, edificar.
construction *n* construcción *f*.
construe *vt* construir; interpretar.
consul *n* cónsul *m*.
consular *adj* consular.
consulate, consulship *n* consulado *m*.
consult *vt* (*vi*) consultar(se); aconsejar(se).
consultant *n* asesor *m*.
consultation *n* consulta, deliberación *f*.
consume *vt* consumir; disipar; * *vi* consumirse.
consumer *n* consumidor/a *m/f*.
consumer goods *npl* bienes de consumo *mpl*.
consumerism *n* consumismo *m*.
consumer society *n* sociedad de consumo *f*.

consummate *vt* consumar, acabar, perfeccionar; * *adj* cumplido/da, consumado/da.
consummation *n* consumación, perfección *f.*
consumption *n* consumo *m.*
contact *n* contacto *m.*
contact lenses *npl* lentes de contacto *fpl.*
contagious *adj* contagioso/sa.
contain *vt* contener, comprender; caber, reprimir, refrenar.
container *n* recipiente *m.*
contaminate *vt* contaminar; corromper; ~d *adj* contaminado/da, corrompido/da.
contamination *n* contaminación *f.*
contemplate *vt* contemplar.
contemplation *n* contemplación *f.*
contemplative *adj* contemplativo/va.
contemporaneous, contemporary *adj* contemporáneo/nea.
contempt *n* desprecio, desdén *m.*
contemptible *adj* despreciable, vil; ~bly *adv* vilmente.
contemptuous *adj* desdeñoso/sa, insolente; ~ly *adv* con desdén.
contend *vi* contender, disputar, afirmar.
content *adj* contento/ta, satisfecho/cha; * *vt* contentar, satisfacer; * *n* contenido *m;* ~s *pl* contenido *m;* tabla de materias *f.*
contentedly *adv* de un modo satisfecho/cha; con paciencia.
contention *n* contención, altercación *f.*
contentious *adj* contencioso/sa, litigioso/sa; ~ly *adv* contenciosamente.
contentment *n* contentamiento, placer *m.*
contest *vt* contestar, disputar, litigar; * *n* concurso *m;* contestación, altercación *f.*
contestant *n* concursante/ta *m/f.*
context *n* contexto *m;* contextura *f.*
contiguous *adj* contiguo/gua, vecino/na.
continent *adj* continente; * *n* continente *m.*
continental *adj.* continental.
contingency *n* contingencia *f;* acontecimiento *m;* eventualidad *f.*
contingent *n* contingente *m;* cuota *f;* * *adj* contingente, casual; ~ly *adv* casualmente.
continual *adj* continuo/nua; ~ly *adv* continuamente.
continuation *n* continuación, serie *f.*
continue *vt* continuar; * *vi* durar, perseverar, persistir.
continuity *n* continuidad *f.*
continuous *adj* continuo/nua, unido/da; ~ly *adv* continuadamente.
contort *vt* torcer.
contortion *n* contorsión *f.*

contour *n* contorno *m.*
contraband *n* contrabando *m;* * *adj* prohibido/da, ilegal.
contraception *n* contracepción *f.*
contraceptive *n* anticonceptivo *m;* * *adj* anticonceptivo/va.
contract *vt* contraer; abreviar; contratar; *vi* contraerse; * *n* contrato, pacto *m.*
contraction *n* contracción *f;* abreviatura *f.*
contractor *n* contratante *m/f.*
contradict *vt* contradecir.
contradiction *n* contradicción, oposición *f.*
contradictory *adj* contradictorio/ria.
contraption *n* artilugio *m.*
contrariness *n* contrariedad, oposición *f.*
contrary *adj* contrario/ria, opuesto/ta; * *n* contrario *m;* on the ~ al contrario.
contrast *n* contraste *m;* oposición *f;* * *vt* contrastar, oponer.
contrasting *adj* opuesto/ta.
contravention *n* contravención *f.*
contributory *adj* contributario/ria.
contribute *vt* contribuir, ayudar.
contribution *n* contribución *f;* tributo *m.*
contributor *n* contribuidor/a *m/f.*
contributory *adj* contribuyente.
contrite *adj* contrito/ta, arrepentido/da.
contrition *n* penitencia, contrición *f.*
contrivance *n* designio *m;* invención *f;* concepto *m.*
contrive *vt* inventar, trazar, maquinar; manejar; combinar.
control *n* control *m;* inspección *f;* * *vt* controlar; manejar; restringir; gobernar.
control room *n* sala de mando *f.*
control tower *n* torre de control *f.*
controversial *adj* polémico/ca.
controversy *n* controversia *f.*
contusion *n* contusión *f,* magullamiento *m.*
conundrum *n* problema *m.*
conurbation *n* conurbación *f.*
convalesce *vi* convalecer.
convalescence *n* convalecencia *f.*
convalescent *adj* convaleciente.
convene *vt* convocar; juntar, unir; * *vi* convenir, juntarse.
convenience *n* conveniencia, comodidad, conformidad *f.*
convenient *adj* conveniente, apto/ta, cómodo/da, propio/pia; ~ly *adv* cómodamente, oportunamente.
convent *n* convento, claustro, monasterio *m.*
convention *n* convención *f;* contrato, tratado *m.*

conventional *adj* convencional, estipulado/ da.
converge *vi* converger.
convergence *n* convergencia *f.*
convergent *adj* convergente.
conversant *adj* versado en; íntimo/ma.
conversation *n* conversación *f, Lat Am* conversa *f.*
converse *vi* conversar; platicar.
conversely *adv* mutuamente, recíprocamente.
conversion *n* conversión, transmutación *f.*
convert *vt* (*vr*) convertir(se); * *n* converso, convertido *m.*
convertible *adj* convertible, transmutable; * *n* descapotable *m.*
convex *adj* convexo/xa.
convexity *n* convexidad *f.*
convey *vt* transportar; transmitir, transferir.
conveyance *n* transporte *m*; conducción *f*; escritura de traspaso *f.*
conveyancer *n* notario *m.*
convict *vt* probar un delito; * *n* convicto/ta *m/f.*
conviction *n* convicción *f.*
convince *vt* convencer, poner en evidencia.
convincing *adj* convincente.
convincingly *adv* de modo convincente.
convivial *adj* sociable; hospitalario/ria.
conviviality *n* sociabilidad *f.*
convoke *vt* convocar, reunir.
convoy *n* convoy *m.*
convulse *vt* conmover, convulsionar.
convulsion *n* convulsión *f*; conmoción *f*; tumulto *m.*
convulsive *adj* convulsivo/va; ~ly *adv* convulsivamente.
coo *vi* arrullar.
cook *n* cocinero/ra *m/f*; * *vt* cocinar; * *vi* cocinar; guisar.
cookbook *n* libro de cocina *m.*
cooker *n* cocina *f.*
cookery *n* arte culinario *m*, cocina *f.*
cookie *n* galleta *f.*
cool *adj* fresco/ca; indiferente; * *n* frescura *f*; * *vt* enfriar, refrescar.
coolly *adv* frescamente; indiferentemente.
coolness *n* fresco *m*; frialdad, frescura *f.*
cooperate *vi* cooperar.
cooperation *n* cooperación *f.*
cooperative *adj* cooperativo/va; cooperante.
coordinate *vt* coordinar.
coordination *n* coordinación, elección *f.*
cop *n* (*col*) poli *m.*

copartner *n* compañero/ra, socio/cia *m/f.*
cope *vi* arreglárselas.
copier *n* copiadora *f.*
copious *adj* copioso/sa, abundante; ~ly *adv* en abundancia.
copper *n* cobre *m.*
coppice, copse *n* bosquecillo *m.*
copulate *vi* copular.
copy *n* copia *f*; original *m*; ejemplar *m*; * *vt* copiar; imitar.
copybook *n* copiador de cartas (libro) *m.*
copying machine *n* copiadora *f.*
copyist *n* copista *m/f.*
copyright *n* propiedad de una obra literaria *f*; derechos de autor *mpl.*
coral *n* coral *m.*
coral reef *n* arrecife de coral *m.*
cord *n* cuerda *f*; cable *m.*
cordial *adj* cordial, de corazón, amistoso/ sa; ~ly *adv* cordialmente.
corduroy *n* pana *f.*
core *n* cuesco *m*; interior, centro, corazón *m*, materia *f*,
cork *n* alcornoque *m*; corcho *m*; * *vt* encorchar.
corkscrew *n* sacacorchos *m invar.*
corn[1] *n* maíz *m*; borona *f*; granos *mpl.*
corn[2] *n* callo *m.*
corncob *n* mazorca *f.*
cornea *n* córnea *f.*
corned beef *n* carne acecinada *f.*
corner *n* rincón *m*; esquina *f.*
cornerstone *n* piedra angular *f.*
cornet *n* corneta *f.*
cornfield *n* maizal *m.*
cornflakes *npl* copos de maíz *mpl.*
cornice *n* cornisa *f.*
cornstarch *n* harina de maíz *f.*
corollary *n* corolario *m.*
coronary *n* infarto *m.*
coronation *n* coronación *f.*
coroner *n* oficial que hace la inspección jurídica de los cadáveres *m.*
coronet *n* corona pequeña *f.*
corporal *n* cabo *m.*
corporate *adj* corporativo/va.
corporation *n* corporación *f*; gremio *m.*
corporeal *adj* corpóreo/rea.
corps *n* cuerpo (de ejército) *m*; regimiento *m.*
corpse *n* cadáver *m.*
corpulent *adj* corpulento/ta, gordo/da.
corpuscle *n* corpúsculo, átomo *m.*
corral *n* corral *m.*
correct *vt* corregir; enmendar; * *adj*

correcto/ta, justo/ta; ~ly adv correctamente.
correction n corrección f; enmienda f; censura f.
corrective adj correctivo/va; * n correctivo m; restricción f.
correctness n exactitud f.
correlation n correlación f.
correlative adj correlativo/va.
correspond vi corresponder; corresponderse.
correspondence n correspondencia f.
correspondent adj correspondiente, conforme; * n corresponsal m.
corridor n pasillo m.
corroborate vt corroborar.
corroboration n corroboración f.
corroborative adj corroborativo/va.
corrode vt corroer.
corrosion n corrosión f.
corrosive adj, n corrosivo m.
corrugated iron n chapa ondulada f.
corrupt vt corromper; sobornar; * vi corromperse, pudrirse; * adj corrompido/da; depravado/da.
corruptible adj corruptible.
corruption n corrupción f; depravación f.
corruptive adj corruptivo/va.
corset n corsé, corpiño m.
cortege n cortejo m.
cosmetic adj cosmético/ca; * n cosmético m.
cosmic adj cósmico/ca.
cosmonaut n cosmonauta m/f.
cosmopolitan adj cosmopolita.
cosset vt mimar.
cost n coste, precio m; * vi costar.
costly adj costoso/sa, caro/ra.
costume n traje m.
cottage n casita, casucha f.
cotton n algodón m.
cotton candy n algodón azucarado m.
cotton mill n hilandería de algodón.
cotton wool n algodón hidrófilo m.
couch n sofá m.
couchette n litera f.
cough n tos f; * vi toser.
council n concilio, consejo m.
councilor n concejal/a m/f.
counsel n consejo, aviso m; abogado/da m/f.
counselor n consejero/ra m/f; abogado/da m/f.
count vt contar, numerar; calcular; to ~ on contar con; * n cuenta f; cálculo m; conde m.

countdown n cuenta atrás f.
countenance n rostro m; aspecto m; (buena/mala) cara f.
counter n mostrador m; ficha f.
counteract vt contrariar, impedir, estorbar; frustrar.
counterbalance vt contrapesar; igualar, compensar; * n contrapeso m.
counterfeit vt contrahacer, imitar, falsear; * adj falsificado/da; fingido/da.
countermand vt contramandar; revocar.
counterpart n parte correspondiente f.
counterproductive adj contraproducente.
countersign vt refrendar; firmar un decreto.
countess n condesa f.
countless adj innumerable.
countrified adj rústico/ca; tosco/ca, rudo/da.
country n país m; campo m; región f; patria f; * adj rústico/ca; campestre, rural.
country house n casa de campo, granja f.
countryman n paisano m; compatriota m.
county n condado m.
coup n golpe m.
coupé n (auto) cupé m.
couple n par m; lazo m; yuntas fpl; * vt unir, parear; casar.
couplet n copla f; par m.
coupon n cupón m.
courage n coraje, valor f.
courageous adj corajudo/da, valeroso/sa; ~ly adv valerosamente.
courier n correo, mensajero/ra m/f, expreso m.
course n curso m; carrera f; camino m; ruta f; método m; of ~ por supuesto, sin duda.
court n corte f; palacio m; tribunal de justicia m, Lat Am corte f; * vt cortejar; solicitar, adular.
courteous adj cortés; benévolo/la; ~ly adv cortésmente.
courtesan n cortesana f.
courtesy n cortesía f; benignidad f.
courthouse n palacio de justicia m.
courtly adj cortesano/na, elegante.
court martial n consejo de guerra m.
courtroom n sala de justicia f.
courtyard n patio m.
cousin n primo m; prima f; first ~ primo hermano m.
cove n (mar) ensenada, caleta f.
covenant n contrato m; convención f; * vi pactar, estipular.
cover n cubierta f; abrigo m; pretexto m; * vt cubrir; tapar; ocultar; proteger.

coverage n alcance m.

coveralls npl mono m; Lat Am overol m.

covering n ropa f; vestido m.

cover letter n carta de explicación f.

covert adj cubierto/ta; oculto/ta, secreto/ta; ~ly adv secretamente.

cover-up n encubrimiento m.

covet vt codiciar, desear con ansia.

covetous adj avariento/ta, sórdido/da.

cow n vaca f.

coward n cobarde m/f.

cowardice n cobardía, timidez f.

cowardly adj, adv cobarde; pusilánime.

cowboy, cowhand n vaquero m.

cower vi agacharse.

cowherd n vaquero m; vaquerizo m.

coy adj recatado/da, modesto/ta; esquivo/va; ~ly adv con esquivez.

coyness n esquivez, modestia f.

cozily adv cómodamente, con facilidad.

cozy adj cómodo/da.

crab n cangrejo m; manzana silvestre f.

crab apple n manzana silvestre f; ~ tree n manzano silvestre m.

crack n crujido m; hendedura, quebraja f; * vt hender, rajar; romper; to ~ down on reprimandar fuertemente;* vi reventar.

cracker n buscapiés m invar; galleta f.

crackle vi crujir, chillar.

crackling n estallido, crujido m.

cradle n cuna f; * vt acunar.

craft n arte m; artificio m; barco m.

craftily adv astutamente.

craftiness n astucia, estratagema f.

craftsman n artífice, artesano m.

craftsmanship n artesanía f.

crafty adj astuto/ta, artificioso/sa.

crag n despeñadero m.

cram vt embutir; engordar; empujar; * vi empollar.

crammed adj atestado/da.

cramp n calambre m; * vt constreñir.

cramped adj apretado/da.

crampon n crampón m.

cranberry n arándano agrio m.

crane n grulla f; grúa f.

crash vi estallar; * vr zamparse; * n estallido m; choque m.

crash helmet n casco m.

crash landing n aterrizaje forzoso m.

crass adj craso/sa, grueso/sa, basto/ta, tosco/ca, grosero/ra.

crate n cesta grande f.

crater n cráter m; boca de volcán f.

cravat n pañuelo m.

crave vt rogar, suplicar.

craving adj insaciable, pedigüeño/ña; * n deseo ardiente m.

crawfish n cangrejo de río m.

crawl vi arrastrar; to ~ with hormiguear.

crayon n lápiz m.

craze n manía f.

craziness n locura f.

crazy adj loco/ca.

creak vi crujir, chirriar.

cream n crema f; * adj color crema.

creamy adj cremoso/sa.

crease n pliegue m; * vt plegar.

create vt crear; causar.

creation n creación f; elección f.

creative adj creativo/va.

creator n creador/a m/f.

creature n criatura f.

credence n creencia, fe f; renombre m.

credentials npl (cartas) credenciales fpl.

credibility n credibilidad f.

credible adj creíble.

credit n crédito m; reputación f; autoridad f; * vt creer, fiar, acreditar.

creditable adj estimable, honorífico/ca; ~bly adv honorablemente.

credit card n tarjeta de crédito f.

creditor n acreedor m.

credulity n credulidad f.

credulous adj crédulo/la; ~ly adv con credulidad.

creed n credo m.

creek n arroyo m.

creep vi arrastrar, serpear; complacer bajamente.

creeper n (bot) enredadera f.

creepy adj horripilante.

cremate vt incinerar cadáveres.

cremation n cremación f.

crematorium n crematorio m.

crescent adj creciente; * n cuarto creciente m.

cress n berro m.

crest n cresta f.

crested adj crestado/da.

crestfallen adj acobardado/da, abatido/da de espíritu.

crevasse n grieta (de glaciar) f.

crevice n raja, hendedura f.

crew n banda, tropa f; tripulación f.

crib n cuna f; pesebre m.

cricket n grillo m; críquet m.

crime n crimen m; culpa f.

criminal adj criminal, reo/rea; ~ly adv criminalmente; * n criminal m/f.

criminality *n* criminalidad *f.*
crimson *adj*, *n* carmesí *m.*
cripple *vt* lisiar; (*fig*) estropear.
crisis *n* crisis *f invar.*
crisp *adj* crujiente.
crispness *n* sequedad *f.*
criss-cross *adj* entrelazado/da.
criterion *n* criterio *m.*
critic *n* crítico *m;* crítica *f.*
critic(al) *adj* crítico/ca; exacto/ta; delicado/
da; ~ally *adv* exactamente, rigurosamente.
criticism *n* crítica *f.*
criticize *vt* criticar, censurar; zaherir; (*fig*)
zurrar.
croak *vi* graznar.
crochet *n* ganchillo *m;* * *vt*, *vi* hacer
ganchillo.
crockery *n* loza *f;* vasijas de barro *fpl.*
crocodile *n* cocodrilo *m.*
crony *n* amigote *m;* compinche *m.*
crook *n* (*col*) ladrón *m;* cayado *m.*
crooked *adj* torcido/da; perverso/sa.
crop *n* cultivo *m;* cosecha *f;* * *vt* recortar.
cross *n* cruz *f;* carga *f;* * *adj* mal humorado/
da; * *vt* atravesar, cruzar; **to ~ over**
traspasar.
crossbar *n* travesaño *m.*
crossbreed *n* raza cruzada *f.*
cross-country *n* carrera a campo traviesa *f.*
cross-examine *vt* preguntar a un testigo.
crossfire *n* fuego cruzado *m.*
crossing *n* cruce *m;* paso a nivel *m.*
cross-purpose *n* disposición contraria *f;*
contradicción *f;* **to be at ~s** entenderse mal.
cross-reference *n* remisión *f.*
crossroad *n* encrucijada *f.*
crosswalk *n* paso de peatones *m.*
crotch *n* entrepierna *f.*
crouch *vi* agacharse, bajarse.
crow *n* cuervo *m;* canto del gallo *m;* * *vi*
cantar el gallo.
crowd *n* público *m;* muchedumbre *f;* * *vt*
amontonar; * *vi* reunirse.
crown *n* corona *f;* cumbre *f;* * *vt* coronar.
crown prince *n* príncipe real *m.*
crucial *adj* crucial.
crucible *n* crisol *m.*
crucifix *n* crucifijo *m.*
crucifixion *n* crucifixión *f.*
crucify *vt* crucificar; atormentar.
crude *adj* crudo/da, imperfecto/ta; ~ly *adv*
crudamente.
cruel *adj* cruel, inhumano/na; ~ly *adv*
cruelmente.
cruelty *n* crueldad *f.*

cruet set/stand *n* vinagreras *fpl.*
cruise *n* crucero *m;* * *vi* hacer un crucero.
cruiser *n* crucero *m.*
crumb *n* miga *f.*
crumble *vt* desmigajar, desmenuzar; * *vi*
desmigajarse.
crumple *vt* arrugar.
crunch *vt* ronzar; * *n* (*fig*) crisis *f invar.*
crunchy *adj* crujiente.
crusade *n* cruzada *f.*
crush *vt* apretar, oprimir; * *n* choque *m.*
crust *n* costra *f;* corteza *f;* zoquete *m.*
crusty *adj* costroso/sa; bronco/ca, áspero/ra.
crutch *n* muleta *f.*
crux *n* lo esencial.
cry *vt*, *vi* gritar; exclamar; llorar; * *n* grito
m; lloro *m;* clamor *m.*
crypt *n* cripta *f.*
cryptic *adj* enigmático/ca.
crystal *n* cristal *m.*
crystal-clear *adj* claro/ra como el agua.
crystalline *adj* cristalino/na; transparente.
crystallize *vt* (*vi*) cristalizar(se).
cub *n* cachorro *m.*
cube *n* cubo *m.*
cubic *adj* cúbico/ca.
cuckoo *n* cuco *m.*
cucumber *n* pepino *m.*
cud *n:* **to chew the ~** rumiar; (*fig*) reflexionar.
cuddle *vt* abrazar; * *vi* abrazarse; * *n*
abrazo *m.*
cudgel *n* garrote, palo *m.*
cue *n* taco (de billar) *m.*
cuff[1] *n* puño *m,* bocamanga *f,* vuelta *f.*
cuff[2] *n* puñada *f.*
culinary *adj* culinario/ria, de la cocina.
cull *vt* escoger, elegir.
culminate *vi* culminar.
culmination *n* colmo *m.*
culpability *n* culpabilidad *f.*
culpable *adj* culpable, criminal; ~bly *adv*
culpablemente, criminalmente.
culprit *n* culpable *m/f.*
cult *n* culto *f.*
cultivate *vi* cultivar, mejorar; perfeccionar.
cultivation *n* cultivo *m.*
cultural *adj* cultural.
culture *n* cultura *f.*
cumbersome *adj* engorroso/sa, pesado/da,
confuso/sa.
cumulative *adj* cumulativo/va.
cunning *adj* astuto/ta; intrigante; ~ly *adv*
astutamente; expertamente; * *n* astucia,
sutileza *f;* ~ **person** zorro *m.*

cup *n* taza, jícara *f*; (*bot*) cáliz *m*.
cupboard *n* armario *m*.
curable *adj* curable.
curate *n* teniente de cura *m*; párroco *m*.
curator *n* curador/a *m/f*; guardián/ana *m/f*.
curb *n* freno *m*; bordillo *m*; * *vt* refrenar, contener, moderar.
curd *n* cuajada *f*.
curdle *vt* (*vi*) cuajar(se), coagular(se).
cure *n* cura *f*; remedio *m*; * *vt* curar, sanar.
curfew *n* toque de queda *m*.
curing *n* curación *f*.
curiosity *n* curiosidad *f*; rareza *f*.
curious *adj* curioso/sa; ~**ly** *adv* curiosamente.
curl *n* rizo de pelo *m*; * *vt* rizar; ondear; * *vi* rizarse.
curling iron *n*, **curling tongs** *npl* tenacillas de rizar *fpl*.
curly *adj* rizado/da.
currant *n* pasa *f*.
currency *n* moneda *f*; circulación *f*; duración *f*.
current *adj* corriente, común; * *n* curso, progreso *m*; marcha *f*; corriente *f*.
current affairs *npl* actualidades *fpl*.
currently *adv* actualmente.
curriculum vitae *n* currículum *m*.
curry *n* curry *m*.
curse *vt* maldecir; * *vi* imprecar; blasfemar; * *n* maldición *f*.
cursor *n* cursor *m*.
cursory *adj* precipitado/da, inconsiderado/da.
curt *adj* sucinto/ta.
curtail *vt* acortar.
curtsy *n* reverencia *f*; * *vi* hacer una reverencia.
curvature *n* curvatura *f*.
curve *vt* encorvar; * *n* curva *f*.

cushion *n* cojín *m*; almohada *f*.
custard *n* natillas *fpl*.
custodian *n* custodio *m*.
custody *n* custodia *f*; prisión *f*.
custom *n* costumbre *f*, uso *m*.
customary *adj* usual, acostumbrado/da, ordinario/ria.
customer *n* cliente *m/f*.
customs *npl* aduana *f*.
customs duty *n* derechos de aduana *mpl*.
customs officer *n* aduanero/ra *m/f*.
cut *vt* cortar; separar; herir; dividir; cortar los naipes; **to ~ short** interrumpir, cortar la palabra; **to ~ teeth** nacerle los dientes (a un niño); * *vi* traspasar; cruzarse; * *n* corte *m*; cortadura *f*; herida *f*; **~ and dried** *adj* rutinario/ria.
cutback *n* reducción *f*.
cute *adj* lindo/da.
cutlery *n* cuchillería *f*.
cutlet *n* chuleta *f*.
cut-rate *adj* a precio reducido.
cut-throat *n* asesino *m*; * *adj* encarnizado/da.
cutting *n* cortadura *f*; * *adj* cortante; mordaz.
cyanide *n* cianuro *m*.
cyberspace *n* ciberespacio *m*.
cycle *n* ciclo *m*; bicicleta *f*; * *vi* ir en bicicleta.
cycling *n* ciclismo *m*.
cyclist *n* ciclista *m/f*.
cyclone *n* ciclón *m*.
cygnet *n* pollo del cisne *m*.
cylinder *n* cilindro *m*; rollo *m*.
cylindric(al) *adj* cilíndrico/ca.
cymbals *n* címbalo *m*.
cynic(al) *adj* cínico/ca; obsceno/na; * *n* cínico *m* (filósofo).
cynicism *n* cinismo *m*.
cypress *n* ciprés *m*.
cyst *n* quiste *m*.
czar *n* zar *m*.

D

dab n pedazo pequeño m; toque m.
dabble vi chapotear.
dad(dy) n papa m.
daddy-long-legs n típula f.
daffodil n narciso m.
dagger n puñal m.
daily adj diario/ria, cotidiano/na; * adv diariamente, cada día; * n diario m.
daintily adv delicadamente.
daintiness n elegancia f; delicadeza f.
dainty adj delicado/da. elegante.
dairy n lechería f.
dairy farm n vaquería f.
dairy produce n productos lácteos mpl.
daisy n margarita, maya f.
dale n valle m.
dally vi tardar.
dam n presa f; * vt represar.
damage n daño m; perjuicio m; * dañar; perjudicar.
damask n damasco m; * adj de damasco.
damn vt condenar; * adj maldito/ta.
damnable adj maldito/ta; ~bly adv terriblemente.
damnation n perdición f.
damning adj irrecusable.
damp adj húmedo/da; * n humedad f; * vt mojar.
dampen vt mojar.
dampness n humedad f.
damson n damascena f (ciruela).
dance n danza f; baile m; * vi bailar.
dance hall n salón de baile m.
dancer n bailarín m, bailarina f.
dandelion n diente de león m.
dandruff n caspa f.
dandy adj mono/na.
danger n peligro, riesgo m.
dangerous adj peligroso/sa; ~ly adv peligrosamente.
dangle vi estar colgado/da.
dank adj húmedo/da.
dapper adj apuesto/ta.
dappled adj rodado/da.
dare vi atreverse; * vt desafiar.
daredevil n atrevido m.
daring n osadía f; * adj atrevido/da; ~ly adv atrevidamente, osadamente.
dark adj oscuro/ra; negro/gra; * n oscuridad f; ignorancia f.
darken vt (vi) oscurecer(se).

dark glasses npl gafas de sol fpl.
darkness n oscuridad f.
darkroom n cuarto oscuro m.
darling n, adj querido m.
darn vt zurcir.
dart n dardo m.
dartboard n diana f.
dash vi irse de prisa; * n pizca f; at one ~ de un golpe.
dashboard n tablero de instrumentos m.
dashing adj gallardo/da.
dastardly adj cobarde.
data n datos mpl.
database n base de datos f.
data processing n proceso de datos m.
date n fecha f; cita f; (bot) dátil m; * vt fechar; salir con.
dated adj anticuado/da.
dative n dativo m.
daub vt manchar.
daughter n hija f; ~ in-law nuera f.
daunting adj desalentador/a.
dawdle vi gastar tiempo.
dawn n alba f; * vi amanecer.
day n día m; luz f; by ~ de día; ~ by ~ de día en día.
daybreak n alba f.
day laborer n jornalero m.
daylight n luz del día, luz natural f; ~ saving time n hora de verano f.
daytime n día m.
daze vt aturdir.
dazed adj aturdido/da.
dazzle vt deslumbrar.
dazzling adj deslumbrante.
deacon n diácono m.
dead adj muerto/ta. marchito/ta; ~wood n lastre m; ~ silence n silencio profundo m; the ~ npl los muertos.
dead-drunk adj borracho como una cuba.
deaden vt amortiguar.
dead heat n empate m.
deadline n fecha tope f.
deadlock n punto muerto m.
deadly adj mortal; * adv terriblemente.
dead march n marcha fúnebre f.
deadness n inercia f.
deaf adj sordo/da.
deafen vt ensordecer.
deaf-mute n sordomudo/da m./f.
deafness n sordera f.

deal *n* convenio *m*; transacción *f*; **a great ~** mucho; **a good ~** bastante; * *vt* distribuir; dar; * *vi* comerciar; **to ~ in/with** tratar en/con.

dealer *n* comerciante *m/f*; traficante *m/f*; mano *f*.

dealings *npl* trato *m*.

dean *n* deán *m*.

dear *adj* querido/da. caro/ra, costoso/sa; **~ly** *adv* caro.

dearness *n* carestía *f*.

dearth *n* escasez *f*.

death *n* muerte *f*.

deathbed *n* lecho de muerte *m*.

deathblow *n* golpe mortal *m*.

death certificate *n* partida de defunción *f*.

death penalty *n* pena de muerte *f*.

death throes *npl* agonía *f*.

death warrant *n* sentencia de muerte *f*.

debacle *n* desastre *m*.

debar *vt* excluir, no admitir.

debase *vt* degradar.

debasement *n* degradación *f*.

debatable *adj* discutible.

debate *n* debate *m*; polémica *f*; * *vt* discutir; examinar.

debauched *adj* vicioso/sa.

debauchery *n* libertinaje *m*.

debilitate *vt* debilitar.

debit *n* debe *m*; * *vt* (*com*) cargar en una cuenta.

debt *n* deuda *f*; obligación *f*; **to get into ~** contraer deudas.

debtor *n* deudor/a *m/f*.

debunk *vt* desacreditar.

decade *n* década *f*.

decadence *n* decadencia *f*.

decaffeinated *adj* descafeinado/da.

decanter *n* garrafa *f*.

decapitate *vt* decapitar, degollar.

decapitation *n* decapitación *f*.

decay *vi* decaer; pudrirse; * *n* decadencia *f*; caries *f*.

deceased *adj* muerto/ta.

deceit *n* engaño *m*.

deceitful *adj* engañoso/sa; **~ly** *adv* falsamente.

deceive *vt* engañar.

December *n* diciembre *m*.

decency *n* decencia *f*; modestia *f*.

decent *adj* decente, razonable; **~ly** *adv* decentemente.

deception *n* engaño *m*.

deceptive *adj* engañoso/sa.

decibel *n* decibelio *m*.

decide *vt, vi* decidir; resolver.

decided *adj* decidido/da.

decidedly *adv* decididamente.

deciduous *adj* (*bot*) de hoja caduca.

decimal *adj* decimal.

decimate *vt* diezmar.

decipher *vt* descifrar.

decision *n* decisión, determinación *f*.

decisive *adj* decisivo/va; **~ly** *adv* de modo decisivo.

deck *n* cubierta *f*; * *vt* adornar.

deckchair *n* tumbona *f*.

declaim *vi* declamar.

declamation *n* declamación *f*.

declaration *n* declaración *f*.

declare *vt* declarar, manifestar.

declension *n* declinación *f*.

decline *vt* (*gr*) declinar; evitar; * *vi* decaer; * *n* decadencia *f*.

declutch *vi* desembragar.

decode *vt* descifrar.

decoder *n* (*TV*) descodificador *m*.

decompose *vt* descomponer.

decomposition *n* descomposición *f*.

decor *n* decoración *f*.

decorate *vt* decorar, adornar.

decoration *n* decoración *f*.

decorative *adj* decorativo/va.

decorator *n* pintor (decorador) *m*.

decorous *adj* decoroso/sa; **~ly** *adv* decorosamente.

decorum *n* decoro, garbo *m*.

decoy *n* señuelo *m*.

decrease *vt* disminuir; * *n* disminución *f*.

decree *n* decreto *m*; * *vt* decretar; ordenar.

decrepit *adj* decrépito/ta.

decry *vt* desacreditar, censurar.

dedicate *vt* dedicar; consagrar.

dedication *n* dedicación *f*; dedicatoria *f*.

deduce *vt* deducir; concluir.

deduct *vt* restar.

deduction *n* deducción *f*; descuento *m*.

deed *n* acción *f*; hecho *m*; hazaña *f*.

deem *vi* juzgar.

deep *adj* profundo/da.

deepen *vt* profundizar.

deep-freeze *n* congeladora *f*.

deeply *adv* profundamente.

deepness *n* profundidad *f*.

deer *n* ciervo *m*.

deface *vt* desfigurar, afear.

defacement *n* desfiguración *f*.

defamation *n* difamación *f*.

default *n* defecto *m*; falta *f*; * *vi* faltar.

defaulter *n* (*law*) moroso/sa *m/f*.

defeat *n* derrota *f*; * *vt* derrotar; frustrar.
defect *n* defecto *m*; falta *f*.
defection *n* deserción *f*.
defective *adj* defectuoso/sa.
defend *vt* defender; proteger.
defendant *n* acusado/da *m/f*.
defense *n* defensa *f*; protección *f*.
defenseless *adj* indefenso/sa.
defensive *adj* defensivo/va; ~ly *adv* de
modo defensivo.
defer *vt* aplazar.
deference *n* deferencia *f*; respeto *m*.
deferential *adj* respetuoso/sa.
defiance *n* desafío *m*.
defiant *adj* insolente.
deficiency *n* defecto *m*; falta *f*.
deficient *adj* insuficiente.
deficit *n* déficit *m*, *Lat Am* faltante *m*.
defile *vt* ensuciar.
definable *adj* definible.
define *vt* definir.
definite *adj* definido/da. preciso/sa; ~ly *adv*
no cabe duda.
definition *n* definición *f*.
definitive *adj* definitivo/va; ~ly *adv*
definitivamente.
deflate *vt* desinflar.
deflect *vt* desviar.
deflower *vt* desvirgar.
deform *vt* desfigurar.
deformity *n* deformidad *f*.
defraud *vt* estafar.
defray *vt* costear.
defrost *vt* deshelar; descongelar.
defroster *n* luneta térmica *f*.
deft *adj* diestro/tra; ~ly *adv* hábilmente.
defunct *adj* difunto/ta.
defuse *vt* desactivar.
degenerate *vi* degenerar; * *adj* degenerado/
da.
degeneration *n* degeneración *f*.
degradation *n* degradación *f*.
degrade *vt* degradar.
degree *n* grado *m*; título *m*.
dehydrated *adj* deshidratado/da.
de-ice *vt* deshelar.
deign *vi* dignarse.
deity *n* deidad, divinidad *f*.
dejected *adj* desanimado/da.
dejection *n* desaliento *m*.
delay *vt* demorar; * *n* retraso *m*.
delectable *adj* deleitoso/sa.
delegate *vt* delegar; * *n* delegado *m*.
delegation *n* delegación *f*.
delete *vt* tachar; borrar.

deliberate *vt* deliberar; * *adj* intencionado/
da; ~ly *adv* a propósito.
deliberation *n* deliberación *f*.
deliberative *adj* deliberativo/va.
delicacy *n* delicadeza *f*.
delicate *adj* delicado/da. exquisito/ta; ~ly
adv delicadamente.
delicious *adj* delicioso/sa. exquisito/ta; ~ly
adv deliciosamente.
delight *n* delicia *f*; gozo, encanto *m*; * *vt*, *vi*
deleitar(se).
delighted *adj* encantado/da.
delightful *adj* encantador/a, ~ly *adv* en
forma encantadora.
delineate *vt* delinear.
delineation *n* delineación *f*.
delinquency *n* delincuencia *f*.
delinquent *n* delincuente *m/f*.
delirious *adj* delirante.
delirium *n* delirio *m*.
deliver *vt* entregar; pronunciar.
deliverance *n* liberación *f*.
delivery *n* entrega *f*; parto *m*.
delude *vt* engañar.
deluge *n* diluvio *m*.
delusion *n* engaño *m*; ilusión *f*.
delve *vi* hurgar.
demagog *n* demagogo/a *m/f*.
demand *n* demanda *f*; reclamación *f*; * *vt*
exigir; reclamar.
demanding *adj* exigente.
demarcation *n* demarcación *f*.
demean *vi* rebajarse.
demeanor *n* conducta *f*.
demented *adj* demente.
demise *n* desaparición *f*.
democracy *n* democracia *f*.
democrat *n* demócrata *m/f*.
democratic *adj* democrático/ca.
Democratic Party *n* Partido Democrático *m*.
demolish *vt* demoler.
demolition *n* demolición *f*.
demon *n* demonio, diablo *m*.
demonstrable *adj* demostrable; ~bly *adv*
manifiestamente.
demonstrate *vt* demostrar, probar; * *vi*
manifestarse.
demonstration *n* demostración *f*; manifestación *f*.
demonstrative *adj* demostrativo/va.
demonstrator *n* manifestante *m/f*.
demoralization *n* desmoralización *f*.
demoralize *vt* desmoralizar.
demote *vt* degradar.

demur *vi* objetar.

demure *adj* modesto/ta; ~ly *adv* modestamente.

den *n* guarida *f*.

denatured alcohol *n* alcohol desnaturalizado *m*.

denial *n* negación *f*.

denims *npl* vaqueros *mpl*.

denomination *n* valor *m*.

denominator *n* (*math*) denominador *m*.

denote *vt* denotar, indicar.

denounce *vt* denunciar.

dense *adj* denso/sa, espeso/sa.

density *n* densidad *f*.

dent *n* abolladura *f*; * *vt* abollar.

dental *adj* dental.

dentifrice *n* dentífrico *m*.

dentist *n* dentista *m/f*.

dentistry *n* odontología *f*.

denture *npl* dentadura postiza *f*.

denude *vt* desnudar, despojar.

denunciation *n* denuncia *f*.

deny *vt* negar.

deodorant *n* desodorante *m*.

deodorize *vt* desodorizar.

depart *vi* partir.

department *n* departamento *m*.

department store *n* gran almacén *m*.

departure *n* partida *f*.

departure lounge *n* sala de embarque *f*.

depend *vi* depender; ~ on/upon contar con.

dependable *adj* seguro/ra, serio/ria.

dependant *n* dependiente *m*.

dependency *n* dependencia *f*.

dependent *adj* dependiente.

depict *vt* pintar, retratar; describir.

depleted *adj* reducido/da.

deplorable *adj* deplorable, lamentable; ~bly *adv* deplorablemente.

deplore *vt* deplorar, lamentar.

deploy *vt* (*mil*) desplegar.

depopulated *adj* despoblado/da.

depopulation *n* despoblación *f*.

deport *vt* deportar.

deportation *n* deportación *f*; destierro *m*.

deportment *n* conducta *f*.

deposit *vt* depositar; * *n* depósito *m*; yacimiento *m*.

deposition *n* deposición *f*.

depositor *n* depositante *m*.

depot *n* depósito *m*.

deprave *vt* depravar, corromper.

depraved *adj* depravado/da.

depravity *n* depravación *f*.

deprecate *vt* lamentar.

depreciate *vi* depreciarse.

depreciation *n* depreciación *f*.

depredation *n* pillaje *m*.

depress *vt* deprimir.

depressed *adj* deprimido/da.

depression *n* depresión *f*.

deprivation *n* privación *f*.

deprive *vt* privar.

deprived *adj* necesitado/da.

depth *n* profundidad *f*.

deputation *n* diputación *f*.

depute *vt* diputar, delegar.

deputize *vi* suplir a.

deputy *n* diputado/da *m/f*.

derail *vt* descarrilar.

deranged *adj* trastornado/da.

derby *n* hongo *m*.

derelict *adj* abandonado/da.

deride *vt* burlar.

derision *n* mofa *f*.

derisive *adj* irrisorio/ria.

derivable *adj* deducible.

derivation *n* derivación *f*.

derivative *n* derivado *m*.

derive *vt* (*vi*) derivar(se).

dermatologist *n* dermatólogo/ga *m/f*.

dermatology *n* dermatología *f*.

derogatory *adj* despectivo/va.

derrick *n* torre de perforación *f*.

desalinate *vt* desalinizar.

desalination plant *n* desalinizadora *f*.

descant *n* (*mus*) discante *m*.

descend *vi* descender.

descendant *n* descendiente *m*.

descent *n* descenso *m*.

describe *vt* describir.

description *n* descripción *f*.

descriptive *adj* descriptivo/va.

descry *vt* divisar.

desecrate *vt* profanar.

desecration *n* profanación *f*.

desert[1] *n* desierto *m*; * *adj* desierto/ta.

desert[2] *vt* abandonar; desertar; * *n* mérito *m*.

deserter *n* desertor/a *m/f*.

desertion *n* deserción *f*.

deserve *vt* merecer, *Lat Am* ameritar; ser digno/na.

deservedly *adv* merecidamente.

deserving *adj* meritorio/ria.

desideratum *n* desiderátum *m*.

design *vt* diseñar; * *n* diseño *m*; dibujo *m*.

designate *vt* nombrar; designar.

designation *n* designación *f*.

designedly *adv* a propósito.

designer *n* diseñador *m*; modisto *m*.

desirability *n* conveniencia *f.*
desirable *adj* deseable.
desire *n* deseo *m;* * *vt* desear.
desirous *adj* deseoso/sa, ansioso/sa.
desist *vi* desistir.
desk *n* escritorio *m.*
desktop publishing *n* autoedición *f.*
desolate *adj* desierto/ta.
desolation *n* desolación *f.*
despair *n* desesperación *f;* * *vi* desesperarse.
despairingly *adj* desesperadamente.
desperado *n* bandido/da *m/f.*
desperate *adj* desesperado/da; ~ly *adv* desesperadamente; sumamente.
desperation *n* desesperación *f.*
despicable *adj* despreciable.
despise *vt* despreciar.
despite *prep* a pesar de.
despoil *vt* despojar.
despondency *n* abatimiento *m.*
despondent *adj* abatido/da.
despot *n* déspota *m/f.*
despotic *adj* despótico/ca, absoluto/ta; ~ally *adv* despóticamente.
despotism *n* despotismo *m.*
dessert *n* postre *m.*
destination *n* destino *m.*
destine *vt* destinar.
destiny *n* destino *m;* suerte *f.*
destitute *adj* indigente.
destitution *n* miseria *f.*
destroy *vt* destruir, arruinar.
destruction *n* destrucción, ruina *f.*
destructive *adj* destructivo/va.
desultory *adj* irregular; sin método.
detach *vt* separar.
detachable *adj* desmontable; de quitapón.
detachment *n* (*mil*) destacamento *m.*
detail *n* detalle *m;* in ~ detalladamente; * *vt* detallar.
detain *vt* retener; detener.
detect *vt* detectar.
detection *n* descubrimiento *m.*
detective *n* detective *m/f.*
detector *n* detector *m.*
detention *n* detención *f.*
deter *vt* disuadir.
detergent *n* detergente *m.*
deteriorate *vt* deteriorar.
deterioration *n* deterioro *m.*
determination *n* resolución *f.*
determine *vt* determinar, decidir.
determined *adj* resuelto/ta.
deterrent *n* fuerza de disuasión *f.*

detest *vt* detestar, aborrecer.
detestable *adj* detestable, abominable.
dethrone *vt* destronar.
dethronement *n* destronamiento *m.*
detonate *vi* detonar.
detonation *n* detonación *f.*
detour *n* desviación *f.*
detract *vt* desvirtuar.
detriment *n* perjuicio *m.*
detrimental *adj* perjudicial.
deuce *n* deuce *m.*
devaluation *n* devaluación *f.*
devastate *vt* devastar.
devastating *adj* devastador.
devastation *n* devastación, ruina *f.*
develop *vt* desarrollar.
development *n* desarrollo *m.*
deviate *vi* desviarse.
deviation *n* desviación *f.*
device *n* mecanismo *m.*
devil *n* diablo, demonio *m.*
devilish *adj* diabólico/ca; ~ly *adv* diabólicamente.
devious *adj* taimado/da.
devise *vt* inventar; idear.
devoid *adj* desprovisto/ta.
devolve *vt* delegar.
devote *vt* dedicar; consagrar.
devoted *adj* fiel.
devotee *n* partidario/a *m/f.*
devotion *n* devoción *f.*
devotional *adj* devoto/ta.
devour *vt* devorar.
devout *adj* devoto/ta, piadoso/sa; ~ly *adv* piadosamente.
dew *n* rocío *m.*
dewy *adj* rociado/da.
dexterity *n* destreza *f.*
dexterous *adj* diestro/tra, hábil.
diabetes *n* diabetes *f.*
diabetic *n* diabético/ca *m/f.*
diabolic *adj* diabólico/ca; ~ally *adv* diabólicamente.
diadem *n* diadema *f.*
diagnosis *n* (*med*) diagnóstico *m.*
diagnostic *adj, n* diagnóstico *m;* ~s *pl* diagnóstica *f.*
diagonal *adj, n* diagonal *f;* ~ly *adv* diagonalmente.
diagram *n* diagrama *m.*
dial *n* cuadrante *m;* disco *m.*
dial code *n* prefijo *m.*
dialect *n* dialecto *m.*
dialog *n* diálogo *m.*
dial tone *n* tono de marcar *m.*

diameter *n* diámetro *m*.
diametrical *adj* diametral; ~ly *adv* diametralmente.
diamond *n* diamante *m*.
diamond-cutter *n* diamantista *m/f*.
diamonds *npl* (cards) diamantes *mpl*.
diaper *n* pañal *m*; **disposable** ~ pañal desechable.
diaphragm *n* diafragma *m*.
diarrhea *n* diarrea *f*.
diary *n* diario *m*.
dice *npl* dados *mpl*.
dictate *vt* dictar; * *n* dictado *m*.
dictation *n* dictado *m*.
dictatorial *adj* autoritativo/va, magistral.
dictatorship *n* dictadura *f*.
diction *n* dicción *f*
dictionary *n* diccionario *m*.
didactic *adj* didáctico/ca.
die[1] *vi* morir; **to** ~ **away** perderse; **to** ~ **down** apagarse.
die[2] *n* dado *m*.
diehard *n* reaccionario/ria *m/f*
diesel *n* diesel *m*.
diet *n* dieta *f*; régimen *m*; * *vi* estar a dieta.
dietary *adj* dictético/ca.
differ *vi* diferenciarse.
difference *n* diferencia, disparidad *f*.
different *adj* diferente; ~ly *adv* diferentemente.
differentiate *vt* diferenciar.
difficult *adj* difícil.
difficulty *n* dificultad *f*.
diffidence *n* timidez *f*.
diffident *adj* desconfiado/da; ~ly *adv* desconfiadamente.
diffraction *n* difracción *f*.
diffuse *vt* difundir, esparcir; * *adj* difuso/sa.
diffusion *n* difusión *f*.
dig *vt* cavar; **to** ~ **ditches** zanjar; * *n* empujón *m*.
digest *vt* digerir.
digestible *adj* digerible.
digestion *n* digestión *f*.
digestive *adj* digestivo/va.
digit *n* dígito *m*.
digital *adj* digital.
digitize *vt* digitalizar.
dignified *adj* grave.
dignitary *n* dignatario *m*.
dignity *n* dignidad *f*.
digress *vi* divagar.
digression *n* digresión *f*.
dike *n* dique *m*.
dilapidated *adj* desmoronado/da.

dilapidation *n* ruina *f*.
dilate *vt*, *vi* dilatar(se).
dilemma *n* dilema *m*.
diligence *n* diligencia *f*.
diligent *adj* diligente, asiduo/dua; ~ly *adv* diligentemente.
dilute *vt* diluir.
dim *adj* turbio/bia; lerdo/da; oscuro/ra; * *vt* bajar.
dime *n* moneda de diez centavos *f*.
dimension *n* dimensión, extensión *f*.
diminish *vt* (*vi*) disminuir(se).
diminution *n* disminución *f*.
diminutive *n* diminutivo *m*.
dimly *adv* indistintamente.
dimmer *n* interruptor *m*.
dimple *n* hoyuelo *m*, *Lat Am* hoyito *m*.
din *n* alboroto *m*.
dine *vi* cenar.
diner *n* restaurante (económico) *m*.
dinghy *n* lancha neumática *f*.
dingy *adj* sombrío/ría.
dinner *n* cena *f*.
dinner-jacket *n* smoking *m*.
dinner time *n* hora de comer *f*.
dinosaur *n* dinosaurio *m*.
dint *n*: **by** ~ **of** a fuerza de.
diocese *n* diócesis *f invar*.
dip *vt* mojar; * *n* zambullida *f*.
diphtheria *n* difteria *f*.
diphthong *n* diptongo *m*.
diploma *n* diploma *m*.
diplomacy *n* diplomacia *f*.
diplomat *n* diplomático/ca *m/f*.
diplomatic *adj* diplomático/ca.
dipsomania *n* dipsomanía *f*.
dipstick *n* (*auto*) varilla de nivel *f*.
dire *adj* calamitoso/sa.
direct *adj* directo/ta; * *vt* dirigir.
direction *n* dirección *f*; instrucción *f*.
directly *adj* directamente; inmediatamente.
director *n* director/a *m/f*.
directory *n* guía *f*.
dirt *n* suciedad *f*; ~ **on clothes** zarpa *f*.
dirtiness *n* suciedad *f*.
dirty *adj* sucio/cia; vil, bajo/ja.
disability *n* discapacidad *f*.
disabled *adj* discapacitado/da.
disabuse *vt* desengañar.
disadvantage *n* desventaja *f*; * *vt* perjudicar.
disadvantageous *adj* desventajoso/sa.
disaffected *adj* descontento/ta.
disagree *vi* no estar de acuerdo.
disagreeable *adj* desagradable; ~bly *adv* desagradablemente.

disagreement *n* desacuerdo *m*.
disallow *vt* rechazar.
disappear *vi* desaparecer; ausentarse.
disappearance *n* desaparición *f*.
disappoint *vt* decepcionar.
disappointed *adj* decepcionado/da.
disappointing *adj* decepcionante.
disappointment *n* decepción *f*.
disapproval *n* desaprobación, censura *f*.
disapprove *vt* desaprobar.
disarm *vt* desarmar.
disarmament *n* desarme *m*.
disarray *n* desarreglo *m*.
disaster *n* desastre *m*.
disastrous *adj* desastroso/sa, calamitoso/sa.
disband *vt* disolver.
disbelief *n* incredulidad *f*.
disbelieve *vt* desconfiar.
disburse *vt* desembolsar, pagar.
discard *vt* descartar.
discern *vt* discernir, percibir.
discernible *adj* perceptible.
discerning *adj* perspicaz.
discernment *n* perspicacia *f*.
discharge *vt* descargar; pagar (una deuda);
cumplir; * *n* descarga *f*; descargo *m*.
disciple *n* discípulo/la *m/f*.
discipline *n* disciplina *f*; * *vt* disciplinar.
disclaim *vt* negar.
disclaimer *n* negación *f*.
disclose *vi* revelar.
disclosure *n* revelación *f*.
discolor *vt* descolorar.
discoloration *n* descolorimiento *m*.
discomfort *n* incomodidad *f*.
disconcert *vt* desconcertar.
disconnect *vt* desconectar.
disconsolate *adj* inconsolable; ~ly *adv*
desconsoladamente.
discontent *n* descontento/ta *m/f*; * *adj*
descontento/ta.
discontented *adj* descontento/ta.
discontinue *vi* interrumpir.
discord *n* discordia *f*.
discordant *adj* discordante.
discotheque, disco *n* discoteca *f*.
discount *n* descuento *m*; rebaja *f*; * *vt*
descontar.
discourage *vt* desalentar, desanimar.
discouraged *adj* desalentado/da.
discouragement *n* desaliento *m*.
discouraging *adj* desalentador/a.
discourse *n* discurso *m*.
discourteous *adj* descortés, grosero/ra; ~ly
adv descortésmente.

discourtesy *n* descortesía *f*.
discover *vt* descubrir.
discovery *n* descubrimiento *m*; revelación *f*.
discredit *vt* desacreditar.
discreditable *adj* ignominioso/sa.
discreet *adj* discreto/ta; ~ly *adv* dis-
cretamente.
discrepancy *n* discrepancia, diferencia *f*.
discretion *n* discreción *f*.
discretionary *adj* discrecional.
discriminate *vt* distinguir.
discrimination *n* discriminación *f*.
discursive *adj* discursivo/va.
discuss *vt* discutir.
discussion *n* discusión *f*.
disdain *vt* desdeñar; * *n* desdén, desprecio *m*.
disdainful *adj* desdeñoso/sa; ~ly *adv*
desdeñosamente.
disease *n* enfermedad *f*.
diseased *adj* enfermo/ma.
disembark *vt, vi* desembarcar.
disembarkation *n* desembarco *m*.
disenchant *vt* desencantar.
disenchanted *adj* desilusionado/da.
disenchantment *n* desilusión *f*.
disengage *vt* soltar.
disentangle *vt* desenredar.
disfigure *vt* desfigurar, afear.
disgrace *n* ignominia *f*; escándalo *m*; * *vt*
deshonrar.
disgraceful *adj* ignominioso/sa; ~ly *adv*
vergonzosamente.
disgruntled *adj* descontento/ta.
disguise *vt* disfrazar; * *n* disfraz *m*.
disgust *n* aversión *f*; * *vt* repugnar.
disgusting *adj* repugnante.
dish *n* fuente *f*; plato *m*; taza *f*; * *vt* servir en
fuente; to ~ up servir.
dishabille *n* deshabillé *m*.
dishcloth *n* paño de cocina *m*.
dishearten *vt* desalentar.
disheveled *adj* desarreglado/da.
dishonest *adj* deshonesto/ta; ~ly *adv*
deshonestamente.
dishonesty *n* falta de honradez *f*.
dishonor *n* deshonra, ignominia *f*; * *vt*
deshonrar.
dishonorable *adj* deshonroso/sa; ~bly *adv*
deshonrosamente.
dishtowel *n* trapo de fregar *m*.
dishwarmer *n* escalfador *m*.
dishwasher *n* lavaplatos *m/f*; lavavajillas
m invar.

disillusion *vt* desilusionar.
disillusioned *adj* desilusionado/da.
disincentive *n* freno *m*.
disinclination *n* aversión *f*.
disinclined *adj* reacio/cia.
disinfect *vt* desinfectar.
disinfectant *n* desinfectante *m*.
disinherit *vt* desheredar.
disintegrate *vi* disgregarse.
disinterested *adj* desinteresado/da; ~ly *adv* desinteresadamente.
disjointed *adj* inconexo/xa.
disk *n* disco.
diskette *n* disco, disquete *m*.
dislike *n* aversión *f*; * *vt* tener antipatía.
dislocate *vt* dislocar.
dislocation *n* dislocación *f*.
dislodge *vt, vi* desalojar.
disloyal *adj* desleal; ~ly *adv* deslealmente.
disloyalty *n* deslealtad *f*.
dismal *adj* triste.
dismantle *vt* desmontar.
dismay *n* consternación *f*.
dismember *vt* despedazar.
dismiss *vt* despedir, *Lat Am* remover.
dismount *vt* desmontar; * *vi* apearse.
disobedience *n* desobediencia *f*.
disobedient *adj* desobediente.
disobey *vt* desobedecer.
disorder *n* desorden *m*; confusión *f*.
disorderly *adj* desarreglado/da, confuso/sa.
disorganization *n* desorganización *f*.
disorganized *adj* desorganizado/da.
disorientated *adj* desorientado/da.
disown *vt* desconocer.
disparage *vt* despreciar.
disparaging *adj* despreciativo/va.
disparity *n* disparidad *f*.
dispassionate *adj* desapasionado/da.
dispatch *vt* enviar; * *n* envío *m*; informe *m*.
dispel *vt* disipar.
dispensary *n* dispensario *m*.
dispense *vt* dispensar; distribuir.
disperse *vt* dispersar.
dispirited *adj* desalentado/da.
displace *vt* desplazar.
display *vt* exponer; * *n* ostentación *f*; despliegue *m*.
displeased *adj* disgustado/da.
displeasure *n* disgusto *m*.
disposable *adj* desechable.
disposal *n* disposición *f*.
dispose *vt* disponer; arreglar.
disposed *adj* dispuesto/ta.
disposition *n* disposición *f*.

dispossess *vt* desposeer.
disproportionate *adj* desproporcionado/da.
disprove *vt* refutar.
dispute *n* disputa, controversia *f*; * *vt* disputar.
disqualify *vt* incapacitar.
disquiet *n* inquietud *f*.
disquieting *adj* inquietante.
disquisition *n* disquisición *f*.
disregard *vt* desatender; * *n* desdén *m*.
disreputable *adj* de mala fama.
disrespect *n* irreverencia *f*.
disrespectful *adj* irreverente; ~ly *adv* irreverentemente.
disrobe *vt* desnudar.
disrupt *vt* interrumpir.
disruption *n* interrupción *f*.
dissatisfaction *n* descontento/ta, disgusto *m*.
dissatisfied *adj* insatisfecho/cha.
dissect *vt* disecar.
dissection *n* disección *f*.
disseminate *vt* diseminar.
dissension *n* disensión *f*.
dissent *vi* disentir; * *n* disensión *f*.
dissenter *n* disidente *m*.
dissertation *n* disertación *f*.
dissident *n* disidente *m*.
dissimilar *adj* distinto/ta.
dissimilarity *n* disimilitud *f*.
dissimulation *n* disimulo *m*.
dissipate *vt* disipar.
dissipation *n* disipación *f*.
dissociate *vt* disociar.
dissolute *adj* libertino/na.
dissolution *n* disolución *f*.
dissolve *vt* disolver; * *vi* disolverse, derretirse.
dissonance *n* disonancia *f*.
dissuade *vt* disuadir.
distance *n* distancia *f*; at a ~ de lejos; * *vt* apartar.
distant *adj* distante.
distaste *n* disgusto *m*.
distasteful *adj* desagradable.
distend *vt* hinchar.
distill *vt* destilar.
distillation *n* destilación *f*.
distillery *n* destilería *f*.
distinct *adj* distinto/ta, diferente; claro/ra; ~ly *adv* distintamente.
distinction *n* distinción *f*.
distinctive *adj* distintivo/va.
distinctness *n* claridad *f*.
distinguish *vt* distinguir; discernir.

distort *vt* retorcer.
distorted *adj* distorsionado/da.
distortion *n* distorción *f.*
distract *vt* distraer.
distracted *adj* distraído/da; ~ly *adj* distraídamente.
distraction *n* distracción *f*; confusión *f.*
distraught *adj* enloquecido/da.
distress *n* angustia *f*; * *vt* angustiar.
distressing *adj* penoso/sa.
distribute *vt* distribuir, repartir.
distribution *n* distribución *f.*
distributor *n* distribuidor *m.*
district *n* distrito *m.*
district attorney *n* fiscal del distrito *m/f.*
distrustful *adj* desconfiado/da. sospechoso/sa.
disturb *vt* molestar.
disturbance *n* disturbio *m.*
disturbed *adj* preocupado/da.
disturbing *adj* inquietante.
disuse *n* desuso *m.*
disused *adj* abandonado/da.
ditch *n* zanja *f.*
dither *vi* vacilar.
ditto *adv* ídem.
ditty *n* cancioneta *f.*
diuretic *adj* (*med*) diurético/ca.
dive *vi* sumergirse; bucear; * *vr* zambullirse; * *n* zambullida *f.*
diver *n* buzo *m.*
diverge *vi* divergir.
divergence *n* divergencia *f.*
divergent *adj* divergente.
diverse *adj* diverso/sa, diferente; ~ly *adv* diversamente.
diversion *n* diversión *f.*
diversity *n* diversidad *f.*
divert *vt* desviar; divertir.
divest *vt* desnudar; despojar.
divide *vt* dividir; * *vi* dividirse.
dividend *n* dividendo *m.*
dividers *npl* (*math*) compás de puntas *m.*
divine *adj* divino/na.
divinity *n* divinidad *f.*
diving *n* salto *m*; buceo *m.*
diving board *n* trampolín *m.*
divisible *adj* divisible.
division *n* (*math*) división *f*; desunión *f.*
divisor *n* (*math*) divisor *m.*
divorce *n* divorcio *m*; * *vi* divorciarse.
divorced *adj* divorciado/da.
divulge *vt* divulgar, publicar.
dizziness *n* vértigo *m.*
dizzy *adj* mareado/da.

DJ *n* pinchadiscos *m.*
do *vt* hacer, obrar.
docile *adj* dócil, apacible.
dock *n* muelle *m*; * *vi* atracar.
docker *n* estibador *m.*
dockyard *n* (*mar*) astillero *m.*
doctor *n* médico/ca *m/f.*
doctrinal *adj* doctrinal.
doctrine *n* doctrina *f.*
document *n* documento *m.*
documentary *adj* documental.
dodge *vt* esquivar.
doe *n* gama *f*; ~ rabbit coneja *f.*
dog *n* perro *m.*
dogged *adj* tenaz; ~ly *adv* tenazmente.
dog kennel *n* perrera *f.*
dogmatic *adj* dogmático/ca; ~ly *adv* dogmáticamente.
doings *npl* hechos *mpl*; eventos *mpl.*
do-it-yourself *n* bricolaje *m.*
doleful *adj* lúgubre, triste.
doll *n* muñeca *f.*
dollar *n* dólar *m.*
dolphin *n* delfín *m.*
domain *n* campo *m.*
dome *n* cúpula *f.*
domestic *adj* doméstico/ca.
domesticate *vt* domesticar.
domestication *n* domesticación *f.*
domesticity *n* domesticidad *f.*
domicile *n* domicilio *m.*
dominant *adj* dominante.
dominate *vi* dominar.
domination *n* dominación *f.*
domineer *vi* dominar.
domineering *adj* dominante.
dominion *n* dominio *m.*
dominoes *npl* dominó *m.*
donate *vt* donar.
donation *n* donación *f.*
done *adj* hecho/cha; cocido/da.
donkey *n* asno, borrico *m.*
donor *n* donante *m/f.*
doodle *vi* garabatear.
doom *n* suerte *f.*
door *n* puerta *f.*
doorbell *n* timbre *m.*
door handle *n* tirador *m.*
doorman *n* portero *m.*
doormat *n* felpudo *m.*
doorplate *n* planchuela *f.*
doorstep *n* peldaño *m.*
doorway *n* entrada *f.*
dormant *adj* latente.
dormer window *n* buhardilla *f.*

dormitory n dormitorio m.
dormouse n lirón m.
dosage n dosis f invar.
dose n dosis f invar, Lat Am dosaje m; * vt disponer la dosis de.
dossier n expediente m.
dot n punto m.
dote vi adorar.
dotingly adv con cariño excesivo.
double adj doble; * vt doblar; duplicar; * n doble m.
double bed n cama matrimonial f.
double-breasted adj cruzado/da.
double chin n papada f.
double-dealing n duplicidad f.
double-edged adj de doble filo.
double entry n (com) partida doble f.
double-lock vt echar la segunda vuelta a la llave a.
double room n habitación doble f.
doubly adj doblemente.
doubt n duda, sospecha f; * vt dudar; sospechar
doubtful adj dudoso/sa.
doubtless adv sin duda.
dough n masa f.
douse vt apagar.
dove n paloma f.
dovecot(e) n palomar m.
dowdy adj mal vestido/da.
down n plumón m; flojel m; * prep abajo; **to sit ~** sentarse; **upside ~** al revés.
downcast adj cabizbajo/ja.
downfall n ruina f.
downhearted adj desanimado/da.
downhill adv cuesta abajo/ja.
down payment n entrada f.
downpour n aguacero m.
downright adj manifiesto/ta.
downstairs adv abajo/ja.
down-to-earth adj práctico/ca.
downtown adv al centro (de la ciudad).
downward(s) adv hacia abajo.
dowry n dote f.
doze vi dormitar.
dozen n docena f.
dozy adj somnoliento/ta.
drab adj gris.
draft n borrador m; quinta f; corriente de aire f.
drafty adj expuesto/ta al aire.
drag vt arrastrar; tirar con fuerza; * n lata f.
dragnet n red barredera f.
dragon n dragón m.
dragonfly n libélula f.
drain vt desaguar; secar; * n desaguadero m.

drainage n desagüe m.
draining board n escurridor m.
drainpipe n desagüe m.
drake n ánade macho m.
dram n traguito m.
drama n drama m.
dramatic adj dramático/ca; **~ally** adv dramáticamente.
dramatist n dramaturgo/ga m/f.
dramatize vt dramatizar.
drape vt cubrir; *n cortina f; telón (en teatro) m; **~s** npl cortinas fpl.
drastic adj drástico/ca.
draw vt tirar; dibujar; **to ~ nigh** acercarse.
drawback n desventaja f.
drawer n cajón m.
drawing n dibujo m.
drawing board n tablero de dibujo m.
drawing room n salón m.
drawl vi hablar con pesadez.
dread n terror, espanto m; * vt temer.
dreadful adj espantoso/sa; **~ly** adv terriblemente.
dream n sueño m; * vi soñar.
dreary adj triste.
dredge vt dragar.
dregs npl heces fpl.
drench vt empapar.
dress vt vestir; vendar; * vi vestirse; * n vestido m.
dresser n aparador m.
dressing n vendaje m; aliño m.
dressing gown n bata f.
dressing room n tocador m.
dressing table n tocador m.
dressmaker n modista f.
dressy adj elegante.
dribble vi caer gota a gota, babear.
dribbling n regateo m.
dried adj seco/ca.
drift n montón m; ventisquero m; significado m; * vi ir a la deriva.
driftwood n madera de deriva f.
drill n taladro m; (mil) instrucción f; * vt taladrar.
drink vt, vi beber; * n bebida f.
drinkable adj potable.
drinker n bebedor/a m/f.
drinking bout n borrachera f.
drinking water n agua potable f.
drip vi gotear; * n gota f; goteo m.
drive vt conducir, Lat Am manejar; empujar; * vi conducir, Lat Am manejar; * n paseo en coche m; entrada f.
drivel n baba f; * vi babear.

driver n conductor/a m/f; Lat Am chofer m.
driver's license n carnet m de conducir, carnet m de manejar.
driveway n entrada f.
driving n conducción f, Lat Am manejo m.
driving instructor n profesor/a de autoescuela m/f.
driving school n autoescuela f.
driving test n examen de conducir, examen de manejo m.
drizzle vi lloviznar.
droll adj gracioso/sa.
drone n zumbido m; zángano m.
drool vi babear.
droop vi decaer.
drop n gota f; * vt dejar caer; * vi bajar; **to ~ out** retirarse.
drop-out n marginado m.
dropper n cuentagotas m invar.
dross n escoria f.
drought n sequía f.
drove n: **in ~s** en tropel.
drown vt anegar; * vi anegarse.
drowsiness n somnolencia f.
drowsy adj somnoliento/ta.
drudgery n trabajo monótono m; zurra f.
drug n droga f; * vt drogar.
drug addict n drogadicto/ta m/f.
drug addiction n drogadicción f.
druggist n farmacéutico/ca m/f.
drugstore n farmacia f.
drug trafficker n narcotraficante m/f.
drum n tambor m; **rural ~** zambomba f; * vi tocar el tambor.
drum majorette n batonista f.
drummer n batería m/f, Lat Am baterista m/f.
drumstick n palillo de tambor m.
drunk adj borracho/cha.
drunkard n borracho m.
drunken adj borracho/cha.
drunkenness n borrachera f.
dry adj seco/ca; * vt secar; * vi secarse.
dry-cleaning n lavado en seco m.
dry-goods store n mercería f.
dryness n sequedad f.
dry rot n podredumbre f.
dual adj doble.
dual-purpose adj de doble uso.
dubbed adj doblado/da.
dubious adj dudoso/sa.
duck n pato m; * vt (vi) zambullir(se).
duckling n patito m.
dud adj estropeado/da.
due adj debido/da, apto/ta; * adv exactamente; * n derecho m.

duel n duelo m.
duet n (mus) dúo m.
dull adj lerdo/da; insípido/da; zopenco/ca; gris; * vt aliviar.
duly adv debidamente; puntualmente.
dumb adj mudo/da; ~ly adv sin chistar.
dumbbell n pesa f.
dumbfounded adj pasmado/da.
dump n montón m; * vt dejar.
dumping n (com) dumping m.
dumpling n bola de masa f.
dumpy adj gordito/ta.
dunce n zopenco m.
dune n duna f.
dung n estiércol m.
dungeon n calabozo m.
dupe n bobo m; * vt engañar, embaucar.
duplex n dúplex m.
duplicate n duplicado m; copia f; * vt multicopiar.
duplicity n duplicidad f.
durability n durabilidad f.
durable adj duradero/ra.
duration n duración f.
during prep mientras, durante el tiempo que.
dusk n crepúsculo m.
dust n polvo m; * vt desempolvar.
duster n plumero m.
dusty adj polvoriento/ta.
Dutch courage n valor fingido m.
duteous adj fiel, leal.
dutiful adj obediente, sumiso/sa; ~ly adv obedientemente.
duty n deber m; obligación f.
duty-free adj libre de derechos de aduana.
dwarf n enano m; enana f; * vt empequeñecer.
dwell vi habitar, morar.
dwelling n habitación f; domicilio m.
dwindle vi mermar, disminuirse.
dye vt teñir; * n tinte m.
dyer n tintorero/ra m/f.
dyeing n tintorería f; tintura f.
dye-works npl taller del tintorero m.
dying adj agonizante, moribundo/da; * n muerte f; **~ moments** postrimerías fpl.
dynamic adj dinámico/ca.
dynamics n dinámica f.
dynamite n dinamita f.
dynamiter n dinamitero/ra m/f.
dynamo n dinamo f, Lat Am dinamo m.
dynasty n dinastía f.
dysentery n disentería f.
dyspepsia n (med) dispepsia f.
dyspeptic adj dispéptico/ca.

E

each *pn* cada uno, cada una; ~ **other** unos a otros, unas a otras, mutuamente.
eager *adj* entusiasmado/da; ~**ly** *adv* con entusiasmo.
eagerness *n* ansia *f*; anhelo *m*.
eagle *n* águila *f*.
eagle-eyed *adj* con vista de lince.
eaglet *n* aguilucho *m*.
ear *n* oreja *f*; oído *m*; espiga *f*; **by ~** de oreja.
earache *n* dolor de oídos *m*.
eardrum *n* tímpano (del oído) *m*.
early *adj* temprano/na; *adv* temprano.
earmark *vt* destinar a.
earn *vt* ganar; conseguir.
earnest *adj* serio/ria; en serio; ~**ly** *adv* seriamente.
earnestness *n* seriedad *f*.
earnings *npl* ingresos *mpl*.
earphones *npl* auriculares *mpl*.
earring *n* zarcillo, pendiente *m*.
earth *n* tierra *f*; * *vt* conectar a tierra.
earthen *adj* de tierra.
earthenware *n* loza de barro *f*.
earthquake *n* terremoto *m*.
earthworm *n* lombriz *f*.
earthy *adj* sensual.
earwig *n* tijereta *f*.
ease *n* comodidad *f*; facilidad *f*; **at ~** con desahogo; * *vt* aliviar; mitigar.
easel *n* caballete *m*.
easily *adv* fácilmente.
easiness *n* facilidad *f*.
east *n* este *m*; oriente *m*.
Easter *n* Pascua de Resurrección; Semana Santa *f*.
Easter egg *n* huevo de Pascua *m*.
easterly *adj* del este.
eastern *adj* del este, oriental.
eastward(s) *adv* hacia el este.
easy *adj* fácil; cómodo/da, ~ **going** acomodadizo/za.
easy chair *n* sillón *m*.
eat *vt* comer; * *vi* alimentarse.
eatable *adj* comestible; * ~**s** *npl* víveres *mpl*.
eaves *npl* alero *m*.
eau de Cologne *n* agua de Colonia *f*.
eavesdrop *vt* escuchar a escondidas.
ebb *n* reflujo *m*; * *vi* menguar; decaer, disminuir.

ebony *n* ébano *m*.
eccentric *adj* excéntrico/ca.
eccentricity *n* excentricidad *f*.
ecclesiastic *adj* eclesiástico/ca.
echo *n* eco *m*; * *vi* resonar, repercutir.
eclectic *adj* ecléctico/ca.
eclipse *n* eclipse *m*; * *vt* eclipsar.
ecologist, environmentalist *n* ecologista *m/f*.
ecology *n* ecología *f*.
e-commerce *n* comercio electrónico *m*.
economic(al) *adj* económico/ca, frugal, moderado/da.
economics *npl* economía *f*.
economist *n* economista *m/f*.
economize *vt* economizar.
economy *n* economía *f*; frugalidad *f*.
ecosystem *n* ecosistema *m*.
ecotax *n* ecotasa *f*.
ecotourism *n* ecoturismo *m*.
ecstasy *n* éxtasis *m*; rapto *m*.
ecstatic *adj* extático/ca; ~**ally** *adv* en éxtasis.
eczema *n* eczema *m*.
eddy *n* reflujo de agua *m*; remolino *m*; * *vi* arremolinarse.
edge *n* filo *m*; punta *f*; margen *m/f*; acrimonia *f*; * *vt* ribetear; introducir.
edgeways, edgewise *adv* de lado.
edging *n* orla, orilla *f*.
edgy *adj* nervioso/sa.
edible *adj* comestible.
edict *n* edicto, mandato *m*.
edification *n* edificación *f*.
edifice *n* edificio *m*; fábrica *f*.
edify *vt* edificar.
edit *vt* dirigir; redactar; cortar.
edition *n* edición *f*; publicación *f*, impresión *f*.
editor *n* director/a *m/f*; redactor/a *m/f*.
editorial *adj*, *n* editorial *m*.
educate *vt* educar; enseñar.
education *n* educación *f*.
eel *n* anguila *f*.
eerie *adj* espeluznante.
efface *vt* borrar, destruir.
effect *n* efecto *m*; realidad *f*; ~**s** *npl* efectos, bienes *mpl*; * *vt* efectuar, ejecutar.
effective *adj* eficaz; efectivo/va; ~**ly** *adv* efectivamente, en efecto.
effectiveness *n* eficacia *f*.

effectual *adj* eficiente, eficaz; ~ly *adv* eficazmente.
effeminacy *n* afeminación *f.*
effeminate *adj* afeminado/da.
effervescence *n* efervescencia *f;* hervor *m.*
effete *adj* estéril.
efficacy *n* eficacia *f.*
efficiency *n* eficiencia, virtud *f.*
efficient *adj* eficaz.
effigy *n* efigie, imagen *f;* retrato *m.*
effort *n* esfuerzo, empeño *m.*
effortless *adj* sin esfuerzo.
effrontery *n* descaro *m;* impudencia, desvergüenza *f.*
effusive *adj* efusivo/va.
egg *n* huevo *m;* * to ~ on *vt* animar.
eggcup *n* huevera *f.*
eggplant *n* berenjena *f.*
eggshell *n* cáscara de huevo *f.*
ego(t)ism *n* egoísmo *m.*
ego(t)ist *n* egoísta *m/f.*
ego(t)istical *adj* egotista.
eiderdown *n* edredón *m.*
eight *adj, n* ocho.
eighteen *adj, n* dieciocho.
eighteenth *adj, n* decimoctavo.
eighth *adj, n* octavo.
eightieth *adj, n* octogésimo/ma.
eighty *adj, n* ochenta.
either *pn* cualquiera; * *conj* o, sea, ya.
ejaculate *vt* exclamar; eyacular.
ejaculation *n* exclamación *f;* eyaculación *f.*
eject *vt* expeler, desechar.
ejection *n* expulsión *f.*
ejector seat *n* asiento eyectable *m.*
eke *vt* alargar; prolongar; hacer crecer.
elaborate *vt* elaborar; * *adj* elaborado/da; ~ly *adv* cuidadosamente.
elapse *vi* pasar, correr (el tiempo).
elastic *adj* elástico/ca.
elasticity *n* elasticidad *f.*
elated *adj* regocijado/da.
elation *n* regocijo *m.*
elbow *n* codo *m;* * *vt* codear.
elbow-room *n* anchura *f;* espacio suficiente *m;* (*fig*) libertad, latitud *f.*
elder *n* saúco *m* (árbol); * *adj* mayor.
elderly *adj* anciano/na.
elders *npl* ancianos, antepasados *mpl.*
eldest *adj* el mayor, la mayor.
elect *vt* elegir; * *adj* elegido/da, escogido/da.
election *n* elección *f.*
electioneering *n* electoralismo *m.*
elective *adj* facultativo/va.
elector *n* elector/a *m/f.*

electoral *adj* electoral, *Lat Am* eleccionario/a.
electorate *n* electorado *m.*
electric(al) *adj* eléctrico/ca; ~ domestic appliance electrodoméstico *m.*
electric blanket *n* manta eléctrica *f.*
electric cooker *n* cocina eléctrica *f.*
electric fire *n* estufa eléctrica *f.*
electrician *n* electricista *m/f.*
electricity *n* electricidad *f.*
electrify *vt* electrizar.
electrocardiogram *n* electrocardiograma *m.*
electron *n* electrón *m.*
electronic *adj* electrónico/ca; ~s *npl* electrónica *f.*
elegance *n* elegancia *f.*
elegant *adj* elegante, delicado/da; ~ly *adv* elegantemente.
elegy *n* elegía *f.*
element *n* elemento *m;* fundamento *m.*
elemental, elementary *adj* elemental.
elephant *n* elefante *m.*
elephantine *adj* inmenso/sa.
elevate *vt* elevar, alzar, exaltar.
elevation *n* elevación *f;* altura *f;* alteza (de pensamientos) *f.*
elevator *n* ascensor *m.*
eleven *adj, n* once.
eleventh *adj, n* undécimo.
elf *n* duende *m.*
elicit *vt* sacar de.
eligibility *n* elegibilidad *f.*
eligible *adj* elegible.
eliminate *vt* eliminar, descartar.
elk *n* alce *m.*
elliptic(al) *adj* elíptico/ca.
elm *n* olmo *m.*
elocution *n* elocución *f.*
elocutionist *n* profesor de elocución *m.*
elongate *vt* alargar.
elope *vi* escapar, huir, evadirse.
elopement *n* fuga, huida, evasión *f.*
eloquence *n* elocuencia *f.*
eloquent *adj* elocuente; ~ly *adv* elocuentemente.
else *pn* otro/ra.
elsewhere *adv* en otra parte.
elucidate *vt* explicar.
elucidation *n* elucidación, explicación *f.*
elude *vt* eludir, evitar.
elusive *adj* esquivo/va.
emaciated *adj* demacrado/da.
e-mail *n* correo electrónico *m.*
emanate (from) *vi* emanar.
emancipate *vt* emancipar; dar libertad.

emancipation *n* emancipación *f.*
embalm *vt* embalsamar.
embankment *n* terraplén *m.*
embargo *n* embargo *m.*
embark *vt* embarcar.
embarkation *n* embarque *m.*
embarrass *vt* avergonzar.
embarrassed *adj* avergonzado/da.
embarrassing *adj* violento/ta; embarazoso/sa.
embarrassment *n* desconcierto *m.*
embassy *n* embajada *f.*
embed *vt* empotrar; clavar.
embellish *vt* hermosear, adornar.
embellishment *n* adorno *m.*
embers *npl* rescoldo *m.*
embezzle *vt* desfalcar.
embezzlement *n* desfalco *m.*
embitter *vt* amargar.
emblem *n* emblema *m.*
emblematic(al) *adj* emblemático/ca, simbólico/ca.
embodiment *n* incorporación *f.*
embody *vt* incorporar.
embrace *vt* abrazar; contener; * *n* abrazo *m.*
embroider *vt* bordar.
embroidery *n* bordado *m*; bordadura *f.*
embroil *vt* embrollar; confundir.
embryo *n* embrión *m.*
emendation *n* enmienda, corrección *f.*
emerald *n* esmeralda *f.*
emerge *vi* salir, proceder.
emergency *n* emergencia *f*; necesidad urgente *f.*
emergency cord *n* timbre de alarma *m.*
emergency exit *n* salida de emergencia *f.*
emergency landing *n* aterrizaje forzoso *m.*
emergency meeting *n* reunión extraordinaria *f.*
emery *n* esmeril *m.*
emigrant *n* emigrante *m/f.*
emigrate *vi* emigrar.
emigration *n* emigración *f.*
eminence *n* altura *f*; eminencia, excelencia *f.*
eminent *adj* eminente, elevado/da; distinguido/da; ~ly *adv* eminentemente.
emission *n* emisión *f.*
emit *vt* emitir; arrojar, despedir.
emolument *n* emolumento, provecho *m.*
emotion *n* emoción *f.*
emotional *adj* emocional.
emotive *adj* emotivo/va.
emperor *n* emperador *m.*
emphasis *n* énfasis *m.*
emphasize *vt* hablar con énfasis.

emphatic *adj* enfático/ca; ~ally *adv* enfáticamente.
empire *n* imperio *m.*
employ *vt* emplear, ocupar.
employee *n* empleado/da *m/f.*
employer *n* patrón *m*; empresario/ria *m/f.*
employment *n* empleo *m*; trabajo *m.*
emporium *n* emporio *m.*
empress *n* emperatriz *f.*
emptiness *n* vaciedad *f*; futilidad *f.*
empty *adj* vacío/cia; vano/na; ignorante; * *vt* vaciar, evacuar.
empty-handed *adj* con las manos vacías.
emulate *vt* emular, competir; imitar.
emulsion *n* emulsión *f.*
enable *vt* capacitar.
enact *vt* promulgar; representar; hacer.
enamel *n* esmalte *m*; * *vt* esmaltar.
enamor *vt* enamorar.
encamp *vi* acamparse.
encampment *n* campamento *m.*
encase *vt* encajar, encajonar.
enchant *vt* encantar.
enchanting *adj* encantador/a.
enchantment *n* encanto *m.*
encircle *vt* cercar, circundar.
enclose *vt* cercar, circunvalar, circundar; incluir.
enclosure *n* cercamiento *m*; cercado *m.*
encompass *vt* abarcar.
encore *adv* otra vez, de nuevo.
encounter *n* encuentro *m*; duelo *m*; pelea *f*; * *vt* encontrar.
encourage *vt* animar, alentar.
encouragement *n* estímulo, patrocinio *m.*
encroach *vt* usurpar, avanzar gradualmente.
encroachment *n* usurpación, intrusión *f.*
encrusted *adj* incrustado/da.
encumber *vt* embarazar, cargar.
encumbrance *n* embarazo, impedimento *m.*
encyclical *adj* encíclico/ca, circular.
encyclopedia *n* enciclopedia *f.*
end *n* fin *m*; extremidad *f*; término *m*; resolución *f*; **to the ~ that** para que; **to no ~** en vano; **on ~** en pie, de pie; * *vt* terminar, concluir, fenecer; * *vi* acabar, terminar.
endanger *vt* peligrar, arriesgar.
endear *vt* encarecer.
endearing *adj* simpático/ca.
endearment *n* ternura *f.*
endeavor *vi* esforzarse; intentar; * *n* esfuerzo *m.*
endemic *adj* endémico/ca.
ending *n* conclusión; *f*; desenlace *m*; terminación *f.*

endive *n* (*bot*) endibia *f.*
endless *adj* infinito/ta, perpetuo/tua; ~**ly**
adv sin fin, perpetuamente.
endorse *vt* endosar; aprobar.
endorsement *n* endoso *m*; aprobación *f.*
endow *vt* dotar.
endowment *n* dote, dotación *f.*
endurable *adj* sufrible, tolerable.
endurance *n* duración *f*; paciencia *f*;
sufrimiento *m.*
endure *vt* sufrir, soportar; * *vi* durar.
endways, endwise *adv* de punta, derecho.
enemy *n* enemigo/ga, antagonista *m/f.*
energetic *adj* enérgico/ca, vigoroso/sa.
energy *n* energía, fuerza *f*; **renewable**
forms of ~ energía renovables.
enervate *vt* enervar, debilitar.
enfeeble *vt* debilitar.
enfold *vt* envolver.
enforce *vt* hacer cumplir.
enforced *adj* forzoso/sa.
enfranchise *vt* emancipar.
engage *vt* llamar; abordar; contratar.
engaged *adj* prometido/da.
engagement *n* empeño *m*; combate *m*;
pelea *f*; obligación *f.*
engagement ring *n* anillo de prometida *m.*
engaging *adj* atractivo/va.
engender *vt* engendrar; producir.
engine *n* motor *m*; locomotora *f.*
engine driver *n* maquinista *m/f.*
engineer *n* ingeniero/ra *m/f*; maquinista
m/f.
engineering *n* ingeniería *f.*
engrave *vt* grabar; esculpir; tallar.
engraving *n* grabado *m*; estampa *f.*
engrossed *adj* absorto/ta.
engulf *vt* sumergir.
enhance *vt* aumentar, realzar.
enigma *n* enigma *m.*
enjoy *vt* gozar; poseer.
enjoyable *adj* agradable; divertido/da.
enjoyment *n* disfrute *m*; placer *m*; fruición *f.*
enlarge *vt* engrandecer, dilatar, extender.
enlargement *n* aumento *m*; ampliación *f*,
soltura *f.*
enlighten *vt* iluminar; instruir.
enlightened *adj* iluminado/da.
Enlightenment *n*: **the** ~ el Siglo de las
Luces *m*, la Ilustración *f.*
enlist *vt* alistar.
enlistment *n* alistamiento *m.*
enliven *vt* animar; avivar; alegrar.
enmity *n* enemistad *f*; odio *m.*
enormity *n* enormidad *f*; atrocidad *f.*

enormous *adj* enorme; ~**ly** *adv* enormemente.
enough *adv* bastante; basta; * *n* bastante *m.*
enounce *vt* declarar.
enquiry *n* pesquisa *f.*
enrage *vt* enfurecer, irritar.
enrapture *vt* arrebatar, entusiasmar;
encantar.
enrich *vt* enriquecer; adornar.
enrichment *n* enriquecimiento *m.*
enroll *vt* registrar; arrollar.
enrollment *n* inscripción *f.*
en route *adv* durante el viaje.
ensign *n* (*mil*) bandera *f*; abanderado *m*;
(*mar*) alférez *m.*
enslave *vt* esclavizar, cautivar.
ensue *vi* seguirse; suceder.
ensure *vt* asegurar.
entail *vt* suponer.
entangle *vt* enmarañar, embrollar.
entanglement *n* enredo *m.*
enter *vt* entrar; admitir; registrar; **to** ~ **for**
presentarse para; **to** ~ **into** establecer;
formar parte de/en; firmar.
enterprise *n* empresa *f.*
enterprising *adj* emprendedor/a.
entertain *vt* divertir; hospedar; mantener.
entertainer *n* artista *m/f.*
entertaining *adj* divertido/da.
entertainment *n* entretenimiento, pasatiempo *m.*
enthralled *adj* encantado/da.
enthralling *adj* cautivador/a.
enthrone *vt* entronizar.
enthusiasm *n* entusiasmo *m.*
enthusiast *n* entusiasta *m/f.*
enthusiastic *adj* entusiasta.
entice *vt* tentar; seducir.
entire *adj* entero/ra, completo/ta, perfecto/
ta; ~**ly** *adv* enteramente.
entitle *vt* intitular; conferir algún derecho.
entitled *adj* titulado/da.
entity *n* entidad, existencia *f.*
entourage *n* séquito *m.*
entrails *npl* entrañas *fpl*; asadura *f.*
entrance *n* entrada *f*; admisión *f*;
principio *m.*
entrance examination *n* examen de
ingreso *m.*
entrance fee *n* cuota *f.*
entrance hall *n* pórtico, vestíbulo *m.*
entrance ramp, on ramp *n* rampa de
acceso *f.*
entrant *n* participante *m*; candidato *m.*
entrap *vt* enredar; engañar.

entreat *vt* rogar, suplicar.
entreaty *n* petición, suplica, instancia *f.*
entrepreneur *n* empresario/ria *m/f.*
entrust *vt* confiar.
entry *n* entrada *f.*
entry phone *n* portero automático *m.*
entwine *vt* entrelazar, enroscar, torcer.
cnumerate *vt* enumerar, numerar.
enunciate *vt* enunciar, declarar.
enunciation *n* enunciación *f.*
envelop *vt* envolver.
envelope *n* sobre *m.*
enviable *adj* envidiable.
envious *adj* envidioso/sa; ~ly *adv* en-
vidiosamente.
environment *n* medio ambiente *m.*
environmental *adj* ambiental, medioa-
mbiental.
environs *npl* vecindad *f;* contornos *mpl.*
envisage *vt* prever; concebir.
envoy *n* enviado/da *m/f;* mensajero/ra *m/f.*
envy *n* envidia, malicia *f;* * *vt* envidiar.
ephemeral *adj* efímero/ra.
epic *adj* épico/ca; * *n* épica *f.*
epidemic *adj* epidémico/ca; * *n* epidemia *f.*
epilepsy *n* epilepsia *f.*
cpileptic *adj* epiléptico/ca.
epilog *n* epílogo *m.*
Epiphany *n* Epifanía *f.*
episcopacy *n* episcopado *m.*
Episcopal *adj* episcopal.
Episcopalian *n* anglicano/na *m/f.*
episode *n* episodio *m.*
epistle *n* epístola *f.*
epistolary *adj* epistolar.
epithet *n* epíteto *m.*
epitome *n* epítome, compendio *m.*
epitomize *vt* epitomar, abreviar.
epoch *n* época *f.*
equable *adj* uniforme; ~bly *adv* unifor-
memente.
equal *adj* igual, justo/ta, semejante; * *n*
igual *m;* compañero *m;* * *vt* igualar;
compensar.
equalize *vt* igualar.
cqualizer *n* igualada *f.*
equality *n* igualdad, uniformidad *f.*
equally *adv* igualmente.
equanimity *n* ecuanimidad *f.*
cquate *vt* equiparar (con).
equation *n* ecuación *f.*
equator *n* ecuador *m.*
equatorial *adj* ecuatorial, ecuatorio/ria.
equestrian *adj* ecuestre.
equilateral *adj* equilátero/ra.

equilibrium *n* equilibrio *m.*
equinox *n* equinoccio *m.*
equip *vt* equipar, pertrechar.
equipment *n* equipaje *m.*
equitable *adj* equitativo/va, imparcial; ~bly
adv equitativamente.
equity *n* equidad, justicia, imparcialidad *f.*
equivalent *adj, n* equivalente *m.*
equivocal *adj* equívoco/ca, ambiguo/gua;
~ly *adv* equivocadamente, ambiguamente.
equivocate *vt* equivocar, usar equívocos.
equivocation *n* equívoco *m.*
era *n* era *f.*
eradicate *vt* desarraigar, extirpar.
eradication *n* extirpación *f.*
erase *vt* borrar.
eraser *n* goma de borrar *f.*
erect *vt* erigir; establecer, * *adj* derecho/ha,
erguido/da, vertical.
erection *n* establecimiento *m;* estructura *f;*
erección *f.*
ermine *n* armiño *m.*
erode *vt* erosionar; corroer.
erotic *adj* erótico/ca.
err *vi* vagar, errar; desviarse.
errand *n* recado, mensaje *m.*
errand boy *n* recadero *m*
errata *npl* fe de erratas *f.*
erratic *adj* errático/ca, errante; irregular.
erroneous *adj* erróneo/nea; falso/sa; ~ly
adv erróneamente.
error *n* error *m;* yerro *m.*
erudite *adj* erudito/ta.
erudition *n* erudición *f;* doctrina *f.*
erupt *vi* entrar en erupción; hacer erupción.
eruption *n* erupción *f.*
escalate *vi* extenderse.
escalation *n* intensificación *f.*
escalator *n* escalera mecánica *f.*
escapade *n* travesura *f.*
escape *vt* evitar; escapar; * *vi* evadirse,
salvarse; * *vr* zafarse; * *n* escapada, huida,
fuga *f;* inadvertencia *f;* to make one's ~
poner los pies en polvorosa.
escapism *n* escapismo *m.*
eschew *vt* huir, evitar, evadir.
escort *n* escolta *f;* * *vt* escoltar.
esoteric *adj* esotérico/ca.
especial *adj* especial; ~ly *adv* especialmente.
espionage *n* espionaje *m.*
esplanade *n* (*mil*) esplanada *f.*
espouse *vt* desposar.
essay *n* ensayo *m.*
essence *n* esencia *f.*

essential *n* esencia *f;* * *adj* esencial, substancial, principal; ~ly *adv* esencialmente.
establish *vt* establecer, fundar, fijar; confirmar.
establishment *n* establecimiento *m;* fundación *f;* institución *f.*
estate *n* estado *m;* hacienda *f;* bienes *mpl.*
esteem *vt* estimar, apreciar; pensar; * *n* estima *f;* consideración *f.*
esthetic *adj* estético/ca; ~s *npl* estética *f.*
estimate *vt* estimar, apreciar, tasar; * *n* presupuesto *m.*
estimation *n* estimación, valuación *f;* opinión *f.*
estrange *vt* extrañar, apartar, enajenar.
estranged *adj* separado/da.
estrangement *n* enajenación *f;* extrañeza, distancia *f.*
estuary *n* estuario *m,* ría *f.*
etch *vt* grabar al aguafuerte.
etching *n* grabado al aguafuerte *m.*
eternal *adj* eterno/na, perpetuo/tua, inmortal; ~ly *adv* eternamente.
eternity *n* eternidad *f.*
ether *n* éter *m.*
ethical *adj* ético/ca; ~ly *adv* moralmente.
ethics *npl* ética *f.*
ethnic *adj* étnico/ca.
ethos *n* genio *m.*
etiquette *n* etiqueta *f.*
etymological *adj* etimológico/ca.
etymologist *n* etimólogo/ga *m/f,* etimologista *m/f.*
etymology *n* etimología *f.*
Eucharist *n* Eucaristía *f.*
eulogy *n* elogio, encomio *m;* alabanza *f.*
eunuch *n* eunuco *m.*
euphemism *n* eufemismo *m.*
euro *n* euro *m.*
Euro MP *n* eurodiputado/da *m/f.*
Europe *n* Europa *f.*
European Community *n* Comunidad Europea *f.*
European Parliament *n* eurocámara *f.*
European Union *n* unión Europea *f.*
Euroskeptic *n* euroescéptico/ca *m/f.*
Eurotunnel, Channel Tunnel *n* eurotúnel *m.*
evacuate *vt* evacuar.
evacuation *n* evacuación *f.*
evade *vt* evadir, escapar, evitar.
evaluate *vt* evaluar; interpretar.
evangelic(al) *adj* evangélico/ca.
evangelist *n* evangelista *m.*

evaporate *vt* evaporar; * *vi* evaporarse; disiparse.
evaporated milk *n* leche evaporada *f.*
evaporation *n* evaporación *f.*
evasion *n* evasión *f;* escape *m.*
evasive *adj* evasivo/va; ~ly *adv* con evasivas.
eve *n* víspera *f.*
even *adj* llano/na, igual; par, semejante; * *adv* aun; aun cuando, supuesto que; no obstante; * *vt* igualar, allanar; * *vi:* to ~ out nivelarse.
even-handed *adj* imparcial, equitativo/va.
evening *n* tarde *f.*
evening class *n* clase nocturna *f.*
evening dress *n* traje de etiqueta *m;* traje de noche *m.*
evenly *adv* igualmente, llanamente.
evenness *n* igualdad *f;* uniformidad *f;* llanura *f;* imparcialidad *f.*
event *n* acontecimiento, evento *m;* suceso *m.*
eventful *adj* lleno de acontecimientos.
eventual *adj* final; ~ly *adv* por fin.
eventuality *n* eventualidad *f.*
ever *adv* siempre; for ~ and ~ siempre jamás, eternamente; ~ since después.
evergreen *adj* de hoja perenne; * *n* árbol de hoja perenne *m.*
everlasting *adj* eterno/na.
evermore *adv* eternamente, para siempre jamás.
every *adj* cada uno, cada una; ~ where en/ por todas partes; ~ thing todo; ~ one, ~ body todos, todo el mundo.
evict *vt* desahuciar.
eviction *n* desahucio *m.*
evidence *n* evidencia *f;* testimonio *m;* prueba *f;* * *vt* evidenciar.
evident *adj* evidente; patente, manifiesto/ ta; ~ly *adv* evidentemente.
evil *adj* malo/la, depravado/da, pernicioso/ sa; dañoso/sa; * *n* mal *m;* maldad *f.*
evil-minded *adj* malicioso/sa, mal intencionado/da.
evocative *adj* sugestivo/va.
evoke *vt* evocar.
evolution *n* evolución *f.*
evolve *vt, vi* evolucionar; desenvolver; desplegarse.
ewe *n* oveja *f.*
exacerbate *vt* exacerbar.
exact *adj* exacto/ta; * *vt* exigir.
exacting *adj* exigente.
exaction *n* exacción, extorsión *f.*

exactly *adj* exactamente.
exactness, exactitude *n* exactitud *f*.
exaggerate *vt* exagerar.
exaggeration *n* exageración *f*.
exalt *vt* exaltar, elevar; alabar; realzar.
exaltation *n* exaltación, elevación *f*.
exalted *adj* exaltado/da; muy animado/da.
examination *n* examen *m*.
examine *vt* examinar; escudriñar.
examiner *n* inspector/a *m/f*.
example *n* ejemplar *m*; ejemplo *m*.
exasperate *vt* exasperar, irritar, enojar, provocar; agravar; amargar.
exasperation *n* exasperación, irritación *f*.
excavate *vt* excavar, ahondar.
excavation *n* excavación *f*.
excavator *n* excavadora *f*.
exceed *vt* exceder; sobrepujar.
exceedingly *adv* extremamente, en sumo grado.
excel *vt* sobresalir, exceder; * *vi* descollar.
excellence *n* excelencia *f*; preeminencia *f*.
Excellency *n* Excelencia (título) *f*.
excellent *adj* excelente; ~ly *adv* excelentemente.
except *vt* exceptuar, excluir; ~(ing) *prep* excepto, a excepción de.
exception *n* excepción, exclusión *f*.
exceptional *adj* excepcional.
excerpt *n* extracto *m*.
excess *n* exceso *m*.
excessive *adj* excesivo/va; ~ly *adv* excesivamente.
exchange *vt* cambiar; trocar, permutar; * *n* cambio *m*; bolsa *f*.
exchange rate *n* tipo de cambio *m*.
excise *n* impuestos sobre el consumo *mpl*.
excitability *n* excitabilidad *f*.
excitable *adj* excitable.
excite *vt* excitar; estimular.
excited *adj* emocionado/da.
excitement *n* estímulo, excitación *f*.
exciting *adj* emocionante.
exclaim *vi* exclamar.
exclamation *n* exclamación *f*; clamor *m*.
exclamation mark *n* punto de admiración *m*.
exclamatory *adj* exclamatorio/ria.
exclude *vt* excluir; exceptuar.
exclusion *n* exclusión, exclusiva, excepción *f*.
exclusive *adj* exclusivo/va; ~ly *adv* exclusivamente.
excommunicate *vt* excomulgar.
excommunication *n* excomunión *f*.

excrement *n* excremento *m*.
excruciating *adj* atroz, enorme, grave.
exculpate *vt* disculpar; justificar.
excursion *n* excursión *f*; digresión *f*.
excusable *adj* excusable.
excuse *vt* disculpar; perdonar; * *n* disculpa, excusa *f*; pretexto *m*; ~ me! *interj* ¡perdón!.
execute *vt* ejecutar.
execution *n* ejecución *f*.
executioner *n* ejecutor/a *m/f*; verdugo *m*.
executive *adj* ejecutivo/va.
executor *n* testamentario/ria, albacea *m/f*.
exemplary *adj* ejemplar.
exemplify *vt* ejemplificar.
exempt *adj* exento/ta.
exemption *n* exención *f*.
exercise *n* ejercicio *m*; ensayo *m*; tarea *f*; practica *f*; * *vi* hacer ejercicio; * *vt* ejercer; valerse de.
exercise book *n* cuaderno *m*.
exert *vt* emplear; to ~ oneself esforzarse.
exertion *n* esfuerzo *m*.
exhale *vt* exhalar.
exhaust *n* escape *m*; * *vt* agotar.
exhausted *adj* agotado/da.
exhaustion *n* agotamiento *m*; extenuación *f*.
exhaustive *adj* comprensivo/va.
exhibit *vt* exhibir; mostrar; * *n* (*law*) objeto expuesto *m*.
exhibition *n* exposición, presentación *f*.
exhilarating *adj* estimulante.
exhilaration *n* alegría *f*; buen humor, regocijo *m*.
exhort *vt* exhortar, excitar.
exhortation *n* exhortación *f*.
exhume *vt* exhumar, desenterrar.
exile *n* destierro *m*; * *vt* desterrar, deportar.
exist *vi* existir.
existence *n* existencia *f*.
existent *adj* existente.
existing *adj* actual, presente.
exit *n* salida *f*; * *vi* hacer mutis.
exit ramp, off ramp *n* vía de acceso *f*.
exodus *n* éxodo *m*.
exonerate *vt* exonerar, descargar.
exoneration *n* exoneración *f*.
exorbitant *adj* exorbitante, excesivo/va.
exorcise *vt* exorcizar, conjurar.
exorcism *n* exorcismo *m*.
exotic *adj* exótico/ca, extranjero/ra.
expand *vt* extender, dilatar.
expanse *n* extensión *f*.
expansion *n* expansión *f*.
expansive *adj* expansivo/va.

expatriate *vt* expatriar.
expect *vt* esperar, aguardar.
expectance, expectancy *n* expectación, esperanza *f*.
expectant *adj* expectante.
expectant mother *n* mujer encinta *f*.
expectation *n* expectación, expectativa *f*.
expediency *n* conveniencia, oportunidad *f*.
expedient *adj* oportuno/na, conveniente; * *n* expediente *m*; ~ly *adv* convenientemente.
expedite *vt* acelerar; expedir.
expedition *n* expedición *f*.
expeditious *adj* pronto/ta, expedito/ta; ~ly *adv* prontamente.
expel *vt* expeler, desterrar.
expend *vt* expender; desembolsar.
expendable *adj* prescindible.
expenditure *n* gasto, desembolso *m*.
expense *n* gasto *m*; coste *m*.
expense account *n* cuenta de gastos *f*.
expensive *adj* caro/ra; costoso/sa; ~ly *adv* costosamente.
experience *n* experiencia *f*; práctica *f*; * *vt* experimentar.
experienced *adj* experimentado/da.
experiment *n* experimento *m*; * *vt* experimentar.
experimental *adj* experimental; ~ly *adv* experimentalmente.
expert *adj* experto/ta, diestro/tra.
expertise *n* pericia *f*.
expiration *n* expiración *f*; muerte *f*.
expire *vi* expirar.
explain *vt* explanar, explicar.
explanation *n* explicación *f*.
explanatory *adj* explicativo/va.
expletive *adj* expletivo/va.
explicable *adj* explicable.
explicit *adj* explícito/ta; ~ly *adv* explícitamente.
explode *vt, vi* estallar, explotar.
exploit *vt* explotar; * *n* hazaña *f*; hecho heroico *m*.
exploitation *n* explotación *f*.
exploration *n* exploración *f*; examen *m*.
exploratory *adj* exploratorio/ria.
explore *vt* explorar, examinar; sondear.
explorer *n* explorador/a *m/f*.
explosion *n* explosión *f*.
explosive *adj*, *n* explosivo *m*.
exponent *n* (*math*) exponente *m*.
export *vt* exportar.
export, exportation *n* exportación *f*.
exporter *n* exportador/a *m/f*.

expose *vt* exponer; mostrar; descubrir; poner en peligro.
exposed *adj* expuesto/ta.
exposition *n* exposición *f*; interpretación *f*.
expostulate *vi* debatir, contender.
exposure *n* exposición *f*; velocidad de obturación *f*; fotografía *f*.
exposure meter *n* fotómetro *m*.
expound *vt* exponer; interpretar.
express *vt* exprimir; representar; * *adj* expreso/sa, claro/ra; a propósito; * *n* expreso, correo *m*; (*rail*) tren expreso *m*.
expression *n* expresión *f*; locución *f*.
expressionless *adj* sin expresión (cara).
expressive *adj* expresivo/va; ~ly *adv* expresivamente.
expressly *adv* expresamente.
expressway *n* autopista *f*.
expropriate *vt* expropiar (por causa de utilidad pública).
expropriation *n* (*law*) expropiación *f*.
expulsion *n* explosión *f*.
expurgate *vt* expurgar.
exquisite *adj* exquisito/ta, perfecto/ta, excelente; ~ly *adv* exquisitamente.
extant *adj* existente.
extempore *adv* de improviso.
extemporize *vi* improvisar.
extend *vt* extender; amplificar; * *vi* extenderse.
extension *n* extensión *f*.
extensive *adj* extenso/sa, dilatado/da; ~ly *adv* extensivamente.
extent *n* extensión *f*.
extenuate *vt* extenuar, disminuir, atenuar.
extenuating *adj* atenuante.
exterior *adj*, *n* exterior *m*.
exterminate *vt* exterminar; extirpar.
extermination *n* exterminación, extirpación *f*.
external *adj* externo/na; ~ly *adv* exteriormente; ~s *npl* exterior *m*.
extinct *adj* extinto/ta; abolido/da.
extinction *n* extinción *f*; abolición *f*.
extinguish *vt* extinguir; suprimir.
extinguisher *n* extintor *m*, *Lat Am* extinguidor *m*.
extirpate *vt* extirpar.
extoll *vt* alabar, magnificar, alzar, exaltar.
extort *vt* sacar por la fuerza.
extortion *n* extorsión *f*.
extortionate *adj* excesivo/va.
extra *adv* extra; * *n* extra *m*.

extract *vt* extraer; extractar; * *n* extracto
m; compendio *m*.
extraction *n* extracción *f*; descendencia *f*.
extracurricular *adj* extraescolar.
extradite *vt* extraditar.
extradition *n* (*law*) extradición *f*.
extramarital *adj* extramatrimonial.
extramural *adj* extraescolar.
extraneous *adj* extraño/ña, ajeno/na.
extraordinarily *adv* extraordinariamente.
extraordinary *adj* extraordinario/ria.
extravagance *n* extravagancia *f*; gastos,
excesivos *mpl*.
extravagant *adj* extravagante, exorbitante;
pródigo/ga; ~ly *adv* extravagantemente.
extreme *adj* extremo/ma, supremo/ma;
último/ma; * *n* extremo *m*; ~ly *adv*
extremamente.
extremist *adj*, *n* extremista *m/f*.
extremity *n* extremidad *f*.

extricate *vt* desembarazar, desenredar.
extrinsic(al) *adj* extrínseco/ca, exterior.
extrovert *adj*, *n* extrovertido *m*.
exuberance *n* exuberancia, suma abundancia *f*.
exuberant *adj* exuberante, abundantísimo/
ma; ~ly *adv* exuberantemente.
exude *vi* transpirar.
exult *vt* exultar, regocijarse, triunfar.
exultation *n* exultación *f*; regocijo *m*.
eye *n* ojo *m*; * *vt* ojear, contemplar, observar.
eyeball *n* globo del ojo *m*.
eyebrow *n* ceja *f*.
eyelash *n* pestaña *f*.
eyelid *n* párpado *m*.
eyesight *n* vista *f*.
eyesore *n* monstruosidad *f*.
eyetooth *n* colmillo *m*.
eyewitness *n* testigo ocular *m*.
eyrie *n* nido de águila *m*.

F

fable *n* fábula *f*; ficción *f*.
fabric *n* tejido *m*.
fabricate *vt* fabricar, edificar.
fabrication *n* fabricación *f*.
fabulous *adj* fabuloso/sa; ~ly *adv* fabulosamente.
facade *n* fachada *f*.
face *n* cara, faz *f*; superficie *f*; fachada *f*; aspecto *m*; apariencia *f*; * *vt* encararse; hacer frente; **to ~ up to** hacer frente a.
face cream *n* crema facial *f*.
face-lift *n* lifting *m*.
face powder *n* polvos *mpl*.
facet *n* faceta *f*.
facetious *adj* chistoso/sa, alegre, gracioso/sa; ~ly *adv* chistosamente.
face value *n* valor nominal *m*.
facial *adj* facial.
facile *adj* fácil, afable.
facilitate *vt* facilitar.
facility *n* facilidad, ligereza *f*; afabilidad *f*.
facing *n* paramento *m*; * *prep* enfrente.
facsimile *n* facsímil *m*; fax *m*.
fact *n* hecho *m*; realidad *f*; **in ~** en efecto.
faction *n* facción *f*; disensión *f*.
factor *n* factor *m*.
factory *n* fábrica *f*.
factual *adj* basado/da en hechos reales.
faculty *n* facultad *f*; personal docente *m*.
fad *n* moda *f*.
fade *vi* decaer, marchitarse, fallecer.
fail *vt* suspender, *Lat Am* reprobar; fallar a; * *vi* suspender; fracasar; fallar; (*fig*) zozobrar.
failing *n* falta *f*; defecto *m*.
failure *n* falta *f*; culpa *f*; descuido *m*; quiebra, bancarrota *f*.
faint *vi* desmayarse, debilitarse; * *n* desmayo *m*; * *adj* débil; ~ly *adv* débilmente.
fainthearted *adj* cobarde, medroso/sa, pusilánime.
faintness *n* flaqueza *f*; desmayo *m*.
fair *adj* hermoso/sa, bello/lla; blanco/ca; rubio/bia; claro/ra, sereno/na; favorable; recto/ta, justo/ta; franco/ca; * *adv* limpio; * *n* feria *f*.
fairly *adv* justamente; completamente.
fairness *n* hermosura *f*; justicia *f*.
fair play *n* juego limpio *m*.
fair trade *n* comercio justo *m*.
fairy *n* hada *f*.

fairy tale *n* cuento de hadas *m*.
faith *n* fe *f*; dogma de fe *m*; fidelidad *f*.
faithful *adj* fiel, leal; ~ly *adv* fielmente.
faithfulness *n* fidelidad, lealtad *f*.
fake *n* falsificación *f*; impostor/a *m/f*; * *adj* falso/sa; * *vt* fingir; falsificar.
falcon *n* halcón *m*.
falconry *n* cetrería *f*.
fall *vi* caer(se); perder el poder; disminuir, decrecer en precio; **to ~ asleep** dormirse; **to ~ back** retroceder; **to ~ back on** recurrir a; **to ~ behind** quedarse atrás; **to ~ down** caerse; **to ~ for** dejarse engañar; enamorarse de; **to ~ in** hundirse; **to ~ short** faltar; **to ~ sick** enfermar; **to ~ in love** enamorarse; **to ~ off** caerse; disminuir; **to ~ out** reñir, disputar; * *n* caída *f*; otoño *m*.
fallacious *adj* falaz, fraudulento/ta; ~ly *adv* falazmente.
fallacy *n* falacia, sofistería *f*; engaño *m*.
fallibility *n* falibilidad *f*.
fallible *adj* falible.
fallow *adj* en barbecho; ~ **deer** *n* gamo *m*.
false *adj* falso/sa; ~ly *adv* falsamente.
false alarm *n* falsa alarma *f*.
falsehood, falseness *n* falsedad *f*.
falsify *vt* falsificar.
falsity *n* falsedad, mentira *f*.
falter *vi* tartamudear; faltar.
faltering *adj* vacilante.
fame *n* fama *f*; renombre *m*.
famed *adj* celebrado/da, famoso/sa.
familiar *adj* familiar; casero/ra; ~ly *adv* familiarmente.
familiarity *n* familiaridad *f*.
familiarize *vt* familiarizar.
family *n* familia *f*; linaje *m*; clase, especie *f*.
family business *n* negocio familiar *m*.
family doctor *n* médico de familia *m*.
famine *n* hambre *f*; carestía *f*.
famished *adj* hambriento/ta.
famous *adj* famoso/sa, afamado/da; ~ly *adv* famosamente.
fan *n* abanico *m*; aficionado *m*; fan *m/f*; * *vt* abanicar; atizar.
fanatic *adj*, *n* fanático/ca *m/ca*.
fanaticism *n* fanatismo *m*.
fan belt *n* correa del ventilador *f*.
fanciful *adj* imaginativo/va, caprichoso/sa; ~ly *adv* caprichosamente.

258

fancy *n* fantasía, imaginación *f*; capricho *m*; * *vt* tener ganas de; imaginarse.

fancy-goods *npl* novedades, modas *fpl*.

fancy-dress ball *n* baile de disfraces *m*.

fanfare *n* (*mus*) fanfarria *f*.

fang *n* colmillo *m*.

fantastic *adj* fantástico/ca; caprichoso/sa; **~ally** *adv* fantásticamente.

fantasy *n* fantasía *f*.

far *adv* lejos, a una gran distancia; * *adj* lejano/na, distante, remoto/ta; **~ and away** con mucho, de mucho; **~ off** lejano/na.

faraway *adj* remoto/ta.

farce *n* farsa *f*.

farcical *adj* burlesco/ca.

fare *n* precio *m*; tarifa *f*; comida *f*; viajero *m*; pasaje *m*.

farewell *n* despedida *f*; **~!** *excl* ¡adiós!

farm *n* finca *f*, granja *f*; * *vt* cultivar.

farmer *n* agricultor/a *m/f*; granjero/ra *m/f*.

farmhand *n* peón *m*.

farmhouse *n* casa de hacienda *f*, granja *f*.

farming *n* agricultura *f*.

farmland *n* tierra de cultivo *f*.

farmyard *n* corral *m*.

far-reaching *adj* de gran alcance.

fart *n* (*col*) pedo; * *vi* tirarse un pedo.

farther *adv* más lejos; más adelante; * *adj* más lejos, ulterior.

farthest *adv* lo más lejos; lo más tarde; a lo más.

fascinate *vt* fascinar, encantar.

fascinating *adj* fascinante.

fascination *n* fascinación *f*; encanto *m*.

fascism *n* fascismo.

fascist *n* fascista *m/f*.

fashion *n* moda *f*; forma, figura *f*; uso *m*; manera *f*; estilo *m*; **people of ~** gente de tono *f*; * *vt* formar, amoldar.

fashionable *adj* a la moda; elegante; **the ~ world** el gran mundo; **~bly** *adv* a/segun la moda.

fashion show *n* desfile de modelos *m*.

fast *vi* ayunar; * *n* ayuno *m*; * *adj* rápido/da; firme, estable; * *adv* rápidamente; firmemente; estrechamente.

fasten *vt* abrochar; afirmar, asegurar, atar; fijar; * *vi* fijarse, establecerse.

fastener, fastening *n* cierre *m*; cerrojo *m*.

fast food *n* comida rápida *f*.

fastidious *adj* fastidioso/sa, desdeñoso/sa; **~ly** *adv* fastidiosamente.

fat *adj* gordo/da; * *n* grasa *f*.

fatal *adj* fatal; funesto/ta; **~ly** *adv* fatalmente.

fatalism *n* fatalismo *m*.

fatalist *n* fatalista *m/f*.

fatality *n* fatalidad, predestinación *f*.

fate *n* hado, destino *m*.

fateful *adj* fatídico/ca.

father *n* padre *m*; **loving (over-indulgent) ~** padrazo *m*.

fatherhood *n* paternidad *f*.

father-in-law *n* suegro *m*.

fatherland *n* patria *f*.

fatherly *adj* paternal.

fathom *n* braza (medida) *f*; * *vt* sondar; penetrar.

fatigue *n* fatiga *f*; * *vt* fatigar, cansar.

fatten *vt*, *vi* engordar.

fatty *adj* graso/sa.

fatuous *adj* fatuo/tua, tonto/ta, imbécil.

faucet *n* grifo *m*, llave *f*.

fault *n* falta, culpa *f*; delito *m*; defecto *m*; yerro *m*.

faultfinder *n* censurador/a *m/f*.

faultless *adj* perfecto/ta, cumplido/da.

faulty *adj* defectuoso/sa.

fauna *n* fauna *f*.

faux pas *n* metedura de pata *f*.

favor *n* favor, beneficio *m*; patrocinio *m*; blandura *f*; * *vt* favorecer, proteger.

favorable *adj* favorable, propicio/cia; **~bly** *adv* favorablemente.

favored *adj* favorecido/da.

favorite *n* favorito/ta *m/f*; * *adj* favorecido/da.

favoritism *n* favoritismo *m*.

fawn *n* cervatillo *m*; * *vi* adular servilmente.

fawningly *adv* lisonjeramente, con adulación servil.

fax *n* facsímil(e) *m*; fax *m*; * *vt* mandar por fax.

fear *vi* temer; * *n* miedo *m*.

fearful *adj* medroso/sa, temeroso/sa; tímido/da; **~ly** *adv* medrosamente, temerosamente.

fearless *adj* intrépido/da, atrevido/da; **~ly** *adv* sin miedo.

fearlessness *n* intrepidez *f*.

feasibility *n* posibilidad *f*.

feasible *adj* factible, viable.

feast *n* banquete, festín *m*; fiesta *f*; * *vi* banquetear.

feat *n* hecho *m*; acción, hazaña *f*.

feather *n* pluma *f*;.

feather bed *n* plumón *m*.

feature *n* característica *f*; rasgo *m*; forma *f*; * *vi* figurar.

feature film *n* largometraje *m*.

February n febrero m.
federal adj federal.
federalist n federalista m/f.
federate vt, vi federar(se).
federation n federación f.
fed-up adj harto/ta.
fee n honorarios mpl; cuota f.
feeble adj flaco/ca, débil.
feebleness n debilidad f.
feebly adv débilmente.
feed vt nutrir; alimentar; **to ~ on** alimentarse de; * vi nutrirse; engordar; * n comida f; pasto m.
feedback n reacción f.
feel vt sentir; tocar; creer; **to ~ around** tantear; * n sensación f; tacto, sentido m.
feeler n antena f; (fig) tentativa f.
feeling n tacto m; sensibilidad f; corazonada f.
feelingly adv sensiblemente.
feign vt inventar, fingir; disimular.
feline adj felino/na.
fellow n tipo, tío m; socio/cia m/f.
fellow citizen n conciudadano/na m/f..
fellow countryman n compatriota m/f.
fellow feeling n simpatía f.
fellow men npl semejantes mpl.
fellowship n compañerismo m; beca (en un colegio) f.
fellow student n compañero/ra de curso m/f.
fellow traveler n compañero/ra de viaje m/f.
felon n criminal m/f.
felony n crimen m.
felt n fieltro m.
felt-tip pen, fiber-tip pen n rotulador m, Lat Am marcador m.
female n hembra f; * adj femenino/na.
feminine adj femenino/na.
feminism n feminismo m.
feminist n feminista m/f.
fence n cerca f, Lat Am cerco m; defensa f; * vt cercar; * vi esgrimir.
fencing n esgrima f.
fender n parachoques m invar.
fennel n (bot) hinojo m.
ferment n agitación f; * vi fermentar.
fern n (bot) helecho m.
ferocious adj feroz; fiero/ra; ~ly adv ferozmente.
ferocity n ferocidad, fiereza f.
ferret n hurón m; * vt huronear; **to ~ out** descubrir, echar fuera.
ferryboat, ferry n transbordador, ferry m; * vt transportar.

fertile adj fértil, fecundo/da.
fertility n fertilidad, fecundidad f.
fertilization n fertilización f.
fertilize vt fertilizar.
fertilizer n abono m.
fervent adj ferviente; fervoroso/sa; ~ly adv con fervor.
fervid adj ardiente, vehemente.
fervor n fervor, ardor m.
fester vi enconarse, inflamarse.
festival n fiesta f; festival m.
festive adj festivo/va.
festivity n festividad f.
fetch vt ir a buscar.
fetching adj atractivo/va.
fete n fiesta f.
fetid adj fétido/da, hediondo/da.
fetus n feto m.
feud n riña, contienda f.
feudal adj feudal.
feudalism n feudalismo m.
fever n fiebre f.
feverish adj febril, Lat Am afiebrado/da.
few adj poco/ca; **a ~** algunos; **~ and far between** pocos.
fewer adj menor; * adv menos.
fewest adj los menos.
fiancé n novio m.
fiancée n novia f.
fib n mentira f; * vi mentir.
fiber n fibra, hebra f.
fiberglass n fibra de vidrio f.
fickle adj voluble, inconstante, mudable, ligero/ra.
fiction n ficción f; invención f.
fictional adj novelesco/ca.
fictitious adj ficticio/cia; fingido/da; ~ly adv fingidamente.
fiddle n violín m; trampa f; * vi tocar el violín.
fiddler n violinista m/f.
fidelity n fidelidad, lealtad f.
fidget vi inquietarse.
fidgety adj inquieto/ta, impaciente.
field n campo m; campaña f; espacio m.
field day n (mil) día de maniobras f.
fieldmouse n ratón de campo m.
fieldwork n trabajo de campo m.
fiend n enemigo m; demonio m.
fiendish adj demoniaco/ca.
fierce adj fiero/ra, feroz; cruel, furioso/sa; ~ly adv furiosamente.
fierceness n fiereza, ferocidad f.
fiery adj ardiente; apasionado/da.
fifteen adj, n quince.

fifteenth *adj, n* decimoquinto/ta.
fifth *adj, n* quinto/ta; **~ly** *adv* en quinto lugar.
fiftieth *adj, n* quincuagésimo/ma.
fifty *adj, n* cincuenta.
fig *n* higo *m.*
fight *vt, vi* reñir; batallar; combatir; * *n* batalla *f*; combate *m*; pelea *f.*
fighter *n* combatiente *m*; luchador/a *m/f*; caza *m.*
fighting *n* combate *m.*
fig-leaf *n* hoja de higuera *f.*
fig tree *n* higuera *f.*
figurative *adj* figurativo/va; **~ly** *adv* figuradamente.
figure *n* figura, forma *f*; imagen *f*; cifra *f*; * *vi* figurar; ser lógico/ca; **to ~ out** comprender.
figurehead *n* testaferro *m.*
filament *n* filamento *m*; fibra *f.*
filch *vi* ratear.
filcher *n* ratero/ra, ladroncillo/lla *m/f.*
file *n* hilo *m*; lista *f*; (*mil*) fila, hilera *f*; lima *f*; carpeta *f*, fichero *m*; * *vt* enhilar; limar, clasificar, presentar; * *vi* **to ~ in/ out** entrar/salir en fila; **to ~ past** desfilar ante.
filing cabinet *n* archivador *m.*
fill *vt* llenar; hartar; **to ~ in** rellenar; **to ~ up** llenar (hasta el borde).
fillet *n* filete *m.*
fillet steak *n* filete de ternera *m.*
fillip *n* (*fig*) estímulo *m.*
filly *n* potra *f.*
film *n* película *f*; film *m*; capa *f*; * *vt* filmar; * *vi* rodar.
film star *n* estrella de cine *f.*
film strip *n* tira de película *f.*
filter *n* filtro *m*; * *vt* filtrar.
filter-tipped *adj* con filtro.
filth(iness) *n* inmundicia, porquería *f*; fango, lodo *m.*
filthy *adj* sucio/cia, puerco/ca.
fin *n* aleta *f.*
final *adj* final, último/ma; **~ly** *adv* finalmente; **~ stages** postrimerías *fpl.*
finale *n* final *m.*
finalist *n* finalista *m/f.*
finalize *vt* concluir.
finance *n* fondos *mpl.*
financial *adj* financiero/ra.
financier *n* financiero/ra *m/f*, *Lat Am* financista *m/f.*
find *vt* hallar, descubrir, *Lat Am* ubicar; **to ~ out** averiguar; descubrir; **to ~ one's self** hallarse; * *n* hallazgo *m.*

findings *npl* fallo *m*; recomendaciones *fpl.*
fine *adj* fino/na; agudo/da, cortante; claro/ra, trasparente; delicado/da; astuto/ta; elegante; bello/lla; * *n* multa *f*; * *vt* multar, *Lat Am* infraccionar.
fine arts *npl* bellas artes *fpl.*
finely *adv* con elegancia.
finery *n* adorno, atavío *m.*
finesse *n* sutileza *f.*
finger *n* dedo *m*; * *vt* tocar, manosear; manejar.
fingernail *n* uña *f.*
fingerprint *n* huella dactilar *f.*
fingertip *n* yema del dedo *f.*
finicky *adj* delicado/da.
finish *vt* acabar, terminar, concluir; **to ~ off** acabar (con); **to ~ up** terminar; * *vi*: **to ~ up** ir a parar.
finishing line *n* línea de llegada, línea de meta *f.*
finishing school *n* academia para señoritas *f.*
finite *adj* finito/ta; conjugado/da.
fir tree *n* abeto *m*
fire *n* fuego *m*; incendio *m*; * *vt* disparar; incendiar; despertar; * *vi* encenderse.
fire alarm *n* alarma de incendios *f.*
firearm *n* arma de fuego *f.*
fireball *n* bola *f* de fuego.
firebreak, fire line *n* cortafuegos *m.*
fire department *n* cuerpo de bomberos *m.*
fire engine *n* coche de bomberos *m.*
fire escape *n* escalera de incendios *f.*
fire extinguisher *n* extintor *m.*
firefly *n* luciérnaga *f.*
fireman *n* bombero *m.*
fireplace *n* hogar, fogón *m.*
fireproof *adj* a prueba de fuego.
fireside *n* chimenea *f.*
fire station, fire house *n* parque de bomberos *m.*
firewater *n* aguardiente *m.*
firewood *n* leña *f.*
fireworks *npl* fuegos artificiales *mpl.*
firing *n* disparos *mpl.*
firing squad *n* pelotón de ejecución *m.*
firm *adj* firme, estable, constante; * *n* (*com*) firma *f*; **~ly** *adv* firmemente.
firmament *n* firmamento *m.*
firmness *n* firmeza *f*; constancia *f.*
first *adj* primero/ra; * *adv* primeramente; **at ~** al principio; **~ly** *adv* en primer lugar.
first aid *n* primeros auxilios *mpl.*
first-aid kit *n* botiquín *m.*
first-class *adj* de primera (clase).

first-hand *adj* de primera mano.
First Lady *n* primera dama *f.*
first name *n* nombre de pila *m.*
first-rate *adj* de primera (clase).
fiscal *adj* fiscal.
fish *n* pez *m;* * *vi* pescar.
fishbone *n* espina *f.*
fisherman *n* pescador *m.*
fish farm *n* piscifactoría *f.*
fishing *n* pesca *f.*
fishing line *n* sedal *m.*
fishing rod *n* caña de pescar *f.*
fishing tackle *n* aparejo *m.*
fish market *n* lonja de pescado *f.*
fishseller *n* pescadero/ra *m/f.*
fish shop *n* pescadería *f.*
fishy *adj* (*fig*) sospechoso/sa.
fissure *n* grieta, hendedura *f.*
fist *n* puño *m.*
fit *n* paroxismo *m;* convulsión *f;* * *adj* en
forma; apto/ta, idóneo/nea, justo/ta; * *vt*
ajustar, acomodar, adaptar; to ~ out
proveer; * *vi* convenir; to ~ in encajarse;
llevarse bien (con todos).
fitness *n* salud *f;* aptitud, conveniencia *f.*
fitted carpet *n* moqueta *f.*
fitted kitchen *n* cocina amueblada *f.*
fitter *n* ajustador *m.*
fitting *adj* conveniente, idóneo/nea, justo/
ta; * *n* conveniencia *f;* ~s *pl* guarnición *f.*
five *adj, n* cinco.
fix *vt* fijar, establecer; to ~ up arreglar.
fixation *n* obsesión *f.*
fixed *adj* fijo/ja.
fixings *npl* equipajes *mpl;* pertrechos *mpl;*
ajuar *m.*
fixture *n* encuentro *m.*
fizz(le) *vi* silbar.
fizzy *adj* gaseoso/sa.
flabbergasted *adj* pasmado/da.
flabby *adj* blando/da, flojo/ja, lacio/cia.
flaccid *adj* flojo/ja, flaco/ca; fláccido/da.
flag *n* bandera *f;* losa *f;* * *vi* debilitarse.
flagpole *n* asta de bandera *f.*
flagrant *adj* flagrante; notorio/ria.
flagship *n* buque insignia *m.*
flag stop *n* parada a petición *f.*
flair *n* aptitud especial *f.*
flak *n* fuego antiaéreo *m;* lluvia de críticas.
flake *n* copo *m;* lámina *f;* * *vi* romperse en
láminas.
flaky *adj* escamoso/sa, desmenuzable.
flamboyant *adj* vistoso/sa.
flame *n* llama *f;* fuego (del amor) *m.*
flamingo *n* flamenco *m.*

flammable *adj* inflamable.
flank *n* ijada *f;* (*mil*) flanco *m;* * *vt* flanquear.
flannel *n* franela, flanela *f.*
flap *n* solapa *f;* hoja *f;* aletazo *m;* * *vt* aletear;
* *vi* ondear.
flare *vi* lucir, brillar; to ~ up encenderse;
encolerizarse; estallar; * *n* llama *f.*
flash *n* flash *m;* relámpago *m;* * *vt* to ~ on
and off encender y apagar.
flashbulb *n* bombilla de flash *f.*
flash cube *n* cubo de flash *m.*
flashlight *n* linterna *f;*antorcha *f.*
flashy *adj* superficial.
flask *n* frasco *m;* botella *f.*
flat *adj* llano/na, plano/na; insípido/da; * *n*
llanura *f;* plano *m;* (*mus*) bemol *m;* ~ly
adv horizontalmente; llanamente; enteramente; de plano, de nivel; francamente.
flatness *n* llanura *f;* insipidez *f.*
flatten *vt* allanar; abatir.
flatter *vt* adular, lisonjear.
flattering *adj* halagüeño/ña, zalamero/ra.
flattery *n* adulación, lisonja *f;* zalamería *f.*
flatulence *n* (*med*) flatulencia *f.*
flaunt *vt* ostentar.
flavor *n* sabor *m;* * *vt* sazonar.
flavored *adj* con sabor (a).
flavorless *adj* soso/sa.
flaw *n* falta, tacha *f;* defecto *m.*
flawless *adj* sin defecto.
flax *n* lino *m.*
flea *n* pulga *f.*
flea bite *n* picadura de pulga *f.*
fleck *n* mota *f;* punto *m.*
flee *vt* huir de; * *vi* escapar; huir.
fleece *n* vellón *m;* * *vt* (*col*) pelar.
fleet *n* flota *f;* escuadra *f.*
fleeting *adj* pasajero/ra, fugitivo/va.
flesh *n* carne *f.*
flesh wound *n* herida superficial *f.*
fleshy *adj* carnoso/sa, pulposo/sa.
flex *n* cordón *m;* * *vt* tensar.
flexibility *n* flexibilidad *f.*
flexible *adj* flexible.
flick *n* golpecito *m;* * *vt* dar un golpecito a.
flicker *vi* aletear; fluctuar.
flier *n* aviador/a *m/f.*
flight *n* vuelo *m;* huida, fuga *f;* bandada (de
pájaros) *f;* (*fig*) elevación *f.*
flight attendant *n* auxiliar de vuelo *m/f.*
flight deck *n* cabina de mandos *f.*
flimsy *adj* débil; fútil.
flinch *vi* encogerse.
fling *vt* lanzar, echar.
flint *n* pedernal *m.*

flip *vt* arrojar, lanzar.
flippant *adj* petulante, locuaz.
flipper *n* aleta *f.*
flirt *vi* coquetear; * *n* coqueta *f.*
flirtation *n* coquetería *f.*
flit *vi* volar, huir; aletear.
float *vt* hacer flotar; lanzar; * *vi* flotar; * *n* flotador *m*; carroza *f*; reserva *f.*
flock *n* manada *f*; rebaño *m*; gentío *m*; * *vi* congregarse.
flog *vt* azotar; (*col*) zurrar.
flogging *n* tunda, zurra *f.*
flood *n* diluvio *m*; inundación *f*, flujo *m*; * *vt* inundar.
flooding *n* inundación *f.*
floodlight *n* foco *m.*
floor *n* suelo, piso *m*; piso (de una casa); * *vt* dejar sin respuesta.
floorboard *n* tabla *f.*
floor lamp *n* lámpara de pie *f.*
floor show *n* cabaret *m.*
flop *n* fracaso *m.*
floppy *adj* flojo/ja
floppy disk *n* floppy *m*, disquete *m.*
flora *n* flora *f.*
floral *adj* floral.
florescence *n* florescencia *f.*
florid *adj* florido/da.
florist *n* florista *m/f.*
florist's (shop) *n* floristería *f.*
flotilla *n* (*mar*) flotilla *f.*
flounder *n* platija (pez de mar) *f*; * *vi* tropezar.
flour *n* harina *f.*
flourish *vi* florecer; gozar de prosperidad; * *n* belleza *f*; lazo *m*; (*mus*) floreo, preludio *m.*
flourishing *adj* floreciente.
flout *vt* burlarse de.
flow *vi* fluir, manar; crecer la marea; ondear; * *n* flujo de la marea *m* ; abundancia *f*; flujo *m.*
flow chart *n* organigrama *m.*
flower *n* flor *f*; * *vi* florear; florecer.
flowerbed *n* parterre *m.*
flowerpot *n* tiesto *m*, maceta *f.*
flowery *adj* florido/da.
flower show *n* exposición de flores *f.*
fluctuate *vi* fluctuar.
fluctuation *n* fluctuación *f.*
fluency *n* fluidez *f.*
fluent *adj* fluido/da; fácil; **-ly** *adv* con fluidez.
fluff *n* pelusa *f*; **~y** *adj* velloso/sa.
fluid *adj*, *n* fluido/da *m.*
fluidity *n* fluidez *f.*
fluke *n* (*col*) chiripa *f.*

fluoride *n* fluoruro *m.*
flurry *n* ráfaga *f*; agitación *f.*
flush *vt*: **to ~ out** levantar; desalojar; * *vi* ponerse colorado/da; * *n* rubor *m*; resplandor *m.*
flushed *adj* ruborizado/da.
fluster *vt* confundir.
flustered *adj* aturdido/da.
flute *n* flauta *f.*
flutter *vi* revolotear; estar en agitación; * *n* confusión *f*; agitación *f.*
flux *n* flujo *m.*
fly *vt* pilotar; transportar; * *vi* volar; huir, escapar; **to ~ away/off** emprender el vuelo; * *n* mosca *f*; bragueta *f.*
flying *n* aviación *f.*
flying saucer *n* platillo volante *m.*
flypast *n* desfile aéreo *m.*
flysheet *n* doble techo *m.*
foal *n* potro *m.*
foam *n* espuma *f*; * *vi* espumar.
foam rubber *n* espuma de caucho *f.*
foamy *adj* espumoso/sa,
focus *n* foco *m.*
fodder *n* forraje *m.*
foe *n* adversario/ria *m/f*, enemigo/ga *m/f.*
fog *n* niebla *f.*
foggy *adj* nebuloso/sa, brumoso/sa.
fog light *n* faro antiniebla *m.*
foible *n* debilidad, parte flaca *f.*
foil *vt* frustrar; * *n* hoja *f*; florete *m.*
fold *n* redil *m*; pliegue *m*; * *vt* plegar; * *vi*: **to ~ up** plegarse, doblarse; quebrar.
folder *n* carpeta *f*; folleto *m.*
folding *adj* plegable.
folding chair *n* silla de tijera *f.*
foliage *n* follaje *m.*
folio *n* folio *m.*
folk *n* gente *f.*
folklore *n* folklore *m.*
folk music *n* folk *m.*
folk song *n* canción folklórica *f.*
follow *vt* seguir; acompañar; imitar; **to ~ up** responder a; investigar; * *vi* seguir, resultar, provenir.
follower *n* seguidor/a *m/f*; imitador/a *m/f*; secuaz, partidario/ria *m/f*; adherente *m*; compañero/ra *m/f.*
following *adj* siguiente; * *n* afición *f.*
folly *n* extravagancia, bobería *f.*
foment *vt* fomentar; proteger.
fond *adj* cariñoso/sa; **~ly** *adv* cariñosamente.
fondle *vt* acariciar.
fondness *n* gusto *m*; cariño *m.*

font n pila bautismal f.
food n comida f.
food mixer n batidora f.
food poisoning n intoxicación alimentaria f.
food processor n robot de cocina m.
foodstuffs npl comestibles mpl.
fool n loco/ca, tonto/ta, Lat Am sonso/sa, Lat Am zonzo/za m/f; * vt engañar.
foolhardy adj temerario/ria.
foolish adj bobo/ba, tonto/ta; ~ly adv tontamente.
foolproof adj infalible.
foolscap n papel tamaño folio m.
foot n pie m; pata f; paso m; on,by ~ a pie.
footage n imágenes fpl.
football n balón m; fútbol m.
footballer n futbolista m/f; jugador/a de fútbol m/f.
footbrake n freno de pie m.
footbridge n puente peatonal m.
foothills npl estribaciones fpl.
foothold n pie firme m.
footing n base f; estado m; condición f; fundamento m.
footlights npl candilejas fpl.
footman n lacayo m; soldado de infantería m.
footnote n nota de pie f.
footpath n senda f.
footprint n huella, pisada f.
footsore adj con los pies doloridos.
footstep n paso m; huella f.
footwear n calzado m.
for prep por, a causa de; para; * conj porque, para que; por cuanto; as ~ me tocante a mí; what ~? ¿para qué?
forage n forraje m; * vt forrajear; saquear.
foray n incursión f.
forbid vt prohibir, vedar; impedir; God ~! ¡Dios no quiera!
forbidding adj inhóspito/ta; severo/ra.
force n fuerza f; poder, vigor m; violencia f; necesidad f; ~s pl tropas fpl; * vt forzar, violentar; esforzar; constreñir.
forced adj forzado/da.
forced march n (mil) marcha forzada f.
forceful adj enérgico/ca.
forceps n fórceps m.
forcible adj fuerte, eficaz, poderoso/sa; ~bly adv fuertemente, forzadamente.
ford n vado m; * vt vadear.
fore n: to the ~ en evidencia.
forearm n antebrazo m.
foreboding n presentimiento m.
forecast vt pronosticar; * n pronóstico m.
forecourt n patio m.

forefather n abuelo, antecesor m.
forefinger n índice m.
forefront n: in the ~ of en la vanguardia de.
forego vt ceder, abandonar; preceder.
foregone adj pasado/da; anticipado/da.
foreground n delantera f.
forehead n frente f; insolencia f.
foreign adj extranjero/ra; extraño/ña.
foreigner n extranjero/ra, forastero/ra m/f.
foreign exchange n divisas fpl.
foreleg n pata delantera f.
foreman n capataz m; (law) presidente del jurado m.
foremost adj principal.
forenoon n mañana f.
forensic adj forense; ~ scientist n forense m/f.
forerunner n precursor/a m/f; predecesor/a m/f.
foresee vt prever.
foreshadow vt pronosticar; simbolizar.
foresight n previsión f; presciencia f.
forest n bosque m; selva f.
forestall vt anticipar; prevenir.
forester n guardabosque m/f.
forestry n silvicultura f.
foretaste n muestra f.
foretell vt predecir, profetizar.
forethought n providencia f; premeditación f.
forever adv para siempre.
forewarn vt prevenir de antemano.
foreword n prefacio m.
forfeit n confiscación f; * vt perder derecho a.
forge n fragua f; fábrica de metales f; * vt forjar; falsificar; inventar; * vi: to ~ ahead avanzar constantemente.
forger n falsificador/a m/f.
forgery n falsificación f.
forget vt olvidar; * vi olvidarse.
forgetful adj olvidadizo/za; descuidado/da.
forgetfulness n olvido m; negligencia f.
forget-me-not n (bot) nomeolvides m.
forgive vt perdonar.
forgiveness n perdón m; remisión f.
fork n tenedor m; horca f, Lat Am horqueta f; * vi bifurcarse; to ~ out (col) desembolsar.
forked adj horcado/da.
fork-lift truck n carretilla elevadora f.
forlorn adj abandonado/da, perdido/da.
form n forma f; modelo m; modo m; formalidad f; método m; molde m; * vt formar.
formal adj formal, metódico/ca; ceremonioso/sa; ~ly adv formalmente.

formality n formalidad f; ceremonia f.
format n formato m; * vt formatear.
formation n formación f.
formative adj formativo/va.
former adj precedente; anterior, pasado/
da; ~ly adv antiguamente, en tiempos
pasados.
formidable adj formidable, terrible.
formula n fórmula f.
formulate vt formular, articular.
forsake vt dejar, abandonar.
fort n castillo m; fortaleza f.
forte adj (mus) fuerte m.
forthcoming adj venidero/ra.
forthright adj franco/ca.
forthwith adj inmediatamente, sin tardanza.
fortieth adj, n cuadragésimo m.
fortification n fortificación f.
fortify vt fortificar; corroborar.
fortitude n fortaleza f; valor m.
fortnight n quince días mpl; dos semanas
fpl, ~ly adj, adv cada quince días.
fortress n (mil) fortaleza f.
fortuitous adj impensado/da; casual; ~ly
adv fortuitamente.
fortunate adj afortunado/da; ~ly adv
felizmente.
fortune n fortuna, suerte f.
fortune-teller n sortílego/ga, adivino/na
m/f.
forty adj, n cuarenta.
forum n foro m.
forward adj avanzado/da; delantero/ra;
presumido/da; ~(s) adv adelante, más allá;
* vt remitir; promover, patrocinar.
forwardness n precocidad f; audacia f.
fossil adj, n fósil m.
foster vt criar, nutrir.
foster child n hijo/ja adoptivo/va m/f.
foster father n padre adoptivo m.
foster mother n madre adoptiva f.
foul adj sucio/cia, puerco/ca; impuro/ra,
detestable; ~ copy n borrador m; ~ly
adv suciamente; ilegítimamente; * vt
ensuciar.
foul play n mala jugada f; muerte violenta f.
found vt fundar, establecer; edificar; fundir.
foundation n fundación f; fundamento m.
founder n fundador/a m/f; fundidor m; * vi
(mar) irse a pique; zozobrar.
foundling n niño/ña expósito/ta m/f.
foundry n fundición f.
fount, fountain n fuente f.
fountainhead n origen de fuente m.

four adj, n cuatro.
fourfold adj cuádruple.
four-poster (bed) n cama de dosel f.
foursome n grupo de cuatro personas m.
fourteen adj, n catorce.
fourteenth adj, n decimocuarto/ta.
fourth adj, n cuarto/ta; * n cuarto m; ~ly
adv en cuarto lugar.
fowl n ave f de corral.
fox n zorra f; (fig) zorro m.
foyer n vestíbulo m.
fracas n riña f.
fraction n fracción f.
fracture n fractura f; * vt fracturar, romper.
fragile adj frágil; débil.
fragility n fragilidad f; debilidad, flaqueza f.
fragment n fragmento m.
fragmentary adj fragmentario/ria.
fragrance n fragancia f.
fragrant adj fragante, oloroso/sa; ~ly adv
con fragancia.
frail adj frágil, débil.
frailty n fragilidad f; debilidad f.
frame n armazón m; marco, cerco m; cuadro
de vidriera m; estructura f; montura f; * vt
encuadrar; componer, construir, formar.
frame of mind n estado de ánimo m.
framework n estructura f; esqueleto m,
armazón f.
franchise n sufragio m; concesión f.
frank adj franco/ca, liberal.
frankly adv francamente.
frankness n franqueza f.
frantic adj frenético/ca, furioso/sa.
fraternal adj, ~ly adv fraternal(mente).
fraternity n fraternidad f.
fraternize vi hermanarse.
fratricide n fratricidio m; fratricida m/f.
fraud n fraude, engaño m.
fraudulence n fraudulencia f.
fraudulent adj fraudulento/ta; ~ly adv
fraudulentamente.
fraught adj cargado/da, lleno/na.
fray n riña, disputa, querella f.
freak n fantasía f; fenómeno m.
freckle n peca f.
freckled adj pecoso/sa.
free adj libre; liberal; suelto/ta; exento/ta;
desocupado/da; gratis; * vt soltar; librar;
eximir; * vr: to ~ oneself from trouble
zafarse de.
freedom n libertad f.
freehold n propiedad absoluta f.
free-for-all n trifulca f.
free gift n prima f.

free kick n tiro libre m.
freelance adj, adv por cuenta propia.
freely adv libremente; espontáneamente;
liberalmente, gratis.
freemason n francmasón m, masón m.
freemasonry n francmasonería f, mas-
onería f.
Freepost™ n franqueo pagado m.
free-range adj de granja.
freethinker n librepensador/a m/f.
freethinking n librepensamiento m.
free trade n libre comercio m.
freeway n autopista f.
freewheel vi ir en punto muerto.
free will n libre albedrío m.
freeze vi helar(se); * vt congelar; helar.
freeze-dried adj liofilizado/da.
freezer n congelador m, Lat Am
freezer m.
freezing adj helado/da.
freezing point n punto de congelación m.
freight n carga f; flete m.
freighter n fletador m.
freight train n tren de mercancías m.
French bean n judía verde f.
French fries npl patatas/papas fritas fpl.
French window n puertaventana f.
frenzied adj loco/ca, delirante.
frenzy n frenesí m; locura f.
frequency n frecuencia f.
frequent adj, ~ly adv frecuente(mente);
* vt frecuentar.
fresco n fresco m.
fresh adj fresco/ca; nuevo/va, reciente; ~
water n agua dulce f.
freshen vt (vi) refrescar(se).
freshly adv nuevamente; recientemente.
freshman n novato m.
freshness n frescura f; fresco m.
freshwater adj de agua dulce.
fret vi agitarse, enojarse.
friar n fraile m.
friction n fricción f.
Friday n viernes m; Good ~ Viernes Santo m.
friend n amigo/ga m/f.
friendless adj sin amigos.
friendliness n amistad, benevolencia,
bondad f.
friendly adj amistoso/sa.
friendship n amistad f.
frieze n friso m.
frigate n (mar) fragata f.
fright n espanto, terror m.
frighten vt espantar.
frightened adj asustado/da.

frightening adj espantoso/sa.
frightful adj espantoso/sa, horrible; ~ly adv
espantosamente, terriblemente.
frigid adj frío/ría, frígido/da; ~ly adv
fríamente.
fringe n franja f.
fringe benefits npl ventajas adicionales fpl.
frisk vt cachear.
frisky adj juguetón/ona.
fritter vt: to ~ away desperdiciar.
frivolity n frivolidad f.
frivolous adj frívolo/la, vano/na.
frizz(le) vt frisar; rizar.
frizzy adj rizado/da.
fro adv: to go to and ~ ir y venir.
frog n rana f.
frolic vi juguetear.
frolicsome adj juguetón/ona, travieso/sa.
from prep de; después; desde.
front n parte delantera f; fachada f; paseo
marítimo m; frente m; apariencias fpl;
* adj delantero/ra; primero/ra.
frontal adj de frente.
front door n puerta principal f.
frontier n frontera f.
front page n primera plana f.
front-wheel drive n (auto) tracción
delantera f.
frost n helada f; hielo m; * vt escarchar.
frostbite n congelación f.
frostbitten adj helado/da, con síntomas de
congelación.
frosted adj deslustrado/da.
frosty adj helado/da, frío/ría como el
hielo.
froth n espuma (de algún líquido) f; * vi
espumar.
frothy adj espumoso/sa.
frown vt mirar con ceño; * n ceño m.
frozen adj helado/da.
frugal adj frugal; económico/ca; sobrio/ria;
~ly adv frugalmente.
fruit n fruta f; fruto m; producto m.
fruiterer n frutero/ra m/f.
fruitful adj fructífero/ra, fértil; provechoso/
sa, útil; ~ly adv con fertilidad.
fruitfulness n fertilidad f.
fruition n realización f.
fruit juice n zumo de fruta m.
fruitless adj estéril; inútil; ~ly adv
vanamente, inútilmente.
fruit salad n ensalada de frutas f, macedonia f.
fruit seller n frutero/ra m.
fruit shop/store n frutería f.

fruit tree n frutal m.
frustrate vt frustrar; anular.
frustrated adj frustrado/da.
frustration n frustración f.
fry vt freír, Lat Am fritar.
frying pan n sartén f.
fuchsia n (bot) fucsia f.
fudge n caramelo blando m.
fuel n combustible m.
fuel tank n depósito de combustible m.
fugitive adj, n fugitivo/va m/f.
fugue n (mus) fuga f.
fulcrum n fulcro m.
fulfill vt cumplir; realizar.
fulfillment n cumplimiento m.
full adj lleno/na, repleto/ta, completo/ta; perfecto/ta; * adv enteramente, del todo.
full-blown adj hecho/cha y derecho/cha.
full-fledged adj hecho/cha y derecho/cha.
full-length adj de cuerpo entero/ra; completo/ta.
full moon n plenilunio m; luna llena f.
fullness n plenitud, abundancia f.
full-scale adj en gran escala; de tamaño natural.
full-time adj de tiempo completo.
fully adv llenamente, enteramente, ampliamente.
fulsome adj exagerado/da.
fumble vi manejar torpemente.
fume vi humear; encolerizarse.
fumes npl humo m.
fumigate vt fumigar, Lat Am humear.
fun n diversión f; alegría f.
function n función f.
functional adj funcional.
fund n fondo m; fondos públicos mpl; * vt costear.
fundamental adj fundamental; ~ly adv fundamentalmente.
fundamentalism n fundamentalismo m.
fundamentalist n fundamentalista m/f.

funeral service n misa de difuntos f, funeral m.
funeral n funeral m.
funereal adj funeral, fúnebre.
fungus n hongo m; seta f.
funnel n embudo m; cañón (de chimenea) m.
funny adj divertido/da; curioso/sa; zumbón/ona.
fur n piel f.
fur coat n abrigo de pieles m.
furious adj furioso/sa, frenético/ca; ~ly adv con furia.
furlong n estadio m; (octava parte de una milla).
furlough n (mil) licencia f; permiso m.
furnace n horno m; hornaza f.
furnish vt amueblar, Lat Am amoblar; facilitar; suministrar.
furniture n muebles mpl.
furrow n surco m; * vt surcar; estriar.
furry adj peludo/da.
further adj nuevo/va; más lejano/na; * adv más lejos, más allá; aún; además; * vt adelantar, promover, ayudar.
further education n educación para adultos f.
furthermore adv además.
furthest adv lo más lejos, lo más remoto.
furtive adj furtivo/va; secreto/ta; ~ly adv furtivamente.
fury n furor m; furia f; ira f.
fuse vt, vi fundir; derretirse; * n fusible m, Lat Am tapón m; mecha f.
fuse box n caja de fusibles f.
fusion n fusión f.
fuss n lío m; alboroto m.
fussy adj jactancioso/sa.
futile adj fútil, frívolo/la.
futility n futilidad, vanidad f.
future adj futuro/ra; * n futuro m; porvenir m.
fuzzy adj borroso/sa; muy rizado/da.

G

gab n (col) charla f.
gabble vi charlar, parlotear; * n algarabía f.
gable n gablete m.
gadget n dispositivo m.
gaffe n plancha f.
gag n mordaza f; chiste m; * vt amordazar.
gage n calibre m; entrevía f; indicador m;
* vt medir.
gaiety n alegría f.
gaily adv alegremente.
gain n ganancia f; interés, provecho m; * vt
ganar; conseguir.
gait n marcha f; porte m.
gala n fiesta f.
galaxy n galaxia f.
gale n vendaval m.
gall n hiel f.
gallant adj galante.
gall bladder n vesícula biliar f.
gallery n galería f.
galley n cocina f; galera f.
gallon n galón m (medida).
gallop n galope m; * vi galopar.
gallows n horca f.
gallstone n cálculo biliar m.
galore adv en abundancia.
galvanize vt galvanizar.
gambit n estrategia f.
gamble vi jugar; especular; * n riesgo m;
apuesta f.
gambler n jugador/a m/f.
gambling n juego m.
game n juego m; pasatiempo m; partido m;
partida f; caza f; * vi jugar.
gamekeeper n guardabosques m invar.
gaming n juego m.
gammon n jamón m.
gamut n (mus) gama f.
gander n ganso m.
gang n pandilla, banda f.
gangrene n gangrena f.
gangster n gángster m.
gangway n pasarela f.
gap n hueco m; claro m; intervalo m.
gape vi boquear; estar con la boca abierta.
gaping adj muy abierto/ta.
garage n garaje m, Lat Am garage m.
garbage cann cubo de la basura m.
garbageman n basurero m.
garbled adj falsificado/da.
garden n jardín m.

garden-hose n regadera f.
gardener n jardinero/ra m/f.
gardening n jardinería f.
gargle vi hacer gárgaras.
gargoyle n gárgola f.
garish adj ostentoso/sa.
garland n guirnalda f.
garlic n ajo m.
garment n prenda f.
garnish vt guarnecer, adornar; * n guarnición f; adorno m.
garret n guardilla f; desván m.
garrison n (mil) guarnición f; * vt (mil)
guarnecer.
garrote vt estrangular.
garrulous adj gárrulo/la, locuaz, charlador/a.
garter n liga f.
garter belt n liguero m.
gas n gas m; gasolina f.
gas burner n mechero de gas m.
gas cylinder n bombona de gas f.
gaseous adj gaseoso/sa.
gas fire n estufa de gas f.
gash n cuchillada f; raja f; * vt acuchillar.
gasket n junta de culata f.
gas mask n careta antigás f.
gas meter n contador de gas m.
gasoline n gasolina f; four-star ~ súper f.
gasp vi jadear; * n boqueada f.
gas pedal n acelerador f.
gas ring n hornillo de gas m.
gassy adj gaseoso/sa.
gas tap n llave del gas f.
gastric adj gástrico/ca.
gastronomic adj gastronómico/ca.
gasworks npl fábrica de gas f.
gate n puerta f.
gateway n puerta f.
gather vt recoger, amontonar; entender;
plegar; * vi juntarse.
gathering n reunión f; colecta f.
gauche adj torpe.
gaudy adj chillón/ona.
gaunt adj flaco/ca, delgado/da.
gauze n gasa f.
gay adj alegre; vivo/va; gay.
gaze vi contemplar, considerar; * n mirada f.
gazelle n gacela f.
gazette n gaceta f.
gazetteer n gacetero m; diccionario
geográfico m.

gear *n* atavío *m*; vestido *m*; aparejo *m*; tirantes *mpl*; velocidad *f.*

gearbox *n* caja de cambios *f.*

gear wheel *n* rueda dentada *f.*

gel *n* gel *m.*

gelatin(e) *n* gelatina, jalea *f.*

gelignite *n* gelignita *f.*

gem *n* gema *f.*

Gemini *n* Géminis *m* (signo del zodiaco).

gender *n* género *m.*

gene *n* gen *m.*

genealogical *adj* genealógico/ca.

genealogy *n* genealogía *f.*

general *adj* general, común, usual; in ~ por lo general; ~ly *adv* generalmente; * *n* general *m*; generala *f.*

general delivery *n* lista de correos *f.*

generality *n* generalidad, mayor parte *f.*

generalization *n* generalización *f.*

generalize *vt* generalizar.

generate *vt* engendrar; producir; causar.

generation *n* generación *f.*

generator *n* generador *m.*

generic *adj* genérico/ca.

generosity *n* generosidad, liberalidad *f.*

generous *adj* generoso/sa.

genetic engineering *n* ingeniería genética *f.*

genetics *npl* genética *f.*

genial *adj* genial, natural; alegre.

genitals *npl* genitales *mpl.*

genitive *n* genitivo *m.*

genius *n* genio *m.*

genteel *adj* refinado/da, elegante.

gentile *n* gentil, pagano/na *m/f.*

gentle *adj* suave, dócil, manso/sa, moderado/ da; benigno/na.

gentleman *n* caballero *m.*

gentleness *n* dulzura, suavidad *f.*

gently *adv* suavemente.

gentry *n* alta burguesía *f.*

gents *n* aseos *mpl.*

genuflection *n* genuflexión *f*, *Lat Am* hincada *f.*

genuine *adj* genuino/na, puro/ra; ~ly *adv* puramente, naturalmente.

genus *n* género *m.*

geographer *n* geógrafo/fa *m/f.*

geographical *adj* geográfico/ca.

geography *n* geografía *f.*

geological *adj* geológico/ca.

geologist *n* geólogo/ga *m/f.*

geology *n* geología *f.*

geometric(al) *adj* geométrico/ca.

geometry *n* geometría *f.*

geranium *n* (*bot*) geranio *m.*

geriatric *n*, *adj* geriátrico/ca *m/f.*

germ *n* germen *m.*

germinate *vi* brotar.

gesticulate *vi* gesticular.

gesture *n* gesto, movimiento expresivo *m.*

get *vt* ganar; conseguir, obtener, alcanzar; coger; agarrar; * *vi* hacerse, ponerse; prevalecer; introducirse; to ~ the better salir vencedor/a, sobrepujar.

geyser *n* géiser *m*; calentador de agua *m.*

ghastly *adj* espantoso/sa.

gherkin *n* pepinillo, cohombrillo *m.*

ghetto *n* gueto *m.*

ghost *n* fantasma *m*, *Lat Am* espanto *m*; espectro *m.*

ghostly *adj* fantasmal.

giant *n* gigante *m.*

gibberish *n* jerigonza *f.*

gibe *vi* escarnecer, burlarse, mofar; * *n* mofa, burla *f.*

giblets *npl* menudillos *mpl.*

giddiness *n* vértigo *m.*

giddy *adj* vertiginoso/sa.

gift *n* regalo *m*; don *m*; dádiva *f*; talento *m.*

gifted *adj* dotado/da.

gift voucher *n* vale de regalo *m.*

gigantic *adj* gigantesco/ca.

giggle *vi* reírse tontamente.

gild *vt* dorar.

gilding, gilt *n* doradura *f.*

gill *n* cuarta parte de pinta *f*; ~s *pl* agallas *fpl.*

gilt-edged *adj* de máxima garantía.

gimmick *n* truco *m.*

gin *n* ginebra *f.*

ginger *n* jengibre *m.*

gingerbread *n* pan de jengibre *m.*

ginger-haired *adj* pelirrojo/ja.

giraffe *n* jirafa *f.*

girder *n* viga *f.*

girdle *n* faja *f*; cinturón *m.*

girl *n* muchacha, chica *f*, zagala *f.*

girlfriend *n* amiga; novia *f.*

girlish *adj* de niña.

giro *n* giro postal *m.*

girth *n* cincha *f*; circunferencia *f.*

gist *n* punto principal *m.*

give *vt*, *vi* dar, donar; conceder; abandonar; pronunciar; aplicarse, dedicarse; to ~ away regalar; traicionar, revelar; to ~ back devolver; to ~ in *vi* ceder; *vt* entregar; to ~ off despedir; to ~ out distribuir; to ~ up *vi* rendir; *vt* renunciar a.

gizzard *n* molleja *f.*

glacial *adj* glacial.

glacier *n* glaciar *m*.

glad *adj* alegre, contento/ta, agradable; **I am ~ to see** me alegro de ver; **~ly** *adv* alegremente.

gladden *vt* alegrar.

gladiator *n* gladiador *m*.

glamor *n* encanto, atractivo *m*.

glamorous *adj* atractivo/va.

glance *n* ojeada *f*; * *vi* mirar; echar una ojeada.

glancing *adj* oblicuo/cua.

gland *n* glándula *f*.

glare *n* deslumbramiento *m*; mirada feroz y penetrante *f*; * *vi* deslumbrar, brillar; echar miradas de indignación.

glaring *adj* deslumbrante; manifiesto/ta; notorio/ria.

glass *n* vidrio *m*, cristal *m*; telescopio *m*; vaso *m*; espejo *m*; **~es** *pl* gafas *fpl*; * *adj* vítreo/rea.

glassware *n* cristalería *f*.

glassy *adj* vítreo/rea, cristalino/na, vidrioso/sa.

glaze *vt* vidriar; embarnizar.

glazier *n* vidriero *m*, cristalero *m*.

gleam *n* relámpago, rayo *m*; * *vi* relampaguear, brillar.

gleaming *adj* reluciente.

glean *vt* espigar; recoger.

glee *n* alegría *f*; gozo *m*; jovialidad *f*.

glen *n* valle *m*; llanura *f*.

glib *adj* con lab; **~ly** *adv* con labia.

glide *vi* resbalar; planear.

gliding *n* vuelo sin motor *m*.

glimmer *n* vislumbre *f*; * *vi* vislumbrarse.

glimpse *n* vislumbre *f*; relámpago *m*; ojeada *f*; * *vt* entrever, percibir.

glint *vi* centellear.

glisten, glitter *vi* relucir, brillar.

gloat *vi* relamerse; saborear.

global *adj* mundial.

globalization *n* globalización *f*.

global warming *n* calentamiento global *m*.

globe *n* globo *m*; esfera *f*.

gloom, gloominess *n* oscuridad *f*; melancolía, tristeza *f*; **~ily** *adv* oscuramente; tristemente.

gloomy *adj* sombrío/ría, oscuro/ra; cubierto de nubes; triste, melancólico/ca.

glorification *n* glorificación, alabanza *f*.

glorify *vt* glorificar, celebrar.

glorious *adj* glorioso/sa, ilustre; **~ly** *adv* gloriosamente.

glory *n* gloria, fama, celebridad *f*.

gloss *n* glosa *f*; lustre *m*; * *vt* glosar, interpretar; **to ~ over** encubrir.

glossary *n* glosario *m*.

glossy *adj* lustroso/sa, brillante.

glove *n* guante *m*.

glove compartment *n* guantera *f*.

glow *vi* arder; inflamarse; relucir; * *n* color vivo *m*; viveza de color *f*; vehemencia de una pasión *f*.

glower *vi* mirar con ceño.

glue *n* cola *f*; *Lat Am* cemento *m*; * *vt* pegar.

gluey *adj* viscoso/sa, pegajoso/sa.

glum *adj* abatido/da, triste.

glut *n* hartura, abundancia *f*.

glutinous *adj* glutinoso/sa, viscoso/sa.

glutton *n* glotón/ona, tragón/ona *m/f*.

gluttony *n* glotonería *f*.

glycerin *n* glicerina *f*.

gnarled *adj* nudoso/sa.

gnash *vt*, *vi* rechinar.

gnat *n* mosquito *m*, *Lat Am* jején *m*.

gnaw *vt* roer.

gnome *n* gnomo *m*.

go *vi* ir, irse, andar, caminar; partir(se), marchar; huir; pasar; **to ~ ahead** seguir adelante; **to ~ away** marcharse; **to ~ back** volver; **to ~ by** pasar; **to ~ for** ir por; gustar; **to ~ in** entrar; **to ~ off** irse; pasarse; **to ~ on** seguir; pasar; **to ~ out** salir; apagarse; **to ~ up** subir.

goad *n* aguijada, aijada *f*, *Lat Am* picana *f*; * *vt* aguijar, *Lat Am* picanear; estimular, incitar.

go-ahead *adj* emprendedor/a; * *n* luz verde *f*.

goal *n* meta *f*; fin *m*.

goalkeeper *n* portero/ra *m/f*, *Lat Am* arquero/ra *m/f*, *Lat Am* guardavallas *m/f invar*.

goalpost *n* poste (de la portería) *m*.

goatherd *n* cabrero/ra *m/f*.

gobble *vt* engullir, tragar; **to ~ down** zampar.

go-between *n* mediador/a *m/f*.

goblet *n* copa *f*.

goblin *n* espíritu ambulante, duende *m*.

God *n* Dios *m*.

godchild *n* ahijado, hijo de pila *m*.

goddaughter *n* ahijada, hija de pila *f*.

goddess *n* diosa *f*.

godfather *n* padrino *m*.

godforsaken *adj* dejado/da de la mano de Dios.

godhead *n* deidad, divinidad *f*.

godless *adj* infiel, impío/pía, sin Dios, ateo/tea.

godlike *adj* divino/na.

godliness *n* piedad, devoción, santidad *f*.

godly *adj* piadoso/sa, devoto/ta, religioso/sa; recto/ta, justificado/da.

godmother *n* madrina *f*.
godsend *n* don del cielo *m*.
godson *n* ahijado *m*.
goggle-eyed *adj* con ojos desorbitados.
goggles *npl* gafas *fpl*; gafas de bucear *fpl*.
going *n* ida *f*; salida *f*; partida *f*; progreso *m*.
gold *n* oro *m*.
golden *adj* áureo/rea, de oro; excelente; ~ **rule** *n* regla de oro *f*.
goldfish *n* pez de colores *m*.
gold-plated *adj* chapado/da en oro.
goldsmith *n* orfebre *m*.
golf *n* golf *m*.
golf ball *n* pelota de golf *f*.
golf club *n* club de golf *m*.
golf course *n* campo de golf *m*.
golfer *n* golfista *m/f*.
gondoller *n* gondolero/ra *m/f*.
gone *adj* ido/da; perdido/da; pasado/da; gastado/da; muerto/ta.
gong *n* atabal chino, gong *m*.
good *adj* bueno/na, benévolo/la, cariñoso/sa, conveniente, apto/ta, * *adv* bien, * *n* bien *m*; prosperidad, ventaja *f*; ~s *pl* bienes muebles *mpl*; mercaderías *fpl*.
goodbye ! *excl* ¡adiós!
Good Friday *n* Viernes Santo *m*.
goodies *npl* golosinas *fpl*.
good-looking *adj* guapo/pa.
good nature *n* bondad *f*.
good-natured *adj* bondadoso/sa.
goodness *n* bondad *f*.
goodwill *n* benevolencia, bondad *f*.
goose *n* ganso *m*; oca *f*.
gooseberry *n* grosella espinosa *f*.
goose bumps, goose flesh *npl* carne de gallina *f*.
goose-step *n* paso de la oca *m*.
gore *n* sangre cuajada *f*; * *vt* cornear.
gorge *n* barranco *m*; * *vt* engullir, tragar.
gorgeous *adj* maravilloso/sa.
gorilla *n* gorila *m*.
gorse *n* aulaga *f*.
gory *adj* sangriento/ta.
goshawk *n* azor *m*.
gospel *n* evangelio *m*.
gossamer *n* vello *m*; pelusa (de frutas) *f*.
gossip *n* cotilleo *m*; * *vi* cotillear.
gothic *adj* gótico/ca.
gout *n* gota *f* (enfermedad).
govern *vt* gobernar, dirigir, regir.
governess *n* gobernadora *f*.
government *n* gobierno *m*; administración publica *f*.
governor *n* gobernador/a *m/f*.

gown *n* toga *f*; vestido de mujer *m*; bata *f*.
grab *vt* agarrar.
grace *n* gracia *f*; favor *m*; merced *f*; perdón *m*; gracias *fpl*; **to say** ~ bendecir la mesa; * *vt* adornar; agraciar.
graceful *adj* gracioso/sa, primoroso/sa; ~ly *adv* elegantemente, con gracia.
gracious *adj* gracioso/sa; favorable; ~ly *adv* graciosamente.
gradation *n* gradación *f*.
grade *n* grado *m*; curso *m*.
grade crossing *n* paso a nivel *m*.
grade school *n* escuela primaria *f*.
gradient *n* (*rail*) pendiente.
gradual *adj* gradual; ~ly *adv* gradualmente.
graduate *vi* graduarse, *Lat Am* egresar.
graduation *n* graduación *f*, *Lat Am* egreso *m*.
graffiti *n* pintadas *fpl*.
graft *n* injerto *m*; * *vt* injertar, ingerir.
grain *n* grano *m*; semilla *f*; cereales *mpl*.
gram *n* gramo *m* (peso).
grammar *n* gramática *f*.
grammatical *adj* gramatical; ~ly *adv* gramaticalmente.
granary *n* granero *m*.
grand *adj* grande, ilustre.
grandchild *n* nieto/ta *m/f*.
granddad *n* abuelo *m*.
granddaughter *n* nieta *f*; **great** ~ bisnieta *f*.
grandeur *n* grandeza *f*; pompa *f*.
grandfather *n* abuelo *m*; **great** ~ bisabuelo *m*.
grandiose *adj* grandioso/sa.
grandma *n* abuelita *f*.
grandmother *n* abuela *f*; **great** ~ bisabuela *f*.
grandparents *npl* abuelos *mpl*.
grand piano *n* piano de cola *m*.
grandson *n* nieto *m*; **great** ~ bisnieto *m*.
grandstand *n* tribuna *f*.
granite *n* granito *m*.
grant *vt* conceder; **to take for** ~ed presuponer; * *n* beca *f*; concesión *f*.
granulate *vt* granular.
granule *n* gránulo *m*.
grape *n* uva *f*; **bunch of** ~s racimo de uvas *m*.
grapefruit *n* toronja *f*, pomelo *m*.
graph *n* gráfica *f*.
graphic(al) *adj* gráfico/ca; pintoresco/ca; ~ally *adv* gráficamente.
graphics *n* artes gráficas *fpl*; gráficos *mpl*.
grapnel *n* (*mar*) arpeo *m*.
grasp *vt* empuñar, asir, agarrar; * *n* puño *m*; comprensión *f*; poder *m*.
grasping *adj* avaro/ra.
grass *n* hierba *f*, *Lat Am* pasto *m*.
grasshopper *n* saltamontes *m invar*.

grassland n pampa, pradera f.
grass-roots adj popular.
grass snake n culebra de agua f.
grassy adj herboso/sa.
grate n reja, verja, rejilla f; * vt rallar; rechinar (los dientes); enrejar.
grateful adj grato/ta, agradecido/da; ~ly adv agradecidamente.
gratefulness n gratitud f.
grater n rallador m.
gratification n gratificación f.
gratify vt contentar; gratificar.
gratifying adj grato/ta.
grating n rejado m; * adj áspero/ra; ofensivo/va.
gratis adv gratis.
gratitude n gratitud f.
gratuitous adj gratuito/ta, voluntario/ria; ~ly adv gratuitamente.
gratuity n gratificación, recompensa f.
grave n sepultura f; * adj grave, serio/ria; ~ly adv con gravedad, seriamente.
grave digger n sepulturero m.
gravel n cascajo m.
gravestone n lápida f.
graveyard n cementerio m.
gravitate vi gravitar.
gravitation n gravitación f.
gravity n gravedad f.
gravy n jugo de la carne f; salsa f.
gray adj gris; cano/na; * n gris m.
gray-haired adj canoso/sa.
grayish adj grisáceo/a; entrecano/na.
grayness n color gris m.
graze vt pastorear; tocar ligeramente; * vi pacer.
grease n grasa f; * vt untar.
greaseproof adj a prueba de grasa.
greasy adj grasiento/ta, Lat Am grasoso/sa.
great adj gran, grande; principal; ilustre; noble; magnánimo/ma; ~ly adv muy, mucho.
greatcoat n sobretodo m.
greatness n grandeza f; dignidad f; poder m; magnanimidad f.
greedily adv vorazmente, ansiosamente.
greediness, **greed** n gula f; codicia f.
greedy adj avaro/ra, codicioso/sa, Lat Am abusador/ra; goloso/sa, glotón/ona.
Greek n griego (idioma) m.
green adj verde, fresco/ca, reciente; no maduro/ra; * n verde m; llanura verde f; ~s pl verduras fpl.
greenback n billete m.
green belt n zona verde f.
green card n carta verde f.
greenery n verdura f.

greenhouse n invernadero m
greenhouse effect n efecto invernadero m.
greenish adj verdoso/sa.
green movement n ecologismo m.
greenness n verdor, vigor m; frescura, falta de experiencia f; novedad f.
greet vt saludar, congratular.
greeting n saludo m.
greeting(s) card n tarjeta de felicitación f.
grenade n (mil) granada f.
grenadier n granadero m.
greyhound n galgo m.
grid n reja f; red f.
gridiron n parrilla f; campo de fútbol americano m.
grief n dolor m; aflicción, pena f.
grievance n pesar m; molestia f; agravio m; injusticia f; perjuicio m.
grieve vt agraviar, afligir; * vi afligirse; llorar.
grievous adj doloroso/sa; enorme, atroz; ~ly adv penosamente; cruelmente.
griffin n grifo m.
grill n parrilla f; * vt interrogar.
grille n reja f.
grim adj feo, fea; horrendo/da; ceñudo/da.
grimace n mueca f.
grime n porquería f.
grimy adj ensuciado/da.
grin n mueca f; * vi sonreír.
grind vt moler; pulverizar; afilar; picar; rechinar los dientes.
grinder n molinero m; molinillo m; amolador m.
grip n asimiento m; asidero m; maletín m; * vt agarrar.
gripping adj absorbente.
grisly adj horroroso/sa.
gristle n tendón, cartílago m.
gristly adj tendinoso/sa, cartilaginoso/sa.
grit n gravilla f; valor m.
groan vi gemir, suspirar; * n gemido, suspiro m.
grocer n tendero/ra, abarrotero/ra m/f.
groceries npl comestibles mpl.
grocery store n tienda de comestibles f.
groggy adj atontado/da.
groin n ingle f.
groom n establero m; criado m; novio m; * vt cuidar, almohazar.
groove n ranura f.
grope vt, vi tentar, buscar a oscuras; andar a tientas.
gross adj grueso/sa, corpulento/ta, espeso/sa; grosero/ra; estúpido/da; ~ly adv enormemente.

grotesque *adj* grotesco/ca.
grotto *n* gruta *f*.
ground *n* tierra *f*; terreno, suelo, pavimento *m*; fundamento *m*; razón fundamental *f*; campo (de batalla) *m*; fondo *m*; * *vt* mantener en tierra; conectar con tierra.
ground floor *n* planta baja *f*.
grounding *n* conocimientos básicos *mpl*.
groundless *adj* infundado/da; ~ly *adv* sin motivo.
ground staff *n* personal de tierra *m*.
groundwork *n* preparación *f*.
group *n* grupo *m*; * *vt* agrupar.
grouse *n* lagópodo escocés *m*; * *vi* quejarse.
grove *n* arboleda *f*.
grovel *vi* arrastrarse.
grow *vt* cultivar; * *vi* crecer, aumentarse; ~ up crecer.
grower *n* cultivador/a *m/f*; productor/a *m/f*.
growing *adj* creciente.
growl *vi* regañar, gruñir; * *n* gruñido *m*.
grown-up *n* adulto/ta *m/f*.
growth *n* crecimiento *m*.
grub *n* gusano *m*.
grubby *adj* sucio/cia.
grudge *n* rencor, odio *m*; envidia *f*; * *vt*, *vi* envidiar.
grudgingly *adv* de mala gana.
grueling *adj* penoso/sa, duro/ra.
gruesome *adj* horrible.
gruff *adj* brusco/ca; ~ly *adv* bruscamente.
gruffness *n* aspereza, severidad *f*.
grumble *vi* gruñir; murmurar.
grumpy *adj* regañón/ona.
grunt *vi* gruñir; * *n* gruñido *m*.
G-string *n* taparrabo *m*.
guarantee *n* garantía *f*; * *vt* garantizar.
guard *n* guardia *f*; * *vt* guardar; defender.
guarded *adj* cauteloso/sa, mesurado/da.
guardroom *n* (*mil*) cuarto de guardia *m*.
guardian *n* tutor/ra *m/f*; curador/a *m/f*; guardián/dana *m/f*.
guardianship *n* tutela *f*.
guerrilla *n* guerrillero/ra *m/f*.
guerrilla group *n* guerrilla *f*.
guerrilla warfare *n* guerra de guerrillas *f*.
guess *vt*, *vi* conjeturar; adivinar; suponer; * *n* conjetura *f*.
guesswork *n* conjeturas *fpl*.
guest *n* huésped/a, convidado/da *m/f*.
guest room *n* cuarto de huéspedes *m*.
guffaw *n* carcajada *f*.
guidance *n* gobierno *m*; dirección *f*.
guide *vt* guiar, dirigir; * *n* guía *m*.
guide dog *n* perro lazarillo *m*.

guidelines *npl* directiva *f*.
guidebook *n* guía *f*.
guild *n* gremio *m*; corporación *f*.
guile *n* astucia *f*.
guillotine *n* guillotina *f*; * *vt* guillotinar.
guilt *n* culpabilidad *f*.
guiltless *adj* inocente, libre de culpa.
guilty *adj* reo, rea, culpable.
guinea pig *n* cobaya *f*, conejillo de Indias *m*.
guise *n* manera *f*.
guitar *n* guitarra *f*.
gulf *n* golfo *m*; abismo *m*.
gull *n* gaviota *f*.
gullet *n* esófago *m*.
gullibility *n* credulidad *f*; simpleza *f*.
gullible *adj* crédulo/la.
gully *n* barranco *m*.
gulp *n* trago *m*; * *vi* tragar saliva; * *vr* tragarse.
gum *n* goma *f*; cemento *m*; encía *f*; chicle *m*; * *vt* pegar con goma.
gum tree *n* árbol gomero *m*.
gun *n* pistola *f*; escopeta *f*.
gunboat *n* cañonera *f*.
gun carriage *n* cureña *f*.
gunfire *n* disparos *mpl*.
gunman *n* pistolero *m*.
gunmetal *n* bronce de cañones *m*.
gunner *n* artillero *m*.
gunnery *n* artillería *f*.
gunpoint *n*: at ~ a punta de pistola; a mano armada.
gunpowder *n* pólvora *f*.
gunshot *n* escopetazo *m*.
gunsmith *n* armero/ra *m/f*.
gurgle *vi* gorgotear.
guru *n* gurú *m*.
gush *vi* brotar; chorrear; * *n* chorro *m*
gushing *adj* superabundante.
gusset *n* escudete *m*.
gust *n* ráfaga *f*; soplo de aire *m*, racha *f*.
gusto *n* entusiasmo *m*.
gusty *adj* tempestuoso/sa.
gut *n* intestino *m*; ~s *npl* valor *m*; * *vt* destripar.
gutter *n* canalón *m*; arroyo *m*.
guttural *adj* gutural.
guy *n* tío *m*; tipo *m*.
guzzle *vt* engullir.
gym(nasium) *n* gimnasio *m*.
gymnast *n* gimnasta *m/f*.
gymnastic *adj* gimnástico/ca; ~s *npl* gimnástica *f*.
gynecologist *n* ginecólogo/ga *m/f*.
Gypsy *n* gitano/na *m/f*.
gypsum *n* yeso *m*.
gyrate *vi* girar.

H

haberdasher *n* camisero/ra *m*/*f*.
haberdashery *n* camisería *f*; mercería *f*; prendas de caballero *fpl*.
habit *n* costumbre *f*.
habitable *adj* habitable.
habitat *n* hábitat *m*.
habitual *adj* habitual; ~ly *adv* por costumbre.
hack *n* corte *m*; gacetillero/ra *m*/*f*; * *vt* tajar, cortar.
hackneyed *adj* trillado/da.
haddock *n* especie de bacalao *f*.
hag *n* bruja *f*.
haggard *adj* ojeroso/sa.
haggle *vi* regatear.
hail *n* granizo *m*; * *vt* saludar; * *vi* granizar.
hailstone *n* piedra de granizo *f*.
hair *n* pelo; cabello *m*.
hairbrush *n* cepillo *m*.
haircut *n* corte de pelo *m*.
hairdresser *n* peluquero/ra *m*/*f*, *Lat Am* peinador/ra *m*/*f*.
hairdryer *n* secador de pelo *m*.
hairless *adj* calvo/va.
hairnet *n* redecilla *f*.
hairpiece *n* tupé *m*.
hairpin *n* horquilla *f*.
hairpin curve *n* curva muy cerrada *f*.
hair remover *n* depilatorio *m*.
hairspray *n* laca *f*.
hairstyle *n* peinado *m*.
hairy *adj* peludo/da, cabelludo/da.
hale *adj* sano/na, vigoroso/sa.
half *n* mitad *f*; * *adj* medio/dia.
half-caste *adj* mestizo/za.
half-hearted *adj* indiferente.
half-hour *n* media hora *f*.
half-moon *n* media luna *f*.
half-price *adj* a mitad de precio.
half step *n* (*mus*) semitono *m*.
half-time *n* descanso *m*.
halfway *adv* a medio camino.
hall *n* vestíbulo *m*; hall *m*, *Lat Am* jol *m*.
hallmark *n* contraste *m*.
hallow *vt* consagrar, santificar.
hallucination *n* alucinación *f*.
halo *n* halo *m*.
halt *vi* parar; * *n* parada *f*; alto *m*.
halve *vt* partir por la mitad.
ham *n* jamón *m*.
hamburger *n* hamburguesa *f*.
hammer *n* martillo *m*; * *vt* martillar.

hammock *n* hamaca *f*.
hamper *n* cesto *f*; * *vt* estorbar.
hamstring *vt* desjarretar.
hand *n* mano *f*; brazo *m*; aguja *f*; at ~ a mano; * *vt* alargar.
handbag *n* cartera *f*, *Lat Am* sobre *m*.
handbell *n* campanilla *f*.
handbook *n* manual *m*.
handbrake *n* freno de mano *m*.
handcuff *n* esposa *f*.
handful *n* puñado *m*.
handicap *n* desventaja *f*.
handicapped *adj* minusválido/da.
handicraft *n* artesanía *f*.
handiwork *n* obra *f*.
handkerchief *n* pañuelo *m*.
handle *n* mango, puño *m*; asa; *Lat Am* manija *f*; * *vt* manejar; tratar.
handlebars *npl* manillar *m*, *Lat Am* manubrio *m*.
handling *n* manejo *m*.
handrail *n* pasamanos *m*.
handshake *n* apretón de manos *m*.
handsome *adj* guapo/pa; ~ly *adv* primorosamente.
handwriting *n* letra *f*.
handy *adj* práctico/ca; diestro/tra.
hang *vt* colgar; ahorcar; * *vi* colgar; ser ahorcado/da.
hanger *n* percha *f*.
hanger-on *n* parásito *m*.
hangings *npl* tapicería *f*.
hangman *n* verdugo *m*.
hangover *n* resaca *f*.
hang-up *n* complejo *m*.
hanker *vi* ansiar, apetecer.
haphazard *adj* fortuito/ta.
hapless *adj* desgraciado/da.
happen *vi* pasar; acontecer, acaecer.
happening *n* suceso *m*.
happily *adv* felizmente.
happiness *n* felicidad *f*.
happy *adj* feliz.
harangue *n* arenga *f*; * *vi* arengar.
harass *vt* cansar, fatigar.
harbinger *n* precursor *m*.
harbor *n* puerto *m*; * *vt* albergar.
hard *adj* duro/ra, firme; difícil; penoso/sa; severo/ra, rígido/da; ~ of hearing medio sordo/da; ~ by muy cerca.
harden *vt* (*vi*) endurecer(se).

274

hard-headed *adj* realista.
hard-hearted *adj* duro de corazón, insensible.
hardiness *n* robustez *f*.
hardly *adv* apenas.
hardness *n* dureza *f*; dificultad *f*; severidad *f*.
hardship *n* penas *fpl*.
hard-up *adj* sin plata.
hardware *n* hardware *m*; quincallería *f*.
hardwearing *adj* resistente.
hardy *adj* fuerte, robusto/ta.
hare *n* liebre *f*.
hare-brained *adj* atolondrado/da.
hare-lipped *adj* labihendido/da.
haricot *n* alubia *f*.
harlequin *n* arlequín *m*.
harm *n* mal, daño *m*; perjuicio *m*; * *vt* dañar.
harmful *adj* perjudicial.
harmless *adj* inocuo/cua.
harmonic *adj* armónico/ca.
harmonious *adj* armonioso/sa; ~ly *adv* armoniosamente.
harmonize *vt* armonizar.
harmony *n* armonía *f*.
harness *n* arreos de un caballo *mpl*; * *vt* enjaezar.
harp *n* arpa *f*.
harpist *n* arpista *m/f*.
harpoon *n* arpón *m*.
harpsichord *n* clavicordio *m*.
harrow *n* grada *f*; rastro *m*.
harry *vt* hostigar.
harsh *adj* duro/ra; austero/ra; ~ly *adv* severamente.
harshness *n* aspereza, dureza *f*; austeridad *f*.
harvest *n* cosecha *f*; * *vt* cosechar.
harvester *n* cosechadora *f*.
hash *n* hachís *m*; picadillo *m*.
hassock *n* cojín de paja *m*.
haste *n* apuro *m*; **to be in** ~ estar apurado/da.
hasten *vt* acelerar, apresurar; * *vi* tener prisa.
hastily *adv* precipitadamente.
hastiness *n* precipitación *f*.
hasty *adj* apresurado/da.
hat *n* sombrero *m*.
hatbox *n* sombrerera *f*.
hatch *vt* incubar; tramar; **to ~ a plot/scheme** zurcir; * *n* escotilla *f*.
hatchback *n* tres puertas, cinco puertas *m invar*.
hatchet *n* hacha *f*.
hatchway *n* (*mar*) escotilla *f*.
hate *n* odio, aborrecimiento *m*; * *vt* odiar, detestar.
hateful *adj* odioso/sa.
hatred *n* odio, aborrecimiento *m*.
hatter *n* sombrerero *m*.
haughtily *adv* orgullosamente.

haughtiness *n* orgullo *m*; altivez *f*.
haughty *adj* altanero/ra, orgulloso/sa.
haul *vt* tirar; * *n* botín *m*.
hauler *n* transportista *m/f*.
haunch *n* anca *f*.
haunt *vt* frecuentar, rondar; * *n* guarida *f*; costumbre *f*.
have *vt* haber, tener, poseer.
haven *n* asilo *m*; puerto *m*.
haversack *n* mochila *f*.
havoc *n* estrago *m*.
hawk *n* halcón *m*; * *vi* cazar con halcón.
hawthorn *n* espino blanco *m*.
hay *n* heno *m*.
hay fever *n* fiebre del heno *f*.
hayloft *n* henil *m*.
haystack *n* almiar *m*.
hazard *n* riesgo *m*; * *vt* arriesgar.
hazardous *adj* arriesgado/da, peligroso/sa.
haze *n* niebla *f*.
hazel *n* avellano *m*; * *adj* castaño/ña.
hazelnut *n* avellana *f*.
hazy *adj* oscuro/ra
he *pn* él.
head *n* cabeza *f*; jefe *m*; juicio *m*; * *vt* encabezar; **to ~ for** dirigirse a.
headache *n* dolor de cabeza *m*.
headdress *n* cofia *f*; tocado *m*.
headland *n* promontorio *m*.
headlight *n* faro *m*, *Lat Am* foco *m*.
headline *n* titular *m*.
headlong *adv* precipitadamente.
headmaster *n* director *m*.
head office *n* oficina central *f*.
headphones *npl* auriculares *mpl*, *Lat Am* audífonos *mpl*.
headquarters *npl* (*mil*) cuartel general *m*; sede central *f*.
headroom *n* altura *f*.
headstrong *adj* testarudo/da, cabezudo/da.
headwaiter *n* maître *m*.
headway *n* progresos *mpl*.
heady *adj* cabezón/ona.
heal *vt*, *vi* curar.
health *n* salud *f*; brindis *m invar*.
healthiness *n* sanidad *f*.
healthy *adj* sano/na.
heap *n* montón *m*; * *vt* amontonar.
hear *vt* oír; escuchar; * *vi* oír; escuchar.
hearing *n* oído *m*.
hearing aid *n* audífono *m*.
hearsay *n* rumor *m*; fama *f*.
hearse *n* coche fúnebre *m*.
heart *n* corazón *m*; **by ~** de memoria; **with all my ~** con toda mi alma.

heart attack n infarto, infarto de miocardio m.
heartbreaking adj desgarrador.
heartburn n ardor de estómago m
heart failure n fallo cardíaco m.
heartfelt adj sincero/ra.
hearth n hogar m.
heartily adv sinceramente, cordialmente.
heartiness n cordialidad, sinceridad f.
heartless adj cruel; ~ly adv cruelmente.
hearty adj cordial.
heat n calor m; * vt calentar.
heater n calentador m.
heather n (bot) brezo m.
heathen n pagano/na m/f; ~ish adj salvaje.
heating n calefacción f.
heat wave n ola de calor f.
heave vt alzar; tirar; * n tirón m.
heaven n cielo m.
heavenly adj divino/na.
heavily adv pesadamente.
heaviness n pesadez f.
heavy adj pesado/da; opresivo/va.
Hebrew n hebreo m.
heckle vt interrumpir.
hectic adj agitado/da.
hedge n seto m; * vt cercar con seto.
hedgehog n erizo m.
heed vt hacer caso de; * n cuidado m; atención f.
heedless adj descuidado/da, negligente; ~ly adv negligentemente.
heel n talón m; **to take to one's ~s** apretar los talones, huir.
hefty adj grande.
heifer n ternera f.
height n altura f; altitud f.
heighten vt realzar; adelantar, mejorar; exaltar.
heinous adj atroz.
heir n heredero/ra m/f; ~ **apparent** heredero/ra forzoso/sa m/f.
heiress n heredera f.
heirloom n reliquia de familia f.
helicopter n helicóptero m.
hell n infierno m.
hellish adj infernal.
helm n (mar) timón m.
helmet n casco m.
help vt, vi ayudar, socorrer; **I cannot ~ it** no puedo remediarlo; no lo puedo evitar; * n ayuda f; socorro, remedio m.
helper n ayudante m/f.
helpful adj útil.
helping n ración f.

helpless adj indefenso/sa; ~ly adv irremediablemente.
helter-skelter adv a trochemoche, en desorden.
hem n ribete m; * vt ribetear.
he-man n macho m.
hemisphere n hemisferio m.
hemorrhage n hemorragia f.
hemorrhoids npl hemorroides mpl.
hemp n cáñamo m.
hen n gallina f.
henchman n secuaz m.
henceforth, henceforward adv de aquí en adelante.
henhouse n gallinero m.
hepatitis n hepatitis f.
her pn su; ella; de ella; a ella.
herald n heraldo m.
heraldry n heráldica f.
herb n hierba f; ~s pl hierbas fpl.
herbaceous adj herbáceo/cea.
herbalist n herbolario m.
herbivorous adj herbívoro/ra.
herd n rebaño m.
here adv aquí, acá.
hereabout(s) adv aquí alrededor.
hereafter adv en el futuro.
hereby adv por esto.
hereditary adj hereditario/ria.
heredity n herencia f.
heresy n herejía f.
heretic n hereje m/f; * adj herético/ca.
herewith adv con esto.
heritage n patrimonio m.
hermetic adj hermético/ca; ~ly adv herméticamente.
hermit n ermitaño/ña m/f.
hermitage n ermita f.
hernia n hernia f.
hero n héroe m.
heroic adj heroico/ca; ~ally adv heroicamente.
heroine n heroína f.
heroism n heroísmo m.
heron n garza f.
herring n arenque m.
hers pn suyo, de ella.
herself pn ella misma.
hesitant adj vacilante.
hesitate vt dudar; tardar.
hesitation n duda, irresolución f.
heterogeneous adj heterogéneo/nea.
heterosexual adj, n heterosexual m.
hew vt tajar; cortar; picar.
heyday n apogeo m.

hi! *excl* ¡hola!
hiatus *n* (*gr*) hiato *m*.
hibernate *vi* invernar.
hiccup *n* hipo *m*; * *vi* tener hipo.
hickory *n* nogal americana *m*.
hide *vt* esconder; * *n* cuero *m*; piel *f*.
hideaway *n* escondite *m*.
hideous *adj* horrible; **~ly** *adv* horriblemente.
hiding place *n* escondite, escondrijo *m*.
hierarchy *n* jerarquía *f*.
hieroglyphic *adj* jeroglífico/ca; * *n* jeroglífico *m*.
hi-fi *n* estéreo, hi-fi *m*.
higgledy-piggledy *adv* confusamente.
high *adj* alto/ta; elevado/da.
high altar *n* altar mayor *m*.
highchair *n* silla alta *f*.
high-handed *adj* despótico/ca.
highlands *npl* tierras montañosas, tierras altas *fpl*.
highlight *n* punto culminante *m*.
highly *adv* en sumo grado.
highness *n* altura *f*; alteza *f*.
high school *n* centro de enseñanza secundaria *m*; escuela secundaria *f*.
highly strung *adj* hipertenso/sa.
high water *n* marea alta *f*.
highway *n* carretera *f*.
hike *vi* ir de excursión.
hijack *vt* secuestrar.
hijacker *n* secuestrador/a *m/f*.
hilarious *adj* alegre.
hill *n* colina *f*.
hillock *n* colina *f*.
hillside *n* ladera *f*.
hilly *adj* montañoso/sa.
hilt *n* puño de espada *m*.
him *pn* le, lo, el.
himself *pn* él mismo, se, si mismo.
hind *adj* trasero/ra, posterior; * *n* cierva *f*.
hinder *vt* impedir.
hindrance *n* impedimento, obstáculo *m*.
hindmost *adj* postrero/ra.
hindquarter *n* cuarto trasero *m*.
hindsight *n*: with ~ en retrospectiva.
hinge *n* bisagra *f*.
hint *n* indirecta *f*; * *vt* insinuar; sugerir.
hip *n* cadera *f*.
hippopotamus *n* hipopótamo *m*.
hire *vt* alquilar; * *n* alquiler *m*.
his *pn* su, suyo, de él.
Hispanic *adj* hispano/na; hispánico/ca; * *n* hispanoamericano/na *m/f*.
hiss *vt*, *vi* silbar.
historian *n* historiador/a *m/f*.

historic(al) *adj* histórico/ca; **~ally** *adv* históricamente.
history *n* historia *f*.
histrionic *adj* teatral.
hit *vt* golpear; alcanzar; zumbar; **to ~ each other** *vr* zumbarse; * *n* golpe *m*; éxito *m*.
hitch *vt* atar; * *n* problema *m*.
hitch-hike *vi* hacer autocstop.
hitch-hiker *n* autoestopista *m/f*.
hitch-hiking *n* autoestop *f*.
hitherto *adv* hasta ahora, hasta aquí.
hive *n* colmena *f*.
HIV-negative *adj* seronegativo/va.
HIV-positive *adj* seropositivo/va.
hoard *n* montón *m*; tesoro escondido *m*; * *vt* acumular.
hoarfrost *n* escarcha *f*.
hoarse *adj* ronco/ca; **~ly** *adv* roncamente.
hoarseness *n* ronquera, carraspera *f*.
hoax *n* trampa *f*; * *vt* engañar, burlar.
hobble *vi* cojear.
hobby *n* pasatiempo *m*, afición *f*.
hobbyhorse *n* caballo de batalla *m*.
hobo *n* vagabundo/da *m/f*.
hockey *n* hockey *m*.
hodgepodge *n* mezcolanza *f*.
hoe *n* azadón *m*; * *vt* azadonar.
hog *n* cerdo, puerco *m*, *Lat Am* chancho *m*; (*col*) cochino *m*.
hoist *vt* alzar; * *n* grúa *f*.
hold *vt* tener; detener; contener; celebrar; **to ~ on to** agarrarse a; * *vi* valer; * *n* presa *f*; poder *m*.
holder *n* poseedor/a *m/f*; titular *m/f*.
holding *n* tenencia, posesión *f*.
stick-up *n* atraco *m*; retraso *m*.
hole *n* agujero *m*.
holiness *n* santidad *f*.
hollow *adj* hueco/ca; * *n* hoyo *m*; * *vt* excavar, ahuecar.
holly *n* (*bot*) acebo *m*.
hollyhock *n* malva hortense *f*.
holocaust *n* holocausto *m*.
holster *n* pistolera *f*.
holy *adj* santo/ta, pío, pía; consagrado/da.
holy water *n* agua bendita *f*.
holy week *n* semana santa *f*.
homage *n* homenaje *m*.
home *n* casa *f*; patria *f*; domicilio *m*; **~ly** *adj* casero/ra.
home address *n* domicilio *m*.
home improvement *n* bricolaje *m*.
homeless *adj* sin casa.
homeliness *n* simpleza *f*.
homely *adj* casero/ra.

home-made adj casero/ra.
homeopathist n homeópata m/f.
homeopathy n homeopatía f.
home shopping program (TV) n teletienda f.
homesick adj nostálgico/ca.
homesickness n nostalgia f.
hometown n ciudad natal f.
homeward adj hacia casa; hacia su país.
homework n deberes mpl.
homicidal adj homicida.
homicide n homicidio m; homicida m/f.
homogeneous adj homogéneo/nea.
homosexual adj, n homosexual m.
honest adj honrado/da; ~ly adv honradamente.
honesty n honradez f.
honey n miel f.
honeycomb n panal m.
honeymoon n luna de miel f.
honeysuckle n (bot) madreselva f.
honor n honra f; honor m; * vt honrar.
honqrable adj honorable; ilustre.
honorably adv honorablemente.
honorary adj honorario/ria.
hood n capo m; capucha f.
hoodlum n matón m.
hoof n pezuña f.
hook n gancho m; anzuelo m; by ~ or by crook de un modo u otro; * vt enganchar.
hooked adj encorvado/da.
hooligan n gamberro/rra m/f.
hoop n aro m.
hop n (bot) lúpulo m; salto m; * vi saltar, brincar.
hope n esperanza f; * vi esperar.
hopeful adj esperanzador/a; ~ly adv con esperanza.
hopefulness n buena esperanza f.
hopeless adj desesperado/da; ~ly adv sin esperanza.
hopscotch n tejo m.
horde n horda f.
horizon n horizonte m.
horizontal adj horizontal; ~ly adv horizontalmente.
hormone n hormona f.
horn n cuerno m; (auto) sirena f.
horned adj cornudo/da.
hornet n avispón m.
horny adj calloso/sa.
horoscope n horóscopo m.
horrendous adj horrendo/da.
horrible adj horrible, terrible.
horribly adv horriblemente; enormemente.
horrid adj horrible.
horrific adj horroroso/sa.
horrify vt horrorizar.

horror n horror, terror m.
horror film n película de horror f.
hors d'oeuvre n entremeses mpl.
horse n caballo m; caballete m.
horseback adv: on ~ a caballo.
horse-breaker n domador/a de caballos m/f.
horse chestnut n castaño de Indias m.
horsefly n moscarda f; moscardón m.
horseman n jinete m.
horsemanship n equitación f.
horsepower n caballo de fuerza m.
horse race n carrera de caballos f.
horseracing n hípica f.
horseradish n rábano silvestre m.
horseshoe n herradura de caballo f.
horsewoman n jineta f.
horticulture n horticultura, jardinería f.
horticulturist n jardinero/ra m/f.
hosepipe n manguera f.
hosiery n calcetería f.
hospitable adj hospitalario/ria.
hospitably adv con hospitalidad.
hospital n hospital m.
hospitality n hospitalidad f.
host n anfitrión m; hostia f.
hostage n rehén m.
hostess n anfitriona f.
hostile adj hostil.
hostility n hostilidad f.
hot adj caliente; cálido/da.
hotbed n semillero m.
hotdog n perro caliente m.
hotel n hotel m.
hotelier n hotelero/ra m/f.
hot-headed adj exaltado/da.
hothouse n invernadero m.
hotline n línea directa f.
hotplate n hornillo m.
hotly adv con calor; violentamente.
hound n perro de caza m.
hour n hora f.
hour-glass n reloj de arena m.
hourly adv cada hora.
house n casa f; familia f; * vt alojar.
houseboat n casa flotante f.
housebreaker n ladrón/ona de casa m/f.
housebreaking n allanamiento de morada m.
household n familia f.
householder n amo de casa, padre de familia m; dueño/ña de la casa m/f.
housekeeper n ama de llaves f.
housekeeping n trabajos domésticos mpl.
house-warming party n fiesta de estreno de una casa f.
housewife n ama de casa f.

housework n faenas de la casa fpl.
housing n vivienda f.
housing development n urbanización f.
hovel n choza, cabaña f.
hover vi flotar.
how adv cómo, como; ~ **do you do!** ¡encantado!
however adv comoquiera, comoquiera que sea; aunque; no obstante.
howl vi aullar; * n aullido m.
hub n centro m.
hubbub n barullo m.
hubcap n tapacubos m invar.
hue n color m; matiz m.
huff n: in a ~ picado/da.
hug vt abrazar; * n abrazo m.
huge adj vasto/ta, enorme; ~ly adv inmensamente.
hulk n (mar) casco m; armatoste m.
hull n (mar) casco m.
hum vi canturrear.
human adv humano/na.
humane adv humano/na; benigno/na; ~ly adv humanamente.
humanist n humanista m/f.
humanitarian adj humanitario/ria.
humanity n humanidad f.
humanize vt humanizar.
humanly adv humanamente.
humble adj humilde, modesto/ta; * vt humillar, postrar.
humbleness n humildad f.
humbly adv con humildad.
humbug n tontcrías fpl.
humdrum adj monótono/na.
humid adj húmedo/da.
humidity n humedad f.
humiliate vt humillar.
humiliation n humillación f.
humility n humildad f.
humming n zumbido m.
humming-bird n colibrí m, Lat Am chupaflor m, Lat Am picaflor m.
humor n sentido del humor m, humor m; jocosidad f; * vt complacer.
humorist n humorista m/f
humorous adj gracioso/sa; ~ly adv con gracia.
hump n giba, joroba f.
hunch n corazonada f; ~**backed** adj jorobado/da, jiboso/sa.
hundred adj ciento; * n centenar m; un ciento.
hundredth adj centésimo.
hundredweight n quintal m.
hunger n hambre f; * vi hambrear.
hunger strike n huelga de hambre f.

hungrily adv con apetito.
hungry adj hambriento/ta, Lat Am hambreado/da.
hunt vt cazar; perseguir; buscar; * vi andar a caza; * n caza f.
hunter n cazador/a m/f.
hunting n caza f.
huntsman n cazador m.
hurdle n valla f.
hurl vt tirar con violencia; arrojar.
hurricane n huracán m.
hurried adj hecho/cha de prisa; ~ly adv con prisa.
hurry vt acelerar, apresurar; * vi apresurarse; * n prisa f.
hurt vt hacer daño; ofender; * n mal, daño m.
hurtful adj dañoso/sa; ~ly adv dañosamente.
hurtle vr zamparse.
husband n marido m.
husbandry n agricultura f.
hush! ¡chitón!, ¡silencio!; * vt hacer callar; * vi estar quieto/ta.
husk n cáscara f.
huskiness n ronquedad f.
husky adj ronco/ca.
hustings n tribuna para las elecciones f.
hustle vt empujar con fuerza.
hut n cabaña, barraca f.
hutch n conejera f.
hyacinth n jacinto m.
hydrant n boca de incendios f.
hydraulic adj hidráulico/ca; ~s npl hidráulica f.
hydroelectric adj hidroeléctrico/ca.
hydrofoil n hidroala f.
hydrogen n hidrógeno m.
hydrophobia n hidrofobia f.
hydroplane n hidroavión m.
hyena n hiena f.
hygiene n higiene f.
hygienic adj higiénico/ca.
hymn n himno m.
hyperbole n hipérbole f; exageración f.
hypermarket n hipermercado m.
hyphen n (gr) guión m.
hypochondria n hipocondria f.
hypochondriac adj, n hipocondríaco/ca m/f.
hypocrisy n hipocresía f.
hypocrite n hipócrita m/f.
hypocritical adj hipócrita.
hypothesis n hipótesis f.
hypothetical adj hipotético/ca; ~ly adv hipotéticamente.
hysterical adj histérico/ca.
hysterics npl histeria f.

I

I *pn* yo; ~ **myself** yo mismo.
ice *n* hielo *m*; * *vt* helar.
ice-axe *n* piqueta *f*.
iceberg *n* iceberg *m*.
ice-bound *adj* rodeado/da de hielos.
icebox *n* nevera *f*.
ice cream *n* helado *m*.
ice rink *n* pista de hielo *f*.
ice skating *n* patinaje sobre hielo *m*.
icicle *n* carámbano *m*.
iconoclast *n* iconoclasta *m/f*.
icy *adj* helado/da; frío/ría.
idea *n* idea *f*.
ideal *adj* ideal; ~**ly** *adv* idealmente.
idealist *n* idealista *m/f*.
identical *adj* idéntico/ca.
identification *n* identificación *f*.
identify *vt* identificar.
identity *n* identidad *f*.
identity card *n* carnet *m* de identidad, *Lat Am* cédula *f* de identidad.
ideology *n* ideología *f*.
idiom *n* idioma *m*.
idiomatic *adj* idiomático/ca.
idiosyncrasy *n* idiosincrasia *f*.
idiot *n* idiota, necio/cia *m/f*.
idiotic *adj* tonto/ta, bobo/ba.
idle *adj* desocupado/da; holgazán/zana; inútil.
idleness *n* pereza *f*.
idler *n* holgazán/zana *m/f*; zángano *m*.
idly *adv* ociosamente; vanamente.
idol *n* ídolo *m*.
idolatry *n* idolatría *f*.
idolize *vt* idolatrar.
idyllic *adj* idílico/ca.
i.e. *adv* esto es.
if *conj* si, aunque; ~ **not** si no.
igloo *n* iglú *m*.
ignite *vt* encender.
ignition *n* (*chem*) ignición *f*; encendido *m*.
ignition key *n* llave de contacto *f*.
ignoble *adj* innoble; bajo/ja.
ignominious *adj* ignominioso/sa; ~**ly** *adv* ignominiosamente.
ignominy *n* ignominia, infamia *f*.
ignoramus *n* ignorante, tonto/ta *m/f*.
ignorance *n* ignorancia *f*.
ignorant *adj* ignorante; ~**ly** *adv* ignorantemente.
ignore *vt* no hacer caso de.

ill *adj* malo/la, enfermo/ma; * *n* mal, infortunio *m*; * *adv* mal.
ill-advised *adj* imprudente.
illegal *adj*, ~**ly** *adv* ilegal(mente).
illegality *n* ilegalidad *f*.
illegible *adj* ilegible.
illegibly *adv* de modo ilegible.
illegitimacy *n* ilegitimidad *f*.
illegitimate *adj* ilegítimo/ma; ~**ly** *adv* ilegítimamente.
ill feeling *n* rencor *m*.
illicit *adj* ilícito/ta.
illiterate *adj* analfabeto/ta.
illness *n* enfermedad *f*.
illogical *adj* ilógico/ca.
ill-timed *adj* inoportuno/na.
ill-treat *vt* maltratar.
illuminate *vt* iluminar.
illumination *n* iluminación *f*.
illusion *n* ilusión *f*.
illusory *adj* ilusorio/ria.
illustrate *vt* ilustrar; explicar.
illustration *n* ilustración *f*; elucidación *f*.
illustrative *adj* explicativo/va.
illustrious *adj* ilustre, insigne.
ill-will *n* rencor *m*.
image *n* imagen *f*.
imagery *n* imágenes *fpl*.
imaginable *adj* concebible.
imaginary *adj* imaginario/ria.
imagination *n* imaginación *f*.
imaginative *adj* imaginativo/va.
imagine *vt* imaginarse; idear, inventar.
imbalance *n* desequilibrio *m*.
imbecile *adj* imbécil, necio/cia.
imbibe *vt* beber.
imbue *vt* infundir.
imitate *vt* imitar, copiar.
imitation *n* imitación, copia *f*.
imitative *adj* imitativo/va.
immaculate *adj* inmaculado/da, puro/ra.
immaterial *adj* poco importante.
immature *adj* inmaduro/ra.
immeasurable *adj* inconmensurable.
immeasurably *adv* inmensamente.
immediate *adj* inmediato/ta; ~**ly** *adv* inmediatamente; ya.
immense *adj* inmenso/sa; vasto/ta; ~**ly** *adv* inmensamente.
immensity *n* inmensidad *f*.
immerse *vt* sumergir.

immersion *n* inmersión *f.*
immigrant *n* inmigrante *m/f.*
immigrate *vi* inmigrar.
immigration *n* inmigración *f.*
imminent *adj* inminente.
immobile *adj* inmóvil.
immobility *n* inmovilidad *f.*
immoderate *adj* inmoderado/da, excesivo/va; ~ly *adv* inmoderadamente.
immodest *adj* inmodesto/ta.
immoral *adj* inmoral.
immorality *n* inmoralidad *f.*
immortal *adj* inmortal.
immortality *n* inmortalidad *f.*
immortalize *vt* inmortalizar, eternizar.
immune *adj* inmune.
immunity *n* inmunidad *f.*
immunize *vt* inmunizar.
immutable *adj* inmutable.
imp *n* diablillo, duende *m.*
impact *n* impacto *m.*
impair *vt* disminuir.
impale *vt* empalar.
impalpable *adj* impalpable.
impart *vt* comunicar.
impartial *adj*, ~ly *adv* imparcial(mente).
impartiality *n* imparcialidad *f.*
impassable *adj* intransitable.
impasse *n* punto muerto *m.*
impassive *adj* impasible.
impatience *n* impaciencia *f.*
impatient *adj*, ~ly *adv* impaciente(mente).
impeach *vt* acusar, denunciar.
impeccable *adj* impecable.
impecunious *adj* indigente.
impede *vt* estorbar.
impediment *n* obstáculo *m.*
impel *vt* impeler, impulsar.
impending *adj* inminente.
impenetrable *adj* impenetrable.
imperative *adj* imperativo/va.
imperceptible *adj* imperceptible.
imperceptibly *adv* imperceptiblemente.
imperfect *adj* imperfecto/ta, defectuoso/sa; ~ly imperfectamente *adv*; * *n* (*gr*) pretérito imperfecto *m.*
imperfection *n* imperfección *f*, defecto *m.*
imperial *adj* imperial.
imperialism *n* imperialismo *m.*
imperious *adj* imperioso/sa; arrogante; ~ly *adv* imperiosamente, arrogantemente.
impermeable *adj* impermeable.
impersonal *adj*, ~ly *adv* impersonal(mente).
impersonate *vt* hacerse pasar por; imitar.

impertinence *n* impertinencia *f*; descaro *m.*
impertinent *adj* impertinente; ~ly *adv* impertinentemente.
imperturbable *adj* imperturbable.
impervious *adj* impermeable.
impetuosity *n* impetuosidad *f.*
impetuous *adj* impetuoso/sa; ~ly *adv* impetuosamente.
impetus *n* ímpetu *m.*
impiety *n* impiedad *f.*
impinge (**on**) *vt* tener influjo en.
impious *adj* impío/pía, irreligioso/sa.
implacable *adj* implacable.
implacably *adv* implacablemente.
implant *vt* implantar; plantear.
implement *n* herramienta *f*; utensilio *m.*
implicate *vt* implicar.
implication *n* implicación *f.*
implicit *adj* implícito/ta; ~ly *adv* implícitamente.
implore *vt* suplicar.
imply *vt* suponer.
impolite *adj* maleducado/da.
impoliteness *n* falta de educación *f.*
impolitic *adj* imprudente; impolítico/ca.
import *vt* importar; * *n* importación *f.*
importance *n* importancia *f.*
important *adj* importante.
importation *n* importación *f.*
importer *n* importador/a *m/f.*
importunate *adj* importuno/na.
importune *vt* importunar.
importunity *n* importunidad *f.*
impose *vt* imponer.
imposing *adj* imponente.
imposition *n* imposición, carga *f.*
impossibility *n* imposibilidad *f.*
impossible *adj* imposible.
impostor *n* impostor *m.*
impotence *n* impotencia *f.*
impotent *adj* impotente; ~ly *adv* sin poder.
impound *vt* embargar.
impoverish *vt* empobrecer.
impoverished *adj* necesitado/da.
impoverishment *n* empobrecimiento *m.*
impracticability *n* inviabilidad *f.*
impracticable *adj* impracticable, inviable.
impractical *adj* poco práctico/ca.
imprecation *n* imprecación, maldición *f.*
imprecise *adj* impreciso/sa.
impregnable *adj* inexpugnable.
impregnate *vt* impregnar.
impregnation *n* fecundación *f*; impregnación *f.*

impress vt impresionar.
impression n impresión f; edición f.
impressionable adj impresionable.
impressive adj impresionante.
imprint n sello m; * vt imprimir; estampar.
imprison vt encarcelar.
imprisonment n encarcelamiento m.
improbability n improbabilidad f.
improbable adj improbable.
impromptu adj de improviso.
improper adj impropio/pia, indecente; ~ly adv impropiamente.
impropriety n impropiedad f.
improve vt, vi mejorar, Lat Am repuntar.
improvement n progreso m, mejora f.
improvident adj impróvido/da, imprudente.
improvise vt improvisar.
imprudence n imprudencia f.
imprudent adj imprudente.
impudence n impudencia f.
impudent adj impudente; ~ly adv desvergonzadamente.
impugn vt impugnar.
impulse n impulso m.
impulsive adj impulsivo/va.
impunity n impunidad f.
impure adj impuro/ra; ~ly adv impuramente.
impurity n impureza f.
in prep en.
inability n incapacidad f.
inaccessible adj inaccesible.
inaccuracy n inexactitud f.
inaccurate adj inexacto/ta.
inaction n inacción f.
inactive adj inactivo/va, perezoso/sa.
inactivity n inactividad f.
inadequate adj inadecuado/da, defectuoso/sa.
inadmissible adj inadmisible.
inadvertently adv sin querer.
inalienable adj inalienable.
inane adj necio/cia.
inanimate adj inanimado/da.
inapplicable adj inaplicable.
inappropriate adj impropio/pia.
inasmuch adv visto que; en tanto en cuanto.
inattentive adj desatento/ta.
inaudible adj inaudible.
inaugural adj inaugural.
inaugurate vt inaugurar.
inauguration n inauguración f.
inauspicious adj poco propicio/cia.
in-between adj intermedio/dia.
inborn, inbred adj innato/ta.

incalculable adj incalculable.
incandescent adj incandescente.
incantation n conjuro m.
incapable adj incapaz.
incapacitate vt inhabilitar.
incapacity n incapacidad f.
incarcerate vt encarcelar.
incarnate adj encarnado/da.
incarnation n encarnación f.
incautious adj incauto/ta; ~ly adv incautamente.
incendiary n bomba incendiaria f.
incense n incienso m; * vt exasperar.
incentive n incentivo m.
inception n principio m.
incessant adj incesante, constante; ~ly adv continuamente.
incest n incesto m.
incestuous adj incestuoso/sa.
inch n pulgada f; ~ by ~ palmo a palmo.
incidence n frecuencia f.
incident n incidente m.
incidental adj casual; ~ly adv a propósito.
incinerator n incinerador m.
incipient adj incipiente.
incise vt tajar, cortar.
incision n incisión f.
incisive adj incisivo/va.
incisor n incisivo m.
incite vt incitar, estimular.
inclement adj feo, fea.
inclination n inclinación, propensión f.
incline vt (vi) inclinar(se); * n cuesta f.
include vt incluir, comprender.
including prep incluso.
inclusion n inclusión f.
inclusive adj inclusivo/va.
incognito adv de incógnito.
incoherence n incoherencia f.
incoherent adj incoherente, inconsecuente; ~ly adv de modo incoherente.
income n renta f; ingresos mpl.
income tax n impuesto sobre la renta m.
incoming adj entrante.
incomparable adj incomparable.
incomparably adv incomparablemente.
incompatibility n incompatibilidad f.
incompatible adj incompatible.
incompetence n incompetencia f.
incompetent adj, ~ly adv incompetente-(mente).
incomplete adj incompleto/ta.
incomprehensibility n incomprensibilidad f.
incomprehensible adj incomprensible.

inconceivable *adj* inconcebible.
inconclusive *adj* no concluyente; ~ly *adv* sin conclusión.
incongruity *n* incongruencia *f.*
incongruous *adj* incongruo/rua; ~ly *adv* incongruamente.
inconsequential *adj* inconsecuente.
inconsiderate *adj* desconsiderado/da; ~ly *adv* desconsideradamente.
inconsistency *n* inconsecuencia *f.*
inconsistent *adj* inconsecuente.
inconsolable *adj* inconsolable.
inconspicuous *adj* discreto/ta.
incontinence *n* incontinencia *f.*
incontinent *adj* incontinente.
incontrovertible *adj* incontrovertible.
inconvenience *n* incomodidad *f*; * *vt* incomodar.
inconvenient *adj* incómodo/da; ~ly *adv* incómodamente.
incorporate *vt* (*vi*) incorporar(se).
incorporated company (inc) *n* sociedad anónima *f*
incorporation *n* incorporación *f.*
incorrect *adj* incorrecto/ta; ~ly *adv* incorrectamente.
incorrigible *adj* incorregible.
incorruptibility *n* incorruptibilidad *f.*
incorruptible *adj* incorruptible.
increase *vt* acrecentar, aumentar; * *vi* crecer; * *n* aumento *m.*
increasing *adj* creciente; ~ly *adv* cada vez más.
incredible *adj* increíble.
incredulity *n* incredulidad *f.*
incredulous *adj* incrédulo/la.
increment *n* incremento *m.*
incriminate *vt* incriminar.
incrust *vt* incrustar.
incubate *vi* incubar.
incubator *n* incubadora *f.*
inculcate *vt* inculcar.
incumbent *adj* obligatorio/ria; * *n* beneficiado/da *m/f.*
incur *vt* incurrir.
incurability *n* lo incurable.
incurable *adj* incurable.
incursion *n* incursión, invasión *f.*
indebted *adj* agradecido/da.
indecency *n* indecencia *f.*
indecent *adj* indecente; ~ly *adv* indecentemente.
indecision *n* irresolución *f.*
indecisive *adj* indeciso/sa.
indecorous *adj* indecente.

indeed *adv* verdaderamente, de veras.
indefatigable *adj* incansable.
indefinite *adj* indefinido/da; ~ly *adv* indefinidamente.
indelible *adj* indeleble.
indelicacy *n* falta de delicadeza, grosería *f.*
indelicate *adj* poco delicado/da.
indemnify *vt* indemnizar.
indemnity *n* indemnidad *f.*
indent *vt* mellar.
independence *n* independencia *f.*
independent *adj* independiente; ~ly *adv* independientemente.
indescribable *adj* indescriptible.
indestructible *adj* indestructible.
indeterminate *adj* indeterminado/da.
index *n* índice *m.*
index card *n* ficha *f.*
indexed *adj* indexado/da.
index finger *n* dedo índice *m.*
indicate *vt* indicar.
indication *n* indicación *f*; indicio *m.*
indicative *adj, n* (gr) indicativo *m.*
indicator *n* indicador *m.*
indict *vt* acusar.
indictment *n* acusación *f.*
indifference *n* indiferencia *f.*
indifferent *adj* indiferente; ~ly *adv* indiferentemente.
indigenous *adj* indígena.
indigent *adj* indigente.
indigestible *adj* indigerible.
indigestion *n* indigestión *f.*
indignant *adj* indignado/da.
indignation *n* indignación *f.*
indignity *n* indignidad *f.*
indigo *n* añil *m.*
indirect *adj* indirecto/ta; ~ly *adv* indirectamente.
indiscreet *adj* indiscreto/ta; ~ly *adv* indiscretamente.
indiscretion *n* indiscreción *f.*
indiscriminate *adj* indistinto/ta; ~ly *adv* sin distinción.
indispensable *adj* indispensable.
indisposed *adj* indispuesto/ta.
indisposition *n* indisposición *f.*
indisputable *adj* indiscutible.
indisputably *adv* indisputablemente.
indistinct *adj* indistinto/ta, confuso/sa; ~ly *adv* indistintamente.
indistinguishable *adj* indistinguible.
individual *adj* individual; ~ly *adv* individualmente; * *n* individuo *m.*
individuality *n* individualidad *f.*

indivisible *adv* indivisible; ~bly *adv* indivisiblemente.
indoctrinate *vt* adoctrinar.
indoctrination *n* adoctrinamiento *m.*
indolence *n* indolencia, pereza *f.*
indolent *adj* indolente; ~ly *adv* con negligencia.
indomitable *adj* indomable.
indoors *adv* dentro.
indubitably *adv* indudablemente.
induce *vt* inducir, persuadir; causar.
inducement *n* aliciente *m.*
induction *n* inducción *f.*
indulge *vt, vi* conceder; ser indulgente.
indulgence *n* indulgencia *f.*
indulgent *adj* indulgente; ~ly *adv* de modo indulgente.
industrial *adj* industrial.
industrialist *n* industrial *m/f.*
industrialization *n* industrialización *f.*
industrialize *vt* industrializar.
industrial park *n* polígono industrial *m.*
industrious *adj* trabajador/a.
industry *n* industria *f.*
inebriated *adj* embriagado/da.
inebriation *n* embriaguez *f.*
inedible *adj* incomestible.
ineffable *adj* inefable.
ineffective, ineffectual *adj* ineficaz; ~ly *adv* sin efecto.
inefficiency *n* ineficacia *f.*
inefficient *adj* ineficaz.
ineligible *adj* ineligible.
inept *adj* incompetente.
ineptitude *n* incompetencia *f.*
inequality *n* desigualdad *f.*
inert *adj* inerte, perezoso/sa.
inertia *n* inercia *f.*
inescapable *adj* ineludible.
inestimable *adj* inestimable, inapreciable.
inevitable *adj* inevitable.
inevitably *adv* inevitablemente.
inexcusable *adj* inexcusable.
inexhaustible *adj* inagotable.
inexorable *adj* inexorable.
inexpedient *adj* imprudente.
inexpensive *adj* económico/ca.
inexperience *n* inexperiencia *f.*
inexperienced *adj* inexperto/ta.
inexpert *adj* inexperto/ta.
inexplicable *adj* inexplicable.
inexpressible *adj* indecible.
inextricably *adv* indisolublemente.
infallibility *n* infalibilidad *f.*

infallible *adj* infalible; indefectible.
infamous *adj* vil, infame; ~ly *adv* infamemente.
infamy *n* infamia *f.*
infancy *n* infancia *f*; pequeñez *f.*
infant *n* niño/ña *m/f.*
infanticide *n* infanticidio *m*; infanticida *m/f.*
infantile *adj* infantil.
infantry *n* infantería *f.*
infatuated *adj* chiflado/da.
infatuation *n* infatuación *f.*
infect *vt* infectar.
infection *n* infección *f.*
infectious *adj* contagioso/sa; infeccioso/sa.
infer *vt* inferir.
inference *n* inferencia *f.*
inferior *adj* inferior; * *n* subordinado/da *m/f.*
inferiority *n* inferioridad *f.*
infernal *adj* infernal.
inferno *n* infierno *m.*
infest *vt* infestar.
infidel *n* infiel, pagano *m.*
infidelity *n* infidelidad *f.*
infiltrate *vi* infiltrarse.
infinite *adj* infinito/ta; ~ly *adv* infinitamente.
infinitive *n* infinitivo *m.*
infinity *n* infinito *m*; infinidad *f.*
infirm *adj* enfermo/ma, débil.
infirmary *n* enfermería *f.*
infirmity *n* fragilidad, enfermedad *f.*
inflame *vt* (*vi*) inflamar(se).
inflammation *n* inflamación *f.*
inflammatory *adj* inflamatorio/ria.
inflatable *adj* inflable.
inflate *vt* inflar, hinchar.
inflation *n* inflación *f.*
inflection *n* inflexión *f*; modulación de la voz *f.*
inflexibility *n* inflexibilidad *f.*
inflexible *adj* inflexible; yerto/ta.
inflexibly *adv* inflexiblemente.
inflict *vt* imponer.
influence *n* influencia *f*; * *vt* influir.
influential *adj* influyente.
influenza *n* gripe *f.*
influx *n* afluencia *f.*
inform *vt* informar.
informal *adj* informal.
informality *n* informalidad *f.*
informant *n* informante *m/f.*
information *n* información *f*; ~ superhighway autopista de la información *f.*
infraction *n* infracción *f.*
infra-red *adj* infrarrojo/ja.

infrastructure *n* infraestructura *f.*
infrequent *adj* raro/ra; ~ly *adv* raramente.
infringe *vt* infringir; violar.
infringement *n* infracción *f.*
infuriate *vt* enfurecer.
infuse *vt* infundir.
infusion *n* infusión *f.*
ingenious *adj* ingenioso/sa; ~ly *adv* ingeniosamente.
ingenuity *n* ingeniosidad *f.*
ingenuous *adj* ingenuo/nua, sincero/ra; ~ly *adv* ingenuamente.
inglorious *adj* ignominioso/sa, vergonzoso/sa; ~ly *adv* ignominiosamente.
ingot *n* lingote *m.*
ingrained *adj* inveterado/da.
ingratiate *vi* congraciarse.
ingratitude *n* ingratitud *f.*
ingredient *n* ingrediente *m.*
inhabit *vt, vi* habitar.
inhabitable *adj* habitable.
inhabitant *n* habitante *m/f.*
inhale *vt* inhalar.
inherent *adj* inherente.
inherit *vt* heredar.
inheritance *n* herencia *f.*
inheritor *n* heredero/a *m/f.*
inhibit *vt* inhibir.
inhibited *adj* cohibido/da.
inhibition *n* inhibición *f.*
inhospitable *adj* inhospitalario/ria.
inhospitality *n* inhospitalidad *f.*
inhuman *adj* inhumano/na, cruel; ~ly *adv* inhumanamente.
inhumanity *n* inhumanidad, crueldad *f.*
inimical *adj* enemigo/ga.
inimitable *adj* inimitable.
iniquitous *adj* inicuo/cua, injusto/ta.
iniquity *n* iniquidad, injusticia *f.*
initial *adj* inicial; * *n* inicial *f.*
initially *adv* al principio.
initiate *vt* iniciar.
initiation *n* principio *m*; iniciación *f.*
initiative *n* iniciativa *f.*
inject *vt* inyectar.
injection *n* inyección *f.*
injudicious *adj* poco juicioso/sa.
injunction *n* entredicho *m.*
injure *vt* herir.
injury *n* daño *m.*
injury time *n* descuento *m.*
injustice *n* injusticia *f.*
ink *n* tinta *f.*
inkling *n* sospecha *f.*

inkstand *n* tintero *m.*
inlaid *adj* taraceado/da.
inland *adj* interior; * *adv* tierra adentro.
in-laws *npl* suegros *mpl.*
inlay *vt* taracear.
inlet *n* ensenada *f.*
inmate *n* preso *m.*
inmost *adj* más íntimo/ma.
inn *n* posada *f*; mesón *m.*
innate *adj* innato/ta.
inner *adj* interior.
innermost *adj* más íntimo/ma.
inner tube *n* cámara *f.*
innkeeper *n* posadero/ra, mesonero/ra *m/f.*
innocence *n* inocencia *f.*
innocent *adj* inocente; ~ly *adv* inocentemente.
innocuous *adj* inocuo/cua; ~ly *adv* inocentemente.
innovate *vt* innovar.
innovation *n* innovación *f.*
innuendo *n* indirecta, insinuación *f.*
innumerable *adj* innumerable.
inoculate *vt* inocular.
inoculation *n* inoculación *f.*
inoffensive *adj* inofensivo/va.
inopportune *adj* inconveniente, inoportuno/na.
inordinately *adv* desmesuradamente.
inorganic *adj* inorgánico/ca.
inpatient *n* paciente interno/na *m/f.*
input *n* entrada *f.*
inquest *n* encuesta judicial *f.*
inquire, enquire *vt, vi* preguntar; **to ~ about** informarse de; **to ~ after** *vt* preguntar por; **to ~ into** *vt* investigar, indagar, inquirir.
inquiry *n* pesquisa *f.*
inquisition *n* inquisición *f.*
inquisitive *adj* curioso/sa.
inroad *n* incursión, invasión *f.*
insane *adj* loco/ca, demente.
insanity *n* locura *f.*
insatiable *adj* insaciable.
inscribe *vt* inscribir; dedicar.
inscription *n* inscripción *f*; dedicatoria *f.*
inscrutable *adj* inescrutable.
insect *n* insecto *m.*
insecticide *n* insecticida *m.*
insecure *adj* inseguro/ra.
insecurity *n* inseguridad *f.*
insemination *n* inseminación *f.*
insensible *adj* inconsciente.
insensitive *adj* insensible.
inseparable *adj* inseparable.
insert *vt* introducir.

insertion n inserción f.
inshore adj costero/ra.
inside n interior m; * adv dentro; Lat Am adentro de.
inside out adv al revés; a fondo.
insidious adj insidioso/sa; ~ly adv insidiosamente.
insight n perspicacia f.
insignia npl insignias fpl.
insignificant adj insignificante, frívolo/la.
insincere adj poco sincero/ra.
insincerity n falta de sinceridad f.
insinuate vt insinuar.
insinuation n insinuación f.
insipid adj insípido/da; insulso/sa; ñoño/ña.
insipidness n ñoñería f.
insist vi insistir.
insistence n insistencia f.
insistent adj insistente.
insole n plantilla f.
insolence n insolencia f.
insolent adj insolente; ~ly adv insolentemente.
insoluble adj insoluble.
insolvency n insolvencia f.
insolvent adj insolvente.
insomnia n insomnio m.
insomuch conj puesto que.
inspect vt examinar, inspeccionar.
inspection n inspección f.
inspector n inspector, superintendente m.
inspiration n inspiración f.
inspire vt inspirar.
instability n inestabilidad f.
install vt instalar.
installation n instalación f.
installment n instalación f; plazo m, Lat Am cuota f.
installment plan n compra a plazos f.
instance n ejemplo m; **for** ~ por ejemplo.
instant adj inmediato/ta; ~ly adv en seguida; * n instante, momento m.
instantaneous adj instantáneo/nea; ~ly adv instantáneamente.
instead (of) prep por, en lugar de, en vez de.
instep n empeine m.
instigate vt instigar.
instigation n instigación f.
instill vt inculcar.
instinct n instinto m.
instinctive adj instintivo/va; ~ly adv por instinto.
institute vt establecer; * n instituto m.
institution n institución f.
instruct vt instruir, enseñar; illustrar.

instruction n instrucción f.
instructive adj instructivo/va.
instructor n instructor/a m/f.
instrument n instrumento m.
instrumental adj instrumental.
insubordinate adj insubordinado/da.
insubordination n insubordinación f.
insufferable adj insoportable.
insufferably adv de modo insoportable.
insufficiency n insuficiencia f.
insufficient adj insuficiente; ~ly adv insuficientemente.
insular adj insular.
insulate vt aislar.
insulating tape n cinta aislante f.
insulation n aislamiento m.
insulin n insulina f.
insult vt insultar; * n insulto m.
insulting adj insultante.
insuperable adj insuperable.
insurance n (com) seguro m.
insurance policy n póliza de seguros f.
insure vt asegurar.
insurgent n insurgente, rebelde m.
insurmountable adj insuperable.
insurrection n insurrección f.
intact adj intacto/ta.
intake n admisión f; entrada f.
integral adj íntegro/gra; (chem) integrante; * n todo m.
integrate vt integrar.
integration n integración f.
integrity n integridad f.
intellect n intelecto m.
intellectual adj intelectual.
intelligence n inteligencia f.
intelligent adj inteligente.
intelligentsia n intelectualidad f.
intelligible adj inteligible.
intelligibly adv inteligiblemente.
intemperate adj inmoderado/da; ~ly adv inmoderadamente.
intend vi tener intención de.
intendant n intendente m.
intended adj deseado/da.
intense adj intenso/sa, hondo/da; ~ly adv intensamente.
intensify vt intensificar.
intensity n intensidad f.
intensive adj intensivo/va.
intensive care unit n unidad de vigilancia intensiva, unidad de cuidados intensivos f.
intent adj atento/ta, cuidadoso/sa; ~ly adv con aplicación; * n designio m.
intention n intención f; designio m.

intentional *adj* intencional; ~ly *adv* a
propósito.
inter *vt* enterrar.
interaction *n* interacción *f.*
intercede *vi* interceder.
intercept *vt* interceptar.
intercession *n* intercesión, mediación *f.*
interchange *n* intercambio *m.*
intercom *n* interfono *m.*
intercourse *n* coito *m.*
interest *vt* interesar; * *n* interés *m.*
interesting *adj* interesante.
interest rate *n* tipo de interés *m.*
interface *n* interfaz, interface *f.*
interfere *vi* entrometerse.
interference *n* interferencia *f.*
interim *adj* provisional.
interior *adj* interior.
interior design *n* interiorismo *m.*
interior designer *n* interiorista *m/f.*
interjection *n* (*gr*) interjección *f.*
interlock *vi* endentarse.
interlocutor *n* interlocutor/a *m/f.*
interloper *n* intruso/sa *m/f.*
interlude *n* intermedio *m.*
intermarriage *n* matrimonio mixto *m.*
intermediary *n* intermediario/ria *m/f.*
intermediate *adj* intermedio/dia.
interment *n* entierro *m*; sepultura *f.*
interminable *adj* inacabable.
intermingle *vt, vi* entremezclar; me-
zclarse.
intermission *n* descanso *m.*
intermittent *adj* intermitente.
intern *n* interno *m.*
internal *adj* interno/na; ~ly *adv* in-
ternamente.
international *adj* internacional.
Internet café *n* cibercafé *m.*
interplay *n* interacción *f.*
interpose *vt* interponer.
interpret *vt* interpretar.
interpretation *n* interpretación *f.*
interpreter *n* intérprete *m/f.*
interracial *adj* interracial.
interregnum *n* interregno *m.*
interrelated *adj* interrelacionado/da.
interrogate *vt* interrogar.
interrogation *n* interrogatorio *m.*
interrogative *adj* interrogativo/va.
interrupt *vt* interrumpir.
interruption *n* interrupción *f.*
intersect *vi* cruzarse.
intersection *n* cruce *m.*
intersperse *vt* esparcir.

intertwine *vt* entretejer.
interval *n* intervalo *m.*
intervene *vi* intervenir; ocurrir.
intervention *n* intervención *f.*
interview *n* entrevista *f*, *Lat Am* reportaje
m; * *vt* entrevistar.
interviewer *n* entrevistador/a *m/f.*
interweave *vt* entretejer.
intestate *adj* intestado/da.
intestinal *adj* intestinal.
intestine *n* intestino *m.*
intimacy *n* intimidad *f.*
intimate *n* amigo/ga íntimo/ma *m/f*; * *adj*
íntimo/ma; ~ly *adv* íntimamente; * *vt*
insinuar, dar a entender.
intimidate *vt* intimidar.
into *prep* en, dentro, adentro.
intolerable *adj* intolerable.
intolerably *adv* intolerablemente.
intolerance *n* intolerancia *f.*
intolerant *adj* intolerante.
intonation *n* entonación *f.*
intoxicate *vt* embriagar.
intoxication *n* embriaguez *f.*
intractable *adj* intratable.
intransitive *adj* (*gr*) intransitivo/va.
intravenous *adj* intravenoso/sa.
in-tray *n* bandeja de entrada *f.*
intrepid *adj* intrépido/da; ~ly *adv* in-
trépidamente.
intrepidity *n* intrepidez *f.*
intricacy *n* complejidad *f.*
intricate *adj* intrincado/da, complicado/da;
~ly *adv* intrincadamente.
intrigue *n* intriga *f*; * *vi* intrigar.
intriguing *adj* fascinante.
intrinsic *adj* intrínseco/ca; ~ally *adv*
intrínsecamente.
introduce *vt* introducir.
introduction *n* introducción *f.*
introductory *adj* introductorio/ria.
introspection *n* introspección *f.*
introvert *n* introvertido/da *m/f.*
intrude *vi* entrometerse.
intruder *n* intruso/sa *m/f.*
intrusion *n* invasión *f.*
intuition *n* intuición *f.*
intuitive *adj* intuitivo/va.
inundate *vt* inundar.
inundation *n* inundación *f.*
inure *vt* acostumbrar, habituar.
invade *vt* invadir.
invader *n* invasor/a *m/f.*
invalid *adj* inválido/da, nulo/la; * *n*
minusválido *m.*

invalidate vt invalidar, anular.
invaluable adj inapreciable.
invariable adj invariable.
invariably adv invariablemente.
invasion n invasión f.
invective n invectiva f.
inveigle vt seducir, persuadir.
invent vt inventar.
invention n invento m.
inventive adj inventivo/va.
inventor n inventor m.
inventory n inventario m.
inverse adj inverso/sa.
inversion n inversión f.
invert vt invertir.
invest vt invertir.
investigate vt investigar.
investigation n investigación, pesquisa f.
investigator n investigador/a m/f.
investment n inversión f.
inveterate adj inveterado/da.
invidious adj odioso/sa.
invigilate vt vigilar.
invigorating adj vigorizante.
invincible adj invencible.
invincibly adv invenciblemente.
inviolable adj inviolable.
invisible adj invisible.
invisibly adv invisiblemente.
invitation n invitación f.
invite vt invitar.
inviting adj atractivo/va.
invoice n (com) factura f.
invoke vt invocar.
involuntarily adv involuntariamente.
involuntary adj involuntario/ria.
involve vt implicar, Lat Am involucrar.
involved adj complicado/da.
involvement n compromiso m.
invulnerable adj invulnerable.
inward adj interior; interno/na; ~, ~s adv hacia dentro.
iodine n (chem) yodo m.
IOU (**I owe you**) n pagaré m.
irascible adj irascible.
irate, ireful adj enojado/da.
iris n iris m.
irksome adj fastidioso/sa.
iron n hierro m, Lat Am fierro m, plancha f; * adj férreo/rea; * vt planchar.
ironic adj irónico/ca; ~ly adv con ironía.
ironing n planchado m.

ironing board n tabla de planchar f.
iron ore n mineral de hierro m.
ironwork n herraje m; ~s pl herrería f.
irony n ironía f.
irradiate vt irradiar.
irrational adj irracional.
irreconcilable adj irreconciliable.
irregular adj, ~ly adv irregular(mente).
irregularity n irregularidad f.
irrelevant adj impertinente.
irreligious adj irreligioso/sa.
irreparable adj irreparable.
irreplaceable adj irreemplazable.
irrepressible adj incontenible.
irreproachable adj irreprensible.
irresistible adj irresistible.
irresolute adj irresoluto/ta; ~ly adv irresolutamente.
irresponsible adj irresponsable.
irretrievably adv irreparablemente.
irreverence n irreverencia f.
irreverent adj irreverente; ~ly adv irreverentemente.
irrigate vt regar.
irrigation n riego m.
irritability n irritabilidad f.
irritable adj irritable.
irritant n (med) irritante m.
irritate vt irritar.
irritating adj fastidioso/sa.
irritation n fastidio m; picazón f.
Islam n islam m.
Islamic adj islámico/ca.
island n isla f.
islander n isleño/ña m/f.
isle n isla f.
isolate vt aislar.
isolation n aislamiento m.
issue n asunto m; * vt expedir; publicar; repartir.
isthmus n istmo m.
it pn él, ella, ello, lo, la, le.
italic n cursiva f.
itch n picazón f; * vi picar.
item n artículo m.
itemize vt detallar, Lat Am itemizar.
itinerant n ambulante, errante m.
itinerary n itinerario m.
its pn su, suyo.
itself pn se, por sí mismo.
ivory n marfil m.
ivy n hiedra f; yedra f.

J

jab *vt* clavar.
jabber *vi* farfullar.
jack *n* gato *m*; sota *f*.
jackal *n* chacal *m*.
jackboots *npl* botas militares *fpl*.
jackdaw *n* grajo *m*.
jacket *n* chaqueta *f*, *Lat Am* saco *m*; funda *f*.
jack-knife *vi* colear.
jackpot *n* premio gordo *m*.
jacuzzi *n* jacuzzi *m*.
jade *n* jade *m*.
jagged *adj* dentado/da.
jaguar *n* jaguar *m*, *Lat Am* tigre *m*.
jail *n* cárcel *f*.
jailbird *n* preso/sa *m/f*.
jailer *n* carcelero/ra *m/f*.
jam *n* conserva *f*; mermelada de frutas *f*; (*auto*) embotellamiento *m*
jangle *vi* sonar.
janitor *n* portero/ra *m/f*, bedel *m*.
January *n* enero *m*.
jar *vi* chocar; (*mus*) discordar; reñir; * *n* jarra *f*.
jargon *n* jerigonza *f*.
jasmine *n* jazmín *m*.
jaundice *n* ictericia *f*
jaunt *n* excursión *f*.
jaunty *adj* alegre.
javelin *n* jabalina *f*.
jaw *n* mandíbula *f*.
jay *n* arrendajo *m*.
jazz *n* jazz *m*.
jealous *adj* celoso/sa; envidioso/sa.
jealousy *n* celos *mpl*; envidia *f*.
jeans *npl* vaqueros *mpl*, jeans *mpl*, *Lat Am* jean *m*.
Jeep™ *n* jeep *m*.
jeer *vi* befar, mofar; * *n* burla *f*.
jelly *n* jalea, gelatina *f*.
jellyfish *n* medusa *f*, aguamar *m*.
jeopardize *vt* arriesgar, poner en riesgo.
jerk *n* sacudida *f*; * *vt* tirar.
jerky *adj* espasmódico/ca.
jersey *n* jersey *m*.
jest *n* broma *f*.
jester *n* bufón/ona *m/f*.
jestingly *adv* de burlas.
Jesuit *n* jesuita *m*.
Jesus *n* Jesús *m*.
jet *n* avión a reacción *m*; azabache *m*.
jet engine *n* motor a reacción *m*, reactor *m*.

jettison *vt* desechar.
jetty *n* muelle *m*.
Jew *n* judío/día *m/f*.
jewel *n* joya *f*.
jeweler *n* joyero/ra *m/f*.
jewelry *n* joyería *f*.
jeweler's (shop/store) *n* joyería *f*.
Jewish *adj* judío/día.
jib *n* (*mar*) foque *m*.
jibe *n* mofa *f*.
jig *n* giga *f*.
jigsaw *n* rompecabezas *m invar*.
jilt *vt* dejar.
jinx *n* gafe *m*.
job *n* trabajo *m*.
jockey *n* jinete *m/f*.
jocular *adj* jocoso/sa, alegre.
jocularity *n* jocosidad *f*.
jog *vi* hacer footing.
jogging *n* footing *m*.
join *vt* juntar, unir; (*fig*) zurcir; to ~ in participar en; * *vi* unirse, juntarse.
joiner *n* carpintero/ra *m/f*.
joinery *n* carpintería *f*.
joint *n* articulación *f*; * *adj* común.
jointly *adv* conjuntamente.
joint-stock company *n* (*com*) sociedad por acciones *f*.
joke *n* broma *f*; * *vi* bromear.
joker *n* comodín *m*.
jollity *n* alegría *f*.
jolly *adj* alegre.
jolt *vt* sacudir; * *n* sacudida *f*.
jostle *vt* codear.
journal *n* revista *f*.
journalism *n* periodismo *m*.
journalist *n* periodista *m/f*.
journey *n* viaje *m*; * *vt* viajar.
jovial *adj* jovial, alegre; ~ly *adv* con jovialidad.
joy *n* alegría *f*; júbilo *m*.
joyful, joyous *adj* alegre, gozoso/sa; ~ly *adv* alegremente.
joystick *n* palanca de control *f*, joystick *m*.
jubilant *adj* jubiloso/sa.
jubilation *n* júbilo/la, regocijo *m*.
jubilee *n* jubileo *m*.
Judaism *n* judaísmo *m*.
judge *n* juez/a *m/f*; * *vt* juzgar.
judgement *n* juicio *m*.

judicial *adj*, ~**ly** *adv* judicial(mente).
judiciary *n* poder judicial *m*, judicatura *f*.
judicious *adj*, prudente.
judo *n* judo *m*.
jug *n* jarro *m*.
juggle *vi* hacer juegos malabares.
juggler *n* malabarista *m/f*.
jugular *adj* yugular.
juice *n* zumo, jugo *m*.
juicy *adj* jugoso/sa.
jukebox *n* gramola *f*.
July *n* julio *m*.
jumble *vt* mezclar; * *n* revoltijo *m*.
jump *vi* saltar, brincar; * *n* salto *m*.
jumper *n* suéter, jersey *m*.
jumpy *adj* nervioso/sa.
juncture *n* coyuntura *f*.
June *n* junio *m*.
jungle *n* selva *f*.
junior *adj* más joven.
juniper *n* (*bot*) enebro *m*.
junk *n* basura *f*; baratijas *fpl*.

junk food *n* comida basura *f*.
junkman *n* trapero *m*.
junta *n* junta *f*.
jurisdiction *n* jurisdicción *f*.
jurisprudence *n* jurisprudencia *f*.
jurist *n* jurista *m/f*.
juror, juryman *n* jurado/da *m/f*.
jury *n* jurado *m*.
just *adj* justo/ta; * *adv* justamente, exactamente; ~ **as** como; ~ **now** ahora mismo.
justice *n* justicia *f*.
justifiably *adv* con justificación.
justification *n* justificación *f*.
justify *vt* justificar.
justly *adv* justamente.
justness *n* justicia *f*.
jut *vi*; **to** ~ **out** sobresalir.
jute *n* yute *m*.
juvenile *adj* juvenil.
juxtapose *vt* yuxtaponer.
juxtaposition *n* yuxtaposición *f*.

K

kaleidoscope *n* caleidoscopio *m.*
kangaroo *n* canguro *m.*
karaoke *n* karaoke *m.*
karate *n* kárate *m.*
kebab *n* pincho *m* moruno.
keel *n* (*mar*) quilla *f.*
keen *adj* agudo/da; vivo/va.
keenness *n* entusiasmo *m.*
keep *vt* mantener; guardar; conservar.
keeper *n* guardián/ana *m/f.*
keepsake *n* recuerdo *m.*
keg *n* barril *m.*
kennel *n* perrera *f.*
kernel *n* fruta *f;* meollo *m.*
kerosene *n* queroseno *m, Lat Am* querosén *m.*
ketchup *n* catsup, ketchup *m.*
kettle *n* hervidor *m.*
kettle-drum *n* timbal *m.*
key *n* llave *f;* (*mus*) clave *f;* tecla *f.*
keyboard *n* teclado *m.*
keyhole *n* ojo de la cerradura *m.*
keynote *n* (*mus*) tónica *f.*
key ring *n* llavero *m.*
keystone *n* piedra clave *f.*
khaki *n* caqui *m.*
kick *vt, vi* patear; * *n* puntapié *m;* patada *f.*
kid *n* chico/ca *m/f.*
kidnap *vt* secuestrar.
kidnaper *n* secuestrador/a *m/f.*
kidnaping *n* secuestro *m;* rapto *m.*
kidney *n* riñón *m.*
killer *n* asesino/na *m/f.*
killing *n* asesinato *m.*
kiln *n* horno *m.*
kilo *n* kilo *m.*
kilobyte *n* kilobyte *m.*
kilogram *n* kilo *m.*
kilometer *n* kilómetro *m.*
kilt *n* falda escocesa *f.*
kin *n* parientes *mpl;* next of ~ pariente próximo *m,* pariente próxima *f.*
kind *adj* cariñoso/sa; * *n* género *m.*
kindergarten *n* parvulario *m.*
kind-hearted *adj* bondadoso/sa.
kindle *vt, vi* encender.
kindliness *n* benevolencia *f.*
kindly *adj* bondadoso/sa.
kindness *n* bondad *f.*

kindred *adj* emparentado/da.
kinetic *adj* cinético/ca.
king *n* rey *m.*
kingdom *n* reino *m.*
kingfisher *n* martín pescador *m.*
king prawn *n* langostino *m.*
kiosk *n* quiosco *m.*
kiss *n* beso *m;* * *vt* besar.
kissing *n* besos *mpl.*
kit *n* equipo *m.*
kitchen *n* cocina *f.*
kitchen garden *n* huerta *f.*
kitchen maid *n* fregona *f.*
kite *n* cometa *f.*
kitten *n* gatito *m.*
knack *n* don *m.*
knapsack *n* mochila *f.*
knave *n* bribón, pícaro *m;* (cards) sota *f.*
knead *vt* amasar.
knee *n* rodilla *f.*
knee-deep *adj* metido hasta las rodillas.
kneel *vi* arrodillarse.
knell *n* toque de difuntos *m.*
knife *n* cuchillo *m.*
knight *n* caballero *m.*
knit *vt, vi* tejer, tricotear; to ~ the brows fruncir el ceño.
knitter *n* calcetero/ra, mediero/ra *m/f.*
knitting needle *n* aguja de tejer *f.*
knitwear *n* prendas de punto *fpl.*
knob *n* bulto *m;* nudo en la madera *m;* botón de las flores *m.*
knock *vt, vi* golpear, tocar; to ~ down derribar; * *n* golpe *m.*
knocker *n* aldaba *f.*
knock-kneed *adj* patizambo/ba; zambo/ba.
knock-out *n* KO *m, Lat Am* nocaut *m.*
knoll *n* cima de una colina *f.*
knot *n* nudo *m;* lazo *m;* * *vt* anudar.
knotty *adj* escabroso/sa.
know *vt, vi* conocer; saber.
know-all *n* sabelotodo *m/f.*
know-how *n* conocimientos *mpl.*
knowing *adj* entendido/da; ~ly *adv* a sabiendas.
knowledge *n* conocimiento *m.*
knowledgeable *adj* bien informado/da.
knuckle *n* nudillo *m.*

L

label *n* etiqueta *f.*
labor *n* trabajo *m*; **to be in** ~ estar de parto;
   * *vt* trabajar.
laboratory *n* laboratorio *m.*
laborer *n* peón *m.*
laborious *adj* laborioso/sa; difícil; ~ly *adv*
   laboriosamente.
labor union *n* sindicato *m*, *Lat Am* gremial *f.*
labor unionist *n* sindicalista *m/f*, *Lat Am*
   gremialista *m/f.*
labyrinth *n* laberinto *m.*
lace *n* cordón; encaje *m*; * *vt* abrochar.
lacerate *vt* lacerar.
lack *vt, vi* faltar; * *n* falta *f.*
lackadaisical *adj* descuidado/da.
lackey *n* lacayo *m.*
laconic *adj* lacónico/ca.
lacquer *n* laca *f.*
lad *n* muchacho *m.*
ladder *n* escalera *f.*
ladle *n* cucharón *m.*
ladleful *n* cucharada *f.*
lady *n* señora *f.*
ladybug *n* mariquita *f.*
lady-killer *n* casanova *m.*
ladylike *adj* fino/na.
ladyship *n* señoría *f.*
lag *vi* quedarse atrás.
lager *n* cerveza (rubia) *f.*
lagoon *n* laguna *f.*
laid-back *adj* relajado/da.
lair *n* guarida *f.*
laity *n* laicado *m.*
lake *n* lago *m*; laguna *f.*
lamb *n* cordero *m*; * *vi* parir.
lame *adj* cojo/ja.
lament *vt* (*vi*) lamentar(se); * *n* lamento *m.*
lamentable *adj* lamentable, deplorable.
lamentation *n* lamentación *f.*
laminated *adj* laminado/da; plastificado/da.
lamp *n* lámpara *f.*
lampoon *n* sátira *f.*
lampshade *n* pantalla *f.*
lance *n* lanza *f*; * *vt* abrir con lanceta.
lancet *n* lanceta *f.*
land *n* país *m*; tierra *f*; * *vt, vi* desembarcar.
land forces *npl* tropas de tierra *fpl.*
land-holder *n* hacendado *m.*
landing *n* desembarco *m.*
landing strip *n* pista de aterrizaje *f.*
landlady *n* propietaria *f.*

landlord *n* propietario *m.*
landlubber *n* marinero de agua dulce *m.*
landmark *n* lugar conocido; hito *m.*
landowner *n* terrateniente *m/f.*
landscape *n* paisaje *m.*
landslide *n* corrimiento de tierras *m*, *Lat*
   Am deslave *m.*
lane *n* callejuela *f.*
langoustine *n* langostino *m.*
language *n* lengua *f*; lenguaje *m.*
languid *adj* lánguido/da, débil; ~ly *adv*
   lánguidamente, débilmente.
languish *vi* languidecer.
lank *adj* lacio/cia.
lanky *adj* larguirucho/cha.
lantern *n* linterna *f*; farol *m.*
lap *n* regazo *m*; * *vt* lamer.
lapdog *n* perro faldero *m.*
lapel *n* solapa *f.*
lapse *n* lapso *m*; * *vi* transcurrir.
laptop *n* portátil *m.*
larceny *n* latrocinio *m.*
larch *n* alerce *m.*
lard *n* manteca de cerdo *f.*
larder *n* despensa *f.*
large *adj* grande; **at** ~ en libertad; ~ly *adv*
   en gran parte.
large-scale *adj* en gran escala.
largesse *n* liberalidad *f.*
lark *n* alondra *f.*
larva *n* larva, oruga *f.*
laryngitis *n* laringitis *f.*
larynx *n* laringe *f.*
lascivious *adj* lascivo/va; ~ly *adv* las-
   civamente.
laser *n* láser *m.*
laser printer *n* impresora láser *f.*
lash *n* latigazo *m*, *Lat Am* cuerazo *m*; * *vt*
   dar latigazos, *Lat Am* cuerear; atar.
lasso *n* lazo *m*, *Lat Am* peal *m.*
last *adj* último/ma; pasado/da; **at** ~ por fin;
   ~ly *adv* finalmente; * *n* horma de zapatero
   f; * *vi* durar.
last-ditch *adj* último/ma.
lasting *adj* duradero/ra, permanente; ~ly
   adv perpetuamente.
last-minute *adj* de última hora.
latch *n* picaporte *m.*
latch-key *n* llave maestra *f.*
late *adj* tarde; difunto/ta; (*rail*) **the train**
   is ten minutes ~ el tren tiene un retraso

de diez minutos; * adv tarde; ~ly adv recientemente.
latecomer n recién llegado/da m/f.
latent adj latente.
lateral adj, ~ly adv lateral(mente).
lathe n torno m.
lather n espuma f.
latitude n latitud f.
latrine n letrina f.
latter adj último/ma; ~ly adv últimamente, recientemente.
lattice n celosía f.
laudable adj loable.
laudably adv loablemente.
laugh vi reir; to ~ at vt reírse de; * n risa f.
laughable adj absurdo/da.
laughing stock n hazmerreír m.
laughter n risa f.
launch vt (vi) lanzar(se); * n (mar) lancha f.
launching n lanzamiento m.
launching pad n plataforma de lanzamiento f.
launder vt lavar.
Launderette™ n lavandería automática f.
laundry n lavandería f.
laurel n laurel m.
lava n lava f.
lavatory n cuarto de baño m.
lavender n (bot) espliego m, lavanda f.
lavish adj pródigo/ga; ~ly adv pródigamente; * vt disipar.
law n ley f; derecho m.
law-abiding adj respetuoso/sa con la ley.
law and order n orden público m.
law court n tribunal m.
lawful adj legal; legítimo/ma; ~ly adv legalmente.
lawless adj anárquico/ca.
lawlessness n anarquía f.
lawmaker n legislador/a m/f.
lawn n pasto m, Lat Am grama f.
lawnmower n cortacésped m.
law school n facultad de derecho f.
lawsuit n proceso m.
lawyer n abogado/da m/f.
lax adj laxo/xa; flojo/ja.
laxative n laxante m.
laxity n laxitud f; flojedad f.
lay vt poner; to ~ claim reclamar; pretender; to ~ into (col) zurrar; * vi poner.
layabout n vago/ga m/f.
layer n capa f.
layette n ajuar de niño m.
layman n lego, seglar m.
layout n composición f.

laze vi holgazanear.
lazily adv perezosamente; lentamente.
laziness n pereza f.
lazy adj perezoso/sa.
lead[1] n plomo m.
lead[2] vt conducir, guiar; * vi mandar.
leader n jefe/fa m/f.
leadership n dirección f; liderazgo m.
leading adj principal; capital; ~ article n artículo principal m.
leaf n hoja f, yema f.
leaflet n folleto m.
leafy adj frondoso/sa.
league n liga, alianza f; legua f.
leak n escape m; * vi (mar) hacer agua.
leaky adj agujereado/da.
lean vt (vi) apoyar(se); * adj magro/ra.
leap vi saltar; * n salto m.
leapfrog n pídola f.
leap year n año bisiesto m.
learn vt, vi aprender.
learned adj docto/ta.
learner n aprendiz m.
learning n erudición f.
lease n arriendo m; * vt arrendar.
leasehold n arriendo m.
leash n correa f.
least adj mínimo/ma; at ~ por lo menos; not in the ~ en absoluto.
leather n cuero m.
leathery adj correoso/sa.
leave n licencia f; permiso m; to take ~ despedirse; * vt dejar, abandonar.
leaven n levadura f; * vt fermentar.
leavings npl sobras fpl.
lecherous adj lascivo/va.
lecture n conferencia f; * vt dar una conferencia.
lecturer n conferenciante m/f; profesor/ra m/f.
ledge n reborde m.
ledger n (com) libro mayor m.
lee n (mar) sotavento m.
leech n sanguijuela f.
leek n (bot) puerro m.
leer vt mirar de manera lasciva.
lees npl sedimento, poso m.
leeward adj (mar) sotavento.
leeway n libertad de acción f.
left adj izquierdo/da; zurdo/da; on the ~ a la izquierda.
left-handed adj zurdo/da.
leftovers npl sobras fpl.
leg n pierna f; pie m.
legacy n herencia f.

legal *adj* legal, legítimo/ma; ~ly *adv* legalmente.
legal holiday *n* fiesta oficial *f.*
legality *n* legalidad, legitimidad *f.*
legalize *vt* legalizar.
legal tender *n* moneda de curso legal *f.*
legate *n* legado *m.*
legatee *n* legado *m.*
legation *n* legación *f.*
legend *n* leyenda *f.*
legendary *adj* legendario/ria.
legible *adj* legible.
legibly *adv* legiblemente.
legion *n* legión *f.*
legislate *vt* legislar.
legislation *n* legislación *f.*
legislative *adj* legislativo/va.
legislator *n* legislador/a *m/f.*
legislature *n* cuerpo legislativo *m.*
legitimacy *n* legitimidad *f.*
legitimate *adj* legítimo/ma; ~ly *adv* legítimamente; * *vt* legitimar.
leisure *n* ocio *m;* ~ly *adj* sin prisa; at ~ desocupado/da.
lemon *n* limón *m.*
lemonade *n* limonada *f.*
lemon tea *n* te con limón *m.*
lemon tree *n* limonero *m.*
lend *vt* prestar.
length *n* largo *m;* duración *f;* at ~ finalmente.
lengthen *vt* alargar; * *vi* alargarse.
lengthways, lengthwise *adv* a lo largo.
lengthy *adj* largo/ga.
lenient *adj* indulgente.
lens *n* lente *f.*
Lent *n* Cuaresma *f.*
lentil *n* lenteja *f.*
leopard *n* leopardo *m;* mallas *fpl.*
leotard *n* leotardo *m.*
leper *n* leproso/sa *m/f.*
leprosy *n* lepra *f.*
lesbian *n* lesbiana *f.*
less *adj* menor; * *adv* menos.
lessen *vt* disminuir; * *vi* disminuirse.
lesser *adj* más pequeño/ña.
lesson *n* lección *f.*
lest *conj* para que no.
let *vt* dejar, permitir; alquilar.
lethal *adj* mortal.
lethargic *adj* letárgico/ca.
lethargy *n* letargo *m.*
letter *n* letra *f;* carta *f.*
letter bomb *n* carta bomba *f.*
lettering *n* letras *fpl.*
letter of credit *n* carta de crédito *f.*

lettuce *n* lechuga *f.*
leukemia *n* leucemia *f.*
level *adj* llano/na, igual; nivelado/da; * *n* nivel *m;* * *vt* allanar; nivelar.
level-headed *adj* sensato/ta.
lever *n* palanca *f.*
leverage *n* influencia *f.*
levity *n* ligereza *f.*
levy *n* leva (de tropas) *f;* * *vt* recaudar.
lewd *adj* obsceno/na.
lexicon *n* lexicón *m.*
liability *n* responsabilidad *f.*
liable *adj* sujeto/ta; responsable.
liaise *vi* enlazar.
liaison *n* enlace *m.*
liar *n* embustero *m.*
libel *n* difamación *f;* * *vt* difamar.
libelous *adj* difamatorio/ria.
liberal *adj* liberal, generoso/sa; ~ly *adv* liberalmente.
liberality *n* liberalidad, generosidad *f.*
liberate *vt* libertar.
liberation *n* liberación *f.*
libertine *n* libertino *m.*
liberty *n* libertad *f.*
Libra *n* Libra *f.*
librarian *n* bibliotecario/ria *m/f.*
library *n* biblioteca *f.*
libretto *n* libreto *m.*
license *n* licencia *f;* permiso *m;* * *vt* autorizar, licenciar.
license plate *n* placa de matrícula *f.*
licentious *adj* licencioso/sa.
lichen *n* (*bot*) liquen *m.*
lick *vt* lamer.
lid *n* tapa *f.*
lie *n* mentira *f;* * *vi* mentir; echarse.
lie down *vi* yacer.
lieu *n:* in ~ of en vez de.
lieutenant *n* lugarteniente *m/f;* teniente *m/f.*
life *n* vida *f;* for ~ para toda la vida.
lifeboat *n* lancha de socorro *f;* bote salvavidas *m.*
lifeguard *n* socorrista *m/f.*
lifeless *adj* muerto/ta; sin vida.
lifelike *adj* natural.
lifeline *n* cordón umbilical *m.*
life preserver *n* chaleco salvavidas *m.*
life sentence *n* cadena perpetua *f.*
life-sized *adj* de tamaño natural.
life span *n* vida *f.*
lifestyle *n* estilo de vida *f.*
life-support system *n* sistema de respiración asistida *m.*

lifetime *n* vida *f*.
lift *vt* levantar.
ligament *n* ligamento *m*.
light *n* luz *f*; * *adj* ligero/ra; claro/ra; * *vt* encender; alumbrar.
light bulb *n* foco *m*; bombilla *f*.
lighten *vi* relampaguear; * *vt* iluminar; aligerar; (*mar*) zafar.
lighter *n* encendedor *m*.
light-headed *adj* mareado/da.
light-hearted *adj* alegre.
lighthouse *n* (*mar*) faro *m*.
lighting *n* iluminación *f*.
lightly *adv* ligeramente.
lightning *n* relámpago *m*.
lightning-rod *n* pararrayos *m invar*.
light pen *n* lápiz óptico *m*.
lightweight *adj* ligero/ra.
light year *n* año luz *m*.
ligneous *adj* leñoso/sa.
like *adj* semejante; igual; * *adv* como, del mismo modo que; * *vt*, *vi* gustar.
likeable *adj* simpático/ca.
likelihood *n* probabilidad *f*.
likely *adj* probable, verosímil.
liken *vt* comparar.
likeness *n* semejanza *f*.
likewise *adv* igualmente.
liking *n* agrado *m*.
lilac *n* lila *f*.
lily *n* lirio *m*; ~ **of the valley** lirio de los valles.
limb *n* miembro *m*.
limber *adj* flexible.
lime *n* cal *f*; lima *f*; ~ **tree** tilo *m*.
limestone *n* piedra caliza *f*; caliza *f*.
limit *n* límite, término *m*; * *vt* restringir.
limitation *n* limitación *f*; restricción *f*.
limitless *adj* inmenso/sa.
limousine *n* limusina *f*.
limp *vi* cojear; * *n* cojera *f*; * *adj* flojo/ja.
limpet *n* lapa *f*.
limpid *adj* claro/ra, transparente.
line *n* línea *f*; raya *f*; * *vt* forrar; revestir.
lineage *n* linaje *m*; filiación *f*.
linear *adj* lineal.
lined *adj* rayado/da; arrugado/da.
linen *n* lino *m*.
liner *n* transatlántico *m*.
linesman *n* juez de línea *m*.
linger *vi* persistir.
lingerie *n* ropa interior *f*.
lingering *adj* lento/ta.
linguist *n* lingüista *m/f*.
linguistic *adj* lingüístico/ca.

linguistics *n* lingüística *f*.
liniment *n* linimento *m*.
lining *n* forro *m*.
link *n* eslabón *m*; * *vt* enlazar.
linnet *n* pardillo *m*.
linoleum *n* linóleo *m*.
linseed *n* linaza *f*.
lint *n* hilas *fpl*.
lintel *n* dintel, tranquero *m*.
lion *n* león *m*.
lioness *n* leona *f*.
lip *n* labio *m*; borde *m*.
liposuction *n* liposucción *f*.
lip read *vi* leer los labios.
lip salve *n* crema protectora para labios *f*.
lipstick *n* lápiz de labios *m*.
liqueur *n* licor *m*.
liquid *adj* líquido/da; * *n* liquido *m*.
liquidate *vt* liquidar.
liquidation *n* liquidación *f*.
liquidize *vt* licuar.
liquor *n* licor *m*.
liquorice *n* regaliz *m*,
lisp *vi* cecear; * *n* ceceo *m*.
list *n* lista *f*; * *vt* hacer una lista de.
listen *vi* escuchar.
listless *adj* indiferente.
litany *n* letanía *f*.
liter *n* litro *m*.
literal *adj*, ~**ly** *adv* literal(mente).
literary *adj* literario/ria.
literate *adj* culto/ta.
literature *n* literatura *f*.
lithe *adj* ágil.
lithograph *n* litografía *f*.
lithography *n* litografía *f*.
litigation *n* litigio *m*.
litigious *adj* litigioso/sa.
litter *n* litera *f*; camada *f*; * *vt* parir.
little *adj* pequeño/ña, poco/ca; ~ **by** ~ poco a poco; * *n* poco *m*.
liturgy *n* liturgia *f*.
live *vi* vivir; habitar; **to** ~ **on** alimentarse de; **to** ~ **up to** *vt* cumplir con; * *adj* vivo/va.
livelihood *n* vida *f*.
liveliness *n* vivacidad *f*; belleza *f*.
lively *adj* vivo/va.
liven up *vt* animar.
liver *n* hígado *m*.
livery *n* librea *f*.
livestock *n* ganado *m*.
livid *adj* lívido/da, cárdeno/na.
living *n* vida *f*; * *adj* vivo/va.
living room *n* sala de estar *f*.

lizard n lagarto m.
load vt cargar; * n carga f.
loaded adj cargado/da.
loaf n pan m.
loafer n holgazán, gandul m.
loam n marga f.
loan n préstamo m.
loathe vt aborrecer; tener hastío; * vi fastidiar.
loathing n aversión f.
loathsome adj asqueroso/sa.
lobby n vestíbulo m.
lobe n lóbulo m.
lobster n langosta f.
local adj local.
local anesthetic n anestesia local f.
local government n gobierno municipal m.
locality n localidad f.
localize vt localizar.
locally adv en la vecindad.
locate vt localizar, Lat Am ubicar.
location n situación f.
loch n lago m.
lock n cerradura f; * vt cerrar con llave.
locker n vestuario m.
locket n medallón m.
lockout n cierre patronal m.
locksmith n cerrajero m.
locomotive n locomotora f.
locust n langosta f.
lodge n casa del guarda f; * vi alojarse.
lodger n inquilino/na m/f.
loft n desván m.
lofty adj alto/ta.
log n leño m.
logbook n (mar) diario de a bordo m.
logic n lógica f.
logical adj lógico/ca.
logo n logotipo m.
loin n lomo m.
loiter vi merodear.
loll vi repantigarse.
lollipop n pirulí m, piruleta f.
loneliness n soledad f.
lonesome adj solitario/ria; solo/la.
long adj largo/ga; * vi anhelar.
long-distance n: ~ call llamada in-
  terurbana f.
longevity n longevidad f.
long-haired adj de pelo largo.
longing n anhelo m.
longitude n longitud f.
longitudinal adj longitudinal.
long jump n salto de longitud m.
long-legged adj zancudo/da.
long-playing record n elepé m.

long-range adj de gran alcance.
long-term adj a largo plazo.
long wave n onda larga f.
long-winded adj prolijo/ja.
look vi mirar; parecer; to ~ after vt cuidar;
  to ~ for vt buscar; to ~ forward to vt esperar
  con impaciencia; to ~ out for vt aguardar;
  * n aspecto m; mirada f.
looking glass n espejo m.
lookout n (mil) centinela f; vigía f.
loom n telar m; * vi amenazar.
loop n lazo m.
loophole n escapatoria f.
loose adj suelto/ta; flojo/ja; ~ly adv
  aproximadamente.
loosen vt aflojar, zafar.
loot vt saquear; * n botín m.
lop vt desmochar.
lop-sided adj desequilibrado/da.
loquacious adj locuaz.
loquacity n locuacidad f.
lord n señor m.
lore n saber popular m.
lose vt perder; * vi perder; to ~ weight vi
  adelgazar.
loss n pérdida f; to be at a ~ no saber qué
  hacer.
lost and found n objetos perdidos mpl.
lot n suerte f; lote m; a ~ mucho.
lotion n loción f.
lottery n lotería, rifa f.
loud adj fuerte; ~ly adv fuerte.
loudspeaker n altavoz m, Lat Am altoparlante m.
lounge n salón m.
louse n (pl lice) piojo m.
lousy adj vil.
lout n gamberro m.
lovable adj amable.
love n amor, cariño m; to fall in ~
  enamorarse; * vt amar; gustar.
love letter n carta de amor f.
love life n vida sentimental f.
lovely adj hermoso/sa.
lover n amante m.
lovesick adj enamorado/da.
loving adj amoroso/sa.
low adj bajo/ja; * vi mugir.
low-cut adj escotado/da.
lower adj más bajo/ja; * vt bajar.
lowest adj más bajo/ja, ínfimo/ma.
lowland n tierra baja f.
lowliness n humildad f.
lowly adj humilde.
low water, low tide n bajamar f.

loyal *adj* leal; fiel; ~ly *adv* lealmente.
loyalty *n* lealtad *f*; fidelidad *f*.
lozenge *n* pastilla *f*.
lubricant *n* lubricante *m*.
lubricate *vt* lubricar.
lucid *adj* lúcido/da.
luck *n* suerte; fortuna *f*.
luckily *adv* afortunadamente.
luckless *adj* desdichado/da.
lucky *adj* afortunado/da.
lucrative *adj* lucrativo/va.
ludicrous *adj* absurdo/da.
lug *vt* arrastrar.
luggage *n* equipaje *m*.
lugubrious *adj* lúgubre, triste.
lukewarm *adj* tibio/bia.
lull *vt* acunar; * *n* tregua *f*.
lullaby *n* nana *f*.
lumbago *n* lumbago *m*.
lumber *n* trastera *f*.
lumberjack *n* maderero/ra *m/f*.
lumber room *n* trastero *m*.
luminous *adj* luminoso/sa.
lump *n* terrón *m*; bulto *m*; chichón *m*; * *vt* juntar.
lump sum *n* suma global *f*.
lunacy *n* locura *f*.
lunar *adj* lunar.
lunatic *adj* loco/ca.
lunch, luncheon *n* almuerzo *m*, comida *f*; * *vt, vi* almorzar.

lungs *npl* pulmones *mpl*.
lurch *n* sacudida *f*.
lure *n* señuelo *m*; cebo *m*; * *vt* inducir.
lurid *adj* sensacional.
lurk *vi* esconderse.
luscious *adj* delicioso/sa.
lush *adj* exuberante.
lust *n* lujuria, sensualidad *f*, concupiscencia *f*; * *vi* lujuriar; to ~ after *vt* codiciar.
luster *n* lustre *m*.
lustful *adj* lujurioso/sa, voluptuoso/sa; ~ly *adv* lujuriosamente.
lustily *adv* vigorosamente.
lusty *adj* fuerte, vigoroso/sa.
lute *n* laúd *m*.
Lutheran *n* luterano/na *m/f*.
luxuriance *n* exuberancia, superabundancia *f*.
luxuriant *adj* exuberante, superabundante.
luxuriate *vi* crecer con exuberancia.
luxurious *adj* lujoso/sa; exuberante; ~ly *adv* lujosamente.
luxury *n* lujo *m*, voluptuosidad *f*; exuberancia *f*.
lying *n* mentiras *fpl*.
lymph *n* linfa *f*.
lynch *vt* linchar.
lynx *n* lince *m*.
lyrical *adj* lírico/ca.
lyrics *npl* letra *f*.

M

macaroni n macarrones mpl.
macaroon n almendrado m.
mace n maza f; macis f invar.
macerate vt macerar; mortificar.
machination n maquinación, trama f.
machine n máquina f.
machine gun n ametralladora f.
machinery n maquinaria, mecánica f.
mackerel n caballa f.
mad adj loco/ca, furioso/sa, rabioso/sa, insensato/ta.
madam n madama, señora f.
madden vt enloquecer.
madder n (bot) rubia f.
madhouse n casa de locos f.
madly adv locamente.
madman n loco m.
madness n locura f.
magazine n revista f; almacén m.
maggot n gusano m.
magic n magia f; * adj mágico/ca; ~ally adv mágicamente.
magician n mago/ga m/f; prestidigitador/a m/f.
magisterial adj magistral; ~ly adv magistralmente.
magistracy n magistratura f.
magistrate n magistrado/da m/f.
magnanimity n magnanimidad f.
magnanimous adj magnánimo; ~ly adv magnanimaménte.
magnet n iman m.
magnetic adj magnetico/ca.
magnetism n magnetismo m.
magnificence n magnificencia f.
magnificent adj magnifico; ~ly adv magníficamente.
magnify vt aumentar; exagerar.
magnifying glass n lupa f.
magnitude n magnitud f.
magpie n urraca f.
mahogany n caoba f.
maid n criada f, Lat Am chinita f.
maiden n doncella f.
maiden name n nombre de soltera m.
mail n correo m.
mailbox n buzón m.
mailing list n lista de direcciones f.
mail order n venta por correo f.
mail train n (rail) tren correo m.
maim vt mutilar.
main adj principal; esencial; in the ~ en general.

mainland n continente m.
main line n (rail) línea principal f.
mainly adv principalmente.
main street n calle mayor f.
maintain vt mantener; sostener.
maintenance n mantenimiento m.
maize n maíz m; borona f.
majestic adj majestuoso/sa; ~ally adv majestuosamente.
majesty n majestad f.
major adj principal; * n (mil) comandante/a m/f.
majority n mayoría f.
make vt hacer, crear; to ~ for dirigirse hacia; to ~ up inventar; to ~ up for compensar; to ~ off with something alzar; * n marca f.
make-believe n invención f.
makeshift adj improvisado.
make-up n maquillaje m.
make-up remover n desmaquillador m.
malady n enfermedad f.
malaise n malestar m.
malaria n malaria f.
malcontent adj, n malcontento/ta m/f.
male adj masculino/na; * n macho m.
malevolence n malevolencia f.
malevolent adj malévolo/la; ~ly adv malignamente.
malfunction n mal funcionamiento, fallo m.
malice n malicia f.
malicious adj malicioso/sa; ~ly adv maliciosamente.
malign adj maligno; * vt calumniar.
malignant adj maligno/na; ~ly adv malignamente.
mall (shopping) n centro comercial; paseo m.
malleable adj maleable.
mallet n mazo m.
mallow n (bot) malva f.
malnutrition n desnutrición f.
malpractice n negligencia f.
malt n malta f.
maltreat vt maltratar.
mammal n mamífero m.
mammoth adj gigantesco/ca.
man n hombre m; * vt (mar) tripular.
manacle n manilla f; ~s npl esposas fpl.
manage vt, vi manejar, dirigir, Lat Am gerenciar.
manageable adj manejable.
management n dirección f.
manager n director/a m/f.

manageress *n* directora *f.*
managerial *adj* directivo/va.
managing director *n* director/a general *m/f.*
mandarin *n* (*bot*) mandarina *f;* mandarín *m.*
mandate *n* mandato *m.*
mandatory *adj* obligatorio/ria.
mane *n* crines *fpl,* melena *f.*
maneuver *n* maniobra *f.*
manfully *adv* valerosamente.
manger *n* pesebre *m.*
mangle *n* rodillo *m;* * *vt* mutilar.
mangy *adj* sarnoso/sa.
manhandle *vt* maltratar.
manhood *n* madurez; hombría *f.*
man-hour *n* hora hombre *f.*
mania *n* manía *f.*
maniac *n* maníaco/ca *m/f.*
manic *adj* frenético/ca.
manicure *n* manicura *f.*
manifest *adj* manifiesto/ta, patente; * *vt* manifestar.
manifestation *n* manifestación *f.*
manifesto *n* manifiesto *m.*
manipulate *vt* manejar; manipular.
manipulation *n* manejo; manipulación *f.*
mankind *n* género humano *m.*
manlike *adj* varonil.
manliness *n* valentía, hombría *f.*
manly *adj* varonil.
man-made *adj* artificial.
manner *n* manera *f;* modo *m;* forma *f;* ~s *pl* modales *mpl.*
manpower *n* mano de obra *f.*
mansion *n* palacio *m,* mansión *f.*
manslaughter *n* homicidio (sin premeditación) *m.*
mantelpiece *n* repisa (de chimenea) *f.*
manual *adj, n* manual *m.*
manufacture *n* fabricación *f;* * *vt* fabricar.
manufacturer *n* fabricante *m/f.*
manure *n* abono *m;* estiércol *m;* fiemo *m;* * *vt* abonar.
manuscript *n* manuscrito *m.*
many *adj* muchos, muchas; ~ **a time** muchas veces; **how** ~? ¿cuantos?; **as** ~ **as** tantos como.
map *n* mapa *m;* * *vt* planear, trazar el mapa de; **to** ~ **out** proyectar.
maple *n* arce *m.*
mar *vt* estropear.
marathon *n* maratón *m.*
marauder *n* merodeador/a *m/f.*
marble *n* mármol *m;* * *adj* marmóreo/rea.
March *n* marzo *m.*
march *n* marcha *f;* * *vi* marchar.
march past *n* desfile *m.*

mare *n* yegua *f.*
margarine *n* margarina *f.*
margin *n* margen *m;* borde *m.*
marginal *adj* marginal.
marigold *n* (*bot*) caléndula *f.*
marijuana *n* marihuana *f.*
marinate *vt* adobar.
marine *adj* marino/na; * *n* infante de marina *m.*
mariner *n* marinero/ra *m/f.*
marital *adj* marital.
maritime *adj* marítimo/ma.
marjoram *n* mejorana *f.*
mark *n* marca *f;* señal *f;* * *vt* marcar.
marker *n* registro *m.*
market *n* mercado *m.*
marketable *adj* vendible.
marketing *n* márketing *m.*
marketplace *n* mercado *m.*
market research *n* análisis de mercados *m invar.*
market value *n* valor de mercado *m.*
marksman *n* tirador *m.*
marmalade *n* mermelada de naranja *f.*
maroon *adj* marrón.
marquee *n* entoldado/da *m/f.*
marriage *n* matrimonio *m;* casamiento *m.*
marriageable *adj* casadero/ra.
marriage certificate *n* partida de casamiento *f.*
married *adj* casado/da; conyugal.
marrow *n* médula *f.*
marry *vi* casarse.
marsh *n* pantano *m.*
marshal *n* mariscal/a *m/f.*
marshy *adj* pantanoso/sa.
marten *n* marta *f.*
martial *adj* marcial; ~ **law** *n* ley marcial *f.*
martyr *n* mártir *m.*
martyrdom *n* martirio *m.*
marvel *n* maravilla *f;* * *vi* maravillar(se).
marvelous *adj* maravilloso/sa; ~**ly** *adv* maravillosamente.
marzipan *n* mazapán *m.*
mascara *n* rímel *m.*
masculine *adj* masculino/na, varonil.
mash *n* mezcla *f.*
mask *n* máscara *f;* * *vt* enmascarar.
masochist *n* masoquista *m/f.*
mason *n* albañil *m.*
masonry *n* mampostería *f.*
masquerade *n* mascarada *f.*
mass *n* masa *f;* misa *f;* montón *m.*
massacre *n* carnicería, matanza *f;* * *vt* hacer una carnicería.
massage *n* masaje *m.*

masseur *n* masajista *m*.
masseuse *n* masajista *f*.
massive *adj* enorme.
mass-media *npl* medios de comunicación de masas *mpl*.
mast *n* mástil *m*.
master *n* amo/ma, dueño/ña *m/f*; maestro/ tra *m/f*; * *vt* dominar.
masterly *adj* magistral.
mastermind *vt* dirigir.
masterpiece *n* obra maestra *f*.
mastery *n* maestría *f*.
masticate *vt* masticar.
mastiff *n* mastín *m*.
mat *n* estera *f*; felpudo *m*.
match *n* fósforo *m*, cerilla *f*; partido *m*, *Lat Am* juego *m*; * *vt* igualar; * *vi* hacer juego.
matchbox *n* caja de fósforos *f*.
matchless *adj* incomparable, sin par.
matchmaker *n* casamentero/ra *m/f*.
mate *n* compañero/ra *m/f*; * *vt* acoplar.
material *adj*, ~ly *adv* material(mente).
materialism *n* materialismo *m*.
maternal *adj* maternal.
maternity clothes *npl* vestido premamá *m*.
maternity hospital *n* hospital de maternidad *m*.
math *n* mates, matemáticas *fpl*.
mathematical *adj* matemático/ca; ~ly *adv* matemáticamente.
mathematician *n* matemático/ca *m/f*.
mathematics *npl* matemáticas *fpl*.
matinee *n* función de la tarde *f*.
mating *n* aparejamiento *m*.
matins *npl* maitines *mpl*.
matriculate *vt* matricular.
matriculation *n* matriculación *f*.
matrimonial *adj* matrimonial.
matte *adj* mate.
matted *adj* enmarañado/da.
matter *n* materia, substancia *f*; asunto *m*; cuestión *f*; what is the ~? ¿qué pasa?; as a ~ of fact en realidad; * *vi* importar.
mattress *n* colchón *m*.
mature *adj* maduro/ra; * *vt* madurar.
maturity *n* madurez *f*.
maul *vt* magullar.
mausoleum *n* mausoleo *m*.
mauve *adj* malva.
maxim *n* máxima *f*.
maximum *n* máximo *m*.
may *vi* poder; ~be acaso, quizá.
May *n* mayo *m*.
Mayday *n* primero de mayo *m*.
mayonnaise *n* mayonesa *f*.

mayor *n* alcalde *m*.
mayoress *n* alcaldesa *f*.
maze *n* laberinto *m*.
me *pn* me; mí.
meadow *n* pradera *f*; prado *m*.
meager *adj* pobre.
meagerness *n* escasez *f*.
meal *n* comida *f*; harina *f*.
mealtime *n* hora de comer *f*.
mean *adj* tacaño/ña; in the ~time, ~while mientras tanto; ~s *npl* medios *mpl*; * *vt, vi* significar.
meander *vi* serpentear.
meaning *n* sentido, significado *m*.
meaningful *adj* significativo/va.
meaningless *adj* sin sentido.
meanness *n* tacañería *f*.
meantime, meanwhile *adv* mientras tanto, *Lat Am* intertanto.
measles *npl* sarampión *m*.
measure *n* medida *f*; (*mus*) compás *m*; * *vt* medir.
measurement *n* medida *f*.
meat *n* carne *f*.
meatball *n* albóndiga *f*.
meaty *adj* sustancioso/sa.
mechanic *n* mecánico/ca *m/f*.
mechanical *adj* mecánico; ~ly *adv* mecánicamente.
mechanics *npl* mecánica *f*.
mechanism *n* mecanismo *m*.
medal *n* medalla *f*.
medallion *n* medallón *m*.
medallist *n* medallero/ra *m/f*.
meddle *vi* entrometerse.
meddler *n* entrometido *m*.
media *npl* medios de comunicación *mpl*.
median strip *n* mediana *f*.
mediate *vi* mediar.
mediation *n* mediación, interposición *f*.
mediator *n* intermediario/ria *m/f*.
medical *adj* médico/ca.
medicate *vt* medicar.
medicated *adj* medicinal.
medicinal *adj* medicinal.
medicine *n* medicina *f*; medicamento *m*.
medieval *adj* medieval.
mediocre *adj* mediocre.
mediocrity *n* mediocridad *f*.
meditate *vi* meditar.
meditation *n* meditación *f*.
meditative *adj* contemplativo/va.
Mediterranean *adj* mediterráneo/nea; the ~ el Mediterráneo/nea *m*.
medium *n* medio *m*; * *adj* mediano/na.

medium wave *n* onda media *f.*
medley *n* mezcla *m.*
meek *adj* manso/sa; ~**ly** *adv* mansamente.
meekness *n* mansedumbre *f.*
meet *vt* encontrar; **to ~ with** reunirse con; * *vi* encontrarse; juntarse.
meeting *n* reunión *f*; congreso *m.*
megaphone *n* megáfono *m.*
melancholy *n* melancolía *f*; * *adj* melancólico/ca.
mellow *adj* maduro/ra; suave; * *vi* madurar.
mellowness *n* madurez *f.*
melodious *adj* melodioso/sa; ~**ly** *adv* melodiosamente.
melody *n* melodía *f.*
melon *n* melón *m.*
melt *vt* derretir; * *vi* derretirse.
melting point *n* punto de fusión *m.*
member *n* miembro *m/f.*
membership *n* número de miembros *m*, *Lat Am* membresía *f.*
membrane *n* membrana *f.*
memento *n* recuerdo *m.*
memo *n* memorándum *m.*
memoir *n* memoria *f.*
memorable *adj* memorable.
memorandum *n* memorándum *m.*
memorial *n* monumento conmemorativo *m.*
memorize *vt* memorizar, aprender de memoria.
memory *n* memoria *f*; recuerdo *m.*
menace *n* amenaza *f*; * *vt* amenazar.
menacing *adj* amenazador/ra.
menagerie *n* casa de fieras *f.*
mend *vt* reparar.
mending *n* reparación *f.*
menial *adj* doméstico/ca.
meningitis *n* meningitis *f.*
menopause *n* menopausia *f.*
menstruation *n* menstruación *f.*
mental *adj* mental, intelectual.
mentality *n* mentalidad *f.*
mentally *adv* mentalmente, intelectualmente.
mention *n* mención *f*; * *vt* mencionar.
mentor *n* mentor *m.*
menu *n* menú *m*; carta *f.*
mercantile *adj* mercantil.
mercenary *adj*, *n* mercenario/ria *m/f.*
merchandise *n* mercancía *f.*
merchant *n* comerciante *m/f.*
merchantman *n* navío mercante *m.*
merchant marine *n* marina mercante *f.*
merciful *adj* compasivo/va.
merciless *adj* despiadado/da; ~**ly** *adv* despiadadamente.
mercury *n* mercurio *m.*

mercy *n* compasión *f.*
mere *adj* mero/ra; ~**ly** *adv* simplemente.
merge *vt* fundir.
merger *n* fusión *f.*
meridian *n* meridiano *m.*
meringue *n* merengue *m.*
merit *n* mérito *m*; * *vt* merecer.
meritorious *adj* meritorio/ria.
mermaid *n* sirena *f.*
merrily *adv* alegremente.
merriment *n* diversión *f*; regocijo *m.*
merry *adj* alegre.
merry-go-round *n* tiovivo *m.*
mesh *n* malla *f.*
mesmerize *vt* hipnotizar.
mess *n* lío *m*, *Lat Am* relajo *m*; mamarracho *m*; (*mil*) comedor *m*; **to ~ up** *vt* desordenar.
message *n* mensaje *m.*
messenger *n* mensajero/ra *m/f.*
metabolism *n* metabolismo *n.*
metal *n* metal *m.*
metallic *adj* metálico/ca.
metallurgy *n* metalurgía *f.*
metamorphosis *n* metamorfosis *f invar.*
metaphor *n* metáfora *f.*
metaphoric(al) *adj* metafórico/ca.
metaphysical *adj* metafísico/ca.
metaphysics *npl* metafísica *f.*
mete (out) *vt* imponer.
meteor *n* meteoro *m.*
meteorological *adj* meteorológico/ca.
meteorology *n* meteorología *f.*
meter[1] *n* contador *m*, *Lat Am* medidor *m.*
meter[2] *n* metro *m.*
method *n* método *m.*
methodical *adj* metódico/ca; ~**ly** *adv* metódicamente.
Methodist *n* metodista *m/f.*
metric *adj* métrico/ca.
metropolis *n* metrópoli *f.*
metropolitan *adj* metropolitano/na.
mettle *n* valor *m.*
mettlesome *adj* brioso/sa.
mew *vi* maullar.
mezzanine *n* entresuelo *m.*
microbe *n* microbio *m.*
microphone *n* micrófono *m.*
microchip *n* microchip *m.*
microscope *n* microscopio *m.*
microscopic *adj* microscópico/ca.
microwave *n* microondas *m invar*; ~ **oven** microondas *m.*
mid *adj* medio/dia.
midday *n* mediodía *m.*
middle *adj* medio/dia; * *n* medio, centro *m.*

middle name *n* segundo nombre *m*.
middleweight *n* peso medio *m*.
middling *adj* mediano/na.
midge *n* mosquito *m*.
midget *n* enano/na *m/f*.
midi system *n* minicadena *f*.
midnight *n* medianoche *f*.
midriff *n* diafragma *m*.
midst *n* medio, centro *m*.
midsummer *n* pleno verano *m*.
midway *adv* a medio camino.
midwife *n* partera *f*.
midwifery *n* obstetricia *f*.
might *n* poder *m*; fuerza *f*.
mighty *adj* fuerte.
migraine *n* jaqueca *f*.
migrate *vi* emigrar, migrar.
migration *n* emigración, migración *f*.
migratory *adj* migratorio/ria.
mike *n* micrófono *m*.
mild *adj* apacible; suave; ~ly *adv* suavemente.
mildew *n* moho *m*.
mildness *n* dulzura *f*.
mile *n* milla *f*.
mileage *n* kilometraje *m*.
milieu *n* ambiente *m*.
militant *adj* militante.
military *adj* militar.
militate *vi* militar.
militia *n* milicia *f*.
milk *n* leche *f*; * *vt* ordenar.
milkshake *n* batido de leche *m*, *Lat Am* malteada *f*.
milky *adj* lechoso/sa; **M~ Way** *n* Via Lactea *f*.
mill *n* molino *m*; * *vt* moler.
millennium *n* milenio *m*.
miller *n* molinero/ra *m/f*.
millet *n* (*bot*) mijo *m*.
milligram *n* miligramo *m*.
milliliter *n* mililitro *m*.
millimeter *n* milímetro *m*.
milliner *n* sombrerero/ra *m/f*.
millinery *n* sombrerería *f*.
million *n* millón *m*.
millionaire *n* millonario/ria *m/f*.
millionth *adj*, *n* millonésimo/ma *m/f*.
millstone *n* piedra de molino *f*.
mime *n* mimo *m*.
mimic *vt* imitar.
mimicry *n* mímica *f*.
mince *vt* picar.
mind *n* mente *f*; * *vt* cuidar; * *vi* molestar.
minded *adj* dispuesto/ta.
mindful *adj* consciente.
mindless *adj* sin motivo.

mine *pn* mío, mía, mi; * *n* mina; * *vi* minar.
minefield *n* campo de minas *m*.
miner *n* minero/ra *m/f*.
mineral *adj*, *n* mineral *m*.
mineralogy *n* mineralogia *f*.
mineral water *n* agua mineral *f*.
minesweeper *n* dragaminas *m invar*.
mingle *vt* mezclar.
miniature *n* miniatura *f*.
minimal *adj* mínimo/ma.
minimize *vt* minimizar.
minimum *n* mínimo *m*.
mining *n* minería *f*.
minion *n* favorito/ta *m/f*.
minister *n* ministro/tro *m/f*; * *vt* servir.
ministerial *adj* ministerial.
ministry *n* ministerio *m*.
mink *n* visón *m*.
minnow *n* vario *m* (pez).
minor *adj* menor; * *n* menor (de edad) *m/f*.
minority *n* minoría *f*.
minstrel *n* juglar *m*.
mint *n* (*bot*) menta *f*; casa de la moneda *f*; * *vt* acuñar.
minus *adv* menos.
minute[1] *adj* diminuto/ta; ~ly *adv* minuciosamente.
minute[2] *n* minuto *m*.
miracle *n* milagro *m*.
miraculous *adj* milagroso/sa.
mirage *n* espejismo *m*.
mire *n* fango *m*.
mirky *adj* turbio/bia.
mirror *n* espejo *m*.
mirth *n* alegría *f*.
mirthful *adj* alegre.
misadventure *n* desgracia *f*.
misanthrope, misanthropist *n* misántropo *m*.
misapply *vt* aplicar mal.
misapprehension *n* error *m*.
misbehave *vi* portarse mal.
misbehavior *n* mala conducta *f*.
miscalculate *vt* calcular mal.
miscarriage *n* aborto (espontáneo) *m*.
miscarry *vi* abortar (espontáneamente); malograrse.
miscellaneous *adj* varios, varias.
miscellany *n* miscelánea *f*.
mischief *n* mal, daño *m*.
mischievous *adj* dañoso/sa; travieso/sa.
misconception *n* equivocación *f*.
misconduct *n* mala conducta *f*.
misconstrue *vt* interpretar mal.
miscount *vt* contar mal.
miscreant *n* malvado/da *m/f*.

misdeed n delito m.
misdemeanor n delito m.
misdirect vt dirigir mal.
miser n avaro/ra m/f.
miserable adj miserable, infeliz.
miserly adj mezquino/na, tacaño/ña.
misery n miseria f.
misfit n inadaptado/da m/f.
misfortune n desgracia f.
misgiving n recelo m; presentimiento m.
misgovern vt gobernar mal.
misguided adj equivocado/da.
mishandle vt manejar mal.
mishap n desgracia f.
misinform vt informar mal, Lat Am malinformar.
misinterpret vt interpretar mal.
misjudge vi juzgar mal.
mislay vt extraviar.
mislead vt engañar.
mismanage vt manejar mal.
mismanagement n mala administración f.
misnomer n nombre inapropriado m.
misogynist n misógino/na m/f.
misplace vt extraviar.
misprint vt imprimir mal; * n errata f.
misrepresent vt representar mal.
Miss n señorita f.
miss vt perder; echar de menos.
missal n misal m.
misshapen adj deforme.
missile n misil m.
missing adj perdido/da; ausente.
mission n misión f.
missionary n misionero/ra m/f.
misspent adj disipado/da.
mist n niebla f.
mistake vt entender mal; * vi equivocarse, engañarse; **to be mistaken** equivocarse; * n equivocación f; error m, Lat Am falla f, yerro m.
Mister n Señor m.
mistletoe n (bot) muérdago m.
mistress n amante f.
mistrust vt desconfiar; * n desconfianza f.
mistrustful adj desconfiado/da.
misty adj nebuloso/sa.
misunderstand vt entender mal.
misunderstanding n malentendido m.
misuse vt maltratar; abusar de.
miter n mitra f.
mitigate vt mitigar.
mitigation n mitigación f.
mittens npl manoplas fpl.
mix vt mezclar.
mixed adj surtido/da; mixto/ta.

mixed-up adj confuso/sa.
mixer n licuadora f.
mixture n mezcla f.
mix-up n confusión f.
moan n gemido m; * vi gemir; quejarse.
moat n foso m.
mob n multitud f.
mobile adj móvil; --/**cell phone** móvil m, Lat Am celular m.
mobile home n caravana f.
mobility n movilidad f.
mobilize vt (mil) movilizar.
moccasin n mocasin m.
mock vt burlarse.
mockery n mofa f.
mode n modo m.
model n modelo m; * vt modelar.
modem n módem m.
moderate adj moderado/da; **~ly** adv medianamente; * vt moderar.
moderation n moderación f.
modern adj moderno/na.
modernize vt modernizar.
modest adj modesto/ta; **~ly** adv modestamente.
modesty n modestia f.
modicum n mínimo m.
modification n modificación f.
modify vt modificar.
modulate vt modular.
modulation n (mus) modulación f.
module n módulo m.
mogul n magnate m/f.
mohair n mohair m.
moist adj húmedo/da.
moisten vt humedecer.
moisture n humedad f.
molars npl muelas fpl.
molasses npl melaza f.
mold n molde m; moho m; * vt moldear.
molder vi decaer.
moldy adj enmohecido/da.
mole n topo m.
molecule n molécula f.
molehill n topera f.
molest vt importunar.
mollify vt apaciguar.
mollusk n molusco m.
mollycoddle vt mimar.
molt vt mudar.
molten adj derretido/da.
moment n momento m.
momentarily adv momentáncamente.
momentary adj momentáneo/nea.
momentous adj importante.
momentum n ímpetu m.

mommy *n* mamá *f.*
monarch *n* monarca *m.*
monarchy *n* monarquía *f.*
monastery *n* monasterio *m.*
monastic *adj* monástico/ca.
Monday *n* lunes *m.*
monetary *adj* monetario/ria.
money *n* dinero *m*, *Lat Am* plata *f.*
money box *n* hucha *f*, *Lat Am* alcancía *f.*
money laundering *n* blanqueo *m.*
money order *n* giro *m.*
Mongol *n* mongólico/ca *m/f.*
mongrel *adj, n* mestizo/za *m/f.*
monitor *n* monitor *m.*
monk *n* monje *m.*
monkey *n* mono *m.*
monochrome *adj* monocromo/ma.
monocle *n* monóculo *m.*
monolog *n* monólogo *m.*
monopolize *vt* monopolizar.
monopoly *n* monopolio *m.*
monosyllable *n* monosílabo *m.*
monotonous *adj* monótono/na.
monotony *n* monotonía *f.*
monsoon *n* (*mar*) monzón *m.*
monster *n* monstruo *m.*
monstrosity *n* monstruosidad *f.*
monstrous *adj* monstruoso/sa; ~ly *adv* monstruosamente.
montage *n* montaje *m.*
month *n* mes *m.*
monthly *adj, adv* mensual(mente).
monument *n* monumento *m.*
monumental *adj* monumental.
moo *vi* mugir.
mood *n* humor *m.*
moodiness *n* mal humor *m.*
moody *adj* malhumorado/da.
moon *n* luna *f.*
moonbeams *npl* rayos lunares *mpl.*
moonlight *n* luz de la luna *f.*
moor *vt* (*mar*) atracar.
mooring rope *n* amarra *f.*
moorland, moor *n* páramo *m.*
moose *n* alce *m.*
mop *n* fregona *f*; * *vt* fregar.
mope *vi* estar triste.
moped *n* ciclomotor *m.*
moral *adj*, ~ly *adv* moral(mente); ~s *npl* moralidad *f.*
morale *n* moral *f.*
moralist *n* moralista *m/f.*
morality *n* ética, moralidad *f.*
moralize *vt, vi* moralizar.
morass *n* pantano *m.*

morbid *adj* morboso/sa.
more *adj, adv* más; **never** ~ nunca más; once ~ otra vez; ~ **and** ~ más y más, cada vez más; **so much the** ~ cuanto más.
moreover *adv* además.
morgue *n* depósito de cadáveres *m.*
morning *n* mañana *f*; **good** ~ buenos días *mpl.*
moron *n* imbécil *m/f.*
morose *adj* hosco/ca.
morphine *n* morfina *f.*
morsel *n* bocado *m.*
mortal *adj* mortal; ~ly *adv* mortalmente; * *n* mortal *m/f.*
mortality *n* mortalidad *f.*
mortar *n* mortero *m.*
mortgage *n* hipoteca *f*; * *vt* hipotecar.
mortgage company *n* banco hipotecario *m.*
mortgager *n* deudor hipotecario *m*, deudora hipotecaria *f.*
mortician *n* director de pompas fúnebres.
mortification *n* mortificación *f.*
mortuary *n* depósito de cadáveres *m.*
mosaic *n* mosaico *m.*
mosque *n* mezquita *f.*
mosquito *n* mosquito *m*; zancudo/da *m.*
moss *n* (*bot*) musgo *m*, *Lat Am* lama *f.*
mossy *adj* cubierto/ta de musgo.
most *adj* la mayoría de; * *adv* sumamente; at ~ a lo sumo; ~ly *adv* principalmente.
motel *n* motel *m.*
moth *n* polilla *f.*
mothball *n* bola de naftalina *f.*
mother *n* madre *f*; **loving** ~ madraza *f.*
motherhood *n* maternidad *f.*
mother-in-law *n* suegra *f.*
motherless *adj* sin madre.
motherly *adj* maternal.
mother-of-pearl *n* nácar *m.*
mother-to-be *n* futura madre *f.*
mother tongue *n* lengua materna *f.*
motif *n* tema *m.*
motion *n* movimiento *m.*
motionless *adj* inmóvil.
motion picture *n* película *f.*
motivated *adj* motivado/da.
motive *n* motivo *m.*
motley *adj* abigarrado/da.
motor *n* motor *m.*
motorbike *n* moto *f.*
motorboat *n* lancha motora *f.*
motorcycle *n* motocicleta *f.*
motor scooter *n* moto *f.*
motor vehicle *n* automóvil *m.*
mottled *adj* multicolor.
motto *n* lema *m.*

mound n montón m.
mount n monte m; * vt subir.
mountain n montaña f.
mountaineer n montañero/ra m/f, alpinista m/f, Lat Am andinista m/f.
mountaineering n montañismo m, alpinismo m, Lat Am andinismo m.
mountainous adj montañoso/sa.
mourn vt lamentar.
mourner n doliente m/f.
mournful adj triste; ~ly adv tristemente.
mourning n luto m.
mouse n (pl **mice**) ratón m.
mouse mat n alfombrilla f.
mousse n mousse f.
mouth n boca f; desembocadura f.
mouthful n bocado m.
mouth organ n harmónica f.
mouthpiece n boquilla f.
mouthwash n enjuague m.
mouthwatering adj apetitoso/sa.
movable adj movible.
move vt mover; proponer; * vi moverse; * n movimiento m.
movement n movimiento m.
movie n película f.
movie camera n cámara cinematográfica f.
movie theater, **movie house** n cine m.
moving adj conmovedor/a.
mow vt segar.
mower n cortacésped m.
Mrs n señora f.
much adj, adv mucho/cha; con mucho.
muck n suciedad f.
mucous adj mocoso/sa.
mucus n moco m.
mud n barro m.
muddle vt confundir m; confusión f.
muddy adj fangoso/sa.
mudguard n guardabarros m invar.
muffle vt embozar.
mug n jarra f.
muggy adj bochornoso/sa.
mulberry n mora f; ~ **tree** morera f.
mule n mulo m, mula f.
mull vt meditar.
multifarious adj múltiple.
multimedia adj multimedia.
multiple adj múltiplo m.
multiplication n multiplicación f; ~ **table** tabla de multiplicar f.
multiply vt multiplicar.
multitude n multitud f.
mumble vt, vi refunfuñar.
mummy n momia f.

mumps npl paperas fpl.
munch vt mascar.
mundane adj trivial.
municipal adj municipal.
municipality n municipalidad f.
munificence n munificencia f.
munitions npl municiones fpl.
mural n mural m.
murder n asesinato m; homicidio m; * vt asesinar.
murderer n asesino/na m/f.
murderess n asesina f.
murderous adj homicida.
murky adj sombrío/ría.
murmur n murmullo m; * vi murmurar.
muscle n músculo m.
muscular adj muscular.
muse vi meditar.
museum n museo m.
mushroom n (bot) seta f; champiñón m.
music n musica f.
musical adj musical; melodioso/sa.
musician n músico/ca m/f.
musk n almizcle m.
muslin n muselina f.
mussel n mejillón m.
must v aux tener que, deber; deber de.
mustache n bigote m.
mustard n mostaza f.
muster vt agregar.
musty adj mohoso/sa, añejo/ja.
mute adj mudo/da, silencioso/sa.
muted adj callado/da.
mutilate vt mutilar.
mutilation n mutilación f.
mutiny n motin, tumulto m; * vi amotinarse, rebelarse.
mutter vt, vi murmurar, musitar; * n murmuración f.
mutton n carnero m.
mutual adj mutuo/tua, mutual, recíproco/ca; ~ly adv mutuamente, recíprocamente.
muzzle n bozal m; hocico m; * vt embozar.
my pn mi, mis; mio, mia; mios, mias.
myriad n miríada f; gran número m.
myrrh n mirra f.
myrtle n mirto, arrayán m.
myself pn yo mismo/ma.
mysterious adj misterioso/sa; ~ly adv misteriosamente.
mystery n misterio m.
mystic(al) adj místico/ca.
mystify vt dejar perplejo/ja.
mystique n misterio m.
myth n mito m.
mythology n mitología f.

N

nab vt agarrar.

nag n jaca f; * vt regañar.

nagging adj persistente; * npl quejas fpl.

nail n uña f; garra f; clavo m; * vt clavar.

nailbrush n cepillo de uñas m.

nailfile n lima de uñas f.

nail polish n esmalte de uñas m.

nail scissors npl tijeras de manicura fpl.

naïve adj ingenuo/nua.

naked adj desnudo/da evidente; puro/ra, simple.

name n nombre m; fama, reputación f; * vt nombrar; mencionar.

nameless adj anónimo/ma.

namely adv a saber.

namesake n tocayo/ya m/f.

nanny n niñera f.

nap n sueño ligero m.

napalm n napalm m.

nape n nuca f.

napkin n servilleta f.

narcissus n (bot) narciso m.

narcotic adj narcótico/ca; * n narcótico m.

narrate vt narrar, relatar.

narrative adj narrativo/va; * n narrativa f.

narrow adj angosto/ta, estrecho/cha; ~ly adv estrechamente; * vt estrechar; limitar.

narrow-minded adj estrecho/cha de miras.

narrow pass n puerto m.

nasal adj nasal.

nasty adj sucio/cia, puerco/ca; obsceno/na; sórdido/da.

natal adj nativo/va; natal.

nation n nación f.

national adj, ~ly adv nacional(mente).

nationalism n nacionalismo m.

nationalist adj, n nacionalista m/f.

nationality n nacionalidad f.

nationalize vt nacionalizar.

nationwide adj a nivel nacional.

native adj nativo/va; * n natural m/f.

native language n lengua materna f.

Nativity n Navidad f.

natural adj natural; sencillo/lla; ~ly adv naturalmente.

natural gas n gas natural m.

naturalist n naturalista m/f.

naturalize vt naturalizar.

nature n naturaleza f; índole f.

naturopath n naturópata m/f.

naught, nought n cero m.

naughty adj malo/la, malvado/da.

nausea n náuseas fpl, gana de vomitar f.

nauseate vt dar náuseas a.

nauseous adj fastidioso/sa.

nautical, naval adj náutico/ca, naval.

nave n nave (de la iglesia) f.

navel n ombligo m.

navigate vi navegar.

navigation n navegación f.

navy n marina f; armada f.

Nazi n nazi m/f.

near prep cerca de, junto a; * adv casi; cerca, cerca de; * adj cercano/na, proximo/ma.

nearby adj cercano/na.

nearly adv casi.

near-sighted adj miope.

neat adj hermoso/sa, pulido/da; puro/ra; neto/ta; ~ly adv elegantemente.

nebulous adj nebuloso/sa.

necessarily adv necesariamente.

necessary adj necesario/ria.

necessitate vt necesitar.

necessity n necesidad f.

neck n cuello m, Lat Am cogote m; * vi besuquearse.

necklace n collar m.

nectar n néctar m.

née, nee adj: ~ Brown de soltera Brown.

need n necesidad f; pobreza f; * vt necesitar.

needle n aguja f.

needless adj superfluo/lua, inútil.

needlework n costura f; bordado de aguja m; obra de punto m.

needy adj necesitado/da, pobre.

negation n negación f.

negative adj negativo/va; ~ly adv negativamente; * n negativa f.

neglect vt descuidar, desatender; * n negligencia f.

negligee n salto de cama m.

negligence n negligencia f; descuido m.

negligent adj negligente, descuidado/da; ~ly adv negligentemente.

negligible adj insignificante.

negotiate vt, vi negociar (con).

negotiation n negociación f; negocio m.

Negress n negra f.

Negro adj negro/gra; * n negro m.

neigh vi relinchar; * n relincho m.

neighbor n vecino/na m/f; * vt confinar.

neighborhood n vecindad f; vecindario m.

neighboring *adj* vecino/na.
neighborly *adj* sociable.
neither *conj* ni; * *pn* ninguno/na, ni uno ni otro, ni una ni otra.
neon *n* neón *m.*
neon light *n* luz de neón *f.*
nephew *n* sobrino *m.*
nepotism *n* nepotismo *m.*
nerve *n* nervio *m*; valor *m.*
nerve-racking *adj* espantoso/sa.
nervous *adj* nervioso/sa; nervudo/da.
nervous breakdown *n* crisis nerviosa *f.*
nest *n* nido *m*; nidada *f.*
nest egg *n* (*fig*) ahorros *mpl.*
nestle *vt* anidarse.
net *n* red *f.*
netball *n* nétbol *m.*
net curtain *n* visillo *m.*
netting *n* mallado *m.*
nettle *n* ortiga *f.*
network *n* red *f*, malla *f.*
neuron *n* neurona *f.*
neurosis *n* neurosis *f invar.*
neurotic *adj*, *n* neurótico/ca *m/f.*
neuter *adj* (*gr*) neutro/tra.
neutral *adj* neutral.
neutrality *n* neutralidad *f.*
neutralize *vt* neutralizar.
neutron *n* neutrón *m.*
neutron bomb *n* bomba de neutrones *f.*
never *adv* nunca, jamás; ~ **mind** no importa.
never-ending *adj* sin fin.
nevertheless *adv* no obstante.
new *adj* nuevo/va, fresco/sca, reciénte; ~**ly** *adv* nuevamente.
newborn *adj* recién nacido/da.
newcomer *n* recién llegado/da *m.*
new-fangled *adj* inventado/da por novedad.
news *npl* novedad, noticias *fpl.*
news agency *n* agencia de noticias *f.*
newscaster *n* presentador/a *m/f.*
newsdealer *n* vendedor/a de periódicos *m/f.*
news flash *n* noticia de última hora *f.*
newsletter *n* boletín *m.*
newspaper *n* periódico *m.*
newsreel *n* noticiario *m.*
New Year *n* Año Nuevo *m*; ~**'s Day** Día de Año Nuevo *m*; ~**'s Eve** Nochevieja *f.*
next *adj* próximo/ma; **the** ~ **day** el día siguiente; * *adv* luego, inmediatamente después.
nib *n* pico *m*; punta *f.*
nibble *vt* picar, mordiscar.
nice *adj* simpático/ca; agradable; lindo/da; ~**ly** *adv* bien.

nice-looking *adj* guapo/pa.
niche *n* nicho *m.*
nick *n* mella *f*; * *vt* (*col*) robar.
nickel *n* níquel *m*; moneda de cinco centavos *f.*
nickname *n* mote, apodo *m*; * *vt* poner apodos.
nicotine *n* nicotina *f.*
niece *n* sobrina *f.*
niggling *adj* insignificante.
night *n* noche *f*; velador *m*; **by** ~ de noche; **good** ~ buenas noches.
nightclub *n* cabaret *m.*
nightfall *n* anochecer *m.*
nightingale *n* ruiseñor *m.*
nightly *adv* por las noches, todas las noches; * *adj* nocturno/na.
nightmare *n* pesadilla *f.*
night school *n* clases nocturnas *fpl.*
night shift *n* turno de noche *m.*
night-time *n* noche *f.*
night work *n* vela *f.*
nihilist *n* nihilista *m/f.*
nimble *adj* ligero/ra, activo/va, listo/ta, ágil.
nine *adj*, *n* nueve.
ninepin *n* bolo *m.*
nineteen *adj*, *n* diecinueve.
nineteenth *adj*, *n* decimonoveno/na.
ninetieth *adj*, *n* nonagésimo/ma.
ninety *adj*, *n* noventa.
ninth *adj*, *n* nono/na, noveno/na.
nip *vt* pellizcar; morder.
nipple *n* pezón *m*; tetilla *f.*
nit *n* liendre *f.*
nitrogen *n* nitrógeno *m.*
no *adv* no; * *adj* ningún, ninguno/na.
nobility *n* nobleza *f.*
noble *adj* noble; insigne; * *n* noble *m/f.*
nobleman *n* noble *m.*
nobody *n* nadie, ninguna persona *f.*
nocturnal *adj* nocturnal, nocturno/na.
nod *n* cabeceo *m*; señal *f*; * *vi* cabecear; amodorrarse.
noise *n* ruido, estruendo *m*; rumor *m.*
noisily *adv* con ruido.
noisiness *n* ruido, tumulto, alboroto *m.*
noisy *adj* ruidoso/sa, turbulento/ta.
nominal *adj*, ~**ly** *adv* nominal(mente).
nominate *vt* nombrar.
nomination *n* nominación *f.*
nominative *n* (*gr*) nominativo *m.*
nominee *n* candidato/ta *m/f.*
nonalcoholic *adj* no alcóholico/ca.
nonaligned *adj* no alineado/da.
nonchalant *adj* indiferente.

noncommittal *adj* reservado/da.
nonconformist *n* inconformista *m/f*.
nondescript *adj* no descrito/ta.
none *adj* nadie, ninguno/na.
nonentity *n* nulidad *f*.
nonetheless *adv* sin embargo.
nonexistent *adj* inexistente.
nonfiction *n* no ficción *f*.
nonplussed *adj* confuso/sa.
nonsense *n* disparate, absurdo *m*, *Lat Am* sonsera *f*.
nonsensical *adj* absurdo/da.
nonsmoker *n* no fumador/a *m/f*.
nonstick *adj* antiadherente.
nonstop *adj* directo/ta; * *adv* sin parar.
noodles *npl* fideos (chinos) *mpl*.
noon *n* mediodía *m*.
noose *n* nudo corredizo *m*.
nor *conj* ni.
normal *adj* normal.
north *n* norte *m*; * *adj* del norte.
North America *n* América del Norte, Norteamérica *f*.
northeast *n* nor(d)este *m*.
northerly, northern *adj* norteño/ña.
North Pole *n* polo norte *m*.
northward(s) *adv* hacia el norte.
northwest *n* nor(d)oeste *m*.
nose *n* nariz *f*; olfato *m*.
nosebleed *n* hemorragia nasal *f*.
nosedive *n* picado vertical *m*.
nostalgia *n* nostalgia *f*.
nostril *n* ventana de la nariz *f*.
not *adv* no.
notable *adj* notable; memorable.
notably *adv* especialmente.
notary *n* notario/ria *m/f*.
notch *n* muesca *f*; * *vt* hacer muescas.
note *n* nota, marca *f*; señal *f*; aprecio *m*; billete *m*; consecuen cia *f*; noticia *f*; indirecta *f*; * *vt* notar, marcar; observar.
notebook *n* cuaderno *m*, libreta *f*.
noted *adj* afamado/da, celebre.
notepad *n* bloc *m*.
notepaper *n* papel de cartas *m*.
nothing *n* nada *f*; good for ~ lo que sirve para nada.
notice *n* noticia *f*; aviso *m*; * *vt* observar.
noticeable *adj* notable, reparable.
notification *n* notificación *f*.
notify *vt* notificar.
notion *n* noción *f*; opinión *f*; idea *f*.
notoriety *n* mala fama *f*.
notorious *adj* tristemente célebre; ~ly *adv* notoriamente.

notwithstanding *conj* no obstante, aunque.
nougat *n* turrón *m*.
noun *n* (*gr*) sustantivo *m*.
nourish *vt* nutrir, alimentar.
nourishing *adj* nutritivo/va.
nourishment *n* nutrimiento, alimento *m*.
novel *n* novela *f*.
novelist *n* novelista *m/f*.
novelty *n* novedad *f*.
November *n* noviembre *m*.
novice *n* novicio/cia *m/f*.
now *adv* ya, ahora, hoy (en) día; ~ and then de vez en cuando.
nowadays *adv* hoy (en) día.
nowhere *adv* en ninguna parte.
noxious *adj* nocivo/va, dañoso/sa.
nozzle *n* boquilla *f*.
nuance *n* matiz *m*.
nuclear *adj* nuclear; ~ power energía nuclear *f*; ~ power station *n* central nuclear *f*.
nucleus *n* núcleo *m*.
nude *adj* desnudo/da, en carnes, en cueros, sin vestido.
nudge *vt* dar un codazo a.
nudist *n* nudista *m/f*.
nudity *n* desnudez *f*.
nuisance *n* daño, perjuicio *m*; incomodidad *f*.
nuke *n* (*col*) bomba atómica *f*; * *vt* atacar con arma nuclear.
null *adj* nulo/la, inválido/da.
nullify *vt* anular, invalidar.
numb *adj* entorpecido/da; * *vt* entorpecer.
number *n* número *m*; cantidad *f*; * *vt* numerar.
numbness *n* entumecimiento *m*.
numeral *n* número *m*.
numerical *adj* numérico/ca.
numerous *adj* numeroso/sa.
nun *n* monja, religiosa *f*.
nunnery *n* convento de monjas *m*.
nuptial *adj* nupcial; ~s *npl* nupcias *fpl*.
nurse *n* enfermera *f*; * *vt* cuidar; amamantar.
nursery *n* guardería infantil *f*; criadero *m*.
nursery rhyme *n* canción infantil *f*.
nursing home *n* clinica de reposo *f*.
nurture *vt* criar, educar.
nut *n* nuez *f*.
nutcrackers *npl* cascanueces *m invar*.
nutmeg *n* nuez moscada *f*.
nutritious *adj* nutritivo/va.
nutshell *n* cascara de nuez *f*.
nylon *n* nylon, nailon *m*; * *adj* de nylon, de nailon.

O

oak *n* roble *m*.

oar *n* remo *m*.

oasis *n* oasis *f invar*.

oath *n* juramento *m*.

oatmeal *n* harina de avena *f*.

oats *npl* avena *f*.

obedience *n* obediencia *f*.

obedient *adj*, ~ly *adv* obediente(mente).

obese *adj* obeso/sa, gordo/da.

obesity *n* obesidad *f*.

obey *vt* obedecer.

obituary *n* necrología *f*.

object *n* objeto *m*; * *vt* objetar.

objection *n* oposición, objeción, réplica *f*.

objectionable *adj* desagradable.

objective *adj* objetivo/va; * *n* objetivo *m*.

obligation *n* obligación *f*.

obligatory *adj* obligatorio/ria.

oblige *vt* obligar; complacer, favorecer

obliging *adj* servicial.

oblique *adj* oblicuo/cua; indirecto/ta; ~ly *adv* oblicuamente.

obliterate *vt* borrar.

oblivion *n* olvido *m*.

oblivious *adj* olvidadizo/za.

oblong *adj* oblongo/ga.

obnoxious *adj* odioso/sa.

oboe *n* oboe *m*.

obscene *adj* obsceno/na, impudico/ca.

obscenity *n* obscenidad *f*.

obscure *adj* oscuro/ra; ~ly *adv* oscuramente; * *vt* oscurecer.

obscurity *n* oscuridad *f*.

observance *n* observancia *f*; reverencia *f*.

observant *adj* observante, respetuoso/sa.

observantly *adv* cuidadosamente, atentamente.

observation *n* observación *f*.

observatory *n* observatorio *m*.

observe *vt* observar, mirar.

observer *n* observador/a *m/f*.

obsess *vt* obsesionar.

obsessive *adj* obsesivo/va.

obsolete *adj* obsoleto/ta.

obstacle *n* obstáculo *m*.

obstinacy *n* tenacidad *f*.

obstinate *adj* obstinado/da; ~ly *adv* obstinadamente.

obstruct *vt* obstruir; impedir.

obstruction *n* obstrucción *f*; impedimento *m*.

obtain *vt* obtener, adquirir; ~ by cunning sonsacar.

obtainable *adj* asequible.

obtrusive *adj* intruso/sa, importuno/na.

obtuse *adj* obtuso/sa, sin punta; lerdo/da, torpe.

obvious *adj* obvio/via, evidente; ~ly *adv* naturalmente.

occasion *n* ocasión *f*; momento oportuno *m*; * *vt* ocasionar, causar.

occasional *adj* ocasional, casual; ~ly *adv* ocasionalmente.

occupant, occupier *n* ocupante *m/f*; poseedor/a *m/f*; inquilino/na *m/f*.

occupation *n* ocupación *f*; empleo *m*.

occupy *vt* ocupar, emplear.

occur *vi* pasar, ocurrir.

occurrence *n* incidente *m*.

ocean *n* océano *m*; alta mar *f*.

ocean-going *adj* de alta mar.

oceanic *adj* oceánico/ca.

ocher *n* ocre *m*.

octave *n* octava *f*.

October *n* octubre *m*.

octopus *n* pulpo *m*.

odd *adj* impar; particular; extravagante; extraño/ña; ~ly *adv* extrañamente.

oddity *n* singularidad, particularidad, rareza *f*.

oddness *n* desigualdad *f*; singularidad *f*.

odds *npl* probabilidades *fpl*; apuestas *fpl*.

odious *adj* odioso/sa.

odometer *n* cuentakilómetros *m invar*.

odor *n* olor *m*; fragancia *f*.

odorous, odoriferous *adj* odorífero/ra.

of *prep* de; tocante; segun.

of course! *interj* ¡naturalmente!

off *adv* desconectado/da; apagado/da; cerrado/da; cancelado/da; ~! *excl* ¡fuera!

offend *vt* ofender, irritar; injuriar; * *vi* pecar.

offender *n* delincuente *m*.

offense *n* ofensa *f*; injuria *f*.

offensive *adj* ofensivo/va; injurioso/sa; ~ly *adv* ofensivamente.

offer *vt* ofrecer; * *n* oferta *f*.

offering *n* sacrificio *m*; oferta *f*.

offhand *adj* descortés; * *adv* de repente.

office *n* oficina *f*; oficio, empleo *m*; servicio *m*.

office building *n* bloque de oficinas *m*.

office hours *npl* horas de oficina *fpl*.

officer *n* oficial/a, empleado/da *m/f.*
office worker *n* oficinista *m/f.*
official *adj* oficial; ~**ly** *adv* de oficio; * *n* empleado *m.*
officiate *vi* oficiar.
officious *adj* oficioso/sa; ~**ly** *adv* oficiosamente.
off-line *adj, adv* fuera de línea.
off-peak *adj* de temporada baja.
off-season *adj, adv* fuera de temporada, en tarifa reducida.
offset *vt* contrarrestar.
offshoot *n* ramificación *f.*
offshore *adj* costero/ra.
offside *adj* fuera de juego.
offspring *n* prole *f*; linaje *m*; descendencia *f.*
offstage *adv* entre bastidores.
off-the-peg *adj* confeccionado/da.
ogle *vt* comerse con los ojos.
oil *n* aceite *m*; óleo *m*; * *vt* engrasar.
oilcan *n* lata de aceite *f.*
oilfield *n* campo petrolífero *m.*
oil filter *n* filtro de aceite *m.*
oil painting *n* pintura al óleo *f.*
oil rig *n* torre de perforación *f.*
oil slick *n* marea negra *f.*
oil tanker *n* petrolero *m.*
oil well *n* pozo petrolífero *m.*
oily *adj* aceitoso/sa; grasiento/ta.
ointment *n* ungüento *m.*
OK, okay *excl* vale, *Lat Am* okey; * *adj* bien; * *vt* dar el visto bueno a.
old *adj* viejo/ja; antiguo/gua.
old age *n* vejez *f.*
old-fashioned *adj* pasado/da de moda.
olive *n* olivo *m*; oliva *f.*
olive oil *n* aceite de oliva *m.*
Olympic Games *npl* las Olímpicos *fpl.*
omelet *n* tortilla (francesa) *f*, *Lat Am* omelet *f.*
omen *n* agüero, presagio *m.*
ominous *adj* ominoso/sa.
omission *n* omisión *f*; descuido *m.*
omit *vt* omitir.
omnipotence *n* omnipotencia *f.*
omnipotent *adj* omnipotente, todopoderoso/sa.
on *prep* sobre, encima, en; de; a; * *adj* encendido/da; prendido/da; abierto/ta; puesto/ta.
once *adv* una vez; **at ~** en seguida; **all at ~** de una vez, en seguida; **~ more** otra vez.
oncoming *adj* que viene de frente.
one *adj* un, uno, una; **~ by ~** uno a uno, una a una, uno por uno, una por una.

one-day excursion *n* billete de ida y vuelta en un día *m.*
one-man *adj* individual.
onerous *adj* oneroso/sa, molesto/ta.
oneself *pn* sí mismo; sí misma.
one-sided *adj* parcial.
one-to-one *adj* de uno a uno; cara a cara.
ongoing *adj* continuo/nua.
onion *n* cebolla *f.*
on line *adj, adv* en línea.
onlooker *n* espectador/a *m/f.*
only *adj* único/ca, solo/la; * *adv* solamente.
onset, onslaught *n* acometida *f*; ataque *m.*
onus *n* responsabilidad *f.*
onward(s) *adv* adelante.
ooze *vi* manar suavemente, rezumar.
opaque *adj* opaco/ca.
open *adj* abierto/ta; patente, evidente; sincero/ra, franco/ca; ~**ly** *adv* con franqueza; * *vt* (*vi*) abrir(se); descubrir(se); **to ~ on to** dar a; **to ~ up** *vt* abrir; *vi* abrirse.
opening *n* abertura *f*; (*com*) salida *f*; principio *m.*
open-minded *adj* de mentalidad abierta.
openness *n* claridad *f*; franqueza, sinceridad *f.*
opera *n* ópera *f.*
opera house *n* teatro de la ópera *m.*
operate *vi* obrar, operar.
operating theater *n* quirófano *m.*
operation *n* operación *f*; efecto *m.*
operational *adj* operacional.
operative *adj* operativo/va.
operator *n* operario/ria *m/f*; operador/a *m/f.*
ophthalmic *adj* oftálmico/ca.
opine *vi* opinar, juzgar.
opinion *n* opinión *f*; juicio *m.*
opinionated *adj* testarudo/da.
opinion poll *n* sondeo *m.*
opponent *n* antagonista *m/f*; adversario/ria *m/f.*
opportune *adj* oportuno/na.
opportunist *n* oportunista *m/f.*
opportunity *n* oportunidad *f.*
oppose *vt* oponerse.
opposing *adj* opuesto/ta.
opposite *adj* opuesto/ta; contrario/ria; * *adv* enfrente; *prep* frente a; * *n* lo contrario.
opposition *n* oposición *f*; resistencia *f*; impedimento *m.*
oppress *vt* oprimir.
oppression *n* opresión *f.*
oppressive *adj* opresivo/va, cruel.
oppressor *n* opresor/a *m/f.*
optic(al) *adj* óptico/ca; ~**s** *npl* óptica *f.*

optician *n* óptico/ca *m/f.*
optimist *n* optimista *m/f.*
optimistic *adj* optimista.
optimum *adj* óptimo/ma.
option *n* opción *f;* deseo *m.*
optional *adj* facultativo/va.
opulent *adj* opulento/ta.
or *conj* o; u.
oracle *n* oráculo *m.*
oral *adj* oral, vocal; ~**ly** *adv* verbalmente, de palabra.
orange *n* naranja *f.*
orator *n* orador/a *m/f.*
orbit *n* órbita *f.*
orchard *n* huerto *m.*
orchestra *n* orquesta *f.*
orchestral *adj* orquestal.
orchid *n* orquídea *f.*
ordain *vt* ordenar; establecer.
ordeal *n* prueba rigurosa *f.*
order *n* orden *m/f;* regla *f;* mandato *m;* serie, clase *f,* * *vt* ordenar, arreglar; mandar.
order form *n* hoja de pedido *f.*
orderly *adj* ordenado/da, regular.
ordinarily *adv* ordinariamente.
ordinary *adj* ordinario/ria.
ordination *n* ordenación *f.*
ordnance *n* armamento *m;* pertrechos *mpl.*
ore *n* mineral *m.*
organ *n* órgano *m.*
organic *adj* orgánico/ca.
organic farming *n* agricultura biológica *f.*
organism *n* organismo *m.*
organist *n* organista *m/f.*
organization *n* organización *f.*
organize *vt* organizar.
orgasm *n* orgasmo *m.*
orgy *n* orgía *f.*
oriental *adj* oriental.
orifice *n* orificio *m.*
origin *n* origen, principio *m.*
original *adj* original, primitivo/va; ~**ly** *adv* originalmente.
originality *n* originalidad *f.*
originate *vi* originar.
ornament *n* ornamento *m;* * *vt* ornamentar, adornar.
ornamental *adj* ornamental, decorativo/va.
ornate *adj* adornado/da, ataviado/da.
ornithology *n* ornitología *f.*
orphan *adj, n* huérfano/na *m/f.*
orphanage *n* orfanato *m.*
orthodox *adj* ortodoxo/xa.
orthodoxy *n* ortodoxia *f.*
orthography *n* ortografía *f.*

orthopedic *adj* ortopédico/ca.
Oscar *n* óscar *m.*
oscillate *vi* oscilar, vibrar.
osprey *n* águila pescadora *f.*
ostensibly *adv* aparentemente.
ostentatious *adj* ostentoso/sa.
osteopath *n* ostéopata *m/f.*
ostracize *vt* condenar al ostracismo.
ostrich *n* avestruz *m.*
other *pn* otro, otra.
otherwise *adv* de otra manera, por otra parte.
otter *n* nutria *f.*
ouch *excl* ¡ay!
ought *v aux* deber, ser menester.
ounce *n* onza *f.*
our, ours *pn* nuestro, nuestra, nuestros, nuestras.
ourselves *pn pl* nosotros mismos, nosotras mismas.
oust *vt* quitar; desposeer.
out *adv* fuera, afuera; apagado/da
outboard *adj:* ~ **motor** fueraborda *m.*
outbreak *n* erupción *f.*
outburst *n* explosión *f.*
outcast *n* paria *m/f.*
outcome *n* resultado *m.*
outcry *n* clamor *m;* griterío *m.*
outdated *adj* fuera de moda.
outdo *vt* exceder a otro, sobrepujar.
outdoor *adj,* ~**s** *adv* al aire libre.
outer *adj* exterior.
outermost *adj* extremo/ma; lo más exterior.
outer space *n* espacio exterior *m.*
outfit *n* vestidos *mpl;* ropa *f.*
outfitter *n* sastre *m.*
outgoing *adj* extrovertido/da.
outgrow *vt* sobrecrecer.
outhouse *n* dependencia (de una casa) *f.*
outing *n* excursión *f.*
outlandish *adj* estrafalario/ria.
outlaw *n* bandido *m;* * *vt* proscribir.
outlay *n* despensa *f,* gastos *mpl.*
outlet *n* salida *f.*
outline *n* contorno *m;* bosquejo *m.*
outlive *vt* sobrevivir.
outlook *n* perspectiva *f.*
outlying *adj* distante, lejos.
outmoded *adj* anticuado/da.
outnumber *vt* superar en número.
out-of-date *adj* caducado/da; pasado/da de moda.
outpatient *n* paciente externo/na *m/f.*
outpost *n* puesto avanzado *m.*

output *n* rendimiento *m*; salida *f.*
outrage *n* ultraje *m*; * *vt* ultrajar.
outrageous *adj* escandaloso/sa; atroz; ~ly *adv* escandalosamente; injuriosamente; enormemente.
outright *adv* absolutamente; * *adj* completo/ta.
outrun *vt* correr más que.
outset *n* principio *m.*
outshine *vt* exceder en brillantez, eclipsar.
outside *n* superficie *f*; exterior *m*; apariencia *f*; * *adv* fuera, *Lat Am* afuera de; * *prep* fuera de.
outsider *n* forástero *m/f.*
outsize *adj* de talla grande.
outskirts *npl* alrededores *mpl.*
outspoken *adj* muy franco/ca.
outstanding *adj* excepcional; pendiente.
outstretch *vt* extenderse, alargar.
outstrip *vt* dejar atrás; superar.
out-tray *n* bandeja de salida *f.*
outward *adj* exterior, externo/na; de ida; ~ly *adv* por fuera; exteriormente.
outweigh *vt* pesar más que.
outwit *vt* burlar.
oval *n* óvalo *m*; * *adj* oval.
ovary *n* ovario *m.*
oven *n* horno *m.*
ovenproof *adj* resistente al horno.
over *prep* sobre, encima; más de; durante; all ~ por todos lados; * *adj* terminado/da; de sobra; ~ again otra vez; ~ and ~ repetidas veces.
overall *adj* total; * *adv* en conjunto.
overalls *npl* mono *m*; *Lat Am* overol *m.*
overawe *vt* imponer respeto.
overbalance *vi* perder el equilibrio.
overbearing *adj* despótico/ca.
overboard *adv* (*mar*) por la borda, al mar.
overbook *vt* sobrereservar.
overcast *adj* encapotado/da.
overcharge *vt* sobrecargar; cobrar de más.
overcoat *n* abrigo *m.*
overcome *vt* vencer; superar.
overconfident *adj* demasiado confiado/da.
overcrowded *adj* atestado/da; superpoblado/da.
overdo *vi* hacer más de lo necesario; exagerar.
overdose *n* sobredosis *f invar.*
overdraft *n* saldo deudor, descubierto *m.*
overdrawn *adj* en descubierto.
overdress *vt* engalanar con exceso.
overdue *adj* retrasado/da.
overeat *vi* comer demasiado.

overestimate *vt* sobreestimar.
overflow *vt*, *vi* inundar; rebosar; * *n* inundación *f*; superabundancia *f.*
overgrown *adj* invadido/da.
overgrowth *n* vegetación exuberante *f.*
overhang *vt* colgar sobre.
overhaul *vt* revisar; * *n* revisión *f.*
overhead *adv* sobre la cabeza, en lo alto.
overhear *vt* oír por casualidad.
overjoyed *adj* muy gozoso/sa.
overkill *n* exceso de medios *m.*
overland *adj*, *adv* por tierra.
overlap *vi* traslaparse.
overleaf *adv* al dorso.
overload *vt* sobrecargar.
overlook *vt* mirar desde lo alto; examinar; repasar; pasar por alto, tolerar; descuidar.
overnight *adv* durante la noche; * *adj* de noche.
overpass *n* paso superior *m.*
overpower *vt* predominar, oprimir.
overpowering *adj* agobiante.
overrate *vt* sobrevalorar.
override *vt* no hacer caso de; anular.
overriding *adj* predominante.
overrule *vt* denegar.
overrun *vt* inundar; infestar; rebasar.
overseas *adv* fuera del país; * *adj* extranjero/ra.
oversee *vt* inspeccionar.
overseer *n* superintendente *m.*
overshadow *vt* eclipsar.
overshoot *vt* excederse.
oversight *n* yerro *m*; equivocación *f.*
oversleep *vi* dormir demasiado.
overspill *n* exceso de población *m.*
overstate *vi* exagerar.
overstep *vt* traspasar, exceder.
overt *adj* abierto/ta; publico/ca; ~ly *adv* abiertamente.
overtake *vt* adelantar, sobrepasar.
overthrow *vt* trastornar; demoler; destruir; * *n* trastorno *m*; ruina, derrota *f.*
overtime *n* horas extra *fpl.*
overtone *n* trasfondo *m.*
overture *n* abertura *f*; (*mus*) obertura *f.*
overturn *vt* subvertir, trastornar.
overweight *adj* demasiado pesado/da.
overwhelm *vt* abrumar; oprimir; sumergir.
overwhelming *adj* arrollador/a; irresistible.
overwork *vi* trabajar demasiado.
owe *vt* deber, tener deudas; estar obligado/da.
owing *adj* que es debido/da; ~ to por causa de.

owl *n* búho *m*.

own *adj* propio/pia; **my** ~ mío, mía; * *vt* tener; poseer; **to** ~ **up** *vi* confesar.

owner *n* dueño/ña, propietario/ria *m/f*.

ownership *n* posesión *f*.

ox *n* buey *m*; ~**en** *pl* ganado vacuno *m*.

oxidize *vt* oxidar.

oxygen *n* oxígeno *m*.

oxygen mask *n* máscara de oxígeno *f*.

oxygen tent *n* tienda de oxígeno *f*.

oyster *n* ostra *f*.

ozone *n* ozono *m*.

P

pa n papá m.
pace n paso m; * vt regular el ritmo de; * vi pasear.
pacemaker n marcapasos m invar.
pacific adj pacífico/ca; P~ Ocean el Pacífico m.
pacification n pacificación f.
pacifier n chupete m.
pacify vt pacificar.
pack n lío, fardo m; baraja (de naipes) f; cuadrilla f; * vt empaquetar; hacer la maleta; llenar.
package n paquete m; acuerdo m.
package tour n viaje organizado m.
packet n paquete m.
packing n embalaje m.
pact n pacto m.
pad n bloc m; plataforma f; (col) casa f; * vt rellenar.
padding n relleno m; paja f.
paddle vivadear; remar; chapotear; * n canalete m.
paddle steamer n vapor de ruedas m.
paddling pool n piscina para niños f.
paddock n corral m.
paddy field n arrozal m.
pagan adj, n pagano/na m/f.
page n página f; paje m.
pageant n espectáculo público m.
pageantry n pompa f.
pail n cubo, pozal m.
pain n pena f; castigo m; dolor m; * vt afligir.
pained adj afligido/da.
painful adj dolorido/da; penoso/sa; ~ly adv dolorosamente, con pena.
painkiller n analgésico m.
painless adj sin pena; indoloro/ra.
painstaking adj laborioso/sa, meticuloso/sa.
paint vt pintar.
paintbrush n pincel m; brocha f.
painter n pintor m/f.
painting n pintura f.
paintwork n pintura f.
pair n par m; yuntas fpl.
pajamas npl pijama m.
pal n compañero/ra m/f.
palatable adj sabroso/sa.
palate n paladar m; gusto m.
palatial adj palatino/na.
palaver n lío m.

pale adj palido/da; claro/ra.
palette n paleta f.
paling n estacada, palizada f.
pall n cortina de humo f; * vi perder el sabor.
palliative adj paliativo/va; * n paliativo m.
pallid adj pálido/da.
pallor n palidez f.
palm n (bot) palma f.
palmistry n quiromancia f.
Palm Sunday n Domingo de Ramos m.
palpable adj palpable; evidente.
palpitation n palpitación f.
paltry adj irrisorio/ria; mezquino/na.
pamper vt mimar.
pamphlet n folleto m.
pan n cazuela f; sartén f; olla f.
panacea n panacea f.
panache n estilo m.
pancake n crepe f, Lat Am panqueque m.
pandemonium n jaleo m.
pane n cristal m.
panel n panel m; paño m.
paneling n paneles mpl.
pang n angustia, congoja f.
panic adj, n pánico/ca m.
panicky adj asustadizo/za.
panic-stricken adj preso/sa del pánico.
pansy n (bot) pensamiento m.
pant vi jadear.
panther n pantera f.
pantihose npl medias fpl.
pants npl bragas fpl.
pantry n despensa f.
papacy n papado m.
papal adj papal.
papaw, pawpaw, papaya n papaya f.
paper n papel m; periódico m; examen m; estudio m; ~s pl escrituras fpl; (com) fondos mpl; * adj de papel; * vt empapelar; tapizar.
paperback n libro en rústica m.
paper bag n bolsa de papel f.
paperclip n clip m.
paperweight n sujetapapeles m invar.
paperwork n papeleo m.
paprika n pimentón m, paprika f.
par n equivalencia f; igualdad f; par m; at ~ (com) a la par.
parable n parábola f.

parachute n paracaídas m invar; * vi lanzarse en paracaídas.

parade n ostentación, pompa f; (mil) parada f; * vt, vi desfilar; pasear; hacer gala.

paradise n paraiso m.

paradox n paradoja f

paradoxical adj paradójico/ca.

paragliding n parapente m.

paragon n dechado m.

paragraph n párrafo m, Lat Am acápite m.

parallel adj paralelo/la; * n línea paralela f; * vt paralelizar; parangonar.

paralyze vt paralizar.

paralysis n parálisis f.

paralytic adj paralítico/ca.

paramedic n auxiliar sanitario/ria m/f.

paramount adj supremo/ma, superior.

paranoid adj paranoico/ca.

paraphernalia n parafernalia f.

parasite n parásito m.

parasol n parasol, quitasol m.

paratrooper n paracaidista m

parcel n paquete m; porción, cantidad f; equipajes, bultos mpl; * vt empaquetar, embalar.

parch vt resecar.

parched adj reseco/ca; muerto/ta de sed.

parchment n pergamino m.

pardon n perdón m; * vt perdonar.

parent n padre m; madre f.

parentage n parentela f; extracción f.

parental adj de los padres.

parenthesis n paréntesis m invar.

parish n parroquia f; * adj parroquial.

parishioner n parroquiano/na m/f.

parity n paridad f.

park n parque m; * vt, vi aparcar, estacionar.

parking n aparcamiento, estacionamiento m.

parking lot n aparcamiento, estacionamiento m.

parking meter n parquímetro m.

parking ticket n multa de estacionamiento f.

parlance n lenguaje m.

parliament n parlamento m.

parliamentary adj parlamentario/ria.

parlor n salón m.

parody n parodia f; * vt parodiar.

parole n: on ~ en libertad bajo palabra.

parricide n parricidio m; parricida m/f.

parrot n papagayo m.

parry vt parar.

parsley n (bot) perejil m.

parsnip n (bot) chirivía f.

part n parte f; partido m; oficio m; papel (de

un actor) m; obligación f; raya f; ~s pl partes fpl; paraje, distrito m; * vt partir, separar, desunir; * vi partirse, separarse; to ~ with entregar; pagar; deshacerse de; ~ly adv en parte.

partial adj, ~ly adv parcial(mente).

participant n concursante m.

participate vi participar (en).

participation n participación f.

participle n (gr) participio m.

particle n partícula f.

particular adj particular, singular; ~ly adv particularmente; * n particular m; particularidad f.

parting n separación, partida f; raya (en los cabellos) f.

partisan n partidario/ria m/f.

partition n partición, separación f; * vt partir, dividir en varias partes.

partner n socio/cia, compañero/ra m/f.

partnership n compañía, sociedad de comercio f.

partridge n perdiz f

party n partido m; fiesta f.

pass vt pasar; traspasar; transferir; adelantarse a; * vi pasar, aprobar; * n permiso m; puerto m; to ~ away vi fallecer; to ~ by vi pasar; vt pasar por alto; to ~ on vt transmitir.

passable adj pasadero/ra, transitable.

passage n pasaje m; travesía f; pasadizo m.

passbook n libreta de depósitos f.

passenger n pasajero/ra m/f.

passer-by n transcúnte m/f.

passing adj pasajero/ra.

passion n pasión f; amor m; celo, ardor m.

passionate adj apasionado/da; ~ly adv apasionadamente; ardientemente.

passive adj pasivo/va; ~ly adv pasivamente

passkey n llava maestra f.

Passover n Pascua f.

passport n pasaporte m.

passport control n control de pasaportes m.

password n contraseña f.

past adj pasado/da; gastado/da; * n (gr) pretérito m; el pasado; * prep más allá de; después de.

pasta n pasta f.

paste n pasta f; engrudo m, * vt engrudar.

pasteurized adj pasteurizado/da.

pastime n pasatiempo m; diversión f.

pastor n pastor m.

pastoral adj pastoril; pastoral.

pastry n pastelería f.

pasture *n* pasto *m*, *Lat Am* potrero *m*.
pasty *adj* pastoso/sa; pálido/da.
pat *vt* dar golpecillos.
patch *n* remiendo *m*; parche *m*; terreno *m*;
* *vt* remendar; to ~ up reparar; hacer las
paces en.
patchwork *n* obra de retacitos *f*; chapu-
cería *f*.
pâté *n* paté *m*.
patent *adj* patente; privilegiado/da; * *n*
patente *f*; * *vt* privilegiar.
patentee *n* poseedor/a de una patente *m/f*.
patent leather *n* charol *m*.
paternal *adj* paternal.
paternity *n* paternidad *f*.
path *n* senda *f*.
pathetic *adj* patético/ca; ~ally *adv*
patéticamente.
pathological *adj* patológico/ca.
pathology *n* patología *f*.
pathos *n* patetismo *m*.
pathway *n* sendero *m*.
patience *n* paciencia *f*.
patient *adj* paciente, sufrido/da, *Lat Am*
aguantador/ra; ~ly *adv* con paciencia; * *n*
enfermo/ma *m/f*.
patio *n* patio *m*.
patriarch *n* patriarca *m*.
patriot *n* patriota *m*.
patriotic *adj* patriotico/ca.
patriotism *n* patriotismo *m*.
patrol *n* patrulla *f*; * *vi* patrullar.
patrol car *n* coche patrulla *m*.
patrolman *n* policía *m*.
patron *n* patrón/ona, protector *m/f*.
patronage *n* patrocinio *m*; patronato,
patronazgo *m*.
patronize *vt* patrocinar, proteger.
patter *n* golpeteo *m*; labia *f*; * *vi* tamborilear.
pattern *n* patrón *m*; dibujo *m*; *Lat Am*
molde *m*.
paunch *n* panza *f*; vientre *m*.
pauper *n* pobre *m/f*.
pause *n* pausa *f*; * *vt* pausar; deliberar.
pave *vt* empedrar; enlosar, embaldosar.
pavilion *n* pabellón *m*.
paving stone *n* ladrillo *m*; losa *f*.
paw *n* pata *f*; garra *f*; * *vt* manosear.
pawn *n* peón *m*; * *vt* empeñar.
pawnbroker *n* prestamista *m/f*.
pawnshop *n* casa de empeños *f*.
pay *vt* pagar; sufrir por; to ~ back *vt*
reembolsar; to ~ for pagar; to ~ off *vt*
liquidar; *vi* dar resultados; * *n* paga *f*;
salario *m*.

payable *adj* pagadero/ra.
payday *n* día de paga *m*.
payee *n* portador/a *m/f*.
pay envelope *n* sobre (de paga) *m*.
paymaster *n* pagador/a *m/f*.
payment *n* paga *f*; pagamento, pago *m*.
payphone *n* teléfono público *m*.
payroll *n* nómina *f*.
pea *n* guisante *m*, *Lat Am* chícharro *m*.
peace *n* paz *f*.
peaceful *adj* tranquilo/la, pacífico/ca.
peach *n* melocotón *m*, *Lat Am* durazno *m*.
peacock *n* pavón, pavo real *m*.
peak *n* cima *f*.
peak hours, peak period *n* horas punta
fpl.
peal *n* campaneo *m*; estruendo *m*.
peanut *n* cacahuete *m*; maní *m*.
pear *n* pera *f*.
pearl *n* perla *f*.
peasant *n* campesino/na *m/f*.
peat *n* turba *f*.
pebble *n* guija *f*; guijarro *m*.
peck *n* picotazo *m*; * *vt* picotear; picar.
pecking order *n* orden de jerarquía *m*.
peculiar *adj* peculiar, particular, singular;
~ly *adv* peculiarmente.
peculiarity *n* particularidad, singularidad *f*.
pedal *n* pedal *m*; * *vi* pedalear.
pedant *n* pedante *m/f*.
pedantic *adj* pedante.
pedestal *n* pedestal *m*.
pedestrian *n* peatón/ona *m/f*; * *adj* pedestre.
pedigree *n* genealogía *f*; * *adj* de raza.
peddler *n* vendedor/a ambulante *m/f*.
peek *vi* mirar de soslayo.
peel *vt* pelar; * *vi* desconcharse; * *n* piel *f*;
cáscara *f*.
peer *n* compañero/ra *m/f*; par *m*.
peerless *adj* incomparable.
peeved *adj* enojado/da.
peevish *adj* regañón/ona, bronco/ca;
enojadizo/za.
peg *n* clavija *f*; gancho *m*; * *vt* clavar.
pelican *n* pelícano *m*.
pellet *n* bolita *f*; ~s perdigones *mpl*.
pelt *n* pellejo, cuero *m*; * *vt* arrojar; * *vi*
llover a cántaros.
pen *n* bolígrafo *m*; pluma *f*; redil *m*.
penal *adj* penal.
penalty *n* pena *f*; castigo *m*; multa *f*.
penance *n* penitencia *f*.
pence *n pl* de penny.
pencil *n* lápiz *m*; lapicero *m*.
pencil case *n* estuche *m*.

pendant *n* pendiente *m*.
pending *adj* pendiente.
pendulum *n* péndulo *m*.
penetrate *vt* penetrar.
penguin *n* pingüino *m*.
penicillin *n* penicilina *f*.
peninsula *n* península *f*.
penis *n* pene *m*.
penitence *n* penitencia *f*.
penitent *adj*, *n* penitente *m*.
penitentiary *n* penitenciaría *f*.
penknife *n* navaja *f*.
pennant *n* banderola *f*.
penniless *adj* sin dinero.
penny *n* penique *m*.
penpal *n* amigo/ga por carta *m/f*.
pension *n* pensión *f*; * *vt* dar pensión a.
pensive *adj* pensativo/va; ~ly *adv* pensativamente.
pentagon *n*: the P~ el Pentágono.
Pentecost *n* Pentecostés *m*.
penthouse *n* ático *m*.
pent-up *adj* reprimido/da.
penultimate *adj* penúltimo/ma.
penury *n* penuria, carestia *f*.
people *n* pueblo *m*; nación *f*; gente *f*; * *vt* poblar.
people mover *n* monovolumen *m*.
pep *n* enérgia *f*; to ~ up *vt* animar.
pepper *n* pimienta *f*; * *vt* sazonar con pimienta.
peppermint *n* menta *f*.
per *prep* por.
per annum *adv* al año.
per capita *adj*, *adv* per cápita.
perceive *vt* percibir, comprender.
percentage *n* porcentaje *m*.
perception *n* percepción, idea, noción *f*.
perch *n* percha *f*.
perchance *adv* acaso, quizá.
percolate *vt* colar; filtrar.
percolator *n* cafetera de filtro *f*.
percussion *n* percusión *f*; golpe *m*.
perdition *n* pérdida, ruina *f*.
peremptory *adj* perentorio/ria; decisivo/va.
perennial *adj* perenne; perpetuo/tua.
perfect *adj* perfecto/ta, acabado/da; puro/ra; ~ly *adv* perfectamente; * *vt* perfeccionar, acabar.
perfection *n* perfección *f*.
perforate *vt* horadar.
perforated *adj* (of stamps) dentado/da.
perforation *n* perforación *f*.
perform *vt* ejecutar; efectuar; * *vi* representar, hacer papel.

performance *n* ejecución *f*; cumplimiento *m*, *Lat Am* performance *m*; obra *f*; representación teatral, función *f*.
performer *n* ejecutor/a *m/f*; actor *m*, actriz *f*.
perfume *n* perfume *m*; fragancia *f*; * *vt* perfumar.
perhaps *adv* quizá, quizás.
peril *n* peligro, riesgo *m*.
perilous *adj* peligroso/sa; ~ly *adv* peligrosamente.
perimeter *n* perímetro *m*.
period *n* período *m*; época *f*; regla *f*.
periodic *adj* periódico/ca; ~ally *adv* periódicamente.
periodical *n* periódico *m*.
peripheral *adj* periférico/ca; * *n* periférico *m*.
perish *vi* perecer.
perishable *adj* perecedero/ra.
perjure *vt* perjurar.
perjury *n* perjurio *m*.
perk *n* extra *m*.
perky *adj* animado/da.
perm *n* permanente *f*.
permanent *adj*, ~ly *adv* permanente(mente).
permeate *vt* penetrar, atravesar.
permissible *adj* lícito/ta, permiso.
permission *n* permiso *m*.
permissive *adj* permisivo/va.
permit *vt* permitir; * *n* permiso *m*.
permutation *n* permutación *f*.
perpendicular *adj*, ~ly *adv* perpendicular(mente); * *n* línea perpendicular *f*.
perpetrate *vt* perpetrar, cometer.
perpetual *adj* perpetuo/tua; ~ly *adv* perpetuamente.
perpetuate *vt* perpetuar, eternizar.
perplex *vt* confundir.
persecute *vt* perseguir, importunar.
persecution *n* persecución *f*.
perseverance *n* perseverancia *f*.
persevere *vi* perseverar.
persist *vi* persistir.
persistence *adj* persistencia *f*.
persistent *adj* persistente.
person *n* persona *f*.
personable *adj* atractivo/va.
personage *n* personaje *m*.
personal *adj*, ~ly *adv* personal(mente).
personal assistant *n* secretario/ria personal *m/f*.
personal column *n* anuncios personales *mpl*.

personal computer *n* ordenador personal *m*, computadora personal *f*.
personality *n* personalidad *f*.
personification *n* personificación *f*.
personify *vt* personificar.
personnel *n* personal *m*.
perspective *n* perspectiva *f*.
perspiration *n* transpiración *f*.
perspire *vi* transpirar.
persuade *vt* persuadir.
persuasion *n* persuasión *f*.
persuasive *adj* persuasivo/va; ~**ly** *adv* de modo persuasivo.
pert *adj* listo/va, vivo/va; petulante.
pertaining: ~ **to** *prep* relacionado/da con.
pertinent *adj* pertinente; ~**ly** *adv* oportunamente.
pertness *n* impertinencia *f*; vivacidad *f*.
perturb *vt* perturbar.
perusal *n* lectura, lección *f*.
peruse *vt* leer; examinar atentamente.
pervade *vt* atravesar, penetrar.
perverse *adj* perverso/sa, depravado/da; ~**ly** *adv* perversamente.
pervert *vt* pervertir, corromper.
pessimist *n* pesimista *m*.
pest *n* plaga *f*; molestia *f*.
pester *vt* molestar, cansar.
pestilence *n* pestilencia *f*.
pet *n* animal doméstico *m*; favorito/ta *m/f*; * *vt* mimar; * *vi* besuquearse.
petal *n* (*bot*) pétalo *m*.
petite *adj* chiquito/ta.
petition *n* presentación, petición *f*; * *vt* suplicar, *Lat Am* peticionar; requerir en justicia.
petrified *adj* horrorizado/da.
petroleum *n* petróleo *m*.
petticoat *n* enaguas *fpl*.
pettiness *n* mezquindad *f*; pequeñez *f*.
petty *adj* mezquino/na; insignificante.
petty cash *n* dinero para gastos menores *m*.
petty officer *n* contramaestre *m*.
petulant *adj* petulante.
pew *n* banco *m*.
pewter *n* peltre *m*.
phantom *n* fantasma *m*.
Pharisee *n* fariseo/sea *m/f*.
pharmaceutical *adj* farmacéutico/ca.
phase *n* fase *f*.
pheasant *n* faisán *m*.
phenomenal *adj* fenomenal.
phenomenon *n* fenómeno *m*.
phial *n* vial *m*.
philanthropic *adj* filantrópico/ca.

philanthropist *n* filántropo/pa *m/f*.
philanthropy *n* filantropía *f*.
philologist *n* filólogo/ga *m/f*.
philology *n* filología *f*.
philosopher *n* filósofo/fa *m/f*.
philosophic(al) *adj* filosófico/ca; ~**ally** *adv* filosóficamente.
philosophize *vi* filosofar.
philosophy *n* filosofía *f*; **natural** ~ filosofía natural *f*.
phlegm *n* flema *f*.
phlegmatic(al) *adj* flemático/ca.
phobia *n* fobia *f*.
phone *n* teléfono *m*; * *vt* telefonear; **to** ~ **back** *vt*, *vi* volver a llamar; **to** ~ **up** llamar por teléfono.
phone book *n* guía telefónica *f*.
phone box *n* cabina telefónica *f*, *Lat Am* monedero *m*.
phone call *n* llamada (telefonica) *f*.
phosphorus *n* fosforo *m*.
photocopier *n* fotocopiadora *f*.
photocopy *n* fotocopia *f*.
photograph *n* fotografía *f*; * *vt* fotografiar.
photographer *n* fotógrafo/fa *m/f*.
photographic *adj* fotográfico/ca.
photography *n* fotografía *f*.
phrase *n* frase *f*; estilo *m*; * *vt* expresar.
phrase book *n* libro de frases *m*.
physical *adj* físico/ca; ~**ly** *adv* físicamente.
physical education *n* educación física *f*.
physician *n* médico/ca *m/f*.
physicist *n* físico/ca *m/f*.
physiological *adj* fisiológico/ca.
physiologist *n* fisiólógo/ga *m/f*.
physiology *n* fisiología *f*.
physiotherapy *n* fisioterapia *f*.
physique *n* físico *m*.
pianist *n* pianista *m/f*.
piano *n* piano *m*.
piccolo *n* flautín *m*.
pick *vt* escoger, elegir; recoger; mondar, limpiar; **to** ~ **on** *vt* meterse con; **to** ~ **out** *vt* escoger; **to** ~ **up** *vi* ir mejor; recobrarse; * *vt* recoger; comprar; aprender; * *n* pico *m*; **the** ~ **of** lo más escogido de.
pickax *n* pico *m*.
picket *n* piquete *m*.
pickle *n* escabeche *m*; *vt* escabechar.
pickpocket *n* carterista *m/f*.
pick-up *n* (*auto*) furgoneta *f*.
picnic *n* picnic *m*.
pictorial *adj* pictórico/ca.
picture *n* pintura *f*; retrato *m*; * *vt* pintar; figurar.

picture book n libro de dibujos m.
picturesque adj pintoresco/ca.
pie n pastel m; tarta f; empanada f.
piece n pedazo m; pieza, obra f; * vt remendar.
piecemeal adv en pedazos; * adj dividido/da.
piecework n destajo m; * vi **to do ~** trabajar a destajo.
pier n pilar m; muelle m.
pierce vt penetrar, agujerear, taladrar.
piercing adj penetrante.
piety n piedad, devoción f.
pig n cerdo m, Lat Am chancho m; (col) cochino m.
pigeon n paloma f; **carrier/homing ~** paloma mensajera f.
pigeonhole n casillero m.
piggy bank n hucha f.
pig-headed adj terco/ca.
pigpen n pocilga f.
pigtail n trenza f.
pike n lucio m; pica f.
pile n estaca f; pila f; montón m; pelo m; pelillo m; **~s** pl almorranas fpl; * vt amontonar, apilar.
pile-up n colisión múltiple f.
pilfer vt hurtar.
pilgrim n peregrino/na m/f.
pilgrimage n peregrinación f.
pill n píldora f.
pillage vt saquear.
pillar n pilar m.
pillion n asiento trasero m.
pillow n almohada f.
pillowcase n funda de almohada f.
pilot n piloto m/f; * vt pilotar; (fig) guiar.
pilot light n piloto m.
pimp n chulo, cafiche m.
pimple n grano m.
pin n alfiler m; **~s and needles** npl hormigueo m; * vt prender con alfileres; fijar con clavija.
pinafore n delantal m.
pinball n flíper m.
pincers n pinzas, tenazuelas fpl.
pinch vt pellizcar; (col) birlar; * vi apretar; * n pellizco m.
pincushion n acerico m.
pine[1] n (bot) pino m.
pine[2] vi ansiar por.
pineapple n piña f, ananás m invar.
ping n sonido agudo m.
pink n rosa f; * adj color de rosa.
pinnacle n cumbre f.

pinpoint vt precisar.
pint n pinta f.
pioneer n pionero/ra m/f.
pious adj pío, pía, devoto/ta; **~ly** adv piadosamente.
pip n pepita f.
pipe n tubo, caño m; pipa f, Lat Am cachimbo m; **~s** cañería f.
pipe cleaner n limpiapipas m invar.
pipe dream n sueño imposible m.
pipeline n tubería f; oleoducto m; gasoducto m.
piper n gaitero/ra m/f.
piping adj hirviente.
pique n pique m; desazón f; ojeriza f.
piracy n piratería f.
pirate n pirata m/f.
pirouette n pirueta; vi piruetear.
Pisces n Piscis m (signo del zodiaco).
piss n (col) meada f; * vi mear.
pistol n pistola f.
piston n émbolo m.
pit n hoyo m; mina f.
pitch n lanzamiento m; tono m; campo m, Lat Am cancha f; * vt tirar, arrojar; * vi caerse; caer de cabeza.
pitch-black adj negro/gra como boca de lobo.
pitcher n cántaro m.
pitchfork n horca f.
pitfall n trampa f.
pithy adj meduloso/sa.
pitiable adj lastimoso/sa.
pitiful adj lastimoso/sa, compasivo/va; **~ly** adv lastimosamente.
pittance n pitanza, ración f; porcioncilla f.
pity n piedad, compasión f; * vt compadecer.
pivot n eje m.
pizza n pizza f.
placard n pancarta f.
placate vt apaciguar.
place n lugar, sitio m; rango, empleo m; * vt colocar; poner.
placid adj plácido/da, quieto/ta; **~ly** adv plácidamente.
plagiarism n plagio m.
plague n peste, plaga f; * vt atormentar; infestar, apestar.
plaice n platija f (pez).
plaid n tartán m.
plain adj liso/so, llano/na, abierto/ta; sincero/ra; puro/ra, simple, común; claro/ra, evidente, distinto/ta; **~ly** adv llanamente; claramente; * n llano m.
plaintiff n (law) demandante m/f.

plait *n* pliegue *m*; trenza *f*; * *vt* plegar; trenzar.

plan *n* plano *m*; plan *m*; * *vt* proyectar.

plane *n* avión *m*; plano *m*; cepillo *m*; * *vt* allanar; acepillar.

planet *n* planeta *m*.

planetary *adj* planetario/ria.

plank *n* tabla *f*.

planner *n* planificador/a *m/f*.

planning *n* planificación *f*.

plant *n* planta *f*; fábrica *f*; maquinaria *f*; * *vt* plantar.

plantation *n* plantación *f*; colonia *f*.

plaque *n* placa *f*.

plaster *n* yeso *m*; emplasto *m*; * *vt* enyesar; emplastar.

plastered *adj* (*col*) borracho/cha.

plasterer *n* yesero/ra *m/f*.

plaster of Paris *n* yeso mate *m*.

plastic *adj* plástico/ca.

plastic surgery *n* cirugía plástica *f*.

plate *n* plato *m*; lámina *f*; placa *f*.

plateau *n* meseta *f*.

plate glass *n* vidrio cilindrado *m*.

platform *n* plataforma *f*.

platinum *n* platino *m*.

platitude *n* tópico *m*.

platoon *n* (*mil*) pelotón *m*.

platter *n* fuente *f*; plato grande *m*.

plaudit *n* aplauso *m*.

plausible *adj* plausible.

play *n* juego *m*; comedia *f*; * *vt*, *vi* jugar; juguetear; representar; (*mus*) tocar; to ~ down *vt* quitar importancia a.

playboy *n* playboy *m*.

player *n* jugador/a *m/f*; comediante/ta *m/f*, actor *m*, actriz *f*.

playful *adj* juguetón/ona, travieso/sa; ~ly *adv* juguetonamente, reto zando.

playmate *n* camarada *m/f*.

playground *n* patio *m*.

playgroup *n* parvulario *m*.

play-off *n* desempate *m*.

playpen *n* corral (de niños) *m*.

plaything *n* juguete *m*.

playwright *n* dramaturgo/ga *m/f*.

plea *n* defensa *f*; excusa *f*; pretexto *m*; * *vt* pretextar.

plead *vt* defender en juicio; alegar.

pleasant *adj* agradable; placentero/ra, alegre; ~ly *adv* alegremente, placenteramente.

please *vt* agradar, complacer.

pleased *adj* contento/ta.

pleasing *adj* agradable, placentero/ra.

pleasure *n* gusto, placer *m*; recreo *m*.

pleat *n* pliegue *m*.

pledge *n* prenda *f*; fianza *f*; * *vt* empeñar, prometer.

plentiful *adj* copioso/sa, abundante.

plenty *n* copia, abundancia *f*.

plethora *n* plétora *f*.

pleurisy *n* pleuresía *f*.

pliable, pliant *adj* flexible, dócil.

pliers *npl* alicates *mpl*.

plight *n* situación difícil *f*.

plinth *n* plinto *m*; zócalo *m*.

plod *vi* afanarse mucho, ajetrearse.

plot *n* terreno *m*; plano *m*; conspiración, trama *f*; estratagema *f*; * *vi* trazar; conspirar; tramar.

plow *n* arado *m*; * *vt* arar, labrar la tierra; to ~ back *vt* reinvertir; to ~ through abrirse paso; roer.

ploy *n* truco *m*.

pluck *vt* tirar con fuerza; arrancar; desplumar; * *n* ánimo *m*.

plucky *adj* gallardo/da.

plug *n* tapón *m*; enchufe *m*; bujía *f*; * *vt* tapar.

plum *n* ciruela *f*.

plumage *n* plumaje *m*.

plumb *n* plomada *f*; * *adv* a plomo; * *vt* aplomar.

plumber *n* fontanero/ra, plomero/ra *m/f*.

plume *n* pluma *f*.

plump *adj* gordo/da, rollizo/za.

plum tree *n* ciruelo *m*.

plunder *vt* saquear, pillar, robar; * *n* pillaje, botín *m*.

plunge *vi* sumergir(se), precipitarse; * *n* zambullida *f*.

plunger *n* desatascador *m*.

pluperfect *n* (*gr*) pluscuamperfecto *m*.

plural *adj*, *n* plural *m*.

plurality *n* pluralidad *f*.

plus *n* signo de más *m*; * *prep* más, y, además de.

plush *adj* de felpa.

plutonium *n* plutonio *m*.

ply *vt* trabajar con ahínco; * *vi* aplicarse; (*mar*) ir y venir.

plywood *n* madera contrachapada *f*.

pneumatic *adj* neumático/ca.

pneumatic drill *n* martillo neumático *m*.

pneumonia *n* pulmonía *f*.

poach *vt* escalfar; cazar en vedado; * *vi* cazar en vedado.

poached *adj* escalfado/da.

poacher *n* cazador furtivo *m*.

poaching *n* caza furtiva *f*.

pocket *n* bolsillo *m*; bolsa *f*; * *vt* embolsar.
pocketbook *n* cartera *f*.
pocket money *n* dinero para gastos *m*.
pod *n* vaina *f*.
podgy *adj* gordinflón/ona.
podiatrist *n* pedicuro/ra *m/f*, *Lat Am* pedicurista *m/f*.
poem *n* poema *m*.
poet *n* poeta *m*, poetisa *f*.
poetic *adj* poético/ca.
poetry *n* poesía *f*.
poignant *adj* punzante.
point *n* punta *f*; punto *m*; promontorio *m*; puntillo *m*; estado *m*; ~ **of view** *n* punto de vista *m*; * *vt* apuntar; aguzar; puntuar; **to ~ a gun** encañonar.
point-blank *adv* directamente.
pointed *adj* puntiagudo/da; epigramático/ca; ~**ly** *adv* sutilmente.
pointer *n* apuntador/a *m/f*; perro de muestra *m*.
pointless *adj* sin sentido.
poise *n* peso *m*; equilibrio *m*.
poison *n* veneno *m*; * *vt* envenenar.
poisoning *n* envenenamiento *m*.
poisonous *adj* venenoso/sa.
poke *vt* hurgar; empujar.
poker *n* atizador *m*; póker *m*.
poker-faced *adj* con cara de póker.
poky *adj* estrecho/cha.
polar *adj* polar.
pole *n* polo *m*; palo *m*; pértiga *f*.
pole bean *n* judía trepadora *f*.
pole vault *n* salto con pértiga *m*.
police *n* policía *f*.
police car *n* coche patrulla *m*.
police officer, policeman *n* policía *m*.
police station *n* comisaría *f*, *Lat Am* destacamento *m* de policía.
policewoman *n* mujer policía *f*.
policy *n* política *f*.
polio *n* polio *f*.
polish *vt* pulir, alisar; limar; **to ~ off** *vt* terminar; despachar; * *n* pulimento *m*.
polished *adj* elegante, pulido/da.
polite *adj* pulido/da, cortés; ~**ly** *adv* cortésmente.
politeness *n* cortesía *f*.
politic *adj* político/ca; astuto/ta.
political *adj* político/ca.
political asylum *n* asilo político *m*.
politician *n* político/ca *m/f*.
politics *npl* política *f*.
polka *n* polca *f*; ~ **dot** *n* lunar *m*.
poll *n* voto *m*; encuesta *f*, sondeo *m*.

pollen *n* (*bot*) polen *m*.
pollute *vt* contaminar.
pollution *n* polución, contaminación *f*.
polo *n* polo *m*.
polyester *n* poliéster *m*.
polyethylene, polythene *n* polietileno *m*.
polygamy *n* poligamia *f*.
polystyrene *n* policstireno *m*.
polytechnic *n* politécnico *m*.
pomegranate *n* granada *f*.
pomp *n* pompa *f*; esplendor *m*.
pompom *n* borla *f*.
pompous *adj* pomposo/sa.
pond *n* estanque *m*.
ponder *vt* ponderar, considerar.
ponderous *adj* ponderoso/sa, pesado/da.
pontiff *n* pontífice, papa *m*.
pontoon *n* pontón *m*.
pony *n* jaca *f*; potro *m*.
ponytail *n* cola de caballo *f*.
pool *n* charca *f*; piscina, alberca *f*; * *vt* juntar; **to form a ~** remansarse.
poor *adj* pobre; humilde; de poco valor; ~**ly** *adv* pobremente; **the ~** *n* los pobres *mpl*.
pop *n* pop *m*; papá *m*; gaseosa *f*; chasquido *m*; * **to ~ in/out** *vi* entrar/salir un momento.
pop concert *n* concierto pop *m*.
popcorn *n* palomitas *fpl*.
Pope *n* Papa *m*.
poplar *n* álamo *m*.
poppy *n* (*bot*) amapola *f*.
populace *n* populacho *m*.
popular *adj*, ~**ly** *adv* popular(mente).
popularity *n* popularidad *f*.
popularize *vt* popularizar.
populate *vi* poblar.
population *n* población *f*.
populous *adj* populoso/sa.
pop video *n* videoclip *m*.
porcelain *n* porcelana, china, loza fina *f*.
porch *n* pórtico, vestíbulo *m*, zaguán *m*.
porcupine *n* puerco espín *m*.
pore *n* poro *m*.
pork *n* carne de cerdo, carne de puerco *f*.
pornography *n* pornografía *f*.
porous *adj* poroso/sa.
porpoise *n* marsopa *f*.
porridge *n* gachas de avena *fpl*.
port *n* puerto *m*; (*mar*) babor *m*; vino de Oporto *m*.
portable *adj* portátil.
portal *n* portal *m*; portada *f*.
porter *n* portero *m*; mozo *m*; conserje *m/f*.
portfolio *n* cartera *f*.

porthole *n* portilla *f.*
portico *n* pórtico, portal *m.*
portion *n* porción, parte *f.*
portly *adj* rollizo/za.
portrait *n* retrato *m.*
portray *vt* retratar.
pose *n* postura *f;* pose *f;* * *vi* posar; * *vt* plantear.
posh *adj* elegante.
position *n* posición, situación *f;* * *vt* colocar.
positive *adj* positivo/va, real, verdadero/ra; ~ly *adv* positivamente; ciertamente.
posse *n* pelotón *m.*
possess *vt* poseer; gozar.
possession *n* posesión *f.*
possessive *adj* posesivo/va.
possibility *n* posibilidad *f.*
possible *adj* posible; ~ly *adv* quizá, quizás.
post *n* correo *m;* puesto *m;* empleo *m;* poste *m;* * *vt* apostar; fijar.
postage *n* franqueo *m.*
postage stamp *n* sello de correos *m; Lat Am* estampilla *f.*
postal box, PO Box *n* apartado de correos *m.*
postcard, postal card *n* tarjeta *f* postal, *Lat Am* carta *f* postal.
post code *n* código postal *m.*
postdate *vt* posfechar.
poster *n* cartel *m, Lat Am* afiche *m.*
posterior *n* trasero *m.*
posterity *n* posteridad *f.*
postgraduate *n* posgraduado/da *m/f.*
posthumous *adj* póstumo/ma.
postman *n* cartero *m.*
postmark *n* matasellos *m.*
postmaster *n* administrador/a de correos *m/f.*
post office *n* correos *m.*
postpone *vt* diferir, suspender; posponer.
postscript *n* posdata *f.*
posture *n* postura *f.*
post-war *adj* de posguerra.
postwoman *n* cartera *f.*
posy *n* ramillete de flores *m.*
pot *n* marmita *f;* olla *f;* (*col*) marihuana *f;* * *vt* preservar en marmitas.
potato *n* patata *f, Lat Am* papa *f.*
potato peeler *n* pelapatatas *m invar, Lat Am* pelapapas *m invar.*
potbellied *adj* panzudo/da.
potent *adj* potente, poderoso/sa, eficaz.
potential *adj* potencial, poderoso/sa.
pothole *n* bache *m.*
potion *n* poción, bebida medicinal *f.*

potted *adj* en conserva; en tiesto.
potter *n* alfarero/ra *m/f.*
pottery *n* cerámica *f.*
potty *adj* chiflado/da.
pouch *n* bolsa *f;* petaca *f;* zurrón *m.*
poultice *n* cataplasma *f.*
poultry *n* aves de corral *fpl.*
pound *n* libra *f;* libra esterlina *f;* corral *m;* * *vt* machacar; * *vi* dar golpes.
pour *vt* echar; servir; * *vi* fluir con rapidez; llover a cántaros.
pout *vi* fruncir el ceño.
poverty *n* pobreza *f.*
powder *n* polvo *m;* pólvora *f;* * *vt* polvorear.
powder compact *n* polvera *f.*
powdered milk *n* leche en polvo *f.*
powder puff *n* borla *f.*
powder room *n* aseos *mpl.*
powdery *adj* polvoriento/ta.
power *n* poder *m;* potestad *f;* imperio *m;* potencia *f;* autoridad *f;* fuerza *f;* * *vt* impulsar.
powerful *adj* poderoso/sa; ~ly *adv* poderosamente, con mucha fuerza.
powerless *adj* impotente.
power station *n* central eléctrica *f.*
practicable *adj* factible; viable.
practical *adj* práctico/ca; ~ly *adv* prácticamente.
practicality *n* viabilidad *f.*
practical joke *n* broma pesada *f.*
practice *n* práctica *f;* uso *m;* costumbre *f;* ~s *pl* intrigas *fpl;* * *vi* practicar, ejercer.
practice *vi* practicar, ejercer.
practitioner (**medical**) *n* médico/ca *m/f.*
pragmatic *adj* pragmático/ca.
prairie *n* pampa *f.*
praise *n* renombre *m;* alabanza *f;* * *vt* celebrar, alabar.
praiseworthy *adj* digno/na de alabanza; laudable.
prance *vi* cabriolar.
prank *n* travesura, extravagancia *f.*
prattle *vi* charlar; * *n* charla *f.*
prawn *n* gamba *f.*
pray *vi* rezar; rogar; orar.
prayer *n* oración, súplica *f.*
prayer book *n* devocionario *m.*
preach *vi* predicar.
preacher *n* pastor/a; predicador/a *m/f.*
preamble *n* preámbulo *m.*
precarious *adj* precario, incierto/ta; ~ly *adv* precariamente.
precaution *n* precaución *fpl.*
precautionary *adj* preventivo/va.

precede *vt* anteceder, preceder.
precedence *n* precedencia *f*.
precedent *adj*, *n* precedente *m*.
precinct *n* límite, lindero *m*; barrio *m*; distrito electoral *m*.
precious *adj* precioso/sa.
precipice *n* precipicio *m*.
precipitate *vt* precipitar; * *adj* precipitado/da.
precise *adj* preciso/sa, exacto/ta; ~ly *adv* precisamente, exactamente.
precision *n* precisión, limitación exacta *f*.
preclude *vt* prevenir, impedir.
precocious *adj* precoz, temprano/na, prematuro/ra.
preconceive *vt* preconcebir.
preconception *n* preconcepción *f*.
precondition *n* condición previa *f*.
precursor *n* precursor/a *m/f*.
predator *n* depredador/a *m/f*.
predecessor *n* predecesor/a, antecesor/a *m/f*.
predestination *n* predestinación *f*.
predicament *n* aprieto *m*; dilema *m*.
predict *vt* predecir.
predictable *adj* previsible.
prediction *n* predicción *f*.
predilection *n* predilección *f*.
predominant *adj* predominante.
predominate *vt* predominar.
preen *vt* limpiarse (las plumas).
prefab *n* casa prefabricada *f*.
preface *n* prefacio *m*.
prefer *vt* preferir.
preferable *adj* preferible.
preferably *adv* de preferencia.
preference *n* preferencia *f*.
preferential *adj* preferente.
preferment *n* promoción *f*; preferencia *f*.
prefix *vt* prefijar; * *n* (*gr*) prefijo *m*.
pregnancy *n* embarazo *m*.
pregnant *adj* embarazada.
prehistoric *adj* prehistórico/ca.
prejudice *n* perjuicio, daño *m*; * *vt* perjudicar, hacer daño.
prejudiced *adj* predispuesto/ta; parcial.
prejudicial *adj* perjudicial, dañoso/sa.
preliminary *adj* preliminar.
prelude *n* preludio *m*.
premarital *adj* premarital.
premature *adj* prematuro/ra; ~ly *adv* anticipadamente.
premeditation *n* premeditación *f*.
premier *n* primer ministro *m*, primera ministra *f*.

première *n* estreno *m*.
premise *n* premisa *f*.
premises *npl* establecimiento *m*.
premium *n* premio *m*; remuneración *f*; prima *f*.
premonition *n* presentimiento *m*.
preoccupied *adj* preocupado/da; ensimismado/da.
prepaid *adj* con el porte pagado.
preparation *n* preparación *f*; cosa preparada *f*.
preparatory *adj* preparatorio/ria.
prepare *vt* (*vi*) preparar(se).
prepared *adj* abonado/da.
preponderance *n* preponderancia *f*.
preposition *n* preposición *f*.
preposterous *adj* absurdo/da.
prerequisite *n* requisito *m*.
prerogative *n* prerrogativa *f*.
prescribe *vi* prescribir; recetar.
prescription *n* prescripción *f*; receta medicinal *f*.
presence *n* presencia *f*, asistencia *f*.
present *n* regalo *m*; * *adj* presente; ~ly *adv* al presente; * *vt* ofrecer, presentar; regalar; acusar.
presentable *adj* decente, decoroso/sa.
presentation *n* presentación *f*.
present-day *adj* actual.
presenter *n* presentador/a *m/f*.
presentiment *n* presentimiento *m*.
preservation *n* preservación *f*.
preservative *n* preservativo *m*.
preserve *vt* preservar, conservar; poner en conserva; * *n* conserva, confitura *f*.
preside *vi* presidir; dirigir.
presidency *n* presidencia *f*.
president *n* presidente *m/f*.
presidential *adj* presidencial.
press *vt* empujar; apretar; compeler; * *vi* apretar; * *n* prensa *f*; armario *m*; apretón *m*; imprenta *f*.
press agency *n* agencia de prensa *f*.
press conference *n* rueda de prensa *f*.
pressing *adj*, ~ly *adv* urgente(mente).
press-up *n* plancha *f*.
pressure *n* presión *f*; opresión *f*.
pressure cooker *n* olla exprés, olla a presión *f*.
pressure group *n* grupo de presión *m*.
pressurized *adj* a presión.
prestige *n* prestigio *m*.
presumable *adj* presumible.
presumably *adv* es de suponer que.
presume *vt* presumir, suponer.

presumption n presunción f.
presumptuous adj presuntuoso/sa.
presuppose vt presuponer.
pretend vi pretender; presumir.
pretender n pretendiente m/f.
pretense n pretexto m; pretensión f.
pretension n pretensión f.
pretentious adj presumido/da; ostentoso/sa.
preterit n preterito m.
pretext n pretexto m; to find a ~ for pretextar.
pretty adj lindo/da, bien parecido/da; hermoso/sa; * adv algo, un poco.
prevail vi prevalecer, predominar.
prevailing adj dominante (uso, costumbre).
prevalent adj predominante, eficaz.
prevent vt prevenir; impedir.
prevention n prevención f.
preventive adj preventivo/va.
previous adj previo/via; antecedente; ~ly adv antes.
prevue n preestreno m.
prewar adj de antes de la guerra.
prey n presa f.
price n precio m.
priceless adj inapreciable.
price list n tarifa, lista de precios f.
pricey adj carero/ra.
prick vt punzar, picar; apuntar; excitar; * n puntura f; pica dura f; punzada f.
prickle n pincho m; espina f.
prickly adj espinoso/sa.
pride n orgullo m; vanidad f; jactancia f.
priest n sacerdote m.
priestess n sacerdotisa f.
priesthood n sacerdocio m.
priestly adj sacerdotal.
priggish adj afectado/da.
prim adj peripuesto/ta, afectado/da.
primacy n primacía f.
primarily adv primariamente, sobre todo.
primary adj primario/ria, principal, primero/ra.
primate n primadoprimate m.
prime n (fig) flor, nata f; primavera f; principio m; * adj primero/ra; primoroso/sa, excelente; * vt cebar.
prime minister n primer ministro m, primera ministra f.
primeval adj primitivo/va.
priming n cebo m; imprimación f.
primitive adj primitivo/va; ~ly adv primitivamente.
primrose n (bot) primavera f.
prince n príncipe m.

princess n princesa f.
principal adj, ~ly adv principal(mente); * n principal, jefe m.
principality n principado/da m.
principle n principio m; causa primitiva f; fundamento, motivo m.
print vt imprimir; * n impresión, estampa, edición f; impreso m; out of ~ vendido/da, agotado/da.
printed matter n impresos mpl.
printer n impresor/a m/f.
printing n imprenta f.
prior adj anterior, precedente; * n prior (prelado) m.
priority n prioridad f.
priory n priorato m.
prism n prisma m.
prison n prisión, carcel f.
prisoner n prisionero/ra m/f.
pristine adj prístino/na, antiguo/gua.
privacy n soledad f.
private adj secreto/ta, privado/da; particular; ~ soldier n soldado raso m; ~ly adv en secreto.
private eye n detective privado/da m/f.
private school n instituto; colegio privado m.
privet n (bot) alheña f.
privilege n privilegio m.
prize n premio m; presa f; * vt apreciar, valuar; to ~ open abrir por fuerza.
prize-giving n entrega de premios f.
prizewinner n premiado/da m/f, Lat Am favorecido/da m/f.
pro prep para.
probability n probabilidad, verosimilitud f.
probable adj probable, verosímil; ~bly adv probablemente.
probation n prueba f.
probationary adj de prueba.
probe n sonda f; encuesta f; * vt sondar; investigar.
problem n problema m.
problematical adj problemático/ca; ~ly adv problemáticamente.
procedure n procedimiento m; progreso, proceso m.
proceed vi proceder; provenir; originarse; ~s npl producto m; rédito m; gross ~s producto íntegro; net ~s producto neto.
proceedings n procedimiento m; proceso m; conducta f.
process n proceso m.
procession n procesión f.
proclaim vt proclamar, promulgar; publicar.

proclamation *n* proclamación *f*; decreto *m*.
procrastinate *vt* diferir, retardar.
proctor *n* censor/a *m/f*.
procure *vt* procurar.
procurement *n* procuración *f*.
prod *vt* empujar.
prodigal *adj* pródigo/ga.
prodigious *adj* prodigioso/sa; ~ly *adv* prodigiosamente.
prodigy *n* prodigio *m*.
produce *vt* producir, criar; causar; * *n* producto *m*; verdura *f*.
produce dealer *n* verdulero/ra *m/f*.
producer *n* productor/a *m/f*.
product *n* producto *m*; obra *f*; efecto *m*.
production *n* producción *f*; producto *m*.
production line *n* línea de producción *f*.
productive *adj* productivo/va.
productivity *n* productividad *f*.
profane *adj* profano/na.
profess *vt* profesar; ejercer; declarar.
profession *n* profesión *f*.
professional *adj* profesional.
professor *n* profesor/a, catedratico/ca *m/f*.
proficiency *n* capacidad *f*.
proficient *adj* proficiente, adelantado/da.
profile *n* perfil *m*.
profit *n* ganancia *f*, *Lat Am* utilidad *f*; provecho *m*; ventaja *f*; * *vi* aprovechar.
profitability *n* rentabilidad *f*.
profitable *adj* provechoso/sa, ventajoso/sa.
profiteering *n* explotación *f*.
profound *adj* profundo/da; ~ly *adv* profundamente.
profuse *adj* profuso/sa, prodigo/ga; ~ly *adv* profusamente.
program *n* programa *m*.
programer *n* programador/a *m/f*.
programing *n* programación *f*.
progress *n* progreso *m*; curso *m*; * *vi* hacer progresos.
progression *n* progresión *f*; adelantamiento *m*.
progressive *adj* progresivo/va; ~ly *adv* progresivamente.
prohibit *vt* prohibir, vedar; impedir.
prohibition *n* prohibición *f*.
project *vt* proyectar, trazar; * *n* proyecto *m*.
projectile *n* proyectil *m*.
projection *n* proyección *f*; estimación *f*.
projector *n* proyector *m*.
proletarian *adj* proletario/ria.
proletariat *n* proletariado *m*.
prolific *adj* prolifico/ca, fecundo/da.

prolog *n* prólogo *m*.
prolong *vt* prolongar; diferir.
prom *n* baile de gala.
promenade *n* paseo *m*.
prominence *n* prominencia *f*.
prominent *adj* prominente, saledizo/za.
promiscuous *adj* promiscuo/cua.
promise *n* promesa *f*; * *vt* prometer.
promising *adj* prometedor/a.
promontory *n* promontorio *m*.
promote *vt* promover.
promoter *n* promotor/a, promovedor/a *m/f*.
promotion *n* promoción *f*.
prompt *adj* pronto/ta; ~ly *adv* prontamente; * *vt* sugerir, insinuar; (*theat*) apuntar.
prompter *n* apuntador/a *m/f*.
prone *adj* inclinado/da.
prong *n* diente *m*.
pronoun *n* pronombre *m*.
pronounce *vt* pronunciar; recitar.
pronounced *adj* marcado/da.
pronouncement *n* declaración *f*.
pronunciation *n* pronunciación *f*.
proof *n* prueba *f*; * *adj* impenetrable; de prueba.
prop *vt* sostener; * *n* apoyo, puntal *m*; sostén *m*.
propaganda *n* propaganda *f*.
propel *vt* impeler.
propeller *n* hélice *f*.
propensity *n* propensión, tendencia *f*.
proper *adj* propio/pia; conveniente; exacto/ta; bien parecido/da; ~ly *adv* propiamente, justamente.
property *n* propiedad *f*.
prophecy *n* profecía *f*.
prophesy *vt* profetizar.
prophet *n* profeta *m*.
prophetic *adj* profético/ca.
proportion *n* proporción *f*; simetría *f*.
proportional *adj* proporcional.
proportionate *adj* proporcionado/da.
proposal *n* propuesta, proposición *f*; oferta *f*.
propose *vt* proponer.
proposition *n* proposición, propuesta *f*.
proprietor *n* propictario/ria *m/f*.
propriety *n* propiedad *f*.
pro rata *adv* de forma prorrateada.
prosaic *adj* prosaico/ca, en prosa.
prose *n* prosa *f*.
prosecute *vt* proseguir.
prosecution *n* prosecución *f*; acusación *f*.
prosecutor *n* fiscal *m/f*.
prospect *n* perspectiva *f*; esperanza *f*; * *vt* explorar; * *vi* buscar.

prospecting *n* prospección *f.*
prospective *adj* probable; futuro/ra.
prospector *n* explorador/a *m/f.*
prospectus *n* prospecto *m.*
prosper *vi* prosperar.
prosperity *n* prosperidad *f.*
prosperous *adj* próspero/ra, feliz.
prostitute *n* prostituta *f.*
prostitution *n* prostitución *f.*
prostrate *adj* postrado/da.
protagonist *n* protagonista *m.*
protect *vt* proteger; amparar.
protection *n* protección *f.*
protective *adj* protectorio/ria.
protector *n* protector/a, patrono/na *m/f.*
protégé(e) *n* protegido/da *m/f.*
protein *n* proteína *f.*
protest *vi* protestar; * *n* protesta *f.*
Protestant *n* protestante *m/f.*
protester *n* manifestante *m/f.*
protocol *n* protocolo *m.*
prototype *n* prototipo *m.*
protracted *adj* prolongado/da.
protrude *vi* sobresalir.
proud *adj* soberbio/bia, orgulloso/sa; ~ly *adv* soberbiamente.
prove *vt* probar, justificar; * *vi* resultar; salir (bien/mal).
proverb *n* proverbio *m.*
proverbial *adj*, ~ly *adv* proverbial- (mente).
provide *vt* proveer; to ~ for mantener a; tener en cuenta.
provided *conj*: ~ that con tal que.
providence *n* providencia *f.*
province *n* provincia *f*; campo de acción *m.*
provincial *adj* provincial; * *n* provincial/a *m/f.*
provision *n* provisión *f*; precaución *f.*
provisional *adj* provisional, *Lat Am* provisorio/a; ~ly *adv* provisionalmente, *Lat Am* provisoriamente.
proviso *n* estipulación *f.*
provocation *n* provocación *f*; apelación *f.*
provocative *adj* provocativo/va.
provoke *vt* provocar; apelar.
prow *n* (*mar*) proa *f.*
prowess *n* proeza, valentía *f.*
prowl *vi* rondar, vagar.
prowler *n* merodeador/a *m/f.*
proximity *n* proximidad *f.*
proxy *n* poder *m*; apoderado/da *m/f.*
prudence *n* prudencia *f.*
prudent *adj* prudente, circunspecto/ta; ~ly *adv* con juicio.

prudish *adj* gazmoño/ña, mojigato/ta.
prune *vt* podar; * *n* ciruela pasa *f.*
prussic acid *n* ácido prúsico *m.*
pry *vi* espiar, acechar; to ~ open *vt* abrir por fuerza.
psalm *n* salmo *m.*
pseudonym *n* seudónimo *m.*
psyche *n* psique *f.*
psychiatric *adj* psiquiátrico/ca.
psychiatrist *n* psiquiatra *m/f.*
psychiatry *n* psiquiatría *f.*
psychic *adj* psíquico/ca.
psychoanalysis *n* psicoanálisis *m.*
psychoanalyst *n* psicoanalista *m/f.*
psychological *adj* psicológico/ca.
psychologist *n* psicólogo/ga *m/f.*
psychology *n* psicología *f.*
puberty *n* pubertad *f.*
public *adj* público/ca; común; notorio/ria; ~ly *adv* publicamente; * *n* público *m.*
public-address system *n* megafonía *f.*
publican *n* publicano *m*; tabernero/ra *m/f.*
publication *n* publicación *f*; edición *f.*
publicity *n* publicidad *f.*
publicize *vt* publicitar; hacer propaganda para.
public opinion *n* opinión pública *f.*
publish *vt* publicar.
publisher *n* editorial *f*; editor/a *m/f.*
publishing *n* industria del libro *f.*
pucker *vt* arrugar, hacer pliegues.
pudding *n* pudín *m*; morcilla *f.*
puddle *n* charco *m.*
puerile *adj* pueril.
puff *n* soplo *m*; bocanada *f*, *Lat Am* pitada *f*; resoplido *m*; * *vt* chupar; * *vi* bufar; resoplar.
puff pastry *n* hojaldre *m.*
puffy *adj* hinchado/da, entumecido/da.
pull *vt* tirar; coger; rasgar, desgarrar; to ~ down derribar; to ~ in parar; llegar a la estación; to ~ off cerrar; to ~ out *vi* irse; salir; * *vt* arrancar; to ~ through salir adelante; to ~ up *vi* parar; * *vt* arrancar; parar; * *n* tirón *m*; sacudida *f.*
pulley *n* polea, garrucha *f.*
pullover *n* jersey *m.*
pulp *n* pulpa *f*; pasta *f.*
pulpit *n* púlpito *m.*
pulsate *vi* pulsar, latir.
pulse *n* pulso *m*; legumbres *fpl.*
pulverize *vt* pulverizar.
pumice *n* piedra pómez *f.*
pummel *vt* aporrear.
pump *n* bomba *f*; zapatilla *f*; * *vt* bombear; sondear; sonsacar.

pumpkin *n* calabaza *f.*

pun *n* juego de palabras *m*; * *vi* hacer juegos de palabras.

punch *n* puñetazo *m*; punzón *m*; taladro *m*; ponche *m*; * *vt* golpear; perforar.

punctual *adj* puntual, exacto/ta; ~ly *adv* puntualmente.

punctuate *vi* puntuar.

punctuation *n* puntuación *f.*

pundit *n* experto/ta *m/f.*

pungent *adj* picante, acre, mordaz.

punish *vt* castigar.

punishment *n* castigo *m*; pena *f.*

punk *n* punk *m/f*; música punk *f*; rufián/ fiana *m/f.*

punt *n* barco llano *m.*

puny *adj* joven, pequeño/ña; inferior.

pup *n* cachorro *m*; * *vi* parir (la perra).

pupil *n* alumno/na *m/f*; pupila *f.*

puppet *n* títere, muñeco *m.*

puppy *n* perrito *m.*

purchase *vt* comprar; * *n* compra *f*; adquisición *f.*

purchaser *n* comprador/a *m/f.*

pure *adj* puro/ra; ~ly *adv* puramente.

purée *n* puré *m.*

purge *vt* purgar.

purification *n* purificación *f.*

purifier *n* depuradora *f.*

purify *vt* purificar.

purist *n* purista *m/f.*

puritan *n* puritano/na *m/f.*

purity *n* pureza *f.*

purl *n* punto del revés *m.*

purple *adj* purpureo/rea; * *n* púrpura *f.*

purport *vi*: to ~ to dar a entender que.

purpose *n* intención *f*; designio, proyecto *m*; to the ~ al propósito; to no ~ inútilmente; on ~ a propósito.

purposeful *adj* resuelto/ta.

purr *vi* ronronear.

purse *n* bolsa *f*; cartera *f*, *Lat Am* sobre *m.*

purser *n* comisario *m/f.*

pursue *vi* perseguir; seguir, acosar.

pursuit *n* perseguimiento *m*; ocupación *f.*

purveyor *n* abastecedor *m.*

push *vt* empujar; estrechar, apretar; to ~ aside apartar; to ~ off (*col*) largarse; to ~ on seguir adelante; * *n* impulso *m*; empujón *m*; esfuerzo *m*; asalto *m.*

pusher (drug) *n* traficante de drogas *m/f.*

put *vt* poner, colocar; proponer; imponer, obligar; to ~ away guardar; to ~ away hurriedly zampar; to ~ down poner en el suelo; sacrificar; apuntar; sofocar; to ~ forward adelantar; to ~ off aplazar; desanimar; to ~ on ponerse; encender; presentar; ganar; echar; to ~ out apagar; extender; molestar; to ~ up alzar; aumentar; alojar.

putrid *adj* podrido/da.

putt *n* putt *m*; *vt* hacer un putt.

putty *n* masilla *f.*

puzzle *n* acertijo *m*; rompecabezas *m inv* ar.

puzzling *adj* extraño/ña.

pylon *n* torre de alta tensión *f.*

pyramid *n* pirámide *f.*

python *n* pitón *m.*

Q

quack vi graznar; * n graznido m; (col) curandero/ra m/f.
quadrangle n cuadrángulo m.
quadrant n cuadrante m.
quadrilateral adj cuadrilátero/ra.
quadruped n cuadrúpedo m.
quadruple adj cuádruplo.
quadruplet n cuatrillizo/za m/f.
quagmire n barrizal m, cenagal m.
quail n codorniz f.
quaint adj pulido/da; exquisito/ta.
quake vi temblar; tiritar.
Quaker n cuáquero/ra m/f.
qualification n calificación f; título m.
qualified adj capacitado/da; titulado/da.
qualify vt calificar; modificar; * vi clasificarse.
quality n calidad f.
qualm n escrupúlo m.
quandary n incertidumbre, duda f.
quantitative adj cuantitativo/va.
quantity n cantidad f.
quarantine n cuarentena f.
quarrel n riña, contienda f; * vi reñir, disputar.
quarrelsome adj pendenciero/ra.
quarry n cantera f.
quarter n cuarto m; cuarta parte f; ~ of an hour cuarto de hora; * vt cuartear.
quarterly adj trimestral; * adv trimestralmente.
quartermaster n (mil) comisario/ria m/f.
quartet n (mus) cuarteto m.
quartz n cuarzo m.
quash vt fracasar; anular, abrogar.
quay n muelle m.
queasy adj nauseabundo/da.
queen n reina f; dama f.
queer adj extraño/ña; ridículo/la; * n (col) maricón m.
quell vt calmar; sosegar.

quench vt apagar; extinguir.
query n cuestión, pregunta f; * vt preguntar.
quest n pesquisa, inquisición, busca f.
question n pregunta f; cuestión f; asunto m; duda f; * vt dudar de; interrogar.
questionable adj cuestionable, dudoso/sa.
questioner n interrogador/a m/f.
question mark n signo de interrogación m.
questionnaire n cuestionario m.
quibble vi buscar evasivas.
quick adj rapido/da; vivo/va; pronto/ta; ágil; ~ly adv rápidamente.
quicken vt apresurar; * vi darse prisa.
quicksand n arenas movedizas f/pl.
quicksilver n azogue, mercurio m.
quick-witted adj agudo/da, perspicaz.
quiet adj callado/da; ~ly adv tranquilamente.
quietness n tranquilidad f.
quinine n quinina f.
quintet n (mus) quinteto m.
quintuple adj quíntuplo.
quintuplet n quintillizo/za m/f.
quip n indirecta f; * vt echar pullas.
quirk n peculiaridad f.
quit vt dejar; desocupar; * vi renunciar; irse; * adj libre, descargado/da.
quite adv bastante; totalmente, enteramente, absolutamente.
quits adv ¡en paz!
quiver vi temblar.
quixotic adj quijotesco/ca.
quiz n concurso m; programa concurso m; * vt interrogar.
quizzical adj burlón/ona.
quota n cuota f.
quotation n citación, cita f.
quotation marks npl comillas f/pl.
quote vt citar.
quotient n cociente m.

R

rabbi *n* rabino/na *m/f.*
rabbit *n* conejo *m.*
rabbit hutch *n* conejera *f.*
rabble *n* gentuza *f.*
rabid *adj* rabioso/sa; furioso/sa.
rabies *n* rabia *f.*
race *n* raza, casta *f;* carrera *f;* * *vt* hacer correr a; competir contra; acelerar; * *vi* correr; competir; latir rápidamente.
racehorse *n* caballo de carreras *m.*
racial *adj* racial.
raciness *n* vivacidad *f.*
racing *n* carreras *fpl.*
racist *adj, n* racista *m/f.*
rack *n* rejilla *f;* estante *m;* * *vt* atormentar; trasegar.
racket *n* ruido *m;* raqueta *f.*
rack-rent *n* alquiler abusivo *m.*
racy *adj* picante, vivo/va.
radiance *n* brillantez *f,* resplandor *m.*
radiant *adj* radiante, brillante, *Lat Am* radioso/sa.
radiate *vt, vi* radiar, irradiar.
radiation *n* radiación *f.*
radiator *n* radiador *m.*
radical *adj* radical; ~ly *adv* radicalmente.
radicalism *n* radicalismo *m.*
radio *n* radio *f.*
radioactive *adj* radioactivo/va; ~ fallout lluvia radioactiva *f.*
radish *n* rábano *m.*
radius *n* radio *f.*
raffle *n* rifa *f* (juego); * *vt* rifar.
raft *n* balsa, almadía *f.*
rafter *n* par *m;* viga *f.*
rafting *n* rafting *m.*
rag *n* trapo, andrajo *m.*
ragamuffin *n* granuja, galopín/ina *m/f.*
rage *n* rabia *f;* furor *m;* * *vi* rabiar; encolerizarse.
ragged *adj* andrajoso/sa.
raging *adj* furioso/sa, rabioso/sa.
ragpicker *n* trapero *m.*
raid *n* incursión *f;* * *vt* invadir.
raider *n* invasor/a *m/f.*
rail *n* baranda, barandilla *f; (rail)* raíl, carril *m;* * *vt* cercar con barandillas.
raillery *n* burlas *fpl.*
railroad *n* ferrocarril *m.*
raiment *n* vestido *m.*
rain *n* lluvia *f;* * *vi* llover.

rainbow *n* arco iris *m.*
rainwater *n* agua de lluvia *f.*
rainy *adj* lluvioso/sa.
raise *vt* levantar, alzar, *Lat Am* parar; fabricar, edificar; elevar.
raisin *n* pasa *f.*
rake *n* rastro, rastrillo *m;* libertino/na *m/f;* * *vt* rastrillar.
rakish *adj* libertino/na, disoluto/ta.
rally *vt (mil)* reunir; * *vi* reunirse.
ram *n* carnero, morueco *m;* ariete *m;* * *vt* chocar con.
ramble *vi* divagar; salir de excursión a pie; * *n* excursión a pie, caminata *f.*
rambler *n* excursionista *m/f.*
ramification *n* ramificación *f.*
ramify *vi* ramificarse.
ramp *n* rampa *f.*
rampant *adj* exuberante.
rampart *n* terraplén *m; (mil)* muralla *f.*
ramrod *n* baqueta *f;* atacador *m.*
ramshackle *adj* en ruina.
ranch *n* hacienda, estancia *f.*
rancid *adj* rancio/cia.
rancor *n* rencor *m.*
random *adj* fortuito/ta, sin orden; at ~ al azar.
range *vt* colocar, ordenar; *vi* vagar; * *n* clase *f;* orden *m;* hilera *f;* cordillera *f;* campo abierto *m;* campo de tiro *m;* reja de cocina *f.*
ranger *n* guardabosques *m invar.*
rank *adj* exuberante; rancio/cia; fétido/da; * *n* fila, hilera, clase *f.*
rankle *vi* doler.
rankness *n* exuberancia *f;* olor/gusto rancio *m.*
ransack *vt* saquear, pillar.
ransom *n* rescate *m.*
rant *vi* vociferar.
rap *vi* dar un golpecito; * *n* golpecito *m.*
rapacious *adj* rapaz; ~ly *adv* con rapacidad.
rapacity, rapaciousness *n* rapacidad *f.*
rape *n* violación *f;* estupro *m; (bot)* colza *f;* * *vt* violar.
rapid *adj* rápido/da; ~ly *adv* rápidamente.
rapidity *n* rapidez *f.*
rapier *n* espadín *m.*
rapist *n* violador *m.*
rapt *adj* arrebatado/da; absorto/ta.
rapture *n* rapto *m;* éxtasis *m invar.*
rapturous *adj* arrebatado/da.

rare *adj* raro/ra, extraordinario/ria; ~**ly** *adv* raramente.
rarity *n* raridad, rareza *f*.
rascal *n* pícaro/ra *m/f*.
rash *adj* precipitado/da, temerario/ria; ~**ly** *adv* temerariamente; * *n* salpullido *m*; erupción (cutánea) *f*.
rashness *n* temeridad *f*.
rasp *n* raspador *m*; * *vt* raspar, escofinar.
raspberry *n* frambuesa *f*; ~ **bush** frambueso *m*.
rat *n* rata *f*.
rate *n* tasa *f*, precio, valor *m*; grado *m*; * *vt* tasar, apreciar.
rather *adv* más bien; antes.
ratification *n* ratificación *f*.
ratify *vt* ratificar.
rating *n* tasación *f*; clasificación *f*; índice *m*.
ratio *n* razón *f*.
ration *n* ración *f*; (*mil*) víveres *mpl*.
rational *adj* racional; razonable; ~**ly** *adv* racionalmente.
rationality *n* racionalidad *f*.
rattan *n* (*bot*) rota *f*.
rattle *vi* golpear; traquetear; * *vt* sacudir; * *n* traqueteo *m*; sonajero *m*.
rattlesnake *n* serpiente de cascabel *f*.
ravage *vt* saquear, pillar; estragar; * *n* saqueo *m*.
rave *vi* delirar.
rave music *n* (*col*) bakalao *m*.
raven *n* cuervo *m*.
ravenous *adj*, ~**ly** *adv* voraz(mente).
ravine *n* barranco *m*.
ravish *vt* encantar; raptar.
ravishing *adj* encantador/a.
raw *adj* crudo/da; puro/ra; novato/ta.
rawboned *adj* huesudo/da; magro/gra.
rawness *n* crudeza *f*; falta de experiencia *f*.
ray *n* rayo de luz *m*; raya *f* (pez).
raze *vt* arrasar.
razor *n* navaja; máquina de afeitar *f*.
reach *vt* alcanzar; llegar hasta; * *vi* extenderse, llegar; alcan zar, penetrar; * *n* alcance *m*.
react *vi* reaccionar.
reaction *n* reacción *f*.
read *vt* leer; * *vi* estudiar.
readable *adj* legible.
reader *n* lector/a *m/f*.
readily *adv* pronto; de buena gana.
readiness *n* voluntad, gana *f*; prontitud *f*.
reading *n* lectura *f*.
reading room *n* sala de lectura *f*.
readjust *vt* reajustar.

ready *adj* listo/ta, pronto/ta; inclinado/da; abonado/da; fácil.
real *adj* real, verdadero/ra; ~**ly** *adv* realmente.
reality *n* realidad *f*.
realization *n* realización *f*.
realize *adv* darse cuenta de; realizar.
realm *n* reino *m*.
ream *n* resma *f*.
reap *vt* segar.
reaper *n* segador/a *m/f*.
reappear *vi* reaparecer.
rear *n* parte trasera *f*; retaguardia *f*; zaga *f*; * *vt* levantar, alzar.
rearmament *n* rearme *m*.
reason *n* razon *f*; causa *f*; * *vt*, *vi* razonar.
reasonable *adj* razonable.
reasonableness *n* lo razonable.
reasonably *adv* razonablemente.
reasoning *n* razonamiento *m*.
reassure *vt* tranquilizar, alentar; (*com*) asegurar.
rebel *n* rebelde *m/f*; * *vi* rebelarse.
rebellion *n* rebelión *f*.
rebellious *adj* rebelde.
rebound *vi* rebotar.
rebuff *n* desaire *m*; * *vt* rechazar.
rebuild *vt* reedificar.
rebuke *vt* reprender; * *n* reprensión *f*.
rebut *vi* repercutir.
recalcitrant *adj* recalcitrante.
recall *vt* recordar; retirar; * *n* retirada *f*.
recant *vt* retractar, desdecirse.
recantation *n* retractación *f*.
recapitulate *vt*, *vi* recapitular.
recapitulation *n* recapitulación *f*.
recapture *n* recobra *f*.
recede *vi* retroceder.
receipt *n* recibo *m*; recepción *f*; ~**s** *npl* ingresos *mpl*.
receivable *adj* por cobrar.
receive *vt* recibir, *Lat Am* recepcionar; aceptar, admitir.
recent *adj* reciente, nuevo/va; ~**ly** *adv* recientemente.
receptacle *n* receptáculo *m*.
reception *n* recepción *f*.
recess *n* descanso *m*; recreo *m*; hueco *m*.
recession *n* retirada *f*; (*com*) recesión *f*.
recipe *n* receta *f*.
recipient *n* recipiente *m*.
reciprocal *adj* recíproco/ca; ~**ly** *adv* recíprocamente.
reciprocate *vi* reciprocar.
reciprocity *n* reciprocidad *f*.

recital *n* recital *m.*
recite *vt* recitar; referir, relatar.
reckless *adj* temerario/ria; ~ly *adv* temerariamente.
reckon *vt* contar, computar; * *vi* calcular.
reckoning *n* cuenta *f*; cálculo *m.*
reclaim *vt* reformar; reclamar.
reclaimable *adj* reclamable.
recline *vt* (*vi*) reclinar(se); recostar(se).
recluse *n* recluso/sa *m/f.*
recognition *n* reconocimiento; recuerdo *m.*
recognize *vt* reconocer.
recoil *vi* recular.
recollect *vt* acordarse de; recordar.
recollection *n* recuerdo *m.*
recommence *vt* empezar de nuevo.
recommend *vt* recomendar.
recommendation *n* recomendación *f.*
recompense *n* recompensa *f*; * *vt* recompensar.
reconcilable *adj* reconciliable.
reconcile *vt* reconciliar.
reconciliation *n* reconciliación *f.*
recondite *adj* recóndito/ta, reservado/da.
reconnaissance *n* (*mil*) reconocimiento *m.*
reconnoiter *vt* (*mil*) reconocer.
reconsider *vt* reconsiderar.
reconstruct *vt* reedificar.
record *vt* registrar; grabar; * *n* registro, archivo *m*; disco; récord *m*; ~s *pl* anales *mpl.*
recorder *n* registrador/a, archivero/ra *m/f*; (*mus*) flauta de pico *f.*
recount *vt* contar de nuevo; relatar.
recourse *n* recurso *m*; remedio *m.*
recover *vt* recobrar; recuperar; restablecer; * *vi* convalecer, restablecerse.
recoverable *adj* recuperable.
recovery *n* convalecencia; recuperación *f.*
recreation *n* recreación *f*; recreo *m.*
recriminate *vi* recriminar.
recrimination *n* recriminación *f.*
recruit *vt* reclutar; * *n* (*mil*) recluta *m/f.*
recruiting *n* recluta *f.*
rectangle *n* rectángulo *m.*
rectangular *adj* rectangular.
rectification *n* rectificación *f.*
rectify *vt* rectificar.
rectilinear *adj* rectilíneo/nea.
rectitude *n* rectitud *f.*
rector *n* rector/a *m/f.*
recumbent *adj* recostado/da, reclinado/da.
recur *vi* repetirse.
recurrence *n* repetición *f.*
recurrent *adj* repetido/da.

recycle *vt* reciclar.
recycled *adj* reciclado/da.
red *adj* rojo/ja; tinto/ta; * *n* rojo *m.*
redden *vt* enrojecer; * *vi* ponerse colorado/da.
reddish *adj* rojizo/za.
redeem *vt* redimir, rescatar.
redeemable *adj* redimible.
redeemer *n* redentor/a *m/f.*
redemption *n* redención *f.*
redeploy *vt* reorganizar.
red-handed *adj*: **to catch somebody ~** pillar a alguien con las manos en la masa.
red-hot *adj* candente, ardiente.
red-letter day *n* dia señalado *m.*
redness *n* rojez, bermejura *f.*
redolent *adj* fragante, oloroso/sa.
redouble *vt* (*vi*) redoblar(se).
redress *vt* corregir; reformar; rectificar; * *n* reparación, compensación *f.*
red tape *n* (*fig*) trámites *mpl.*
reduce *vt* reducir; disminuir; rebajer.
reducible *adj* reducible.
reduction *n* reducción *f*; rebaja *f.*
redundancy *n* despido *m.*
redundant *adj* superfluo/lua.
reed *n* caña *f.*
reedy *adj* lleno de canas.
reef *n* (*mar*) rizo *m*; arrecife *m.*
reek *n* mal olor *m*; * *vi* humear; vahear.
reel *n* carrete *m*; bobina *f*; rollo *m*; * *vi* tambalear(se).
re-election *n* reelección *f.*
re-engage *vt* empeñar de nuevo.
re-enter *vt* volver a entrar.
re-establish *vt* restablecer, volver a establecer.
re-establishment *n* restablecimiento *m*; restauración *f.*
refectory *n* refectorio; comedor *m.*
refer *vt, vi* referir, remitir; referirse.
referee *n* arbitro/ra *m/f*, *Lat Am* referí *m/f.*
reference *n* referencia, relación *f.*
refine *vt* refinar, purificar.
refinement *n* refinación *f*; refinadura *f*; cultura *f.*
refinery *n* refinería *f.*
refit *vt* reparar; (*mar*) reparar.
reflect *vt, vi* reflejar; reflexionar.
reflection *n* reflexión, meditación *f.*
reflector *n* reflector *m*; captafaros *m invar.*
reflex *adj* reflejo.
reform *vt* (*vi*) reformar(se).
reform, reformation *n* reformación *f.*

reformer *n* reformador/a *m/f.*
reformist *n* reformista *m/f.*
refract *vt* refractar.
refraction *n* refracción *f.*
refrain *vi:* to ~ from something abstenerse de algo.
refresh *vt* refrescar.
refreshment *n* refresco, refrigerio *m.*
refrigerator *n* nevera *f*; refrigerador *m.*
refuel *vi* repostar (combustible).
refuge *n* refugio, asilo *m.*
refugee *n* refugiado/da *m/f.*
refund *vt* devolver; * *n* reembolso *m.*
refurbish *vt* restaurar, renovar.
refusal *n* negativa *f.*
refuse¹ *vt* rehusar.
refuse² *n* basura *f.*
refuse collector *n* basurero *m.*
refute *vt* refutar.
regain *vt* recobrar, recuperar.
regal *adj* real.
regale *vt* regalar.
regalia *n* insignias *fpl.*
regard *vt* estimar; considerar; * *n* consideración *f*; respeto *m.*
regarding *pr* en cuanto a.
regardless *adv* a pesar de todo.
regatta *n* regata *f.*
regency *n* regencia *f.*
regenerate *vt* regenerar; * *adj* regenerado/da.
regeneration *n* regeneración *f.*
regent *n* regente *m/f.*
regime *n* régimen *m.*
regiment *n* regimiento *m.*
region *n* región *f.*
register *n* registro *m*; * *vt* registrar.
registrar *n* registrador/a *m/f.*
registration *n* registro *m.*
registry *n* registro *m.*
regressive *adj* regresivo/va.
regret *n* sentimiento *m*; remordimiento *m*; pensión *f*; * *vt* sentir.
regretful *adj* pesaroso/sa.
regular *adj* regular; ordinario/ria; ~ly *adv* regularmente; * *n* regular *m.*
regularity *n* regularidad *f.*
regulate *vt* regular, ordenar; *Lat Am* normar.
regulation *n* regulación *f*; arreglo *m.*
regulator *n* regulador *m.*
rehabilitate *vt* rehabilitar.
rehabilitation *n* rehabilitación *f.*
rehearsal *n* repetición *f*; ensayo *m.*
rehearse *vt* repetir; ensayar.

reign *n* reinado, reino *m*; * *vi* reinar; prevalecer.
reimburse *vt* reembolsar.
reimbursement *n* reembolso *m.*
rein *n* rienda *f*; * *vt* refrenar.
reindeer *n* reno *m.*
reinforce *vt* reforzar.
reinstate *vt* reintegrar.
reinsure *vt* (*com*) reasegurar.
reissue *n* reedición *f.*
reiterate *vt* reiterar.
reiteration *n* reiteración, repetición *f.*
reject *vt* rechazar.
rejection *n* rechazo *m.*
rejoice *vt* (*vi*) regocijar(se).
rejoicing *n* regocijo *m.*
relapse *vi* recaer; * *n* reincidencia *f*; recaída *f.*
relate *vt, vi* relatar, referirse.
related *adj* emparentado/da.
relation *n* relación *f*; pariente *m.*
relationship *n* parentesco *m*; relación *f.*
relative *adj* relativo/va; ~ly *adv* relativamente; * *n* pariente *m/f.*
relax *vt, vi* relajar; descansar.
relaxation *n* relajación *f*; descanso *m*; relax *m.*
relay *n* relevo *m*; * *vt* retransmitir.
release *vt* soltar, libertar; * *n* liberación *f*; descargo *m.*
relegate *vt* relegar.
relegation *n* relegación *f*, descenso *m.*
relent *vi* ablandarse.
relentless *adj* implacable.
relevant *adj* pertinente.
reliable *adj* fiable, de confianza, *Lat Am* confiable.
reliance *n* confianza *f.*
relic *n* reliquia *f.*
relief *n* relieve *m*; alivio *m.*
relieve *vt* aliviar, consolar; socorrer.
religion *n* religión *f.*
religious *adj* religioso/sa; ~ly *adv* religiosamente.
relinquish *vt* abandonar, dejar.
relish *n* sabor *m*; gusto *m*; salsa *f*; * *vt* gustar de, agradar.
reluctance *n* repugnancia *f.*
reluctant *adj* reticente.
rely *vi* confiar en; contar con.
remain *vi* quedar, restar, permanecer, durar.
remainder *n* resto, residuo *m.*
remains *npl* restos, residuos *mpl*; sobras *fpl.*
remand *vt:* to ~ in custody mantener bajo prisión preventiva.

remark n observación, nota f; * vt notar, observar.
remarkable adj notable, interesante.
remarkably adv notablemente.
remarry vi volver a casarse.
remedial adv curativo/va.
remedy n remedio, recurso m; * vt remediar.
remember vt acordarse de; recordar.
remembrance n memoria f; recuerdo m.
remind vt recordar.
reminiscence n reminiscencia f.
remiss adj negligente.
remission n remisión f.
remit vt, vi remitir, perdonar; disminuir.
remittance n remesa f.
remnant n resto, residuo m.
remodel vt remodelar.
remonstrate vi protestar.
remorse n remordimiento m; compunción f.
remorseless adj implacable.
remote adj remoto/ta, lejano/na; ~ly adv remotamente, lejos.
remote control n mando a distancia m.
remoteness n alejamiento m; distancia f.
removable adj de quita y pon, de quitapón.
removal n remoción f; mudanza f.
remove vt quitar; * vi mudarse.
remunerate vt remunerar.
remuneration n remuneración f.
render vt devolver, restituir; traducir; rendir.
rendezvous n cita f; lugar de encuentro m.
renegade n renegado/da m/f.
renew vt renovar, restablecer.
renewal n renovación f.
rennet n cuajo m.
renounce vt renunciar.
renovate vt renovar.
renovation n renovación f.
renown n renombre m; celebridad f.
renowned adj célebre.
rent n renta f; arrendamiento m; alquiler m; * vt alquilar.
rental n alquiler m.
renunciation n renuncia f.
reopen vt reabrir.
reorganization n reorganización f.
reorganize vt reorganizar.
repair vt reparar; resarcir; * n reparación f.
reparable adj reparable.
reparation n reparación f.
repartee n réplica aguda/picante f.
repatriate vt repatriar.
repay vt devolver; pagar, restituir.

repayment n pago m.
repeal vt abrogar, revocar; * n revocación, anulación f.
repeat vt repetir.
repeatedly adv repetidamente.
repeater n reloj de repetición m.
repel vt repeler, rechazar.
repent vi arrepentirse.
repentance n arrepentimiento m.
repentant adj arrepentido/da.
repertory n repertorio m.
repetition n repetición, reiteración f.
replace vt reemplazar, reponer.
replenish vt llenar, surtir.
replete adj repleto/ta, lleno/na.
reply n respuesta f; * vi responder.
report vt referir, contar; dar cuenta de; * n informe m; reportaje m; relación f.
reporter n reportero/ra m/f.
repose vt, vi reposar; * n reposo m.
repository n depósito m.
repossess vt reobrar.
reprehend vt reprender.
reprehensible adj reprensible.
represent vt representar.
representation n representación f.
representative adj representativo/va; * n representante m/f.
repress vt reprimir, domar.
repression n represión f.
repressive adj represivo/va.
reprieve vt suspender una ejecución; indultar; * n indulto m.
reprimand vt reprender, corregir; * n reprensión f; repri menda f.
reprint vt reimprimir.
reprisal n represalia f.
reproach n improperio, oprobio m; * vt hacer reproches a.
reproachful adj ignominioso/sa; ~ly adv ignominiosamente.
reproduce vt reproducir.
reproduction n reproducción f.
reptile n reptil m.
republic n república f.
republican adj, n republicano/a m/f.
republicanism n republicanismo m.
Republican Party n Partido Republicano m.
repudiate vt repudiar.
repugnance n repugnancia f.
repugnant adj repugnante; ~ly adv con repugnancia.
repulse vt repulsar, desechar; * n repulsa f; rechazo m.

repulsion *n* repúlsion, repulsa *f.*
repulsive *adj* repulsivo/va.
reputable *adj* honroso/sa.
reputation *n* reputación *f.*
repute *vt* reputar.
request *n* petición, súplica *f, Lat Am* pedido *m;* * *vt* rogar, suplicar.
require *vt* requerir, demandar.
requirement *n* requisito *m;* exigencia *f.*
requisite *adj* necesario/ria, indispensable; * *n* requisito *m.*
requisition *n* petición, demanda *f.*
requite *vt* recompensar.
rescind *vt* rescindir, abrogar.
rescue *vt* librar, rescatar; * *n* libramiento, recobro *m.*
research *vt* investigar; * *n* investigación *f.*
resemblance *n* semejanza *f.*
resemble *vt* asemejarse.
resent *vt* resentirse.
resentful *adj* resentido/da; vengativo/va; ~ly *adv* con resentimi ento.
resentment *n* resentimiento *m.*
reservation *n* reserva *f.*
reserve *vt* reservar; * *n* reserva *f.*
reservedly *adv* con reserva.
reservoir *n* depósito *m;* pantano *m.*
reside *vi* residir, morar.
residence *n* residencia, morada *f.*
resident *adj* residente.
residuary *adj* sobrado/da; ~ **legatee** *n* (*law*) legatario/ria universal *m/f.*
residue *n* residuo, resto *m.*
resign *vt, vi* resignar, renunciar, ceder; resignarse, rendirse.
resignation *n* resignación *f;* dimisión *f.*
resin *n* resina *f.*
resinous *adj* resinoso/sa.
resist *vt* resistir, oponerse.
resistance *n* resistencia *f.*
resolute *adj* resuelto/ta; ~ly *adv* resueltamente.
resolution *n* resolución *f.*
resolve *vt* (*vr*) resolver(se); (*fig*) zanjar.
resonance *n* resonancia *f.*
resonant *adj* resonante.
resort *vi* recurrir, frecuentar; * *n* recurso *m;* resorte *m.*
resound *vi* resonar.
resource *n* recurso *m;* expediente *m.*
respect *n* respecto *m;* respeto *m;* motivo *m;* ~s *pl* recuerdos *mpl;* * *vt* apreciar; respetar; venerar.
respectability *n* respetabilidad *f.*

respectable *adj* respetable; considerable; ~bly *adv* notablemente.
respectful *adj* respetuoso/sa; ~ly *adv* respetuosamente.
respecting *prep* con respecto a.
respective *adj* respectivo/va, relativo/va; ~ly *adv* respectivamente.
respirator *n* respirador *m.*
respiratory *adj* respiratorio/ria.
respite *n* suspensión *f;* respiro *m;* * *vt* suspender, diferir.
resplendence *n* resplandor, brillo *m.*
resplendent *adj* resplandeciente.
respond *vt* responder; corresponder.
respondent *n* (*law*) defensor/a *m.*
response *n* respuesta, réplica *f.*
responsibility *n* responsabilidad *f.*
responsible *adj* responsable.
responsive *adj* sensible.
rest *n* reposo *m;* sueño *m;* quietud *f;* (*mus*) pausa *f;* resto, residuo *m;* * *vt* descansar; apoyar; *vi* dormir, reposar; descansarse.
restaurant *n* restaurante, restorán *m.*
resting place (last) *n* última morada *f.*
restitution *n* restitución *f.*
restive *adj* inquieto/ta; obstinado/da.
restless *adj* insomne; inquieto/ta.
restoration *n* restauración *f.*
restorative *adj* restaurativo/va.
restore *vt* restaurar, restituir.
restrain *vt* restringir, restriñir.
restraint *n* refrenamiento, constreñimiento *m.*
restrict *vt* restringir, limitar.
restriction *n* restricción *f.*
restrictive *adj* restrictivo/va.
result *vi* resultar; * *n* resultado *m.*
resume *vt* resumir; empezar de nuevo.
resurrection *n* resurrección *f.*
resuscitate *vt* resucitar.
retail *vt* vender al por menor; * *n* venta por menor *f.*
retain *vt* retener, guardar.
retainer *n* adherente, partidario/ria *m/f;* ~s *pl* comitiva *f;* séquito *m.*
retake *vt* volver a tomar.
retaliate *vt* tomar represalias.
retaliation *n* represalias *fpl.*
retardation *n* retraso *m.*
retarded *adj* retrasado/da.
retch *vi* tener arcadas.
retention *n* retención *f.*
retentive *adj* retentivo/va.
reticence *n* reticencia *f.*
retina *n* retina *f.*

retire *vt* (*vi*) retirar(se); jubilar(se).
retired *adj* apartado/da, retirado/da; jubilado/da.
retirement *n* retiro *m*, jubilación *f*.
retort *vt* replicar; * *n* réplica *f*.
retouch *vt* retocar.
retrace *vt* volver a trazar.
retract *vt* retraer; retractar.
retrain *vt* reciclar.
retraining *n* reciclaje profesional *m*.
retreat *n* retirada *f*; * *vi* retirarse.
retribution *n* retribución, recompensa *f*.
retrievable *adj* recuperable; reparable.
retrieve *vt* recuperar, recobrar.
retriever *n* sabueso *m*.
retrograde *adj* retrógrado/da.
retrospect, retrospection *n* reflexión *f*.
retrospective *adj* retrospectivo/va.
return *vt* retribuir; restituir; devolver; * *n* retorno *m*; vuelta *f*; recompensa, rendimiento *m*; recaída *f*.
reunion *n* reunión *f*.
reunite *vt* (*vi*) reunir(se).
reveal *vi* revelar.
revel *vi* andar de juerga.
revelation *n* revelación *f*.
reveler *n* juerguista *m/f*.
revelry *n* juerga *f*.
revenge *vt* vengar; * *n* venganza *f*.
revengeful *adj* vengativo/va.
revenue *n* renta *f*; rédito *m*.
reverberate *vt*, *vi* reverberar; resonar, retumbar.
reverberation *n* rechazo *m*; reverberación *f*.
revere *vt* reverenciar, venerar.
reverence *n* reverencia *f*; * *vt* reverenciar.
reverend *adj* reverendo/da; venerable; * *n* padre *m*.
reverent, reverential *adj* reverencial, respetuoso/sa.
reversal *n* revocación *f*; cambio total *m*.
reverse *vt* trastrocar; abolir; poner en marcha atrás; * *n* vicisi tud *f*; contrario *m*; reverso *m* (de una moneda).
reversible *adj* revocable; reversible.
reversion *n* reversión *f*.
revert *vt*, *vi* trastrocar; volverse atrás.
review *vt* rever; (*mil*) revistar; * *n* revista *f*; reseña *f*.
reviewer *n* revisor/a *m/f*; crítico/ca *m/f*.
revile *vt* ultrajar; difamar.
revise *vt* rever; repasar.
reviser *n* revisor/a *m/f*.
revision *n* revisión *f*.
revisit *vt* volver a visitar.

revival *n* restauración *f*; restablecimiento *m*.
revive *vt* avivar; restablecer; * *vi* revivir.
revocation *n* revocación *f*.
revoke *vt* revocar, anular.
revolt *vi* rebelarse; * *n* rebelión *f*.
revolting *adj* asqueroso/sa.
revolution *n* revolución *f*.
revolutionary *adj*, *n* revolucionario/a *m/f*.
revolve *vt* revolver; meditar; * *vi* girar.
revolver *n* revólver *m*.
revolving *adj* giratorio/ria.
revue *n* revista *f*.
revulsion *n* revulsión *f*.
reward *n* recompensa *f*; * *vt* recompensar.
rhapsody *n* rapsodia *f*.
rhetoric *n* retórica *f*.
rhetorical *adj* retórico/ca.
rheumatic *adj* reumático/ca.
rheumatism *n* reumatismo *m*.
rhinoceros *n* rinoceronte *m*.
rhomboid *n* romboide *m*.
rhombus *n* rombo *m*.
rhubarb *n* ruibarbo *m*.
rhyme *n* rima *f*, poema *m*; * *vi* rimar.
rhythm *n* ritmo *m*.
rhythmical *adj* rítmico/ca.
rib *n* costilla *f*.
ribald *adj* escabroso/sa.
ribbon *n* listón *m*; cinta *f*.
rice *n* arroz *m*.
rich *adj* rico/ca; opulento/ta; abundante; ~ly *adv* ricamente.
riches *npl* riqueza *f*.
richness *n* riqueza *f*; abundancia *f*.
rickets *n* raquitismo *m*.
rickety *adj* raquítico/ca.
rid *vt* librar, desembarazar.
riddance *n*: good ~! ¡enhoramala!
riddle *n* enigma *m*; criba *f*; * *vt* cribar.
ride *vi* cabalgar; andar en coche; * *n* paseo a caballo/en coche *m*.
rider *n* caballero/ra, jinete *m*, amazona *f*.
ridge *n* espinazo, lomo *m*; cumbre *f*; * *vt* formar lomos/surcos.
ridicule *n* ridiculez *f*; ridiculo *m*; * *vt* ridiculizar.
ridiculous *adj* ridículo/la; ~ly *adv* ridiculamente.
riding *n* equitación *f*.
riding habit *n* traje de amazona *m*.
riding school *n* picadero *m*.
rife *adj* común, frecuente.
riffraff *n* desecho, desperdicio *m*.
rifle *vt* robar, pillar; estriar, rayar; * *n* rifle *m*.

rifleman *n* fusilero *m*.

rig *vt* ataviar; (*mar*) aparejar; * *n* torre de perforación *f*; **oil ~** plataforma petrolera *f*.

rigging *n* (*mar*) aparejo *m*.

right *adj* derecho/cha, recto/ta; justo/ta; honesto/ta; ~! ¡bien!, ¡bueno!; **~ly** *adv* rectamente, justamente; * *n* justicia *f*; razón *f*; derecho *m*; mano derecha *f*; * *vt* hacer justicia.

righteous *adj* justo/ta, honrado/da; **~ly** *adv* justamente.

righteousness *n* equidad *f*; honradez *f*.

rigid *adj* rígido/da; austero/ra, severo/ra; yerto/ta; **~ly** *adv* con rigidez.

rigidity *n* rigidez, austeridad *f*.

rigmarole *n* galimatías *m*.

rigor *n* rigor *m*; severidad *f*.

rigorous *adj* riguroso/sa; **~ly** *adv* rigorosamente.

rim *n* margen *m/f*; orilla *f*.

rind *n* corteza *f*.

ring *n* círculo, cerco *m*; anillo *m*; campaneo *m*; * *vt* sonar; * *vi* retiñir, retumbar; **to ~ the bell** pulsar el timbre.

ringer (bell) *n* campanero/ra *m/f*.

ringleader *n* cabecilla *m/f*.

ringlet *n* anillejo *m*.

ringworm *n* (*med*) tina favosa *f*.

rink *n* (*also* **ice ~**) pista de hielo *f*.

rinse *vt* lavar, limpiar.

riot *n* tumulto, bullicio *m*; * *vi* amotinarse.

rioter *n* amotinado/da *m/f*.

riotous *adj* bullicioso/sa, sedicioso/sa; disoluto/ta; **~ly** *adv* disolutamente.

rip *vt* rasgar, lacerar; descoser.

ripe *adj* maduro/ra, sazonado/da.

ripen *vt*, *vi* madurar.

ripeness *n* madurez *f*.

rip-off *n* (*col*): **it's a ~!** ¡es una estafa!

ripple *vi* rizarse; * *vt* rizar; * *n* onda *f*, rizo *m*.

rise *vi* levantarse; nacer, salir; rebelarse; ascender; hincharse; elevarse; resucitar; * *n* levantamiento *m*; elevación *f*; subida *f*; salida (del sol) *f*; causa *f*.

rising *n* salida (del sol) *f*; fin (de una junta/sesión) *m*.

risk *n* riesgo, peligro *m*; * *vt* arriesgar.

risky *adj* peligroso/sa, *Lat Am* riesgoso/sa.

rissole *n* croqueta *f*.

rite *n* rito *m*.

ritual *adj*, *n* ritual *m*.

rival *adj*, *n* rival *m/f*; * *vt* competir, emular.

rivalry *n* rivalidad *f*.

river *n* río *m*.

riverside *adj* ribereño/ña.

rivet *n* remache *m*; * *vt* remachar, roblar.

rivulet *n* riachuelo *m*.

road *n* camino *m*.

road sign *n* señal de trafico *f*.

roadstead *n* (*mar*) rada *f*.

roadworks *npl* obras *fpl*.

roam *vt*, *vi* corretear; vagar.

roan *adj* ruano/na.

roar *vi* rugir, aullar; bramar; * *n* rugido *m*; bramido, truendo *m*; mugido *m*.

roast *vt* asar; tostar.

roast beef *n* rosbif *m*.

rob *vt* robar, hurtar.

robber *n* ladrón/ona *m/f*.

robbery *n* robo *m*.

robe *n* manto *m*; toga *f*; * *vt* vestir de gala.

robin (redbreast) *n* petirrojo *m*.

robust *adj* robusto/ta.

robustness *n* robustez *f*.

rock *n* roca *f*; escollo *m*; rueca *f*; * *vt* mecer; arrullar; ape drear; * *vi* bambolear.

rock and roll *n* rocanrol *m*.

rock crystal *n* cuarzo *m*.

rocking chair *n* mecedora *f*.

rocket *n* cohete *m*, *Lat Am* cuete *m*.

rock salt *n* sal gema *f*.

rocky *adj* peñascoso/sa.

rod *n* varilla, verga, cana *f*.

rodent *n* roedor/a *m/f*.

roe[1] *n* corzo *m*.

roe[2] *n* hueva *f*.

roebuck *n* corzo *m*.

rogation *n* rogaciones *fpl*.

rogue *n* bribón/ona, pícaro/ra, villano/na *m/f*.

roguish *adj* pícaro/ra.

roll *vt* rodar; volver; arrollar; * *vi* rodar; girar; * *n* rodadura *f*; rollo *m*; lista *f*; catalogo *m*; bollo *m*; panecillo *m*.

roller *n* rodillo, cilindro *m*.

roller skates *npl* patines de rueda *mpl*.

rolling pin *n* rodillo de cocina *m*.

Roman Catholic *adj*, *n* católico/ca *m/f* (romano/na).

romance *n* romance *m*; ficción *f*; cuento *m*; fábula *f*.

romantic *adj* romántico/ca.

romp *vi* retozar.

roof *n* tejado *m*; paladar *m*; * *vt* techar.

roofing *n* techado, tejado *m*.

rook[1] *n* grajo *m*.

rook[2] *n* torre *f* (en el juego de ajedrez).

room *n* habitación, sala *f*; lugar, espacio *m*; aposento *m*.

roominess *n* espaciosidad, capacidad *f.*
roomy *adj* espacioso/sa.
roost *n* pértiga del gallinero *f;* * *vi* dormir en una pértiga.
root *n* raíz *f;* origen *m;* * *vt, vi:* **to ~ out** desarraigar; arraigar.
rooted *adj* inveterado/da.
rope *n* cuerda *f;* cordel *m;* * *vi* hacer hebras.
rope maker *n* cordelero/ra *m/f.*
rosary *n* rosario *m.*
rose *n* rosa *f.*
rose bed *n* campo de rosales *m.*
rosebud *n* capullo de rosa *m.*
rosemary *n* (*bot*) romero *m.*
rose tree *n* rosal *m.*
rosette *n* roseta *f.*
rosé wine *n* vino rosado *m.*
rosewood *n* palo de rosa *m.*
rosiness *n* color rosado *m.*
rosy *adj* rosado/da.
rot *vi* pudrirse; * *n* putrefacción *f.*
rotate *vt, vi* girar.
rotation *n* rotación *f.*
rote *n* uso *m,* práctica *f.*
rotten *adj* podrido/da, corrompido/da.
rottenness *n* podredumbre, putrefacción *f.*
rotund *adj* rotundo/da, redondo/da, circular, esférico/ca.
rouge *n* arrebol, colorete *m.*
rough *adj* áspero/ra, tosco/ca; bronco/ca, bruto/ta, brusco/ca; tempestuoso/sa; **~looking** zarrapastroso/sa; **~ly** *adv* rudamente.
roughcast *n* mezcla gruesa *f.*
roughen *vt* poner áspero/ra.
roughness *n* aspereza *f;* rudeza, tosquedad *f;* tempestad *f.*
roulette *n* ruleta *f.*
round *adj* redondo/da; cabal; franco/ca, sincero/ra; * *n* círculo *m;* redondez *f;* vuelta *f;* giro *m;* escalón *m;* ronda *f;* andanada de canones *f;* descarga *f;* * *adv* alrededor; por todos lados; **~ly** *adv* redondamente; francamente; * *vt* cercar, rodear; redondear.
roundabout *adj* amplio/lia; indirecto/ta, vago/ga; * *n* tiovivo *m.*
roundness *n* redondez *f.*
rouse *vt* despertar; excitar.
rout *n* derrota *f;* * *vt* derrotar.
route *n* ruta *f;* camino *m.*
routine *adj* rutinario/ria; * *n* rutina *f;* número *m.*
rove *vi* vagar, vaguear.
rover *n* vagabundo/da *m/f;* pirata *m/f.*
row[1] *n* camorra *f;* rina *f.*
row[2] *n* hilera, fila *f.*

row[3] *vt* (*mar*) remar, bogar.
rowdy *n* alborotador/a, bullanguero/ra *m/f.*
rower *n* remero/ra *m/f.*
royal *adj* real; regio/gia; **~ly** *adv* regiamente.
royalist *n* realista *m/f.*
royalty *n* realeza, dignidad real *f;* honorarios que paga el editor al autor por cada ejemplar vendido de su obra *mpl.*
royalties *npl* regalías *fpl.*
rub *vt* estregar, fregar, frotar; raspar; * *n* frotamiento *m;* (*fig*) embarazo *m;* dificultad *f.*
rubber *n* caucho *m,* goma *f;* (*col*) condón *m.*
rubber-band *n* goma, gomita *f.*
rubbish *n* basura *f;* tonterías *fpl;* escombro *m;* ruinas *fpl.*
rubble *n* escombros *mpl,* cascote *m.*
ruble *n* rublo *m.*
rubric *n* rúbrica *f.*
ruby *n* rubí *m.*
rucksack *n* mochila *f.*
rudder *n* timón *m.*
ruddiness *n* tez encendida; rubicundez *f.*
ruddy *adj* colorado/da, rubio/bia.
rude *adj* rudo/da, brutal, rústico/ca, grosero/ra; tosco/ca; **~ly** *adv* rudamente, groseramente.
rudeness *n* descortesía *f;* rudeza, insolencia *f.*
rudiment *n* rudimentos *mpl.*
rue *vi* compadecerse; * *n* (*bot*) ruda *f.*
rueful *adj* lamentable, triste.
ruffian *n* malhechor/a, bandolero/ra *m/f;* * *adj* brutal.
ruffle *vt* desordenar, desazonar; rizar.
rug *n* alfombra *f.*
rugby *n* rugby *m.*
rugged *adj* áspero/ra, tosco/ca; brutal; peludo/da.
ruin *n* ruina *f;* perdición *f;* escombros *mpl;* * *vt* arruinar; destruir.
ruinous *adj* ruinoso/sa.
rule *n* mando *m;* regla *f;* regularidad *f;* dominio *m;* * *vt* gobernar; reglar, arreglar, dirigir.
ruler *n* gobernador/a *m/f;* regla *f.*
rum *n* ron *m.*
rumble *vi* crujir, rugir.
ruminate *vt* rumiar.
rummage *vt* rebuscar.
rumor *n* rumor *m;* * *vt* rumorearse.
rump *n* ancas *fpl.*
run *vt* dirigir; organizar; llevar; pasar; **to ~ the risk** aventurar, arriesgar; * *vi* correr; fluir, manar; pasar rápidamente; proceder; ir; desteñirse; ser candidato/ta; * *n* corrida,

carrera *f*; paseo *m*; curso *m*; serie *f*; moda *f*; ataque *m*.

runaway *n* fugitivo/va, desertor/a *m/f*.

rung *n* escalón, peldaño *m* (de escalera de mano).

runner *n* corredor/a *m/f*; correo, mensajero/ra *m/f*.

running *n* carrera, corrida *f*; curso *m*.

runway *n* pista de aterrizaje *f*.

rupture *n* rotura *f*; hernia, quebradura *f*; * *vt* reventar, romper.

rural *adj* rural, campestre, rústico/ca.

ruse *n* astucia, maña *f*.

rush *n* junco *m*; ráfaga *f*; ímpetu *m*; * *vt* apresurar; * *vi* abalanzarse, tirarse.

rusk *n* galleta *f*.

russet *adj* bermejo/ja.

rust *n* herrumbre *f*; * *vi* oxidarse.

rustic *adj* rústico/ca; * *n* patán/ana, rústico/ca *m/f*.

rustiness *n* herrumbre *f*.

rustle *vi* crujir, rechinar; * *vt* hacer crujir.

rustling *n* estruendo *m*; crujido *m*.

rusty *adj* oriniento/ta, mohoso/sa; oxidado/da.

rut *n* celo *m*; carril *m*.

ruthless *adj* cruel, insensible; ~ly *adv* inhumanamente.

rye *n* (*bot*) centeno *m*.

S

Sabbath n sábado m.
sable n cebellina f.
sabotage n sabotaje m.
saber n sable m.
saccharin n sacarina f.
sachet n sobrecito m.
sack n saco m; * vt despedir; saquear.
sacrament n sacramento m; Eucaristía f.
sacramental adj sacramental.
sacred adj sagrado/da, sacro/cra; inviolable.
sacredness n santidad f.
sacrifice n sacrificio m; * vt, vi sacrificar.
sacrificial adj de sacrificio.
sacrilege n sacrilegio m.
sacrilegious adj sacrílego/ga.
sad adj triste, melanólico/ca; infausto/ta; obscuro/ra; ~ly adv tristemente.
sadden vt entristecer.
saddle n silla f; sillín m; * vt ensillar.
saddlebag n alforja f.
saddler n sillero m/f.
sadness n tristeza f.
safari n safari m.
safe adj seguro/ra; ileso/sa; fuera de peligro; de fiar; ~ly adv seguramente; ~ and sound sano y salvo; * n caja fuerte f.
safe-conduct n salvoconducto m.
safeguard n salvaguardia f; * vt proteger, defender.
safety n seguridad f; salvamento m.
safety belt n cinturón (de seguridad) m.
safety match n cerilla f.
safety pin n imperdible, seguro m.
saffron n azafrán m.
sage n (bot) salvia f; sabio/bia m/f; * adj sabio/bia; ~ly adv sabiamente.
Sagittarius n Sagitario m (signo del zodíaco).
sago n (bot) sagú m.
sail n vela f; * vt gobernar; * vi dar a la vela, navegar.
sailing n navegación f.
sailing boat n yate m.
sailor n marinero/ra m/f.
saint n santo/ta m/f.
sainted, saintly adj santo/ta.
sake n causa, razón f; for God's ~ por amor de Dios.
salable adj vendible.
salad n ensalada f.
salad bowl n ensaladera f.

salad dressing n aliño m.
salad oil n aceite para ensaladas m.
salamander n salamandra f.
salary n sueldo m.
sale n venta f; liquidación f.
salesman n vendedor m.
saleswoman n vendedora f.
salient adj saliente, saledizo/za.
saline adj salino/na.
saliva n saliva f.
sallow adj cetrino/na, pálido/da.
sally n (mil) salida, surtida f; * vi salir.
salmon n salmón m.
salmon trout n trucha salmonada f.
saloon n bar m.
salt n sal f; * vt salar.
salt cellar n salero m.
salting n saladura f.
saltpeter n salitre m.
saltworks npl salinas fpl.
salubrious adj salubre, saludable.
salubrity n salubridad f.
salutary adj salubre, salutífero/ra.
salutation n salutación f.
salute vt saludar; * n saludo m.
salvage n (mar) salvamento, rescate m.
salvation n salvación f.
salve n emplasto, ungüento m.
salver n salvilla, bandeja f.
salvo n salva, excusa f.
same adj mismo/ma, idéntico/ca.
sameness n identidad f.
sample n muestra f; ejemplo m; * vt probar.
sampler n muestra f; dechado, modelo m.
sanctify vt santificar.
sanctimonious adj santurrón/ona.
sanction n sanción f; * vt sancionar.
sanctity n santidad f.
sanctuary n santuario m; asilo m.
sand n arena f; * vt lijar.
sandal n sandalia f.
sandbag n (mil) saco de tierra m.
sandpit n arenal m.
sandstone n arenisca f.
sandwich n bocadillo, sandwich m, Lat Am sánduche m.
sandy adj arenoso/sa.
sane adj sano/na.
sanguinary adj sanguinario/ria.
sanguine adj sanguíneo/nea.
sanitarium n sanatorio m.

339

sanitary napkin *n* compresa *f*, *Lat Am* toalla *f* higiénica.

sanity *n* juicio sano, sentido común *m*.

sap *n* savia *f*; * *vt* minar.

sapient *adj* sabio/bia, cuerdo/da.

sapling *n* arbolito *m*.

sapper *n* (*mil*) zapador *m*.

sapphire *n* zafiro *m*.

sarcasm *n* sarcasmo *m*.

sarcastic *adj* sarcástico/ca; ~ally *adv* sarcásticamente.

sarcophagus *n* sarcófago, sepulcro *m*.

sardine *n* sardina *f*.

sash *n* cingulo *m*, cinta *f*.

sash window *n* ventana/vidriera corrediza *f*.

Satan *n* Satanás *m*.

satanic(al) *adj* diabólico/ca.

satchel *n* mochila *f*.

satellite *n* satélite *m*.

satellite dish *n* antena parabólica *f*.

satiate, sate *vt* saciar, hartar.

satin *n* raso *m*; * *adj* de raso.

satire *n* satira *f*.

satiric(al) *adj* satírico/ca; ~ly *adv* satíricamente.

satirist *n* autor satírico *m*, autora satírica *f*.

satirize *vt* satirizar.

satisfaction *n* satisfacción *f*.

satisfactorily *adv* satisfactoriamente.

satisfactory *adj* satisfactorio/ria.

satisfy *vt* satisfacer; convencer.

saturate *vt* saturar.

Saturday *n* sábado *m*.

saturnine *adj* saturnino/na, melancólico/ca.

satyr *n* sátiro *m*.

sauce *n* salsa *f*; crema *f*; compota de frutas *f*; * *vt* condimentar.

saucepan *n* cazo *m*.

saucer *n* platillo *m*.

saucily *adv* desvergonzadamente.

sauciness *n* insolencia, impudencia *f*.

saucy *adj* insolente.

saunter *vi* callejear, corretear.

sausage *n* salchicha *f*.

savage *adj* salvaje, bárbaro/ra; ~ly *adv* bárbaramente; * *n* salvaje *m/f*.

savageness *n* salvajería, *f*; crueldad *f*.

savagery *n* crueldad *f*.

savanna(h) *n* sabana *f*.

save *vt* salvar; economizar; ahorrar; evitar; conservar; * *adv* salvo, excepto; * *n* parada *f*, *Lat Am* atajada *f*.

saveloy sausage *n* chorizo *m*.

saver *n* ahorrador/a *m/f*.

saving *adj* frugal, económico/ca; * *prep* fuera de, excepto; * *n* salvamiento *m*; ~s *pl* ahorro *m*, economía *f*.

savings account *n* cuenta de ahorros *f*.

savings bank *n* caja de ahorros *f*.

Savior *n* Salvador *m*.

savior *n* libertador/a *m/f*.

savor *n* olor *m*; sabor *m*; * *vt* gustar, saborear.

savoriness *n* paladar; sabor *m*.

savory *adj* sabroso/sa.

saw *n* sierra *f*; * *vt* serrar, *Lat Am* serruchar.

sawdust *n* serrín *m*.

sawfish *n* pez sierra *m*.

sawmill *n* aserradero *m*.

sawyer *n* aserrador/a *m/f*.

saxophone *n* saxofóno *m*.

say *vt* decir, hablar.

saying *n* dicho, proverbio *m*.

scab *n* roña *f*; roñoso *m*.

scabbard *n* vaina (de espada) *f*; cobertura *f*.

scabby *adj* sarnoso/sa.

scaffold *n* tablado *m*; cadalso *m*.

scaffolding *n* andamio *m*.

scald *vt* escaldar; * *n* escaldadura *f*.

scale *n* balanza *f*; escama *f*; escala *f*; gama *f*; * *vt*, *vi* escalar; descostrarse.

scallop *n* vieira *f*; festón *m*; * *vt* festonear.

scalp *n* cuero cabelludo *m*; * *vt* escalpar.

scamp *n* bribón/ona, ladrón/ona *m/f*.

scamper *vi* escapar, huir.

scampi *npl* gambas *fpl*.

scan *vt* escudriñar; registrar; escandir; escanear.

scandal *n* escándalo *m*; infamia *f*.

scandalize *vt* escandalizar.

scandalous *adj* escandaloso/sa; ~ly *adv* escandalosamente.

scanner *n* escáner *m*.

scant, scanty *adj* escaso/sa, parco/ca.

scantily *adv* escasamente, estrechamente.

scantness *n* estrechez, escasez *f*.

scapegoat *n* chivo expiatorio *m*.

scar *n* cicatriz *f*; * *vt* dejar cicatriz en.

scarce *adj* raro/ra; ~ly *adv* apenas.

scarcity *n* escasez *f*; raridad *f*.

scare *vt* espantar; * *n* susto *m*.

scarecrow *n* espantapájaros *m invar*.

scarf *n* bufanda *f*.

scarlet *n* escarlata *f*; * *adj* escarlata.

scarlet fever *n* escarlatina *f*.

scarp *n* escarpa *f*.

scat *interj* (*col*) ¡zape!

scatter *vt* esparcir; disipar.

scavenger *n* basurero/ra *m/f*; carroñero/ra *m/f*.

scenario n argumento m; guión m; (fig) escenario m.

scene n escena f; panorama m; escándalo m; paisaje m.

scenery n vista f; decoración (de teatro) f.

scenic adj escénico/ca.

scent n olfato m; olor m; rastro m; * vt oler.

scent bottle n frasco de perfume m.

scentless adj sin olfato; inodoro/ra.

scepter n cetro m.

schedule n horario m; programa m; lista f.

scheme n proyecto, plan m; esquema m; sistema m; modelo m; * vt proyectar; * vi intrigar.

schemer n proyectista, intrigante m/f.

schism n cisma m.

schismatic adj cismático/ca.

scholar n estudiante m/f; erudito/ta m/f, escolástico/ca m/f.

scholarship n ciencia f; erudición f.

scholastic adj escolástico/ca.

school n escuela f, colegio m; * vt enseñar.

schoolboy n alumno m.

schoolgirl n alumna f.

schooling n instrucción f.

schoolmaster n maestro de escuela m.

schoolmistress n maestra de niños/niñas f.

schoolteacher n maestro/tra m/f; profesor/ra m/f.

schooner n (mar) goleta f.

sciatica n ciática f.

science n ciencia f.

scientific adj científico/ca; ~ally adv científicamente.

scientist n científico/ca m/f.

scimitar n cimitarra f.

scintillate vi chispear, centellar.

scintillating adj brillante, ingenioso/sa.

scissors npl tijeras fpl.

scoff vi mofarse, burlarse.

scold vt, vi regañar, reñir, refunfuñar.

scoop n cucharón m; pala f; exclusiva f; * vt cavar, socavar.

scooter (child's) n patinete m.

scope n objeto, intento, designio, blanco, espacio m; alcance m; libertad f.

scorch vt quemar; tostar; * vi quemarse, secarse.

score n muesca, canalita f; consideración f; cuenta f; puntuación f; razón f; motivo m; veintena f; * vt ganar; señalar con una línea; * vi marcar.

scoreboard n marcador m.

scorn vt, vi despreciar; mofar; * n desdén, menosprecio m.

scornful adj desdeñoso/sa; ~ly adv con desdén.

Scorpio n Escorpión m (signo del zodíaco).

scorpion n escorpión m.

scotch vt descartar.

Scotch n whisky escocés m.

scoundrel n pícaro/ra m/f.

scour vt fregar, estregar; limpiar; * vi corretear.

scourge n azote m; castigo m; * vt azotar, castigar.

scout n (mil) explorador/a m/f; espía m/f; * vi ir de reconocimiento.

scowl vi fruncir el ceño; * n ceño, semblante ceñudo m.

scragginess n flaqueza, aspereza f.

scraggy adj áspero/ra; macilento/ta.

scramble vi arrapar; trepar; disputar; * n disputa f; subida f.

scrap n migaja f; sobras fpl; pedacito m; riña f; chatarra f.

scrape vt, vi raer, raspar; arañar; tocar mal un instrumento; * n embarazo m; dificultad f.

scraper n rascador m.

scratch vt rascar, raspar; raer, garrapatear; * n rasguño m, Lat Am rasguñón m.

scrawl vt, vi garrapatear; * n garabatos mpl.

scream, screech vi chillar, dar alaridos; * n chillido, grito, alarido m.

screen n pantalla f; biombo m; mampara f; abanico de chimenea m; * vt abrigar, esconder; proyectar; cribar, cerner.

screenplay n guión m, Lat Am libreto m.

screw n tornillo m; * vt atornillar; forzar, apretar, estrechar.

screwdriver n destornillador m.

scribble vt escarabajear; * n escrito de poco mérito m.

scribe n escritor/a m/f; escriba m/f.

scrimmage n tumulto m, scrimmage m.

script n guión m; letra f.

scriptural adj bíblico/ca.

Scripture n Sagrada Escritura f.

scroll n rollo (de papel/pergamino) m.

scrounger n mamón/ona m/f.

scrub vt restregar; anular; * n maleza f.

scruffy adj desaliñado/da.

scruple n escrúpulo m.

scrupulous adj escrupuloso/sa; ~ly adv escrupulosamente.

scrutinize vt escudriñar, examinar.

scrutiny n escrutinio, examen m.

scuffle n quimera, riña f; * vi reñir, pelear.

scull n barquillo m.

sculptor *n* escultor/a *m/f.*
sculpture *n* escultura *f*; * *vt* esculpir.
scum *n* espuma *f*; escoria *f*; canalla *m/f.*
scurrilous *adj* vil, bajo/ja; injurioso/sa; ~ly *adv* injuriosamente.
scurvy *n* escorbuto *m*; * *adj* escorbútico/ca; vil, despreciable.
scuttle[1] *n* carbonera *f.*
scuttle[2] *vt* barrenar.
scythe *n* guadaña *f.*
sea *n* mar *m/f*; * *adj* de mar; heavy ~ oleada *f.*
sea breeze *n* viento de mar *m.*
seacoast *n* costa marítima *f.*
sea fight *n* combate naval *m.*
seafood *n* mariscos *mpl.*
sea front *n* paseo marítimo *m.*
sea-green *adj* verdemar.
seagull *n* gaviota *f.*
sea horse *n* caballito de mar *m.*
seal *n* sello *m*; foca *f*; * *vt* sellar.
sealing wax *n* lacre *m.*
seam *n* costura *f*; * *vt* coser.
seaman *n* marinero *m.*
seamanship *n* pericia en la navegación *m.*
seamstress *n* costurera *f.*
seamy *adj* sórdido/da.
seaport *n* puerto de mar *m.*
sear *vt* cauterizar.
search *vt* examinar; escudriñar; inquirir, tentar; investigar, buscar; * *n* pesquisa *f*; busca *f*, Lat Am procura *f*; buscada *f.*
searchlight *n* reflector *m.*
seashore *n* ribera *f*, litoral *m.*
seasick *adj* mareado/da.
seasickness *n* mareo *m.*
seaside *n* orilla/ribera del mar *f.*
season *n* estación *f*; tiempo oportuno *m*; sazón *f*; * *vt* sazonar; imbuir.
seasonable *adj* oportuno/na, a propósito.
seasonably *adv* oportunamente.
seasoning *n* condimento *m.*
season ticket *n* abono *m.*
season ticket holder *n* abonado/da *m/f.*
seat *n* asiento *m*; silla *f*; escaño *m*; situación *f*; * *vt* situar; colocar; asentar.
seat belt *n* cinturón de seguridad *m.*
seaward *adj* del litoral; ~s *adv* hacia el mar.
seaweed *n* alga marina *f.*
seaworthy *adj* en condiciones de navegar.
secede *vi* apartarse, separarse.
secession *n* secesión *f*; separación *f.*
seclude *vt* apartar, excluir.
seclusion *n* separación *f*; exclusión *f.*
second *adj* segundo/da; ~(ly) *adv* en segundo

lugar; * *n* defensor/a *m/f*; segundo *m*; (mus) segunda *f*; * *vt* ayudar; segundar.
secondary *adj* secundario/ria.
secondary school *n* escuela secundaria *f.*
secondhand *adj* de segunda mano.
secrecy *n* secreto *m*, confidencialidad *f.*
secret *adj* secreto/ta; * *n* secreto *m*; ~ly *adv* secretamente.
secretary *n* secretario/ria *m/f.*
secrete *vt* esconder; (med) secretar.
secretion *n* secreción *f.*
secretive *adj* misterioso/sa.
sect *n* secta *f.*
sectarian *n* sectario/ria *m/f.*
section *n* sección *f.*
sector *n* sector *m.*
secular *adj* secular, seglar.
secularize *vt* secularizar.
secure *adj* seguro/ra; salvo/va; ~ly *adv* seguramente; * *vt* asegurar; salvar.
security *n* seguridad *f*; defensa *f*; confianza *f*; fianza *f.*
sedan, saloon *n* sedán *m.*
sedate *adj* sosegado/da, tranquilo/la; ~ly *adv* tranquilamente.
sedateness *n* tranquilidad *f.*
sedative *n* sedativo *m.*
sedentary *adj* sedentario/ria.
sedge *n* (bot) juncia *f.*
sediment *n* sedimento *m*; hez *f*; poso *m.*
sedition *n* sedición *f*; tumulto, alboroto, motín *m*; revuelta *f.*
seditious *adj* sedicioso/sa.
seduce *vt* seducir; engañar.
seducer *n* seductor/a *m/f.*
seduction *n* seducción *f.*
seductive *adj* seductor/a.
sedulous *adj* asiduo/dua; ~ly *adv* asiduamente.
see *vt, vi* ver, observar, descubrir; advertir; conocer, juzgar; comprender; ~! ¡mira!
seed *n* semilla, simiente *f*; * *vi* granar.
seedling *n* plantón *m.*
seedsman *n* tratante en semillas *m.*
seedy *adj* desaseado/da.
seeing *conj*: ~ that visto que, ya que.
seek *vt, vi* buscar; pretender.
seem *vi* parecer, semejarse.
seeming *n* apariencia *f*; ~ly *adv* al parecer.
seemliness *n* decensia *f.*
seemly *adj* decente, propio/pia.
seer *n* profeta *m*, profetisa *f.*
seesaw *n* vaivén *m*; * *vi* balancear.
seethe *vi* hervir, bullir.
segment *n* segmento *m.*

seize *vt* asir, agarrar; secuestrar (bienes/ efectos).
seizure *n* captura *f*; secuestro *m*.
seldom *adv* raramente, rara vez.
select *vt* elegir, escoger; * *adj* selecto/ta, escogido/da.
selection *n* selección *f*.
self *n* uno/na mismo/ma; **the** ~ el yo; * *pref* auto-.
self-command *n* autocontrol *m*.
self-conceit *n* presunción *f*.
self-confident *adj* que tiene confianza en sí mismo/ma.
self-defense *n* defensa propia *f*.
self-denial *n* abnegación de sí mismo/ma *f*.
self-employed *adj* autónomo/ma, *Lat Am* cuentapropista.
self-evident *adj* obvio/via.
self-governing *adj* autónomo/ma.
self-interest *n* interés propio *m*.
selfish *adj* egoísta; ~**ly** *adv* interesadamente.
selfishness *n* egoísmo *m*.
self-medication *n* automedicación *f*.
self-pity *n* lástima de sí mismo/ma *f*.
self-portrait *n* autorretrato *m*.
self-possession *n* sangre fría, tranquilidad de ánimo *f*.
self-reliant *adj* independiente.
self-respect *n* amor propio *m*.
selfsame *adj* mismísimo/ma.
self-satisfied *adj* pagado/da de sí mismo/ ma.
self-seeking *adj* egoísta.
self-service *adj* de autoservicio.
self-styled *adj* autoproclamado/da.
self-sufficient *adj* autosuficiente.
self-taught *adj* autodidacta.
self-willed *adj* obstinado/da.
sell *vt, vi* vender; traficar.
seller *n* vendedor/a *m/f*.
selling-off *n* privatización *f*.
Sellotape™ *n* celo *m*.
semblance *n* semejanza, apariencia *f*.
semen *n* semen *m*.
semester *n* semestre *m*.
semicircle *n* semicírculo *m*.
semicircular *adj* semicircular.
semicolon *n* punto y coma *m*.
semiconductor *n* semiconductor *m*.
semifinal *n* semifinal *f*.
seminarist *n* seminarista *m*.
seminary *n* seminario *m*.
semitone *n* (*mus*) semitono *m*.
senate *n* senado *m*.

senator *n* senador/a *m/f*.
senatorial *adj* senatorio/ria.
send *vt* enviar, despachar, mandar; enviar; producir.
sender *n* remitente *m/f*.
senile *adj* senil.
senility *n* senectud *f*; vejez *f*.
senior *n* mayor *m*; * *adj* mayor; superior.
seniority *n* antigüedad, ancianidad *f*.
senna *n* (*bot*) sena *f*.
sensation *n* sensación *f*.
sense *n* sentido *m*; entendimiento *m*; razón *f*, juicio *m*; sentimiento *m*.
senseless *adj* insensible; insensato/ta; ~**ly** *adv* insensatamente.
senselessness *n* tontería, insensatez *f*.
sensibility *n* sensibilidad *f*.
sensible *adj* sensato/ta; juicioso/sa.
sensibly *adv* sensatamente.
sensitive *adj* sensible.
sensual, sensuous *adj*, ~**ly** *adv* sensual(mente).
sensuality *n* sensualidad *f*.
sentence *n* oración *f*; sentencia *f*; * *vt* sentenciar, condenar.
sententious *adj* sentencioso/sa; ~**ly** *adv* sentenciosamente.
sentient *adj* sensitivo/va.
sentiment *n* sentimiento *m*; opinión *f*.
sentimental *adj* sentimental.
sentinel, sentry *n* centinela *m*.
sentry box *n* garita *f*.
separable *adj* separable.
separate *vt* (*vi*) separar(se); * *adj* separado/ da; distinto/ta; ~**ly** *adv* separadamente.
separation *n* separación *f*.
September *n* septiembre *m*.
septennial *adj* sieteñal.
septuagenarian *n* septuagenario/ria *m/f*.
sepulchre *n* sepulcro *m*.
sequel *n* continuación *f*; consecuencia *f*.
sequence *n* serie, continuación *f*.
sequester, sequestrate *vt* secuestrar.
sequestration *n* secuestro *m*.
seraglio *n* serallo *m*.
seraph *n* serafín *m*.
serenade *n* serenata *f*; * *vt* dar serenatas.
serene *adj* sereno/na; ~**ly** *adv* serenamente.
serenity *n* serenidad *f*.
serf *n* siervo/va, esclavo/va *m/f*.
serge *n* sarga *f*.
sergeant *n* sargento/ta *m/f*; alguacil *m/f*.
serial *adj* consecutivo/va, en serie; * *n* serial *m*; telenovela *f*.
series *n* serie *f*.

serious *adj* serio/ria, grave; ~ly *adv* seriamente.

sermon *n* sermón *f*; oración evangélica *f*.

serpent *n* serpiente, sierpe *f*.

serpentine *adj* serpentino/na; * *n* (*chem*) serpentina *f*.

serrated *adj* serrado/da.

serum *n* suero *m*.

servant *n* criado *m*; criada *f*.

servant girl *n* criada *f*.

serve *vt, vi* servir; asistir (a la mesa); hacer; cumplir; sacar; ser a propósito; to ~ a warrant ejecutar un auto de prisión.

service *n* servicio *m*; servidumbre, utilidad *f*; culto divino *m*; acomodo *m*; * *vt* mantener; reparar.

serviceable *adj* servible; oficioso/sa.

service station *n* estación de servicio *f*; gasolinera *f*.

servile *adj* servil.

servitude *n* servidumbre, esclavitud *f*.

session *n* junta *f*; sesión *f*.

set *vt* poner, colocar, fijar; establecer, determinar; * *vi* ponerse (el sol/los astros); cuajarse; aplicarse; * *n* juego, conjunto *m*; servicio (de plata) *m*; conjunto/agregado de muchas cosas *m*; decorado *m*; set *m*; cuadrilla, bandada *f*; * *adj* puesto/ta, fijo/ja; listo/ta; decidido/da.

settee *n* sofá *m*.

setter *n* setter *m*.

setting *n* establecimiento *m*; marco *m*; montadura *f*; ~ of the sun puesta del sol *f*.

settle *vt* colocar, fijar, afirmar; arreglar; calmar; * *vi* repo sarse; establecerse; sosegarse.

settlement *n* establecimiento *m*; domicilio *m*; contrato *m*; empleo *m*; poso *m*; colonia *f*.

settler *n* colono/na *m/f*.

set-to *n* riña *f*; combate *m*.

seven *adj, n* siete.

seventeen *adj, n* diecisiete.

seventeenth *adj, n* decimoséptimo/ma.

seventh *adj, n* séptimo/ma.

seventieth *adj, n* septuagésimo/ma.

seventy *adj, n* setenta.

sever *vt, vi* separar.

several *adj, pn* varios/as, algunos/nas.

severance *n* separación *f*.

severe *adj* severo/ra, riguroso/sa, áspero/ra, duro/ra; ~ly *adv* severamente.

severity *n* severidad *f*.

sew *vt, vi* coser.

sewer *n* alcantarilla *f*.

sewerage *n* alcantarillado *m*.

sewing machine *n* máquina de coser *f*.

sex *n* sexo *m*.

sexist *adj, n* sexista *m/f*.

sextant *n* sextante *m*.

sexton *n* sepulturero/ra *m/f*.

sexual *adj* sexual.

sexy *adj* sexy.

shabbily *adv* vilmente, mezquinamente.

shabbiness *n* miseria *f*.

shabby *adj* desharrapado/da, zarrapastroso/sa.

shackle *vt* poner grilletes; ~s *npl* grilletes *mpl*.

shade *n* sombra, oscuridad *f*; matiz *m*; sombrilla *f*; * *vt* dar sombra a; abrigar; proteger.

shadiness *n* sombraje *m*; umbría *f*.

shadow *n* sombra *f*; protección *f*.

shadowy *adj* umbroso/sa; oscuro/ra; quimerico/ca.

shady *adj* opaco/ca, oscuro/ra, sombrío/ría.

shaft *n* flecha, saeta *f*; fuste de columna *m*; pozo *m*; hueco *m*; rayo *m*.

shag *n* tabaco picado *m*; cormorán moñudo *m*.

shaggy *adj* lanoso/sa.

shake *vt* sacudir; agitar; to ~ vigorously zarandear; to ~ hands darse las manos; * *vi* vacilar; temblar; * *n* sacudida *f*, *Lat Am* sacudón *m*; vibración *f*.

shaking *n* temblor *m*.

shaky *adj* titubeante.

shallow *adj* somero/ra, superficial; trivial.

shallowness *n* poca profundidad *f*; necedad *f*.

sham *vt* engañar; * *n* fingimiento *m*; impostura *f*; * *adj* fingido/da, disimulado/da.

shambles *npl* confusión *f*.

shame *n* vergüenza *f*; deshonra *f*; * *vt* avergonzar, deshonrar.

shamefaced *adj* vergonzoso/sa, pudoroso/sa.

shameful *adj* vergonzoso/sa; deshonroso/sa; ~ly *adv* ignominiosamente.

shameless *adj* desvergonzado/da; ~ly *adv* desvergonzadamente.

shamelessness *n* desvergüenza, impudencia *f*.

shammy, chamois *n* gamuza *f*.

shampoo *vt* lavar con champú; * *n* champú *m*.

shamrock *n* trébol *m*.

shank *n* caña *f*; asta (de ancla) *f*; cañón (de pipa) *m*.

shanty *n* chabola *f*.
shanty town *n* barrio de chabolas *m*, *Lat Am* barriada *f*.
shape *vt*, *vi* formar; proporcionar; concebir; * *n* forma, figura *f*; modelo *m*.
shapeless *adj* informe.
shapely *adj* bien hecho/cha.
share *n* parte, porción *f*; (*com*) acción *f*; reja del arado *f*; * *vt*, *vi* repartir; compartir.
sharer *n* partícipe *m/f*.
shark *n* tiburón *m*.
sharp *adj* agudo/da, aguzado/da; afilado/da, *Lat Am* filoso/sa; astuto/ta; perspicaz; penetrante; acre, mordaz, severo/ra, rígido/da; vivo/va, violento/ta; * *n* (*mus*) sostenido *m*; * *adv* en punto.
sharpen *vt* afilar, aguzar.
sharply *adv* con filo; severamente, agudamente; ingenios amente.
sharpness *n* agudeza *f*; sutileza, perspicacia *f*; acrimonia *f*.
shatter *vt* destrozar, estrellar; * *vi* hacerse pedazos.
shave *vt* afeitar, rasurar; * *vi* afeitarse, rasurarse; * *n* afeite *m*, *Lat Am* afeitada *f*.
shaver *n* máquina de afeitar *f*.
shaving *n* rasurado *m*.
shaving brush *n* brocha de afeitar *f*.
shaving cream *n* crema de afeitar *f*.
shawl *n* chal *m*, *Lat Am* rebozo *m*.
she *pn* ella.
sheaf *n* gavilla *f*; haz *m*.
shear *vt* atusar; tundir; ~s *npl* tijeras de podar *fpl*.
sheath *n* vaina *f*.
shed *vt* verter, derramar; esparcir; * *n* tejadillo *m*; cabaña *f*.
sheen *n* resplandor *m*.
sheep *n* oveja *f*.
sheepfold *n* redil *m*.
sheepish *adj* vergonzoso/sa; tímido/da.
sheepishness *n* timidez, cortedad de genio *f*.
sheepskin *n* piel de carnero *m*; zamarra *f*; ~ jacket zamarra *f*.
sheer *adj* puro/ra, claro/ra, sin mezcla; escarpado/da; * *adv* verticalmente.
sheet *n* sábana *f*; lámina *f*; pliego de papel *f*; (*mar*) escota *f*.
sheet anchor *n* áncora mayor de un navio *f*.
sheeting *n* tela para sábanas *f*.
sheet iron *n* chapa de hierro batido *f*.
sheet lightning *n* relampagueamiento *m*.
shelf *n* anaquel *m*; (*mar*) arrecife *m*; escollera *f*; on the ~ desecho/cha.

shell *n* cáscara *f*; proyectil *m*; concha *f*; corteza *f*; * *vt* descas carar, descortezar; bombardear; * *vi* descascararse.
shellfish *npl invar* crustáceo *m*; marisco *m*.
shelter *n* guardia *f*; amparo, abrigo *m*; asilo, refugio *m*; * *vt* guarecer, abrigar; acoger; * *vi* abrigarse.
shelve *vt* echar a un lado, arrinconar.
shelving *n* estantería *f*.
shepherd *n* pastor *m*.
shepherdess *n* pastora *f*.
sherbet *n* sorbete *m*.
sheriff *n* sheriff *m/f*.
sherry *n* jerez *m*.
shield *n* escudo *m*; patrocinio *m*; * *vt* defender.
shift *vi* cambiarse; moverse; * *vt* mudar, cambiar; transpor tar; * *n* cambio *m*; turno *m*.
shinbone *n* espinilla *f*.
shine *vi* lucir, brillar, resplandecer; * *vt* lustrar; * *n* brillo *m*.
shingle[1] *n* guijarros *mpl*.
shingle[2] *n* letrero con nombre del dueno *m*.
shingles *npl* (*med*) herpes *m invar*.
shining *adj* resplandeciente; * *n* esplendor *m*.
shiny *adj* brillante, luciente.
ship *n* nave *f*; barco *m*; navío, buque *m*; * *vt* embarcar; transportar.
shipbuilding *n* construcción naval *f*.
shipmate *n* (*mar*) ayudante *m/f*.
shipment *n* cargamento *mf*.
shipowner *n* naviero/ra *m/f*.
shipwreck *n* naufragio *m*.
shirt *n* camisa *f*.
shit *excl* (*col*) ¡mierda!
shiver *vi* tiritar de frío.
shoal *n* banco *m*.
shock *n* choque *m*; descarga *f*; susto *m*; * *vt* asustar; ofender.
shock absorber *n* amortiguador *m*.
shoddy *adj* de pacotilla.
shoe *n* zapato *m*; herradura *f*; * *vt* calzar; herrar.
shoe factory *n* zapatería *f*.
shoehorn *n* calzador *m*.
shoelace *n* cordón de zapato *m*.
shoemaker *n* zapatero/ra *m/f*.
shoemaking *n* zapatería *f*.
shoe shop/store *n* zapatería *f*.
shoestring *n* lazo de zapato *m*.
shoot *vt* tirar, arrojar, lanzar, disparar, *Lat Am* balacear, *Lat Am* balear; * *vi* brotar, germinar; sobresalir; lanzarse; * *n* vástago *m*.

shooter *n* tirador *m*.
shooting *n* caza con escopeta *f*; tiroteo *m*.
shop front, shop window *n* escaparate *m*, *Lat Am* vidriera *f*, *Lat Am* vitrina *f*.
shopkeeper *n* tendero/ra *m/f*.
shoplifter *n* ladrón/ona de tiendas *m/f*.
shopper *n* comprador/a *m/f*.
shopping *n* compras *fpl*.
shopping center *n* centro comercial *m*.
shopping mall *n* paseo *m*.
shore *n* costa, ribera, playa *f*.
short *adj* corto/ta, breve, sucinto/ta, conciso/sa; ~**ly** *adv* brevemente; pronto; en pocas palabras.
shortcoming *n* insuficiencia *f*; déficit *m*.
shorten *vt* acortar; abreviar.
shortness *n* cortedad *f*; brevedad *f*.
short-sighted *adj* miope, corto de vista.
short-sightedness *n* miopía *f*.
short wave *n* onda corta *f*.
shot *n* tiro *m*; alcance *m*; perdigones *mpl*; tentativa *f*; toma *f*.
shotgun *n* escopeta *f*.
shoulder *n* hombro *m*; brazuelo *m*; * *vt* cargar al hombro.
shout *vi* gritar, aclamar; * *vt* gritar; * *n* aclamación *f*, grito *m*.
shouting *n* gritos *mpl*.
shove *vt*, *vi* empujar; impeler; * *n* empujon *m*.
shovel *n* pala *f*; * *vt* traspalar.
show *vt* mostrar; descubrir, manifestar; probar, ensenar, explicar; * *vi* parecer; * *n* espectaculo *m*; muestra *f*; exposición, parada *f*.
show business *n* el mundo del espectaculo *m*.
shower *n* nubada *f*; llovizna *f*; ducha *f*, *Lat Am* baño *m*; (*fig*) abundancia *f*; * *vi* llover.
showery *adj* lluvioso/sa.
showjumping *n* hípica *f*.
showroom *n* sala de muestras *f*.
showy *adj* ostentoso/sa, suntuoso/sa.
shred *n* cacho, pedazo pequeño *m*; * *vt* hacer trizas.
shrew *n* mujer de mal genio *f*; musaraña *f*.
shrewd *adj* astuto/ta; maligno/gna; ~**ly** *adv* astutamente.
shrewdness *n* astucia *f*.
shriek *vt*, *vi* chillar; * *n* chillido *m*.
shrill *adj* agudo/da, penetrante.
shrillness *n* aspereza (del sonido/de la voz) *f*.
shrimp *n* camarón *m*; enano/na *m/f*, hombrecillo *m*.

shrine *n* relicario *m*.
shrink *vi* encogerse; angostarse, acortarse.
shrivel *vi* arrugarse, encogerse; * *vt* encoger.
shroud *n* cubierta *f*; mortaja *f*; * *vt* cubrir, defender; amortajar; proteger.
Shrove Tuesday *n* martes de carnaval *m*.
shrub *n* arbusto *m*.
shrubbery *n* plantio de arbustos *m*.
shrug *vt* encogerse de hombros; * *n* encogimiento de hombros *m*.
shudder *vi* estremecerse; * *n* temblor *m*.
shuffle *vt* desordenar; barajar.
shun *vt* huir, evitar.
shunt *vt* (*rail*) maniobrar.
shut *vt* cerrar, encerrar; *vi* cerrarse.
shutter *n* contraventana *f*.
shuttle *n* lanzadera *f*.
shuttlecock *n* volante, rehilete *m*.
shy *adj* tímido/da; reservado/da; vergonzoso/sa, contenido/da; ~**ly** *adv* tímidamente.
shyness *n* timidez *f*.
sibling *n* hermano/na *m/f*.
sibyl *n* sibila, profetisa *f*.
sick *adj* malo/la, enfermo/ma; disgustado/da.
sicken *vt* enfermar; * *vi* caer enfermo/ma.
sickle *n* hoz *f*.
sick leave *n* baja por enfermedad *f*.
sickliness *n* indisposición habitual *f*.
sickly *adj* enfermizo/za.
sickness *n* enfermedad *f*.
sick pay *n* subsidio por enfermedad *m*.
side *n* lado *m*; costado *m*; facción *f*; partido *m*; * *adj* lateral; oblicuo/cua; * *vi* unirse.
sideboard *n* aparador *m*; alacena *f*.
sidelight *n* luz lateral *f*.
sidelong *adj* lateral.
sidewalk *n* acera *f*.
sideways *adv* de lado, al través.
siding *n* toma de partido *f*; (*rail*) aguja *f*.
sidle *vi* ir de lado.
siege *n* (*mil*) sitio *m*.
sieve *n* tamiz *m*; criba *f*; colador *m*; * *vt* cribar.
sift *vt* cerner; cribar; examinar; investigar.
sigh *vi* suspirar, gemir; * *n* suspiro *m*.
sight *n* vista *f*; mira *f*; espectáculo *m*.
sightless *adj* ciego/ga.
sightly *adj* vistoso/sa, hermoso/sa.
sightseeing *n* excursionismo, turismo *m*.
sign *n* señal *f*, indicio *m*; letrero *m*; signo *m*; firma *f*; seña *f*; * *vt* firmar.
signal *n* señal *f*, aviso *m*; * *adj* insigne, señalado/da.
signalize *vt* señalar.
signal lamp *n* (*rail*) reflector de señales *m*.

signalman *n* (*rail*) guardavía *m*.
signature *n* firma *f*.
signet *n* sello *m*.
significance *n* importancia *f*.
significant *adj* significante.
signify *vt* significar.
signpost *n* indicador *m*.
silence *n* silencio *m*; * *vt* imponer silencio.
silent *adj* silencioso/sa; ~ly *adv* silenciosamente.
silex *n* sílex *m*.
silicon chip *n* chip de silicio *m*.
silk *n* seda *f*.
silken *adj* hecho/cha de seda; sedeño/ña.
silkiness *n* blandura, molicie *f*.
silkworm *n* gusano de seda *m*.
silky *adj* hecho/cha de seda; sedoso/sa.
sill *n* repisa *f*; umbral de puerta *m*.
silliness *n* simpleza, bobería, tontería, necedad *f*.
silly *adj* tonto/ta, imbécil; ñoño/ña.
silver *n* plata *f*; * *adj* de plata.
silversmith *n* platero/ra *m/f*.
silvery *adj* plateado/da.
similar *adj* similar; semejante; ~ly *adv* del mismo modo.
similarity *n* semejanza *f*.
simile *n* símil *m*.
simmer *vi* hervir a fuego lento.
simony *n* simonía *f*.
simper *vi* sonreír; * *n* sonrisa *f*.
simple *adj* simple, puro/ra, sencillo/lla.
simpleton *n* simplón/ona, simplonazo/za *m/f*.
simplicity *n* sencillez *f*; simpleza *f*.
simplification *n* simplificación *f*.
simplify *vt* simplificar.
simply *adv* sencillamente; solo.
simulate *vt* simular, fingir.
simulation *n* simulación *f*.
simultaneous *adj* simultáneo/nea.
sin *n* pecado *m*; * *vi* pecar, faltar.
since *adv* desde, entonces, después; * *prep* desde; * *conj* desde que; ya que.
sincere *adj* sencillo/lla; sincero/ra; ~ly *adv* sinceramente; yours ~ly le saluda atentamente.
sincerity *n* sinceridad *f*.
sinecure *n* sinecura *f*.
sinew *n* tendón *m*; nervio *m*.
sinewy *adj* nervioso/sa, robusto/sa.
sinful *adj* pecaminoso/sa, malvado/da; ~ly *adv* malvadamente.
sinfulness *n* corrupción *f*.
sing *vi*, *vt* cantar; gorjear; (*poet*) celebrar.

singe *vt* chamuscar.
singer *n* cantante *m/f*.
singing *n* canto *m*.
single *adj* sencillo/lla, simple, solo/la; soltero/ra; * *n* billete sencillo *m*; sencillo *m*; * *vt* singularizar; separar.
singly *adv* separadamente.
singular *adj* singular, peculiar; * *n* singular *m*; ~ly *adv* singularmente.
singularity *n* singularidad *f*.
sinister *adj* siniestro/tra, izquierdo/da; infeliz, funesto/ta.
sink *vi* hundirse; sumergirse; bajarse; arruinarse, decaer; * *vt* hundir, echar a lo hondo; destruir; * *n* fregadero *m*.
sinking fund *n* fondo de amortización *m*.
sinner *n* pecador/a *m/f*.
sinuosity *n* sinuosidad *f*.
sinuous *adj* sinuoso/sa.
sinus *n* seno *m*.
sip *vt* sorber; * *n* sorbo *m*.
siphon *n* sifón *m*.
sir *n* señor *m*.
sire *n* caballo padre *m*.
siren *n* sirena *f*.
sirloin *n* solomillo *m*.
sister *n* hermana *f*.
sisterhood *n* hermandad *f*.
sister-in-law *n* cuñada *f*.
sisterly *adj* de hermana.
sit *vi* sentarse; estar situado/da; * *vi* presentarse a.
sitcom *n* telecomedia *f*.
site *n* sitio *m*; situación *f*.
sit-in *n* ocupación *f*.
sitting *n* sesión, junta *f*; sentada *f*.
sitting room *n* sala de estar *f*.
situated *adj* situado/da.
situation *n* situación *f*.
six *adj*, *n* seis.
sixteen *adj*, *n* dieciséis.
sixteenth *adj*, *n* decimosexto/ta.
sixth *adj*, *n* sexto/ta.
sixtieth *adj*, *n* sexagésimo/ma.
sixty *adj*, *n* sesenta.
size *n* tamaño, talle *m*; calibre *m*; dimensión *f*; estatura *f*; condición *f*.
sizeable *adj* considerable.
skate *n* patín *m*; * *vi* patinar.
skateboard *n* monopatín *m*.
skating *n* patinaje *m*.
skating rink *n* pista de patinaje *f*.
skein *n* madeja *f*.
skeleton *n* esqueleto *m*.
skeleton key *n* llave maestra *f*.

skeptic n escéptico/ca m/f.
skeptic(al) adj escéptico/ca.
skepticism n escepticismo m.
sketch n esbozo m; esquicio m; * vt esquiciar, bosquejar.
skewer n aguja de lardear f; espetón m; * vt espetar.
ski n esquí m; * vi esquiar.
ski boot n bota de esquí f.
skid n patinazo m; * vi patinar.
skier n esquiador/a m/f.
skiing n esquí m.
skill n destreza, arte, pericia f.
skilled adj práctico/ca, instruido/da.
skillful adj práctico/ca, diestro/tra; ~ly adv diestramente.
skillfulness n destreza f.
skim vt espumar; tratar superficialmente.
skimmed milk n leche desnatada f.
skimmer, skimming ladle n espumadera f.
skin n piel f; cutis m; * vt desollar.
skin diving n buceo m.
skinned adj desollado/da.
skinny adj flaco/ca, macilento/ta.
skip vi saltar, brincar; * vt pasar, omitir; * n salto, brinco m; cuba f.
ski pants npl pantalones de esquí mpl.
skipper n capitán/ana m/f.
skirmish n escaramuza f; * vi escaramuzar.
skirt n falda, orla f; * vt orillar.
skit n burla, zumba f.
skittish adj espantadizo/za, retozón/ona; terco/ca; inconstante; ~ly adv caprichosamente.
skulk vi escuchar, acechar.
skull n cráneo m.
skullcap n casquete m.
sky n cielo, firmamento m.
skylight n claraboya f.
skyrocket n cohete m.
skyscraper n rascacielos m invar.
slab n losa f.
slack adj flojo/ja, perezoso/sa, negligente, lento/ta.
slack(en) vt, vi aflojar; ablandar; entibiarse; decaer; relajar; aliviar.
slacker n zángano m.
slackness n flojedad, remisión f; descuido m.
slag n escoria f.
slam vt cerrar de golpe; * vi cerrarse de golpe.
slander vt calumniar, infamar; * n calumnia f.
slanderer n calumniador/a, maldiciente m/f.

slanderous adj calumnioso/sa; ~ly adv calumniosamente.
slang n argot m; jerigonza f.
slant vi pender oblicuamente; * n sesgo m; interpretación f.
slanting adj sesgado/da, oblicuo/cua.
slap n manotazo m; bofetada f; * adv directamente; * vt golpear, dar una bofetada.
slash vt acuchillar; * n cuchillada f.
slate n pizarra f.
slater n pizarrero/ra m/f.
slating n techo de pizarras m.
slaughter n carnicería, matanza f; * vt matar atrozmente; hacer una matanza de.
slaughterer n matador/a, asesino/na m/f.
slaughterhouse n matadero m, Lat Am cuadro m.
slave n esclavo/va m/f; * vi trabajar como esclavo/va.
slaver n baba f; * vi babosear.
slavery n esclavitud f.
slavish adj servil, humilde; ~ly adv servilmente.
slavishness n bajeza, servidumbre f.
slay vt matar, quitar la vida.
slayer n matador/a m/f.
sleazy adj de mala fama.
sled, sleigh n trineo m.
sledgehammer n mazo m.
sleek adj liso/sa, brunido/da.
sleep vi dormir; * n sueño m.
sleeper n durmiente m.
sleepily adv con somnolencia/torpeza.
sleepiness n sueño m.
sleeping bag n saco m de dormir, Lat Am bolsa f de dormir.
sleeping pill n somnífero m.
sleepless adj desvelado/da.
sleepwalking n sonambulismo m.
sleepy adj soñoliento/ta.
sleet n aguanieve f.
sleeve n manga f.
sleight n: ~ of hand escamoteo m.
slender adj delgado/da, débil, pequeño/ña, escaso/sa; ~ly adv delgadamente.
slenderness n delgadez f; tenuidad f; pequeñez f.
slice n rebanada f; espátula f; * vt rebanar.
slide vi resbalar, deslizarse; correr por encima del hielo; * n resbalón m; corredera f; diapositiva f; tobogán m.
sliding adj corredizo/za.
slight adj ligero/ra, leve, pequeño/ña; * n descuido m; * vt despreciar.

slightly *adv* ligeramente.
slightness *n* debilidad *f*; negligencia *f*.
slim *adj* delgado/da; * *vi* adelgazar.
slime *n* lodo *m*, *Lat Am* lama *f*; substancia viscosa *f*.
sliminess *n* viscosidad *f*.
slimming *n* adelgazamiento *m*.
slimy *adj* viscoso/sa, pegajoso/sa.
sling *n* honda *f*; cabestrillo *m*; * *vt* tirar.
slink *vi* escaparse; esconderse.
slip *vi* resbalar; escapar, huirse; * *vt* deslizar; * *n* resbalón *m*, *Lat Am* resbalada *f*; tropiezo *m*; escapada *f*; papelito *m*.
slipper *n* zapatilla *f*.
slippery *adj* resbaladizo/za.
slipshod *adj* descuidado/da.
slipway *n* grada *f*, gradas *fpl*.
slit *vt* rajar, hender; * *n* raja, hendedura *f*.
slobber *n* baba *f*.
sloe *n* endrina *f*.
slogan *n* eslogan, lema *m*.
sloop *n* (*mar*) balandro *m*.
slop *n* aguachirle *f*; lodazal *m*; ~s *pl* gachas *fpl*.
slope *n* cuesta *f*; sesgo *m*; declivio *m*; escarpa *f*; * *vt* sesgar.
sloping *adj* oblicuo/cua; en declive.
sloppy *adj* descuidado/da; desaliñado/da.
sloth *n* pereza *f*.
slouch *vt, vi* estar cabizbajo/ja; bambolearse pesadamente.
slovenliness *n* desaliño *m*; porquería *f*.
slovenly *adj* desaliñado/da, puerco/ca, sucio/cia.
slow *adj* tardío/día, lento/ta, torpe, perezoso/sa; ~ly *adv* lentamente, despacio.
slowness *n* lentitud, tardanza, pesadez *f*.
slowworm *n* lución *m*.
slug *n* holgazán/ana *m/f*, zángano *m*; babosa *f*; ficha *f*; trago *m*.
sluggish *adj* perezoso/sa; lento/ta; ~ly *adv* perezosamente.
sluggishness *n* pereza *f*.
sluice *n* compuerta *f*; * *vt* soltar la compuerta de.
slum *n* tugurio *m*; barrio bajo *m*.
slumber *vi* dormitar; * *n* sueño ligero *m*.
slump *n* depresión *f*.
slur *vt* ensuciar; calumniar; pronunciar mal; * *n* calumnia *f*.
slush *n* lodo, barro, cieno *m*.
slut *n* marrana *f*.
sly *adj* astuto/ta; ~ly *adv* astutamente.
slyness *n* astucia, maña *f*.
smack *n* sabor, gusto *m*; beso fuerte (que se

oye) *m*; chasquido de latigo *m*; * *vi* saber; besar con ruido; * *vt* golpear.
small *adj* pequeño/ña, menudo/da.
smallish *adj* algo pequeño/ña.
smallness *n* pequeñez *f*.
smallpox *n* viruelas *fpl*.
small talk *n* charla, prosa *f*.
smart *adj* elegante; listo/ta, ingenioso/sa; vivo/va; * *vi* escocer.
smartly *adv* agudamente, vivamente; elegantemente; inteligentemente.
smartness *n* agudeza, viveza, sutileza *f*.
smash *vt* romper, quebrantar; estrellar; batir; * *vi* hacerse pedazos; estrellarse; * *n* fracaso *m*; choque *m*.
smattering *n* conocimiento superficial *m*.
smear *n* mancha *f*; (*med*) frotis *m invar*; ~ test *Lat Am* Papanicolau *m*; * *vt* untar; difamar.
smell *vt, vi* oler; * *n* olfato *m*; olor *m*; hediondez *f*.
smelly *adj* maloliente.
smelt *n* espirenque de mar *m*; † *vt* fundir (el metal).
smelter *n* fundidor/a *m/f*.
smile *vi* sonreír; * *n* sonrisa *f*.
smirk *vi* sonreír.
smite *vt* herir; afligir.
smith *n* herrero/rra *m/f*.
smithy *n* herrería *f*.
smock *n* camisa de mujer *f*.
smoke *n* humo *m*; vapor *m*; * *vt, vi* ahumar; humear; fumar.
smoked herring, kipper *n* arenque ahumado *m*.
smokeless *adj* sin humo.
smoker *n* fumador/a *m/f*.
smoking: no ~ prohibido fumar.
smoky *adj* humeante; humoso/sa.
smooth *adj* liso/sa, pulido/da, llano/na; suave; afable; * *vt* allanar; alisar; lisonjear.
smoothly *adv* llanamente; con blandura.
smoothness *n* lisura *f*; llanura *f*; suavidad *f*.
smother *vt* sofocar; suprimir.
smolder *vi* arder debajo la ceniza.
smudge *vt* manchar; * *n* mancha *f*.
smug *adj* presumido/da.
smuggle *vt* pasar de contrabando.
smuggler *n* contrabandista *m/f*.
smuggling *n* contrabando *m*.
smut *n* tiznón *m*; suciedad *f*.
smuttiness *n* obscenidad *f*.
smutty *adj* tiznado/da; obsceno/na.
snack *n* bocado, bocadillo *m*, pinchito *m*.
snack bar *n* cafetería *f*.

snag *n* problema *m*.

snail *n* caracol *m*.

snake *n* serpiente, culebra *f*.

snaky *adj* serpentino/na.

snap *vt, vi* romper; agarrar; morder; insultar; to ~ one's fingers castañetear; * *n* estallido *m*; foto *f*.

snapdragon *n* (*bot*) boca de dragón *f*.

snare *n* lazo *m*; trampa *f*.

snarl *vi* regañar, gruñir.

snatch *vt* arrebatar; agarrar; * *n* arrebatamiento *m*; robo *m*; bocado *m*.

sneak *vi* arrastrar; * *n* soplón/ona *m/f*.

sneakers *npl* zapatillas de lona *fpl*.

sneer *vi* hablar con desprecio.

sneeringly *adv* con desprecio.

sneeze *vi* estornudar.

sniff *vt* oler; * *vi* resollar con fuerza.

snigger *vi* reír disimuladamente.

snip *vt* tijeretear; * *n* tijeretada *f*, pedazo pequeño *m*; porción *f*.

snipe *n* agachadiza *f*; zopenco *m*.

sniper *n* francotirador/a *m/f*.

snivel *n* moquita *f*; * *vi* moquear.

sniveler *n* lloraduelos *m invar*.

snob *n* (e)snob *m/f*.

snobbish *adj* esnob.

snooze *n* sueño ligero *m*; * *vi* echar una siesta.

snore *vi* roncar.

snorkel *n* (tubo)respirador *m*.

snort *vi* resoplar.

snout *n* hocico *m*; morro *m*.

snow *n* nieve *f*; * *vi* nevar.

snowball *n* bola de nieve *f*.

snowdrop *n* (*bot*) campanilla blanca *f*.

snowman *n* muñeco de nieve *m*.

snowplow *n* quitanieves *m invar*.

snowy *adj* nevoso/sa; nevado/da.

snub *vt* reprender, regañar.

snub-nosed *adj* chato/ta; ñato/ta.

snuff *n* rapé *m*.

snuffbox *n* tabaquera *f*.

snuffle *vi* ganguear, hablar gangoso.

snug *adj* abrigado/da; conveniente, cómodo/da, agradable, grato/ta.

so *adv* así; de este modo; tan.

soak *vi, vt* remojarse; calarse; empapar, remojar.

so-and-so *n* zutano/na *m/f*.

soap *n* jabón *m*; * *vt* jabonar.

soap bubble *n* burbuja de jabón *f*.

soap opera *n* telenovela *f*.

soap powder *n* jabón en polvo *m*.

soapsuds *n* jabonaduras *fpl*.

soapy *adj* jabonoso/sa.

soar *vi* remontarse, sublimarse.

sob *n* sollozo *m*; * *vi* sollozar.

sober *adj* sobrio/ria; serio/ria; ~ly *adv* sobriamente; juiciosamente.

sobriety *n* sobriedad *f*; seriedad, sangre fria *f*.

soccer *n* fútbol *m*.

sociability *n* sociabilidad *f*.

sociable *adj* sociable, comunicativo/va.

sociably *adv* sociablemente.

social *adj* social, sociable; ~ly *adv* sociablemente.

socialism *n* socialismo *m*.

socialist *n* socialista *m/f*.

social work *n* asistencia social *f*.

social worker *n* asistente/ta social *m/f*.

society *n* sociedad *f*; compañia *f*.

sociologist *n* sociólogo/ga *m/f*.

sociology *n* sociología *f*.

sock *n* calcetín *m*; media *f*.

socket *n* enchufe *m*, Lat Am tomacorriente *f*.

socket *n* enchufe *m*.

sod *n* césped *m*.

soda *n* sosa *f*; gaseosa *f*.

sofa *n* sofá *m*.

soft *adj* blando/da, suave; benigno/na, tierno/na; afeminado/da; mullido/da; ~ly *adv* suavemente; paso a paso.

soften *vt* ablandar, mitigar; enternecer.

soft-hearted *adj* compasivo/va.

softness *n* blandura, dulzura *f*.

soft-spoken *adj* de voz suave.

software *n* (*comput*) software *m*.

soil *vt* ensuciar, emporcar; * *n* mancha, porquería *f*; terreno *m*; tierra *f*.

sojourn *vi* residir, morar; * *n* morada *f*; residencia *f*.

solace *vt* solazar, consolar; * *n* consuelo *m*.

solar *adj* solar; ~ energy energía solar *f*.

solder *vt* soldar; * *n* soldadura *f*.

soldier *n* soldado/da *m/f*; militar *m*.

soldierly *adj* soldadesco/ca.

sole *n* planta (del pie) *f*; suela (del zapato) *f*; lenguado *m*; * *adj* único/ca, solo/la.

solecism *n* (*gr*) solecismo *m*.

solemn *adj*, ~ly *adv* solemne(mente).

solemnity *n* solemnidad *f*.

solemnize *vt* solemnizar.

solicit *vt* solicitar; implorar.

solicitation *n* solicitación *f*.

solicitor *n* representante, agente *m/f*.

solicitous *adj* solícito/ta, diligente; ~ly *adv* solícitamente.

solicitude *n* solicitud *f*.

solid adj sólido/da, compacto/ta; * n sólido m; ~ly adv sólidamente.
solidify vt solidificar.
solidity n solidez f.
soliloquy n soliloquio m.
solitaire n solitario m.
solitary adj solitario/ria, retirado/da; * n ermitaño/ña m/f.
solitude n soledad f; vida solitaria f.
solo n (mus) solo/la m.
solstice n solsticio m.
soluble adj soluble.
solution n solución f.
solve vt resolver.
solvency n solvencia f.
solvent adj solvente; n (chem) solvente m.
some adj algo de, un poco, algún, alguno, alguna, unos, pocos, ciertos.
somebody n alguien m.
somehow adv de algún modo.
someplace adv en alguna parte; a alguna parte.
something n alguna cosa, algo.
sometime adv algún día.
sometimes adv a veces.
somewhat adv algo; algún tanto, un poco.
somewhere adv en alguna parte; a alguna parte.
somnambulism n sonambulismo m.
somnambulist n sonámbulo/la m/f.
somnolence n somnolencia f.
somnolent adj somnoliento/ta.
son n hijo m.
sonata n (mus) sonata f.
song n canción f.
son-in-law n yerno m.
sonnet n soneto m.
sonorous adj sonoro/ra.
soon adv ya, pronto; as ~ as luego que.
sooner adv antes, más pronto.
soot n hollín m.
soothe vt adular; calmar.
soothsayer n adivino/na m/f.
sop n sopa f.
sophism n sofisma m.
sophist n sofista m/f.
sophistical adj sofístico/ca.
sophisticate vt sofisticar; falsificar.
sophisticated adj sofisticado/da.
sophistry n sofisteria f.
soporific adj soporífero/ra.
sorcerer n hechicero m.
sorceress n hechicera f.
sorcery n hechizo, encanto m.

sordid adj sórdido/da, sucio/cia; asqueroso/sa.
sordidness n sordidez, suciedad f.
sore n llaga, úlcera f; * adj doloroso/sa, penoso/sa; resentido/da; ~ly adv penosamente.
sorrel n (bot) acedera f; * adj alazán rojo/ja.
sorrow n pesar m; tristeza f; * vi entristecerse.
sorrowful adj pesaroso/sa, afligido/da; ~ly adv con aflicción.
sorry adj triste, afligido/da; arrepentido/da; 1 am ~ lo siento.
sort n suerte f; género m; especie f; calidad f; manera f; * vt separar en distintas clases; escoger, elegir.
soul n alma f; esencia f; persona f.
sound adj sano/na; entero/ra; puro/ra; firme; ~ly adv sanamente, vigo rosamente; * n sonido, ruido m; estrecho m; * vt sonar; tocar; celebrar; sondar; * vi sonar, resonar; parecer.
sounding board n diapasón m; sombrero de púlpito m.
sound effects npl efectos sonoros mpl.
soundings npl (mar) sondeo m; (mar) surgidero m.
soundness n sanidad f; fuerza, solidez f.
soundtrack n banda sonora f.
soup n sopa f.
sour adj agrio/ria, ácido/da; cortado/da; áspero/ra; ~ly adv agriamente; * vt, vi agriar, acedar; agriarse.
source n manantial m; principio m.
sourness n acedía, agrura f; acrimonia f.
souse n (col) borracho/cha m/f; * vt escabechar; chapuzar.
souvenir n recuerdo m.
south n sur m; * adj del sur; * adv al sur.
southerly, southern adj del sur, meridional.
southward(s) adv hacia el sur.
southwester n (mar) viento de sudoeste m; sombrero grande de los marineros m.
sovereign adj, n soberano/na m/f.
sovereignty n soberanía f.
sow[1] n puerca, marrana f.
sow[2] vt sembrar; esparcir.
sowing time n sementera, siembra f.
soybean n semilla de soja f.
space n espacio m; intersticio m; * vt espaciar.
spacecraft n nave espacial f.
spaceman n astronauta m.
spacewoman n astronauta f.

spacious *adj* espacioso/sa, amplio/lia; **~ly** *adv* con bastante espacio.

spaciousness *n* espaciosidad *f.*

spade *n* laya, azada *f;* pica (en los naipes) *f.*

spaghetti *n* espaguetis *mpl.*

span *n* palmo *m;* envergadura *f;* * *vt* cruzar; abarcar.

spangle *n* lentejuela *f;* * *vt* adornar con lentejuelas.

spaniel *n* perro de aguas *m.*

Spanish *adj, n* español/a *m/f;* ~ **musical comedy/light opera** zarzuela *f.*

Spanish America *n* Hispanoamérica *f.*

Spanish American *adj* hispanoamericano/na; * *n* hispanoamericano/na *m/f.*

spar *n* palo *m;* * *vi* entrenarse.

spare *vt, vi* ahorrar, economizar; perdonar; pasarse sin; vivir con economía; * *adj* de más; de reserva.

sparing *adj* escaso/sa, raro/ra, económico/ca; **~ly** *adv* parcamente, frugalmente.

spark *n* chispa *f.*

sparkle *n* centella, chispa *f;* * *vi* chispear; espumar.

spark plug *n* bujía *f.*

sparrow *n* gorrión *m.*

sparrowhawk *n* gavilán *m.*

sparse *adj* delgado/da; tenue; **~ly** *adv* tenuemente.

spasm *n* espasmo *m.*

spasmodic *adj* espasmódico/ca.

spatter *vt* salpicar, manchar.

spatula *n* espátula *f.*

spawn *n* freza *f;* * *vt, vi* desovar; engendrar.

spawning *n* freza *f.*

speak *vt, vi* hablar; decir; conversar; pronunciar.

speaker *n* altavoz *m, Lat Am* parlante *m;* bafle *m;* orador/a *m/f.*

spear *n* lanza *f;* arpón *m;* * *vt* herir con lanza.

special *adj* especial, particular; **~ly** *adv* especialmente.

specialty *n* especialidad *f.*

species *n* especie *f.*

specific *adj* específico/ca; * *n* específico *m.*

specifically *adv* específicamente.

specification *n* especificación *f.*

specify *vt* especificar.

specimen *n* muestra *f;* prueba *f.*

specious *adj* especioso/sa.

speck(le) *n* mácula, tacha *f;* * *vt* abigarrar, manchar.

spectacle *n* espectáculo *m.*

spectacles *npl* gafas *fpl.*

spectator *n* espectador/a *m/f.*

spectral *adj* espectral; ~ **analysis** *n* análisis espectral *m invar.*

specter *n* espectro *m.*

speculate *vi* especular; reflexionar.

speculation *n* especulación *f;* especulativa *f;* meditación *f.*

speculative *adj* especulativo/va, teórico/ca.

speculum *n* espéculo *m.*

speech *n* habla *m;* discurso *m;* lenguaje *m;* conversación *f.*

speechify *vi* arengar.

speechless *adj* sin habla.

speed *n* prisa *f;* velocidad *f;* * *vt* apresurar; despachar; * *vi* darse prisa.

speedboat *n* lancha motora *f.*

speedily *adv* aceleradamente, deprisa.

speediness *n* celeridad, prontitud, precipitación *f.*

speed limit *n* límite de velocidad *m,* velocidad maxima *f.*

speedometer *n* velocímetro *m.*

speedway *n* pista de carreras *f.*

speedy *adj* veloz, pronto/ta, diligente.

spell *n* hechizo, encanto *m;* período *m;* * *vt, vi* escribir correc tamente; deletrear; hechizar, encantar.

spelling *n* ortografía *f.*

spend *vt* gastar; pasar; disipar; consumir.

spendthrift *n* despilfarrador/a *m/f.*

spent *adj* agotado/da.

sperm *n* esperma *f.*

spermaceti *n* espermaceti *m.*

spew *vi* (*col*) vomitar.

sphere *n* esfera *f.*

spherical *adj* esférico/ca; **~ly** *adv* en forma esférica.

spice *n* especia *f;* * *vt* especiar.

spick-and-span *adj* aseado/da, (bien) arreglado/da.

spicy *adj* aromático/ca.

spider *n* araña *f.*

spigot *n* grifo *m.*

spike *n* espiga de grano *f;* espigón *m;* * *vi* clavar con espi gones.

spill *vt* derramar, verter; * *vi* derramarse.

spin *vt* hilar; alargar, prolongar; girar; * *vi* dar vueltas; * *n* vuelta *f;* paseo (en coche) *m.*

spinach *n* espinaca *f.*

spinal *adj* espinal.

spindle *n* huso *m;* quicio *m.*

spine *n* espinazo *m,* espina *f.*

spineless *adj* ñoño/ña.

spinet *n* (*mus*) espineta *f.*

spinner *n* hilador/a *m/f;* hilandero/ra *m/f.*

spinning top *n* trompa *f.*

spinning wheel *n* rueca *f.*
spin-off *n* derivado, producto secundario *m.*
spinster *n* soltera *f.*
spiral *adj* espiral; ~ly *adv* en figura de espiral.
spire *n* espira *f;* pirámide *m;* aguja *f* (de una torre).
spirit *n* aliento *m;* espíritu *m;* ánimo, valor *m;* brío *m;* humor *m;* fantasma *m;* * *vt* incitar, animar; **to ~ away** quitar secretamente.
spirited *adj* vivo/va, brioso/sa; ~ly *adv* con espíritu.
spirit lamp *n* velón/quinque de alcohol *m.*
spiritless *adj* abatido/da, sin espíritu.
spiritual *adj,* ~ly *adv* espiritual(mente).
spiritualist *n* espiritista *m/f.*
spirituality *n* espiritualidad *f.*
spit *n* asador *m;* saliva *f;* * *vt, vi* espetar; escupir.
spite *n* rencor *m,* malevolencia *f;* **in ~ of** a pesar de, a despe cho; * *vt* dar pesar.
spiteful *adj* rencoroso/sa, malicioso/sa; ~ly *adv* malignamente, con tirria.
spitefulness *n* malicia *f;* rencor *m.*
spittle *n* saliva *f;* baba *f,* esputo *m.*
splash *vt* salpicar, enlodar; * *vi* chapotear; * *n* chapoteo *m;* mancha *f.*
spleen *n* bazo *m;* esplín *m.*
splendid *adj* espléndido/da, magnífico/ca; ~ly *adv* espléndidamente.
splendor *n* esplendor *m;* pompa *f.*
splice *vt* (*mar*) empalmar, empleitar.
splint *n* tablilla *f.*
splinter *n* cacho *m;* astilla *f;* brisna *f;* * *vt* (*vi*) hender(se).
split *n* hendedura *f;* división *f;* * *vt* hender, rajar; * *vi* hen derse.
splutter, sputter *vi* escupir con frecuencia; babosear; barbotar.
spoil *vt* despojar; arruinar; mimar.
spoiled *adj* pasado/da; cortado/da.
spoke *n* radio (de la rueda) *m.*
spokesman *n* portavoz *m,* *Lat Am* personero *m,* *Lat Am* vocero *m.*
spokeswoman *n* portavoz *f,* *Lat Am* personera *f,* *Lat Am* vocera *f.*
sponge *n* esponja *f;* * *vt* limpiar con esponja; * *vi* meterse de mogollón.
sponger *n* mogollón *m.*
sponginess *n* esponjosidad *f.*
spongy *adj* esponjoso/sa.
sponsor *n* patrocinador/a *m/f;* padrino *m;* madrina *f.*
sponsorship *n* patrocinio *m.*

spontaneity *n* espontaneidad, voluntariedad *f.*
spontaneous *adj* espontáneo/nea; ~ly *adv* espontaneamente.
spool *n* carrete *m;* canilla, broca *f.*
spoon *n* cuchara *f.*
spoonful *n* cucharada *f.* ·
sporadic(al) *adj* esporádico/ca.
sport *n* deporte *m;* juego, retozo *m;* juguete, divertimiento, recreo, pasatiempo *m.*
sports car *n* coche deportivo *m.*
sports coat, sports jacket *n* chaqueta deportiva *f.*
sportsman *n* deportista *m.*
sportswear *n* ropa de deporte/sport *f.*
sportswoman *n* deportista *f.*
spot *n* mancha *f;* borrón *m;* sitio, lugar *m;* grano *m;* * *vt* notar; manchar.
spotless *adj* limpio/pia, inmaculado/da.
spotlight *n* foco, reflector *m.*
spotted, spotty *adj* lleno/na de manchas; con granos.
spouse *n* esposo/a *m/f.*
spout *vi* borbotar; chorrear; * *vt* arrojar; vomitar; (*fig*) declamar; * *n* piton *m,* pico *m.*
sprain *adj* descoyuntar; * *n* dislocación *f.*
sprat *n* meleta, nuesa (pez) *f.*
sprawl *vi* revolcarse.
spray *n* rociada *f;* espray *m;* ramita *f;* espuma de la mar *f.*
spread *vt* extender, desplegar; esparcir, divulgar; * *vi* extenderse, desplegarse; * *n* extensión, dilatación *f.*
spree *n* fiesta *f;* juerga *f.*
sprig *n* ramito *m.*
sprightliness *n* alegría, vivacidad *f.*
sprightly *adj* alegre, despierto/ta, vivaracho/cha.
spring *vi* brotar, arrojar; nacer, provenir; dimanar, origi narse; saltar, brincar; * *n* primavera *f;* elasticidad *f;* muelle, resorte *m;* salto *m;* manantial *m.*
springiness *n* elasticidad *f.*
spring onion *n* cebolleta *f.*
springtime *n* primavera *f.*
spring water *n* agua de fuente *f.*
springy *adj* elástico/ca; mullido/da.
sprinkle *vt* rociar.
sprinkling *n* rociadura *f.*
sprout *n* vástago, renuevo *m;* ~s *npl* coles de Bruselas *fpl;* * *vi* brotar.
spruce *adj* pulido/da, gentil; ~ly *adv* bellamente, lindamente; * *vr* vestirse con afectación.

spruceness *n* lindeza, hermosura *f.*
spur *n* espuela *f;* espolón (del gallo) *m;* estímulo *m;* * *vt* espolear, *Lat Am* talonear; estimular.
spurious *adj* espurio/ria, falso/sa; contrahecho/cha; supuesto/ta; bastardo/da.
spurn *vt* despreciar.
spy *n* espía *m/f;* * *vt, vi* espiar.
squabble *vi* reñir, disputar; * *n* riña, disputa *f.*
squad *n* escuadra *f;* brigada *f;* equipo *m.*
squadron *n* (*mil*) escuadrón *m.*
squalid *adj* sucio/cia, puerco/ca.
squall *n* ráfaga *f;* chubasco *m;* * *vi* chillar.
squally *adj* borrascoso/sa.
squalor *n* porquería, suciedad *f.*
squander *vt* malgastar, disipar.
square *adj* cuadrado/da, cuadrángulo/la; exacto/ta; cabal; * *n* cuadro *m;* plaza *f;* escuadra *f;* * *vt* cuadrar; ajustar, arreglar; * *vi* ajustarse.
squareness *n* cuadratura *f.*
squash *vt* aplastar; * *n* squash *m.*
squat *vi* agacharse; * *adj* agachado/da; rechoncho/cha.
squatter *n* ocupante ilegal *m/f; (col)* okupa *m/f.*
squaw *n* mujer de un indio *f.*
squeak *vi* plañir, chillar; * *n* grito, plañido *m.*
squeal *vi* plañir, gritar.
squeamish *adj* fastidioso/sa; demasiado delicado/da.
squeeze *vt* apretar, comprimir; estrechar; * *n* presión *f;* apre ton *m;* restricción *f.*
squid *n* calamar *m.*
squint *adj* bizco/ca; * *vi* bizquear; * *n* estrabismo.
squirrel *n* ardilla *f.*
squirt *vt* jeringar; * *n* jeringa *f;* chorro *m;* pisaverde *m.*
stab *vt* apuñalar; * *n* puñalada *f.*
stability *n* estabilidad, solidez *f.*
stable *n* establo *m;* * *vt* poner en el establo; * *adj* estable.
stack *n* pila *f;* * *vt* hacinar.
staff *n* personal *m,* plantilla *f;* palo *m;* apoyo *m.*
stag *n* ciervo *m.*
stage *n* etapa *f;* escena *f;* tablado *m;* teatro *m;* parada *f;* escalón *m.*
stagger *vi* vacilar, titubear; estar incierto/ta; * *vt* asustar; esca lonar.
stagnant *adj* estancado/da.
stagnate *vi* estancarse.

stagnation *n* estancamiento *m.*
staid *adj* grave, serio/ria.
stain *vt* manchar; empañar la reputación de; * *n* mancha *f;* deshonra *f.*
stainless *adj* limpio/pia; inmaculado/da.
stair *n* escalón *m;* ~s *pl* escalera *f.*
staircase *n* escalera *f.*
stake *n* estaca *f;* apuesta (en el juego) *f;* * *vt* estacar; apostar.
stale *adj* añejo/ja, viejo/ja, rancio/cia, *Lat Am* zocato/ta.
staleness *n* vejez *f;* rancidez *f.*
stalk *vi* andar con paso majestuoso; * *n* tallo, pie, tronco *m;* troncho *m* (de ciertas hortalizas).
stall *n* pesebre *m;* puesto *m;* tabanco *m;* emplazamiento *m;* * *vt* parar; * *vi* pararse; buscar evasivas.
stallion *n* semental *m;* caballo entero *m.*
stalwart *n* partidario/ria leal *m/f.*
stamen *n* estambre *m;* fundamento *m.*
stamina *n* resistencia *f.*
stammer *vi* tartamudear; * *n* tartamudeo *m.*
stamp *vt* patear; estampar, imprimir; acuñar; andar con mucha pesadez; * *vi* patear; * *n* cuño *m;* sello *m;* impresión *f;* huella *f; Lat Am* estampilla *f;* zapatazo *m.*
stampede *n* estampida *f.*
stand *vi* estar de pie; ponerse de pie, *Lat Am* pararse; sostenerse; permanecer; pararse, hacer alto, estar situado/da; hallarse; erizarse (el pelo); * *vt* poner; aguantar; sostener, defender; * *n* puesto, sitio *m;* posición, situación *f;* parada *f;* estado *m* (fijo); tribuna *f;* stand *m.*
standard *n* estandarte *m;* modelo *m;* precio ordinario *m;* norma *f;* * *adj* normal.
standing *adj* permanente, fijado/da, establecido/da; de pie, *Lat Am* parado/da; estancado/da; * *n* duración *f;* posición *f;* puesto *m.*
standstill *n* pausa *f;* alto *m.*
staple *n* grapa *f;* * *adj* básico/ca, establecido/da; * *vt* grapar, *Lat Am* engrapar.
star *n* estrella *f;* asterisco *m.*
starboard *n* estribor *m.*
starch *n* almidón *m;* * *vt* almidonar.
stare *vi:* **to ~ at** clavar la vista en; * *n* mirada fija *f.*
stark *adj* fuerte, áspero/ra; puro/ra; * *adv* del todo.
starling *n* estornino *m.*
starry *adj* estrellado/da.
start *vi* empezar; sobrecogerse, sobresaltarse; levantarse de repente; salir; * *vt* empezar;

causar; fundar; poner en marcha; * *n*
principio *m;* salida *f;* sobresalto *m;* ímpetu
m; paso primero *m.*
starter *n* estárter *m;* juez de salida *m.*
starting point *n* punto de partida *m.*
startle *vt* sobresaltar.
startling *adj* alarmante.
starvation *n* hambre, inanición *f.*
starve *vi* pasar hambre.
state *n* estado *m;* condición *f;* estado
(político); pompa, gran deza *f;* the S~s los
Estados Unidos *mpl;* * *vt* afirmar; exponer.
stateliness *n* grandeza, pompa *f.*
stately *adj* augusto/ta, majestuoso/sa.
statement *n* afirmación, cuenta *f.*
statesman *n* estadista, político *m.*
statesmanship *n* política *f.*
static *adj* estático/ca; * *n* parásitos *mpl.*
station *n* estación *f;* emisora *f;* empleo,
puesto *m;* situación *f;* condición *f;* (*rail*)
estación; * *vt* apostar.
stationary *adj* estacionario/ria, fijo/ja.
stationer *n* papelero/ra *m/f.*
stationery *n* papelería *f.*
station wagon *n* ranchera *f.*
statistical *adj* estadístico/ca.
statistics *npl* estadística *f.*
statuary *n* estatuario/ria, escultor/a *m/f.*
statue *n* estatua *f.*
stature *n* estatura, talla *f.*
statute *n* estatuto *m;* reglamento *m.*
stay *n* estancia *f, Lat Am* estadía *f;* ~s *npl*
corsé, justillo *m;* * *vi* quedarse, estarse;
detenerse; esperarse; to ~ in quedarse en
casa; to ~ on quedarse; to ~ up velar.
steadfast *adj* firme, estable, sólido/da; ~ly
adv firmemente, con constancia.
steadily *adv* firmemente; invariablemente.
steadiness *n* firmeza, estabilidad *f.*
steady *adj* firme, fijo/ja; * *vt* hacer firme.
steak *n* filete *m;* bistec *m.*
steal *vt, vi* robar.
stealth *n* hurto *m;* by ~ a hurtadillas.
stealthily *adv* furtivamente.
stealthy *adj* furtivo/va.
steam *n* vapor *m;* humo *m;* * *vt* cocer al
vapor; * *vi* echar humo.
steam-engine *n* máquina de vapor *f.*
steamer, steamboat *n* vapor, buque de vapor *m.*
steel *n* acero *m;* * *adj* de acero.
steelyard *n* romana *f.*
steep *adj* escarpado/da; excesivo/va; * *vt*
empapar.
steeple *n* torre *f;* campanario *m.*

steeplechase *n* carrera de obstáculos *f.*
steepness *n* lo escarpado; lo abrupto.
steer[1] *n* novillo *m.*
steer[2] *vt* manejar, conducir; dirigir; gobernar;
* *vi* conducir.
steering *n* dirección *f.*
steering wheel *n* volante *m.*
stellar *adj* estrellado/da.
stem *n* vástago, tallo *m;* estirpe *f;* pie *m;*
cañón *m;* * *vt* cortar la corriente.
stench *n* hedor *m.*
stencil *n* cliché *m.*
stenographer *n* taquígrafo/fa *m/f.*
stenography *n* taquigrafía *f.*
step *n* paso, escalón *m;* huella *f;* * *vi* dar un
paso; andar.
stepbrother *n* hermanastro *m.*
stepdaughter *n* hijastra *f.*
stepfather *n* padrastro *m.*
stepmother *n* madrastra *f.*
stepping stone *n* pasadera *f.*
stepsister *n* hermanastra *f.*
stepson *n* hijastro *m*
stereo *n* estéreo *m.*
stereotype *n* estereotipo *m;* * *vt* estereotipar.
sterile *adj* estéril.
sterility *n* esterilidad *f.*
sterling *adj* esterlín/ina, genuino/na,
verdadero/ra; * *n* libras esterlinas *fpl.*
stern *adj* austero/ra, rígido/da, severo/ra;
* *n* (*mar*) popa *f;* ~ly *adv* austeramente.
stethoscope *n* (*med*) estetoscopio *m.*
stevedore *n* (*mar*) estibador/a *m/f.*
stew *vt* estofar; * *n* estufa, olla *f.*
steward *n* mayordomo *m;* (*mar*) des-
pensero *m.*
stewardess *n* azafata *f, Lat Am* aeromoza *f.*
stewardship *n* mayordomía *f.*
stick *n* palo, palillo, bastón *m;* vara *f;* * *vt*
pegar, hincar; aguantar; picar; * *vi* pegarse;
detenerse; perseverar; dudar.
stickiness *n* viscosidad, gomosidad *f.*
sticking plaster *n* esparadrapo *m.*
stick shift *n* palanca de cambios *f.*
stick-up *n* asalto, atraco *m.*
sticky *adj* viscoso/sa, tenaz.
stiff *adj* tieso/sa; duro/ra, torpe; rígido/da;
yerto/ta; obstinado/da; ~ly *adv* obstinadamente.
stiffen *vt* atiesar, endurecer; * *vi* en-
durecerse.
stiff neck *n* tortícolis *m.*
stiffness *n* tesura, rigidez *f;* obstinación *f.*
stifle *vt* suofocar.

stifling *adj* bochornoso/sa.
stigma *n* estigma *m.*
stigmatize *vt* estigmatizar.
stile *n* portillo con escalones *m* (para pasar de un cercado a otro).
stiletto *n* estilete *m;* tacón de aguja *m.*
still *vt* aquietar, aplacar; destilar; * *adj* silencioso/sa, tranquilo/la; * *n* alambique *m;* * *adv* todavía; hasta ahora; no obstante; aún así.
stillborn *adj* nacido/da muerto/ta.
stillness *n* calma, quietud *f.*
stilts *npl* zancos *mpl.*
stimulant *n* estimulante *m.*
stimulate *vt* estimular, aguijonear.
stimulation *n* estímulo *m;* estimulación *f.*
stimulus *n* estímulo *m.*
sting *vt* picar/morder (un insecto); * *vi* escocer; * *n* aguijón *m;* punzada, picadura, picada *f;* timo *m.*
stingily *adv* avaramente.
stinginess *n* tacañería, avaricia *f.*
stingy *adj* mezquino/na, tacaño/ña, avaro/ra.
stink *vi* heder; * *n* hedor *m.*
stint *n* tarea *f.*
stipulate *vt* estipular.
stipulation *n* estipulación *f;* condición *f.*
stir *vt* remover; agitar; incitar; * *vi* moverse; * *n* tumulto *m;* turbulencia *f.*
stirrup *n* estribo *m.*
stitch *vt* coser; * *n* punzada *f;* punto *m.*
stoat *n* armiño *m.*
stock *n* existencias *fpl;* ganado *m;* caldo *m;* estirpe *f,* linaje *m;* capital, principal *m;* fondo *m;* ~s *pl* acciones en los fondos públicos *fpl;* * *vt* proveer, abastecer.
stockade *n* prisión militar *f.*
stockbroker *n* agente de bolsa *m/f.*
stock exchange *n* bolsa *f.*
stockholder *n* accionista *m/f.*
stocking *n* media *f.*
stock market *n* bolsa *f.*
stoic *n* estoico/ca *m/f.*
stoical *adj* estoico/ca; ~ly *adv* estoicamente.
stoicism *n* estoicismo *m.*
stole *n* estola *f.*
stomach *n* estómago *m;* apetito *m;* * *vt* aguantar.
stone *n* piedra *f;* pepita *f;* hueso de fruta *m;* * *adj* de piedra; * *vt* apedrear; deshuesar; empedrar; trabajar de albañil.
stone deaf *adj* sordo/da como una tapia.
stoning *n* apedreamiento *m.*

stony *adj* de piedra, pétreo/rea; duro/ra.
stool *n* banquillo, taburete *m.*
stoop *vi* encorvarse, inclinarse; bajarse; * *n* inclinación hacia abajo *f.*
stop *vt* detener, parar; tapar; * *vi* pararse, hacer alto; * *n* parada *f;* punto *m;* pausa *f;* obstáculo *m.*
stopover *n* parada; rescala *f.*
stoppage *n* obstrucción *f;* impedimiento *m.*
stopwatch *n* cronómetro *m.*
storage *n* almacenamiento *m;* almacenaje *m.*
store *n* abundancia *f;* provisión *f;* almacén *m,* taller *m,* tienda *f;* * *vt* surtir, proveer, abastecer.
store front, store window *n* escaparate *m.*
store owner *n* tendero/ra *m/f.*
storm *n* tempestad, borrasca *f;* asalto *m;* * *vt* tomar por asalto; * *vi* rabiar.
stormily *adv* violentamente.
stormy *adj* tempestuoso/sa; violento/ta.
story[1] *n* historia *f;* chiste *m.*
story[2] *n* piso (de una casa) *m.*
stout *adj* robusto/ta, corpulento/ta, vigoroso/sa; terco/ca; ~ly *adv* valientemente; obstinadamente.
stork *n* cigüeña *f.*
stoutness *n* valor *m;* fuerza *f;* corpulencia *f.*
stove *n* cocina *f;* estufa *f.*
stow *vt* ordenar, colocar; (*mar*) estibar.
straggle *vi* rezagarse.
straggler *n* rezagado/da *m/f.*
straight *adj* derecho/cha; estrecho/cha; franco/ca; * *adv* directamente.
straightaway *adv* inmediatamente.
straighten *vt* enderezar.
straightforward *adj* derecho/cha; franco/ca; leal.
straightforwardness *n* derechura *f,* franqueza *f.*
strain *vt* colar, filtrar; apretar (a uno contra sí); forzar, violen tar; * *vi* esforzarse; * *n* tensión *f;* retorcimiento *m;* raza *f;* linaje *m;* estilo *m;* sonido *m;* armonía *f.*
strainer *n* colador *m,* Lat Am coladera *f.*
strait *n* estrecho *m;* aprieto, peligro *m;* penuria *f.*
straitjacket *n* camisa de fuerza *f.*
strand *n* hebra *f;* costa, playa *f.*
strange *adj* raro/ra; extraño/ña; ~ly *adv* extrañamente, extraordinariamente.
strangeness *n* rareza *f;* extrañeza *f.*
stranger *n* desconocido/da *m/f;* extranjero/ra *m/f.*
strangle *vt* estrangular.

strangulation n estrangulamiento m.

strap n correa, tira de cuero f; tirante de bota m; * vt atar con correa.

strapping adj abultado/da, corpulento/ta.

stratagem n estratagema f; astucia f.

strategic adj estratégico/ca.

strategy n estrategia f.

stratum n estrato m.

straw n paja m; pajita f.

strawberry n fresa f.

stray vi extraviarse; perder el camino; * adj extraviado/da; perdido/da.

streak n raya, lista f; vena f; * vt rayar.

stream n arroyo m, río m, Lat Am quebrada f, torrente m; * vi correr.

streamer n serpentina f.

street n calle f.

strength n fuerza, robustez f; vigor m; fortaleza f.

strengthen vt fortificar; corroborar.

strenuous adj arduo/dua; ágil.

stress n presión f; estrés m; fuerza f; peso m; importancia f; acento m; * vt subrayar; acentuar.

stretch vt, vi extender, alargar; estirar; extenderse; esforzarse; * n extensión f; trecho m; estirón m.

stretcher n camilla f.

strew vt esparcir; sembrar.

strict adj estricto/ta, estrecho/cha; exacto/ta, riguroso/sa, severo/ra; ~ly adv exactamente, con severidad.

strictness n exactitud f; severidad f, Lat Am estrictez f, estrechez f.

stride n tranco m; zancada f; * vi atrancar.

strife n contienda, disputa f.

strike vt, vi golpear; herir; castigar; tocar; chocar; sonar; cesar de trabajar; * n ataque m; descubrimiento m; huelga f, Lat Am paro m.

striker n huelguista m/f.

striking adj llamativo/va; notorio/ria; ~ly adv sorprendentemente.

string n cordón m; hilo m; cuerda f; hilera f; fibra f; * vt encordar; enhilar; estirar.

stringent adj astringente.

stringy adj fibroso/sa.

strip vt desnudar, despojar; * vi desnudarse; * n tira f; franja f; faja f; cinta f.

stripe n raya, lista f; azote m; * vt rayar.

strive vi esforzarse; empeñarse; disputar, contender; oponerse.

stroke n golpe m; toque (en la pintura) m; sonido (del reloj) m; plumada f; acaricia f; apoplejía f; * vt acariciar.

stroll n paseo; * vi dar un paseo.

strong adj fuerte, vigoroso/sa, robusto/ta; poderoso/sa; violento/ta; ~ly adv fuertemente, con violencia.

strongbox n caja fuerte f.

stronghold n plaza fuerte f.

strophe n estrofa f.

structure n estructura f; edificio m.

struggle vi esforzarse; luchar; agitarse; * n lucha f.

strum vt (mus) rasguear.

strut vi pavonearse; * n contoneo m.

stub n talón m; colilla f; tronco m.

stubble n rastrojo m; cerda f.

stubborn adj obstinado/da, testarudo/da, Lat Am necio/a; ~ly adv obstinadamente.

stubbornness n obstinación, pertinacia f.

stucco n estuco m.

stud[1] n corchete m; taco m.

stud[2] caballeriza f.

student n estudiante m/f; * adj estudiantil.

studio n estudio m.

studio flat n estudio m.

studious adj estudioso/sa; diligente; ~ly adv estudiosamente, diligentemente.

study n estudio m; aplicación f; meditación profunda f; * vt estudiar; observar; * vi estudiar; aplicarse.

stuff n materia f; material m; estofa f; * vt henchir, llenar; disecar.

stuffing n relleno m.

stuffy adj cargado/da; de miras estrechas.

stumble vi tropezar; * n traspié, tropiezo m.

stumbling block n tropiezo m; escollo m.

stump n tronco m; tocón m; muñón m.

stun vt aturdir, ensordecer.

stunner n cosa estupenda f.

stunt n vuelo acrobático m; truco publicitario m; * vt no dejar crecer.

stuntman n especialista m.

stuntwoman n especialista f.

stupefy vt atontar, atolondrar.

stupendous adj estupendo/da, maravilloso/sa.

stupid adj estúpido/da; very ~ zopenco/ca; ~ly adv estúpidamente.

stupidity n estupidez f.

stupor n estupor m.

sturdily adv fuertemente.

sturdiness n fuerza, fortaleza f; obstinación f.

sturdy adj fuerte, tieso/sa, robusto/ta; bronco/ca, insolente.

sturgeon n esturión m.

stutter *vi* tartamudear.
sty *n* zahurda *f*; pocilga *f*.
stye, sty *n* orzuelo *m*.
style *n* estilo *m*; moda *f*; * *vt* titular; nombrar; estilizar.
stylish *adj* elegante, en buen estilo.
suave *adj* afable.
subdivide *vt* subdividir.
subdivision *n* subdivisión *f*.
subdue *vt* sojuzgar, sujetar; conquistar; mortificar.
subject *adj* sujeto/ta; sometido/da; * *n* sujeto *m*; súbdito/ta *m/f*; tema *m*; * *vt* sujetar; exponer.
subjection *n* sujeción *f*.
subjugate *vt* sojuzgar, subyugar.
subjugation *n* subyugación *f*.
subjunctive *n* subjuntivo *m*.
sublet *vt* subarrendar.
sublimate *vt* sublimar.
sublime *adj* sublime, excelso/sa; ~**ly** *adv* de modo sublime; * *n* sublime *m*.
sublimity *n* sublimidad *f*.
submachine gun *n* metralleta *f*.
submarine *adj* submarino/na; * *n* submarino *m*.
submerge *vt* sumergir.
submersion *n* inmersión *f*; zambullida *f*.
submission *n* sumisión *f*.
submissive *adj* sumiso/sa, obsequioso/sa; ~**ly** *adv* con sumisión.
submissiveness *n* obsequio *m*; sumisión *f*.
submit *vt* (*vi*) someter(se).
subordinate *adj* subordinado/da, inferior; * *vt* subordinar.
subordination *n* subordinación *f*.
subpoena *n* citación *f*; * *vt* citar.
subscribe *vt, vi* suscribir, certificar con su firma; consentir.
subscriber *n* suscriptor/a *m/f*.
subscription *n* suscripción *f*.
subsequent *adj*, ~**ly** *adv* subsiguiente-(mente).
subservient *adj* subordinado/da; servil.
subside *vi* sumergirse, irse a fondo.
subsidence *n* derrumbamiento *m*.
subsidiary *adj* subsidiario/ria.
subsidize *vt* subvencionar, dar subsidios.
subsidy *n* subvención *f*; subsidio, socorro *m*.
subsist *vi* subsistir; existir.
subsistence *n* existencia *f*; subsistencia *f*.
substance *n* substancia *f*; entidad *f*; esencia *f*.
substantial *adj* substancial; real, material; substancioso/sa; fuerte; ~**ly** *adv* substancialmente.

substantiate *vt* probar.
substantive *n* sustantivo *m*.
substitute *vt* sustituir; * *n* suplente *m/f*.
substitution *n* sustitución *f*.
substratum *n* sustrato *m*.
subterfuge *n* subterfugio *m*; evasión *f*.
subterranean *adj* subterráneo/nea.
subtitle *n* subtítulo *m*.
subtle *adj* sutil, astuto/ta.
subtlety *n* sutileza, astucia *f*.
subtly *adv* sutilmente.
subtract *vt* (*math*) sustraer.
suburb *n* zona residencial *f*.
suburban *adj* suburbano/na.
subversion *n* subversión *f*.
subversive *adj* subversivo/va.
subvert *vt* subvertir, destruir.
succeed *vt, vi* seguir; conseguir, lograr, tener exito.
success *n* éxito *m*.
successful *adj* exitoso/sa; próspero/ra, dichoso/sa; ~**ly** *adv* con éxito; prósperamente.
succession *n* sucesión *f*; descendencia *f*; herencia *f*.
successive *adj* sucesivo/va; ~**ly** *adv* sucesivamente.
successor *n* sucesor/a *m/f*.
succinct *adj* sucinto/ta, compendioso/sa; ~**ly** *adv* con brevedad.
succulent *adj* suculento/ta, jugoso/sa.
succumb *vi* sucumbir.
such *adj* tal, semejante; ~ **as** tal como.
such and such a one *n* zutano/na y fulano *m/f*.
suck *vt, vi* chupar; mamar.
suckle *vt* amamantar.
suckling *n* mamantón/ona *m/f*.
suction *n* (*med*) succión *f*.
sudden *adj* repentino/na, no previsto/ta; ~**ly** *adv* de repente, súbitamente.
suddenness *n* precipitación *f*.
sue *vt* demandar.
suede *n* ante *m*, gamuza *f*.
suet *n* sebo *m*.
suffer *vt, vi* sufrir, padecer; tolerar, permitir.
suffering *n* pena *f*; dolor *m*.
suffice *vi* bastar, ser suficiente.
sufficiency *n* suficiencia *f*; capacidad *f*.
sufficient *adj* suficiente; ~**ly** *adv* bastante.
suffocate *vt* asfixiar; sofocar; * *vi* asfixiarse.
suffocation *n* asfixia *f*.
suffrage *n* sufragio, voto *m*.
suffuse *vt* difundir, derramar.
sugar *n* azúcar *m*; * *vt* azucarar.

sugar beet n remolacha f.
sugar cane n caña de azúcar f.
sugar loaf n pan de azúcar m.
sugary adj azucarado/da.
suggest vt sugerir.
suggestion n sugestión f.
suicidal adj suicida.
suicide n suicidio m; suicida m/f.
suit n conjunto m; petición f; traje m; pleito m; surtido m; * vt convenir; sentar a; adaptar.
suitable adj conforme, conveniente.
suitably adv convenientemente.
suitcase n maleta, valija f.
suite n suite f; serie f; tren m, comitiva f.
suitor n suplicante m; amante, cortejo m; pleiteante m/f; galanteador m.
sulkiness n mal humor m.
sulky adj regañon, terco/ca.
sullen adj hosco/ca; intratable; ~ly adv de mal humor; tercamente.
sullenness n hosquedad f; obstinación, pertinacia, terquedad f.
sulfur n azufre m.
sulfurous adj sulfureo, azufroso/sa.
sultan n sultán m.
sultana n sultana f; pasa f.
sultry adj caluroso/sa; sofocante.
sum n suma f; total m; * **to ~ up** vt sumar; recopilar; * vi hacer un resumen.
summarily adv sumariamente.
summary adj sumario/ria; * n sumario m.
summer n verano, estío m.
summerhouse n glorieta de jardín f.
summit n ápice m; cima f.
summon vt citar, requerir por auto de juez; convocar, convidar; (mil) intimar la rendición.
summons n citación f; requerimiento m.
sumptuous adj suntuoso/sa; ~ly adv suntuosamente.
sun n sol m.
sunbathe vi tomar el sol.
sunburnt adj quemado/da por el sol.
Sunday n domingo m; * adj dominical; **done/worn on** ~ dominguero/ra.
Sunday driver n dominguero/ra m/f.
sundial n reloj de sol, cuadrante m.
sundry adj diversos/sas.
sunflower n girasol m.
sunglasses npl gafas de sol fpl.
sunless adj sin sol; sin luz.
sunlight n luz del sol f.
sunny adj soleado/da; brillante.
sunrise n salida del sol f; amanecer m.

sunroof n techo corredizo m.
sunset n puesta del sol f.
sunshade n quitasol m.
sunshine n solana f; claridad del sol f.
sunstroke n insolación f.
suntan n bronceado m.
suntan oil n aceite bronceador m.
super adj (col) bárbaro/ra.
superannuated adj añejado/da; pensionado/da.
superannuation n pensión, jubilación f; retiro m.
superb adj magnífico/ca; ~ly adv magníficamente.
supercargo n (mar) sobrecargo m.
supercilious adj arrogante, altanero/ra; ~ly adv con altivez.
superficial adj, ~ly adv superficial(mente).
superfluity n superfluidad f.
superfluous adj superfluo/lua.
superhuman adj sobrehumano/na.
superintendent n superintendente m/f.
superior adj superior; * n superior/a m/f.
superiority n superioridad f.
superlative adj superlativo/va; * n superlativo m; ~ly adv superlativamente, en sumo grado.
supermarket n supermercado m.
supernatural adj sobrenatural.
supernumerary adj supernumerario/ria.
superpower n superpotencia f.
supersede vt sobreseer; sustituir; invalidar.
supersonic adj supersónico/ca.
superstition n superstición f.
superstitious adj supersticioso/sa; ~ly adv supersticiosamente.
superstructure n supcrestructura f.
supertanker n superpetrolero m.
supervene vi sobrevenir.
supervise vt supervisar, revistar.
supervision n supcrvisión f.
supervisor n supervisor/a m/f.
supine adj supino/na; negligente.
supper n cena f.
supplant vt suplantar.
supple adj flexible, manejable; blando/da.
supplement n suplemento m.
supplementary adj adicional.
suppleness n flexibilidad f.
supplicant, suppliant n suplicante m/f.
supplicate vt suplicar.
supplication n súplica, suplicación f.
supplier n proveedor/a m/f.
supply vt suministrar; suplir, completar; surtir; * n provisión f; suministro m.

support *vt* sostener; soportar, asistir; * *n* apoyo *m*.

supportable *adj* soportable.

supporter *n* partidario/ria *m/f*; aficionado/ da *m/f*.

suppose *vt, vi* suponer.

supposition *n* suposición *f*.

suppress *vt* suprimir.

suppression *n* supresión *f*.

supremacy *n* supremacía *f*.

supreme *adj* supremo/ma; ~ly *adv* supremamente.

surcharge *vt* sobrecargar; * *n* sobretasa *f*.

sure[1] *adj* seguro/ra, cierto/ta; firme; estable; **to be** ~ estar seguro/ra; ~ly *adv* ciertamente, seguramente, sin duda.

sure![2] *interj* ¡ya!

sureness *n* certeza, seguridad *f*.

surety *n* seguridad *f*; fiador *m/f*.

surf *n* (*mar*) resaca *f*.

surface *n* superficie *f*; * *vt* revestir; * *vi* salir a la superficie.

surfboard *n* plancha de surf *f*.

surfeit *n* exceso *m*.

surge *n* ola, onda *f*; * *vi* avanzar en tropel.

surgeon *n* cirujano/na *m/f*.

surgery *n* cirugía *f*.

surgical *adj* quirúrgico/ca.

surliness *n* mal humor *m*.

surly *adj* hosco/ca.

surmise *vt* sospechar; * *n* sospecha *f*.

surmount *vt* sobrepujar; (*fig*) zanjar.

surmountable *adj* superable.

surname *n* apellido, sobrenombre *m*.

surpass *vt* sobresalir, sobrepujar, exceder, aventajar.

surpassing *adj* sobresaliente.

surplice *n* sobrepelliz *f*.

surplus *n* excedente *m*; sobrante *m*; * *adj* sobrante.

surprise *vt* sorprender; * *n* sorpresa *f*.

surprising *adj* sorprendente.

surrender *vt, vi* rendir; ceder; rendirse; * *n* rendición *f*.

surreptitious *adj* subrepticio/cia; ~ly *adv* subrepticiamente.

surrogate *vt* subrogar; * *n* subrogado/da *m/f*.

surrogate mother *n* madre de alquiler *f*.

surround *vt* circundar, cercar, rodear.

surrounding area *n* inmediaciones *fpl*.

survey *vt* inspeccionar, examinar; apear; * *n* inspección *f*; apeo (de tierras) *m*.

survive *vi* sobrevivir; * *vt* sobrevivir a.

survivor *n* superviviente *m/f*.

susceptibility *n* susceptibilidad *f*.

susceptible *adj* susceptible.

suspect *vt, vi* sospechar; * *n* sospechoso/sa *m/f*.

suspend *vt* suspender.

suspense *n* suspense *m*, *Lat Am* suspenso *m*; detención *f*; incertidumbre *f*.

suspension *n* suspensión *f*.

suspension bridge *n* puente colgante *m*.

suspicion *n* sospecha *f*.

suspicious *adj* suspicaz; ~ly *adv* sospechosamente.

suspiciousness *n* suspicacia *f*.

sustain *vt* sostener, sustentar, mantener; apoyar; sufrir.

sustenance *n* sostenimiento, sustento *m*.

suture *n* sutura, costura *f*.

swab *n* algodón *m*; frotis *m invar*.

swaddle *vt* fajar.

swaddling-clothes *npl* pañales *mpl*.

swagger *vi* baladronear.

swallow *n* golondrina *f*; * *vt* tragar, engullir.

swamp *n* pantano *m*.

swampy *adj* pantanoso/sa.

swan *n* cisne *m*.

swap *vt* canjear; * *n* intercambio *m*.

swarm *n* enjambre *m*; gentío *m*; hormiguero *m*; * *vi* enjambrar; hormiguear de gente; abundar.

swarthy *adj* atezado/da.

swarthiness *n* tez morena *f*.

swashbuckling *adj* fanfarrón/ona.

swathe *vt* fajar.

sway *vt* mover; * *vi* ladearse, inclinarse; * *n* balanceo *m*; poder, imperio, influjo *m*.

swear *vt, vi* jurar; hacer jurar; juramentar.

sweat *n* sudor *m*; * *vi* sudar; trabajar con fatiga.

sweater, sweatshirt *n* suéter *m*.

sweep *vt, vi* barrer; arrebatar; deshollinar; pasar/tocar liger amente; oscilar; * *n* barredura *f*; vuelta *f*; giro *m*.

sweeping *adj* rápido/da; ~s *pl* barreduras *fpl*.

sweepstake *n* lotería *f*.

sweet *adj* dulce, grato/ta, gustoso/sa; suave; oloroso/sa; melodioso/sa; hermoso/sa; amable; * *adv* dulcemente, suavemente; * *n* dulce, caramelo *m*.

sweetbread *n* mellejas de ternera *fpl*.

sweeten *vt* endulzar; suavizar; aplacar; perfumar.

sweetener *n* edulcorante *m*.

sweetheart *n* novio/via *m/f*; querida *f*.

sweetmeats *npl* dulces secos *mpl*.

sweetness *n* dulzura, suavidad *f*.
swell *vi* hincharse; ensoberbecerse; embravecerse; * *vt* hinchar, inflar, agravar; * *n* marejada *f*; * *adj* (*col*) estupendo/da, fenomenal.
swelling *n* hinchazón *f*; tumor *m*.
swelter *vi* ahogarse de calor.
swerve *vi* vagar; desviarse.
swift *adj* veloz, ligero/ra, rápido/da; * *n* vencejo *m*.
swiftly *adv* velozmente.
swiftness *n* velocidad, rapidez *f*.
swill *vt* beber en exceso; * *n* bazofia *f*.
swim *vi* nadar; abundar en; * *vt* pasar a nado; * *n* nadada *f*.
swimming *n* natación *f*.
swimming pool *n* piscina *f*.
swimsuit *n* traje de baño *m*.
swindle *vt* estafar.
swindler *n* estafador/a *m/f*.
swine *n* puerco, cochino *m*.
swing *vi* balancear, columpiarse; vibrar; agitarse; * *vt* colum piar: balancear; girar; * *n* vibración *f*; balanceo *m*.
swinging *adj* (*col*) alegre.
swing (ing) door *n* puerta giratoria *f*.
swirl *n* remolino.
switch *n* varilla *f*; interruptor *m*; (*rail*) aguja *f*; * *vt* cambiar de; **to ~ off** apagar; parar; **to ~ on** encender, *Lat Am* prender.
switchboard *n* centralita *f*, *Lat Am* conmutador *m*.
swivel *vt* girar.
swoon *vi* desmayarse; * *n* desmayo, deliquio, pasmo *m*.
swoop *vi* calarse; * *n* calada; redada *f*; **in one ~** de un golpe.
sword *n* espada *f*.
swordfish *n* pez espada *f*.

swordsman *n* guerrero, espadachín *m*.
sycamore *n* sicomoro *m* (árbol).
sycophant *n* sicofante *m*.
syllabic *adj* silábico/ca.
syllable *n* sílaba *f*.
syllabus *n* programa de estudios *m*.
syllogism *n* silogismo *m*.
sylph *n* silfio *m*; sílfide *f*.
symbol *n* simbolo *m*.
symbolic(al) *adj* simbólico/ca.
symbolize *vt* simbolizar.
symmetrical *adj* simétrico/ca; ~**ly** *adv* con simetría.
symmetry *n* simetría *f*.
sympathetic *adj* simpático/ca; ~**ally** *adv* simpáticamente.
sympathize *vi* compadecerse.
sympathy *n* simpatía *f*.
symphony *n* sinfonía *f*.
symposium *n* simposio *m*.
symptom *n* síntoma *m*.
synagogue *n* sinagoga *f*.
synchronism *n* sincronismo *m*.
syndicate *n* sindicato *m*.
syndrome *n* síndrome *m*.
synod *n* sínodo *m*.
synonym *n* sinónimo *m*.
synonymous *adj* sinónimo/ma; ~**ly** *adv* con sinonimia.
synopsis *n* sinopsis *f invar*; sumario *m*.
synoptic *adj* sinóptico/ca.
syntax *n* sintaxis *f*.
synthesis *n* síntesis *f invar*.
syringe *n* jeringa, lavativa *f*; * *vt* jeringar.
system *n* sistema *m*.
systematic *adj* sistemático/ca; ~**ally** *adv* sistemáticamente.
systems analyst *n* analista de sistemas *m/f*.

T

tab *n* lengüeta *f*; etiqueta *f*.
tabernacle *n* tabernáculo *m*.
table *n* mesa *f*; tabla *f*; * *vt* someter a discusión; poner sobre la mesa; ~ d'hôte menu *m*.
tablecloth *n* mantel *m*.
tablespoon *n* cuchara para comer *f*.
tablet *n* tableta *f*; pastilla *f*; comprimido *m*.
table tennis *n* ping-pong, tenis de mesa *m*.
taboo *adj* tabú; * *n* tabú *m*; * *vt* interdecir.
tabular *adj* tabular.
tachometer *n* cuentarrevoluciones *m invar*.
tacit *adj* tácito/ta; ~ly *adv* tácitamente.
taciturn *adj* taciturno/na, callado/da.
tack *n* bordo *m*; *n* tachuela *f*; * *vt* atar; pegar; * *vi* virar.
tackle *n* equipo *m*, aparejos *mpl*; placaje *m*; (*mar*) cordaje *m*, jarcia *f*.
tact *n* tacto *m*.
tactician *n* táctico/ca *m/f*.
tactics *npl* táctica *f*.
tadpole *n* renacuajo *m*.
taffeta *n* tafetán *m*.
tag *n* herrete *m*; * *vt* herretear.
tail *n* cola *f*; rabo *m*; * *vt* vigilar a.
tailgate, tailboard *n* puerta trasera *f*.
tailor *n* sastre *m*.
tailoring *n* corte *m*.
tailor-made *adj* hecho/cha a la medida.
tailwind *n* viento de cola *m*.
taint *vt* tachar, manchar; viciar; * *n* mancha *f*.
tainted *adj* contaminado/da; manchado/da.
take *vt* tomar, coger, asir; recibir, aceptar; pillar; prender; admitir; entender; * *vi* prender el fuego; to ~ apart *vt* descoser; to ~ away quitar; llevar; to ~ back devolver; retractar; to ~ down derribar; apuntar; to ~ in entender, abarcar; acoger; to ~ off *vi* despegar, *Lat Am* decolar; *vt* quitar; imitar; to ~ on aceptar; contratar; desafiar; to ~ out sacar; quitar; to ~ to encariñarse con; to ~ up acortar; ocupar; dedicarse a; * *n* toma *f*.
takeoff *n* despegue *m*, *Lat Am* decolaje *m*.
takeover *n* absorción *f*; ~ bid opa *f*.
takings *npl* ingresos *mpl*.
talc *n* talco *m*.
talent *n* talento *m*; capacidad *f*.
talented *adj* con talento.
talisman *n* talismán *m*.

talk *vi* hablar, conversar; charlar; * *n* habla *f*; charla *f*, *Lat Am* conversa *f*; fama *f*.
talkative *adj* locuaz.
talk show *n* programa de entrevistas *m*.
tall *adj* alto/ta, elevado/da; robusto/ta.
tally *vi* corresponder.
talon *n* garra *f*.
tambourine *n* pandereta *f*.
tame *adj* amansado/da, domado/da, domesticado/da; ~ly *adv* mansamente; bajamente; * *vt* domar, domesticar.
tameness *n* domesticidad *f*; sumisión *f*.
tamper *vi* tocar.
tampon *n* tampón *m*.
tan *vt* broncear; * *vi* broncearse, ponerse moreno/na; * *n* bronceado *m*.
tang *n* sabor fuerte *m*.
tangent *n* tangente *f*.
tangerine *n* mandarina *f*.
tangible *adj* tangible.
tangle *vt* enredar, embrollar.
tank *n* cisterna *f*; aljibe *m*.
tanker *n* petrolero *m*; camión cisterna *m*.
tanned *adj* bronceado/da.
tantalizing *adj* tentador/a.
tantamount *adj* equivalente.
tantrum *n* rabieta *f*.
tap *vt* tocar ligeramente; utilizar; intervenir; zapatear; * *n* grifo *m*; palmada suave *f*; toque ligero *m*; espita *f*.
tape *n* cinta *f*; * *vt* grabar.
tape measure *n* metro *m*.
taper *n* cirio *m*.
tape recorder *n* grabadora *f*.
tapestry *n* tapiz *m*; tapicería *f*.
tar *n* brea *f*, alquitrán *m*.
target *n* blanco *m* (para tirar).
tariff *n* tarifa *f*.
tarnish *vt* deslustrar.
tarpaulin *n* alquitranado *m*.
tarragon *n* (*bot*) estragón *m*.
tart *adj* acedo/da, acre; * *n* tarta, torta *f*; (*col*) zorra *f*.
tartan *n* tela escocesa *f*.
tartar *n* tártaro *m*.
task *n* tarea *f*.
tassel *n* borlita *f*.
taste *n* gusto *m*; sabor *m*; saboreo *m*; ensayo *m*; * *vt*, *vi* gustar; probar; experimentar; agradar; tener sabor.
tasteful *adj* sabroso/sa; ~ly *adv* sabrosamente.

tasteless *adj* insípido/da, sin sabor.
tasty *adj* sabroso/sa.
tattoo *n* tatuaje *m*; * *vt* tatuar.
taunt *vt* mofar; ridiculizar; * *n* mofa, burla *f*.
Taurus *n* Tauro *m* (signo del zodíaco).
taut *adj* tieso/sa.
tautology *n* tautología *f*.
tawdry *adj* jarifo/fa, vistoso/sa, chabacano/na.
tax *n* impuesto *m*; contribución *f*; * *vt* gravar; poner a prueba.
taxable *adj* sujeto/ta a impuestos.
taxation *n* imposición de impuestos *f*.
tax collector *n* recaudador/a *m/f* de impuestos.
tax-free *adj* libre de impuestos.
taxi *n* taxi *m*; * *vi* rodar por la pista.
taxi driver *n* taxista *m/f*.
taxi rank *n* parada de taxis *f*.
tax payer *n* contribuyente *m/f*.
tax relief *n* desgravación fiscal *f*.
tax return *n* declaración de la renta *f*.
tea *n* té *m*
teach *vt* enseñar, instruir, *Lat Am* dictar; * *vi* enseñar.
teacher *n* profesor/a *m/f*; maestro/tra *m/f*.
teaching *n* enseñanza *f*.
teacup *n* taza de té *f*.
teak *n* teca *f* (árbol).
team *n* equipo *m*.
teamster *n* camionero/ra *m/f*.
teamwork *n* trabajo de equipo *m*.
teapot *n* tetera *f*.
tear[1] *vt* despedazar, rasgar; to ~ up hacer trizas.
tear[2] *n* lágrima *f*; gota *f*.
tearful *adj* lloroso/sa; ~ly *adv* con lloro.
tear gas *n* gas lacrimógeno *m*.
tease *vt* tomar el pelo.
tea service, tea set *n* servicio para té *m*.
teasing *adj* zumbón/ona; * *n* zumba *f*.
teaspoon *n* cucharita *f*.
teat *n* ubre, teta *f*.
technical *adj* técnico/ca.
technicality *n* detalle técnico *m*.
technician *n* técnico/ca *m*
technique *n* técnica *f*.
technological *adj* tecnológico/ca.
technology *n* tecnología *f*.
teddy (bear) *n* osito de felpa *m*.
tedious *adj* tedioso/sa, fastidioso/sa; ~ly *adv* fastidiosamente.
tedium *n* tedio, fastidio *m*.
tee *n* tee *m*.
teem *vi* rebosar de.

teenage *adj* juvenil; ~r *n* adolescente *m/f*.
teens *npl* adolescencia *f*.
tee-shirt, T-shirt *n* camiseta *f*.
teeth *npl* de tooth.
teethe *vi* echar los dientes.
teetotal *adj* abstemio/mia, sobrio/ria.
teetotaler *n* abstemio/mia *m/f*.
telegram *n* telegrama *m*.
telegraph *n* telégrafo *m*.
telegraphic *adj* telegráfico/ca.
telegraphy *n* telegrafía *f*.
telepathy *n* telepatía *f*.
telephone *n* teléfono *m*.
telephone banking *n* telebanca *f*.
telephone booth *n* cabina telefónica *f*.
telephone call *n* llamada telefónica *f*, *Lat Am* telefonema *m*.
telephone directory *n* guía *f* telefónica.
telephone number *n* número de teléfono *m*.
telescope *n* telescopio *m*.
telescopic *adj* telescópico/ca.
televise *vt* televisar.
television *n* televisión *f*.
television news *n* telediario *m*.
television set *n* televisor *m*.
teleworker *n* teletrabajador/ra *m/f*.
teleworking *n* teletrabajo *m*.
tell *vi* decir; informar, contar.
teller *n* cajero/ra *m/f*.
telling *adj* contundente; revelador/a.
telltale *adj* indicador/a.
temper *vt* templar, moderar; * *n* mal genio *m*.
temperament *n* temperamento *m*.
temperance *n* templanza, moderación *f*.
temperate *adj* templado/da, moderado/da, sobrio/ria.
temperature *n* temperatura *f*.
tempest *n* tempestad *f*.
tempestuous *adj* tempestuoso/sa.
template *n* plantilla *f*.
temple *n* templo *m*; sien *f*.
temporarily *adv* temporalmente, *Lat Am* temporariamente.
temporary *adj* temporal, *Lat Am* temporario/ria.
tempt *vt* tentar; provocar.
temptation *n* tentación *f*.
tempting *adj* tentador/a.
ten *adj*, *n* diez.
tenable *adj* defendible.
tenacious *adj*, ~ly *adv* tenaz(mente).
tenacity *n* tenacidad *f*; porfía *f*.
tenancy *n* tenencia *f*.

tenant n arrendatario/ria, inquilino/na m/f.
tend vt guardar, velar; * vi tener tendencia a.
tendency n tendencia f.
tender adj tierno/na, delicado/da; sensible; ~ly adv tiernamente; * n oferta f; * vt ofrecer; estimar.
tenderness n ternura f.
tendon n tendón m.
tendril n zarcillo m.
tenement n casa de pisos f.
tenet n dogma m; aserción f.
tennis n tenis m.
tennis court n cancha de tenis f.
tennis player n tenista m/f.
tennis racket n raqueta de tenis f.
tennis shoes npl zapatillas de tenis fpl.
tenor n (mus) tenor m; contenido m; substancia f.
tense adj tieso/sa, tenso/sa; * n (gr) tiempo m.
tension n tensión, tirantez f.
tent n tienda de campaña f, Lat Am carpa f.
tentacle n tentáculo m.
tentative adj de ensayo, de prueba; ~ly adv como prueba.
tenth adj, n décimo/ma.
tenuous adj tenue.
tenure n tenencia f.
tepid adj tibio/bia.
term n término m; dicción f; vocablo m; condición, estipulación f; * vt nombrar, llamar.
terminal adj mortal; * n terminal m; terminal f.
terminate vt terminar.
termination n terminación, conclusión f.
terminus n terminal f.
terrace n terraza f.
terrain n terreno m.
terrestrial adj terrestre, terreno/na.
terrible adj terrible.
terribly adv terriblemente.
terrier n terrier m.
terrific adj fantástico/ca; maravilloso/sa.
terrify vt aterrar, espantar.
territorial adj territorial.
territory n territorio, distrito m.
terror n terror m.
terrorism n terrorismo m.
terrorist n terrorista m/f.
terrorist attack n atentado m.
terrorize vt aterrorizar.
terse adj tajante.
test n examen m; prueba f; * vt probar; examinar.
testament n testamento m.

tester n ensayador/a m/f.
testicles npl testículos mpl.
testify vt testificar, atestiguar.
testimonial n atestación f.
testimony n testimonio m.
test pilot n piloto de pruebas m/f.
test tube n probeta f.
testy adj tétrico/ca.
tetanus n tétanos m invar.
tether vt atar.
text n texto m.
textbook n libro de texto m.
textiles npl textiles mpl.
textual adj textual.
texture n textura f; tejido m.
than adv que, de.
thank vt agradecer, dar las gracias a.
thankful adj grato/ta, agradecido/da; ~ly adv con gratitud.
thankfulness n gratitud f.
thankless adj ingrato/ta.
thanks npl gracias fpl.
Thanksgiving n día de acción de gracias m.
that pn aquel, aquello, aquella; que; este; * conj porque; para que; **so** ~ de modo que.
thatch n techo de paja m; * vt techar con paja.
thaw n deshielo m; * vi deshelarse.
the art el, la, lo; los, las.
theater n teatro m.
theatergoer n aficionado/da al teatro m/f.
theatrical adj teatral.
theft n robo m.
their pn su, suyo, suya; de ellos, de ellas; ~s el suyo, la suya, los suyos, las suyas; de ellos, de ellas.
them pn los, las, les; ellos, ellas.
theme n tema m.
themselves pn pl ellos mismos, ellas mismas; sí mismos; se.
then adv entonces, después; en tal caso; * conj en ese caso; * adj entonces; **now and** ~ de vez en cuando.
theologian n teólogo/ga m/f.
theological adj teológico/ca.
theology n teología f.
theorem n teorema m.
theoretic(al) adj teórico/ca; ~ly adv teóricamente.
theorist n teórico/ca m/f.
theorize vt teorizar.
theory n teoría f.
therapist n terapeuta m/f.
therapy n terapia f.
there adv allí, allá.
thereabout(s) adv por ahí, acerca de.

thereafter *adv* después; según.
thereby *adv* así; de ese modo.
therefore *adv* por eso, por lo tanto.
thermal *adj* termal.
thermometer *n* termómetro *m*.
thermostat *n* termostato *m*.
thesaurus *n* diccionario de sinónimos *m*.
these *pn pl* éstos, éstas; *adj* estos, estas.
thesis *n* tesis *f invar*.
they *pn pl* ellos, ellas.
thick *adj* espeso/sa, denso/sa; grueso/sa; torpe.
thicken *vi* espesar, condensar; condensarse.
thicket *n* espesura *f*.
thickness *n* espesor *m*.
thickset *adj* grueso/sa; rechoncho/cha.
thick-skinned *adj* duro/ra de pellejo.
thief *n* ladrón/ona *m/f*.
thigh *n* muslo *m*.
thimble *n* dedal *m*.
thin *adj* delgado/da, delicado/da, flaco/ca; claro/ra, * *vt* atenuar; adelga zar; aclarar.
thing *n* cosa *f*, objeto *m*, chisme *m*.
think *vi* pensar, imaginar, meditar, considerar; creer, juzgar; **to ~ over** reflexionar; **to ~ up** imaginar.
thinker *n* pensador/a *m/f*.
thinking *n* pensamiento *m*; juicio *m*; opinión *f*.
third *adj* tercero/ra; * *n* tercio *m*; **~ly** *adv* en tercer lugar.
third rate *adj* mediocre.
thirst *n* sed *f*.
thirsty *adj* sediento/ta.
thirteen *adj*, *n* trece.
thirteenth *adj*, *n* decimotercero/ra.
thirtieth *adj*, *n* trigésimo/ma.
thirty *adj*, *n* treinta.
this *adj* este, esta; * *pn* éste, ésta, esto.
thistle *n* cardo *m*.
thorn *n* espino *m*; espina *f*.
thorny *adj* espinoso/sa; arduo/dua.
thorough *adj* entero/ra, perfecto/ta; **~ly** *adv* enteramente, profundamente.
thoroughbred *adj* de sangre, de casta.
thoroughfare *n* paso, tránsito *m*.
those *pn pl* ésos, ésas; aquéllos, aquéllas; * *adj* esos, esas; aquellos, aquellas.
though *conj* aunque, no obstante; * *adv* sin embargo.
thought *n* pensamiento, juicio *m*; opinión *f*; cuidado *m*.
thoughtful *adj* pensativo/va.
thoughtless *adj* descuidado/da; insensato/ta; **~ly** *adv* descuidadamente, sin reflexión.

thousand *adj*, *n* mil.
thousandth *adj*, *n* milésimo/ma.
thrash *vt* golpear; derrotar.
thread *n* hilo *m*; rosca *f*; * *vt* enhebrar.
threadbare *adj* raído/da, muy usado/da.
threat *n* amenaza *f*.
threaten *vt* amenazar.
three *adj*, *n* tres.
three-dimensional *adj* tridimensional.
three-monthly *adj* trimestral.
threshold *n* umbral *m*.
thrifty *adj* económico/ca.
thrill *vt* emocionar; * *n* emoción *f*.
thriller *n* película/novela de suspense *f*.
thrive *vi* prosperar; crecer.
throat *n* garganta *f*.
throb *vi* palpitar; vibrar; dar punzadas.
throne *n* trono *m*.
throng *n* tropel de gente *m*; * *vt* venir en tropel.
throttle *n* acelerador *m*; * *vt* estrangular.
through *prep* por; durante; mediante; * *adj* directo/ta; * *adv* completamente.
throughout *prep* por todo; * *adv* en todas partes.
throw *vt* echar, arrojar, tirar, lanzar; * *n* tiro *m*; golpe *m*; **to ~ away** tirar; **to ~ off** desechar; **to ~ out** tirar; **to ~ up** vomitar, devolver.
throwaway *adj* desechable.
thrush *n* tordo (ave) *m*.
thrust *vt* empujar, introducir; * *vr* zamparse; * *n* empuje *m*.
thud *n* ruido sordo *m*; zarpazo *m*.
thug *n* gamberro/rra *m/f*.
thumb *n* pulgar *m*.
thumbtack *n* chincheta *f*, *Lat Am* chinche *f*.
thump *n* golpe *m*; * *vt*, *vi* golpear.
thunder *n* trueno *m*; * *vi* tronar.
thunderbolt *n* rayo *m*.
thunderclap *n* trueno *m*.
thunderstorm *n* tormenta *f*.
thundery *adj* tormentoso/sa.
Thursday *n* jueves *m invar*.
thus *adv* así, de este modo.
thwart *vt* frustrar.
thyme *n* (*bot*) tomillo *m*.
thyroid *n* tiroides *m invar*.
tiara *n* tiara *f*.
tic *n* tic *m*.
tick *n* tictac *m*; palomita *f*; marca *f*; * *vt* marcar; **to ~ over** girar en marcha; ir tirando.
ticket *n* billete, *Lat Am* boleto *m*; etiqueta *f*; tarjeta *f*.
ticket collector *n* (*rail*) revisor/a *m/f*.

ticket office *n* taquilla *f*, *Lat Am* boletería *f*;
Lat Am despacho *m* de boletos.
tickle *vt* hacer cosquillas.
ticklish *adj* con cosquillas, *Lat Am*
cosquilloso/sa.
tidal *adj* de marea.
tidal wave *n* maremoto *m*.
tidbit *n* golosina *f*; pedazo *m*.
tide *n* curso *m*; marea *f*.
tidy *adj* ordenado/da; arreglado/da; aseado/
da.
tie *vt* anudar, atar; * *vi* empatar; to ~ up
envolver; atar; amarrar; concluir; * *n*
atadura *f*; lazo *m*; corbata *f*; empate *m*.
tier *n* grada *f*; piso *m*.
tiger *n* tigre *m*.
tight *adj* tirante, tieso/sa, tenso/sa; cerrado/
da; apretado/da; * *adv* con fuerza.
tighten *vt* tirar, estirar.
tightfisted *adj* tacaño/ña.
tightly *adv* muy fuerte.
tightrope *n* cuerda floja *f*.
tigress *n* tigresa *f*.
tile *n* teja *f*; baldosa *f*; azulejo *m*; * *vt* tejar.
tiled *adj* embaldosado/da.
till¹ *n* caja registradora *f*.
till² *vt* cultivar, labrar.
tiller *n* cana del timón *f*.
tilt *vt* inclinar; * *vi* inclinarse.
timber *n* madera de construcción *f*; árboles
mpl.
time *n* tiempo; época *f*; hora *f*; momento
m; (*mus*) compás *m*; in ~ a tiempo; from
~ to ~ de vez en cuando; * *vt* medir el
tiempo; cronometrar.
time bomb *n* bomba de relojería *f*.
time lag *n* desfase *m*.
timeless *adj* eterno/na.
timely *adj* oportuno/na.
time off *n* tiempo libre *m*.
timer *n* interruptor *m*; programador
horario *m*.
time scale *n* escala de tiempo *f*.
time trial *n* contrarreloj *f*.
time zone *n* huso horario *m*.
timid *adj* tímido/da, temeroso/sa; ~ly *adv*
con timidez.
timidity *n* timidez *f*.
timing *n* cronometraje *m*; oportunidad *f*.
tin *n* estaño *m*; hojalata *f*.
tinder *n* yesca *f*.
tinfoil *n* papel de estaño *m*.
tinge *n* matiz *m*.
tingle *vi* zumbar; latir, punzar.
tingling *n* zumbido *m*; latido *m*.

tinkle *vi* tintinear.
tin plate *n* hojalata *f*.
tinsel *n* oropel *m*.
tint *n* tinte *m*; * *vt* teñir.
tinted *adj* teñido/da; ahumado/da.
tiny *adj* pequeño/ña, chico/ca.
tip¹ *n* punta, extremidad *f*.
tip² propina *f*; consejo *m*; * *vt* dar una
propina a.
tip³ *vt* inclinar; vaciar.
tip-off *n* advertencia *f*.
tipsy *adj* alegre.
tiptop *adj* excelente, perfecto/ta.
tirade *n* invectiva *f*.
tire¹ *vt* cansar, fatigar; * *vi* cansarse;
fastidiarse.
tire² *n* neumático *m*; llanta *f*.
tireless *adj* incansable.
tire pressure *n* presión de los neumáticos *f*.
tiresome *adj* tedioso/sa, molesto/ta.
tiring *adj* cansado/da.
tissue *n* tejido *m*; pañuelo de papel *m*.
tissue paper *n* papel de seda *m*.
titillate *vt* estimular.
title *n* título *m*.
title deed *n* derecho de propiedad *m*.
title page *n* portada *f*.
titter *vi* reírse disimuladamente; * *n* risa
disimulada *f*.
titular *adj* titular.
to *prep* a; para; por; de; hasta; en; con; que.
toad *n* sapo *m*.
toadstool *n* (*bot*) seta venenosa *f*.
toast *vt* tostar; brindar; * *n* tostada *f*;
brindis *m*.
toaster *n* tostadora *f*.
tobacco *n* tabaco *m*.
tobacconist *n* tabaquero/ra, estanquero/ra
m/f.
tobacconist's (shop) *n* estanco *m*, tabaquería *f*, *Lat Am* cigarrería *f*.
tobacco pouch *n* petaca *f*.
toboggan *n* tobogán *m*.
today *adv* hoy.
toddler *n* niño/ña (que empieza a andar)
m/f.
toe *n* dedo del pie *m*; punta *f*.
toffee *n* caramelo *m*.
together *adv* juntamente, juntos; al mismo
tiempo.
toil *vi* fatigarse, trabajar mucho; afanarse;
* *n* trabajo *m*; fatiga *f*; afán *m*.
toilet *n* servicios *mpl*; sanitario *m*; * *adj* de
aseo.
toilet bag *n* bolsa de aseo *f*.

toilet bowl *n* taza del retrete *f*.
toilet paper *n* papel higiénico *m*.
toiletries *npl* artículos de aseo *mpl*.
token *n* senal *f*; muestra *f*; recuerdo *m*; vale *m*; ficha *f*.
tolerable *adj* soportable; pasable.
tolerance *n* tolerancia *f*.
tolerant *adj* tolerante.
tolerate *vt* tolerar.
toll[1] *n* peaje *m*; número de victimas *m*.
toll[2] *vi* doblar.
tomato *n* tomate *m*.
tomb *n* tumba *f*; sepulcro *m*, sepultura *f*.
tomboy *n* muchachota *f*.
tombstone *n* piedra sepulcral *f*.
tomcat *n* gato *m*.
tomorrow *adv* mañana; * *n* mañana *f*.
ton *n* tonelada *f*.
tone *n* tono *m*; acento *m*; * *vi* armonizar; to ~ down suavizar.
tone-deaf *adj* sin oído musical.
tongs *npl* tenacillas *fpl*.
tongue *n* lengua *f*.
tongue-tied *adj* mudo/da.
tongue-twister *n* trabalenguas *m invar*.
tonic *n* (*med*) tónico *m*.
tonight *adv*, *n* esta tarde (*f*).
tonnage *n* tonelaje *m*.
tonsil *n* amígdala *f*; ~s *npl* agallas *fpl*.
tonsillitis *n* agalla *f*.
tonsure *n* tonsura *f*.
too *adv* demasiado; también.
tool *n* herramienta *f*; utensilio *m*.
tool box *n* caja de herramientas *f*.
toot *vi* tocar la bocina.
tooth *n* diente *m*.
toothache *n* dolor de muelas *m*.
toothbrush *n* cepillo de dientes *m*.
toothless *adj* desdentado/da.
toothpaste *n* pasta de dientes *f*.
toothpick *n* palillo *m*.
top *n* cima, cumbre *f*; último grado *m*; lo alto; superficie *f*; tapa *f*; cabeza *f*; * *adj* de arriba; primero/ra; * *vt* elevarse por encima; sobrepujar, exceder; to ~ off llenar.
topaz *n* topacio *m*.
top floor *n* último piso *m*.
top-heavy *adj* inestable.
topic *n* tema *m*; ~al *adj* actual.
top-level *adj* al más alto nivel.
topmost *adj* lo más alto.
topographic(al) *adj* topográfico/ca.
topography *n* topografía *f*.
topple *vt* derribar; * *vi* volcarse.
top-secret *adj* de alto secreto.

topsy-turvy *adv* al revés.
torment *vt* atormentar; * *n* tormento *m*.
tornado *n* tornado *m*.
torrent *n* torrente *m*.
torrid *adj* apasionado/da.
tortoise *n* tortuga *f*.
tortoiseshell *adj* de carey.
tortuous *adj* tortuoso/sa, sinuoso/sa.
torture *n* tortura *f*; * *vt* torturar.
toss *vt* tirar, lanzar, arrojar; agitar, sacudir.
total *adj* total, entero/ra; ~ly *adv* totalmente.
totalitarian *adj* totalitario/ria.
totality *n* totalidad *f*.
totter *vi* vacilar.
touch *vt* tocar, palpar; to ~ on aludir a; to ~ up retocar; * *n* contacto *m*; tacto *m*; toque *m*; prueba *f*.
touch-and-go *adj* arriesgado/da.
touchdown *n* aterrizaje *m*; ensayo *m*.
touched *adj* conmovido/da; chiflado/da.
touching *adj* patético/ca, conmovedor/a.
touchstone *n* piedra de toque *f*.
touchy *adj* quisquilloso/sa.
tough *adj* duro/ra; difícil; resistente; fuerte; * *n* gorila *m*.
toughen *vt* endurecer.
toupee *n* tupé *m*.
tour *n* viaje *m*; visita *f*; * *vt* visitar.
touring *n* viajes turísticos *mpl*.
tourism *n* turismo *m*; bicycle ~ cicloturismo; rural ~ turismo rural.
tourist *n* turista *m/f*.
tourist office *n* oficina de turismo *f*.
tournament *n* torneo *m*.
tow *n* remolque *m*; * *vt* remolcar.
toward(s) *prep*, *adv* hacia, con dirección a; cerca de, respecto a.
towel *n* toalla *f*.
toweling *n* toalla *f*.
towel rack *n* toallero *m*.
tower *n* torre *m*.
towering *adj* imponente.
town *n* ciudad *f*.
town clerk *n* secretario/ria del ayuntamiento *m/f*.
town hall *n* ayuntamiento *m*.
towrope *n* cable de remolque *m*.
toy *n* juguete *m*.
toy store *n* juguetería *f*.
trace *n* huella, pisada *f*; * *vt* trazar, delinear; encontrar.
track *n* vestigio *m*; huella *f*; camino *m*; vía *f*; pista *f*; canción *f*; * *vt* rastrear.
tracksuit *n* chándal *m*.

tract *n* región, comarca *f*; serie *f*; tratado *m*.
traction *n* tracción *f*.
trade *n* comercio, tráfico *m*; negocio, trato *m*; ocupación *f*; * *vi* comerciar, traficar.
trade fair *n* feria de muestras *f*.
trademark *n* marca comercial *f*.
trade name *n* nombre comercial *m*.
trader *n* comerciante, traficante *m*.
tradesman *n* tendero *m*.
trading *n* comercio *m*; * *adj* comercial.
tradition *n* tradición *f*
traditional *adj* tradicional.
traffic *n* tráfico *m*; tránsito *m*; * *vi* traficar, comerciar.
traffic circle *n* glorieta *f*.
traffic jam *n* embotellamiento *m*, aglomeración *f* de tráfico.
trafficker *n* traficante, comerciante *m/f*.
traffic lights *npl* semáforo *m*.
tragedy *n* tragedia *f*.
tragic *adj* trágico/ca; ~ally *adv* trágicamente.
tragicomedy *n* tragicomedia *f*.
trail *vt*, *vi* rastrear; arrastrar; * *n* rastro *m*; pista *f*; cola *f*.
trailer *n* tráiler *m*; remolque *m*; avance *m*.
train *vt* entrenar; amaestrar, enseñar, criar, adiestrar; disciplinar; * *vr* ejercitarse; * *n* tren *m*; cola *f*; serie *f*; **high-speed** ~ tren de alta velocidad *m*.
trained *adj* cualificado/da; amaestrado/da.
trainee *n* aprendiz/a *m/f*.
trainer *n* entrenador/a *m/f*.
training *n* entrenamiento *m*; formación *f*.
trait *n* rasgo *m*.
traitor *n* traidor/a *m/f*.
tram *n* tranvía *f*.
trample *vt* pisotear.
trampoline *n* cama elástica *f*.
trance *n* rapto *m*; éxtasis *m*.
tranquil *adj* tranquilo/la.
tranquilize *vt* tranquilizar.
tranquilizer *n* tranquilizante *m*.
transact *vt* negociar.
transaction *n* transacción *f*; negociación *f*.
transatlantic *adj* transatlántico/ca.
transcend *vt* trascender, pasar; exceder.
transcription *n* transcripción *f*.
transfer *vt* transferir, trasladar; * *n* transferencia *f*; traspaso *m*; calcomanía *f*.
transform *vt* transformar.
transformation *n* transformación *f*.
transfusion *n* transfusión *f*.
transient *adj* pasajero/ra, transitorio/ria.
transit *n* tránsito *m*.

transition *n* tránsito *m*; transición *f*.
transitional *adj* de transición.
transitive *adj* transitivo/va.
translate *vt* traducir.
translation *n* traducción *f*.
translator *n* traductor/ra *m/f*.
transmission *n* transmisión *f*.
transmit *vt* transmitir.
transmitter *n* transmisor *m*; emisora *f*.
transparency *n* transparencia *f*.
transparent *adj* transparente, diáfano/na.
transpire *vi* resultar; ocurrir.
transplant *vt* trasplantar; * *n* trasplante *m*.
transport *vt* transportar; * *n* transporte *m*.
transportation *n* transporte *m*.
trap *n* trampa *f*; * *vt* atrapar, bloquear.
trap door *n* trampilla *f*; escotillón *m*.
trapeze *n* trapecio *m*.
trappings *npl* adornos *mpl*.
trash *n* basura *f*; tonterías *fpl*.
trash can *n* cubo de la basura *m*.
trashy *adj* vil, despreciable, de ningún valor.
travel *vi* viajar; * *vt* recorrer; * *n* viaje *m*.
travel agency *n* agencia de viajes *f*.
travel agent *n* agente de viajes *m*.
traveler *n* viajante, viajero/ra *m/f*.
traveler's check *n* cheque de viaje *m*.
travel-sickness *n* mareo *m*.
travesty *n* parodia *f*.
trawler *n* arrastrero *m*.
tray *n* bandeja *f*; cajón *m*.
treacherous *adj* traidor/a, perfido/da.
treachery *n* traición *f*.
tread *vi* pisar; pistoear; * *n* pisada *f*; ruido de pasos *m*; banda de rodadura *f*.
treason *n* traición *f*; **high** ~ alta traición *f*.
treasure *n* tesoro *m*; * *vt* atesorar.
treasurer *n* tesorero/ra *m/f*.
treat *vt* tratar; regalar; * *n* regalo *m*; placer *m*.
treatise *n* tratado *m*.
treatment *n* trato *m*.
treaty *n* tratado *m*.
treble *adj* triple; * *vt* (*vi*) triplicar(se); * *n* (*mus*) tiple *m*.
treble clef *n* clave de sol *f*.
tree *n* árbol *m*.
trek *n* caminata *f*; expedición *f*.
trellis *n* enrejado *m*.
tremble *vi* temblar.
trembling *n* temor *m*; trino *m*.
tremendous *adj* tremendo/da; enorme; estupendo/da.
tremor *n* temblor *m*.
trench *n* foso *m*; (*mil*) trinchera *f*; zanja *f*.
trend *n* tendencia *f*; curso *m*; moda *f*.

trendy *adj* de moda.
trepidation *n* inquietud *f.*
trespass *vt* transpasar, violar.
tress *n* trenza *f;* rizo de pelo *m.*
trestle *n* caballete de serrador *m.*
trial *n* proceso *m;* prueba *f;* ensayo *m;* desgracia *f.*
triangle *n* triángulo *m.*
triangular *adj* triangular.
tribal *adj* tribal.
tribe *n* tribu *f;* raza, casta *f.*
tribulation *n* tribulación *f.*
tribunal *n* tribunal *m.*
tributary *adj, n* tributario/ria *m/f.*
tribute *n* tributo *m.*
trice *n* momento, tris *m.*
trick *n* engaño, fraude *m;* burla *f;* baza *f;* zancadilla *f;* * *vt* engañar.
trickery *n* engaño *m.*
trickle *vi* gotear; * *n* reguero *m.*
tricky *adj* difícil; delicado/da.
tricycle *n* triciclo *m.*
trifle *n* bagatela, nineria *f;* * *vi* bobear; juguetear.
trifling *adj* frívolo/la, inútil.
trigger *n* gatillo *m;* * to ~ off *vt* desencadenar.
trigonometry *n* trigonometría *f.*
trill *n* trino *m;* * *vi* trinar.
trillion *n* billón *m.*
trim *adj* aseado/da; en buen estado; arreglado/da; * *vt* arreglar; recortar; adornar.
trimester *n* trimestre *m.*
trimmings *npl* accesorios *mpl.*
Trinity *n* Trinidad *f.*
trinket *n* joya, alhaja *f;* adorno *m.*
trio *n* (*mus*) trío *m.*
trip *vt* hacer caer; * *vi* tropezar; resbalar; * *n* resbalón *m;* viaje corto *m, Lat Am* paseo *m;* zancadilla *f.*
tripe *n* callos *mpl;* bobadas *fpl.*
triple *adj* triple; * *vt* triplicar.
triplets *npl* trillizos/zas *m/fpl.*
triplicate *n* triplicado *m.*
tripod *n* trípode *m.*
trite *adj* trivial; usado/da.
triumph *n* triunfo *m;* * *vi* triunfar.
triumphal *adj* triunfal.
triumphant *adj* triunfante; victorioso/sa; ~ly *adv* en triunfo.
trivia *npl* trivialidades *fpl.*
trivial *adj* trivial, vulgar; ~ly *adv* trivialmente.
triviality *n* trivialidad *f.*
trolley *n* carrito *m.*

trombone *n* trombón *m.*
troop *n* grupo *m;* ~s *npl* tropas *fpl.*
trooper *n* soldado a caballo *m.*
trophy *n* trofeo *m.*
tropical *adj* trópico/ca.
trot *n* trote *m;* * *vi* trotar.
trouble *vt* afligir; molestar; * *n* problema *m;* disturbio *m;* inquietud *f;* aflicción, pena *f.*
troubled *adj* preocupado/da; agitado/da.
troublemaker *n* agitador/a *m/f.*
troubleshooter *n* conciliador/a *m/f.*
troublesome *adj* molesto/ta.
trough *n* abrevadero *m;* comedero *m.*
troupe *n* grupo *m.*
trousers *npl* pantalones *mpl.*
trout *n* trucha *f.*
trowel *n* paleta *f.*
truce *n* tregua *f.*
truck *n* camión *m;* vagón *m.*
truck driver *n* camionero/ra *m/f.*
truculent *adj* truculento/ta, cruel.
trudge *vi* andar fatigosamente, andar con dificultad.
true *adj* verdadero/ra, cierto/ta; sincero/ra; exacto/ta.
truelove *n* amor verdadero *m.*
truffle *n* trufa *f.*
truly *adv* en verdad; sinceramente.
trump *n* triunfo (en el juego de naipes) *m.*
trumpet *n* trompeta *f.*
trunk *n* baúl, cofre *m;* trompa *f.*
truss *n* braguero *m;* * *vt* atar; espetar.
trust *n* confianza *f;* trust *m;* fideicomiso *m;* * *vt* tener confianza en; confiar algo a.
trusted *adj* de confianza.
trustee *n* fideicomisario/ria, curador/a *m/f.*
trustful *adj* fiel; confiado/da.
trustily *adv* fielmente.
trusting *adj* confiado/da.
trustworthy *adj* digno/na de confianza.
trusty *adj* fiel, leal; seguro/ra.
truth *n* verdad *f;* fidelidad *f;* realidad *f;* in ~ en verdad.
truthful *adj* verídico/ca; veraz.
truthfulness *n* veracidad *f.*
try *vt* examinar, ensayar, probar; experimentar; tentar; inte ntar; juzgar; * *vi* probar; to ~ on probarse; to ~ out probar; * *n* tentativa *f;* ensayo *m.*
trying *adj* pesado/da; cansado/da.
tub *n* balde *m,* barreño *m,* cubo *m;* tina *f.*
tuba *n* tuba *f.*
tube *n* tubo, cañon, canuto *m.*
tuberculosis *n* tuberculosis *f invar.*
tubing *n* caería *f.*

tuck n pliegue m; * vt poner.
Tuesday n martes m invar.
tuft n mechón m; manojo m.
tug vt remolcar; * n remolcador m.
tuition n matrícula f; enseñanza f.
tulip n tulipán m.
tumble vi caer, hundirse; revolcarse; * vt revolver; volcar; * n caída f; vuelco m.
tumbledown adj destartalado/da.
tumbler n vaso m.
tummy n barriga f.
tumor n tumor m.
tumultuous adj tumultuoso/sa.
tuna n atún m.
tune n tono m; armonia f; aria f; * vt afinar; sintonizar.
tuneful adj armonioso/sa, acorde, melodioso/sa.
tuner n sintonizador/a m.
tunic n túnica f.
tuning fork n (mus) diapasón m.
tunnel n túnel m; * vt construir un tunel por.
turban n turbante m.
turbine n turbina f.
turbulence n turbulencia, confusión f.
turbulent adj turbulento/ta, tumultuoso/sa.
tureen n sopera f.
turf n césped m; * vt cubrir con césped.
turgid adj pesado/da.
turkey n pavo m.
turmoil n disturbio m; baraúnda f.
turn vi volver; cambiar; girar; dar vueltas; volverse a, mudarse, transformarse; **to ~ around** volverse; girar; **to ~ back** volverse; **to ~ down** rechazar; doblar; **to ~ in** acostarse; **to ~ off** vi desviarse; vt apagar; parar; **to ~ on** encender, prender; poner en marcha; **to ~ out** apagar; **to ~ over** vi volverse; vt volver; **to ~ up** vi llegar; aparecer; vt subir; * n vuelta f; giro m; rodeo m; turno m; vez f; inclinación f.
turncoat n desertor/a, renegado/da m/f.
turning n vuelta f.
turnip n nabo m.
turn-off n salida f.
turnout n concurrencia f.
turnover n facturación f.
turnpike n autopista de peaje f.
turnstile n torniquete m.
turntable n plato m.
turpentine n trementina f.
turquoise n turquesa f.
turret n torrecilla, torreta f.

turtle n tortuga marina f.
turtledove n tórtola f.
tusk n colmillo m.
tussle n pelea f.
tutor n tutor/a m/f; profesor/a m/f; * vt enseñar, instruir.
tuxedo n smoking m.
twang n gangueo m; sonido agudo m.
tweezers npl tenacillas fpl.
twelfth adj, n duodécimo/ma.
twelve adj, n doce.
twentieth adj, n vigésimo/ma.
twenty adj, n veinte.
twice adv dos veces.
twig n ramita f; * vi caer en la cuenta.
twilight n crepúsculo m.
twin n gemelo/la m/f.
twine vi entrelazarse; caracolear; * n bramante m.
twinge vt punzar, pellizcar; * n dolor agudo/ punzante m; punzada f.
twinkle vi centellear; parpadear.
twirl vt dar vueltas a; * vi piruetear; * n rotación f.
twist vt torcer, retorcer; entretejer; * vi serpentear; * n torsión f; vuelta f; doblez f.
twit n (col) tonto/ta m/f.
twitch vi moverse nerviosamente; * n tirón; tic m.
twitter vi gorjear; * n gorjeo m.
two adj, n dos.
two-door adj de dos puertas.
two-faced adj falso/sa.
twofold adj doble, duplicado/da; * adv al doble.
two-seater n avión/coche de dos plazas m.
twosome n pareja f.
tycoon n magnate m.
type n tipo m; letra f; modelo m; * vt escribir a máquina, Lat Am tipear.
typecast adj encasillado/da.
typeface n tipo m.
typescript n texto mecanografiado m.
typewriter n máquina de escribir f.
typewritten adj mecanografiado/da.
typical adj típico/ca.
typographer n tipógrafo m.
typographical adj tipógrafico/ca.
typography n tipografía f.
tyrannical adj tiránico/ca.
tyranny n tiranía f; crueldad f.
tyrant n tirano/na m/f.

U

ubiquitous *adj* ubicuo/cua.
udder *n* ubre *f.*
ugh *excl* ¡puaj!
ugliness *n* fealdad *f.*
ugly *adj* feo, fea; peligroso/sa.
ulcer *n* úlcera *f.*
ulterior *adj* ulterior.
ultimate *adj* último/ma; ~ly *adv* al final; a fin de cuentas.
ultimatum *n* ultimátum *m.*
ultramarine *n* ultramar *m;* * *adj* ultramarino/na.
ultrasound *n* ultrasonido *m.*
ultrasound scan *n* ecografía *f*
umbilical cord *n* cordón umbilical *m.*
umbrella *n* paraguas *m invar.*
umpire *n* árbitro/tra *m/f.*
umpteen *adj* enésimos/mas.
unable *adj* incapaz.
unaccompanied *adj* solo/la, sin acompañamiento.
unaccomplished *adj* incompleto/ta, no acabado/da.
unaccountable *adj* inexplicable, extraño/ña.
unaccountably *adv* extrañamente.
unaccustomed *adj* desacostumbrado/da, desusado/da.
unacknowledged *adj* desconocido/da; negado/da.
unacquainted *adj* desconocido/da; ignorado/da.
unadorned *adj* sin adorno.
unadulterated *adj* genuino/na, puro/ra; sin mezcla.
unaffected *adj* sincero/ra, sin afectación.
unaided *adj* sin ayuda.
unaltered *adj* invariado/da.
unambitious *adj* poco/ca ambicioso/sa.
unanimity *n* unanimidad *f.*
unanimous *adj* unánime; ~ly *adv* unánimemente.
unanswerable *adj* incontrovertible, incontestable.
unanswered *adj* no contestado/da.
unapproachable *adj* inaccesible.
unarmed *adj* inerme, desarmado/da.
unassuming *adj* nada presuntuoso/sa, modesto/ta.
unattached *adj* independiente; disponible.
unattainable *adj* inasequible.

unattended *adj* sin atender.
unauthorized *adj* no autorizado/da.
unavoidable *adj* inevitable.
unavoidably *adv* inevitablemente.
unaware *adj* ignorante.
unawares *adv* inadvertidamente; de improviso.
unbalanced *adj* desequilibrado/da; trastornado/da.
unbearable *adj* insoportable.
unbecoming *adj* indecente, indecoroso/sa.
unbelievable *adj* increíble.
unbend *vi* relajarse; * *vt* enderezar.
unbiased *adj* imparcial.
unblemished *adj* sin mancha, sin tacha, irreprensible.
unborn *adj* no nacido/da.
unbreakable *adj* irrompible.
unbroken *adj* intacto/ta; indómito/ta; entero/ra; no batido/da.
unbutton *vt* desabotonar.
uncalled-for *adj* fuera de lugar.
uncanny *adj* extraordinario/ria.
unceasing *adj* sin cesar, continuo/nua.
unceremonious *adj* brusco/ca.
uncertain *adj* incierto/ta, dudoso/sa.
uncertainty *n* incertidumbre *f.*
unchangeable *adj* inmutable.
unchanged *adj* no alterado/da.
unchanging *adj* inalterable, immutable.
uncharitable *adj* nada caritativo/va, duro/ra.
unchecked *adj* desenfrenado/da, incontrolado/da.
unchristian *adj* poco cristiano/na.
uncivil *adj* grosero/ra, descortés.
uncivilized *adj* tosco/ca, salvaje, incivilizado/da.
uncle *n* tío.
uncomfortable *adj* incómodo/da; molesto/ta.
uncomfortably *adv* incómodamente; inquietantemente.
uncommon *adj* raro/ra, extraordinario/ria.
uncompromising *adj* irreconciliable.
unconcerned *adj* indiferente.
unconditional *adj* sin condiciones, incondicional.
unconfined *adj* libre, ilimitado/da.
unconfirmed *adj* no confirmado/da.

unconnected *adj* inconexo/xa.
unconquerable *adj* invencible, insuperable.
unconscious *adj* inconsciente; ~**ly** *adv* inconscientemente.
unconstrained *adj* libre, voluntario/ria.
uncontrollable *adj* incontrolable; desenfrenado/da.
unconventional *adj* poco convencional.
unconvincing *adj* no convincente.
uncork *vt* destapar.
uncorrected *adj* sin corregir, no corregido/da.
uncouth *adj* grosero/ra, zafio/fia.
uncover *vt* descubrir.
uncultivated *adj* inculto/ta.
uncut *adj* no cortado/da, entero/ra.
undamaged *adj* ileso/sa, libre de daño.
undaunted *adj* intrépido/da.
undecided *adj* indeciso/sa.
undefiled *adj* impoluto/ta, puro/ra.
undeniable *adj* innegable, incontestable; ~**bly** *adv* indubitablemente.
under *prep* debajo de; menos de; segun; * *adv* debajo.
under-age *adj* menor de edad.
undercharge *vt* cobrar de menos.
underclothing *n* ropa íntima *f.*
undercoat *n* primera mano *f.*
undercover *adj* clandestino/na.
undercurrent *n* corriente subyacente *f.*
undercut *vt* vender más barato que.
underdeveloped *adj* subdesarrollado/da.
underdog *n* desvalido/da *m/f.*
underdone *adj* poco cocido/da.
underestimate *vt* subestimar.
undergo *vt* sufrir; sostener.
undergraduate *n* estudiante universitario/ria *m/f.*
underground *n* movimiento clandestino *m.*
undergrowth *n* soto *m,* maleza *f.*
underhand *adv* clandestinamente; * *adj* secreto/ta, clandestino/na.
underlie *vi* estar debajo.
underline *vt* subrayar.
undermine *vt* minar.
underneath *adv* debajo; * *prep* debajo de.
underpaid *adj* mal pagado/da.
underpants *npl* calzoncillos *mpl.*
underprivileged *adj* desvalido/da.
underrate *vt* menospreciar.
undersecretary *n* subsecretario/ria *m/f.*
undershirt *n* camiseta *f.*
underside *n* revés *m.*
understand *vt* entender, comprender.
understandable *adj* comprensible.

understanding *n* entendimiento *m;* inteligencia *f;* conocimiento *m;* correspondencia *f;* * *adj* comprensivo/va.
understatement *n* subestimación *f;* modestia *f.*
undertake *vt, vi* emprender.
undertaking *n* empresa *f;* empeño *m.*
undervalue *vt* menospreciar.
underwater *adj* submarino/na; * *adv* bajo el agua.
underwear *n* ropa íntima *f.*
underworld *n* hampa *f.*
underwrite *vt* suscribir; asegurar contra riesgos.
underwriter *n* asegurador/a *m/f.*
undeserved *adj* inmerecido/da; ~**ly** *adv* sin haberlo merecido.
undeserving *adj* indigno/na.
undesirable *adj* indeseable.
undetermined *adj* indeterminado/da, indeciso/sa.
undigested *adj* no digerido/da.
undiminished *adj* entero/ra, no disminuido/da.
undisciplined *adj* indisciplinado/da.
undisguised *adj* sin disfraz, cándido/da, sincero/ra.
undismayed *adj* intrépido/da.
undisputed *adj* incontestable.
undisturbed *adj* quieto/ta, tranquilo/la.
undivided *adj* indiviso/sa, entero/ra.
undo *vt* deshacer, destar, descoser.
undoing *n* ruina *f.*
undoubted *adj* indudable; ~**ly** *adv* indudablemente.
undress *vi* desnudarse.
undue *adj* indebido/da; injusto/ta.
undulating *adj* ondulante.
unduly *adv* indebidamente.
undying *adj* inmortal.
unearth *vt* desenterrar.
unearthly *adj* inverosímil.
uneasiness *n* inquietud *f;* zozobra *f.*
uneasy *adj* inquieto/ta, desasosegado/da; incomodo/da.
uneducated *adj* ignorante.
unemployed *adj* desmpleado/da, parado/da; ~ **person** parado/da *m/f.*
unemployment *n* desempleo, paro *m.*
unending *adj* interminable.
unenlightened *adj* no iluminado/da.
unenviable *adj* poco envidiable.
unequal *adj,* ~**ly** *adv* desigual(mente).
unequaled *adj* incomparable.
unerring *adj,* ~**ly** *adv* infalible(mente).

uneven adj desigual; impar; ~ly adv desigualmente.

unexpected adj inesperado/da; inopinado/da; ~ly adv de repente; inopinadamente.

unexplored adj inexplorado/da, no descubierto/ta.

unfailing adj infalible, seguro/ra.

unfair adj falso/sa; injusto/ta; ~ly adv injustamente.

unfaithful adj infiel, pérfido/da.

unfaithfulness n infidelidad, perfidia f.

unfaltering adj firme, asegurado/da.

unfamiliar adj desacostumbrado/da, poco común.

unfashionable adj pasado/da de moda; ~bly adv contra la moda.

unfasten vt desatar, soltar, aflojar.

unfathomable adj insondable, impenetrable.

unfavorable adj desfavorable.

unfeeling adj insensible, duro/ra de corazón.

unfinished adj imperfecto/ta, no acabado/da.

unfit adj indispuesto/ta; incapaz.

unfold vt desplegar; revelar; * vi abrirse.

unforeseen adj imprevisto/ta.

unforgettable adj inolvidable.

unforgivable adj imperdonable.

unforgiving adj implacable.

unfortunate adj desafortunado/da, infeliz; ~ly adv por desgracia, infelizmente.

unfounded adj sin fundamento.

unfriendly adj antipático/ca.

unfruitful adj estéril; infructuoso/sa.

unfurnished adj sin muebles; desprovisto/ta.

ungainly adj desmañado/da.

ungentlemanly adj indigno/na de un hombre bien criado.

ungovernable adj indomable, ingobernable.

ungrateful adj ingrato/ta; desagradable; ~ly adv ingratamente.

ungrounded adj infundado/da.

unhappily adv infelizmente.

unhappiness n infelicidad f.

unhappy adj infeliz.

unharmed adj ileso/sa, sano/na y salvo/va.

unhealthy adj malsano/na; enfermizo/za.

unheard-of adj inaudito/ta, extraño/ña, sin ejemplo.

unheeding adj negligente; distraído/da.

unhitch vt desaparejar.

unhook vt desenganchar; descolgar; desabrochar.

unhoped (for) adj inesperado/da.

unhurt adj ileso/sa.

unicorn n unicornio m.

uniform adj, ~ly adv uniforme(mente); * n uniforme m.

uniformity adj uniformidad f.

unify vt unificar.

unimaginable adj inimaginable.

unimpaired adj no disminuido/da, no alterado/da.

unimportant adj poco importante.

uninformed adj desinformado/da.

uninhabitable adj inhabitable.

uninhabited adj inhabitado/da, desierto/ta.

uninjured adj ileso/sa, no dañado/da.

unintelligible adj ininteligible.

unintelligibly adv de modo ininteligible.

unintentional adj involuntario/ria, no intencionado/da.

uninterested adj desinteresado/da.

uninteresting adj poco interesante.

uninterrupted adj sin interrupción, continuo/nua.

uninvited adj no convivado/da.

union n unión f; sindicato m.

unionist n sindicalista m/f.

unique adj único/ca, uno/na, singular.

unison n unísono m.

unit n unidad f.

Unitarian n unitario/ria m/f.

unite vt (vi) unir(se); juntarse; (fig) zurcir.

unitedly adv unidamente, de acuerdo.

United States (of America) npl Estados Unidos (de América) mpl.

unity n unidad, concordia, conformidad f.

universal adj, ~ly adv universal(mente).

universe n universo m.

university n universidad f.

unjust adj injusto/ta; ~ly adv injustamente.

unkempt adj despeinado/da; descuidado/da.

unkind adj poco amable; severo/ra.

unknowingly adv sin saberlo.

unknown adj incógnito/ta.

unlawful adj ilegal; ~ly adv ilegalmente.

unlawfulness n ilegalidad f.

unleash vt desencadenar.

unless conj a menos que, si no.

unlicensed adj sin licencia.

unlike, unlikely adj diferente; improbable; inverosímil.

unlikelihood n inverisimilitud f.

unlimited adj ilimitado/da.

unlisted adj que no viene en la guía.

unload vt descargar.

unlock vt abrir.

unluckily *adv* desafortunadamente.
unlucky *adj* desafortunado/da.
unmanageable *adj* inmanejable, intratable.
unmannered *adj* rudo/da, brutal, grosero/ra.
unmannerly *adj* malcriado/da, descortés.
unmarried *adj* soltero/ra.
unmask *vt* desenmascarar.
unmentionable *adj* que no se puede mencionar.
unmerited *adj* desmerecido/da.
unmindful *adj* olvidadizo/za, negligente.
unmistakable *adj* inconfundible; ~ly *adv* indudablemente.
unmitigated *adj* absoluto/ta.
unmoved *adj* inmoto, firme.
unnatural *adj* antinatural; perverso/sa; afectado/da.
unnecessary *adj* inútil, innecesario/ria.
unneighborly *adj* poco atento/ta con sus vecinos; descortés.
unnoticed *adj* inadvertido/da.
unnumbered *adj* innumerable.
unobserved *adj* no observado/da.
unobtainable *adj* inconseguible; inexistente.
unobtrusive *adj* modesto/ta.
unoccupied *adj* desocupado/da.
unoffending *adj* sencillo/lla, inocente.
unofficial *adj* no oficial.
unorthodox *adj* heterodoxo/xa.
unpack *vt* desempacar; desenvolver.
unpaid *adj* no pagado/da, *Lat Am* impago/ga.
unpalatable *adj* desabrido/da, desgradable.
unparalleled *adj* sin paralelo; sin par.
unpleasant *adj* , ~ly *adv* desagradable(mente).
unpleasantness *n* desagrado *m*.
unplug *vt* desconectar.
unpolished *adj* que no está pulido/da; rudo/da, grosero/ra.
unpopular *adj* impopular.
unpracticed *adj* inexperto/ta, no versado/da.
unprecedented *adj* sin precedentes.
unpredictable *adj* imprevisible.
unprejudiced *adj* imparcial.
unprepared *adj* no preparado/da.
unprofitable *adj* inútil, vano/na; poco lucrativo/va.
unprotected *adj* desvalido/da, sin protección.
unpublished *adj* no publicado/da; inédito/ta.
unpunished *adj* impune.
unqualified *adj* sin títulos; total.
unquestionable *adj* indubitable, indisputable; ~ly *adv* sin duda, sin disputa.

unquestioned *adj* incontestable, no preguntado/da.
unravel *vt* desenredar.
unread *adj* no leído/da; ignorante.
unreal *adj* irreal.
unrealistic *adj* poco realista.
unreasonable *adj* poco razonable; disparatado/da.
unreasonably *adv* poco razonablemente; disparatadamente.
unrelated *adj* sin relación; inconexo/xa.
unrelenting *adj* implacable.
unreliable *adj* poco fiable.
unremitting *adj* constante, incansable.
unrepentant *adj* impenitente.
unreserved *adj* sin restricción; franco/ca; ~ly *adv* abiertamente.
unrest *n* malestar *m*; disturbios *mpl*.
unrestrained *adj* desenfrenado/da; ilimitado/da.
unripe *adj* inmaduro/ra.
unrivaled *adj* sin rival, sin igual.
unroll *vt* desenrollar.
unruliness *n* turbulencia *f*; desenfreno *m*.
unruly *adj* desenfrenado/da.
unsafe *adj* inseguro/ra, peligroso/sa.
unsatisfactory *adj* insatisfactorio/ria.
unsavory *adj* desabrido/da, insípido/da.
unscathed *adj* ileso/sa.
unscrew *vt* destornillar.
unscrupulous *adj* sin escrúpulos.
unseasonable *adj* intempestivo/va, fuera de propósito.
unseemly *adj* indecente.
unseen *adj* invisible.
unselfish *adj* desinteresado/da.
unsettle *vt* perturbar.
unsettled *adj* inquieto/ta; inestable; variable.
unshaken *adj* firme, estable.
unshaven *adj* sin afeitar.
unsightly *adj* desagradable a la vista, feo/a.
unskillful *adj* inhábil, poco mañoso/sa.
unskilled *adj* no cualificado/da.
unsociable *adj* insociable, intratable.
unspeakable *adj* inefable, indecible.
unstable *adj* instable, inconstante.
unsteadily *adv* ligeramente, inconstantemente.
unsteady *adj* inestable.
unstudied *adj* no estudiado/da; no premeditado/da.
unsuccessful *adj* infeliz, desafortunado/da; ~ly *adv* sin éxito.
unsuitable *adj* inapropiado/da; inoportuno/na.
unsure *adj* inseguro/ra.

unsympathetic *adj* poco comprensivo/va.
untamed *adj* indomado/da.
untapped *adj* sin explotar.
untenable *adj* insostenible.
unthinkable *adj* inconcebible.
unthinking *adj* desatento/ta, irreflexivo/va.
untidiness *n* desaliño *m*.
untidy *adj* desordenado/da; sucio/cia.
untie *vt* desatar, deshacer, soltar, zafar.
until *prep* hasta; * *conj* hasta que.
untimely *adj* intempestivo/va.
untiring *adj* incansable.
untold *adj* nunca dicho/cha; indecible; incalculable.
untouched *adj* intacto/ta.
untoward *adj* impropio/pia; adverso/sa.
untried *adj* no ensayado/da/probado/da.
untroubled *adj* no perturbado/da, tranquilo/la.
untrue *adj* falso/sa.
untrustworthy *adj* indigno/na de confianza.
untruth *n* falsedad, mentira *f*.
unused *adj* sin usar, no usado/da.
unusual *adj* inusual, inusitado/da, raro/ra; ~ly *adv* inusitadamente, raramente.
unveil *vt* quitar el velo, descubrir.
unwavering *adj* inquebrantable.
unwelcome *adj* desagradable, inoportuno/na.
unwell *adj* enfermizo/za, malo/la.
unwieldy *adj* pesado/da.
unwilling *adj* desinclinado/da; ~ly *adv* de mala gana.
unwillingness *n* mala gana, repugnancia *f*.
unwind *vt* desenredar, desenmarañar; * *vi* relajarse.
unwise *adj* imprudente.
unwitting *adj* inconsciente.
unworkable *adj* poco práctico/ca.
unworthy *adj* indigno/na.
unwrap *vt* desenvolver.
unwritten *adj* no escrito/ta.
up *adv* arriba, en lo alto; levantado/da; * *prep* hacia; hasta.
upbraid *vt* zaherir.
upbringing *n* educación *f*.
update *vt* poner al dia.
upheaval *n* agitación *f*.
uphill *adj* difícil, penoso/sa; * *adv* cuesta arriba.
uphold *vt* sostener, apoyar.
upholstery *n* tapicería *f*.
upkeep *n* mantenimiento *m*.
uplift *vt* levantar.
upon *prep* sobre, encima.
upper *adj* superior; más elevado/da.
upper-class *adj* de la clase alta.

upper-hand *n* (*fig*) superioridad *f*.
uppermost *adj* más alto/ta, supremo/ma; to be ~ predominar.
upright *adj* derecho/cha, perpendicular, recto/ta; puesto/ta en pie; honrado/da.
uprising *n* sublevación *f*.
uproar *n* tumulto, alboroto *m*.
uproot *vt* desarraigar.
upset *vt* trastornar; derramar, volcar; * *n* revés *m*; trastorno *m*; * *adj* molesto/ta; revuelto/ta.
upshot *n* remate *m*; fin *m*; conclusión *f*.
upside-down *adv* al revés.
upstairs *adv* arriba.
upstart *n* advenedizo/za *m/f*.
uptight *adj* nervioso/sa.
up-to-date *adj* al día.
upturn *n* mejora *f*.
upward *adj* ascendente; ~s *adv* hacia arriba.
urban *adj* urbano/na.
urbane *adj* cortés.
urchin *n* golfillo/lla *m/f*.
urge *vt* animar; * *n* impulso *m*; deseo *m*.
urgency *n* urgencia *f*.
urgent *adj* urgente.
urinal *n* orinal *m*.
urinate *vi* orinar.
urine *n* orina *f*.
urn *n* urna *f*.
us *pn* nos; nosotros, nosotras.
usage *n* tratamiento *m*; uso *m*.
use *n* uso *m*; utilidad, práctica *f*; * *vt* usar, emplear.
used *adj* usado/da.
useful *adj* , ~ly *adv* útil(mente).
usefulness *n* utilidad *f*.
useless *adj* inútil; ~ly *adv* inútilmente.
uselessness *n* inutilidad *f*.
user-friendly *adj* fácil de utilizar.
usher *n* ujier *m/f*; acomodador/a *m/f*.
usherette *n* acomodadora *f*.
usual *adj* usual, común, normal; ~ly *adv* normalmente.
usurer *n* usurero/ra *m/f*.
usurp *vt* usurpar.
usury *n* usura *f*.
utensil *n* utensilio *m*.
uterus *n* útero *m*.
utility *n* utilidad *f*.
utilize *vt* utilizar.
utmost *adj* extremo/ma, sumo/ma; último/ma.
utter *adj* total; todo; entero/ra; * *vt* proferir; expresar; publicar.
utterance *n* expresion *f*.
utterly *adv* enteramente, del todo.

V

vacancy *n* cuarto libre *m*, vacante *f*.
vacant *adj* vacío/cía; desocupado/da; vacante.
vacant lot *n* solar *m*.
vacate *vt* desocupar; dejar.
vacation *n* vacaciones *fpl*.
vaccinate *vt* vacunar.
vaccination *n* vacunación *f*.
vaccine *n* vacuna *f*.
vacuous *adj* vacío/cía, vacuo/cua.
vacuum *n* vacío *m*.
vacuum flask *n* termo *m*.
vagina *n* vagina *f*.
vagrant *n* vagabundo/da *m/f*.
vague *adj* vago/ga; ~ly *adv* vagamente.
vain *adj* vano/na, inútil; vanidoso/sa.
valet *n* criado *m*.
valiant *adj* valiente, valeroso/sa.
valid *adj* válido/da.
valley *n* valle *m*.
valor *n* valor, aliento, brío, esfuerzo *m*.
valuable *adj* valioso/sa; ~s *npl* objetos de valor *mpl*.
valuation *n* tasa, valuación *f*.
value *n* valor, precio *m*; * *vt* valuar, *Lat Am* avaluar; estimar, apreciar.
valued *adj* apreciado/da.
valve *n* válvula *f*.
vampire *n* vampiro *m*.
van *n* camioneta *f*.
vandal *n* gamberro/rra *m/f*.
vandalism *n* vandalismo *m*.
vandalize *vt* dañar.
vanguard *n* vanguardia *f*.
vanilla *n* vainilla *f*.
vanish *vi* desvanecerse, desaparecer.
vanity *n* vanidad *f*.
vanity case *n* neceser *m*.
vanquish *vt* vencer, conquistar.
vantage point *n* punto panorámico *m*.
vapor *n* vapor *m*; exhalación *f*.
variable *adj* variable; voluble.
variance *n* discordia, desavenencia *f*.
variation *n* variación *f*.
varicose vein *n* variz *f*, *Lat Am* várice *f*.
varied *adj* variado/da.
variety *n* variedad *f*.
variety show *n* espectáculo de variedades *m*.
various *adj* vario/ria, diverso/sa, diferente.
varnish *n* barniz *m*; * *vt* barnizar.

vary *vt*, *vi* variar; cambiar.
vase *n* florero, jarrón *m*.
vast *adj* vasto/ta; inmenso/sa.
vat *n* tina *f*.
vault *n* bóveda *f*; cueva *f*; caverna *f*; * *vt* saltar.
veal *n* ternera *f*.
veer *vi* (*mar*) virar.
vegetable *adj* vegetal; * *n* vegetal *m*; ~s *pl* verduras *fpl*.
vegetable garden *n* huerta *f*.
vegetarian *n* vegetariano/na *m/f*.
vegetate *vi* vegetar.
vegetation *n* vegetación *f*.
vehemence *n* vehemencia, violencia *f*.
vehement *adj* vehemente, violento/ta; ~ly *adv* vehementemente.
vehicle *n* vehículo *m*; all-terrain ~ todoterreno *m*.
veil *n* velo *m*; * *vt* encubrir, ocultar.
vein *n* vena *f*; cavidad *f*; inclinación del ingenio *f*.
velocity *n* velocidad *f*.
velvet *n* terciopelo *m*.
vending machine *n* máquina expendedora *f*.
vendor *n* vendedor/a *m/f*.
veneer *n* chapa *f*; barniz *m*.
venerable *adj* venerable.
venerate *vt* venerar, honrar.
veneration *n* veneración *f*.
venereal *adj* venéreo.
vengeance *n* venganza *f*.
venial *adj* venial.
venison *n* (carne de) venado *f*.
venom *n* veneno *m*.
venomous *adj* venenoso/sa; ~ly *adv* venenosamente.
vent *n* respiradero *m*; salida *f*; * *vt* desahogar.
ventilate *vt* ventilar.
ventilation *n* ventilación *f*.
ventilator *n* ventilador *m*.
ventriloquist *n* ventrílocuo/cua *m/f*.
venture *n* empresa *f*; * *vi* aventurarse; * *vt* aventurar, arriesgar.
venue *n* lugar de reunión, local *m*.
veranda(h) *n* terraza *f*, porche *m*.
verb *n* (*gr*) verbo *m*.
verbal *adj* verbal, literal; ~ly *adv* verbalmente.
verbatim *adv* literalmente.

verbose adj verboso/sa.
verdant adj verde.
verdict n (law) veredicto m; opinión f.
verification n verificación f.
verify vt verificar.
veritable adj verdadero/ra.
vermicelli npl fideos mpl.
vermin n bichos mpl.
vermouth n vermut m.
versatile adj versátil; polifacético/ca.
verse n verso m; versículo m.
versed adj versado/da.
version n versión f.
versus prep contra.
vertebra n vértebra f.
vertebral, vertebrate adj vertebral.
vertex n cenit, vértice m.
vertical adj , ~ly adv vertical(mente).
vertigo n vértigo m.
verve n brío m.
very adj idéntico/ca, mismo/ma; * adv muy, mucho, sumamente.
vessel n vasija f; vaso m; barco m.
vest n chaleco m.
vestibule n vestíbulo m.
vestige n vestigio m.
vestment n vestido m; vestidura f.
vestry n sacristía f.
veteran adj, n veterano/na m/f.
veterinarian, vet n veterinario/ria m/f.
veterinary adj veterinario/ria.
veterinary science n veterinaria f.
veto n veto m; * vt vetar.
vex vt molestar.
vexed adj molesto/ta; controvertido/da.
via prep por.
viaduct n viaducto m.
vial n ampolla f, vial m.
vibrate vi vibrar.
vibration n vibración f.
vicarious adj sustituto/ta.
vice n vicio m; culpa f; tornillo m.
vice-chairman n vice-presidente m.
vice-chancellor (of a university) n rector/ra m/f.
vice-chancellorship n rectorado m.
vice versa adv viceversa.
vicinity n vecindad, proximidad f; **immediate** ~ inmediaciones fpl.
vicious adj vicioso/sa; ~ly adv de manera viciosa.
victim n víctima f.
victimize vt victimizar.
victor n vencedor/a m/f.
victorious adj victorioso/sa.

victory n victoria f.
video n vídeo m, Lat Am video m.
video camera n videocámara f.
video cassette n videocasete m.
video game n videojuego m.
video tape n cinta de vídeo f.
vie vi competir.
view n vista f; perspectiva f; aspecto m; opinión f; paisaje m; * vt mirar, ver; examinar.
viewer n televidente m/f.
viewfinder n visor m.
viewpoint n punto de vista m.
vigil n vela f; vigilia f.
vigilance n vigilancia f.
vigilant adj vigilante, atento/ta.
vigorous adj vigoroso/sa; ~ly adv vigorosamente.
vigor n vigor m; energía f.
vile adj vil, bajo/ja; asqueroso/sa.
vilify vt envilecer.
villa n chalet m; casa de campo f.
village n aldea f.
villager n aldeano/na m/f.
villain n malvado/da m/f.
vindicate vt vindicar, defender.
vindication n vindicación f; justificación f.
vindictive adj vengativo/va.
vine n vid f.
vinegar n vinagre m.
vineyard n viña f.
vintage n vendimia f.
vinyl n vinilo m.
viola n (mus) viola f.
violate vt violar.
violation n violación f.
violence n violencia f.
violent adj violento/ta; ~ly adv violentamente.
violet n (bot) violeta f.
violin n (mus) violín m.
violinist n violinista m/f.
violoncello, cello n (mus) violoncelo, violonchelo m.
VIP n vip m/f.
viper n víbora f.
virgin n virgen f; * adj virgen.
virginity n virginidad f.
Virgo n Virgo f (signo del zodiaco).
virile adj viril.
virility n virilidad f.
virtual adj, ~ly adv virtual(mente).
virtue n virtud f.
virtuous adj virtuoso/sa.
virulent adj virulento/ta.

virus *n* virus *m invar.*
visa *n* visado *m*, visa *f.*
vis-à-vis *prep* con respecto a.
viscous *adj* viscoso/sa, glutinoso/sa.
visibility *n* visibilidad *f.*
visible *adj* visible.
visibly *adv* visiblemente.
vision *n* vista *f*; visión *f.*
visit *vt* visitar; * *n* visita *f.*
visitation *n* visitación, visita *f.*
visiting hours *npl* horas de visita *fpl.*
visitor *n* visitante *m/f*; turista *m/f.*
visor *n* visera *f.*
vista *n* vista, perspectiva *f.*
visual *adj* visual.
visual aid *n* medio visual *m.*
visualize *vt* imaginarse.
vital *adj* vital; esencial; imprescindible; ~ly
  adv vitalmente; ~s *npl* partes vitales *fpl.*
vitality *n* vitalidad *f.*
vital statistics *npl* medidas vitales *fpl.*
vitamin *n* vitamina *f.*
vitiate *vt* viciar, corromper.
vivacious *adj* vivaz.
vivid *adj* vivo/va; gráfico/ca; intenso/sa; ~ly
  adv vivamente; gráficamente.
vivisection *n* vivisección *f.*
vixen *n* zorra *f.*
vocabulary *n* vocabulario *m.*
vocal *adj* vocal.
vocation *n* vocación *f*; oficio *m*; carrera,
  profesión *f*; ~al *adj* profesional.
vocative *n* vocativo *m.*
vociferous *adj* vocinglero/ra, clamoroso/sa.
vodka *n* vodka *m.*

vogue *n* moda *f*; boga *f.*
voice *n* voz *f*; * *vt* expresar.
void *adj* nulo* *n* vacio *m.*
volatile *adj* volátil; voluble.
volcanic *adj* volcánico/ca.
volcano *n* volcán *m.*
volition *n* voluntad *f.*
volley *n* descarga *f*; salva *f*; rociada *f*; volea *f.*
volleyball *n* voleibol *m*, *Lat Am*
  vóleibol *m.*
volt *n* voltio *m.*
voltage *n* voltaje *m.*
voluble *adj* locuaz.
volume *n* volumen *m*; libro *m.*
voluntarily *adv* voluntariamente.
voluntary *adj* voluntario/ria.
volunteer *n* voluntario/ria *m/f*; * *vi*
  ofrecerse voluntariamente.
voluptuous *adj* voluptuoso/sa.
vomit *vt, vi* vomitar; * *n* vómito *m.*
voracious *adj*, ~ly *adv* voraz(mente).
vortex *n* remolino, torbellino *m.*
vote *n* voto, sufragio *m*; votación *f*; * *vt*
  votar, *Lat Am* sufragar.
voter *n* votante *m/f.*
voting *n* votación *f.*
voucher *n* vale *m.*
vow *n* voto *m*; * *vi* jurar.
vowel *n* vocal *f.*
voyage *n* viaje *m*; travesía *f.*
vulgar *adj* vulgar, ordinario/ria; de mal gusto.
vulgarity *n* vulgaridad *f*, grosería *f*; mal
  gusto *m.*
vulnerable *adj* vulnerable.
vulture *n* buitre *m.*

W

wad n fajo m; bolita f.
waddle vi anadear.
wade vi vadear.
wafer n galleta f; oblea f.
waffle n gofre m.
waft vt hacer flotar; * vi flotar.
wag vt menear; * vi menearse.
wage n salario m.
wage earner n asalariado/da m/f.
wager n apuesta f; * vt apostar.
wages npl salario m.
waggish adj zumbón/ona.
waggle vt menear.
wagon n carro m; (rail) vagón m.
wail n lamento, gemido m; * vi gemir.
waist n cintura f.
waistline n talle m.
wait vi esperar; * n espera f; pausa f.
waiter n camarero m.
waiting list n lista de espera f.
waiting room n sala de espera f.
waive vt suspender.
wake[1] vi despertarse; * vt despertar; * n vela f.
wake[2] n (mar) estela f.
wakefulness n vela f.
waken vt (vi) despertar(se).
walk vt, vi pasear, ir; andar, caminar; * n paseo m; caminata f.
walker n paseante m/f.
walkie-talkie n walkie-talkie m.
walking n paseos mpl.
walking stick n bastón m.
walkout n huelga f.
walkover n (col) pan comido m.
walkway n paseo m.
wall n pared f; muralla f; muro m.
walled adj amurallado/da.
wallflower n (bot) alhelí m.
wallow vi revolcarse.
wallpaper n papel pintado m.
walnut n nogal m; nuez f.
walrus n morsa f.
waltz n vals m invar.
wan adj pálido/da.
wand n varita mágica f.
wander vt, vi errar; vagar.
wane vi menguar.
want vt querer; necesitar; faltar; * n necesidad f; falta f.
wanting adj falto/ta, defectuoso/sa.
wanton adj lascivo/va; juguetón/ona.

war n guerra f.
ward n sala f; pupilo/la m/f.
wardrobe n guardarropa f, ropero m.
warehouse n almacén m.
warfare n guerra f.
warhead n ojiva f.
warily adv prudentemente.
wariness n cautela, prudencia f.
warm adj cálido/da; caliente; efusivo/va; * vt calentar; to ~ up vi calentarse; entrar en calor; acalorarse; vt calentar.
warm-hearted adj afectuoso/sa.
warmly adv con calor, ardientemente.
warmth n calor m.
warn vt avisar; advertir.
warning n aviso m.
warning light n luz de advertencia f.
warp vi torcerse; * vt torcer; pervertir.
warrant n orden judicial f; mandamiento judicial m
warranty n garantía f.
warren n conejero m.
warrior n guerrero/ra, soldado/da m/f.
warship n barco de guerra m.
wart n verruga f.
wary adj cauto/ta, prudente.
wash vt lavar; bañar; * vi lavarse; * n lavado m; baño m.
washable adj lavable.
washbowl, washbasin n lavabo m.
washcloth n manopla f.
washer n arandela f.
washing n ropa sucia f; colada f.
washing machine n lavadora f.
washing-up n fregado m.
wash out n (col) fracaso m.
washroom n aseos mpl.
wasp n avispa f.
wastage n desgaste m; pérdida f.
waste vt malgastar; destruir, arruinar; perder; * vi gastarse; * n desperdicio m; destrucción f; despilfarro m; basura f; yermo m.
wasteful adj destructivo/va; pródigo/ga; ~ly adv pródigamente.
wasteland n yermo m.
waste paper n papel usado m.
waste pipe n tubo de desagüe m.
watch n reloj m; centinela f; guardia f; * vt mirar; ver; vigilar; tener cuidado; * vi ver; montar guardia.
watchdog n perro guardián m.

379

watchful *adj* vigilante; **~ly** *adv* vigilantemente.

watchmaker *n* relojero/ra *m/f.*

watchman *n* sereno *m*; vigilante *m.*

watchtower *n* atalaya, garita *f.*

watchword *n* santo *y* seña *m.*

water *n* agua *f*; * *vt* regar, humedecer, mojar; * *vi* hacerse agua.

water closet, WC *n* váter *m.*

watercolor *n* acuarela *f.*

waterfall *n* cascada *f.*

water heater *n* calentador de agua *m.*

watering-can *n* regadera *f.*

water level *n* nivel del agua *m.*

water lily *n* ninfea *f.*

water line *n* línea de flotación *f.*

waterlogged *adj* anegado/da.

water main *n* cañería del agua *f.*

watermark *n* filigrana *f.*

water melon *n* sandía *f.*

watershed *n* momento crítico *m.*

watertight *adj* impermeable.

waterworks *npl* depuradora de agua *f.*

watery *adj* aguado/da, *Lat Am* aguachento/ta; desvaído/da; lloroso/sa.

watt *n* vatio *m.*

wave *n* ola, onda *f*; oleada *f*; senal *f*; * *vi* agitar la mano; ondear; * *vt* agitar.

wavelength *n* longitud de onda *f.*

waver *vi* vacilar, balancear.

wavering *adj* inconstante.

wavy *adj* ondulado/da.

wax *n* cera *f*; * *vt* encerar; * *vi* crecer.

wax paper *n* papel de cera *m.*

waxworks *n* museo de cera *m.*

way *n* camino *m*; vía *f*; ruta *f*; modo *m*; recorrido *m*; **to give ~** ceder.

waylay *vt* salir al paso.

wayward *adj* caprichoso/sa.

we *pn* nosotros, nosotras.

weak *adj* , **~ly** *adv* débil(mente).

weaken *vt* debilitar.

weakling *n* enclenque *m/f.*

weakness *n* debilidad *f*; punto débil *m.*

weal, wheal *n* roncha *f.*

wealth *n* riqueza *f*; bienes *mpl.*

wealthy *adj* rico/ca.

wean *vt* destetar.

weapon *n* arma *f.*

wear *vt* gastar, consumir; usar, llevar; * *vi* consumirse; **to ~ away** *vt* gastar; *vi* desgastarse; **to ~ down** gastar; agotar; **to ~ off** pasar; **to ~ out** desgastar; agotar; * *n* uso *m*; desgaste *m.*

weariness *n* cansancio *m*; fatiga *f*; enfado *m.*

wearisome *adj* tedioso/sa.

weary *adj* cansado/da, fatigado/da; tedioso/sa.

weasel *n* comadreja *f.*

weather *n* tiempo *m*; * *vt* (out) sufrir, superar.

weather-beaten *adj* curtido/da.

weather cock *n* gallo de campanario *m*; veleta *f.*

weather forecast *n* boletín meteorológico *m.*

weave *vt* tejer; trenzar; (*fig*) zurcir.

weaving *n* tejido *m.*

web *n* telarana *f*; membrana *f*; red *f.*

wed *vt* (*vi*) casar(se).

wedding *n* boda *f*; nupcias *fpl*; casamiento *m.*

wedding day *n* día de la boda *m.*

wedding dress *n* traje de novia *m.*

wedding present *n* regalo de boda *m.*

wedding ring *n* alianza *f.*

wedge *n* cuña *f*; * *vt* acuñar; apretar.

wedlock *n* matrimonio *m.*

Wednesday *n* miércoles *m invar.*

wee *adj* pequeñito/ta.

weed *n* mala hierba *f*; * *vt* escardar.

weedkiller *n* herbicida *m.*

weedy *adj* lleno/na de malas hierbas.

week *n* semana *f*; **tomorrow ~** mañana en una semana; **yesterday ~** ayer hace ocho dias.

weekday *n* día laborable *m.*

weekend *n* fin de semana *m.*

weekly *adj* semanal; * *adv* semanalmente, por semana.

weep *vt*, *vi* llorar; lamentar.

weeping willow *n* sauce llorón *m.*

weigh *vt*, *vi* pesar.

weight *n* peso *m.*

weightily *adv* pesadamente.

weightlifter *n* levantador/a *m/f* de pesas, *Lat Am* fierrero/ra *m/f.*

weighty *adj* ponderoso/sa; importante.

welcome *adj* bienvenido/da; **~!** ¡bienvenido!; * *n* bienvenida *f*; * *vt* dar la bienvenida a.

weld *vt* soldar; * *n* soldadura *f.*

welfare *n* prosperidad *f*; bienestar *m*; subsidio de paro *m.*

welfare state *n* estado del bienestar *m.*

well *n* fuente *f*; manantial *m*; pozo *m*; * *adj* bueno/na, sano/na; * *adv* bien, felizmente; favorablemente; suficientemente; convenientemente; **as ~ as** así como, además de, lo mismo que.

well-behaved *adj* bien educado/da.

wellbeing *n* felicidad, prosperidad *f.*

well-bred *adj* bien criado/da, bien educado/da.

well-built *adj* fornido/da.

well-deserved *adj* merecido/da.

well-dressed adj bien vestido/da.
well-known adj conocido/da.
well-mannered adj educado/da.
well-meaning adj bien intencionado/da.
well-off adj acomodado/da.
well-to-do adj acomodado/da.
well-wisher n partidario/ria m/f.
wench n mozuela, cantonera f.
west n oeste, occidente m; * adj occidental;
   * adv hacia el oeste.
westerly, western adj occidental.
westward adv hacia el oeste.
wet adj húmedo/da, mojado/da; * n humedad
   f; * vt mojar, hume decer.
wet-nurse n ama de leche f.
wet suit n traje de buzo m.
whack vt aporrear; * n golpe m.
whale n ballena f.
wharf n muelle m.
what pn que, ;¿qué?, el que, la que, lo que;
   * adj ¿qué?; * excl ¡cómo!
whatever pn cualquier, cualquiera cosa que,
   lo que sea.
wheat n trigo m.
wheedle vt halagar, engañar con lisonjas,
   sonsacar.
wheedler n zalamero/ra m/f.
wheel n rueda f; volante m; timón m; * vt
   (hacer) rodar; volver, girar; * vi rodar.
wheelbarrow n carretilla f.
wheelchair n silla de ruedas f.
wheel clamp n cepo m.
wheeze vi jadear.
when adv ¿cuándo?; mientras que; * conj cuando.
whenever adv cuando; cada vez que.
where adv ¿dónde?; * conj donde; any~ en
   cualquier parte; every~ en todas partes.
whereabout(s) adv ¿dónde?
whereas conj mientras que; pues que, ya que.
whereby pn por lo cual, con lo cual.
whereupon conj con lo cual.
wherever adv dondequiera que.
wherewithal npl recursos mpl.
whet vt excitar.
whether conj si.
which pn qué; lo que; el que, el cual; cuál;
   * adj ¿qué?; cuyo.
whiff n bocanada de humo f.
while n rato m; vez f; * conj durante;
   micntras; aunquc.
whim n antojo, capricho m.
whimper vi sollozar, gemir.
whimsical adj caprichoso/sa, fantástico/ca.
whine vi llorar, lamentar; * n quejido,
   lamento m.

whinny vi relinchar.
whip n azote m; látigo m, Lat Am chicote
   m, Lat Am cuero m; * vt azotar; batir.
whipped cream n nata montada f.
whirl vt, vi girar; hacer girar; mover(se)
   rápidamente.
whirlpool n remolino m.
whirlpool bath n hidromasaje m.
whirlwind n torbellino m.
whisky n whisky m.
whisper vi cuchichear; susurrar.
whispering n cuchicheo m; susurro m.
whistle vi silbar; * n silbido m.
white adj blanco/ca, pálido/da; cano/na; puro/
   ra; * n color blanco m; clara del huevo f.
white elephant n maula f.
white-hot adj incandescente.
white lie n mentirijilla f.
whiten vt, vi blanquear; emblanquecerse.
whiteness n blancura f; palidez f.
whitewash n enlucimiento m; * vt encalar;
   jalbegar.
whiting n pescadilla f
whitish adj blanquecino/na.
who pn ¿quién?, que.
whoever pn quienquiera, cualquiera.
whole adj todo/da, total, sano/na, entero/
   ra; * n total m; conjunto m.
wholehearted adj sincero/ra.
wholesale n venta al por mayor f, Lat Am
   mayoreo m.
wholesome adj sano/na, saludable.
wholewheat adj integral.
wholly adv enteramente.
whom pn ¿quién?; que.
whooping cough n tos ferina f.
whore n puta f; (col) zorra f.
why n ¿por qué?; * conj por qué; * excl ¡hombre!
wick n mecha f.
wicked adj malvado/da, perverso/sa; ~ly
   adv malamente.
wickedness n perversidad, malignidad f.
wicker n mimbre m; * adj tejido/da de mimbre.
wide adj ancho/cha, vasto/ta; grande; ~ly
   adv muy; far and ~ por todos lados.
wide-awake adj despierto/ta.
widen vt ensanchar, extender.
wide open adj de par en par.
widespread adj extendido/da.
widow n viuda f.
widower n viudo m.
width n anchura f.
wield vt manejar, empuñar.
wife n esposa f; mujer f
wig n peluca f; tupé m.

wiggle *vt* menear; * *vi* menearse.

wild *adj* silvestre, feroz; desierto/ta; descabellado/da; salvaje.

wilderness *n* desierto *m*; yermo *m*.

wild life *n* fauna *f*.

wildly *adv* violentamente; locamente; desatinadamente.

willful *adj* deliberado/da; testarudo/da.

willfulness *n* obstinación *f*.

wiliness *n* fraude, engaño *m*.

will *n* voluntad *f*; testamento *m*; * *vt* querer, desear.

willing *adj* inclinado/da, dispuesto/ta; ~ly *adv* de buena gana.

willingness *n* buena voluntad, buena gana *f*.

willow *n* sauce *m* (árbol).

willpower *n* fuerza de voluntad *f*.

wilt *vi* marchitarse.

wily *adj* astuto/ta.

win *vt* ganar, conquistar; alcanzar; lograr.

wince *vi* encogerse, estremecerse.

winch *n* torno *m*.

wind *n* viento *m*; aliento *m*; flatulencia *f*.

wind *vt* enrollar; envolver; dar cuerda a; * *vi* serpentear.

windfall *n* golpe de suerte *m*.

wind farm *n* parque eólico *m*.

winding *adj* tortuoso/sa.

windmill *n* molino de viento *m*.

window *n* ventana *f*.

window box *n* jardinera de ventana *f*.

window cleaner *n* limpiacristales *m invar*.

window ledge *n* repisa *f*.

windowpane *n* cristal *m*.

windowsill *n* repisa *f*.

windpipe *n* tráquea *f*.

windshield *n* parabrisas *m invar*.

windshield washer *n* lavaparabrisas *m invar*.

windshield wiper *n* limpiaparabrisas *m invar*.

windsurfer *n* windsurfista *m/f*.

windsurfing *n* windsurf *m*.

wind turbine *n* aerogenerador *m*.

windy *adj* de mucho viento.

wine *n* vino *m*.

wine cellar *n* bodega *f*.

wine glass *n* copa de vino *f*.

wine list *n* carta de vinos *f*.

wine merchant *n* vinatero/ra *m/f*.

wine-tasting *n* degustación de vinos *f*.

wing *n* ala *f*.

winged *adj* alado/da.

winger *n* extremo *m*.

wink *vi* guiñar; * *n* pestañeo *m*; guino *m*.

winner *n* ganador/a *m/f*; vencedor/a *m/f*.

winning post *n* meta *f*.

winter *n* invierno *m*; * *vi* invernar.

winter sports *npl* deportes de invierno *mpl*.

wintry *adj* invernal.

wipe *vt* limpiar; borrar.

wire *n* alambre *m*; telegrama *m*; * *vt* instalar el alambrado en; conectar.

wiring *n* alambrada *m*, *Lat Am* alambrado *m*.

wiry *adj* delgado/da y fuerte.

wisdom *n* sabiduría, prudencia *f*.

wisdom teeth *npl* muelas del juicio *fpl*.

wise *adj* sabio/bia, docto/ta, juicioso/sa, prudente.

wisecrack *n* broma *f*.

wish *vt* querer, desear, anhelar; * *n* anhelo, deseo *m*.

wishful *adj* deseoso/sa.

wisp *n* mechón *m*; voluta *f*.

wistful *adj* pensativo/va, atento/ta.

wit *n* entendimiento, ingenio *m*.

witch *n* bruja, hechicera *f*.

witchcraft *n* brujería *f*; sortilegio *m*.

with *prep* con; por, de, a.

withdraw *vt* quitar; privar; retirar; * *vi* retirarse, apartarse.

withdrawal *n* retirada *f*.

withdrawn *adj* reservado/da.

wither *vi* marchitarse, secarse.

withhold *vt* detener, impedir, retener.

within *prep* dentro de, adentro; * *adv* interiormente; en casa.

without *prep* sin.

withstand *vt* resistir.

witless *adj* necio/cia, tonto/ta, falto/ta de ingenio.

witness *n* testimonio *m*; testgo *m/f*; * *vt* atestiguar, testificar.

witness stand *n* estrado de los testigos *m*.

witticism *n* ocurrencia *f*.

wittily *adv* ingeniosamente.

wittingly *adv* adrede, de propósito.

witty *adj* ingenioso/sa, agudo/da, chistoso/sa.

wizard *n* brujo, hechicero *m*.

wobble *vi* tambalearse.

woe *n* dolor *m*; miseria *f*.

woeful *adj* triste, funesto/ta; ~ly *adv* tristemente.

wolf *n* lobo *m*; **she** ~ loba *f*.

woman *n* mujer *f*.

womanish *adj* mujeril.

womanly *adj* mujeril, mujeriego/ga.

womb *n* útero *m*.

women's lib *n* la liberación de la mujer *f*.

wonder *n* milagro *m*; maravilla *f*; asombro *m*; * *vi* maravil larse de; preguntarse si.

wonderful *adj* maravilloso/sa; ~ly *adv* maravillosamente.

wondrous *adj* maravilloso/sa.
won't *abbrev* will not.
wont *n* uso *m*; costumbre *f*.
woo *vt* cortejar.
wood *n* bosque *m*; selva *f*; madera *f*; leña *f*.
wood alcohol *n* alcohol metílico *m*.
wood carving *n* tallado en madera *m*.
woodcut *n* estampa de madera *f*.
woodcutter *n* leñador/a *m/f*; grabador en láminas de madera, xilógrafo *m/f*.
wooded *adj* arbolado/da.
wooden *adj* de madera.
wood engraver *n* xilógrafo *m*.
wooden shoe *n* zueco *m*.
woodland *n* arbolado *m*.
woodlouse *n* cochinilla *f*.
woodpecker *n* pájaro carpintero *m*.
woodsman *n* cazador *m*; guardabosque *m*.
woodwind *n* intrumento de viento de madera *m*.
woodwork *n* carpintería *f*.
woodworm *n* carcoma *f*.
wool *n* lana *f*.
woolen *adj* de lana.
woolens *npl* géneros de lana *mpl*.
woolly, wooly *adj* lanudo/da, lanoso/sa.
word *n* palabra *f*; noticia *f*; * *vt* expresar; componer en escri tura.
wordiness *n* verbosidad *f*.
wording *n* redacción *f*.
word processing *n* tratamiento de textos *m*.
word processor *n* procesador de textos *m*.
wordy *adj* verboso/sa.
work *vi* trabajar; obrar; estar en movimiento/ en acción; fermentar; * *vt* trabajar, labrar; fabricar, manufacturar; to ~ out *vi* salir bien; * *vt* resolver; * *n* trabajo *m*; fábrica *f*; obra *f*; empleo *m*.
workable *adj* práctico/ca.
workaholic *n* trabajador obsesivo *m*, trabajadora obsesiva *f*.
worker *n* trabajador/a *m/f*; obrero/ra *m/f*.
workforce *n* mano de obra *f*.
working-class *adj* obrero/ra, de clase trabajadora.
workman *n* labrador *m*.
workmanship *n* manufactura *f*; destreza del artífice *f*.
workmate *n* compañero/ra de trabajo *m/f*.
workshop *n* taller, obrador *m*.
world *n* mundo *m*; * *adj* del mundo; mundial.
worldliness *n* mundanería *f*.
worldly *adj* mundano/na, terreno/na
worldwide *adj* mundial.

worm *n* gusano *m*; (*tec*) rosca de tornillo *f*.
worn-out *adj* gastado/da; rendido/da.
worried *adj* preocupado/da.
worry *vt* preocupar; * *n* preocupación *f*; pensión *f*.
worrying *adj* inquietante.
worse *adj*, *adv* peor; ~ and ~ cada vez peor; * *n* lo peor.
worship *n* culto *m*; adoración *f*; your ~ su señoría; * *vt* adorar, venerar.
worst *adj* el/la peor; * *adv* peor; * *n* lo peor *m*.
worth *n* valor, precio *m*; mérito *m*.
worthily *adv* dignamente, convenientemente.
worthless *adj* sin valor; inútil.
worthwhile *adj* que vale la pena; valioso/sa.
worthy *adj* digno/na; respetable; honesto/ta.
would-be *adj* aspirante.
wound *n* herida, llaga *f*; * *vt* herir, llagar.
wrangle *vi* reñir; * *n* riña *f*.
wrap *vt* envolver.
wrath *n* ira, rabia, cólera *f*.
wreath *n* corona, guirnalda *f*.
wreck *n* naufragio *m*; ruina *f*; destrucción *f*; navío naufragado *m*; * *vt* naufragar; arruinar.
wreckage *n* restos *mpl*; escombros *mpl*.
wren *n* chochín *m*.
wrench *vt* arrancar; dislocar; torcer; * *n* llave inglesa *f*; tirón *m*.
wrest *vt* arrancar, arrebatar.
wrestle *vi* luchar; disputar.
wrestling *n* lucha *f*.
wretched *adj* infeliz, miserable.
wriggle *vi* menearse, agitarse.
wring *vt* torcer; arrancar; estrujar.
wrinkle *n* arruga *f*; * *vt* arrugar; * *vi* arrugarse.
wrist *n* muñeca *f*.
wristband *n* puno de camisa *m*.
wristwatch *n* reloj de pulsera *m*.
writ *n* escrito *m*; escritura *f*; orden *f*.
write *vt* escribir; componer; to ~ down apuntar; to ~ off borrar; desechar; to ~ up redactar.
write-off *n* pérdida total *f*.
writer *n* escritor/a, *m/f*; autor/a *m/f*.
writhe *vi* retorcerse.
writing *n* escritura *f*; letra *f*; obras *fpl*; escrito *m*.
writing desk *n* escritorio *m*.
writing paper *n* papel para escribir *m*.
wrong *n* injuria *f*; injusticia *f*; perjuicio *m*; error *m*; * *adj* malo/la; injusto/ta; equivocado/da, inoportuno/na; falso/sa; * *adv* mal, equivocadamente; * *vt* agraviar, injuriar.
wrongful *adj* injusto/ta.
wrongly *adv* injustamente.
wry *adj* irónico/ca.

XYZ

xenophobia *n* xenofobia *f.*
Xmas *n* Navidad *f.*
X-ray *n* radiografía *f.*
xylographer *n* xilógrafo *m.*
xylophone *n* xilófano *m.*

yacht *n* yate *m.*
yachting *n* vela *f.*
Yankee *n* yanqui *m/f.*
yard *n* corral *m*; yarda *f.*
yardstick *n* criterio *m.*
yarn *n* estambre *m*; hilo de lino *m.*
yawn *vi* bostezar; * *n* bostezo *m.*
yawning *adj* muy abierto/ta.
yeah *adv* sí.
year *n* año *m.*
yearbook *n* anuario *m.*
yearling *n* añal *m.*
yearly *adj* anual; * *adv* anualmente, todos los años.
yearn *vi* añorar.
yearning *n* añoranza *f.*
yeast *n* levadura *f.*
yell *vi* aullar; * *n* aullido *m.*
yellow *adj* amarillo/lla; * *n* amarillo *m.*
yellowish *adj* amarillento/ta.
yelp *vi* latir, gañir; * *n* aullido *m.*
yes *adv* sí; * *n* sí *m.*
yesterday *adv* ayer; * *n* ayer *m.*
yet *conj* sin embargo; pero; * *adv* todavía.
yew *n* tejo *m.*
yield *vt* dar, producir; rendir; * *vi* rendirse; ceder el paso; * *n* producción *f*; cosecha *f*; rendimiento *m.*
yoga *n* yoga *m.*
yogurt *n* yogur *m.*
yoke *n* yugo *m*; yunta *f.*
yolk *n* yema (de huevo) *f.*

yonder *adv* allá.
you *pn* vosotros/tras, tú, usted, *Lat Am* vos, ustedes.
young *adj* joven, mozo/za; ~er *adj* menor.
youngster *n* jovencito/ta *m/f*; joven *m/f.*
your(s) *pn* tuyo, tuya, vuestro, vuestra, suyo, suya.
yourself *pn* tú mismo, tú misma, usted mismo, usted misma.
yourselves *pn pl* vosotros mismos, vosotras mismas, ustedes mismos, ustedes mismas.
youth *n* juventud, adolescencia *f*; joven *m/f.*
youthful *adj* juvenil.
youthfulness *n* juventud *f.*
yuppie *adj*, *n* yupi *m/f.*

zany *adj* estrafalario/ria.
zap *vt* borrar.
zeal *n* celo *m*; ardor *m.*
zealous *adj* celoso/sa.
zebra *n* cebra *f.*
zenith *n* cénit *m.*
zero *n* zero, cero *m.*
zest *n* ánimo *m.*
zigzag *n* zigzag *m*; * *adj* zigzag; * *vi* zigzaguear.
zinc *n* zinc *m.*
zipper *n* cremallera *f*; cierre de cremallera *m.*
zodiac *n* zodíaco *m.*
zone *n* banda, faja *f*; zona *f.*
zoo *n* zoo, zoológico *m.*
zoological *adj* zoológico/ca.
zoologist *n* zoólogo/ga *m/f.*
zoology *n* zoología *f.*
zoom *vi* zumbar.
zoom lens *n* zoom *m.*